Eleanor Roosevelt

Eleanor Roosevelt in 1934. Courtesy of *Newsweek* (October 13, 1934).

ELEANOR ROOSEVELT

A Comprehensive Bibliography

Compiled by
John A. Edens

Bibliographies and Indexes in American History, *Number 29*

GREENWOOD PRESS
Westport, Connecticut • London

Library of Congress Cataloging-in-Publication Data

Edens, John A.
    Eleanor Roosevelt : a comprehensive bibliography / compiled by
John A. Edens.
       p. cm.—(Bibliographies and indexes in American history,
ISSN 0742–6828 ; no. 29)
    Includes bibliographical references and index.
    ISBN 0–313–26050–8 (alk. paper)
    1. Roosevelt, Eleanor, 1884–1962—Bibliography. I. Title.
II. Series.
Z8757.27.E33   1994
[E807.1]
016.973917′092—dc20   94–25906

British Library Cataloguing in Publication Data is available.

Library of Congress Catalog Card Number: 94–25906
ISBN: 0–313–26050–8
ISSN: 0742–6828

First published in 1994

Greenwood Press, 88 Post Road West, Westport, CT 06881
An imprint of Greenwood Publishing Group, Inc.

Printed in the United States of America

The paper used in this book complies with the
Permanent Paper Standard issued by the National
Information Standards Organization (Z39.48–1984).

10 9 8 7 6 5 4 3 2 1

For

Nancy W. Davis

and

Sara W. Smith

Contents

Introduction and Acknowledgments xi

Chronology. xv

A. Bibliographies and Guides to Archival Material about Eleanor Roosevelt

    Bibliographies 1
    Guides to Archival Material 2

B. Books, Book Sections, and Periodical Articles by Eleanor Roosevelt

    Books and Pamphlets 5
    Book Sections and Periodical Articles 11
    Translations of Her Writings 65

C. Major Periodical Columns by Eleanor Roosevelt

    "Passing Thoughts of Mrs. Franklin D. Roosevelt." *Women's*
        Democratic News (1933-1935) 71
    "Mrs. Roosevelt's Page." *Woman's Home Companion* (1933-1935) 73
    "Dear Mrs. Roosevelt:" *Democratic Digest* (1937-1941) 75
    "If You Ask Me." *Ladies' Home Journal* (1941-1949),
        McCall's (1949-1962) 78

D. Addresses, Remarks, and Other Statements by Eleanor Roosevelt 101

E. Reviews of the Writings of Eleanor Roosevelt 141

F. Writings about Eleanor Roosevelt

Major Biographical Works 157
Biographical Sketches
    Major Biographical Sketches 162
    Brief Overviews of Her Life and Work 169
Private Life 174
Emergence as a Public Figure 201
First Lady, Contemporary Writings 212
First Lady, Later Writings 238
Eleanor Roosevelt and World War II 264
Social Reformer
    General 276
    Human Welfare 282
    Race Relations 292
    Women's Rights 304
    Young Americans and Their Problems 313
Cardinal Spellman and Parochial Schools
    Background and General Accounts 321
    Writings in Support of Spellman 323
    Writings in Support of Roosevelt 324
First Lady of the World
    UN Delegate: As Reported in United Nations Publications 326
    UN Delegate: As Reported in Department of State Publications 329
    UN Delegate: Other Accounts 333
    Universal Declaration of Human Rights and the Covenants:
        Chronology as Reported in UN Publications 340
    Universal Declaration of Human Rights and the Covenants:
        Chronology as Reported in Department of State Publications 344
    Universal Declaration of Human Rights and the Covenants:
        Other Accounts 347
    American Association for the United Nations 354
    World Figure 354
Political Activities after the Death of FDR 362
Writer, Public Speaker, and Media Personality 370
The Death of Eleanor Roosevelt 381
Eleanor Roosevelt Centennial 395
Miscellaneous Tributes and Assessments 404

G. Interviews with Eleanor Roosevelt 411

H. Eleanor Roosevelt in Recordings, Films, and Computer Software

Recordings and Films of Radio and Television Appearances
    Recordings 429
    Films 430

Recordings and Films Featuring Eleanor Roosevelt
Recordings 432
Films 433
Recordings and Films about Eleanor Roosevelt
Recordings 434
Films 435
Computer Software 438

I. Writings about Eleanor Roosevelt for Younger Readers

Books 439
Sections of Books and Periodical Articles 441

J. Eleanor Roosevelt in Fiction, Poetry, and Song

Fiction 449
Poetry 452
Song 453

Author Index 455

Subject Index 473

Introduction and Acknowledgments

How the wife of the President of the United States approaches her role as First Lady is watched with interest and suspicion. Her public actions and statements are reported. Her private life and the influence which she is suspected of having on the President become the subject of speculation and gossip. All aspects of a First Lady's life, both public and private, can eventually be subjected to the scholar's interpretation. This has proved to be particularly true in regard to Eleanor Roosevelt.

First ladies are criticized for exercising too much influence or for not being sufficiently involved. They can be considered too outspoken. They can be recognized for being stylish or derided for being preoccupied with clothing and appearance. A First Lady can be accused of being extravagant or for appearing to neglect making the White House a home for her husband and children. While serving in a position for which no defined duties exist, most first ladies receive more criticism than praise. Some criticism and suspicion of first ladies is linked to the belief that as First Lady, someone not elected to any public office, a woman should restrict herself to being a wife and mother and White House hostess. Not until a woman assumes the duties of chief executive is this belief likely to disappear.

Eleanor Roosevelt broke many precedents as First Lady, and, not surprisingly, much criticism and ridicule were heaped upon her. There may never be consensus on the extent to which she influenced her husband's thinking and the part she played in defining New Deal programs and establishing or influencing policy in the Roosevelt administration. But as to the significance of her role as spokesperson for the New Deal, there is little disagreement.

Unlike most First Ladies before and after her, Mrs. Roosevelt was a public figure before her husband assumed the presidency. Born Anna Eleanor Roosevelt in New York City on October 11, 1884, she was the niece of Theodore Roosevelt. She married her distant cousin Franklin Delano Roosevelt in 1905 and between 1906 and 1916 bore six children (one died as an infant). Among the factors which may have contributed to her desire to create a life separate from that of her husband and her eventual emergence as a public figure were learning of Franklin Roosevelt's relationship with Lucy Page Mercer, the impact of her husband's crippling illness together with her subsequent desire to see him return to public life, and the extent to which she was influenced by the women with whom she formed friendships in the 1920s.

By the time Franklin Roosevelt was elected President Mrs. Roosevelt had become a powerful force in the Democratic Party in both New York State and at the national level. She was part owner of Val-Kill Industries and the Todhunter School for Girls. She had edited a Democratic Party newsletter for women and a magazine for new mothers and had been actively involved in numerous organizations which were concerned with social welfare issues and promoting an expanded public role for women. She had served four years as First Lady of New York. The ways of politics had been learned. Valuable friendships had been formed. She knew what it took to make a speech, write an article, or participate in a political debate. She knew what it was like to respond to a reporter's questions. Criticism was something which she had already experienced.

Eleanor Roosevelt had the preparation necessary to become an active First Lady, but apparently her husband did not envision such a role for her. For reasons which may never be fully known she entered into activities which kept her highly visible and subject to constant derision for all of the twelve years the Roosevelts were in the White House. Her regular press conferences, the books and many articles which she wrote, her radio series, magazine columns, speeches, and lectures, and her frequent travels made her the subject of almost daily newspaper and radio reporting. After her column "My Day" was launched in December 1935, it was almost a certainty that for most Americans, whether they liked it or not, Eleanor Roosevelt would be part of their lives each and every day.

During the seventeen years which followed Franklin Roosevelt's death Mrs. Roosevelt continued to lead an active public life. As a delegate to the United Nations, chair of the United Nations Human Rights Commission, one of the framers of the Universal Declaration of Human Rights, an active participant in the Democratic Party, a founder of the Americans for Democratic Action, and a writer and speaker, she was highly visible to the American people and throughout the world. "My Day" continued almost until her death, and the column along with her radio and eventual television series were vehicles for communicating her opinions and ideas. As such a visible and outspoken figure she continued to be the subject of harsh criticism, some of which was more vicious than that which she had experienced as First Lady. But when she died on November 7, 1962, her life and career were praised by her fellow citizens of all walks of life.

Eleanor Roosevelt was always modest about her contributions. She preferred to downplay her own significance and influence and to give credit to others. Disagreement about the extent of her influence during the Roosevelt administration, the significance of her contributions to the United Nations and to the cause of human rights, whether she aided or hindered equal rights for women and basic civil rights for all, and whether her insight into the post-World War II war was perceptive or merely foolish is certain to continue.

Numerous scholarly monographs and doctoral dissertations about Mrs. Roosevelt include useful, but incomplete lists of published works by or about her. Earlier bibliographies devoted to her are highly selective. The present bibliography of works by and about Mrs. Roosevelt is the most comprehensive one compiled to date. It includes monographs which were written or edited by her as well as chapters in monographs written or edited by others. It includes prefaces, forewords, and introductions which Mrs. Roosevelt wrote for monographs written or edited by others. It includes periodical articles and book reviews written by her. Her periodical columns are included, but this bibliography does not include a listing of her "My Day" columns which appeared over a twenty-six year period.

Included are the full or partial texts of many addresses and remarks made by Mrs. Roosevelt which were published by her as articles or excerpted in periodical articles written by others. However, no attempt has been made to document all of the many thousands of speeches, addresses, lectures, and other public statements which she made. A listing of these providing date, place, audience, and source--published or unpublished--would be a valuable addition to the literature.

Monographs and periodical articles which have Mrs. Roosevelt as their subject as well as those which pay particular attention to her are included. An extensive number of articles from the *New York Times* are included, but there are many other articles of lesser significance which can be identified through the *New York Times Index*. No attempt has been made to include broad coverage from newspapers other than the *New York Times*. Works about Franklin D. Roosevelt and events and personalities in the New Deal and post-war eras which pay substantive attention to her are included. Dissertations and theses which have Mrs. Roosevelt as their theme can be found in this bibliography. Separate chapters list works written for younger readers and works of fiction and poetry about her. Also in a separate chapter are films and recordings about her or which feature her.

Two basic arrangements for organizing entries are followed. Chapters which list the writings or addresses of Mrs. Roosevelt are arranged by year of publication, and use is made of subentries designated by letters (a, b, etc.) to identify other editions or excerpts. Other chapters devoted to works about her are arranged by topical sections and then by author or title. This bibliography is fully annotated except for some biographical sketches for which annotations would not provide any useful additional information and a small number of works which could not be located. In numerous instances similar or related works are cited only as part of the annotations for other works.

The preparation of this bibliography was supported in part by grants from the National Endowment for the Humanities and the New York State / United University Professions Development and Study Leave Grant Program for Professional Employees. Acknowledgment is made for the invaluable assistance provided by staff at the Franklin D. Roosevelt Library and the Buffalo and Erie County Public Library and in General Libraries Interlibrary Loan at the State University of New York at Buffalo. The assistance of colleagues at the State University of New York at Buffalo, most notably Christopher Densmore, Kimberly Doyle, Elizabeth Felmet, Shonnie Finnegan, Ellen Greenblatt, Judith Hopkins, and Elizabeth Syracuse is also gratefully acknowledged. Marilyn Kramer and David Nuzzo demonstrated unusual patience while this bibliography was being compiled. The guidance and encouragement of Mildred Vasan of Greenwood Press kept this project going. All errors, omissions, and other shortcomings are the fault of the compiler.

Chronology

1884	Born in New York City, October 11
1889	Birth of brother Elliott Roosevelt, Jr. (d. 1893)
1891	Birth of brother Gracie Hall Roosevelt
1892	Death of mother Anna Hall Roosevelt
1894	Death of father Elliott Roosevelt
1899-1902	Attends Allenswood school
1902	Joins National Consumers League and works in New York City settlement house
1905	Marries Franklin D. Roosevelt
1906	Birth of daughter Anna
1907	Birth of son James
1909	Birth of son Franklin, Jr. (d. 1909)
1910	Birth of son Elliott
	Franklin D. Roosevelt elected to New York State Senate
1913	Franklin D. Roosevelt named Assistant Secretary of the the Navy
1914	Birth of son Franklin, Jr.
1916	Birth of son John
1917	Works as Red Cross volunteer

1920s	Is active in the League of Women Voters, Women's City Club of New York, the Women's Trade Union League, and the Democratic Party
1923	Serves on American Peace Award committee
1924	Chairs group charged with recommending Democratic Party platform planks of interest to women
1925-1928	Edits *Women's Democratic News*
1926	Establishes Val-Kill Industries and becomes part owner of Todhunter School for Girls
1928	Heads Democratic Party Women's Division
	Franklin D. Roosevelt elected Governor of New York
1932	Franklin D. Roosevelt elected President
1933	Begins White House press conferences
1935	Begins "My Day"
1936	Franklin D. Roosevelt elected to a second term as President
1939	Resigns from the Daughters of the American Revolution
1940	Addresses Democratic National Convention
	Franklin D. Roosevelt elected to a third term as President
1941	Named assistant director of the Office of Civilian Defense
1942	Makes wartime visit to England
1943	Makes wartime visit to the South Pacific
1944	Franklin D. Roosevelt elected to a fourth term as President
1945	Death of Franklin D. Roosevelt, April 12
	Appointed member of the United States delegation to the United Nations
1946	Elected chair of the Commission on Human Rights
1947	Co-founds the Americans for Democratic Action
1948	Universal Declaration of Human Rights adopted by the United Nations General Assembly

1953   Resigns as member of the United States delegation to the United Nations

Begins work with the American Association for the United Nations

1961   Named chair of the President's Commission on the Status of Women

1962   Dies in New York City, November 7

A

Bibliographies and Guides to Archival Material about Eleanor Roosevelt

BIBLIOGRAPHIES

A1   Boulard, Garry. "Roosevelt, Eleanor." *St. James Guide to Biography*. Ed. Paul E. Schellinger. Chicago: St. James, 1991. 674-75.
   A critique of major works about ER and *This Is My Story*. Considers Joseph Lash's works about ER not well documented and concludes that the definitive study about her has yet to appear.

A2   Edelstein, Pauline. "Bibliography of Eleanor Roosevelt: First Lady of the Land." Class paper. Simmons College, 1940. n.pag.
   No known extant copy.

A3   Kemp, Barbara H. *Eleanor Roosevelt Centenary Bibliography*. [Washington]: Smithsonian Institution, National Museum of American History, Dept. of Public Programs, 1984. 11p. Typescript.
   "Reflects all [English language] listings under the heading 'Roosevelt, Eleanor,' at the Library of Congress." Annotated.

A4   *Mrs. Eleanor (Roosevelt) Roosevelt (Mrs. Franklin D. Roosevelt): A List of References*. Washington: Library of Congress, General Reference and Bibliography Division, 1948. 4p. Typescript.
   A brief list without annotations.

A5   Myers, R. David, and Margaret L. Morrison and Marguerite D. Bloxom. *First Lady: A Bibliography of Selected Material by and about Eleanor Roosevelt*. Washington: Library of Congress, 1984. ix + 46p. Index.
   "Compiled on the occasion of the centenary of her birth." Annotated entries in the following arrangement: "Works by Eleanor Roosevelt" with topical subdivisions; "Works About Eleanor Roosevelt" arranged by decades.

A6   *Periodical Articles by Eleanor Roosevelt, 1923-1971*. Rev. 1979. [Hyde Park]: The Franklin D. Roosevelt Library, 1979. 33 + 2p.
   A chronological listing of published articles and speeches. Revision of 1965 ed. plus an addendum. Most entries are available at FDRL. Some entries are for writings about her. Not annotated.

GUIDES TO ARCHIVAL MATERIAL

A7 *Eleanor Roosevelt: A Register of Her Papers*. 2 Pts. Hyde Park: The Franklin D. Roosevelt Library, 1971-1972. Typescript.

A8 *A Guide to Manuscripts in the Presidential Libraries*. Comp. and ed. Dennis A. Burton, et. al. College Park: Research Materials, 1985. xxiii + 451p. Index.
   Description, extent, and location of manuscript collections related to ER in presidential libraries.

A9 *Guide to the National Archives of the United States*. Washington: National Archives and Records Admin., 1987. xxxii + 896p. Index.
   Descriptions of National Archives collections which include recordings of speeches and interviews by or featuring ER.

A10 *A Guide to the Papers of Eleanor Roosevelt, 1933-1945*. Research Collections in Women's Studies. Frederick: University Publications of America, 1986. xxv + 45p. Subject Index.
   Contains a description of each of the 20 reels in the microfilm collection drawn from the ER Papers at FDRL.

A11 *Historical Materials in the Franklin D. Roosevelt Library*. 10th ed. [Hyde Park]: The Franklin D. Roosevelt Library, National Archives and Records Admin., 1993. 38p.
   Brief descriptions of library holdings and information on use of collections. New eds. issued frequently.

A12 Lester, DeeGee. *Roosevelt Research: Collections for the Study of Theodore, Franklin, and Eleanor*. Bibliographies and Indexes in American History, 23. Westport: Greenwood, 1992. x + 194p. Index.
   A guide to collections of published works, films, recordings, and manuscript material.

A13 *The National Union Catalog of Manuscript Collections*. 1959/1961 to date. Washington: Library of Congress, 1962 to date.
   The description and location of manuscript holdings on ER. New entries are now included in both RLIN and OCLC.

A14 Research Libraries Group.
   The Research Libraries Information Network (RLIN) of the Research Libraries Group contains many records for manuscript material by and about ER. Also of value are the records for the same type of material available in the bibliographic database of OCLC.

A15 Seeber, Frances M. "'I Want You to Write to Me': The Papers of Eleanor Roosevelt." *Modern First Ladies: Their Documentary History*. Comp. and ed. Nancy Kegan Smith and Mary C. Ryan. Washington: National Archives and Records Admin., 1989. 59-70. Notes.
   Seeber describes the content and organization of the Franklin D. Roosevelt Library's collection of letters to and from ER, articles, "My Day" columns, speeches, manuscripts, and related collections of papers.

A16 Schick, Frank L. "The Franklin D. Roosevelt Library and Museum in Hyde Park, New York." *Records of the Presidency: Presidential Papers and Libraries from Washington to Reagan.* By Frank L. Schick, et. al. Phoenix: Oryx, 1989. 150-67. Bibliography. Notes.

The history of the Franklin D. Roosevelt Library and brief descriptions of the collections including audiovisual material related to ER (pp. 162-67).

A17 *Women's History Sources: A Guide to Archives and Manuscript Collections in the United States.* 2 Vols. Ed. Andrea Hinding. Index ed. Suzanna Moody. New York: Bowker, 1979. Index.

Location of manuscript material about ER.

B

Books, Book Sections, and Periodical Articles by Eleanor Roosevelt

BOOKS AND PAMPHLETS

1927

B1 *1927 Legislative Program of the Women's City Club of New York.* New York: Women's City Club of New York, 1927. [7]p.
  Unsigned but believed to have been written by ER as chair of the club's Committee on Legislation.

1928

B2 *Mrs. Alfred E. Smith as I Know Her.* New York: Democratic National Committee, [1928]. 8p.
  She is a charming woman who has been effective as the wife of the Gov. of N.Y. She will be equally effective as the nation's First Lady.

B3 *Our Legislative Platform for 1928.* New York: Women's City Club of New York, 1928. [5]p.
  Why the club is supporting some current state legislation. Unsigned but believed to have been written by ER as chair of the club's Committee on Legislation.

1932

B4 *Hunting Big Game in the Eighties: The Letters of Elliott Roosevelt, Sportsman.* Ed. Eleanor Roosevelt. New York: Scribner's, 1932. x + 182p.
  Through his letters she points to the value of her father's brief life and illustrates the lasting impact which he had on her. Foreword, preface, and explanatory notes by ER.

B4a *Hunting Big Game in the Eighties: The Letters of Elliott Roosevelt, Sportsman.* Ed. Eleanor Roosevelt. New York: Scribner's, 1933. x + 182p.

B5 *When You Group Up to Vote.* Boston: Houghton Mifflin; Cambridge: Riverside, 1932. 64p.

1933

B6   *It's Up to the Women.* New York: Stokes, 1933. x + 263p.
   Compilation of articles and speeches emphasizing the role of women in time of depression. They provide advice to the homemaker and encouragement for women to participate in the political process. Excludes sources and dates.

1935

B7   *A Trip to Washington with Bobby and Betty.* New York: Dodge, 1935. 91p.
   Work of fiction for younger readers telling the story of two children who tour Washington and have lunch with the President.

1937

B8   *This Is My Story.* New York: Harper, 1937. x + 365p.
   Autobiographical account through the 1924 presidential election.

B8a   *This Is My Story.* Philadelphia: Curtis, 1937. 8p.
   Preview of the first installment of *This Is My Story* published in the Apr. 1937 issue of the *Ladies' Home Journal.*

B8b   *The Lady of the White House.* London: Hutchinson, 1938. 287p. Index.
   British edition of *This Is My Story.*

B8c   *This Is My Story.* New York: Garden City, 1939. viii + 365p.

B8d   *The Lady of the White House.* London: Hutchinson, 1942. 183p. Index.

B8e   *This Is My Story.* New York: Bantam, 1950. 278p.

B8f   *The Lady of the White House.* Corgi Books, 846. London: Transworld, 1951. 278p.

B8g   *This Is My Story.* Dolphin Books, C264. Garden City: Dolphin-Doubleday, 1961. 270p.

1938

B9   *My Days.* New York: Dodge, 1938. 254p.
   Selected "My Day" columns from the period Jan. 1936-May 1938.

B10   *This Troubled World.* New York: Kinsey, 1938. 47p.
   Relates peace to individual citizens and their desire for it.

1940

B11   *Christmas: A Story.* New York: Knopf, 1940. 42p.
   A story for children about a Dutch girl's first Christmas Eve without her father. Published originally as "Christmas 1940: A Short Story." *Liberty* (28 Dec. 1940): 10-13.

B11a *Christmas 1940*. New York: St. Martin's, 1986. 61p.
With a foreword by Elliott Roosevelt.

B12 *The Moral Basis of Democracy*. New York: Howell, Soskin, 1940. 82p.
An attempt to make others think about what democracy means to them.

B12a *The Moral Basis of Democracy*. Cleveland: Cleveland Chapter, American Red Cross, 1941. 68p.
"Transcribed and presented by Belle Olenberg."

B12b *The Moral Basis of Democracy*. London: Hodder and Stoughton, 1941. 62p.

1942

B13 *This Is America*. By Eleanor Roosevelt and Frances Cooke Macgregor. New York: Putnam's, 1942. [191]p.
The people and freedoms of America are celebrated through words and photographs. In the introduction ER celebrates the accomplishments of the nation and calls for a commitment to build a future which will provide equal opportunity for all.

1946

B14 *If You Ask Me*. New York: Appleton-Century, 1946. 156p.
Answers to questions from prominent citizens about national affairs, social concerns, and personal matters.

B14a *If You Ask Me*. London: Hutchinson, 1948. 136p.

1948

B15 *Fifty Years of Community Service*. Society for Ethical Culture, 1948. 7p.
Copy not examined.

1949

B16 *Franklin D. Roosevelt and Hyde Park: Personal Recollections of Eleanor Roosevelt*. Washington: GPO, 1949. 18p.
ER's account of life at Hyde Park. Consists primarily of edited recollections which FDR wrote in 1945.

B16a *Franklin D. Roosevelt and Hyde Park: Personal Recollections of Eleanor Roosevelt*. Pamphlets in American History. Group 1. Biography, B1932. Glen Rock: Microfilming Corp. of America, 1978. 1 microfiche.

B16b *Franklin D. Roosevelt and Hyde Park: Personal Recollections of Eleanor Roosevelt*. Washington: GPO, 1980. 18p.

B17 *This I Remember*. New York: Harper, 1949. x + 387p. Index.
Autobiographical account for the period 1921 through 1945.

B17a   *This I Remember.* New York: Bantam, 1950. 278p. Index.

B17b   *This I Remember.* London: Hutchinson, 1950. 304p. Index.

B17c   *This I Remember.* Dolphin Books, C263. Garden City: Dolphin-Doubleday, 1961. Index. 305p.

B17d   *This I Remember.* Westport: Greenwood, 1975. x + 387p. Index.

1950

B18   *Partners: The United Nations and Youth.* By Eleanor Roosevelt and Helen Ferris. Garden City: Doubleday, 1950. 206p. Index. Bibliography.
   As illustrated by letters, field reports, and published accounts youth throughout the world are partners in the activities of the UN and its related organizations. For younger readers.

B18a   *Partners: The United Nations and Youth.* By Eleanor Roosevelt with Helen Ferris. Garden City: Junior Literary Guild-Doubleday, [1951?] 206p.

1953

B19   *India and the Awakening East.* New York: Harper, 1953. xvi + 237p. Index.
   Anecdotes and reports of conversations make this account of her 1952 trip to India and the East personal and informative. In the conclusion she sees the need for India to be the leader in the East while recognizing that the future of China is the most critical concern.

B19a   *India and the Awakening East.* London: Hutchinson, 1954. 168p.

B20   *UN: Today and Tomorrow.* By Eleanor Roosevelt with William De Witt. New York: Harper, 1953. xiv + 236p.
   Popular introduction to the UN including questions and answers about the organization and its charter and about the Universal Declaration of Human Rights.

1954

B21   *It Seems to Me.* New York: Norton, 1954. 188p.
   Arranged according to 24 topics about world affairs and social concerns, the book includes her responses to questions which she had originally answered in her column "If You Ask Me" between 1946 and 1951.

B21a   *It Seems to Me.* Ed. with notes by Yasuo Deguchi. Kenkyusha's Spoken English Readers. Senior Series, 13. Tokyo: Kenkyusha, 1964. iv + 94p.
   Preface and notes in Japanese.

B22   *Ladies of Courage.* By Eleanor Roosevelt and Lorena A. Hickok. New York: Putnam's, 1954. 312p. Index.
   The achievements of women in public office.

1955

B23 *United Nations: What You Should Know about It*. By Jean S. Picker. Ed. Eleanor Roosevelt. New London: Croft, 1955. [54]p.

Simple guide to how the UN works. Contains untitled concluding statement by ER emphasizing that the actions of UN member states are more important than the organization itself. 1957, 1958, 1959, 1961, and 1971 eds. are adapted from the original 1955 ed.

1958

B24 *On My Own*. New York: Harper, 1958. xii + 241p. Index.

The account of her activities from 1945 until 1958.

B24a *On My Own*. London: Hutchinson, 1959. 287p. Index.

B24b *On My Own: The Years since the White House*. New York: Dell, 1959. 288p. Index.

1960

B25 *Growing Toward Peace*. By Regina Tor and Eleanor Roosevelt. New York: Random House, 1960. 83p. Index. Bibliography.

A survey of civilization emphasizing efforts to maintain peace and promote the dignity of man precedes a discussion of the goals of the UN and its related organizations. For younger readers.

B25a *Growing Toward Peace*. Delhi: Rajkamal Prakashan, 1962.

B26 *You Learn by Living*. New York: Harper, 1960. xii + 211p. Index.

Enthusiasm for life and its experiences is necessary if one is to face responsibility, use time wisely, adjust to change, and avoid fears. Draws on experiences from her own life. Elinore Denniston was collaborating author.

B26a *You Learn by Living*. London: Hutchinson, 1961. 190p.

B26b *You Learn by Living*. Dolphin Book, C407. Garden City: Dolphin-Doubleday, 1963. xii + 145p.

B26c *You Learn by Living*. Philadelphia: Westminster, 1983. xii + 211p. Index.

With a new introduction by Mildred McAfee Horton.

1961

B27 *The Autobiography of Eleanor Roosevelt*. New York: Harper, 1961. xix + 454p. Index.

Revised and abbreviated versions of *This Is My Story*, *This I Remember*, and *On My Own* to which has been added the "Search for Understanding" covering her activities for 1958 through 1960.

B27a *The Autobiography of Eleanor Roosevelt*. London: Hutchinson, 1962. 368p.

B27b *The Autobiography of Eleanor Roosevelt.* Barnes & Noble Book ed. New York: Harper, 1978. 454p. Index.

B27c *The Autobiography of Eleanor Roosevelt.* Boston, Hall, 1984. xxv + 454p. Index.
    With a new introduction by her grandson John Boettiger.

B27d *The Autobiography of Eleanor Roosevelt.* New York: Da Capo, 1992. xix + 454p. Index.
    An exact reissue of the 1961 Harper ed.

B28 *Your Teens and Mine.* By Eleanor Roosevelt with Helen Ferris. Garden City: Doubleday, 1961. 189p.
    Utilizing material from *This Is My Story*, *This I Remember*, *On My Own*, and *You Learn by Living* this work deals with some of ER's greatest concerns: gaining self-confidence, the importance of family life, the value of books, and the obligations of citizenship.

B28a *Your Teens and Mine.* Kingswood, Surrey: World's Work, 1963. 215p.

B28b *Your Teens and Mine.* Kingswood, Surrey: World's Work, 1966. 216p.

1962

B29 *Eleanor Roosevelt's Book of Common Sense Etiquette.* By Eleanor Roosevelt with the assistance of Robert O. Ballou. New York: Macmillan, 1962. xi + 591p. Index. Bibliography.
    Morality, law, and kindness dictate etiquette.   A comprehensive guide to contemporary etiquette.

B30 *The Wisdom of Eleanor Roosevelt.* New York: McCall, 1962. 112p.
    Selections from her column "If You Ask Me" from the period 1954 through 1962.

1963

B31 *Eleanor Roosevelt's Christmas Book.* New York: Dodd, Mead, 1963. xi + 338p.
    Contains her "Christmas at Hyde Park," "Christmas in the White House," and "Christmas: A Story" plus some of her favorite writings about Christmas.

B32 *Tomorrow Is Now.* New York: Harper, 1963. xvii + 139p.
    We make our history today. Urges long-range world planning and a strengthened role for the UN.

B32a *Tomorrow Is Now.* London: Hutchinson, 1964. 144p.

B32b *Tomorrow Is Now.* New York: Perennial-Harper, 1964. xviii + 141p.

1982

B33 *Love, Eleanor: Eleanor Roosevelt and Her Friends.* Ed. Joseph P. Lash. Garden City: Doubleday, 1982. xvi + 534p. Index.

The first of two collections of ER's personal letters. This volume covers the period through 1943 and includes an introduction and commentary by Lash. Sometimes referred to as *Eleanor Roosevelt and Her Friends*. Vol. 1. Prior to publication title announced as *Eleanor, Letters of Love: Her Life as Seen Through Her Letters, 1932-1943*. Continued by *A World of Love*. A lengthy annotation is available in Joyce D. Goodfriend, *The Published Diaries and Letters of American Women*, p. 175 (Boston: Hall, 1987).

B34   *Mother & Daughter: The Letters of Eleanor and Anna Roosevelt*. Ed. Bernard Asbell. New York: Coward, McCann & Geoghegan, 1982. 366p. Index.
The letters which they exchanged between 1916 and 1962 with background material by the editor. Intended by Asbell as a possible substitute for the memoir which Anna never wrote. Annotation in Joyce D. Goodfriend, *The Published Diaries and Letters of American Women*, pp. 184-85 (Boston: Hall, 1987).

B34a   *Mother & Daughter: The Letters of Eleanor and Anna Roosevelt*. Ed. Bernard Asbell. New York: Fromm, 1988. 366p. Index.

1984

B35   *A World of Love: Eleanor Roosevelt and Her Friends, 1943-1962*. Ed. Joseph P. Lash. Garden City: Doubleday, 1984. xxxi + 610p. Index.
A collection of her personal letters with an introduction and commentary by Lash. Sometimes referred to as *Eleanor Roosevelt and Her Friends*. Vol. 2. Continues *Love, Eleanor*. A lengthy annotation is in Joyce D. Goodfriend, *The Published Diaries and Letters of American Women*, pp. 199-200 (Boston: Hall, 1987).

1989-1991

B36   *Eleanor Roosevelt's My Day*. 3 vols. New York: Pharos, 1989-1991. Index.
A sampling of her columns are presented in chronological order. The editors' commentary provides historical perspective. [Vol. 1] ed. by Rochelle Chadakoff. Vols. 2-3 ed. by David Emblidge. Name on v. 3 printed incorrectly as "Elmblidge."

BOOK SECTIONS AND PERIODICAL ARTICLES

1921

B37   "Common Sense Versus Party Regularity." *News Bulletin* (League of Women Voters of New York State) (16 Sept. 1921).
Today voters are more concerned with the qualifications of candidates than with party affiliation. Copy not examined. Cited in Hilda R. Watrous, *In League with Eleanor*, p. 3 (New York: Foundation for Citizen Education, League of Women Voters of New York State, 1984).

1922

B38   "The Fall Election." *L.W.V. Weekly News* (New York League of Women Voters) (1922).

Copy not examined. Cited in Hilda R. Watrous, *In League with Eleanor*, p. 6 (New York: Foundation for Citizen Education, League of Women Voters of New York State, 1984).

B39   "Organizing County Women for a Political Party." *L.W.V. Weekly News* (New York League of Women Voters) (1922).
Copy not examined. Cited in Hilda R. Watrous, *In League with Eleanor*, p. 6 (New York: Foundation for Citizen Education, League of Women Voters of New York State, 1984).

1923

B40   "American Peace Award." *Ladies' Home Journal* 40 (Oct. 1923): 54.
Edward Bok established the prize to solicit possible plans on how the U.S. should cooperate with the rest of the world in establishing a lasting peace.

B41   *L.W.V. Weekly News* (New York League of Women Voters) (12 Oct. 1923).
Copy not examined. Untitled article cited in Hilda R. Watrous, *In League with Eleanor*, p. 12 (New York: Foundation for Citizen Education, League of Women Voters of New York State, 1984).

B42   "Why I Am a Democrat." *Junior League Bulletin* 10 (Nov. 1923): 18-19.
It is important to decide which of the political parties is more concerned with human welfare. Reviews the achievements of the Democratic Party in N.Y. where numerous social welfare reforms have been introduced.

B42a   "I Am a Democrat." *Women's Democratic Campaign Manual, 1924.* Washington: Democratic Party, National Committee 1924-1928, 1924. 85.
Issued with statements by others under the common title "Why I Am a Democrat."

B42b "Why I Am a Democrat." *Junior League Magazine* 26 (Sept. 1939): 29, 60.

1924

B43   "How to Interest Women in Voting." *Women's Democratic Campaign Manual, 1924.* Washington: Democratic Party, National Committee 1924-1928, 1924. 102-3.
There is a need to interest women in voting and government. Identifies goals which Democratic women should strive for.

B44   "M'Adoo [sic] Mobilizes His Forces Here." *New York Times* 8 June 1924: 5.
Includes a lengthy excerpt from an "article" by ER. We need a leader who can explain to the people just what are the country's problems and needs. Al Smith has done that in N.Y.

B45   "Statement of Policy Committee." *The Winning Plan Selected by the Jury of the American Peace Award*. New York: n.p., 1924. 4-6.
Highlights the selected plan and outlines the procedures which were followed in the voting. Signed by ER and others.

B46 "What Has Politics Gained by the Women's Vote?" *National Democratic Magazine* 1 (Apr. 1924): 21.
Women are new to politics, and they have to learn the importance of government.

1925

B47 "New York Rebuilt." *Women's City Club Bulletin* (June 1925): 5-6.
City officials will want the help which the club's City Planning Dept. of the Committee on Transit can provide.

B48 *Women's Democratic News*. Ed. Eleanor Roosevelt.
ER served as editor May 1925-Nov. 1928. Editorials which appeared during that period are unsigned. In a farewell statement she expresses her regrets in giving up the editorship (Nov. 1928, p. 6). Two of her biographers believe that ER wrote the editorials which appeared during her editorship. See Joseph P. Lash, *Eleanor and Franklin*, pp. 308 and Blanche Wiesen Cook, *Eleanor Roosevelt, 1884-1933*, pp. 382, 384. Cook claims that ER continued to control the publication's content and write the editorials after her name no longer appeared on the publication. The collaboration of Louis Howe is acknowledged by Lash.
Manuscript copies of some of the editorials are in the ER Papers, Box 3025, FDRL.

1926

B49 "The Democratic Platform." *Women's City Club of New York* (Oct. 1926): 14-15.
Unlike the Republicans, Democrats in N.Y. are specific about the issues of the work week for women and minors, prohibition, and aid to rural schools. One of three articles issued under the common title "What Every Voter Should Know" (pp. 14-16).

1927

B50 "As a Practical Idealist." *North American Review* 224 (Nov. 1927): 472-75.
ER's contribution is the second of a two-part article issued as "Why Democrats Favor Smith." After warning against an over emphasis on materialistic concerns she criticizes the Wilson, Harding, and Coolidge administrations and portrays Al Smith as a leader who trained for the presidency as Gov. of N.Y.

B51 *Congressional Record* (6 Jan. 1927): 1154.
ER wrote a letter in support of legislation for aid to health care for mothers and infants. Text of 5 Jan. letter on behalf of the Women's Activities [Division] of the Democratic State Committee.
She continued to send letters and telegrams to members of Congress about matters which interested her. See annual indexes to the *Congressional Record* for other communications of this type.

B52 *L.W.V. Weekly News* (New York League of Women Voters) (Dec. 1927).
Women should be nominated for state office, and other women should be allowed to select the nominees. Copy not examined. Annotation based on citation in Hilda

R. Watrous, *In League with Eleanor*, pp. 19-20 (New York: Foundation for Citizen Education, League of Women Voters of New York State, 1984).

B53   "On Albany Hill." *Quarterly* (Women's City Club of New York) (June 1927): 40-42.
The annual report of the club's Committee on Legislation describes the year as one "of great achievement."   Believed to have been written by ER as chair of the committee.

B54   "What I Want Most Out of Life." *Success Magazine* 11 (May 1927): 16-17, 70.
To be happy by being able to do something useful. "As told to Catharine Brody."

B55   "What Is Being Done in Albany." *Quarterly* (Women's City Club of New York) (Mar. 1927): 10-11.
About pending state legislation. Believed to have been written by ER as chair of the club's Committee on Legislation.

1928

B56   "Committee on Legislation." *Quarterly* (Women's City Club of New York) (June 1928): 28-29.
Annual report of the club's Committee on Legislation.

B57   "Governor Smith." *Junior League Magazine* 15 (Nov. 1928): 23, 110.
After comparing Herbert Hoover and Al Smith she supports Smith's presidential campaign because of his emphasis on the "human side of government."

B58   "Governor Smith and Our Foreign Policy." *Woman's Journal* n.s. 13 (Oct. 1928): 21.
Unlike Herbert Hoover, Al Smith has the vision to explore ways to improve the image of the U.S. and to encourage citizens to take an interest in international problems as a step toward peace. Article written in response to an invitation from the Democratic National Committee.

B59   "Jeffersonian Principles the Issue in 1928." *Current History* 28 (June 1928): 354-57.
One of 11 articles issued as "The Presidential Campaign of 1928." After discussing the effect of eight years of Republican control of domestic and foreign affairs she concludes that the Republican Party is allied with special interest groups. Calls for a return to government which has more concern for people.

B60   "News of Democrats and Their Activities." *Bulletin* (Women's National Democratic Club) 3 (Dec. 1928): 18-19.
In this article about ER's activities as chair of the Women's Activities and Advisory Committee is her report of activities during the 1928 campaign.

B61   "Women Must Learn to Play the Game as Men Do." *Red Book Magazine* 50 (Apr. 1928): 78-79, 141-42.
Women must learn more about history and government, devote time to politics, and be willing to sacrifice if they wish to succeed in politics.

B61a "Mrs. F.D. Roosevelt for Women Bosses." *New York Times* 10 Mar. 1928: 3.
Extensive excerpts.

B62 "The Women's City Club at Albany." *Quarterly* (Women's City Club of New York) (Mar. 1928): 16-17.
Report of the club's Committee on Legislation.

1929

B63 "Education for Girls." *Independent Education* 3 (Dec. 1929): 7-8.
Modern conveniences give women more time to pursue activities other than caring for home and children. The type of education which young women receive must change so that they are prepared to understand the forces of history, work to ensure that the world is not ruled by physical force, and seek solutions to economic and social problems.

1930

B64 "Building Character." *Childhood and Character* 7 (May 1930): 6-7.
Parents and teachers are important in the development of a child's character and the elimination of fear from the child's life.

B65 "Good Citizenship: The Purpose of Education." *Pictorial Review* 31 (Apr. 1930): 4, 94, 97.
Students should receive the preparation necessary to participate in politics.

B66 "The Ideal Education." *Woman's Journal* n.s. 15 (Oct. 1930): 8-10, 36.
Considers vision, curiosity, and a joy in reading as attributes of a ideal education and emphasizes role of the home in the educational process.

B67 Introduction. *Margaret Fuller.* By Margaret Bell. New York: Boni, 1930. 13-14.
Fuller's value was not in what she wrote but in the life which she led.

B68 "Mrs. Franklin D. Roosevelt Looks at this Modern Housekeeping." *Modern Priscilla* 44 (Apr. 1930): 13, 64.
Today's homemakers have more conveniences, but planning and organization are still essential for maintaining a home which provides the proper atmosphere for children.

B69 "Servants." *Forum* 83 (Jan. 1930): 24-28.
What is needed is a school for training domestic workers, proper training for the mistress of the house, and the recognition that servants should be treated as human beings whose labor is respected.

B70 "A Summer Trip Abroad." *Women's Democratic News* 5 (April 1930): 2, 12, 16; 6 (May 1930): 6, 13; 6 (June 1930): 16; 6 (Aug. 1930): 6, 16; 6 (Oct. 1930): 14, 24; 6 (Dec. 1930): 16; 6 (Feb. 1931): 14; 6 (Apr. 1931): 7, 16; 7 (May 1931): 16; 7 (July 1931): 2.
Account of her Summer 1929 trip to England and Europe with Nancy Cook, Marion Dickerman, and sons Franklin and John. Title varies. Aug., Oct., and Dec.

1930; May and July 1931: "A Democrat Abroad." Feb. 1931: "My Trip Abroad." Apr. 1931: "Travels of a Democrat."

B71   "Women in Politics." *Women's City Club of New York Quarterly* (Jan. 1930): 5-7.

It is sensible for women to enter politics as officers of political party organizations and members of groups interested in political questions, but they must feel that they have equal opportunity to establish policy and direction. Women should master the issues and try to change the belief that the only way to settle international disputes is through war.

1931

B72   "Building Character: An Editorial." *Parents' Magazine* 6 (June 1931): 17.

Children should learn self-restraint and how to entertain themselves, work, and overcome problems.

B73   "Let Every Child Have His Own Library." *Wings* (Literary Guild of America) 5 (Jan. 1931): 16-17.

Having books of one's own can make a strong impression on a child. Every child should be encouraged to start a library.

B74   "Mrs. Franklin D. Roosevelt Tells the Story in a Nutshell: A Word to the Woman in the Home and to the Woman in Business by the First Lady of New York." *Baltimore and Ohio Magazine* 19 (May 1931): 21.

Brief statement about the importance of the roles which women play in the home and in business.

B75   "Ten Rules for Success in Marriage." *Pictorial Review* 33 (Dec. 1931): 4, 36, 44.

The ten rules call for maturity of both husband and wife. It is important to bring up children in a way which will give them the maturity needed for marriage.

B76   "This Question of Jobs." *Junior League Magazine* 17 (Jan. 1931): 14.

Girls from Junior League families should strive for positions which create "work for others" instead of being satisfied with those types of jobs which are needed by girls who have had fewer advantages and must support themselves. It would be wonderful if all Junior League girls could accept their obligation to serve others through work or volunteer activities.

1932

B77   Introduction. *Alice's Adventures in Wonderland, Through the Looking-Glass, and The Hunting of the Shark.* Jacket Library. By Lewis Carroll. Washington: National Home Library Foundation, 1932. [2].

Children should enjoy the nonsense and then as adults better understand the meaning of it.

B77a "Mrs. Roosevelt Lauds 'Alice in Wonderland.'" *New York Times* 25 July 1932: 17.

Reprints her introduction.

B78   *Babies-Just Babies*. Ed. Eleanor Roosevelt. 1-2 (Oct. 1932-June 1933). No issue published for Mar. 1933.

B79   "Be Curious-and Educated!" *Liberty* 9 (2 July 1932): 30-31.
To be educated and lead a satisfying life, one must be curious.

B80   "Christmas." *New York American* 24 Dec. 1932.
Christmas traditions in the Roosevelt family. From photocopy at FDRL. Page no. lacking.

B80a Moses, Belle. *Franklin Delano Roosevelt: The Minute Man of '33*. New York: Appleton-Century, 1933. ix + 201p.
Most of her article from the *New York American* is reprinted (pp. 176-81).

B81   "Grandmothers Can Still Be Young." *Liberty* 9 (20 Feb 1932): 38-40.
Grandmothers can stay youthful by trying to keep mind and body young.

B81a "Grandmothers Can Still Be Young." *Life in the Liberty Years: A Nostalgic Look at the '20s, '30s, and '40s*. Selected by Shifra Stein. Kansas City: Hallmark, 1973. 44-47.
Abridged ed.

B82   "Grow Old Gracefully." *Reader's Digest* 21 (Sept. 1932): recto and verso of back cover.
Youth have good ideas and being around them can refresh the older person.

B83   "How to Choose a Candidate." *Liberty* 9 (5 Nov. 1932): 16-17.
Consider the candidate's character. How honest is he? Does he have what it takes to lead others in support of his program? At different times in our history we have needed different types of leaders. What kind do we need now? As a woman you can play an important role in the political process by involving yourself in the selection of local party leaders, the people who have the real political power.

B84   Introduction. *John Martin's Book: Tell Me a Story*. Jacket Library, 1932.
Copy not examined.

B85   "Make Them Believe in You: An Editorial." *Babies-Just Babies* 1 (Nov. 1932): 3.
Parents should establish a feeling of trust in children and give reasons for everything demanded of them, although quick discipline without explanation is sometimes required.

B86   "Merry Christmas! An Editorial." *Babies-Just Babies* 1 (Dec. 1932): 3.
Describes Christmas in her home as an example of the traditions of the holiday.

B87   "Mrs. Roosevelt Finds Politics Give Chance to Serve Humanity." *New York Times* 4 Dec. 1932, sect. 2: 1, 4.
Young people should become interested in politics either as well-informed citizens or as active participants in political parties. Enter the political arena to help others, not to seek fortune or fame. Written for the North American Newspaper Alliance. Title and date may vary according to the paper in which it was published.

B88 [Newspaper articles]. King Features, North American Newspaper Alliance, McNaught Syndicate, and Columbia Syndicate.

She wrote a series of syndicated articles beginning in Dec. 1932 and continuing through 1935. Articles were published on different dates and issued with various titles according to the newspapers in which they appeared.

Included in this bibliography are "Mrs. Roosevelt Finds Politics Give Chance to Serve Humanity" (1932), "Depicts Home Life in the White House" (1933), and "White House to Mrs. Roosevelt" (1933) all written for the North American Newspaper Alliance.

The ER Papers, FDRL document probable dates for the articles. King Features Syndicate, Dec. 1932-Feb. 1933 (Boxes 3023-24); North American Newspaper Alliance, Apr. 1933-Sept. 1933 (Box 3026); McNaught Syndicate, Nov.? 1933-May? 1934 (Box 3028); and Columbia Syndicate, Nov.? 1934-Apr.? 1935 (Box 3028).

In Box 3023 there are typescript copies of eight articles which indicate that they were written for King Features Syndicate. Some of the typescripts are numbered: 2, 3, VI, VII (twice), and VIII.

Possible publication dates for articles for the McNaught Syndicate include 3 Dec. 1933 (a visit to W.Va.), 10 Dec. (about wives of miners), 13 Jan. 1934 (on working women), 20 Jan. 1934 (on crime), 2 Feb. 1934 (on parks and recreation), and 19 Mar. 1934 (on prisons).

Columbia Syndicate asked United Features to take over the series, and it became "My Day."

B89 "Preparing the Child for Citizenship." *New York Times* 24 Apr. 1932, sect. 3: 7.

By their example parents teach the child the responsibilities of citizenship. In the home children learn the standards which they will uphold for the rest of their lives and the relationship which they will have with government. One of a series of articles about the principles put forth by the White House Conference on Child Health and Protection.

B90 "Presenting 'Babies-Just Babies.'" *Babies-Just Babies* 1 (Oct. 1932): 5-6.

Photographs, true stories, and detailed instructions on child rearing are planned for this new magazine.

B91 "Today's Girl and Tomorrow's Job." *Woman's Home Companion* 59 (June 1932): 11-12.

Education should prepare the girl for the roles which she will fill: wife, mother, citizen, political participant. Includes a description of her own childhood and education. Signed "Anna Roosevelt" but written by ER.

B92 "What Are the Movies Doing to Us?" *Modern Screen* 4 (Nov. 1932): 26-27, 102.

Movies can be educational if those who make them realize the power which they have to inform and teach.

B93 "What Religion Means to Me." *Forum* 88 (Dec. 1932): 322-24.

After describing the role of religion in her childhood and youth she urges the need for a belief in a greater power during troubled times such as these.

B94   "What Ten Million Women Want." *Home Magazine* 5 (Mar. 1932): 19-21, 86.
Today's women do not want a woman as President, but they do want representation, fair legislation, better living conditions, and a peaceful world. To achieve this, women must be active in their communities.

B95   "Wives of Great Men." *Liberty* 9 (1 Oct. 1932): 12-16.
Recalls how as a young adult she knew nothing about politics. Since both husband and wife cannot have political careers, the wife must keep her political views to herself.

B96   "Women's Political Responsibility." *Democratic Bulletin* 7 (Jan. 1932): 12.
To help select leaders and shape policies women should join men in working at the various levels of the political party organization.

1933

B97   "The Camp for Unemployed Women: A Novel American Experiment Under the Relief Administration." *World Today: Encyclopaedia Britannica* 1 (Oct. 1933): 1.
About Camp Tera, named for the State Temporary Relief Admin. in N.Y., and the type of life the young women lead there.

B98   "A Child Belongs in the Country: An Editorial." *Babies-Just Babies* 1 (Apr. 1933): 3.
All the lessons of life can be learned from nature.

B99   "Consider the Babies: An Editorial." *Babies-Just Babies* 2 (May 1933): 3.
The importance of helping children and families in need.

B100   "Depicts Home Life in the White House." *New York Times* 30 Apr. 1933, sect. 4: 7.
FDR's day starts with a succession of meetings while he is still in bed. An article syndicated by the North American Newspaper Alliance. Date and title can vary.

B101   "A Happy New Year: An Editorial." *Babies-Just Babies* 1 (Jan. 1933): 3.
Resolve to make our homes better places to bring up children.

B102   "Has Life Been Too Easy for Us?" *Liberty* 10 (4 Feb. 1933): 4-7.
Modern conveniences can make life too easy. Our children must be taught the role which physical hardship and adversity play in building character. So that the quality of life can be improved for all they must learn the value of sacrificing.

B103   "In Appreciation of Anne Alive!" [Foreword] *Anne Alive! A Year in the Life of a Girl of New York State.* By Margaret Doane Fayerweather. New York: Junior Literary Guild & McBridge. 1933. vii-ix.
Encourages the young to become interested in government.

B104   "Lives of Great Men: An Editorial." *Babies-Just Babies* 1 (Feb. 1933): 3.
By studying the lives of great men and the influence of their parents today's parents and their children can realize how they can handle difficult situations.

B105 "Mobilization for Human Needs." *Democratic Digest* 8 (Nov. 1933): 3.
Since government cannot do it alone, contributions must be made to charities which work to improve human welfare.

B106 "Mrs. Roosevelt Replies to the Letter of an Unknown Woman." *McCall's* 60 (Mar. 1933): 4.
In these difficult times all that some people have to give others is friendship and advice.

B107 "Mrs. Roosevelt Urges Women to Have Courage of Convictions and to Stand on Own Feet." *Clubwoman GFWC (General Federation of Womens's Clubs)* 13 (Feb. 1933): 10.
Women should make themselves aware of the nation's problems and prepare for holding public office. Issued with an article by FDR under the common title "Mr. and Mrs. Roosevelt on Citizenship."

B107a "Mrs. Roosevelt Says Women Must Fit Selves for Office." *New York Times* 1 Feb. 1933: 14.
Excerpts.

B108 "The State's Responsibility for Fair Working Conditions." *Scribner's Magazine* 93 (Mar. 1933): 140.
Appeals for reduced workdays to allow more workers to be employed and for better protection of the health of all of those who work. One of two articles issued under the common title "Protect the Worker."

B109 "What I Hope to Leave Behind." *Pictorial Review* 34 (Apr. 1933): 4, 45.
A better world in which youth will receive joy from living and be interested in giving of themselves.

B110 "When Nature Smiles: An Editorial." *Babies-Just Babies* 2 (June 1933): 3.
Easter is the time to consider what we can give to children which is of value to their health and education. Asks readers to understand that the pressure of her duties as First Lady may force her to give up the editorship of the magazine. Publication ceased with this issue.

B111 "White House to Mrs. Roosevelt." *New York Times* 2 Apr. 1933, sect. 2: 1-2.
The First Lady faces the same problem as other homemakers: how to live within a household budget. Also describes how rooms in the living quarters of the White House are being used by the Roosevelts. Syndicated by the North American Newspaper Alliance. Title and date can vary.

1934

B112 "Adventures with Early American Furniture." *House & Garden* 65 (Feb. 1934): 21-23.
The founding and operation of the Val-Kill furniture manufactory.

B113 "Appreciations." *Miss Wylie of Vassar.* Ed. Elisabeth Woodbridge Morris. New Haven: Yale Univ. Pr. for the Laura J. Wylie Memorial Associates. 149-55.

ER and others pay tribute to the life and work of Laura Wylie. ER's contribution is on pp. 154-55.

B114 "Exposition Farms: A New Idea in Experimental Farming." *Consumers' Guide* 1 (13 Aug. 1934): 3-4.
Owners of rural estates should allow their land to be used as experimental farms by state agricultural colleges.

B115 Foreword. *Getting Acquainted with Your Children*. By James W. Howard. New York: Leisure League of America, 1934. 5-6.
Parents who read this book will profit from its advice. There may be no better use of leisure time than to spend it with one's children.

B116 "Learning to Teach." *Virginia Teacher* 15 (May 1934): 100-101.
Excerpts column "Mrs. Roosevelt's Page" from the *Woman's Home Companion*.

B116a "Learning to Teach." *Circular* (Educational Research Service, National Education Association) 3 (Apr. 1934): 8-9.
Excerpts.

B117 "Mrs. Franklin D. Roosevelt." *Guidebook for the Women's Crusade*. New York: National Women's Committee of the 1934 Mobilization for Human Needs, n.d. 8.
In the last campaign women were successful in convincing their neighbors that help must be provided at the local level. The federal government cannot do it all. Available in ER Pamphlet Collection, FDRL.

B117a "Mrs. Roosevelt Asks Aid in Social Work" *New York Times* 12 Sept. 1934: 25.
Reprints text.

B118 "On Education." *School Life* 19 (Jan. 1934): 102-3.
Brief statements by ER, FDR, and cabinet members. Her statement is an unidentified quotation stressing the importance of education and a need for all citizens to be concerned about the quality of the educational system (p. 102).

B119 "The Power of Knowledge." *Circular* (Educational Research Service, National Education Association) 3 (Apr. 1934): 5.
Excerpts column "Mrs. Roosevelt's Page" from the *Woman's Home Companion*.

B120 "Subsistence Farmsteads." *Forum* 91 (Apr. 1934): 199-201.
If the Arthurdale project is successful, it will be the model for other subsistence farming projects and will help solve the problems of unemployment and poor urban living conditions.

B121 "The Women Go After the Facts about Milk Consumption." *Consumers' Guide* 1 (28 May 1934): 3-5.
Women should make the excessive profit made by milk distributors and the resulting under-consumption of milk by children a special concern (p. 3). This separate section by ER begins the article.

1935

B122 "Because the War Idea Is Obsolete." *Why Wars Must Cease.* Ed. Rose Young. New York: Macmillan, 1935. 20-29.
War is an obsolete means of settling disputes. One of 10 essays issued by the National Committee on the Cause and Cure of War.

B123 "Can a Woman Ever Be President of the United States?" *Cosmopolitan* (Oct. 1935): 22-23, 120-21.
A woman will not be elected President until women gain more political experience and accept the challenges and pressures which men have been more inclined to accept.

B124 "Children." *Hearst's International-Cosmopolitan* (Jan. 1935): 24-27.
ER and others discuss changes which occurred during the last five years. Depressed economic conditions have affected children, and those most affected will present medical and social problems for the nation. Issued with statements by others under the common title "Five Years: What Have They Done to Us?"

B125 "Facing the Problems of Youth." *National Parent-Teacher* 29 (Feb. 1935): 30.
Older persons must learn of the problems of youth and then help the young to face the realities of the world in which they will have to live.

B125a "Facing the Problems of Youth." *Journal of Social Hygiene* 21 (Oct. 1935): 393-94.

B126 "In Defense of Curiosity." *Saturday Evening Post* 208 (24 Aug. 1935): 8-9, 64-66.
Curiosity can open the mind and the heart.

B126a "Curiosity in Women Urged by First Lady." *New York Times* 20 Aug. 1935: 17.
Excerpts.

B126b "In Defense of Curiosity." *Saturday Evening Post* 248 (July/Aug. 1976): 59.
Reprints her 1935 article.

B127 "Jane Addams." *Democratic Digest* 12 (June 1935): 3.
A brief statement of appreciation for Addams' work and her encouragement of others.

B128 "La Labor de la Union Panamericana." *Boletin de la Union Panamericana* 69 (Feb. 1935): 101-3.
From the *Washington Herald* of 2 Dec. 1934 and various other periodical publications. In Spanish.

B129 "Mountains of Courage." *This Week* (4 Nov. 1935): 7, 25.
ER visits an old woman in the Va. mountains and hears the account of her life.

B130 "Mrs. Roosevelt Believes in Paroles and Providing Jobs for Released Men." *Periscope* (U.S.N.E.P. Lewisburg, Pa.) 3 (Oct. 1935): 5-6.

Parolees need close supervision but also a chance to make a better life for themselves. Reprinted from the *Beacon-Journal* [Akron, Ohio].

B131 "My Day."
Her syndicated column appeared between 30 Dec. 1935 and 27 Sept. 1962. Manuscript copies are in the ER Papers, FDRL. Only the columns for 1957 are indexed. Final columns were entitled "By Eleanor Roosevelt."
On numerous occasions the column was entered into the *Congressional Record*. Consult the annual indexes to the *Congressional Record*. Selected columns are reprinted in *Eleanor Roosevelt's My Day*. 3 vols. (New York: Pharos, 1989-1991).

B132 "We Can't Wait for the Millennium." *Liberty* (1935): 18-20.
While subsistence homesteads such as Arthurdale are expensive, they have already provided significant strides toward a higher standard of living.

B133 "We Need Private Charity." *Current Controversy* (Nov. 1935): 6, 47.
Charities must help the government correct the current social ills. It will cost us less to contribute to charities than to bear the greater public expense of trying to correct the damage which life in a slum can cause.

1936

B134 "About State Institutions." *Caswell News* (Caswell Training School, Kinston, N.C.) 1 (May 1936): 3, 8.
Excerpts "My Day" of 8 May 1936 about District of Columbia Training School for Delinquent Girls (p. 3).

B135 "Are We Overlooking the Pursuit of Happiness?" *Parents' Magazine* 11 (Sept. 1936): 21, 67.
Government must provide old age pensions, unemployment insurance, and equal educational opportunities so that people can pursue happy and meaningful lives.

B136 *Bulletin* (National Committee on Household Employment) 4 (Jan. 1936): page nos. lacking.
The residences provided our public officials should maintain the type of living conditions which should be expected for all domestic help regardless of where they work. Copy not examined. Annotation based on excerpt in Phyllis Palmer, *Domesticity and Dirt: Housewives and Domestic Servants in the Untied States, 1920-1945*, p. 123 (Philadelphia: Temple Univ. Pr., 1989).

B137 "A Fortnight in the White House." *Women's Democratic News* (New York State Section of the Democratic Digest) (Feb. 1936): 3-4.
Official and family events in the White House during 1935/36 holiday season.

B138 "Goal Kicks for '36." *School Life* 21 (Jan. 1936): 105.
Her wish for education in 1936 is that all adults would take an interest in the public schools in their neighborhoods. One of several brief statements.

B139 "The Homesteads Are Making Good." *Democratic Digest* 13 (Mar. 1936): 10.
Praise for the progress which has been made in the establishment of homesteads. Uses Arthurdale as an example.

B140   "A Month at the White House." *Women's Democratic News* (New York State Section of the Democratic Digest) (June 1936): 3.
   Travels, visitors, and engagements for the period Mar.-Apr., 1936.

B141   "Safeguard the Children." *American Child* 18 (Jan. 1936): 1.
   Congress will not use the amendment as the means of telling parents how to raise their children. A response to critics of the Child Labor Amendment.

B142   "The White House and Here and There." *Women's Democratic News* (New York State Section of the Democratic Digest) (July 1936): 3.
   Travels, visitors, and engagements for the period mid-April through May 1936.

1937

B143   "A Busy Month in and out of the White House." *Women's Democratic News* (New York State Section of the Democratic Digest) (July 1937): 2.
   During May she saw the play *The Women* but did not enjoy it. Christened airplane inaugurating hourly service between Washington and New York and talked over new telephone line to China.

B144   "A Christmas Letter." *Post-Intelligencer* [Seattle, Wash.] 25 Nov. 1937.
   The meaning of Christmas and memories of family holiday traditions. A letter to daughter Anna. From photocopy, ER Papers, Box 3037, FDRL. Page no. lacking.

B145   "A Christmas-Spirited Housecleaning." *Reader's Digest* 31 (31 Dec. 1937): verso of front cover, recto and verso of back cover.
   Get the entire family involved in doing "spring" housecleaning before Christmas. Your holiday spirit will benefit from giving unwanted items around your home to the needy.

B145a   "A Christmas Reminder." *Reader's Digest* 32 (Dec. 1938): verso of front cover.
   An abbreviated version of "A Christmas-Spirited Housecleaning."

B146   "Health Care Stressed." *New York Times* 26 Apr. 1937: 11.
   Excerpts an article from *Neighborhood Health* (New York City Dept. of Health) in which she calls for mothers to be better informed about how to maintain their health and the health of their children. Typescript of article in ER Papers, Box 3033, FDRL.

B147   "Highlights of a Busy Month." *Women's Democratic News* (New York Section of the Democratic Digest) (May 1937): 2.
   Lecture trip through the South and Southwest. Easter at the White House.

B148   "Highlights of a Month at the White House." *Women's Democratic News* (New York State Section of the Democratic Digest) (Aug. 1937): 2, 4.
   Visitors, engagements, and trips for June 1937. Includes discussion of Emil Ludwig's visit to research book on FDR.

B149   "Highlights of the Past Few Months." *Women's Democratic News* (New York State Section of the Democratic Digest) (Mar. 1937): 2.
FDR's inauguration and other occasions for entertaining.

B150   "In Praise of Molly Dewson." *Democratic Digest* 14 (Nov. 1937): 15.
Congratulates Dewson for her appointment to the Social Security Board but regrets her departure from the Women's Division of the Democratic National Committee.

B151   "A Month in the White House." *Women's Democratic News* (New York State Section of the Democratic Digest) (Apr. 1937): 2, 4.
Her activities during Feb. 1937.

B152   "Mrs. Roosevelt as 'Copywriter.'" *New York Times* 22 July 1937: 38.
The Sept. 1937 issue of *True Story* will contain an advertisement written by her for the movie *Stella Dallas*. Copy in *True Story* not examined.

B153   "My Month." *Women's Democratic News* (New York State Section of the Democratic Digest) (Dec. 1937): 3.
An account of her activities for Oct. 1937 including numerous references to speeches, none of which are dated.

B154   "A Peaceful Month in the Country." *Women's Democratic News* (New York State Section of the Democratic Digest) (Oct. 1937): 2, 4.
A vacation trip and activities for the months of Aug. and Sept. 1937. Attended a meeting at Vassar about women as jurors.

B155   "Questions." *Progressive Education* 14 (Oct. 1937): 407.
Ten questions about education and its future. Introduces a series of articles by educators who answer the questions.

B156   "Should Wives Work?" *Good Housekeeping* 105 (Dec. 1937): 28-29. 211-12.
The question must be considered carefully by both husband and wife. They must ask themselves what they want out of life.

B156a "Should Wives Work?" *The Good Housekeeping Marriage Book: Twelve Ways to a Happy Marriage*. New York: Prentice-Hall, 1938. 43-53.

B156b "Should Wives Work?" *The Good Housekeeping Marriage Book: Twelve Ways to a Happy Marriage*. Garden City: Garden City, 1946. 43-53.

B156c "Should Wives Work?" *The Good Housekeeping Marriage Book: Twelve Ways to a Happy Marriage*. Garden City: Garden City, 1949. 43-53.

B157   "South by Motor and West by Plane." *Women's Democratic News* (New York State Section of the Democratic Digest) (July 1937): 2.
Visited CCC camps while driving through the South. Flew to San Francisco and saw the newly-completed Golden Gate Bridge.

B158   "This Is My Story." *Ladies' Home Journal* 54 (Apr. 1937): 11-13 48, 50, 53, 55; 54 (May 1937): 14-15, 47-48, 50, 52-53; 54 (June 1937): 14-15, 100, 102-4, 106-7; 54 (July 1937): 22, 76-80; 54 (Aug. 1937): 29, 68-70, 72; 54 (Sept. 1937): 30, 52-53,

55-56; 54 (Oct. 1937): 18, 88, 90, 93, 95; 54 (Nov. 1937): 19, 55-56, 58-60, 63; 54 (Dec. 1937): 29, 49, 51-52, 54-55; 55 (Jan. 1938): 23, 55-57.
   Serialized version of the book.

B159 "A Vacation Month Spent in Guest House at the Val-Kill Cottages." *Women's Democratic News* (New York State Section of the Democratic Digest) (Sept. 1937): 2, 4.
   Activities, travels, and visitors for July 1937. Includes a tribute to the late Sen. Joseph T. Robinson.

B160 Foreword. *The White House: An Informal History of Its Architecture, Interiors and Gardens.* By Ethel Lewis. New York: Dodd, Mead, 1937. v-vi.
   What she likes best about living in the White House is the view of the Washington Monument at night.

1938

B161 "Americans I Admire." *Woman's Day* 1 (Sept. 1938): 4-5, 43-44; 2 (Nov. 1938): 8-9, 42; 2 (Jan. 1939): 8-9, 43; 2 (Mar. 1939): 16, 49.
   Through visits and letters ER came to know and admire Americans who are fighting adversities.

B162 "Cherry Blossom Time in Washington." *Reader's Digest* 32 (Apr. 1938): 57-58.
   Enthusiasm for the cherry trees in Washington and how they came to be planted there.

B162a "Cherry-Blossom Time." *Reader's Digest* 82 (Apr. 1963): 228c.

B163 "A Christmas Letter." *Post-Intelligencer* [Seattle, Wash.] 24 Nov. 1938.
   The joy of giving. A letter to daughter Anna. From photocopy, ER Papers, Box 3037, FDRL. Page no. lacking. A typescript copy of a 1939 letter in the same box.

B164 "Divorce." *Ladies' Home Journal* 55 (Apr. 1938): 16.
   Divorce can be necessary in spite of the numerous examples of couples who stay together through adversity. Stresses the importance of a couple's premarital understanding of what makes a marriage successful.

B165 "Education, a Child's Life." *Progressive Education* 15 (Oct. 1938): 451.
   Education is a constant process, at all times and in all places.

B166 "Henry Street's Pioneer." Rev. of *Lillian Wald: Neighbor and Crusader* by R.L. Duffus. *Survey Graphic* 27 (Dec. 1938): 616.
   This story of Wald's life will inspire old and young to embrace life and fight for what they think is right.

B167 "Lady Bountiful Rolls Up Her Sleeves." *Reader's Digest* 32 (Mar. 1938): 53-55.
   Throughout the country Junior League members are performing community work which benefits local communities and the women who participate.

B168 "Mi Vida Diaria." *Boletin Seccion Servicio Social PRRA* 1 (31 Dic. 1938): 2.
   Copy not examined.

B169   "Mrs. Roosevelt Answers Mr. Wells on 'The Future of the Jews.'" *Liberty* 15 (31 Dec. 1938): 4-5.

Rebuttal of H.G. Wells' article in *Liberty* 15 (24 Nov. 1938): 6-7. ER feels that oppression of the Jews results from the fear that they are superior. While Jews may be to blame in part, it is others who must rid themselves of fear.

B170   "My Children." *McCall's* (Apr. 1938): 4, 75.

We must remember that our children are independent persons, and that to become their friend is something to strive for. Concludes that she was not an ideal parent.

B171   "My Day." *Consumers' Cooperative* 24 (Feb. 1938): 19.

From a "My Day" column describing her 17 Dec. 1937 visit to the Cooperative League.

B172   "My Days." *Quote* 1 (Nov. 1938): 36-37.

Excerpts book *My Days*.

B173   "My Home." *McCall's* (Feb. 1938): 4, 46, 132.

Describes life in the White House. As in any home one has to go about life in an orderly fashion and strive for a house filled with love.

B174   "My Job." *McCall's* (Mar. 1938): 4, 68.

How she adjusted to her duties as White House hostess. By late 1933 she felt that she could be useful by visiting impoverished areas and prisons.

B175   "My Month." *Women's Democratic News* (New York State Section of Democratic Digest) (Feb. 1938): 2, 4.

Activities for Dec. 1937 including a Christmas visit with daughter Anna in Seattle.

B176   "On Teachers and Teaching." *Harvard Educational Review* 8 (Oct. 1938): 423-24.

What makes a teacher great is the ability to inspire.

B177 "Resolutions I Wish Consumers Would Make for 1938: A Dozen Targets for Consumers Who Want to Make Their Buying Power Count Toward a Better New Year." *Consumers' Guide* 4 (3 Jan. 1938): 3-8.

Women should know more about what they purchase and the "conditions under which these goods were produced." One of 12 brief statements published under a common title (p. 3).

B178 "Should Married Women Work? A Californian Asks Mrs. Roosevelt to Explain Her Statement in the Democratic Digest." *Democratic Digest* 15 (May 1938): 24.

Responding to a question in "Dear Mrs. Roosevelt:" of Dec. 1937 a businessman states that when a married woman works she is denying a man the opportunity. ER responds that most married women work out of financial necessity, and that while women should stay at home with small children, juvenile delinquency results from economic factors, not because of the mother's absence.

B179 "Success Formula for Public-Spirited Women." *Democratic Digest* 15 (Aug. 1938): 39.

Training and courage are among the five points for women to remember if they want to be successful in community and national affairs.

B180   "Youth." *Hearst's International Cosmopolitan* (Feb. 1938): 26-27, 134-36.
In every community we must be aware of the aspirations of youth and help young people achieve their goals.

1939

B181   "American Democracy and Youth." *New University* (Mar. 1939): 7-8.
Federal programs have done much to help youth, but we must also work at the community level for the concerns of the young.

B182   *Common Sense Neutrality.* Ed. Paul Comly French. New York: Hastings, 1939. 182-97.
In an untitled contribution ER discusses the importance of showing the rest of the world that people can govern themselves and solve their problems.   Advocates disarmament and a world organization to promote peace.

B183   "Conquer Fear and You Will Enjoy Living." *Look* 3 (23 May 1939): 6-11.
Examples of fears which we have as a nation and as individuals. Consists mainly of illustrations.

B184   "Current Quotations." *Education Digest* 4 (May 1939): 7.
Unidentified statement praising teachers.

B185   "Do Our Young People Need Religion?" *Liberty* 16 (17 June 1939): 12-13.
Although the honesty of the young can make us question the value of religion as practiced by some adults, the problems of the world, and those of youth in particular, make religion important.

B186   "Eleanor Roosevelt Says." *Educational Music Magazine* 18 (Jan./Feb. 1939): 6-7.
Teachers should remember that music is important to the life of the nation.

B187   "Flying Is Fun." *Collier's* 103 (22 Apr. 1939): 15, 88-89.
In celebration of traveling by commercial aircraft.

B188   "Food in America." *Woman's Day* (Oct. 1939): 27-29, 33.
American food can be imaginative.

B189   "Good Manners." *Ladies' Home Journal* 56 (June 1939): 21, 116-17.
Kindness is behind good manners regardless of time or culture.

B190   "Government Becomes Alive." *Daily Times* [Chicago, Ill.] 6 Sept. 1939: 55.
In the last 10 years government has become more responsive by improving the lives of its citizens.   Written on the occasion of the 10th anniversary of the newspaper.

B191   "Keepers of Democracy." *Virginia Quarterly Review* 15 (Jan. 1939): 1-5.
Criticizes those who lack the moral courage and the necessary appreciation of democracy to overcome fears of communism and religions different from their own.

B192 "Mrs. Roosevelt on Democratic Women's Day." *Democratic Digest* 16 (Dec. 1939): 29.

It is a woman's obligation to raise funds for a political party and to explain why it is needed. From "My Day" of 14 Oct. 1939.

B193 "Our American Homes." *Child Study* 16 (May 1939): 182.

A child's home life is the basis upon which all else is built, including the training for life in a democracy. An editorial introducing a special issue on the home.

B194 "Security Begins Beyond the City Limits." *Hearst's International-Cosmopolitan* 106 (May 1939): 38-39, 90-91.

Farms are of such importance that we must improve the quality of rural education, health, and nutrition, and, in turn, the security of the nation.

B195 *To Enrich Young Life: Ten Years with the Junior Literary Guild in the Schools of Our Country.* Garden City: Junior Literary Guild, 1939. [24].

Reading is an excellent way for children to learn proper values and how to think for themselves. An untitled contribution. For a description of her qualifications to serve as a reviewer for the Junior Literary Guild, see pp. 16-17.

B196 "A Vision for Today." *New York Times Magazine* 24 Dec. 1939: 4.

The birth and life of the Christ child is more than history. It should be the vision which leads our lives. When that happens there will peace on earth.

B197 "War! What the Women of America Can Do to Prevent It." *Woman's Day* 2 (Apr. 1939): 4-5, 46-47.

We must teach our children that there are ways other than force to settle difficulties and that we are a world of nations which must work together. One of 20 statements made by women (p. 5).

B198 Introduction. *Washington, Nerve Center.* The Face of America. By Edwin Rosskam; Ruby A. Black, co-editor. New York: Alliance, 1939. 5-6.

This book is a guide to the sights of Washington and the federal government. It is intended to educate citizens to become better participants in the democratic process.

B199 "Why I Am Against the People's Vote on War." *Liberty* 16 (8 Apr. 1939): 7-8.

The Ludlow amendment providing for a referendum on war would be a mistake. Rebuttal of an article by Rose Wilder Lane in *Liberty* 16 (1 Apr. 1939): 11-12.

B200 "The Women of America Must Fight." *This Week Magazine* 16 (2 July 1939): 7.

Women should launch a crusade for law and order and try to reduce the incidents of crime.

B200a "You Can Prevent Crime." *Woman* (Nov. 1939): 36-37.

Condensation of "The Women of America Must Fight."

1940

B201   Foreword. *American Youth: An Enforced Reconnaissance*. Ed. Thacher Winslow and Frank P. Davidson. Cambridge: Harvard Univ. Pr., 1940. ix-xi.
We must be concerned about the problems which face young people. As much as the National Youth Admin. and the Civilian Conservation Corps have helped more is needed, and that help must be within the context of democracy.

B202   Foreword. *American Youth Today*. By Leslie A. Gould. New York: Random House, 1940. vii-viii.
Gould's study presents the facts about the American Youth Congress. He has not treated FDR kindly, however.

B203   "Christmas 1940: A Short Story." *Liberty* (28 Dec. 1940): 10-13.
A story for children about a Dutch girl's first Christmas Eve without her father.

B203a "Christmas-A Story." *Eleanor Roosevelt's Christmas Book*. New York: Dodd, Mead. 1963. 3-5.

B203b "Christmas 1940, A Short Story." *The Liberty Years, 1924-1950: An Anthology*. Ed. Allen Churchill. Englewood Cliffs: Prentice-Hall, 1969. 297-300.

B203c "Christmas." *A Christmas Treasury*. Ed. Jack Newcombe. New York: Viking, 1982. 382-89.

B203d "Christmas 1940: A Short Story." *McCall's* 114 (Jan. 1987): 95-97.
Includes excerpt from Elliott Roosevelt's introduction to the 1986 publication of the story in book form.

B203e "Christmas." *A New Christmas Treasury*. Ed. Jack Newcombe. New York: Viking, 1991. 438-46.

B204   "Eleanor Roosevelt on Recreation." *Recreation* 34 (Dec. 1940): 570.
Some of our youth point to the lack of recreational facilities. While they are right, they also overlook activities such as reading and group singing which do not require special facilities. From a "My Day" column.

B205   "Farm Youth of Today." *American Farm Youth* 6 (Nov. 1940): 3.
Today farming requires skill and knowledge.

B206   "Fear Is the Enemy." *Nation* 150 (10 Feb. 1940): 173.
Those who fear unpopular ideas have never learned the real meaning of a democratic society and their responsibility for making it work.

B207   "A Guest Editorial." *Opportunity* 18 (Mar. 1940): 66.
Supports the efforts of *Opportunity* to interest black youth in vocational guidance. Looks forward to the time when there is equal opportunity for all types of education.

B208   Foreword. *Happy Times in Czechoslovakia*. By Libushka Bartusek. New York: Knopf, 1940. [iii].

The traditions and culture of Czechoslovakia will live on through books and children.

B209 "Helping Them to Help Themselves." *Rotarian* 56 (Apr. 1940): 8-11.
"Self-help co-operatives" keep people busy providing the essentials of life and developing skills of value to industry.

B209a "Helping People to Help Themselves." *Ladies' Home Journal* 57 (Aug. 1940): 12.

B210 "Homes for Americans: An Editorial." *Woman's Day* 3 (Apr. 1940): 3.
Home ownership is part of the independent American spirit, and the building industry and government must work together to make it possible for the low income family to own a home.

B211 "In Appreciation." *Synagogue Light* 8 (Oct. 1940): 4.
Brief statement of appreciation for the work of the late Cyrus Adler.

B212 "Insuring Democracy." *Collier's* 105 (15 June 1940): 70, 87-88.
Since the first White House Conference on Children in 1909 steps have been taken to provide proper living conditions and educational opportunities for children. Now we must add the problems of youth.

B213 "Intolerance." *Cosmopolitan* (Feb. 1940): 24-25, 102-3.
Intolerance of certain groups is a result of fear that they are better prepared to survive economically. We could eliminate much of that intolerance by providing more employment opportunities for all.

B214 "The Man from Jail." *World Digest* 12 (June 1940): 61-62.
The man who has been released from prison should be afforded the opportunity to work, and he should be able to expect the understanding of his neighbors. Condensed from *St. Anthony Messenger*.

B215 "Men Have to Be Humored." *Woman's Day* 3 (Aug. 1940): 12-13, 58.
She provides examples from family life and public affairs to prove her point that men are more emotional than women. A response to Raymond Clapper's "Women Are Too Emotional" which appeared in the July 1940 issue.

B216 "Mrs. Roosevelt Speaks." *Democratic Digest* 17 (Aug. 1940): 16.
Quotations from "My Day" for May-Aug. 1940 are substituted for the monthly "Dear Mrs. Roosevelt:" column.

B217 "My Advice to American Youth." *Look* 4 (27 Aug. 1940): 56-58.
Youth are concerned about health, jobs, and education. By volunteering their services to local communities youth can use their energy and enthusiasms to improve our standard of living and be participants in the democratic process.

B218 "Read the Bill of Rights." *Democratic Digest* 17 (Jan. 1940): 12.
The Bill of Rights guarantees rights for the accused criminal. Perhaps those accused only by the press deserve similar protection. Reprint of "My Day" for 13 Dec. 1939.

B219 "Shall We Enroll Aliens? No." *Liberty* 17 (3 Feb. 1940): 13.
Legislation which would allow illegal aliens to apply for citizenship is preferable. ER takes the opposite stance from Sen. James J. Davis who argues in favor of a periodic enrollment of aliens.

B220 "A Spanking." *Liberty* 17 (22 June 1940): 6-8.
It is important for her to befriend members of the American Youth Congress even if she does not agree with all of their actions and policies. Response to article by Archie Roosevelt and Murray Plavner, "Why We Know the Youth Congress is Pro-Stalin." *Liberty* 17 (27 Apr. 1940): 12-14.

B221 "Twenty-four Hours." *Ladies' Home Journal* 57 (Oct. 1940): 20, 58, 60.
By describing some of her typical days she explains how she uses her time to accomplish more.

B222 "What Value Has the Ballot for Women?" *Democratic Digest* 17 (June/July 1940): 25.
Women owe it to themselves and to the country to exercise their right to vote.

B223 "The White House Speaks." *Ladies' Home Journal* 57 (June 1940): 21, 121-24.
Through ER the White House "speaks" about its famous inhabitants with the most lengthy discussion being about herself.

B223a "The White House Speaks." *Washington: A Reader, the National Capital As Seen Through the Eyes of Thomas Jefferson [and Others].* Comp. Bill Adler. New York: Meredith, 1967. 117-32.

B224 "Why I Still Believe in the Youth Congress." *Liberty* 17 (20 Apr. 1940): 30-32.
Critics of the American Youth Congress should recognize the economic and political events which led to the concerns of youth.

B225 "Women in Politics." *Good Housekeeping* 110 (Jan. 1940): 8-19, 150; 110 (Mar. 1940): 45, 68; 110 (Apr. 1940): 45, 201-3.
Leaders of the suffrage movement and trailblazing women in public office are celebrated. Written on the occasion of the 20th anniversary of women's suffrage.

B226 "Women in Politics." *Woman's Press* (Y.W.C.A.) (Apr. 1940): 165.
In the community civic duties are important. Get involved in politics at the local level, affiliate with a political party, and work to make the party responsive to your concerns and ideas.

B227 Foreword. *Youth-Millions Too Many? A Search for Youth's Place in America.* By Bruce L. Melvin. New York: Association Pr., 1940. 5-6.
We must provide opportunities for youth to learn and work.

1941

B228 [Review]. *The American Presidency: An Interpretation.* By Harold J. Laski. *Harvard Law Review* 54 (June 1941): 1413-14.
This book provides insight into the presidency and will help ordinary citizens understand their responsibility to our democratic society.

B229 "Appreciating the Great Outdoors." *Student Life* 7 (May 1941): 2.
Learning about nature can bring a lifetime of enjoyment.

B230 "Defense and Girls." *Ladies' Home Journal* 58 (May 1941): 25, 54.
Compulsory community service for girls would be good for the community and the girl. A preview of her column "If You Ask Me" which began in the June 1941 issue of the *Ladies' Home Journal.*

B230a "Defense and Girls." *Women in America: Half of History*. Ed. Mary Kay Tetreault. Boston: Houghton Mifflin, 1978. 60-63.

B230b "Girls and National Defense." *Women in America: Half of History*. Ed. Mary Kay Tetreault. Chicago: Rand McNally, 1978. 60-64.
A reprinting of "Defense and Girls."

B231 "First Lady Addresses Workers' Wives." *Trade Union Courier* 6 (1 Sept. 1941): 6.
American women are playing an important role in the defense effort and are defending the liberties we enjoy and want to guarantee to peoples everywhere. An article written at the request of the *Trade Union Courier.*

B232 "If I Were a Freshman...." *Threshold* 1 (Oct. 1941): 5-6.
I would study foreign languages and take courses which would develop my mind. I would seek out inspirational professors and lasting friendships.

B233 "Important as Ever." *Our Bill of Rights: What It Means to Me, a National Symposium*. By James Waterman Wise. New York: Bill of Rights Sesqui-centennial, 1941. 116.
By practicing the principles of the Bill of Rights we can eliminate racial and religious prejudice.

B234 "An Inspiration to All." *Opinion* 12 (Nov. 1941): 12.
The life of Louis Brandeis was an inspiration. Brief statement in Brandeis memorial issue.

B235 "Larder for the Democracies." *Democratic Digest* 18 (Oct. 1941): 7.
Women should grow food for their families thus making more commercially produced foodstuffs available for shipment to foreign countries which are at war.

B236 "My Week." *Our Country* 1 (May 1941): 16.
Covers several topics: rural electrification, current reading, and her travels. Appears to be a reprint of a United Features column "My Week." Date supplied by FDRL.

B237 Foreword. *The New Program of the United States Committee of International Student Service*. New York: The Committee, 1941. 4-5.
The work of the International Student Service is important to the future of our country. There should be ISS centers on all campuses where students and faculty can discuss important issues. Hopefully, this pamphlet will create more interest in the work of the ISS.

B238 "Our Widening Horizon." *Democratic Digest* 18 (Feb. 1941): 9.
Party workers must be attracted at all levels, and then they should work together to demonstrate that a democracy is still possible in the world today.

B239 "Shall We Draft American Women?" *Liberty* 18 (13 Sept. 1941): 10-11.
A defense and explanation of her proposal for young women to devote a year to public service.

B240 "Tower Club." *The Tower: Yearbook of the Tower Club, Ohio State University, 1941.* 2.
Praises the use of space under the Ohio State stadium for low-cost student housing. Reprint of "My Day" for 17 Nov. 1938.

B241 "Weaving: An Old American Handicraft." *Woman's Day* (Feb. 1941): 27-28.
Weaving can bring pleasure, beautify the home, and be a source of income.

B242 "What Does Pan-American Friendship Mean?" *Liberty* 18 (4 Oct. 1941): 10-11, 35.
It means political, economic, and cultural relations.

B242a "What Does Pan-American Friendship Mean? *Congressional Record Appendix* (22 Oct. 1941): A4784-85.

B243 "What Is the Matter with Women?" *Liberty* 18 (3 May 1941): 12-13.
Unless women get involved in their communities and in politics they will continue to let men rule the world.

B244 "What's Wrong with the Draft." *Look* 5 (15 July 1941): 23-25.
The age limit should be lowered. Draft boards should make their decisions public, and there should be more uniformity among boards.

B245 *Women in Defense*. Motion Picture. Office of Emergency Management Blackhawk Films, 1941. 10 min. b & w.
A film about the role of women in the war effort. Written by ER.

B245a "Women in Defense: A Script by Mrs. Roosevelt." *New York Times* Magazine 7 Dec. 1941: 6-7.
Narrative and photographic excerpts.

1942

B246 Foreword. "Born in the USA." *Baby Talk* 7 (July 1942): 11.
We should provide medical care for the children of our enlisted men since these children will make up the world we are trying to preserve.

B247 "The Democratic Effort." *Common Ground* 2 (Spring 1942): 9-10.
We must demonstrate that democracy works by uniting the country against discrimination toward aliens and people with foreign-sounding names.

B248 "Education Is the Cornerstone on Which We Must Build Liberty." *Education for Victory* 1 (1 Apr. 1942): 1.
Discussion of the value of education to a democracy.

B249 "For American Unity." *American Unity* 1 (Oct. 1942): 3.
Children must learn that in a democracy citizens are entitled to political, economic, and religious rights.

B250 "How about Your Vacation?" *Cosmopolitan* (Apr. 1942): 28-29.
In uncertain times such as these a vacation is advisable.

B251 "The Issue Is Freedom." Rev. of *American Unity and Asia* by Pearl Buck. *New Republic* 107 (3 Aug. 1942): 147-48.
In this series of wartime articles and speeches the real issue is freedom for Asians as well as for Europeans and black Americans.

B252 "Kedgeree." *Sincerely Yours: A Collection of Favorite Recipes of Well-Known Persons.* Comp. Bess Boardman. San Francisco, Grabhorn, 1942. 45.
A recipe for whitefish.

B253 "Let Us Earn a True Peace." *Country Gentleman* 112 (Dec. 1942): 9, 52-53.
The peace must also be achieved here at home. We must assume more responsibility as citizens and better prepare ourselves for life in an international world.

B254 "Let Us Have Faith in Democracy." *Land Policy Review* 5 (Jan. 1942): 20-22.
Democracy requires educated and informed citizens who take responsibility for their communities and their government.

B255 "Marching...with Eleanor Roosevelt: This Month Your Government Asks That You...." *McCall's* 69 (Mar. 1942): 57.
Signed "ER" as assistant director of the Office of Civilian Defense. Lists and describes eight things which women are asked to do for the defense effort. States that column will appear monthly, but this was the only issue.

B256 "Messages." *Free World* 4 (Oct. 1942): 7-18.
Best wishes to *Free World*. Reproduction of a brief letter (p. 8). One of several congratulatory messages.

B257 "Mobilizing Human Skills." *Common Sense* 11 (July 1942): 240-42.
We need to better utilize the skills of all citizens and to make educational opportunities available to them. In the post-war years Americans will take more advantage of government services to better realize their potential.

B258 "Mrs. Roosevelt Sends Columbus Day Message to Jewish People Through Jewish Mirror." *Jewish Mirror* 1 (Oct. 1942): 3.
Encourages European Jews to settle in this hemisphere.

B259 "Must We Hate To Fight? No." *Saturday Review of Literature* 25 (4 July 1942): 13.
In an companion article Norman Cousins believes that the answer is "yes," but ER

argues that if men must hate in order to kill can we expect them to stop hating once the war is over.

B259a "Must We Hate to Fight?" *The Saturday Review Treasury*. New York: Simon and Schuster, 1957. 233-34.

B260   "My Day." *Democratic Digest* 19 (Sept. 1942): 14.
   In the years following World War I Americans showed weakness of character and morality. If we want to build a better world and justify the present sacrifices of youth, these failings must not be repeated.

B261   "My Day-The Polish Day." *Pulaski Foundation Bulletin* 1 (Dec. 1942): 3.
   Reports on radio broadcast on the occasion of the third anniversary of the fall of Poland in which she, Dorothy Thompson, Pearl Buck, Clare Boothe Luce, and Marianne Moore participated. Excerpts "My Day" of 25 Sept. 1942.

B262   *Pour la Victoire* (10 Jan. 1942): 1
   An untitled congratulatory statement to the editors of the new French weekly praising their courage and sharing in their hope for victory in the war. In French.

B263   "Race, Religion and Prejudice." *New Republic* 106 (11 May 1942): 630.
   Americans have formed attitudes about certain groups, and it is for black Americans that we should be concerned first as evidence that we provide equality for our citizens while fighting for the same for all peoples of the world.

B264   Preface. *Refugees at Work*. Comp. Sophia M. Robinson. New York: King's Crown, 1942. [v]-vi.
   She requested that this study be undertaken to allay fears Americans have of refugees and to demonstrate the refugees' skills and willingness to work.

B265   Special Issue on Morale. Ed. Eleanor Roosevelt. *Saturday Review of Literature* 25 (4 July 1942).

B266   "To Care for Him Who Shall Have Borne the Battle." *Collier's* 110 (28 Nov. 1942): 20.
   When visiting military hospitals she wishes that the wounded men could see the women they love instead of her.

B267   "What Is Morale." Editorial. *Saturday Review of Literature* 25 (4 July 1942): 12.
   The source of morale is character which has been built at work, home, and school. Also discusses Virginius Dabney's "Press and Morale" (pp. 5-6, 24-25) by stating that if morale is built in the home it is not surprising that members of the Negro race can lack it. Urges white citizens to provide equal opportunity to all of our citizens, something which has been promised for all races of the world.

B268   "What We Are Fighting For." *American Magazine* 134 (July 1942): 16-17, 60-62.
   We are fighting for freedom and a better world which the "United Nations" will create at the end of the war. Written at the request of the editor of *American Magazine*.

1943

B269 "Abolish Jim Crow!" *New Threshold* 1 (Aug. 1943): 4, 34.
While we are fighting a war so that peoples of all nations will have freedom we must provide all of our citizens, regardless of race, the right to equality before the law, equality of education, economic equality, and equality of expression.

B269a "First Lady Adds to Four Freedoms." *New York Times* 15 July 1943: 13.
Extensive excerpts from "Abolish Jim Crow!"

B269b "The Four Equalities." *Negro Digest* 1 (Sept. 1943): 81-83.
Condensation of "Abolish Jim Crow!"

B270 "The Case Against the Negro Press. Con." *Negro Digest* 1 (Feb. 1943): 53.
A weakness of black newspapers is that reporting the news is not their main objective. One of five short articles about the Afro-American press. Condensation from the *Chicago Times*.

B271 "A Challenge to American Sportsmanship." *Collier's* 112 (16 Oct. 1943): 21, 71.
Loyal Americans of Japanese descent are citizens who should be accepted by others. Disloyal Japanese-Americans should be held under tight security and deported to Japan after the war.

B272 "Eleanor Roosevelt Visits the South Pacific: As the First Lady Views It." *Democratic Digest* 20 (Sept. 1943): 8-9.
Excerpts from several "My Day" columns written during her 1943 trip.

B273 "Freedom: Promise or Fact." *Negro Digest* 1 (Oct. 1943): 8-9.
The black woman, like women of all races, does not have equality. If she were black she would do her best under the circumstances and continue working for economic and social equality while not letting her spirit be hurt.

B274 "Greetings!" *Bridge* (The Credit Union National Association) 7 (Jan. 1943): 4.
Credit unions are a good example of cooperative efforts.

B275 "Gumbo Z' Herbes (New Orleans)." *Bundles for America: Selected Recipes with Culinary Herbs.* Columbus: Bundles for America, 1943. 21-22.
Recipe followed by instructions which state that some of the ingredients are not essential and the exact amounts used need not be firm.

B276 "How Britain Is Treating Our Soldier Boys and Girls." *Ladies' Home Journal* 60 (Feb. 1943): 24-25, 125-26.
Written after her 1942 trip she praises the British for the hospitality extended to the American military.

B277 "It's a Ladies' Fight." *Kelly Magazine* (San Antonio Air Service Command) 1 (Christmas 1943): 7.
Women at home have roles to play producing goods, rationing food, and maintaining better homes.

B278 "It's Patriotic to Teach." *Educational Leadership* 1 (Oct. 1943): 3.
Teachers will play an important role in shaping the post-war world.

B278a "It's Patriotic to Teach." *Teacher's Digest* 4 (Feb. 1944): 56.

B279 "A Message to the Mountain Folk." *Arcadian Life Magazine* 2 (Spring/Summer 1943): 5.
While fighting on foreign soil your sons may realize for the first time the interdependence of nations.

B280 "Monthly Posters Are Vital in War Bond Sale." *Minute Man* 2 (15 May 1943): 5.
Attractive posters help promote sales. Excerpts "My Day" of 30 Mar. 1943.

B281   "Mrs. Roosevelt's Article: My Day." *Union of Two Peoples: Monterrey Conference.* War Emergency ed. Ed. Jose G. Morales. Mexico City: Mexican Associated Pr., 1943. 31-32.
ER accompanied FDR to a meeting held 20 Apr. 1943 in Monterrey. Early on 21 Apr. abroad their train she wrote her "My Day" column. It was a busy day, she wrote, and she hopes that two of her grandchildren who made the trip received their first lesson in Pan-American friendship. Also issued in Spanish.

B282 "My Day." *Answer* 1 (7 Sept. 1943): 21.
We must try to stop the persecution of Jews in Europe. From "My Day" of 14 Aug. 1943.

B283 "Noted Women Write on World We Want--First Article by Mrs. Roosevelt." *Christian Science Monitor* 5 Jan. 1943, Atlantic ed.: 8.
In the post-war era women want a world free of aggression, an international body to help resolve difficulties which arise between nations, a world economic system, the availability of good jobs for all, religion as an important part of everday life, and a world where women realize that they can play an important role in addressing the problems which face all nations. The first of a series of articles by women about the post-war world.

B283a "The World We Want." *Letter from America* 13 (22 Jan. 1943): 1.
Abridged version.

B284 "The Red Cross in the South Seas." *Ladies' Home Journal* 60 (Dec. 1943): 30, 158-60.
Nature of the work done by the Red Cross.

B285 "Studying Spanish." *Saturday Review of Literature* 26 (10 Apr. 1943): 10.
Since there will be closer ties with Latin America in the post-war years, more people should learn Spanish.

B286 "They Talk Our Language Differently." *Collier's* 111 (27 Feb. 1943): 18, 20, 22.
Many Americans consider the British to be peculiar, but during my visit there I found that American soldiers had developed respect for their hosts.

B287 "Trained Minds and Trained Hearts." *Smith Alumnae Quarterly* 34 (May 1943): 125.

Demands on the country's future are great, and students can no longer be satisfied to just "get by." Forms part of "The Challenge to Education" (pp. 125-26, 150) with the opposing side defended by Marjorie Hope Nicolson.

B288 "Women at War in Great Britain." *Ladies' Home Journal* 60 (Apr. 1943): 22-25, 70, 72.

British women are meeting the demands of war.

B289 "Women Students-the Men Are Counting on You!" *Intercollegian* 61 (Dec. 1943): 7.

Women must prepare themselves for what lies ahead and be active participants in creating a world which makes the men's sacrifices more meaningful.

1944

B290 "American Red Cross 'Down Under.'" *American Lawn Tennis* 37 (Apr. 1944): 16-17.

In her interview of Mary K. Browne at the Red Cross at War Rally in New York on 29 Feb. 1944 ER raises questions about the work of the Red Cross in the South Pacific.

B291 "American Women in the War." *Reader's Digest* 44 (Jan. 1944): 42-44.

Praises the role of women, in and out of uniform, and suggests that more should be done to help married women with child care and shopping. Concludes that the war has changed the lives of most women.

B292 "As Johnny Thinks of Home: He Idealizes What He Left Behind." *Social Action* 10 (15 Mar. 1944): 5-7.

Young soldiers are concerned about the opportunities which will exist when they return home, and we must make sure that chances for education and employment will exist for them. One of several articles prefaced by "As Johnny Thinks of Home."

B293 "Eleanor Roosevelt Says." *Ammunition* (UAW-CIO) 2 (Aug. 1944): 1.

Women are to be commended for assuming difficult jobs during wartime. They should participate in union affairs, further the common interests of labor and community, and then use this training to promote their roles as citizens.

B294 "Henry Wallace's Democracy." Rev. of *Democracy Reborn* by Henry Wallace. *New Republic* 111 (7 Aug. 1944): 165-66.

This collection of speeches helps one to better understand Wallace the realist and the dreamer. She agrees with him about the need to support the common good and for religious belief to be behind the democratic role of America.

B295 "How to Take Criticism." *Ladies' Home Journal* 61 (Nov. 1944): 155, 171.

As a public figure she is subject to criticism no matter what she does. It is better to be honest with one's self and not worry about the critics.

B295a "Mrs. Roosevelt, Despite Criticism, Prefers a Life of Service to Role of a Dresden Doll." *New York Times* 25 Oct. 1944: 23.
Lengthy excerpts of "How to Take Criticism."

B296 "I Will Get Well." *This Week Magazine* (14 May 1944).
ER promised a young soldier in the South Pacific that she would visit his mother if he promised to get well.

B297 "If You Ask Me." *Reader's Digest* 45 (Sept. 1944): 100-101.
Excerpts from her question and answer column.

B298 "In Unity There Is Strength." *Workmen's Circle Call* 12 (July 1944): 10.
Labor should unite with all races and work together to set an example for the rest of the country and the world. One of two articles under the common title "Equality Is Labor's Cause."

B299 "Is the Human Race Worth Saving?" *Liberty* 21 (23 Dec. 1944): 15, 54.
The human race has material and spiritual needs, and the first may depend on the second. She goes into detail about the need to rebuild or improve economic conditions and the standard of living in all nations after the war. The U.S. may have to give up some of its manufacturing capacity in order to improve the world economy and increase foreign demand for U.S. goods. The roles which youth, education, and the spiritual life can play give her hope for the future of the human race.

B300 "New Stepping Stones in the Pacific." *Survey Graphic* 33 (Jan. 1944): 5.
The Pacific area will be of great interest and value in the years ahead. Praises the work of the Red Cross in the South Pacific. Her article serves as a foreword to an article about the organization.

B301 "The South in Postwar America." *Southern Patriot* 2 (June 1944): 1-2.
The South will prosper if it realizes that the Civil War is over, accepts the idea that we are one nation, improves education, diversifies agriculture, and pays its workers more.

B302 "To the Women of the B & O Family." *Baltimore and Ohio Magazine* 30 (June 1944): 3.
During wartime women have made important contributions by taking up the jobs of men. Prepare yourselves for being an active participant in the democratic process, because even if you leave your jobs and return to your homes after the war you will still have a contribution to make.

B303 "We Must Have Compulsory Service." *Parents' Magazine* 19 (Nov. 1944): 16-18.
After the war has ended we must still have a year of compulsory service, because some countries must be prepared to enforce the peace. Her statement is one of several which make up the article "Shall We Have Compulsory Military Training After the War?"

B303a "Should the U.S. Adopt Peacetime Compulsory Military Training? Pro." *Congressional Digest* 24 (Jan. 1945): 16.

Reprint of "We Must Have Compulsory Service." One of several statements (pp. 3-32).

B304 "What I Saw in the South Seas." *Ladies' Home Journal* 61 (Feb. 1944): 26-27, 88-90.
   Praises the actions of Australian and New Zealand women in the war effort and of Americans in uniform in the South Pacific.

B305 "What Kind of World Are We Fighting For?" *Canadian Home Journal* (Jan. 1944): 12-13.
   Look to a new democracy after the war characterized by equality, an adequate number of jobs, and the arts. "As told to Nelson Ingersoll."

B306 "What Will Happen to Women War Workers in Post-War America." *Southern Patriot* 2 (Apr. 1944): 1-2.
   If we plan for full employment, men returning from the war can find jobs and women who wish to do so can continue working. But our social customs will change as more women enter the workforce.

B307 "What Will Victory Bring?" *Argosy* 318 (Apr. 1944) 16-17.
   We must commit ourselves to working for an enduring peace (p. 16). One of six statements by prominent figures about the post-war world.

B308 "Woman's Place After the War." *Click* 7 (Aug. 1944): 17-19.
   After the war most women will return to their main jobs as wife and mother, but those who need or want to work should be able to do so. Government and business should work together to assure jobs for both men and women.

B309 "Women at the Peace Conference." *Reader's Digest* 44 (Apr. 1944): 48-49.
   In many areas of the world there are women who are qualified to participate in the peace talks and plan the post-war society.

B310 Foreword. "Women in the Postwar World." *Journal of Educational Sociology* 17 (Apr. 1944): 449-50.
   After the war many women plan to keep their jobs. We must expand our global economy to allow for enough jobs for both men and women. Article introduces coverage of symposium on women in the post-war world.

B311 "Young Men Must Look Forward." *Future* 6 (June 1944): 9.
   Young men should be included in the peace talks and planning for the post-war world.

1945

B312 "From the Melting Pot-An American Race." *Liberty* 22 (14 July 1945): 17, 89.
   There are still obstacles to our having a unified country: language, foreign names (she suggests that those with foreign names change them), customs, and religious beliefs.

B313 [Greetings to Girls of Todhunter]. *Todhunter Alumnae Bulletin* 1 (Jan. 1945): 5.

Sends her best wishes in an undated letter and thanks them for their wartime sacrifices. Title supplied by FDRL.

B314 "If You Ask Me." *Negro Digest* 3 (Feb. 1945): 9-10.
Selected questions and answers about race relations from her column "If You Ask Me."

B315 "Mrs. Roosevelt Resumes News Column; She Calls on People to Achieve Objectives." *New York Times* 18 Apr. 1945: 17.
FDR, like Abraham Lincoln and Woodrow Wilson, died before his work was finished. It is now up to those of us who remain to work for a peaceful world. Text of "My Day" of 17 Apr. 1945, the first written after FDR's death.

B315a "My Day." *Franklin Delano Roosevelt: A Memorial.* Ed. Donald Porter Geddes. New York: Dial, 1945. 83-84.

B315b "One of Many." *Reader's Digest* 46 (June 1945): 26.
From "My Day" of 17 Apr. 1945.

B315c "Personal Sorrow Lost in Humanity's Sadness." *Democratic Digest* 22 (June 1945): 9.

B316 "Mrs. Roosevelt Says." *Bayonet* 1 (Jan. 1945): 16.
ER and others were asked to respond to three questions. "What are some of the essentials of enduring peace?" Equal opportunity. "How might we achieve economic equality without intensifying racial prejudices?" Through legislation and the efforts of labor unions. "How might the suggestions made best be related to community activities?" Interracial forums sponsoring activities for all races. Forms part of article "Symposium." (pp. 16-17).

B317 "Music in the White House." *Your Music* (Nov. 1945).
The best musical events at the White House are the simple presentations for a few friends. Programs of folk music are particularly enjoyable. Copy not examined. Annotation based on the following entry.

B317a "Folk Music in the White House." *Folk Music in the Roosevelt White House: A Commemorative Program Presented by the Office of Folklife Programs at the National Museum of American History, Smithsonian Institution, Washington, D.C., January 31, 1982.* Washington: Smithsonian Institution, [1982]. 8-9.
Excerpts from "Music in the White House."

B318 "Now for the World We Are Fighting For." *Modern Mystic and Monthly Science Review* 5 (July 1945): 124-25.
Those nations hurt most by the war will need our help in the form of food. But if there is to be a lasting peace, we must solve the spiritual problems which face mankind.

B319 Forword. *Orbit, 1945* (Franklin Delano Roosevelt High School, Hyde Park, N.Y.).
Once the war has been won you will be living in an exciting time. Democracy requires obligations such as being involved in one's community and working to ensure

the benefits of democracy to all citizens. Available as typescript in ER Papers, Box 3050, FDRL.

B320 "This Is My America." *True Confessions* 44 (Feb. 1945): 27.
America means individual rights, equality of opportunity, and feeling at home anywhere in the country.

B320a "This Is My America." *Fawcett Digest* (1945).
Condensation. Copy not examined.

B321 "Tolerance Is an Ugly Word." *Coronet* 18 (July 1945): 118.
"Tolerance" must be eliminated from our vocabularies. We should accept and respect, not simply tolerate, our neighbors at home and peoples everywhere.

B321a "Tolerance Is an Ugly Word." *Negro Digest* 3 (Oct. 1945): 7-8.
Condensation.

B322 Introduction. *The White House Conference on Rural Education, October 3, 4, and 5, 1944.* Washington: National Education Assoc. of the U.S., n.d. 11-13.
To the benefits of growing up in a rural area must be added schools which are equipped to prepare the child for the modern world.

B323 "You Can't Pauperize Children." *Ladies' Home Journal* 62 (Sept. 1945): 128-29.
Adequate assistance to dependent children is necessary for the child to grow up healthy and secure.

1946

B324 Foreword. *As He Saw It*. By Elliott Roosevelt. New York: Duell, Sloan and Pearce, 1946. vii-ix.
Elliott's account of conferences attended by FDR during World War II and of father and son conversations about the post-war world are important as a record of those events, but his interpretations may differ from those of others.

B324a Foreword. *As He Saw It*. By Elliott Roosevelt. Bombay: Asia, 1947. vii-ix

B324b Foreword. *As He Saw It*. By Elliott Roosevelt. Westport: Greenwood, 1974. vii-ix.

B325 *Congressional Record* (18 July 1946): 9401.
ER and nine other women issued a statement opposing the Equal Rights Amendment on the grounds that it would not provide equal opportunity while eliminating protective legislation for women. Text of statement.

B326 "Eleanor Roosevelt to the German American." *German American* 5 (15 Oct. 1946): 3.
The Democratic Party has tried harder to provide equal opportunity for minorities and to support legislation that improves housing and conditions for workers, veterans, and farmers.

B327 "For an International Bill of Rights." *Democratic Digest* 23 (July 1946): 4-5.
Describes the establishment and work of the Nuclear Commission on Human Rights and the Subcommission on the Status of Women.

B328 "Frau Roosevelt fur eine starke Arbeiterbewegung." *Der Sozialdemokrat* 1 (3 June 1946): 1.
A strong labor movement in Germany will help liberate the country.   One of several brief messages in the inaugural issue.   In German.

B328a "Mrs. Roosevelt Hails Berlin Party's Paper." *New York Times* 3 June 1946: 8.
Reprinting of her message in English.

B329 "If You Ask Mrs. Roosevelt." *Practical English* 2 (17 Mar. 1947): 7.
Excerpts the book *If You Ask Me.*

B330 Preface. *The Jew in American Life.* By James Waterman Wise. New York: Messner, 1946. 5-6.
Jewish citizens have made outstanding contributions to the life of the nation. Calls for understanding of, and respect for, all groups.

B331 "A Message to American Girls." *American Girl* 29 (Feb. 1946): 4.
The Girl Scouts help to inform us about the needs of children everywhere.

B332 "The Minorities Question." *Toward a Better World*. Ed. William Scarlett. Philadelphia: Winston, 1946. 35-39.
Black citizens must be accepted as full partners and allowed to develop their potential. One of 11 articles written at the request of the Joint Commission on Social Reconstruction of the Protestant Episcopal Church.

B332a "The Minorities Question." *Christianity Takes a Stand: An Approach to the Issues of Today, a Symposium*. Penguin, 612. Ed. William Scarlett. New York: Penguin, 1946. 72-76.

B333 "Mrs. Roosevelt Speaks." *Summary* (Elmira, N.Y. Reformatory) 64 (29 Mar. 1946): 2.
The war is over, and we won. But we need the UN to foster better relations with other nations and to help create the climate which will enable other countries to buy our goods.

B334 "My Father and I." *New York Times Magazine* 16 June 1946: 28.
Her father was a great horseman, and she enjoyed riding with him in a horse-drawn cart. ER was among those asked to write about their fathers in an article by Leonard White.

B335 "The People Interview Mrs. Roosevelt." *Saturday Review of Literature* 29 (23 Mar. 1946): 24.
Excerpts the book *If You Ask Me.*

B336 "Why I Do Not Choose to Run." *Look* 10 (9 July 1946): 25-26.
She is not interested in elective office because she is too old, women do not have the necessary backing, and she would lose some of her freedom. It is better to help

younger people achieve office and to continue furthering FDR's ideas through the UN.

B337   "Why I Travel." *Holiday* (Apr. 1946): 24-26.
Travel better prepares one to live with others. Contains a candid account of her travels as a child.

1947

B338   Foreword. *F.D.R. Columnist: The Uncollected Columns of Franklin D. Roosevelt*. Ed. Donald Scott Carmichael. Chicago: Pellegrini & Cudahy, 1947. [ii-iii].
FDR's 1920 newspaper columns illustrate his concern for people and their living conditions as well as his life-long interest in the land, forests, and his native Hudson Valley.

B339   Foreword. *F.D.R.: His Personal Letters, Early Years*. Ed. Elliott Roosevelt. New York: Duell, Sloan and Pearce, 1947. xv-xvi.
These letters shed light on his background, education, and early training. This and subsequent volumes also published, London: Harrap, 1949-52.

B340   "Getting Over Having a Baby." *Babies Keep Coming: An Anthology*. Ed. Rebecca Reyher. New York: Whittlesey House-McGraw-Hill, 1947. 400-401.
Brief statement about her life during the 10 years when she bore her children. Excerpt from *This Is My Story*, pp. 163-64.

B341   "I Tell My Life Story in Pictures." *Look* 11 (16 Sept. 1947): 26-33.
Private and public photographs captioned by ER.

B342   "If I Had It All to Do Over Again." *Babies Keep Coming: An Anthology*. Ed. Rebecca Reyher. New York: Whittlesey House-McGraw-Hill, 1947. 321-23.
She wishes that she had taken care of her children during their early years without the help of servants. Excerpt from *This Is My Story*, pp. 144-46.

B343   "In Pursuit of Happiness." *Woman's Journal* 11 (Aug. 1947): 20.
Happiness results only when one is able to enjoy a variety of activities and survive life's problems and disappointments.

B344   "International Bill of Human Rights." *Methodist Woman* 8 (Nov. 1947): 14.
Progress in drafting the Universal Declaration of Human Rights.

B345 "Message from Mrs. Franklin D. Roosevelt, Chairman, Commission on Human Rights." *United Nations Weekly Bulletin* 2 (25 Feb. 1947): 170.
Brief report on the first meeting of the commission.

B346   "Roosevelt Christening Charm." *Babies Keep Coming: An Anthology*. Ed. Rebecca Reyher. New York: Whittlesey House-McGraw-Hill, 1947. 123-24.
About FDR's small Russian gold charm worn by his children and grandchildren at their christenings. Excerpt from *This Is My Story*, p. 241.

B347   "Roosevelt, Franklin Delano." *10 Eventful Years: A Record of Events of the Years Preceding Including and Following World War II, 1937 through 1946.* Vol. 3. Ed. Walter Yust. Chicago: Encyclopaedia Britannica, 1947. 810-13.
A biographical sketch written "in part" by ER (v. 1, p. xvii).

B348   "The Russians Are Tough." *Look* 11 (18 Feb. 1947): 65-69.
They are distrustful and persistent and will try to win a dispute regardless of what they have to do. We should be just as determined to promote democracy. Drawn from her early experiences at the UN.

B349   "Should a Negro Boy Ask a White Girl to Dance?" *Negro Digest* 6 (Dec. 1947): 41-42.
Yes, if they are friends. From her column "If You Ask Me" of Sept. 1947.

1948

B350   "A Comment by the Commission Chairman: Mrs. Franklin D. Roosevelt." *United Nations Bulletin* 5 (1 July 1948): 521.
Reports that the final draft of the Universal Declaration of Human Rights has been completed but is disappointed that the covenant was not completed since it is the covenant which will make the declaration enforceable.

B351   "A Decade of Democratic Women's Days." *Democratic Digest* 25 (Aug. 1948): 16.
Financial support should be given to the Democratic National Committee Women's Division for its effort to educate women about democracy and the responsibilities which they have to their communities.

B352   Foreword. *F.D.R.: His Personal Letters, 1905-1928.* Ed. Elliott Roosevelt and James N. Rosenau. New York: Duell, Sloan and Pearce, 1948. xvii-xix.
Letters from this period address his formative years in public service and his affliction with polio.

B352a   "He Learned to Bear It." *The Roosevelt Treasury.* Ed. James N. Rosenau. Garden City: Doubleday, 1951. 74-75.
Excerpt from foreword to *F.D.R.: His Personal Letters, 1905-1928.*

B353   "Plain Talk about Wallace." *Democratic Digest* 25 (Apr. 1948): 2.
Never a good politician, Henry Wallace is naive about Communists and totalitarianism. Excerpts a "My Day" column.

B354   "The Promise of Human Rights." *Foreign Affairs* 26 (Apr. 1948): 470-77.
An analysis of the work of the Commission on Human Rights and of specific articles in the Universal Declaration of Human Rights.

B355   "Toward Human Rights Throughout the World." *Democratic Digest* 25 (Feb. 1948): 14-15.
Reports on the progress of the Commission on Human Rights in drafting the Universal Declaration of Human Rights.

1949

B356 Editorial. *ADA World* 3 (20 Apr. 1949): 2.
The ADA has "done much to awaken the conscience of America." From an untitled message to the 1949 ADA convention.

B357 Introduction. *Freedom's Charter: The Universal Declaration of Human Rights.* Headline Series, 76. By O. Frederick Nolde. New York: Foreign Policy Assoc., 1949. 3-4.
Nolde's conclusion is correct that tensions in the world can be lessened by broader adherence to principles of human rights.

B357a Introduction. *Freedom's Charter: The Universal Declaration of Human Rights.* Headline Series, 76. By O. Frederick Nolde. Millwood: Kraus Reprint, 1973. 3-4.

B358 "Human Rights." *Peace on Earth*. New York: Hermitage House, 1949. 65-71.
The development of the Universal Declaration of Human Rights.

B359 "If You Ask Me." *Negro Digest* 7 (July 1949): 20-23.
Selected questions and answers pertaining to race relations from her column "If You Ask Me."

B360 "Importance of the Covenant." *United Nations Bulletin* 7 (1 July 1949): 3.
Status of the development of the covenant. Issued with Charles Malik's "The Covenant on Human Rights" (pp. 3-4).

B360a "Importance of the Covenant." *The Covenant on Human Rights*. By Charles Malik and Mrs. Franklin D. Roosevelt. New York: International Documents Service, 1949. 4-5.
Consists of both the ER and Malik articles from the *United Nations Bulletin*.

B361 Foreword. *Mark Twain and Franklin D. Roosevelt*. By Cyril Clemens. Webster Groves: International Mark Twain Society, 1949. [11].
FDR's visit with Cyril Clemens confirmed his interest in the writings of Mark Twain.

B362 "A Message to College Men." *Prologue* (Bowdoin College) 2 (May 1949): 7.
Begin your college work although you may be called into the military. Your education is important, because it will prepare you for the role you must play in trying to build a peaceful world where all nations are free to pursue the type of government which they prefer.

B363 "Messages on Human Rights." *United Nations Bulletin* 7 (15 Dec. 1949): 743-45, 747-49.
Each year the anniversary of the Universal Declaration of Human Rights should be the time when nations gauge the progress which has been made in improving individual rights and relations between nations (p. 748). One of several statements.

B364 "This I Remember." *McCall's* 76 (June 1949): 11-15, 116-28, 138-39, 141-42, 144-49, 156, 159, 163-64; 76 (July 1949): 16-19, 95-98, 101-2, 109-12, 120, 123-24, 127-28; 76 (Aug. 1949): 14-15, 99-102, 109-13, 116, 119-20, 123-24, 127-28; 76 (Sept.

1949): 16-17, 111-16, 128, 130, 132-39, 143-45, 148; 77 (Oct. 1949): 18-19, 33-34, 36-38, 40-42, 44, 46, 59-60, 62, 66-70, 80; 77 (Nov. 1949): 20-21, 112-26, 136; 77 (Dec. 1949): 20-23, 80, 82, 84, 86, 88-89, 91.
Serialized version of the book with minor changes in wording from the original text.

B365 "Universal Declaration of Human Rights." *School Life* 31 (Mar. 1949): 8-10.
Hopes the U.S. will take a leadership role in accepting a covenant of human rights. Brief statement introducing the text of the Universal Declaration of Human Rights (p. 8).

B366 "What I Think of the United Nations." *United Nations World* 3 (Aug. 1949): 39-41, 48.
Counters criticisms of the UN by stating that it was intended to help maintain the peace, not to make it. Discusses the UN's problems of language and cultural barriers and lack of authority.

B366a "Eleanor Roosevelt: The United Nations." *Annals of America.* Vol. 16. Chicago: Encyclopaedia Britannica, 1968. 613-17.

1950

B367 "A Brief History of the Drafting of the Universal Declaration of Human Rights and of the Draft Covenant on Human Rights." *Negro History Bulletin* 14 (Nov. 1950): 29-30, 46.
A description of the formation and work of the Commission on Human Rights and of the drafting of the human rights documents.

B368 "Continue the Fight for Better Schools." *School Life* 33 (Dec. 1950): 33-34.
Consists of brief statements by Warren Austin, Bernard Baruch, Dwight Eisenhower, and ER. In her statement she endorses the report of the National Citizens Commission for the Public Schools and calls for more support for education in order to develop an enlightened citizenry (p. 34).

B368a "War or No War...the Battle for Better Schools Must Be Won." *Parents' Magazine* 26 (Apr. 1951): 40-41, 102.
ER's statement is on p. 41.

B369 Foreword. *F.D.R.: His Personal Letters, 1928-1945.* Ed. Elliott Roosevelt and Joseph P. Lash. New York: Duell, Sloan and Pearce, 1950. xvii.
These letters should help historians to better understand FDR.

B370 "A Front on Which We May Serve." *United Nations World* 4 (June 1950): 50-51.
Through the efforts of Brooks Mendell the UN and the World Health Organization are working with developing countries to reduce disease.

B371 "Huckleberry Pudding." *"As We Like It": Cookery Recipes by Famous People.* Ed. Kenneth Downey. London: Barker, 1950. 137.
A recipe.

B372 "If I Were a Republican Today." *Cosmopolitan* 128 (June 1950): 29, 172.
The failure of Republicans to develop a position on the issues has diluted our two party system; therefore, if I were a Republican I would want my party to take a stand.

B373 "A Message to Boys' Village...and You!" *Southwest Louisiana Boys' Village News* 3 (Aug. 1950): cover.
As young boys you should learn more about our natural resources, the values of our democratic way of life, and how to live in harmony with other races.

B374 "Mrs. Roosevelt Discusses Human Rights." *United Nations Reporter* 3 (Apr. 1950): 3.
The importance of developing the covenant and the problems which will be faced with enforcing it.

B374a "Mrs. Roosevelt Discusses Human Rights." *American Association for the United Nations-United Nations Reporter* 22 (Apr. 1950): 3.

B375 Foreword. *Pandit Nehru's Discovery of America.* By Philip Pothens. Madras: Indian Press, 1950. 9.
Nehru's visit to U.S. helped improve our knowledge of India.

B376 "The Real Perle Mesta." *Flair* 1 (Oct. 1950): 31, 110.
Mesta was not named Ambassador to Luxembourg as a political favor. Her background in the steel industry made her an appropriate choice for a major steel-producing country, and she is carrying out her duties in an outstanding manner.

B377 "Reason...Must...Dominate...." *United Nations Bulletin* 8 (1 Apr. 1950): 327.
The spring 1950 session of the Commission on Human Rights was a productive one. Members of the commission should maintain contact with governments of nations not represented and stress the importance of human rights for all.

B378 "This I Remember." *Omnibook* 12 (May 1950): 1-45.
Condensation of the book.

B379 "United Nations: All of Us Can Help." *Book of Knowledge 1950 Annual.* New York: Grolier Society, 1950. 161-62.
The UN is our best hope for world peace and for avoiding the possibility of a war which could take place on U.S. soil.

B380 "What Liberty Means to Me." *Liberty* (1950).
Liberty means that the people have control of their government. Copy not examined. Annotation based on the following entry.

B380a "What Liberty Means to Me." *The Liberty Years, 1924-1940.* Ed. Allen Churchill. Englewood Cliffs: Prentice-Hall, 1969. 426-27.

B381 "Women Have Come a Long Way." *Harper's* 201 (Oct. 1950): 74-76.
I was not brought up to lead the type of life which I have. Today women enjoy much more equality than they did when I was young, and their presence in the UN

may be the best example of this. We do not need the Equal Rights Amendment, just elimination of state laws which discriminate against women.

B381a "Women Have Come a Long Way, Writes Mrs. Eleanor Roosevelt." *Senior Scholastic* 57 (11 Oct. 1950): 13.
Excerpts.

B382 Introduction. *The World We Saw.* By Mary Bell Decker. New York: R. Smith, 1950. 3.
During the world tour of the radio program *America's Town Meeting of the Air* the participants served as U.S. ambassadors.

1951

B383 "A Collector's Characteristics." *The Roosevelt Treasury.* Ed. James N. Rosenau. Garden City: Doubleday, 1951. 199-201.
Excerpt from Chapter 10 of *This Is My Story.*

B384 "The Elementary Teacher as a Champion of Human Rights." *Instructor* 61 (Sept. 1951): 7.
In the elementary school classroom children should be taught democracy, citizenship, human rights, and respect for all of our freedoms.

B385 "Esperance pour l'Europe." *Notre Europe* 3 (Mar. 1951): 5-6.
Increased collaboration between the U.S. and France is a positive change. The U.S. needs to work more closely with all of its European allies because of the threat of Soviet aggression. Someday there will be a common military force under the direction of the UN. In French.

B386 "The Faces of the People." *The Roosevelt Treasury.* Ed. James N. Rosenau. Garden City: Doubleday, 1951. 445-49.
Excerpt from Chapter 20 of *This I Remember.*

B387 "Franklin Was a Practical Politician." *The Roosevelt Treasury.* Ed. James N. Rosenau. Garden City: Doubleday, 1951. 380-81.
Excerpt from Chapter 1 of *This I Remember.*

B388 "He Disliked Being Disagreeable." *The Roosevelt Treasury.* Ed. James N. Rosenau. Garden City: Doubleday, 1951. 155-57.
Excerpts from Chapters 1 and 5 of *This I Remember.*

B389 "The Home: A Citadel of Freedom." *Jewish Parents Magazine* (Apr. 1951): 4-5.
The home should be comfortable. While no one should dominate the atmosphere, children should be taught discipline and good taste in the home. The home is where training for life in a democracy should begin.

B390 Introduction. *No Time for Tears.* By Charles H. Andrews. Garden City: Doubleday, 1951. 7-8.
The greatest assets of polio victims are faith and confidence in the future. Those qualities enabled FDR to meet the challenges of his presidency.

B391 "Redrafting the Human Rights Covenant." *United Nations Bulletin* 10 (15 Apr. 1951): 386.
   The UN Economic and Social Council has asked the Commission on Human Rights to revise the draft covenant. A report on commission activities.

B392 "Report on the Covenant." *United Nations World* 5 (Aug. 1951): 17-18.
   At the conclusion of the last meeting of the Commission on Human Rights no one was entirely satisfied, but there is a willingness for the Third Committee to write the covenant or give advice to the commission.

B392a "A Report on the Covenant of Human Rights." *Delhi Mirror* 1 (24 Feb. 1952): 4, 13.

B393 "The Role of the Elder Statesman Appealed to Him." *The Roosevelt Treasury*. Ed. James N. Rosenau. Garden City: Doubleday, 1951. 190-92
   Excerpt from Chapter 13 of *This I Remember*.

B394 "The Seven People Who Shaped My Life." *Look* 15 (19 June 1951): 54-56, 58.
   Her parents, Aunt Pussie (Mrs. Forbes Morgan), Marie Souvestre, Sara Roosevelt, Louis Howe, and FDR.

B395 Foreword. *The Story of My Life*. By Helen Keller. 1951. 7-8.
   The life and work of Helen Keller is a tribute to the human spirit.

B395a Foreword. *The Story of My Life*. By Helen Keller. New York: Dell, 1961. 7-8.

B395b Foreword. *The Story of My Life*. By Helen Keller. Dell, 8296. New York: Dell, 1972. 7-8.

B396 "That Was Characteristic of Franklin." *The Roosevelt Treasury*. Ed. James N. Rosenau. Garden City: Doubleday, 1951. 116-17.
   Excerpt from Chapter 6 of *This I Remember*.

B397 "To My Complete Surprise." *The Roosevelt Treasury*. Ed. James N. Rosenau. Garden City: Doubleday, 1951. 186-87.
   Excerpt from Chapter 1 of *This I Remember*.

B398 [Introduction]. *The World's Favorite Recipes*. Ed. The American Home Economics Assoc. New York: Harper, 1951. [i].
   Sharing recipes can foster improved relations between nations.

1952

B399 Foreword. *Beauty Behind Barbed Wire: The Arts of the Japanese in Our War Relocation Camps*. By Allen H. Eaton. New York: Harper, 1952. xi-xii.
   The book provides insight into the character of the Japanese people.

B400 Introduction. *The Diary of a Young Girl*. By Anne Frank. Garden City: Doubleday, 1952. 7-8.
   The diary is a monument to Anne's spirit and to all who work for peace.

B400a Introduction. *The Diary of a Young Girl*. By Anne Frank. New York: Modern Library, 1952. 7-8.

B401 Foreword. *A Fair World for All: The Meaning of the Declaration of Human Rights*. By Dorothy Canfield Fisher. New York: Whittlesey House, 1952. 5-6.
  This is a simple, easy to understand discussion of the Universal Declaration of Human Rights. Young people can learn about their responsibilities as world citizens from this book.

B402 "Growth That Starts from Thinking." *This I Believe [1]: The Living Philosophies of One Hundred Thoughtful Men and Women in All Walks of Life*. Ed. Edward P. Morgan. New York: Simon & Schuster, 1952. 155-56.
  Live each day with courage.

B403 Foreword. *To Win These Rights: A Personal Story of the CIO in the South*. By Lucy Randolph Mason. New York: Harper, 1952. [ix].
  Considers the stories included in this book to be an important part of history.

B403a Foreword. *To Win These Rights: A Personal Story of the CIO in the South*. By Lucy Randolph Mason. Westport: Greenwood, 1970. [ix].

B404 "UN: Good U.S. Investment." *Foreign Policy Bulletin* 32 (1 Oct. 1952): 1-2.
  There are many benefits to be gained from the specialized agencies. Responds to attacks on the UN and urges Americans to learn more about the organization and its work.

B405 "The United Nations and You." *See* 11 (Nov. 1952): 10-13.
  The UN allows us to understand other nations and give hope to all peoples, both of which are necessary for a peaceful world. A description of the UN and related organizations and the positive things which are being accomplished.

1953

B406 "The Education of an American." *House & Garden* 104 (Aug. 1953): 60-61, 94-98.
  College provides new intellectual interests at the time when most young people are maturing into adulthood (p. 61). ER, Ralph Bunche, and Bernard Baruch were asked to discuss the value of a college education to accompany Robert Maynard Hutchins' article.

B407 "The Japan I Saw." *Minneapolis Sunday Tribune Picture Roto Magazine* 11 Oct. 1953: 4-5.
  Impressions from her visit. Based on "My Day" columns.

B408 Foreword. *Peace Through Strength: Bernard Baruch and a Blueprint for Security*. By Morris V. Rosenbloom. Washington: American Survey Assoc.-Farrar, Straus and Young. 1953. 23-26.
  Calls Baruch a "practical visionary" and outlines his contributions.

B409 Foreword. *Roosevelt and the Warm Springs Story.* By Turnley Walker. New York: Wyn, 1953. [v].
The book is delightful.

B410 "Should UN Remain a Major Plank in U.S. Policy?" *Foreign Policy Bulletin* 33 (15 Oct. 1953): 4-5.
Yes, because the UN provides the opportunity for better understanding among nations (p. 4).

B411 "Some of My Best Friends Are Negro." *Ebony* 9 (Feb. 1953): 16-20, 22, 24-26.
Recalls many of her close associations with blacks, discusses the public reaction to her support of racial equality, and defends FDR as an independent thinker on the issue.

B411a "Some of My Best Friends Are Negro." *White on Black: The Views of Twenty-one White Americans on the Negro.* Ed. Era Bell Thompson and Herbert Nipson. Chicago, Johnson, 1963. 3-17.

B411b "Some of My Best Friends Are Negro." *Ebony* 31 (Nov. 1975): 72-78.

B412 "Speaking of Teaching." *National Parent-Teacher* 48 (Nov. 1953): 20.
We need good, dedicated teachers who are rewarded for their ability and dedication.

B413 "To Answer Their Needs...." *United Nations Bulletin* 14 (15 Jan. 1953): 92.
UNICEF should become a permanent part of the UN. A defense of UNICEF's programs.

1954

B414 Foreword. *The Captains and the Kings.* By Edith Benham Helm. New York: Putnam's, 1954. v-vii.
Appreciation for her White House social secretary and this account of the Wilson, Roosevelt, and Truman administrations.

B415 "Churchill as a Guest." *Churchill by His Contemporaries.* Ed. Charles Eade. New York: Simon and Schuster, 1954. 186-92.
Excerpt from *This I Remember.* Describes Churchill's White House visits of Dec. 1941-Jan. 1942 and June 1942.

B416 Foreword. *G.P.A. Healy, American Artist: An Intimate Chronicle of the Nineteenth Century.* By Marie De Mare. New York: McKay, 1954. xv-xvi.
Praise for the work and life of Healy.

B417 Foreword. *The Man Behind Roosevelt: The Story of Louis McHenry Howe.* By Lela Stiles. Cleveland: World, 1954. [vii].
It took someone close to Howe to write this intimate account of the devotion which he had for FDR.

B418 "Memo to the Field." *AAUN News* 26 (Nov. 1954): 7.
Reports on her recent trip to the West. Urges readers to help increase AAUN membership.

B419 "The Need for Intellectual Freedom." *Say: The Alumni Magazine of Roosevelt College* 5 (Spring 1954): 4.
None of our freedoms will exist if we are afraid to lead free lives. Brief article accompanying statements attributed to FDR under the caption "The Need for Intellectual Freedom."

B420 "Negotiate with Russia: Never Use the H-Bomb." *Time* 64 (30 Aug. 1954): 16.
While keeping our armaments, we should concentrate on diplomacy.

B421 "Roosevelt Day Greetings." *ADA World* 9 (Feb. 1954): 2M.
It would please FDR that his beliefs are being commemorated.

B422 Preambulo. *Roosevelt y la Buena Vecindad*. By Francisco Cuevas Cancino. Mexico City: Fondo de Cultura Economica, 1954. 7.
Pleased that a book has been written about FDR's Good Neighbor Policy and encourages the continuation of efforts of the U.S. and Latin American countries to work together to promote democracy and resolve economic problems. In Spanish.

B423 "Should You Help Your Children?" *Lifetime Living* 3 (Dec. 1954): 26.
Young married couples should be able to expect some help from their parents.

B424 "The U.S. and the U.N." *Guide to Politics, 1954*. Ed. Quincy Howe and Arthur M. Schlesinger, Jr. New York: Dial, 1954. 60-64.
In this Americans for Democratic Action guide to the issues of the 1954 elections she sees no reason why the UN should be an issue. Lengthy rebuttal to six criticisms of the UN.

B425 "Why Are We Co-operating with Tito?" *Look* 18 (5 Oct. 1954): 80, 82-83.
We should cooperate with Tito because he is an enemy of Soviet imperialism.

1955

B426 "Children of Israel." *Midstream* 1 (Autumn 1955): 110-11.
Public and private funds are being used to improve the quality of life for the children of Israel.

B427 "Memo from the Field." *AAUN News* 27 (Mar. 1955): 7.
Travels to the Midwest and Southwest.

B428 "Memo from the Field." *AAUN News* 27 (May 1955): 7.
Reports on new AAUN officers and praises the activities of the United Nations Youth of Maryland.

B429 "Memo from the Field." *AAUN News* 27 (June 1955): 7.
A variety of association activities are reported.

B430 "Memo from the Field." *AAUN News* 27 (Sept. 1955): 7.
  Reports on new chapters established. Announces plans to attend meeting of World Federation of United Nations Associations in Bangkok on 5-11 Sept.

B431 "Memo from the Field." *AAUN News* 27 (Oct. 1955): 7.
  As part of our celebration of the 10th anniversary of the UN we should dedicate ourselves to making it an even stronger body during the next decade. Upcoming AAUN travels.

B432 "Memo to the Field." *AAUN News* 27 (Feb. 1955): 7.
  Reports on her travels in the eastern states on behalf of the AAUN.

B433 "Obligation of Leadership." *Childhood Education* 32 (Sept. 1955): 2-3.
  Teachers have the difficult task of preparing students for the new world in which they will live and work with other races, to accept the responsibilities of living in a democracy, and to better understand people elsewhere in the world.

B434 "Report to the Membership." *AAUN News* 27 (Dec. 1955/Jan. 1956): 1.
  The original ideas of the UN will be realized during the next 10 years.

B435 "Social Responsibility for Individual Welfare." *National Policies for Education, Health and Social Services*. Ed. James Earl Russell. Columbia University Bicentennial Conference Series. Garden City: Doubleday, 1955. xxxv-xxxvii.
  Discusses the real meaning of "welfare state" and defends the social programs initiated during the New Deal.

B435a "Social Responsibility for Individual Welfare." *National Policies for Education, Health and Social Services*. Ed. James Earl Russell. Columbia University Bicentennial Conference Series. New York: Russell & Russell, 1955. xxxv-xxxvii.

B436 "Your United Nations." *Bulletin of the American Library Association* 49 (Oct. 1955): 491.
  Librarians can promote understanding of the UN through books, films, and exhibits.

1956

B437 "Attorney General's List and Civil Liberties: Replies to an Anvil Questionnaire." *Anvil and Student Partisan* 7 (Spring/Summer 1956): 17.
  Her responses to questions about the U.S. Attorney General's subversive list are terse.

B438 "Do the Kind Thing." *Every Week* 23 (15-19 Oct. 1956): 48.
  Regardless of whether you know the customs of a country, you can never go wrong by being kind.

B439 "If You Ask Me." *Ladies' Home Journal Treasury*. New York: Simon & Schuster, 1956. 314-16.
  Selections from her column "If You Ask Me."

B440 "Memo from the Field." *AAUN News* 28 (Mar. 1956): 7.
Reports on trip to the Southwest.

B441 "Memories of F.D.R.." *Look* 20 (17 Apr. 1956): 101.
FDR was a pragmatist who had concern for the average citizen and an appreciation for human suffering.

B442 "Prayer for a Better World." *Parents' Magazine* 31 (June 1956): 76.
A prayer for achieving peace with our brothers everywhere through understanding and courage.

B443 "The Right to Vote." *Voting Guide, 1956: How to Make Your Vote Count.* Washington: Americans for Democratic Action, 1956. 4-5.
Study the issues and decide how you wish to vote. Serves as an introduction to a non-partisan guide to the issues in the 1956 elections.

B444 "Roosevelt Day Greetings." *ADA World* 11 (Feb. 1956): 2M.
It would please FDR that his beliefs are being commemorated. Same as the message issued in 1954.

B445 "Salute to Montgomery." *Liberation* 1 (Dec. 1956): 4-5.
The Montgomery, Ala. busing protest was a great example of peaceful resistance (p. 4). One of several statements.

B446 "This Is My Story." *Ladies' Home Journal Treasury.* New York: Simon & Schuster, 1956. 262-67.
Excerpts from the book pertaining to her childhood.

1957

B447 "F.D.R. as Seen by Eleanor Roosevelt." *Wisdom* 2 (July 1957): 30.
Brief statements about FDR excerpted from *My Days*, *It Seems to Me*, and *If You Ask Me*.

B448 "From the Wisdom of Eleanor Roosevelt." *Wisdom* 2 (July 1957): 31.
Brief excerpts from *My Days*, *It Seems to Me*, and *If You Ask Me*.

B449 Introduction. *Letters from Jerusalem.* By Mary Clawson. London, New York: Abelard-Schuman, 1957. [xiii].
Brief statement about a book of letters written by American women living in Israel.

B450 "Roosevelt Day Greetings." *ADA World* 12 (Feb. 1957): 2M.
The ADA has been effective in promoting the ideas of the New Deal.

B451 "Schoolday Tips from Mrs. Roosevelt." *Sunday Star Magazine* [Washington] 25 Aug. 1957: 28-29.
Brief statement about her education. Tips for today's student: study a foreign language, study the arts and history for lifelong pleasure, develop curiosity, develop ability to explain your local and national governments to a foreigner, and prepare yourself for accepting the responsibilities of living in a democracy.

B452   Foreword. *300,000 New Americans: The Epic of a Modern Immigrant-Aid Service*. By Lyman Cromwell White. New York: Harper, 1957. ix.
   To appreciate the work of refugee organizations this book is required reading.

B453   Introduction. *Youth Aliyah: Past, Present and Future*. By Moshe Kol. F.I.C.E. Documents 1, Israel. Jerusalem: International Federation of Children's Communities, 1957. 7-8.
   As World Patron of Youth Aliyah she provides a brief introduction to the history of an organization which fosters the immigration of youth to Israel.

1958

B454   "Among My Favorites: A Massachusetts Coast Scene by Ludwig Bemelmans." *Art in America* 46 (Spring 1958): 39.
   The two paintings by Bemelmans which she has at Val-Kill remind her of coastal waters.

B455   "A Brief Message to Japanese Women." *Today's Japan* 3 (Sept. 1958): 16.
   You should work hard, as women everywhere must do, for what you want to accomplish.

B456   "How to Get the Most Out of Life." *Star Weekly Magazine* [Toronto] 30 Aug. 1958: 3-4.
   Decide on what is important and emphasize it. Describes her daily routine and includes recollections of summers at Campobello and life with her children when they were young.

B457   "On My Own." *Saturday Evening Post* 230 (8 Feb. 1958): 19-21, 66, 68-70; (15 Feb. 1958): 32-33, 106-8; (22 Feb. 1958): 30-31, 56-57, 60-62; (1 Mar. 1958): 30, 95-96, 98; (8 Mar. 1958): 32-33, 72-74.
   Abridged ed. of the book. 15 Feb. also entitled "Hostess at Hyde Park"; 22 Feb., "I Learn about Communists"; 1 Mar., "My Round-the-World Adventures"; 8 Mar., "Of Stevenson, Truman and Kennedy."

B458   [Foreword]. *The Shook-up Generation*. By Harrison E. Salisbury. New York: Harper & Row: 1958. [5].
   Although this country has not dealt adequately with juvenile delinquency, we must remember that we can solve the problem if we start in our own communities and homes.

B459   Foreword. *Talks with Teachers*. By Alice Keliher. Darien: Educational Publishing, 1958. 3-4.
   Teachers are important in shaping the future of the young, and they should strive to improve themselves and their position in the community.

B460   "The Value of Human Personality." *Intercollegian* (YMCA) 76 (Sept. 1958): 4.
   Learn to use your mind, develop curiosity and integrity, and have respect for all peoples. Part of "11 Voices in the Third Great Revolution" (pp. 3-7, 22).

B461 "Values to Live By." *Jewish Heritage* 1 (Spring 1958): 44-45, 54.
Duty has been the most important factor in my life. Religion has also been important to me as it was to FDR who felt that he could ask and receive divine guidance. Thankful for her early work in a settlement house which exposed her to poverty, she hopes that she can continue working for peace and better understanding between nations.

B462 Foreword. *World Youth and the Communists: The Facts about Communist Penetration of WFDY and IUS*. By Nils M. Apeland. London: Phoenix House, 1958. [7-8].
In this work about the World Federation of Democratic Youth and the International Union of Students ER argues that since the future rests with the young they should be aware of how Communists infiltrate youth organizations.

1959

B463 "A Dessert Mother's Helper Can Prepare." *Kids' Stuff* (Fall 1959): 11.
A recipe for a huckleberry desert.

B464 Preface. *From the Morgenthau Diaries, Years of Crisis, 1928-1938*. By John Morton Blum. Boston: Houghton Mifflin, 1959. [v].
Brief statement about FDR's relationship with Henry Morgenthau, Jr. which reveals the conflicts which developed between FDR and his Secretary of the Treasury.

B465 Introduction. *Give Us the Tools*. By Henry Viscardi. New York: Eriksson, 1959. xvii-xix.
Introduction to Viscardi's account of helping the handicapped perform complex, work-related tasks.

B466 *The Meaning of Freedom*. New York: Freedom Fund, 1959?
To be free is to be able to think about any subject, be curious, associate with whomever you wish, and worship as you choose. It also entails the obligation to participate in our democracy and assure that all enjoy the same rights. Published in English and Russian. Copy not examined. Annotation based on the following entry.

B466a "The Meaning of Freedom." *This Week Magazine* (3 May 1959): 2.

B467 "Mrs. Roosevelt Reports on Her Trip to Russia." *Equity* 44 (May 1959): 3.
Her impressions of the arts in Russia. Written after her trip to Russia, it complements an interview also published in *Equity*.

B468 "On Reaching Her 75th Birthday Eleanor Roosevelt Praises Television's Contribution to the Senior Citizen." *TV Guide* 7 (17 Oct. 1959): 6-8.
Television can be a companion to older persons. It can keep them informed and help them to relate to the young.

B469 "Segregation." *Educational Forum* 24 (Nov. 1959): 5-6.
Democracy cannot exist without equality, and there can be no equality as long as

segregation and discrimination persist. Warns that communism can beat out democracy in developing nations if it is more sensitive to the effects of segregation.

B470 "What Are We Here For?" By Eleanor Roosevelt and Huston Smith. *The Search for America.* Ed. Huston Smith. Englewood Cliffs: Prentice-Hall, 1959. 3-12. Suggested Readings.
The U.S. needs a leader with the vision to reverse the decline in its world position. U.S. foreign policy should abandon the passive goal of containing communism and once again promote peace and prosperous democracies.

B471 "Where I Get My Energy." *Harper's* 218 (Jan. 1959): 45-47.
She credits her energy to strong ancestors, learning that one must meet obligations, and having many interests.

B471a "Where I Get My Energy." *Reader's Digest* 74 (Mar. 1959): 52-53.
Condensation.

B472 "Why I Am Opposed to 'Right to Work' Laws." *American Federationist* 66 (Feb. 1959): 5-7.
Right-to-work laws are not good for the worker or the country, because their real intent is to weaken unionism.

1960

B473 "Education Is Essential." *Bryn Mawr Alumnae Bulletin* 40 (Winter 1960): 7.
Women throughout the world are recognizing the importance of education, and more than men they will improve living conditions wherever they live.

B474 [Foreword]. *FDR Speaks.* Ed. Henry Steele Commager. Washington: Washington Records, 1960. 3.
This collection of FDR's presidential speeches contains much which is relevant to today's issues. Introduces recordings of speeches by FDR.

B475 "Mrs. Roosevelt's Page." *Woman* 47 (26 Nov. 1960): 17; 47 (3 Dec. 1960): 21; 47 (10 Dec. 1960): 25; 47 (17 Dec. 1960): 21; 47 (24 Dec. 1960): ?; 47 (31 Dec. 1960): 23; 48 (7 Jan. 1961): 23; 48 (14 Jan. 1961): 16; 48 (21 Jan. 1961): 18.
Excerpts from *You Learn by Living.* 10 Dec. 1960 and later parts entitled "Mrs. Roosevelt's Friendly Page."

B476 "My Advice to the Next First Lady." *Redbook* 116 (Nov. 1960): 18-21, 95-96.
Her advice on clothing, making the White House a home, fulfilling the duties of White House hostess, and living in the public eye. While giving advice to the next First Lady ER provides an intimate view of her own years in the White House.

B477 "You Learn by Living." *True Story* 83 (Oct. 1960): 37, 112-16; 83 (Nov. 1960): 56-59, 98.
Condensation of the book.

1961

B478 [Review]. *Dag Hammarskjold: Custodian of a Brushfire Peace*. By Joseph P. Lash. Garden City: Doubleday, 1961. 304p. Index.
Reading this book makes one want to know Dag Hammarskjold. A brief review printed on the dust jacket.

B479 "The Joy of Reading." *Coronet* 50 (Sept. 1961): 74-75, 80.
Adults should instill in the young an appreciation for books as objects of beauty and sources of knowledge. Reading is important in order to better understand the world in which we live.

B480 "A Policy Toward Castro's Cuba." *Current* 14 (June 1961): 19.
Neither the U.S. nor the Soviet Union should provide military aid to Cuba. Instead they should participate in economic trade which would improve the internal situation in Cuba. From "My Day" of 30 Apr. 1961.

B481 "A President's Planning." *Saturday Review* 44 (8 July 1961): 10.
Recalls the careful preparations which FDR made for conferences, even those which he was not to attend.

B482 "What Has Happened to the American Dream?" *Atlantic* 207 (Apr. 1961): 46-50.
The Soviets have succeeded in inspiring their youth to carry the message of communism, and we must make our young feel they are needed in conquering new challenges and spreading the American dream of democracy.

B482a "What Has Happened to the American Dream?" *Modern Composition*. Book 6. By Wallace Stegner, et al. New York: Holt, Rinehart and Winston, 1965. 250-61.
Used as an example of persuasive writing.

1962

B483 Introduction. *The Adventure of America*. By John Tobias and Savin Hoffecker. New York: Geis, 1962. vii.
The history of the U.S. is told through literature. For young readers.

B484 Foreword. *Brutal Mandate: A Journey to South West Africa*. By Allard K. Lowenstein. New York: Macmillan, 1962. [v]-vi.
Praises Lowenstein's abilities and his fact-finding trip.

B485 Foreword. *From the Eagle's Wing: A Biography of John Muir*. By Hildegarde Hoyt Swift. New York: Morrow, 1962. 7-8.
This book should convince us of the need to conserve our natural resources.

B486 Foreword. *The Long Shadow of Little Rock: A Memoir*. By Daisy Bates. New York: D. McKay, 1962. xiii-xv.
The 1957 school integration crisis in Little Rock, Ark. was an example of the beast in man. Fears that the types of actions and attitudes discussed in the book will continue to occur.

B487 "Modern Children and Old-Fashioned Manners." *Redbook* 119 (Oct. 1962): 47, 122, 124-25, 127-28.
Condensation of pp. 31-49 of *Eleanor Roosevelt's Book of Common Sense Etiquette*.

B488 Foreword. *The Road to the White House. F.D.R.: The Pre-Presidential Years.* By Lorena A. Hickok. Philadelphia: Chilton, 1962. vii-viii.
Hickok has presented FDR's courage and imagination in a way which should appeal to young readers.

B489 "Statement of Mrs. Eleanor Roosevelt, Chairman of the President's Commission on the Status of Women." *Congressional Record* (15 Feb. 1962): 2281.
Our work will help women benefit from the economic and social changes which are occurring. "In the years ahead many of the outmoded barriers to women's aspirations will disappear."

B490 Foreword. *This Is Our Strength: Selected Papers of Golda Meir.* Ed. Henry M. Christman. New York: Macmillan, 1962. ix-xiv.
The character and determination of Mrs. Meir and of Israel can be seen in Mrs. Meir's words. Extensive quotations from the book.

B491 "To All AAUN Members West of the Mississippi:" *AAUN News* 34 (Mar. 1962): 6.
Support the UN by joining the American Association for the United Nations.

B492 "A Woman for the Times." *Boston Sunday Globe Magazine* 27 May 1962: 3.
Women are important assets, and their talents should not be wasted. A First Lady must be intelligent, disciplined, and dedicated to the public good, and Jacqueline Kennedy has those qualities. Forms part of "The President's Wife: Jacqueline Kennedy, Her Life Story in Pictures."

B493 [Review]. *The Young Citizens: The Story of the Encampment for Citizenship.* By Algernon D. Black. New York: Ungar, 1962.
The encampment made democracy dynamic for young people. A brief review printed on the dust jacket.

B494 Introduction. *You're the Boss: The Practice of American Politics.* By Edward J. Flynn. New York: Collier, 1962. 7-9.
Brief introduction consisting primarily of quotations from the book. Joins Flynn in promoting broader participation in politics. Introduction written for the 1962 ed.

1963

B495 "Eleanor Roosevelt from This Is My Story." *A Reader for Parents: A Selection of Creative Literature About Childhood.* New York: Norton, 1963. 61-69.
Excerpts several sections of *This Is My Story* in which she writes about her parents and childhood.

B495a "Eleanor Roosevelt from This Is My Story." *Insights: A Selection of Creative Literature About Childhood.* New York: Aronson, 1973. 61-69.

B496 "I Remember Hyde Park: A Final Reminiscence." *McCall's* 90 (Feb. 1963): 71-73, 162-63.

Memories of Hyde Park home emphasizing that it was Sara Roosevelt's and not hers, changes made to accommodate a crippled FDR, disputes with her mother-in-law about the rearing of the Roosevelt children, New York and Val-Kill homes, and the visit of the British royal couple.

B496a "I Remember Hyde Park." *Reader's Digest* 82 (June 1963): 95-100.
Condensation.

B496b "I Remember Hyde Park." *Reader's Digest 50th Anniversary Treasury: A Selection of the Best of 50 Years from the Reader's Digest.* Pleasantville: Reader's Digest Assoc., 1972. 157-62.
Condensation.

B497 "Israel Will Become a Great Nation." *The Mission of Israel.* Ed. Jacob Baal-Teshuva. New York: Speller, 1963. 32.

As the state of Israel reaches its 13th year of existence, it is a nation moving toward maturity.

B498 Introduction. *My Darling Clementine: The Story of Lady Churchill.* By Jack Fishman. New York: McKay, 1963. 1-5.

Discusses the life of the wife of a public figure, Mrs. Churchill's and her own.

B499 Foreword. *Planning Community Services for Children in Trouble.* By Alfred J. Kahn. New York: Columbia Univ. Pr., 1963. vii-viii.

Services which are available to help children and families must be connected in some way. Dated Sept. 1962.

B500 "Tomorrow Is Now." *Ladies' Home Journal* 80 (Sept. 1963): 39-45.
Excerpts the book and its foreword.

B501 "A Visit to Campobello." *Ford Times* 56 (Apr. 1963): 2-6.

She spends a few days with son John and his family in the former Roosevelt cottage. Recalls FDR's days there.

1964

B502 Preface. *Letters of a Javanese Princess.* By Raden Adjeng Kartini. Ed. Hildred Geertz. Unesco Collection of Representative Works. Indonesian Series. New York: Norton Library-Norton, 1964. 5-6.

These letters provide insight into the life and customs of late 19th century Java.

1965

B503 "Churchill at the White House." *Atlantic* 215 (Mar. 1965): 77-80.

One of a series of articles in an issue about Churchill. Recalls visits from and to Churchill beginning with his Christmas 1941 visit to the White House. Discusses her sense of inadequacy when around him and leaves the impression that their association was not a comfortable one. Written in 1959 and revised for publication shortly before her death.

1966

B504 *The Common Sense Wisdom of Three First Ladies*. Ed. Bill Adler. New York: Citadel, 1966. 160p.
  Arranged by topics including marriage, bringing up children, and education, there are brief quotations by ER, Jacqueline Kennedy, and Lady Bird Johnson. Some quotations are dated. No sources provided.

B504a "Wise and Warm Thoughts from Eleanor Roosevelt." *Good Housekeeping* 162 (June 1966): 95.
  Excerpts from *The Common Sense Wisdom of Three First Ladies*.

B505 "Uniting for Peace." By Regina Tor and Eleanor Roosevelt. *Into New Worlds*. Macmillan Reading into New Worlds Program. London: Macmillan, 1966. 322-29.
  Excerpt from *Growing Toward Peace*.

1967

B506 "Eleanor Roosevelt: Marriage." *Franklin Delano Roosevelt*. Great Lives Observed. Ed. Gerald D. Nash. Englewood Cliffs: Prentice-Hall, 1967. 76-78.
  Excerpt from *This Is My Story*, pp. 124-27.

B507 "Mrs. Roosevelt Wins a Victory." *The Human Side of American History*. Ed. Richard C. Brown. Boston: Ginn, 1967. 289-91.
  An abridgement of pp. 49-52 of *On My Own* which discusses her debate at the UN with Soviet delegate Andrei Vishinsky.

1970

B508 "Little Nell." *Dear Father: Warm and Witty Writings about Fathers*. Selected by Dean Walley. Kansas City: Hallmark, 1970. 56-58.
  Abridged excerpt from *The Autobiography of Eleanor Roosevelt* about recollections of her father.

B509 "Little Nell." *To Father with Love*. Selected by Aileene Herrbach Neighbors. Kansas City: Hallmark, 1970. 42-43.
  Abridgment of pp. 5-6 of *The Autobiography of Eleanor Roosevelt*.

1971

B510 "A Reform-Minded President's Wife." *The American Woman: Who Was She?* Eyewitness Accounts of American History Series. Ed. Anne Firor Scott. Englewood Cliffs: Spectrum-Prentice-Hall, 1971. 119-21.
  From *This I Remember*, pp. 125-27.

1975

B511 "On Living." *Step to the Music You Hear*. Vol. II. Philosophical Poems by Modern Authors. Ed. Susan Polis Schutz. Boulder: Blue Mountain Arts, 1975.
  Think about others, not yourself and do the best you can with what life sends your way. Taken from her "If You Ask Me" column of Sept. 1957.

1976

B512 "If You Ask Me." *The Journal of the Century*. Comp. Bryan Holme. New York: Studio Book-Viking, 1976. 221-23.
A selection of questions and answers from several of her columns presented as if a single column.

B513 "If You Ask Me." *McCall's* 103 (Apr. 1976): 40-41.
Selections from her columns for June 1949-Nov. 1962.

1977

B514 "Eleanor Roosevelt Works to End the Depression." *We, the American Women: A Documentary History*. By Beth Millstein and Jeanne Bodin. Chicago: Science Research Assocs., 1977. 242-43.
An abridgement of pp. 162-64 of *This I Remember*. Also published 1976 and 1977 (New York: Ozer). The 1977 Ozer publication is by Beth Millstein Kava and Jeanne Bodin.

1982

B515 "Eleanor Roosevelt." *The Quotable Woman, 1800-1981*. Comp. and ed. Elaine Partnow. New York: Facts on File, 1982. 190-94.
Documented quotations from her writings and speeches.

B515a "Eleanor Roosevelt." *The New Quotable Woman*. Comp. and ed. Elaine Partnow. New York: Facts on File, 1992. 278-81.
The number of quotations is reduced.

1984

B516 "Eleanor Roosevelt on the Challenges of Citizenship." *Social Education* 48 (Nov./Dec. 1984): 531.
Excerpts from *Tomorrow Is Now* selected to illustrate "moral imperatives."

1986

B517 *Seeds of Peace: A Catalogue of Quotations*. Comp. Jeanne Larson and Madge Micheels-Cyrus. Philadelphia: New Society, 1986. xi + 276p. Index.
Includes four quotations from her writings. An undated statement in which she expresses her belief in peace and the need to work for it (p. 209), two undated ones in which she states that peace will come about only through the efforts of women and youth (pp. 221, 226), and a quotation from *It's Up to the Women* about the role which women can play in creating a peaceful world (p. 256).

1988

B518 "A Challenge for the West." *Women on War: Essential Voices for the Nuclear Age*. Ed. Daniela Gioseffi. New York: Simon & Schuster-Touchstone, 1988. 156-58.
Since the Soviet Union has made great strides in improving the lives of its citizens, underdeveloped countries may look to communism. The West must demonstrate that

democracy can also improve the material aspects of life. Excerpts pp. 231-33 of *On My Own*.

1990

B519 "Eleanor Roosevelt: 'I Had a Point of View of My Own....'" *Women of Valor: The Struggle against the Great Depression as Told in Their Own Life Stories*. Ed. with commentary by Bernard Sternsher and Judith Sealander. Chicago: Dee, 1990. 48-66.
    Excerpts *This I Remember*.

B520 "Having Learned to Stare Down Fear." *American Women: Their Lives in Their Words*. By Doreen Rappaport. New York: Crowell, 1990. 221-23.
    She overcame fear and became her own person. Excerpts pp. 411-12 of *The Autobiography of Eleanor Roosevelt*.

TRANSLATIONS OF HER WRITINGS

The Autobiography of Eleanor Roosevelt. 1961

B521 *Autobiografía*. Mexico: Ed. Novaro, 1964. 252p.
    Translation into Spanish.

B522 *Eleanor: Atmakahini*. Calcutta: Asia, 1966. 193p.
    Translation into Bengali.

B523 *Eleanor Roosevelt*. Dacca: Popular, 1966. ii + 222p.
    Translation into Bengali.

B524 *Eleanor Roosevelt Jijoden*. Tokyo: Jiji tsushinsha, 1964? 262p.
    Translation into Japanese.

B525 *Eleanor Roosevelt--Ni Atma Katha*. Bombay: Vora, 1967. 216p.
    Translation into Gujarati.

B526 *Elrinoeo Ruzeuvelteu Jaseojeon*. Seoul: Jeonghyangsa, 1963? 716p.
    Translation into Korean.

B527 *Ma Vie*. Paris: Gonthier, 1965. 285p.
    Translation into French.

B528 *As Memorias de Eleanor Roosevelt*. 2 vols. Belo Horizante: Difusao Pan-Americana do Livro, 1961.
    Translation into Portuquese.

B529 *Srimati Eleanor Rooseveltnka Atmacharita*. Cuttack: Cuttack Trading Co., 1965. iv + 198p.
    Translation into Oriya.

"Churchill at the White House." 1965

B530 "Churchill at the White House." *Fair Lady* [Tokyo] (June 1965): 86-90.
Translation into Japanese.

Eleanor Roosevelt's Book of Common Sense Etiquette. **1962**

B531 *Etiquette.* Tokyo: Hakusuisha, 1969?
Translation into Japanese.

Growing Toward Peace. **1960**

B532 *A Luta Pela Paz.* Rio de Janeiro: Distribuidora Record, 1964.
Translation into Portuguese.

B533 *La Marche Vers la Paix.* Strasbourg: Istra, 1962. 126p.
Translation into French.

B534 *La Marche Vers la Paix.* Coll. Nouveaux Horizons, E.2.
Paris: Nouveaux horizons, 1963. 125p.
Translation into French.

B535 *Nyeinchanthayar Bawata.* Rangoon: U Than Htun, 1963? 110p.
Translation into Burmese.

India and the Awakening East. **1953**

B536 *Indien und der Erwachende Osten.* Bern: A. Scherz, 1954. 231p.
Translation into German.

On My Own. **1958**

B537 *Allenn Verder.* Antwerpen: Diogemes, 1959. 283p.
Translation into Dutch.

B538 *Allenn Verder.* Bussum: Ruys, 1959. 283p.
Translation into Dutch.

B539 *On My Own: The Years Since the White House.* Seoul: Korea Legal Aid Center
for Family Relations, 1980. 359p.
Translation into Korean. Added title in English.

B540 *Veien fra det Hvite Hus.* Oslo: Ansgar, 1959? 264p.
Translation into Norwegian.

Partners: The United Nations and Youth. **1950**

B541 *Kawan: Perserikatan Bangsa-Bangsa dan Pemuda.* Bandung:
Masa Baru, 1952. 174p.
Translation into Indonesian.

This I Remember. 1949

B542 "Dette Jusker jeg." *Alt for Damerne* (20 Dec. 1949): 6-7, 29-31.
Excerpts in Danish.

B543 *Ik Herinner Mij.* Amsterdam: Keesing, 1949. 359p.
Translation into Dutch.

B544 *Jag Minns.* Stockholm: Tidens, 1950. 415p.
Translation into Swedish.

B545 *Lo-ssu-fu fu Jen Hui i Lu.* Chin jih shih chieh tsung shu, 1. Hsiang-kang: Jen jih shih chieh she, 1949? 24p.
Condensation and translation into Chinese.

B546 *...Minner og Mennesker.* Oslo: Bergendahls, 1950. 272p.
Translation into Norwegian.

B547 *...Questo io Ricordo.* Milan: Garzanti, 1950. 475p.
Translation into Italian.

B548 "Roosevelt was Myn Man." *Margriet* (28 Jan. 1950): 3; (4 Feb. 1950): 3-5, 42, 47; (11 Feb. 1950): 3-5; (18 Feb. 1950): 11-13, 45; (25 Feb. 1950): 12-13, 44; (4 Mar. 1950): 10-12, 31; (11 Mar. 1950): 18-19; (18 Mar. 1950): 5-7; (25 Mar. 1950): 28-29; (1 Apr. 1950): 20-21; (8 Apr. 1950): 10-11; (15 Apr. 1950): 14-15; (22 Apr. 1950): 14-15, 36; (29 Apr. 1950): 13-15; (6 May 1950): 12-13; (13 May 1950): 11-13; (20 May 1950): 6-7; (27 May 1950): 16-17; (3 June 1950): 34-35, 37; (10 June 1950): 32-34; (17 June 1950): 20-22; (24 June 1950): 12-13.
Serialized condensation in Dutch.

B549 *Wie ich es sah.* Wien: Humboldt, 1951. 389p.
Translation into German.

B550 *Wie ich es sah.* Zurich: Atlantis-Verlag, 1951. 389p.
Translation into German.

B551 *Wie ich es sah*: Politisches und privates um Franklin D. Roosevelt. Stuttgart: Humboldt-Verlag, 1951. 389p.
Translation into German.

This Is My Story. 1937

B552 *Beetey Din.* Lahore: West Pakistan Pub. Co., 1955? 256p.
Translation into Urdu.

B553 *Fru Roosevelt Segir Fra; Sjalfrsaevisaga.* Reykjavik: E. Bjarnason, 1942. 283p.
Translation into Icelandic.

B554 "Her er min Historie." *Alt for Damerne* (Sept. 1948): 4-5, 23.
ER's childhood. Excerpted from Chapter 1 of *This Is My Story.* In Danish.

B555 *Itu Jnan Orkkunnu*. Alleppey: Vidyarambham, 1956. 167p.
Translation into Malayalam.

B556 *Khaphachao Yang Cham Dai*. 1952. 397p.

B557 *Lo Shu fu fu Jen Hui I lu*. Taiwan: Hsin Ya, 1965. 128p.
Translation into Chinese.

B558 *Maim bhula na Sakungi*. New Delhi: Adhunik Sahitya Prakashan, 1956? 150p.
Translation into Hindi.

B559 *Mane Pade*. Calcutta: Candrasekhara Pustakalaya, 1955? 172p.
Translation into Oriya.

B560 *Mhat Mi Se To*. Rankun: Rhu ma va Caup tuik, 195?.
Translation into Burmese.

B561 *Moj muz Franklin Ruzvelt*. Subotica: Minerva, 1953. 117p.
Translation into Serbo-Croatian.

B562 *Ninaivu Alaikai*. 1957. 175p.
Translation into Tamil.

Tomorrow Is Now. 1963

B563 *Imorgen er Na*. Oslo: Ansgar, 1964? 172p.
Translation into Norwegian.

"Where I Get My Energy." 1959

B564 "Waar Haal Ik Mijn Energie Vandaan?" *Vrij Nederland* (10 Okt. 1959).
Translation into Dutch.

B565 "Zrodlo Mojej Energii." *Ameryka* 16 (1960): 16-17.
Translation into Polish.

Preface. World Youth and the Communists. 1958.

B566 Preface. *Le Communisme et la Jeunesse, la Penetration Communiste dans les Organisations Internationales*. By Nils M. Apeland. Paris: S.P.E.P.H.E., 1959.
Translation into French.

You Learn by Living. 1960

B567 *Aprendiendo a Vivir*. Buenos Aires: Ed. Central, 1965. 239p.
Translation into Spanish.

B568 *Elama Opettaa*. Helsinki: Otava, 1964. 223p.
Translation into Finnish.

B569 *Jagnam Mhanje Sikanam*. Bombay: Vora, 1963? ii + 164p.
Translation into Marathi.

B570 *Laer av Livet*. Oslo: Angsar, 1960. 204p.
Translation into Norwegian.

B571 *Lekah ha-hayyim*. Tel-Aviv: Iddit, 1961. 232p.
Translation into Hebrew.

B572 *Ningal Jivichu Kontu Pathikkunnu*. Kozhikode: Mathrubhumi, 1962. xii +
254p.
Translation into Malayalam.

B573 *Ya Kichhu Peyechhi*. Calcutta: Mitra & Ghosh, 1962. ii + 166p.
Translation into Bengali.

B574 *Yeoseongeui Saranggawa Haengbog*. Seoul: Samsinseojeog, 1974? 255p.
Translation into Korean.

Your Teens and Mine. 1961

B575 *Anata to Watashi no Judai*. Tokyo: Akimoto shobo, 1963? 167p.
Translation into Japanese.

C

Major Periodical Columns by Eleanor Roosevelt

"Passing Thoughts of Mrs. Franklin D. Roosevelt." *Women's Democratic News* **(1933-1935).**

C1   8 (Feb. 1933): 6. She will try to report on her activities as First Lady. Urges women to take an interest in unemployment relief work and the quality of nutrition available to children in their communities.

C2   8 (Mar. 1933): 6. A brief history of the White House.

C3   8 (Apr. 1933): 6-7. Allies are meeting with FDR to seek solutions to the world's economic and political problems. We must try to improve the conditions of people everywhere.

C4   8 (May 1933): 6. Reports on a trip to the boyhood homes of Robert E. Lee and George Washington.

C5   9 (June 1933): 6-7. A trip to Charlottesville, Va. and to the West.

C6   9 (July 1933): 6-7. White House renovations. A visit to CCC camps while touring in the South.

C7   9 (Aug. 1933): 6-7. In Abingdon, Va. was impressed with efforts to revive early American folk music. She met some of the friends her father had made when he lived there. Visited a CCC camp for blacks.

C8   9 (Sept. 1933): 6. To observe how relief measures are working she made an unannounced trip to W.Va. Her interest in conditions in mining communities dates to 1915 when she learned that reports about adverse conditions usually went unattended. Tribute to Ike Hoover. Spoke to Salvation Army in Boston.

C9   9 (Oct. 1933): 6. Trip to Chicago with FDR.

C10   9 (Nov. 1933): 6-7. On 30 Oct. attended Chicago meeting of the Women's Crusade of the Mobilization for Human Needs. Praises groups which support community social service activities.

C11   9 (Dec. 1933): 6-7. White House entertaining. Went to Reedsville, W. Va. and considers it a good site for the first subsistence homesteads project.

C12   9 (Jan. 1934): 6-7. Christmas in the White House.

C13   9 (Feb. 1934): 6-7. White House entertaining. Went to Williamsburg, Va. and describes progress with the restoration.

C14   9 (Mar. 1934): 6. A trip to Reedsville, W. Va. and an update on the Arthurdale project.

C15   9 (Apr. 1934): 6-7. Her trip to Puerto Rico.

C16   10 (May 1934): 6-7. White House entertaining. All of the problems of the country have not been solved, but there is a feeling of hope since people are once again thinking about summer vacations.

C17   10 (June 1934): 6-7. Opened the Institute on International Relations at Duke Univ. In an observation of the workings of Congress concludes that "the eternal boy...lies buried in every man."

C18   10 (July 1934): 6-7. Went to southeastern states with Nancy Cook and Marion Dickerman to observe the making of crafts and in Tenn. saw TVA sites and subsistence homesteads at Crossville. Visited Berea College and then Chicago to make a radio broadcast.

C19   10 (Aug. 1934): 6-7. Vacations in the West while FDR visits U.S. island possessions.

C20   10 (Sept. 1934): 6-7. Travels from the West coast and visits Booneville and Grand Coulee dams. Observes that unlike in the East, people have ideas about how to accomplish things in their communities.

C21   10 (Oct. 1934): 6. White House renovations. Support for Caroline O'Day's campaign for U.S. congresswoman from N.Y.

C22   10 (Nov. 1934): 6. On a trip with FDR to Tenn. observes housing and school experiments in the new towns and visits TVA dams which she describes as evidence of what private industry can do to bring about a better way of life.

C23   10 (Jan. 1935): 6. FDR's annual message to Congress "laid down principles of what should be a very great change in American life." Anecdote about John Nance Garner.

C24   10 (Feb. 1935): 6. On 19 Jan. spoke at a District of Columbia League of Women Voters luncheon. White House entertaining.

C25   10 (Mar. 1935): 6, 16. Amused that White House gold flatware was used for the annual Supreme Court dinner at the time when the gold decision was pending before the court.

C26 10 (Apr. 1935): 6, 14. On 30 Mar. spoke at a meeting inaugurating the campaign for the early detection of tuberculosis. Also a trip to Reedsville, W. Va.

C27 10 (May 1935): 6-7. Spoke to a meeting of blacks in Washington and attended a meeting on housing.

C28 11 (June 1935): 6-7. Spoke at an International Society for Crippled Children banquet. Reports on a conference on social education as a means of preventing crime held at the White House, 17-18 May.

C29 11 (July 1935): 6-7. Presided at dinner in Montreal given by public welfare organizations. Visited Camp Tera for girls.

C30 11 (Aug. 1935): 6-7. Attended conference organized by Rexford Tugwell in Buck Hill Falls, Pa. on subsistence homesteads. Her travel to Campobello.

C31 11 (Sept. 1935): 6-7. After driving through New England and seeing so many automobiles concludes that people once again have a feeling of hope. On 22 Aug. while driving to Chautauqua, N.Y. makes an unexpected speech to a Young Democrats' club in DuBois, Pa. Spoke at Chautauqua. N.Y. on 23 Aug. and to a women's club near Hyde Park, N.Y. in early Sept.

C32 11 (Oct. 1935): 6-7. Describes a train trip to the West with FDR and preparations which must be made when the President travels. In early Oct. spoke for the Mobilization for Human Needs in Ft. Worth, Tex. Takes a trip to the foot of Boulder Dam.

C33 11 (Nov. 1935): 6-7. White House renovations. Travels of FDR. On 1 Nov. spoke at the Blackstone Forum in Chicago.

C34 11 (Dec. 1935): 6. Thanksgiving at Warm Springs. Preparations for Christmas. Description of the new White House kitchen.

"Mrs. Roosevelt's Page." *Woman's Home Companion* **(1933-1935).**

C35 "I Want You to Write to Me." 60 (Aug. 1933): 4. Write and tell me about your problems. Discusses child nutrition and the importance of youth.

C36 "Ratify the Child Labor Amendment." 60 (Sept. 1933): 4. Background of the amendment and progress toward ratification.

C37 "Setting Our House in Order." 60 (Oct. 1933): 4. By objecting to the conditions under which goods are manufactured, one can influence which ones are on the market. A woman's conscience can influence labor conditions in a small factory community. Proper way to handle servants.

C38 "The Married Woman in Business." 60 (Nov. 1933): 14. Today women should work only when economic conditions dictate.

C39   "I Answer Two Questions." 60 (Dec. 1933): 24. Identifies those agencies which will help save a home or farm. Associates spirit with caring for others as much as for oneself.

C40   "Recreation." 61 (Jan. 1934): 4. The types of recreation and toys which children enjoy can be an influence on their lives.

C41   "Too Old for the Job." 61 (Feb. 1934): 4. American ingenuity can find ways to employ the older worker and provide meaningful lives for older citizens.

C42   "The Power of Knowledge." 61 (Mar. 1934): 4. We must prepare our teachers properly and then pay them adequate salaries. Women should work to reduce money spent on arms and to increase funding for education.

C43   "Learning to Teach." 61 (Apr. 1934): 4. Teachers are important and so is their preparation for the job. Teachers should travel extensively.

C44   "Youth Facing the Future." 61 (May 1934): 4. Unemployed youth should be given the opportunity to volunteer at camps where they can learn a trade.

C45   "I Have Confidence in Our Common Sense." 61 (June 1934): 4. The critics are wrong when they say that the Child Labor Amendment would give Congress too much authority over children.

C46   "Rural Homes." 61 (July 1934): 4. Today farming is a cooperative venture between men and women, and those in rural areas need to understand the interdependence between city and farm. We must put more emphasis on rural schools and better utilize the radio and automobile as means of improving rural life.

C47   "By Car & Tent." 61 (Aug. 1934): 4. Camping can be a way of enjoying an inexpensive vacation.

C48   "Traditional Holidays." 61 (Sept. 1934): 4. There are lessons to be learned from our national holidays.

C49   "Our Island Possessions." 61 (Oct. 1934): 4. Recalls her recent trip to the Caribbean and discusses conditions in Puerto Rico.

C50   "Let Us Be Thankful." 61 (Nov. 1934): 14. There is still much to be thankful for. Out of this depression we have learned that it is time to plan for ways in which as a nation we can prosper.

C51   "The Right to Give." 61 (Dec. 1934): 21. Children should learn the value of giving.

C52   "Facing Forward." 62 (Jan. 1935): 4. While many of our citizens are having to live under unfortunate conditions, we as a nation are capable of solving our problems.

C53   "Building for the Future." 62 (Feb. 1935): 4. Current conditions make it difficult for young people to have homes of their own or even to find jobs.

C54   "Gardens." 62 (Mar. 1935): 4. Gardens and gardening can provide much pleasure.

C55   "Woman's Work Is Never Done." 62 (Apr. 1935): 4. Women who go into domestic work should be trained, and their employers should maintain standards for living conditions and the length of the workday.

C56   "In Everlasting Remembrance." 62 (May 1935): 4. Memorial Day can be a time to pay tribute to those whose efforts have improved our lives.

C57   "Maternal Mortality." 62 (June 1935): 4. We must do more to reduce the number of mothers and babies who die.

C58   "Tree Worship." 62 (July 1935): 4. The importance of trees and customs about them.

"Dear Mrs. Roosevelt:" *Democratic Digest* (1937-1941).

C59   14 (Aug. 1937): 25. Membership in the League of Women Voters is a good way to become involved in public affairs. Social Security for farm workers. Working women. The types of public issues which appeal to women are human interest ones.

C60   14 (Sept. 1937): 25. Working women. Older women in the workforce. Appointment of women to positions with federal projects. The Girl Scouts. How to interest women in government.

C61   14 (Oct. 1937): 5. There will always be some people who will need to be on relief. Social Security. Marriage laws. Self-help cooperatives. War propaganda. Vocational training.

C62   14 (Nov. 1937): 5. Parents should discuss political issues with children, but not influence their views. School lunch program. Women's involvement in politics.

C63   14 (Dec. 1937): 7. The State Dept. works for peace. The U.S. and war in Europe. The value of CCC camps. Giving the right to vote to residents of the District of Columbia. Democracy.

C64   15 (Jan. 1938): 7. Women have proven to be intelligent voters. The topic mentioned most often by those who write is the problems of youth. Minimum wage. Women as public office holders.

C65   15 (Feb. 1938): 9. Equal rights for women are advanced by those who do their best at jobs new to women. No opinion on proposal to create a Dept. of Conservation. Peace and fairness can exist in a free enterprise system.

C66   15 (Mar. 1938): 8. We need not fear the presence of Communists or Fascists as long as we can provide our citizens with a proper standard of living. Financing health care. Civil service and the strength of political parties. Political participation of women. National referendum on war.

C67   15 (Apr. 1938): 6. If domestic workers find WPA jobs more attractive, then wages for domestics are too low. Supports idea of a federal agency for consumers. Students should learn about the causes of war and previous efforts to maintain the peace. Vocational training for youth.

C68   15 (May 1938): 6. Union affiliation presents no threat to higher education. Federal involvement in providing care for mothers and newborn infants. Wages of industrial workers. A national theater. Young people who want to enter politics should establish themselves first in a line of work which they can always return to.

C69   15 (June 1938): 7. Social Security. Older workers. Employee ownership of businesses. WPA, CCC, and federal agencies involved with housing.

C70   15 (July 1938): 7. Social Security, welfare, unemployment, and the minimum wage.

C71   15 (Aug. 1938): 6. If citizens would take more interest in who is elected to public office, politics would be viewed more favorably. Domestic and farm workers should be covered by Social Security. Accomplishments of women in Congress.

C72   15 (Sept. 1938): 7. Child labor provisions of the wage and hour bill are not a substitute for the Child Labor Amendment. Economic problems of the South.

C73   15 (Oct. 1938): 9. Industry cannot exploit our natural resources if informed citizens do not want it to happen. National Labor Relations Board. Consumer cooperatives.

C74   15 (Nov. 1938): 7. Detailed explanation of why women are not taking jobs away from men. The Munich Conference. Utopian pension plans and Social Security.

C75   15 (Dec. 1938): 7. Not interested in the nomination for herself if FDR does not run in 1940, because it is doubtful that a woman could be elected or even nominated. What women can do to help prevent war. The sale of military planes to Great Britain.

C76   16 (Jan. 1939): 9. In a democracy we do not need to fear Nazi, Fascist, or Communist propaganda. Women as public speakers. The WPA and Social Security as coercion of voters.

C77   16 (Feb. 1939): 11. An adequate defense is not encouragement to engage in war. Public opinions polls. Political education of youth. The radio need not standardize the opinions of youth.

C78   16 (Mar. 1939): 9. My speeches are planned in advance but not written. A creative woman can make contributions in the home or the community. The duties of a citizen. Dangers to democracy.

C79   16 (Apr. 1939): 16. Differences between men and women as voters. Women as candidates and officer holders. Definition of a "liberal." People are concerned with the problems in their local communities.

C80   16 (May 1939): 10.   Refugees have little effect on unemployment problems. Defines "liberty" and concludes that its preservation is the result of "individual responsibility."   The role of the individual in preventing war.   Means of achieving greater solidarity with Latin American countries.

C81   16 (June 1939): 11.   Lengthy defense of admitting refugee children. Referendum on declaring war.   Cordell Hull and neutrality laws.

C82   16 (Aug. 1939): 9.   Preparing the young for playing an active role in government.   Residents of the District of Columbia and their right to vote.   Laws regarding married women in government employment.

C83   16 (Sept. 1939): 7.   Has not seen evidence of subversive activities during her domestic travels.   Problems of migratory workers.   Voting age.

C84   16 (Oct. 1939): 11.   The role of the individual in keeping the country out of war.   Conservation in wartime.   Democratic Party in Puerto Rico.   The politics of foreign relations should be "adjourned" while there is a European war.

C85 16 (Nov. 1939): 8. We should not abridge the liberties of foreign born groups. Recent improvements in economic conditions are not the result of a European war boom.   Higher education does not always succeed in training young people to work.

C86   16 (Dec. 1939): 8.   Military training for those in the CCC.   Detailed explanation of functions of the Women's Democratic Club and the Women's Division of the Democratic National Committee.

C87   17 (Feb. 1940): 10. Public relief. Agricultural policy. How Americans feel about the European war.

C88   17 (Mar. 1940): 22. Hatch Act. Social Security.

C89   17 (Apr. 1940): 18.   Cooperating with the rest of the world and solving our domestic problems are the best contributions which the U.S. can make.   Promoting interest in government and New Deal programs are the significant accomplishments of the last seven years.   The important issues in the 1940 campaign will be international affairs and unemployment.

C90   17 (June-July 1940): 24.   Preventing war should be of equal concern to both men and women.   Poll tax.

C91   17 (Sept. 1940): 13. Strong defense of the draft. The most important issue in the 1940 campaign is whether we want a government in which no group dominates. Resisting propaganda.

C92   18 (Jan. 1941): 14.   How can women plan for a lasting peace? By promoting a body which can consider disputes between nations and by developing in their communities the desire to see justice prevail throughout the world. Defense industry workers. Subversive activities. Congress should prepare for the defense of our democracy through arms and programs which serve the needs of all citizens. Women should not be drafted, but a year of community service is advisable.

"If You Ask Me." *Ladies' Home Journal* **(1941-1949),** *McCall's* **(1949-1962).**

C93   58 (June 1941): 23.   She congratulated a group of women for their effort to win better working conditions, not because they went on strike. Marriage and family life, religion in American life, and FDR and the third term.

C94   58 (July 1941): 29.   Food for occupied countries. Alexander Woollcott's White House visits, racial equality, FDR's most successful social reforms, and jokes and cartoons about her.

C95   58 (Aug. 1941): 24, 101.   Detailed explanation of how her sons received military commissions. Prohibition, racial equality, and marriage and family. The presence of Communists and Fascists in defense plants. Charles Lindbergh. Hitler.

C96   58 (Sept. 1941): 21.   Answers questions about her agreement with FDR's ideas. Racial equality, interracial marriage, married life, religion, and her family's earnings.

C97   58 (Oct. 1941): 25, 133.   When asked about her plan for world peace she states that we must realize that war brings suffering, that armaments are a temptation to engage in war, and that there is a need for an international peacekeeping force. Whether FDR is of Jewish descent, "My Day" as a trial balloon for FDR's ideas, young people and alcohol, and religious beliefs and medical treatment. Marriage and family, divorce, personal relationship with FDR, and use of public funds for social reforms rather than defense needs.

C98   58 (Nov. 1941): 33, 156, 158.   FDR's remarks about Americans fighting in a foreign war. Joseph Lash and the International Student Service, American Student Union, and American Youth Congress. Morale of the military. Her philosophy of life. How she would like to be remembered.

C99   58 (Dec. 1941): 29, 48.   When asked why her sons cannot grow up and stop riding the coattails of their father she explains the problems of being a President's child. Anti-Semitism in the U.S. can be overcome if Jews are not too aggressive or ingratiating.   Marriage and children, rumors about separation from FDR, and treatment of the British in history texts. Pope Pius XII's five points for peace and Clarence Strait's Union Now plan.

C100 59 (Jan. 1942): 25, 87.   Considers Marie Souvestre, Theodore Roosevelt, and FDR the most interesting persons in her life. The Townsend Plan, Harry Bridges, marriage and children, and sex education. Prostitution and venereal disease. The differences between men and women.

C101 59 (Feb. 1942): 29.   For Jews to belong to Jewish organizations is not being aggressive, but to pursue one's own interests at the expense of the needs of the community at large is. The need for an organization to keep the peace after the war. Divorce, women in the military, strikes by defense workers, and her earnings from writing and speaking.

C102 59 (Mar. 1942): 29. Why were we not prepared for war? We had convinced ourselves that there would never be another war. Conservation in wartime, defense bonds, religion and marriage, Jews, women and the war, Churchill, and her sons in the military.

C103 59 (Apr. 1942): 19, 126. Defends herself against Westbrook Pegler's criticism that she would not cross a picket line. The presence of sons of the rich and prominent including the Roosevelts in the military. Childbearing in time of war, soldiers and religion, women in the military, punishment of negligent officers at Pearl Harbor, and the Red Cross.

C104 59 (May 1942): 17, 86. Regulation of labor unions, censorship, farmers and the draft, and Office of Civilian Defense. Duke and Duchess of Windsor, women in the post-war world, conservation in wartime, and negligent officers at Pearl Harbor.

C105 59 (June 1942): 23, 87. Asked if she had "colored" blood. Racial equality, child rearing, religion, conservation in wartime, U.S. in the post-war world, defense bonds, and Jews and women in the war effort.

C106 59 (July 1942): 25. Defends a New England family for inviting a black soldier to their home. The Red Cross, women and the military, defense bonds, and negligent officers at Pearl Harbor.

C107 59 (Aug. 1942): 26. Considers Florence Nightingale, Marie Curie, and Harriet Beecher Stowe the greatest symbols of women's development. Conscientious objectors after the war, child rearing, Judaism, and Billy Mitchell. Labor unions, tax deductions for medical expenses, and her influence on FDR.

C108 59 (Sept. 1942): 27, 131. She responds to a charge that she and FDR maintain 10 homes. Ethics, Roosevelt family in American wars, Alexander de Seversky, and morality of public officials. Indians and convicted criminals and the draft.

C109 59 (Oct. 1942): 23, 153. Eleanor Roosevelt Clubs, Harry Hopkins' family, fighting on foreign soil, college attendance, conservation in wartime, and FDR and state politics.

C110 59 (Nov. 1942): 33. Defense bonds, 18 and 19 year-olds and the draft. Marriage and child rearing. Prayer. Conservation in wartime.

C111 59 (Dec. 1942): 31. The right to vote should be extended to 18 year-olds. Refutes claim that there are no Jews in the military. The draft, Hitler, women and the war effort, and child rearing.

C112 60 (Jan. 1943): 31. Women who go into the military are not trying to imitate men. Strikers should not be drafted because they may be needed more in industry. Childbearing in wartime, Pearl Harbor, and sterilization of San Quentin inmates.

C113 60 (Feb. 1943): 28. Her 1942 trip to England was at the invitation of the Queen. We should seek a just peace not a vindictive one. Landlords should not discriminate against children. Income tax, military allotments for wives, and childbearing and conservation in wartime.

C114 60 (Mar. 1943): 35. Government planning and food shortages. Minimum age of women in the military, women doctors and the military, feeding the military, labor unions, and conservation in wartime.

C115 60 (Apr. 1943): 29. Responds to a father who allowed his son to enter military and now wants him released because of immoral behavior of other soldiers. College attendance, labor unions, conservation in wartime, defense bonds, and compulsory military training in time of peace.

C116 60 (May 1943): 39. Communists in the U.S. FDR and the radio. Aid to children in Europe. Farmers and factory workers in the war effort. Childbearing. Conservation in wartime.

C117 60 (June 1943): 30. Eddie Rickenbacker on drafting "slackers" in the defense industry, economic cycles, and Mme. Chiang Kai-shek. Also several topics in relation to the military: physicians, waste of food, gambling, and liquor.

C118 60 (July 1943): 32. Her sons receive no privileges that others in the military do not receive. The Supreme Court, conservation in wartime, inevitability of war, and eligibility of those in the military to run for public office.

C119 60 (Aug. 1943): 39. FDR and a fourth term, marriage, conservation in wartime, opening of union financial accounts, the radio and censorship, women in the military, and the opportunity of the military to vote.

C120 60 (Sept. 1943): 36. Labor unions, allotments for dependent families, childbearing, conservation in wartime, college attendance, women in the military, and the Supreme Court.

C121 60 (Oct. 1943): 39. Jews and blacks and the draft, son James and the military, prisoners of war on Bataan, women and the military, China and the war, marriage, and divorce.

C122 60 (Nov. 1943): 41. A lengthy discussion of the differences between nazism, fascism, communism, and socialism. Allotments for dependent families, conservation in wartime, the draft, and defense workers.

C123 60 (Dec. 1943). Defends her 1943 trip to the South Pacific. Westbrook Pegler, labor unions, defense workers, allotments for dependent families, and women in the peace negotiations.

C124 61 (Jan. 1944): 33. Juvenile delinquency is a community problem, and the home and school cannot bear all of the blame. Drafting of fathers and high school boys. College attendance. Her wearing a Red Cross uniform. Childbearing. Conservation in wartime.

C125 61 (Feb. 1944): 39. Denies that John L. Lewis has power to keep FDR from stopping wartime strikes. FDR's Four Freedoms and racial equality. Marriage, soldiers and divorce. Women and the military. Women's role in the domestic war effort. Payments to German and American prisoners of war.

C126 61 (Mar. 1944): 41. Defends bombing of Berlin. Jews in Nazi-dominated countries, equal pay for women, Sen. Hugh Butler on aid to South American nations, and food for occupied countries.

C127 61 (Apr. 1944): 35. Would she vote for a black for President? One should vote for the best qualified. Compulsory military training for men and women in time of peace. Japanese-Americans, conservation in wartime, teachers' salaries, and women and the military.

C128 61 (May 1944): 30. Democrats, not Republicans, are more interested in helping the average citizen. Sharing FDR birthday collections for the National Foundation for Infantile Paralysis with Sister Elizabeth Kenny. Women in the military, conservation in wartime, and who writes FDR's speeches.

C129 61 (June 1944): 38. Conscientious objectors and family allotments, young people and alcohol, and FDR and music. Fathers and the draft, ration points for the White House and the Hyde Park home, and conservation in wartime.

C130 61 (July 1944): 34. Does not own stock in southern textile mills and if she did that would not explain her interest in the rights of blacks. Believes in planned parenthood but not when used to avoid having any children. The role of retired presidents, age of presidential candidates, young mothers working outside the home, religion and family, and conservation in wartime.

C131 61 (Aug. 1944): 33. Women still have few choices about their lives. Defense bonds, venereal disease, morale of the military, unionization of household workers, conservation in wartime, and public schools and the education of her children.

C132 61 (Sept. 1944): 41. Qualities FDR considers responsible for his success. Religious education in schools, race relations, working mothers, harmony within her family, marriage, and her interest in youth movements. The draft.

C133 61 (Oct. 1944): 43. Democratic Party and machine politics, race relations, defense bonds, treatment of a conquered Germany, the draft, and conservation in wartime.

C134 61 (Nov. 1944): 41. Whether one must hate the enemy. Prayer, Japanese Americans and the military, pre-draft age boys and problem behavior, newspaper treatment of FDR, women in the post-war world, and means of keeping the peace.

C135 61 (Dec. 1944): 41. Abortion, racial equality, discrimination against married female teachers, and FDR and the disciplining of their children.

C136 62 (Jan. 1945): 26. It is no more appropriate to teach German prisoners of war the American way of life than to want Americans to learn Nazi teachings. Marriage, divorce, education in the U.S., and the draft and 18 year-olds.

C137 62 (Feb. 1945): 38. Defends Arthurdale project and explains transfer of Hyde Park home to the federal government. Child rearing, the Red Cross, Army nurses and Germans as prisoners of war, and supplies for the military.

C138 62 (Mar. 1945): 39. Conservation in wartime, foreign prisoners of war, and compulsory service in time of peace. Marriage, family size, child care centers, and adoption of children. The Democratic Party.

C139 62 (Apr. 1945): 41. Planned Parenthood League, child rearing, fighting a foreign war, and defense workers and the draft. Women in defense plants and black nurses in the military.

C140 62 (May 1945): 38. The Soviet Union, unlike Germany, does want to make other countries such as Poland subservient. How she ignores criticism. Marriage, conservation in wartime, and allotments for families. American prisoners of war, the war with Japan, and the end of war in Europe.

C141 62 (June 1945): 31. Taxation of soldiers' pay and wives' allotments and earnings. Divorce, child rearing, Social Security for domestic workers, and the Oleomargarine Act.

C142 62 (July 1945): 31. Suffering helped make FDR great because he learned the importance of courage. Reading, women and politics, divorce, religion, the Red Cross, and conservation in wartime.

C143 62 (Aug. 1945): 23. Health, military discharges, childbearing, and defense bonds. The transfer of the Hyde Park home to the federal government.

C144 62 (Sept. 1945): 39. To be "born equal" is to have equal opportunity to make the most of our abilities. Disabilities and the draft, military discharges, Communist Party in the U.S., defense bonds, conservation in wartime, and FDR's grave.

C145 62 (Oct. 1945): 28. FDR's health and his estate. Childbearing and rearing of children, the Red Cross, and morale of the military.

C146 62 (Nov. 1945): 24. Denies that she said that military dischargees should be in rehabilitation centers until they have readjusted. The radio, conscientious objectors, and the impossibility of nominating a woman for President.

C147 62 (Dec. 1945): 37. When a reader refers to her article "You Can't Pauperize Children" and asks how the war nursery program can be continued, she states that the need for child care has always existed and that only industry or the government can provide it. Believes that HST is pursuing his own policies, but some of them are the same as FDR's. Death of Hitler, women and politics, and the United Nations Rehabilitation and Relief Administration. The role of reading in child rearing.

C148 63 (Jan. 1946): 39. The public should be informed of labor negotiations so that wages, prices, and profits are known. She hopes that her granddaughter will know and accept all races. Compulsory community service and the importance of peace in one's own neighborhood as part of worldwide peace.

C149 63 (Feb. 1946): 33. Comparing men and women she feels that while women are too sensitive they can be more committed and decisive. How many more wars will there be? No one knows just as no one knows if the UN will be used to build a peaceful world. Child rearing. Youth.

C150 63 (Mar. 1946): 32. When asked if as a UN delegate she will be guided by her own principles or allegiance to her country, responds that she will work for the good of the entire world. The UN should continue regardless of whether more atomic bombs are manufactured. Palestine war criminals, HST's policies, aid to Germans, child rearing, and sex education.

C151 63 (Apr. 1946): 43. For the present the atomic bomb has advanced civilization. Marriage, income tax, child care for working mothers, planned parenthood, divorce, and federal funds for medical research. Occupied France, Sweden as a neutral nation, and internationalizing of the Ruhr.

C152 63 (May 1946): 45. The UN, marriage, domestic workers and day care for children, child rearing, age discrimination, war brides, and defense bonds.

C153 63 (June 1946): 28. Does not consider herself qualified to serve as ambassador to Russia. To maintain control over politics Americans cannot be indifferent. War, child rearing, and New York *Social Register*.

C154 63 (July 1946): 41. Occupation forces as teachers of democracy. Divorce, federal aid to education, religion, venereal disease, and alcohol and youth.

C155 63 (Aug. 1946): 28. An organization of women will not end war. Artificial insemination, college attendance, adoption of European orphans, and child rearing. Working mothers, Anti-Semitism, and marriage.

C156 63 (Sept. 1946): 49. Labor unions, teachers' salaries, college attendance, child rearing and marriage.

C157 63 (Oct. 1946): 31. Tells young readers that war is not inevitable. Occupied Japan, anti-Semitism, Andrei Gromyko, marriage, child rearing, and federal aid for health care.

C158 63 (Nov. 1946): 54. It is healthy to analyze one's actions and motives. Social Security, day care for the elderly, draft of college age youth, women and the political process, and Palestine.

C159 63 (Dec. 1946): 48. She does not have a troubled conscience about being born to comfortable means. Marriage between blacks and whites must be considered only by those willing to face criticism and prejudice. Child rearing.

C160 64 (Jan. 1947): 46. Defends son Elliott's book *As He Saw It* but insists that FDR and Churchill had a friendly relationship while their approaches may have differed. Lengthy response to question about whether U.S. and Britain will be able to work with Russia. Russia is a young, insecure country, and only time and a stronger UN will improve the situation. Favors minimum income level for families rather than payments to offset cost of raising a family.

C161 64 (Feb. 1947): 49. All citizens can make their opinions known. Child rearing. Housing.

C162 64 (Mar. 1947): 26. Government control over the press cannot be justified. Recalls Mme. Chiang Kai-shek's visits. Child rearing. Housing for displaced persons.

C163 64 (Apr. 1947): 26. Political Citizens Assoc. and Americans for Democratic Action do not want to be political parties. Adoption of war orphans, child rearing, and causes of war.

C164 64 (May 1947): 26. Problems of the elderly, sex education, cancer, family size, marriage, and the mentally retarded.

C165 64 (June 1947): 26. Supports a common world language. Child rearing, racial equality, Georgia Warm Springs Foundation, marriage, and domestic workers.

C166 64 (July 1947): 26. When asked if her thinking about Communists has changed, she says that she has always felt that they were a minor threat and that it is more important to make democracy work. Defends the right of New Deal officials to write about their government service. Value of public schools and need for higher salaries for teachers. British royal family, Fala, and the need for better informed public officials and voters.

C167 64 (Aug. 1947): 26. The U.S. must be interested in the affairs of other countries. The problems of minorities in this country result from prejudice. Assessment of her ability as a public speaker. Religion. College attendance.

C168 64 (Sept. 1947): 26. One might oppose interracial marriage but accept social contact between the races. The 1948 presidential election and a third party candidate. James Farley. Juvenile delinquency.

C169 64 (Oct. 1947): 65. Agrees that there is tension between the U.S. and Soviet Union but refutes Sen. Joseph McCarthy's claim that the two are at war. Turning education over to the federal government would be neither wise nor the way to end racial discrimination. A national lottery, marriage, and business ethics.

C170 64 (Nov. 1947): 50. The U.S. is dependent on the rest of the world for its prosperity. Future wars as unthinkable. Religion, marriage, and child rearing.

C171 64 (Dec. 1947): 51. Explains involvement with Hanns Eisler case. Marriage, communism and religion, freedom of speech, and differences between Democratic and Republican parties.

C172 65 (Jan. 1948): 46. Disagrees with Walter Winchell that the Soviet Union is preparing to attack the U.S. Russians as individuals and as representatives of their government. Food for Europeans, child rearing, and marriage.

C173 65 (Feb. 1948): 70. Prefers to promote the UN instead of the concept of a world government. Freedom of speech for Communists in the U.S., marriage, and food sent abroad.

C174 65 (Mar. 1948): 72. Describes how UN delegates decide how to vote. Whether she has Negro blood, child rearing, FDR's stamp collection, value of European aid as a weapon against communism, and President's Commission on Civil Rights.

C175 65 (Apr. 1948): 77. Loyalty tests, the FBI, and Communists. Favors compulsory public service for both sexes. The Marshall Plan and propaganda about it, choosing a political party, and child rearing.

C176 65 (May 1948): 67. The country must decide if it is to be a nation without racial prejudice. Form of government in a partitioned Palestine, the UN, mothers-in-law and child rearing, and reading.

C177 65 (June 1948): 68. Churchill's "iron curtain" speech was a mistake. Reading, freedom of speech, mothers-in-law including reference to Sara Roosevelt, and world government and the UN.

C178 65 (July 1948): 44. Compares 19th and 20th century liberalism. Child rearing. Social Security for domestic workers.

C179 65 (Aug. 1948): 44. Conditions are not right for American and Russian women to work together to prevent war. Discusses how ignorant she once was about politics and government. Child rearing and marriage.

C180 65 (Sept. 1948): 52. Denies that she considers her work with UN as a sacrifice. Defends partition of Palestine and the creation of a Jewish state. Henry Wallace, defense of the peacetime draft, FDR and Warm Springs, adoption, and child rearing.

C181 65 (Oct. 1948): 45. How FDR wrote his speeches. Atheism in the Soviet Union, education for citizenship, and child rearing.

C182 65 (Nov. 1948): 69. Women's clubs could be more effective by addressing domestic and international problems. William Bullitt on FDR and Communists. Mme. Kasenkina. Race relations.

C183 65 (Dec. 1948): 40. Sara Roosevelt was a great influence on FDR, but, except for ideas about social issues, she herself was not. Urges making democracy work rather than worrying about communism. Religion and public schools, reading, child rearing, and the Soviet Union as an immature nation.

C184 66 (Jan. 1949): 23. Westbrook Pegler, Communists in the U.S., freedom of religion in the Soviet Union, adoption, Townsend Pension Plan, and Mme. Chiang Kai-shek's White House visits.

C185 66 (Feb. 1949): 59. Opposes National Committee for American Education's desire to remove textbooks considered to be Communist or Socialist propaganda. The Constitution and Congress allowed FDR to be given special powers to deal with domestic conditions. The Soviet Union as a World War II ally. Post-war military service.

C186 66 (Mar. 1949): 53. Explains background of selecting the wording "all human beings are born free and equal" in the Universal Declaration of Human Rights. Explains her position about rights of children in the draft of the covenant. Birth control. Shifts in balance of power between political parties.

C187 66 (Apr. 1949): 40. She signed a manifesto on the anniversary of the deaths of Sacco and Vanzetti, because their deaths were a result of hysteria not unlike that of the present time. Freedom of speech and rights of individuals. Christianity in the U.S. and relationships between churches and the UN. Marriage, adoption of European orphans, and the Communist Party in the U.S.

C188 66 (May 1949): 45. In her final column for the *Ladies' Home Journal* she responded to questions about the extent to which she and FDR had supported aid for American Indians. HST and the investigation of un-American activities, current status of blacks in the U.S., college attendance, Bible study in public schools, American businesses in Communist countries, and the relationship between the UN and a country's propaganda measures against other countries. In discussing activities of American clubwomen she stated that they should support democracy and worry less about communism.

C189 76 (June 1949): 28, 115. She transferred her column to *McCall's* because the publisher of the *Ladies' Home Journal* had wanted her to seek assistance in making revisions to the manuscript of *This I Remember*. She concludes that the switch was a good business move. In her first column she responded to numerous questions. The press was able to report fully on FDR's death. FDR's casket was kept closed because he had asked that it be that way, and only she saw it open. Prayer and the UN, girls and the Boys' Club of America. Voting age, marriage, support for national health insurance, and employment opportunities for the physically handicapped.

C190 76 (July 1949): 28. We must watch post-war Germany carefully and not let an undesirable force develop. Her definition of a "liberal," the Catholic Church and war, the North Atlantic Pact, agricultural policy, and child rearing.

C191 76 (Aug. 1949): 28, 83. In the 1930s she tried to help youth see that there was a future in a democracy, but she has never supported communism. Henrietta Nesbitt, college attendance, U.S. and Soviet Union as world leaders, and how FDR's many interests helped him live with his paralysis.

C192 76 (Sept. 1949): 28, 86. Disagrees that the government is dominated by military men trying to militarize industry. Hopes that we learned that greed caused the last depression. Marshall Plan. The afterlife.

C193 77 (Oct. 1949): 30, 116. Defends her position on Franco. The UN cannot decree English as a common language. Working women, marriage, and child rearing. She and FDR never had a marital separation.

C194 77 (Nov. 1949): 28. Refutes James Farley's claim that she said that FDR was comfortable only with those of his own social standing. Cardinal Mindszenty. Juvenile delinquency. The mentally ill. She has become philosophical about her children's problems.

C195 77 (Dec. 1949): 28. President Hoover may have returned his salary, but FDR did not. Her White House entertaining. Relations with Japan before World War II. Communism.

C196 77 (Jan. 1950): 30. FDR often supplemented the prepared texts of his speeches. How she handles critical letters. Higher education. When giving a concert Paul Robeson should sing, not make political speeches.

C197 77 (Feb. 1950): 28. The slowness of reform in a democracy might appear to be a disadvantage, but it is really a strength. The UN is the only means of achieving cooperation between nations and peace in the world. The older worker and Social Security laws. The White House. Supports the direct election of Presidents.

C198 77 (Mar. 1950): 25. Harry Hopkins and U.S. wartime aid to Russia. FDR never received a salary from the National Foundation for Infantile Paralysis. Guards at FDR's grave.

C199 77 (Apr. 1950): 25. FDR believed that he would live to complete his fourth term. HST was not looked upon as a successor, simply the choice of the party for Vice President. The quality of education can be improved by paying teachers adequate salaries and by parents taking an interest in the schools. Our present tax structure should support new businesses and high employment. Fala.

C200 77 (May 1950): 27. Congress has never voted her a pension. Cannot imagine being a man and having a choice of careers. The UN is the only way of achieving world agreement on armaments. Rings worn by FDR.

C201 77 (June 1950): 23. The UN is becoming a stronger organization, but a lasting peace will never be possible until we see better relations between the U.S. and the Soviet Union. Marshall Plan. Child rearing. Hydrogen bomb.

C202 77 (July 1950): 19. Presidents' vacations. Interracial marriages. Cardinal Mindszenty. The trial of Robert Vogeler illustrates that justice as we know it is not practiced in Communist controlled countries.

C203 77 (Aug. 1950): 19. Not interested in being President. Before a woman can achieve that office we must see many other offices held by women and a gender-free public attitude about candidates. Labor unions. Social Security. Equal pay for women.

C204 77 (Sept. 1950): 27. Son John says that he is a Republican, but I do not know how he votes. If we want more teachers we must increase the opportunities for teacher education and then pay teachers more. Amelia Earhart. White House receiving lines. College attendance.

C205 78 (Oct. 1950): 25. "Red Day" in Mosinee, Wisc., Malvina Thompson, the U.S. Census, U.S. Postal Service, and food for China. Problems which New York City would encounter in the event of atomic attack, the White House, and the education of royalty.

C206 78 (Nov. 1950): 25. Many Americans do not vote because they think that their vote has no effect. Religion in the Soviet Union, divorce, her youth, and veterans' benefits for members of the Merchant Marine. Differences between Democrats and Republicans. Intimate biographies of presidents and their families are more readily accepted than those of royalty.

C207 78 (Dec. 1950): 19. Women and the draft, marriage, Karl Marx, aid to Spain, and child rearing and sex education. Her youth. The White House Conference on Children and Youth.

C208 78 (Jan. 1951): 21. China should not be admitted to the UN at this time. Books about FDR, education of her children, how she learned to speak French, and American women compared with other women. Financial assistance to her sons when they were young. How the Commission on Human Rights has the authority to help rescue Greek children abducted by Communist guerrillas.

C209 78 (Feb. 1951): 23. Voice of America broadcasts, image of the U.S., Kinsey report, marriage, U.S.-Soviet relations, and her 1948 gifts to the British royal family.

C210 78 (Mar. 1951): 25. Atom bomb, working women, child rearing, and adoption. Churchill's reaction to son Elliott's published comments about Churchill's relationship with Charles de Gaulle.

C211 78 (Apr. 1951): 25. FDR when he was angry and how he dealt with criticism. The draft, J. Edgar Hoover on homosexuals, and a defense of the benefits which women have received as a result of their right to vote.

C212 78 (May 1951): 23. U.S. troops in Korea, religion, conscientious objectors, and the relationship between FDR and Churchill.

C213 78 (June 1951): 23. FDR's disability, troops in Korea, Stalin, working mothers, child rearing, and Fala.

C214 78 (July 1951): 19. War, HST, and Hanns Eisler.

C215 78 (Aug. 1951): 23. What does she think about the Soviet Union's charge that the U.S. government is corrupt? It may be corrupt, but it is not decadent. Portraits and photographs of FDR. FDR and physical pain. HST. Sororities and fraternities.

C216 78 (Sept. 1951): 25. Her perception of Soviet delegates to the UN, retirement, FDR's plans for retirement, and recollections of life in the White House.

C217 79 (Oct. 1951): 27. The ambitions of her youth, William O'Dwyer, and a movie about FDR.

C218 79 (Nov. 1951): 27. Jews in the Soviet Union, intelligence tests, religion, and the rearing of her children.

C219 79 (Dec. 1951): 21. Bernard Baruch, reading, Santa Claus, and an assessment of some of her public statements.

C220 79 (Jan. 1952): 21. The characteristics of an ideal First Lady are those which are important in anyone. Unfaithful husbands and wives, her influence on FDR, her speaking engagements, Dean Acheson, and Marion Davies and William Randolph Hearst.

C221 79 (Feb. 1952): 25. What FDR told her about his meetings with Stalin, a movie about FDR, and those who influenced FDR. Sen. Joseph McCarthy, religion, and the rearing of her children.

C222 79 (Mar. 1952): 29. Accusations that she is a Communist do not bother her. FDR's health in 1944, who will portray her in movie about FDR, dogs as pets, cremation, and the Red Cross.

C223 79 (Apr. 1952): 29. Communists misrepresent the U.S. as imperialistic and not interested in humanitarian concerns. Jesse Jones' published memoirs and FDR's feelings about war. The 1952 presidential election. Death.

C224 79 (May 1952): 25. Some of her actions may explain why people think that she lacks religious conviction. Treatment of blacks in France, support for the vote for 18 year-olds, and the 1952 presidential election.

C225 79 (June 1952): 23. She does not see the need for the U.S. to have an ambassador to the Vatican. Defends the fact that FDR had to get along with political bosses. Her salary as a UN delegate, college attendance, and women in the Soviet delegation to the UN.

C226 79 (July 1952): 19. She did not encourage FDR to run for any office, including the fourth term. The 1952 presidential election. Her opinion about the Bible.

C227 79 (Aug. 1952): 21. The 1952 presidential election, what the Middle East likes and dislikes about the U.S. FDR and Alger Hiss. How FDR felt about Sen. Robert Taft and Dean Acheson.

C228 79 (Sept. 1952): 29. FDR and Wendell Willkie did not plan to establish a third political party. Agrees with Edith Sampson that the living conditions of American blacks are far superior to those of many peoples elsewhere. Herbert Hoover's published comments about FDR can be explained because he resents that FDR succeeded where he failed.

C229 80 (Oct. 1952): 29. In his published comments about ER's role in the New Deal Samuel Rosenman states that if she had had her way there would have been more compromises and fewer accomplishments. ER responds by stating that FDR thought she was too impatient to be a good politician. FDR was one of our five great Presidents. Her earnings, child rearing, and FDR's liberalism.

C230 80 (Nov. 1952): 25. Sen. John Sparkman, psychoanalysis, marriage, use of her picture in advertisements, and pros and cons of a military person as President.

C231 80 (Dec. 1952): 21. UNESCO is not a Communist organization, Spain, Westbrook Pegler, and Stalin.

C232 80 (Jan. 1953): 19. HST has been a courageous and wise President. Does not agree with critics as to her mistakes as First Lady. U.S.-Soviet relations. A national lottery.

C233 80 (Feb. 1953): 25. Defends New York City as headquarters for the UN. Contemporary youth, censorship, capital punishment, and her own retirement.

C234 80 (Mar. 1953): 27. Disagrees with son John's comment that FDR would be ashamed of the Democratic Party today. U.S.-Soviet relations, religion in the schools, and ending the military involvement in Korea.

C235 80 (Apr. 1953): 29. No longer has her own radio or television program because she travels too much and advertisers consider her too controversial. Rearing of her own children. Peace.

C236 80 (May 1953): 25. Atheists should be allowed to teach. It has never been worthwhile to worry about what columnists say about her and her family. Soviet propaganda. Critics of UNESCO.

C237 80 (June 1953): 25. There is no truth to the idea that FDR lacked confidence in the potential of the UN.

C238 80 (July 1953): 21. Labor unions and liberals in the fight against communism, the McCarthy committee, FDR and Communists in the State Dept. She broke her ties with the American Youth Congress because some of the leaders lied to her.

C239 80 (Aug. 1953): 21. Soviets have not made acceptable peace offers in the UN because they have never been willing to accept essential safeguards to peace. President Eisenhower's position on Sen. McCarthy is not clear, and it is too early to assess him as President. FDR's birthday celebrations. His church attendance.

C240 80 (Sept. 1953): 21. The Daughters of the American Revolution is still a narrow organization afraid of change. The greatest danger of communism as it is practiced in Soviet bloc countries is the police state atmosphere. The White House isolated the Roosevelts from gossip. U.S. support of the UN.

C241 81 (Oct. 1953): 56. She received the Most Admired Award from the American Institute of Public Opinion because of the admiration people still have for FDR. FDR did as much as he could to end racial discrimination, and he never tried to stop her efforts. Nazi sympathizers, maturity, Tito, teaching about communism, and U.S.-Soviet relations.

C242 81 (Nov. 1953): 27. When the actions of the American Youth Congress leaders proved that they were under Communist domination, she stopped supporting them. Religion in Yugoslavia, contemporary Christian spiritual leaders, and demonstrations against her in Japan.

C243 81 (Dec. 1953): 50. Communist Party in U.S. The Kinsey report. Queen Elizabeth II is knowledgeable about international affairs.

C244 81 (Jan. 1954): 21. Our former enemies should be admitted to the UN. Former American prisoners of war who have embraced communism should be shown the benefits of democracy. Opposes using atom bomb in the Far East.

C245 81 (Feb. 1954): 23. She has made strong attacks on communism in her UN speeches. Only the UN can negotiate problems between Israel and Jordan. Christianity, capital punishment, and FDR's ancestry.

C246 81 (Mar. 1954): 56. The split between James Farley and FDR was the result of minor disputes culminated by FDR's third term decision. FDR and religion, Mme. Chiang Kai-shek, income tax, and race relations. Not everyone who is taking advantage of the Fifth Amendment is a spy.

C247 81 (Apr. 1954): 54. Did not interfere during FDR's presidency and is surprised to hear that high officials had to do things because of her wishes. Current hysteria about Communists makes government officials fearful and untrusting. Rearing of her children, Communists in U.S., and Harold Ickes.

C248 81 (May 1954): 52. President Eisenhower has courage and integrity, but he lacks persistence. FDR thought that she had no sense about money. She accepts blame for poor White House meals.

C249 81 (June 1954): 46. Churches do help in the fight against communism, but labor unions do more. China in the UN.

C250 81 (July 1954): 42. Fees for speaking engagements. FDR was a natural public speaker and never took lessons. Explains Sen. Herbert Lehman's support of funding for congressional committees while opposing Sen. McCarthy and his committee.

C251 81 (Aug. 1954): 52. Women do not now have equal recognition, because the government positions which they hold lack the decision making authority of positions held by men. She has written all of her publications except a few for the UN. FDR and Pearl Harbor. Polio gave FDR patience and courage. Religion in her life and her contributions to political causes.

C252 81 (Sept. 1954): 70. While President Eisenhower could have done more to stop Sen. McCarthy, it was the Senate's responsibility. Sara Roosevelt's desire for FDR to retire after his polio attack.

C253 82 (Oct. 1954): 58. The South is better able to set a positive example for desegregation. Adlai Stevenson as the 1956 Democratic nominee. Sen. McCarthy, rearing of her own children, and the Catholic Church's fight against communism in France and Italy.

C254 82 (Nov. 1954): 68. Has she ever made important changes in her thinking? Before 1934 she felt that only the opportunity to receive an education was what was needed for most to achieve their potential, but she has come to realize that government must protect citizens from the effects of adverse economic conditions. She still believes in the rights of labor, but labor must accept some responsibilities as well. Son John's association with President Eisenhower. Chiang Kai-shek. Divorce.

C255 82 (Dec. 1954): 56. The time may come when the Panama Canal and other such passageways should be under UN control. Activities of the Roosevelts on day of Pearl Harbor attack. Adlai Stevenson and the 1956 election. Candidacies of son John and Averell Harriman for Gov. of N.Y. Juvenile delinquency, Westbrook Pegler, and a clothing allowance for first ladies.

C256 82 (Jan. 1955): 60. Credits Marguerite Hoyle for much of the research on, and rewriting of, *India and the Awakening East*. Martin Dies on ER and Joseph Lash. Hitler, hydrogen bomb, and her sons' involvement in politics.

C257 82 (Feb. 1955): 60. Still believes that FDR's policies were sound and necessary. The FBI is more capable of protecting us from communism than any congressional committee. Segregation.

C258 82 (Mar. 1955): 72. The American people are not fighting hard enough for individual freedom. Comic books may be a cause of juvenile delinquency. Re-arming of Germany. Robert Oppenheimer. Desegregation.

C259 82 (Apr. 1955): 76. Defends her earlier statement about comic books and juvenile delinquency. Harold Ickes and his aspirations for the presidency. Movie about FDR's life. The Bible. Pierre Mendes-France.

C260 82 (May 1955): 72. Still has high regard for President Eisenhower as a soldier. Girl Scouts. The UN. Atheists.

C261 82 (June 1955): 68. Labor disputes. Day care for children. Henry Cabot Lodge on the Soviet Union in the UN. Prejudice is not limited to the blacks. FDR may have offered to send six million Jews to Saudi Arabia.

C262 82 (July 1955): 60. Criticism of her as First Lady was not abusive. FDR's health when he went to Yalta.

C263 82 (Aug. 1955): 44. Comments about Mamie Eisenhower's health are less harmful than some comments made during FDR's administration. Origin of Westbrook Pegler's dislike for her. Constitution of the Soviet Union. Education of contemporary political figures.

C264 82 (Sept. 1955): 60. The Dixon-Yates Project is supported by those who feel that private enterprise can better provide the services now received through the TVA.

C265 83 (Oct. 1955): 72. The International Rescue Committee is trying to help Eastern Europeans escape communism, and Senators Herbert Lehman and John Kennedy are trying to change the McCarran-Walter Immigration Act, but there is little public enthusiasm for these efforts. Her children are doing a better job as parents than she has done. Her children received many of FDR's great qualities. FDR received more newspaper criticism than President Eisenhower is receiving. Herbert Hoover's efforts to solve the problems of the depression. The most important things about her life are her work with the UN and the part she played in the life of a great man.

C266 83 (Nov. 1955): 66. During wartime FDR traveled on naval ships, but it was not appropriate for her to travel with him. FDR made adjustments to our capitalist system in order to preserve it. FDR let her speak her mind. Plans to support Adlai Stevenson as the Democratic nominee in 1956. Compares John Foster Dulles with Dean Acheson.

C267 83 (Dec. 1955): 64. Had she been in HST's place she would have used the atom bomb. Queen Juliana, statue of FDR in London, and FDR and the Secret Service.

C268 83 (Jan. 1956): 62. Earl Warren would make a good nominee for the Republicans; Richard Nixon would not. Her judgments of Alger Hiss and William O'Dwyer were appropriate at the time. Her recollections of HST's reaction to FDR's death. What attracted FDR to her. She has burned letters written during their courtship.

C269 83 (Feb. 1956): 58. Averell Harriman is not under the influence of Carmine De Sapio. Herbert Hoover could have pursued reform measures in spite of a Democratic congress. Would not consider being a candidate for Vice President. Would consider remarrying if the opportunity arose. FDR and political bosses, Social Security, marriage, and child rearing.

C270 83 (Mar. 1956): 66. The establishment of the UN has been the most important event of the century. Neither FDR nor HST were naive about Communists. Democrats can use corruption and agricultural issues against the Republicans in 1956. A woman as Vice President. Child rearing.

C271 83 (Apr. 1956): 72. Supports admitting Spain to the UN. FDR as a father.

C272 83 (May 1956): 62. She signed a petition seeking the release of Communists jailed under the Smith Act since the act allows imprisonment because of ideas not actions. Herself as mother and grandmother. Cannot explain why Henry Wallace is supporting President Eisenhower. Religion.

C273 83 (June 1956): 60. Criticizes Richard Nixon for his Senate campaign against Helen Gahagan Douglas. Frank Freidel's study of FDR is the most comprehensive. HST on Adlai Stevenson's 1952 campaign.

C274 83 (July 1956): 54. A good personal portrait of FDR is John Gunther's *Roosevelt in Retrospect*. The vice presidency would not be good training for a woman. When she would support a Republican presidential candidate. Interracial marriage, childbearing, and student exchanges between Harvard and the Univ. of Moscow.

C275 83 (Aug. 1956): 68. How she judges a man's character. Race relations. Admission of Spain to the UN.

C276 83 (Sept. 1956): 68. Compares Democrats and Republicans. Young people are more conservative today because of the McCarthy investigations.

C277   84 (Oct. 1956): 70. Gives possible reasons for son John being a Republican. Agrees with Adlai Stevenson that the testing of the hydrogen bomb should be outlawed. FDR's plans after leaving the White House. Prayer.

C278   84 (Nov. 1956): 72. Marriage is an individual matter. No one can prevent interracial marriages. Accomplishments and failures of the Eisenhower administration. Federal support for the arts. Jokes about FDR.

C279   84 (Dec. 1956): 64. Fads of the young need not be taken seriously. Travel to China. Death and young children. Unitarians.

C280   84 (Jan. 1957): 58. Without the NAACP and efforts of Thurgood Marshall there would have been less progress in gaining rights for blacks. Alger Hiss. Averell Harriman.

C281   84 (Feb. 1957): 78. Republicans want big business to control government, but men like Herbert Lehman, Averell Harriman, and Adlai Stevenson want government to be stronger than big business. Mamie Eisenhower, political unification of Ireland, and race relations.

C282   84 (Mar. 1957): 80. Current U.S. relations with Britain and France have given the Soviet Union the impression of a weakened NATO and may have encouraged their actions in Hungary. President Eisenhower. Possibilities for 1960 Democratic nominee.

C283   84 (Apr. 1957): 92. Prohibition was a mistake. A defense of today's youth. FDR as a father and his personal library.

C284   84 (May 1957): 88. Supports the objectives and goals of the Americans for Democratic Action. The Roosevelts' income during the early years of their marriage. The Bible. The financial burden of being President.

C285   84 (June 1957): 76. A President should not be limited to two terms. Disputes claim of Josephine Truslow Adams and Frank Meyer that FDR and Earl Browder were political friends. President Eisenhower and his vacations. Possibilities for 1960 Democratic nominee. Marriage.

C286   84 (July 1957): 70. FDR was never wealthy, but he had enough money to allow him the freedom to pursue public office. Fraternities and sororities should not exclude on the basis of race or religion. FDR on Wayne Morse. Her father's letters about his world travels. Faith healers.

C287   84 (Aug. 1957): 66. She will have no say in who will play her and FDR in Sunrise at Campobello. Would prefer to see a united but unarmed Germany. What it takes to be a UN representative.

C288   84 (Sept. 1957): 78. Billy Graham and other revivalists do not appeal to her. Britain should be free to trade with China regardless of what the U.S. thinks. Salaries of public officials should be tax exempt. The Bible. Possibilities for 1960 Democratic nominee. Defense of today's youth. Her philosophy of life is to do one's best and to think of others rather than one's self.

C289 85 (Oct. 1957): 86. She voted for Al Smith because she believed in what he stood for. On neither domestic nor foreign issues has President Eisenhower done a good job. FDR's favorite presidents were Jefferson, Jackson, Lincoln, and Wilson. Medical care for all citizens. Prejudice.

C290 85 (Nov. 1957): 74. There is no problem in beginning the school day with the Lord's Prayer as long as it not compulsory. Since she does not consider herself qualified to do the necessary research, she has no plans to write a book about FDR. FDR, Jr. has provided legal representation for the Dominican Republic, not Trujillo. Child rearing.

C291 85 (Dec. 1957): 58. The press is kinder to her now since she is old. FDR's most troublesome secret was the development of the atom bomb. She still has negative feelings about Richard Nixon. Coping with grief and emotional distress, rearing of her own children, and an assessment of President Eisenhower's second term.

C292 85 (Jan. 1958): 52. Details about her trip to Russia. At his best Khrushchev can exhibit many fine qualities. No comment as to why Irene Dunne was appointed to the UN.

C293 85 (Feb. 1958): 64. The country has no sense of direction since neither President Eisenhower nor the Senate led by Lyndon Johnson are establishing policies. Russia has moved ahead in space technology because they realize the value of scientific research. Her trip to Russia. Child rearing.

C294 85 (Mar. 1958): 66. Women must care for their families before participating in community affairs. Discusses her shyness and fear of not living up to what is expected of her. Walter Reuther has some of the qualities needed for a good President. FDR's health in 1945. Elsa Maxwell.

C295 85 (Apr. 1958): 66. The country needs to be committed to funding scientific research. Refuses to speculate as to type of President JFK would make. FDR was never anti-Semitic. Government should never be dominated by religion.

C296 85 (May 1958): 70. The *Christian Science Monitor* is our most objective newspaper. John Foster Dulles does not appear to relate well to foreign leaders. The March of Dimes.

C297 85 (June 1958): 54. FDR may have felt that he had divine guidance when making some difficult decisions. Defends son John's providing public relations for Haiti. Portrayal of herself in *Sunrise at Campobello*, recognition of China, and her relationship with Churchill.

C298 85 (July 1958): 56. If Adlai Stevenson is not the Democratic nominee in 1960, the nominee should take advantage of his abilities. FDR as an educated, but very practical person. Sees little difference between Stalin and Khrushchev. Walter Reuther.

C299 85 (Aug. 1958): 58. Better economic leadership and a more imaginative agricultural policy could have prevented the recession. Advises reader to stay in the

Daughters of the American Revolution and fight its stand against the UN. Cardinal Spellman's attack on her should be forgotten. Churchill as an artist.

C300 85 (Sept. 1958): 56. In the fall elections the Democrats should emphasize the need for positive foreign policy and better agricultural and economic policies. Marriage, birth control, childhood education, and prayer.

C301 86 (Oct. 1958): 16, 18. She would not consider running for President, because no woman is ready for the office. It is the attitude of adults toward education, not progressive education, that is to blame for the poor performance of students. A Catholic as President, advice for widows, gifts received when in the White House, and blacks as her friends.

C302 86 (Nov. 1958): 60. Defends the U.S. presence in Lebanon but blames the Republicans for making it necessary. We need to see less corruption in government, not attempts to blame either party. College attendance.

C303 86 (Dec. 1958): 74. Right-to-work laws allow for the exploitation of labor. U.S.-Soviet bans on nuclear testing. President Eisenhower should not resign and let Richard Nixon succeed him. Suicide. FDR's loss of temper.

C304 86 (Jan. 1959): 50. As is the case with many women, her greatest contribution may be her children. Disputes claim that no civil rights legislation was passed under FDR and HST. Atheism, study of foreign languages, and a national lottery.

C305 86 (Feb. 1959): 47. Referring to published comments by James Byrnes, FDR did not promise to support him for the 1944 vice presidential nomination. Orval Faubus, Westbrook Pegler, race relations, and Adlai Stevenson as Secretary of State.

C306 86 (Mar. 1959): 81. The cost of a housekeeper should be a tax deduction for working mothers. Mamie Eisenhower. Boris Pasternak.

C307 86 (Apr. 1959): 36. Fala. Labor strikes. Equality of opportunity for women.

C308 86 (May 1959): 50. We do not need the Committee on Un-American Activities because we have the FBI. Does not approve of James Hoffa's attempt to unionize New York City police. Her secretaries.

C309 86 (June 1959): 38. Because the U.S. has failed to adopt the Universal Declaration of Human Rights other nations doubt our sincerity to end segregation. U.S. agricultural policy, nuclear attack, and the rearing of her own children.

C310 86 (July 1959): 30. It would be foolish to have a law forbidding public officials from hiring their family members. Why she did a television commercial. Relationships between wives and mothers-in-law.

C311 86 (Aug. 1959): 88. Role of the Secretary of State. We have the right to know about the health of public officials, but some details should be spared.

C312 86 (Sept. 1959): 90. The volume of her mail and how it is answered. Labor strikes.

C313 87 (Oct. 1959): 44. In a lengthy response to her 1933 statement about young women and drinking she explains that what she said was that young women should learn their tolerance to alcohol at home, not in public. Her opinion about Prohibition. Censorship of books. Marriage. A President's right to select his cabinet members.

C314 87 (Nov. 1959): 42. Divorce alone is not a cause for juvenile delinquency, because the quality of home life is an important factor whether there has been a divorce or not. Americans are too complacent, and they fail to recognize the contributions of other countries. Charities, U.S.-Soviet relations, and political candidates.

C315 87 (Dec. 1959): 48, 158. The Roosevelts' celebration of Christmas in the White House.

C316 87 (Jan. 1960): 28. Disagrees with Samuel S. Leibowitz that tighter immigration laws would reduce juvenile delinquency. Khrushchev's visit to Hyde Park.

C317 87 (Feb. 1960): 14. There should not be a universal language. Refuses to state her preference for the 1960 Democratic nominee. A sense of humor is essential for anyone in public life. Children do not owe their parents any more than to do their best. Senate investigation of quiz shows, the value of work, and the writing of her books and articles.

C318 87 (Mar. 1960): 16. Does not plan to attend the Democratic National Convention and hopes that nothing makes it necessary for her to do so. At the local level she votes for the candidate, but with the party in national elections. We could learn from the Russian educational system and its respect for learning and emphasis on foreign languages. Nursery school for the very young can be good discipline. Manners. Rearing of her own children.

C319 87 (Apr. 1960): 16. If she had chosen a career it would have been in the social welfare area. Opposes idea of New York City being a separate state. Religion. Cancer. Office of Vice President. Study of foreign languages. Richard Nixon.

C320 87 (May 1960): 16. The most difficult task for the new First Lady will be to live her own life. U.S.-Arab relations, polio vaccine, Charles de Gaulle, widowhood, and U.S.-Soviet competition in space exploration. The scheduling of her lectures.

C321 87 (June 1960): 16. In a lengthy discussion about U.S.-Latin American relations states that the Cuban revolution was justified but now Castro seems unable to establish a government. Still no plans to attend the Democratic National Convention, and Richard Nixon is still not seen as an acceptable President. Rent control. Clare Boothe Luce. HST. President Eisenhower. Still takes lessons in breath control from Elizabeth von Hesse.

C322 87 (July 1960): 18, 132. Recollections of Democratic National Conventions beginning with 1912 when she had no interest in who the nominee would be, through 1920, 1932, 1940 with a description of why she addressed the convention, 1952, and

1956. FDR, Louis Howe, Ed Flynn, James Farley, Frances Perkins, Henry Wallace, HST, Adlai Stevenson, and son Elliott are mentioned.

C323 87 (Aug. 1960): 16. Since conditions have changed, the role of NATO must be re-examined. Nicknames for political figures. Study of foreign languages. U.S.-South Korean relations and Syngman Rhee. Child rearing.

C324 87 (Sept. 1960): 14. President Eisenhower's "open skies" proposal should be discussed by the UN. Greer Garson should do an admirable job of portraying her in *Sunrise at Campobello*. West Germany, women in the clergy, housing for the elderly, and her opposition to capital punishment.

C325 88 (Oct. 1960): 18. Disagrees with HST that a business owner should be able to deny service to anyone. In national and state elections she votes for the Democratic candidate even if the Republican is superior. Cuba is making an error in seizing foreign assets. War can be more inevitable if children do not learn to get along with one another.   Electoral college vs. popular vote, trade boycott against South Africa, ethics of public officials, wiretapping, Adlai Stevenson as Secretary of State, a national lottery, and revision of civil service laws.

C326 88 (Nov. 1960): 14. Agreeing that national conventions are rigged to some extent she thinks that there could be a more democratic way to choose presidential candidates. Bomb shelters and nuclear war, segregation in the North and South, American people and demagogues, selection of cabinet members, and ethics and privileges of public officials.

C327 88 (Dec. 1960): 18. Christmas celebrations during her childhood and in the pre-White House years.

C328 88 (Jan. 1961): 16. Public criticism of the U.S. government and the country's image, Khrushchev on war, relocation of UN headquarters, and teachers' salaries.

C329 88 (Feb. 1961): 14. Argues for compulsory medical care for the elderly under Social Security. Presidents Eisenhower's support of Richard Nixon in 1960, Khrushchev, television cameras in the courtroom, the hungry in the U.S., government aid to farmers, and developing African nations and the UN.

C330 88 (Mar. 1961): 16. It is good for a President to serve only two terms, but the people should be free to re-elect him as often as they wish. Value of public school attendance and of parents working to improve the schools. Her secretarial assistance while First Lady. Carmine De Sapio.

C331 88 (Apr. 1961): 16. William Dawson's declination of a cabinet post under JFK, ethics of public officials, electoral college vs. popular vote, education for life of public service, FDR's health in 1944, and the value of community activities for young mothers.

C332 88 (May 1961): 16. Government doing what is necessary to improve the welfare of its citizens is the American tradition. The Supreme Court and censorship of movies, appointment or election of public officials on the basis of race or religion,

Formosa after the death of Chiang Kai-shek, U.S. relations with Cuba, New York City mayoralty candidates, and television.

C333 88 (June 1961): 22. The Monroe Doctrine is no longer relevant because the U.S. and South American countries are equals. Any fight against communism must be waged by the South American countries themselves. Disagrees with David Ben-Gurion that Jews should emigrate to Israel. Her work as a current UN delegate, JFK's record of ambassadorship appointments, the Peace Corps, *Sunrise at Campobello*, her mother, picket lines, Internal Revenue Service and informants, and religion and prayer.

C334 88 (July 1961): 14. Praises Kennedy presidency and agrees that there are similarities between his approach and that of FDR. Coverage of international news by American newspapers, funding for American embassies, U.S. relations with China, the federal government and support for the arts, juvenile delinquency, unions and length of workday, and U.S. postal service as inferior to that of some other countries.

C335 88 (Aug. 1961): 18. Does not favor instituting a WPA type program to put unemployed back to work. Peace marches are not Communist-backed. South Africa, unions and reduced work week, and teachers' salaries.

C336 88 (Sept. 1961): 24. Opposes Soviet Union's proposal for a three-person committee to head the UN Security Council. Her experience with the need to use personal resources to help finance White House entertaining. Her charitable contributions. Fala.

C337 89 (Oct. 1961): 32. JFK should make periodic speeches to the nation to explain problems he considers important. Space exploration, New York City mayoralty candidates, Val-Kill furniture manufactory, and Khrushchev on Castro.

C338 89 (Nov. 1961): 26. Loyalty to the Democratic Party would not prevent her from speaking against JFK's policies. Divorce, Food for Peace, and differences between the Democratic and Republican parties.

C339 89 (Dec. 1961): 20. ER describes Christmas at Hyde Park when her children were young.

C340 89 (Jan. 1962): 16. She defends the need for a political organization when asked about Carmine De Sapio and Tammany Hall but speaks against control by one person. Explains what a "liberal" is. Divorce, censorship of military officers' speeches, and Frank Sinatra.

C341 89 (Feb. 1962): 20. Prefers the UN to Sen. William Fulbright's idea of working through a group of free nations. Medical profession, relations between China and the Soviet Union, a national lottery, bomb shelters, and the Peace Corps in Nigeria.

C342 89 (Mar. 1962): 18. Teachers should be free to unionize and strike. Opposes Konrad Adenauer's stance on NATO forces and the use of nuclear weapons. Divorce, women in politics, and older women and community service.

C343 89 (Apr. 1962): 16. The U.S. should join the UN in condemning Portugal for colonial policies in Africa even if the loss of bases in the Azores is at risk. Jawaharlal Nehru and the invasion of Goa, former Nazi party members in the West German government, assessment of Kennedy presidency, New York City transit strikes, coverage of international news by the American press, and what the housewife can do to achieve world peace.

C344 89 (May 1962): 18. A literacy test is an appropriate prerequisite for voting. FDR's membership in private clubs, peace marches, U.S. relations with Cuba, mailing of Communist propaganda, and bomb shelters.

C345 89 (June 1962): 20. The Daughters of the American Revolution, child rearing, nuclear testing, disarmament talks with the Russians, space exploration, bomb shelters, and middle and low-income housing.

C346 89 (July 1962): 16. Defends JFK's statement that nuclear weapons will be used if Soviets attack Berlin. Washington as a cultural center, college professors who work for the government or the UN, education of American leaders, Khrushchev's agricultural problems, Algeria and the threat of Communism, and her foreign travels as First Lady.

C347 89 (Aug. 1962): 16. How Ralph Bunche would be treated if he were a U.S. senator. She would not have been a conscientious objector. Boxing, child rearing, and JFK and the business community.

C348 89 (Sept. 1962): 16. Corruption in business and government results from lack of education and an over dependence on material possessions. Organization of the military, China, prejudice, equality for women, comparison of her early work with UN with her present work there, image of U.S. abroad, and FDR and the opposition press.

C349 90 (Oct. 1962): 16. Today mental illness is in the open, but it was hidden when she was a child. Supports raising the legal drinking age in N.Y. The teaching of foreign languages in Russian schools. Co-educational colleges.

C350 90 (Nov. 1962): 18. Marriage. John Birch Society. Financial exchange between U.S. and Soviet Union, integration, training of women for employment, and communication satellites. Abortion.

D

Addresses, Remarks, and Other Statements by Eleanor Roosevelt

1921

D1   Watrous, Hilda R. *Eleanor Roosevelt: Some of Her Days in Onondaga County.* Syracuse: Onondaga County Public Library. 1984. [11]p.
   Women should develop an interest in politics. Excerpts address "Legislative Record of the 1921 Season" to Syracuse League of Women Voters, 4 May (p. [1]). This pamphlet excerpts other speeches which she made in Syracuse, N.Y. through 1956.

1922

D2   ---. *In League with Eleanor: Eleanor Roosevelt and the League of Women Voters, 1921-1962.* New York: Foundation for Citizen Education of League of Women Voters of New York State, 1984. 25p.
   Numerous addresses at league meetings and other groups beginning in 1922 are cited. Most lack exact date of address. Some are not excerpted (pp. 7-23 passim).

1924

D3   "Campaign on Today to Get Out the Vote." *New York Times* 6 Oct. 1924: 5.
   Includes text of ER's appeal for increased voter registration. Since so many citizens do not vote we have a minority government.

D4   "Miscellaneous Mention." *Time* 4 (29 Sept. 1924): 5.
   Brief report on speech to Southampton, L.I. women Democrats on the difference between Republicans and Democrats. Republicans join the President's cabinet to make money; Democrats leave it to do so.

1925

D5   "Appeal for Child Labor." *New York Times* 2 Mar. 1925: 3.
   N.Y. state legislators are warned that if they do not honor their party's platforms and support the Child Labor Amendment their failure could become a major campaign issue. Excerpts testimony to the N.Y. legislature.

1928

D6   "Mrs. F.D. Roosevelt Hits Woman's Plank." *New York Times* 10 Oct. 1928: 7.
Women in the workplace need more protection than men. Text of statement on behalf of Women's Advisory Committee of the Democratic National Committee challenging the position of the Woman's Party that both men and women need the same protective legislation.

D7   "Mrs. Roosevelt Holds Real Issue Is Equality." *New York Times* 17 Oct. 1928: 3.
The most important issues in the election are those of equality and freedom. Excerpts radio address in support of Al Smith to the New York Section of the Council of Jewish Women, 16 Oct.

D8   "Two Women Leaders Explain Dry Planks." *New York Times* 8 Aug. 1928: 3.
ER explains the position of presidential candidate Al Smith and the Democratic Party on prohibition and enforcement of the current law. Excerpts radio address "What the Platforms Say on Prohibition," 7 Aug. Also including excerpts of her public statements in support of Smith are "Lauds Smith's Record." *New York Times* 22 Sept. 1928: 3 and "Talk to 1,000 at Barnard." *New York Times* 31 Oct. 1928: 9.

1929

D9   "Club Meeting on Legislative Program." *Quarterly* (Women's City Club of New York) 11 (Mar. 1929): 28-30.
She misses her work with the club and lack of "direct political responsibility." Excerpts ER's remarks at Women's City Club of New York luncheon in her honor, 9 Jan.

D10   "Dry Policy Urged by Mrs. Roosevelt." *New York Times* 18 Oct. 1929: 12.
More important than obeying the law is the desire of the individual to do the right thing for himself and for others. Text of speech to State Woman's Christian Temperance Union convention, Binghamton, N.Y., 17 Oct.

D11   "Where Are We Going in Our Public Schools?" *School Parent* 9 (Nov. 30, 1929): 6-7, 14.
Education is the training of the mind, and we must recognize the contributions of teachers to the process. Text of address at United Parents' Associations luncheon, New York, 9 Nov.

D12   *Women's Democratic News* 4 (Apr. 1929): 8.
"I never give my husband advice. And I shall follow the example of my predecessor [Mrs. Al Smith] who always smiled, was always grateful and who never spoke in public." Text of remarks at Jeffersonian Club of Dutchess County dinner honoring FDR upon assuming the governorship of N.Y., Poughkeepsie, N.Y., 6 Apr.

1930

D13   "Dinner for Mrs. Roosevelt." *Quarterly* (Women's City Club of New York) (Mar. 1930): 16.

Women should get into politics. It is more important for them to know the sources of information than to try to be fully informed on all of the issues. Excerpts ER's remarks at Women's City Club of New York dinner in her honor, 13 Jan.

1931

D14   "Mrs. Roosevelt Looks at the College Graduate." *Russell Sage Alumnae Quarterly* 2 (Jan. 1931): 1-3.
   The female college graduate should not make a career out of a job which can be performed by a woman who lacks higher education. It is unfortunate that women must struggle to earn the same salary as men for the same type of work. Based on her address to the Albany, N.Y. chapter of the Russell Sage Alumnae Assoc., 10 Jan.

1932

D15   "Charity Not Enough, Says Mrs. Roosevelt." *New York Times* 13 Jan. 1932: 8.
   Emergency relief is admirable, but we must find permanent solutions to the problems which face the nation. These solutions will require basic changes to our way of life. Excerpts address to New York City League of Women Voters, 12 Jan.

D16   "The Crisis in Industry." *New York Times* 18 Dec. 1932, sect. 9: 2.
   Economic conditions have never been as bad. Drastic changes are needed if we are to realize "a new deal" in a country which should not tolerate many of the conditions which exist today. Abridged version of address to the National Consumers' League of New York.

D17   "Economic Readjustment Necessary." *Democratic Bulletin* 7 (Aug. 1932): 14, 27.
   We need to readjust our economic system so that American workers receive a fair wage. Partial text of address, Chautauqua, N.Y., 12 July.

D18   "Girls' Drinking Hit by Mrs. Roosevelt." *New York Times* 10 Dec. 1932: 3.
   Prohibition has failed to protect the weak from the abuses of alcohol. Girls today drink, and because of the automobile young people can go more places and see more people than girls of my generation. Today's girls should determine how much alcohol they can tolerate. Excerpts radio address, 9 Dec.
   For reactions from women's and prohibition groups, see "Assail Liquor Talk by Mrs. Roosevelt." *New York Times* 14 Dec. 1932: 16, "On Girls Learning to Drink." *Literary Digest* 115 (7 Jan. 1933): 20, and "Criticize Wet View of Mrs. Roosevelt." *New York Times* 20 Jan. 1933: 3.

D19   "Mrs. Roosevelt Urges Courage in Crisis." *New York Times* 15 Jan. 1932: 13.
   We need to be more like our ancestors who founded this country and have the courage to face new problems and seek new solutions. Excerpts address to meeting of Congress of State Societies, New York, 14 Jan.

1933

D20 "Aid to Youth Urged by Mrs. Roosevelt." *New York Times* 19 Oct. 1933: 21.
Your organizations can give spiritual help to youth. Text of a message sent to an 18 Oct. meeting of the Young Men's and Young Women's Christian Associations, New York, 18 Oct.

D21 "Child Aids Listed by Mrs. Roosevelt." *New York Times* 2 May 1933: 14.
Even in difficult economic times there is no reason to neglect the health of children. Simple housing, food, and recreation can help keep children healthy. Text of radio address on Child Health Day, 1 May.

D22 "Children of School Age." *School Life* 18 (Mar. 1933): 121-22.
Parents should remember that school age children are preparing themselves for the life and work ahead of them. Parents and teachers need to cooperate in the process. Based on radio address, 13 Jan.

D23 "A Message to Parents and Teachers." *Progressive Education* 11 (Jan./Feb. 1934): 38-39.
In educating the child to be the citizen of tomorrow the teacher is more important than the quality of the school building or the curriculum. Abstract of address at Progressive Education Association Regional Conference, New York, 26 Nov.

D24 "Mrs. Franklin D. Roosevelt." *"This Crisis in History": Report of the Third Annual New York Herald Tribune Women's Conference on Current Problems, the Waldorf-Astoria, New York City, October 12th and 13th, 1933.* New York: New York Herald Tribune, 1933. 102-6.
Like youth, our country is young. She hopes that both will face the problems which are before them now. Text of address, 12 Oct. Listed in table of contents as "Young Americans."

D25 "Mrs. Roosevelt Advises Organization and Publicity." *Life and Labor Bulletin* [2nd ser.] 1 (Apr. 1933): 3.
All members of the Women's Trade Union League should be concerned about the problems faced by women workers and share their concern with the public. Text of address made at conference on union identification labels for women's clothing, Washington, 11 Apr.

D26 "Mrs. Roosevelt to Be 'Contact' for Public in White House, She Says at Chicago." *New York Times* 22 Jan. 1933: 1, 6.
When a man is elected President the people also expect something from his wife, and I think that they deserve more than have come to expect in the past. The President will not be able to answer all of his mail. I can help him with that, and I also want people to write and tell me what is going on in the country. Excerpts address to the Illinois League of Women Voters, Chicago, 21 Jan.

D27 "Recreation as a Preparation for Life." *Recreation* 27 (Nov. 1933): 374, 394.
It is a good use of public funds to provide playgrounds because in larger cities they can make for a better life for all. Text of address at New York City Recreation Conference, 3 Oct. 1933.

D28 "Roosevelt Party Brings Throngs to League on February 14th." *Monthly Bulletin* (New York Women's Trade Union League) (Mar. 1933): 2.

She hopes to be an effective First Lady and improve conditions for women. Excerpts ER's remarks at dinner in her honor. A skit was presented about her anticipated activities as First Lady.

D29 "Sparks Struck from Council Speeches." *League News of the National League of Women Voters* 7 (May 1933): 3-5.

The young develop an interest in government and public affairs in the home and school (p. 3). One of several excerpts of speeches from General Council of League of Women Voters meeting, Washington, Apr.

D30 United States. Federal Emergency Relief Administration. *Proceedings of the Conference on Emergency Needs of Women.* Washington: GPO, 1933. 38p.

Brief introductory remarks by ER (p. 5) and her introductions of Harry Hopkins and Ellen Woodward. A discussion (p. 15-28) presided over by ER concluded the morning session and reveals the breadth of ER's knowledge of the problems faced by women and the types of public programs considered necessary. Did not preside over the afternoon session and may not have been present. Text of remarks, Washington, 22 Nov.

D31 "The Woman's Crusade." *Daughters of the American Revolution Magazine* 68 (Jan. 1934): 8-10.

In order to help those in need we must know what their problems are and then support relief agencies at the local level. Based on address to Washington branch of the Woman's Crusade, 9 Nov.

1934

D32 "Address." *Delegate's Worksheet* (Ninth Conference on the Cause and Cure of War) 3 (18 Jan. 1934): 1.

We have to face up to the causes of war: greed and hatred. Text of address, Washington, 17 Jan. Available in the ER Pamphlet Collection, FDRL.

D33 "Blind Partisanship." "The Philosophy of Social Reform in the Speeches of Eleanor Roosevelt." By Eleanor Janice Bilsborrow. Diss. Univ. of Denver, 1957. 187-88.

Women must help lead the nation out of its problems, not the least being the difficulties facing our young people. Text of address, Rye, N.Y., 7 May.

D34 "First Lady Pleads for Old Age Pensions." *Social Security* 8 (Feb. 1934): 3-4.

We owe it to our older citizens to provide them with pensions. Text of address at meeting sponsored by District of Columbia branch of the American Assoc. for Social Security, Council of Social Agencies, and Monday Evening Club, Washington, 5 Jan.

D35 *Helping Your Children to Success.* New York: Typewriter Educational Research Bureau, 1934. 28p.

Based on radio broadcasts, Nov.-Dec. 1934.

D36 "Johnson Meets NRA Critics, Proposes 12-Point Revision; J.W. Davis Scores New Deal." *New York Times* 28 Feb. 1934: 1, 11.

Text of ER's statement in support of small community businesses in a report on the National Recovery Administration's "field day" for comments and criticism.

D37   "Living and Preparation for Life through Recreation." *Recreation* 28 (Nov. 1934): 366-69.
Recreation is important for persons of all ages, and it can help one achieve "success," which is really the extent to which one enjoys life.   Text of address to National Recreation Assoc.

D38   "Mrs. Franklin D. Roosevelt Addresses Coordination Conference." *Council Review* (Council for Exceptional Children) 1 (Feb. 1935): 77-79.
It is better to tailor the education of the exceptional child to the child's needs and abilities than to finance help for that child as an adult. Excerpts address, Nov.

D38a   "Since We Last Met." *School Life* 20 (Dec. 1934): 73, 89.
Excerpts.

D39   "Mrs. Roosevelt Addresses Board." *Clubwoman GFWC* (General Federation of Women's Clubs) 14 (Feb. 1934): 4, 17-18.
Women should take more interest in government, support education and the arts, and not forget about the homeless.   Partial text of ER's address at dinner in her honor, Washington, 12 Jan.

D40   "Mrs. Roosevelt on Home Demonstration Work." *Extension Service Review* 5 (May 1934): [81].
Brief statement of appreciation for Martha Van Renselaer and others in the home demonstration field who have helped us achieve more satisfactory lives.   From address at Cornell Univ., 15 Feb.

D41   "Mrs. Roosevelt Tells 'Em." *Jeffersonian* (Apr. 1934): 5.
Women look to newspapers for more than homemaking hints. They are interested in their government and what it is doing about social problems, but newspaper editors have yet to realize this. Excerpts address to American Newspaper Publishers' Assoc., New York.

D42   "The National Conference on the Education of Negroes." *Journal of Negro Education* 3 (Oct. 1934): 573-75.
The best possible educational opportunities are deserved by all children including the black child who has much to contribute to the artistic development of the nation. Text of address, Washington, 11 May.

D42a   "An Educational Conference." *Opportunity* 12 (18 June 1934): 166-67.
Excerpts.

D42b   "Excerpts from Address of Mrs. Franklin D. Roosevelt." *Fundamentals in the Education of Negroes*. Bulletin (U.S. Office of Education) 1935, no.6. Washington: GPO, 1935. 9-10.

D43   "The New Government Interest in the Arts." *Proceedings of the Twenty-fifth Convention of the American Federation of Arts, Washington, D.C., May 14, 15, 16, 1934*. Washington: American Federation of Arts, 1934. 47.

Out of the nation's current crisis may come greater interest in the arts as we learn to cherish and support the skill and insight of the artist. Text of address concluding the convention, 16 May. Issued as *American Magazine of Art*, v. 27, no. 9, pt. 2.

D44 "Opening Address." *"Changing Standards": Report of the Fourth Annual New York Herald Tribune Women's Conference on Current Problems, Hotel Waldorf-Astoria, New York, September 26th and 27th, 1934.* New York: New York Herald Tribune, 1934. 15-17.
Events of great importance are also bringing changes in some of our standards. We are beginning to realize that the best way to control crime is to correct those conditions in our society which cause people to want to pursue such a way of life. There is also greater acceptance of the role of women in public life. The need for capable leaders in the labor movement is critical. Text of address, 26 Sept.

D45 *Proceedings of the Spring Conference of the Eastern-States Association of Professional Schools for Teachers.* Problems in Teacher Training, 9. Ed. Alonzo F. Myers. New York: Prentice-Hall, 1934. 201.
Those who become teachers must accept the responsibility of shaping the leaders of tomorrow. Text of letter read at the joint convention of the Eastern States Assoc. of Professional Schools for Teachers and the Junior High School Conference, New York, 13 Apr.

D45a "Urges College Idle in Apprentice Jobs." *New York Times* 14 Apr. 1934: 17.
Text of letter.

D46 "What Does the Public Expect from Nursing?" *American Journal of Nursing* 34 (July 1934): 637-40.
We expect skill and dedication. They serve a teaching function by demonstrating to parents that health care is available. Text of address at convention of national nursing organizations, Washington, 24 Apr.

1935

D47 "Fame Is a Nuisance: Travel Difficulties of Mrs. Roosevelt." *Democratic Digest* 12 (Nov. 1935): 13.
Get to know your country first before going abroad. Traveling as First Lady can be difficult since one is so easily recognized. Excerpts address at the Brooklyn Institute of Arts and Sciences.

D48 "First Lady Speaks." *Crisis* 42 (June 1935): 184.
We should recognize the contributions of all races and the need to provide equal opportunity. Excerpts address to NAACP District of Columbia branch, Washington, 14 Apr.

D49 "Mrs. Franklin D. Roosevelt." *America Faces a Changing World: Report of the Fifth Annual New York Herald Tribune Forum on Current Problems, Held at the Waldorf-Astoria Hotel, New York City, October 15th, 16th and 17th, 1935.* New York: New York Herald Tribune, 1935. 9-12.
These are difficult times, and we should be glad that our form of government allows us to experiment with solutions at the state level. Also expresses hope in the potential of women to be leaders. Text of address, 15th Oct.

D50 "The Outlook for Peace." *Delegate's Worksheet* (Tenth Conference on the Cause and Cure of War) 2 (23 Jan. 1935): 1.

Wars can be prevented if they are no longer profitable, if women throughout the world work together to promote better understanding among nations just as they do in their own homes, and as a nation we believe in something and work to promote it.   In the end we have to decide if we cherish material gain or humanitarian concerns.   Text of address, Washington, 22 Jan.   Available in ER Pamphlet Collection, FDRL.

D51 "Peace-o-graphs." *Peace Action* 1 (May 1935): 15.

"You were a pioneer and still are pioneering…and perhaps this is most evident in your work for peace." Excerpts remarks at dinner in honor of Jane Addams, 2 May. Article covers a variety of topics.

D52 "The Place of Women in the Community." *Proceedings of the Seventy-third Annual Meeting, National Education Association of the United States, 30 June-5 July, 1935.* Washington: National Education Assoc. of the United States, 1935. 313-16.

Stresses the importance of being part of the community in which one lives and the role of the educator in demonstrating that to young women.   Text of address at meeting of the Dept. of Deans of Women, Denver.

D53 "Youth Today Is Tomorrow's Nation." "Eleanor Roosevelt and Federal Responsibility to Youth, the Negro, and Others in Time of Depression." By Mildred Abramowitz. Diss. New York Univ., 1970. 49.

Why are young people going without basic necessities and are unable to find work? What are we going to do about it?   Abbreviated text of remarks, Cornell Univ. Based on article in *Cornell Farm and Home Weekly*, 14 Feb. 1935.

D53a "First Lady Doubts Townsend or Long Can Put All to Work."
Congressional Record (15 Feb. 1935): 2002

Partial text.   Appeared originally in the *Washington Evening Star*, 14 Feb. 1935.

1936

D54 "Banquet Address." *Public Speaking for Women.* By J.V. Garland. New York: Harper, 1938. 105-9.

The peace effort begins in one's own community, and once the public's opinion is influenced locally it can have an impact at the national level.   Text of address at the 11th Conference on the Cause and Cure of War, Washington, 21 Jan.

D55 *Democratic Digest* 13 (July 1936): 5.

Credits *Democratic Digest* and leaders of the Women's Division of the Democratic National Committee for teaching women how to get political work accomplished. Untitled congratulatory statement to women at the 1936 Democratic National Convention.

D56 Eads, Jane. "First Lady Stresses Courage." *Equal Rights* 2 (6 June 1936): 112.

If women want to succeed in politics they cannot take things   personally, bear grudges, or get discouraged, and they must learn how to get the facts and make their own decisions. Women have much to offer the political life of the country. Excerpts address to Political Study Club, Washington, 24 May. Appeared originally in the *Washington Herald*, 25 May 1936.

D56a "Good Advice from Mrs. Roosevelt." *Women's Democratic News* (New York State Section of the Democratic Digest) (July 1936): 3.
  Excerpts.

D57 "Greetings of Mrs. Franklin Delano Roosevelt, Delivered at Constitution Hall, June 1, 1936." *Associated Country Women of the World. Proceedings of the Third Triennial Conference, Held at Washington, May 31-June 11, 1936*. Dept. of State Publication, 1092. Conference Series, 34. Washington: GPO, 1937. 211.
  "A better understanding of the problems facing rural women in other countries will help good international relationships" and reinforce the fact that the farm can no longer be independent. Text of address. ER was honorary chair of the conference.

D58 Lazell, Louise T. "7,000 Farmers Give Mrs. Roosevelt a Picnic." *Democratic Digest* 13 (Aug. 1936): 21.
  She makes a "plea for youth, for education, and for the active conservation of our national resources." Excerpts address, Grayville, Ill., Summer 1936.

D59 *Lecture on 'A Typical Day in the White House.'* N.p.: n.p., n.d. 9p. Typescript.
  Describes life in the White House. Text of address at Sinai Temple Lecture Forum, Chicago, 16 Nov. Available in ER Pamphlet Collection, FDRL.

D60 "Microphone Duet." *Independent Woman* 15 (May 1936): 145, 151.
  Marie Souvestre opened her eyes to social issues. Text of discussion between ER and Charl Ormond Williams on the occasion of the 9th annual celebration of National Business Women's Week. Radio broadcast, 18 Mar. For a discussion of the broadcast, see Pauline E. Mandigo, "Business Women's Week--1936 Model." *Independent Woman* 15 (May 1936): 146-47.

D61 "Mrs. Franklin D. Roosevelt." *Report of the Sixth Annual New York Herald Tribune Forum on Current Problems on "The New Way of Living" and "The Political Issues Which America Faces in 1936," Waldorf-Astoria, New York City, September 22nd and 23rd, 1936*. New York: New York Herald Tribune, 1936. 16-17.
  Today's women have made progress in realizing the benefits of "the new way of living," and as always women are concerned about improving conditions for all. Text of a letter sent to the forum in lieu of an address.

D62 "The Negro and Social Change." *Opportunity* 14 (Jan. 1936): 22-23.
  All races must live together peacefully. Blacks must improve their standard of living and through education for blacks of all ages they will become better citizens. Text of address at Baltimore celebration of the 25th anniversary of the founding of the National Urban League, 12 Dec.

D62a "The Negro and Social Change." *The Negro American: A Documentary History*. By Leslie H. Fishel, Jr., and Benjamin Quarles. Glenview: Scott, Foresman, 1967. 460-62.

D62b "The Negro and Social Change." *The Black American: A Documentary History*. By Leslie H. Fishel, Jr., and Benjamin Quarles. New York: Morrow, 1970. 460-62.

D63 "Persistance Wins Says Mrs. Roosevelt: Experience Gives Weight to Words." *School Press Review* 12 (Oct. 1936): 1-2.
Working on a school paper can be good training for citizenship. Text of address at annual convention of the Columbia Scholastic Press Assoc., New York, 14 Mar.

D64 "The Roosevelt New Deal and the Colored Citizen." *Congressional Record* (20 June 1936): 10839.
Included is an abridgment of ER's address to the conference Fundamentals in the Education of Negroes, Washington, 9 May. Children of all races deserve a good education. All races have unique contributions which they can make, and if we do not work together to solve our problems we will fail together.

D65 Studebaker, J.W. "First Lady Outstanding Forum Leader." *School Life* 21 (Mar. 1936): 177-78.
Work is good for all people, and women who want to work should have the opportunity to do so. Excerpts presentation "Should Women Be Allowed to Work," Washington's Town Hall, 2 Feb. She also responded to questions from a panel and the audience.

D66 "The Unemployed Are Not a Strange Race." *Democratic Digest* 13 (June 1936): 19.
If we all citizens are to lead decent lives, we must educate everyone about the less fortunate. Excerpts address to convention of directors of WPA women's and professional projects, Washington, 4 May.

D67 *What Libraries Mean to the Nation*. Chicago: Published for the District of Columbia Library Assoc. by the American Library Assoc., 1936. 7p.
Education depends on libraries, and in all areas of the country, no matter how remote, there should be easy access to books as sources of education and relaxation. Text of address to District of Columbia Library Assoc., Washington, Apr. 1936.

D67a "What Libraries Mean to the Nation." *Bulletin of the American Library Association* 30 (June 1936): 477-79.

D68 "Young America Looks Forward." *America's Town Meeting of the Air* 18 (27 Feb. 1936): 5-32.
In her opening statement she remarks that all countries are facing the problems of youth and the need for persons of all ages to work together to solve them (pp. 6-7). She introduces and thanks other participants (pp. 8, 13-14, 19-20, 24, 32). Text of NBC radio broadcast of 27 Feb. moderated by ER.

1937

D69 "Address by Mrs. Franklin D. Roosevelt." *Hearing News* 5 (Dec. 1937): 1-3.
Children with handicaps should be made to feel normal. Text of address to American Society for the Hard of Hearing, 1937.

D70 "Conscience or Chaos." *"The Second Discovery of America:" Report of the Seventh Annual New York Herald Tribune Forum on Current Problems, the Waldorf-Astoria, New York City, October 4th and 5th, 1937*. New York: New York Herald Tribune, 1937. 7-9.

Our youth have been successful in dealing with the problems of today, and we should be glad that they can also dream about a happier future. Text of address, 4 Oct.

D71   "Mrs. Roosevelt at New Haven." *American Teacher* 21 (Mar./Apr. 1937): 4-5.
Like other groups, teachers can work together to strengthen the union movement and the American way of life. Excerpts address to New Haven chapter of the American Federation of Teachers, 23 Feb.

D72   "Three Americans Plead for Peace." *Democratic Digest* 14 (May 1937): 17.
For civilization to survive we must end war, and American women must work with women elsewhere to accomplish this. Excerpts from address for Emergency Peace Campaign. Also includes excerpts from addresses of Richard E. Byrd and Harry Emerson Fosdick.

D73   "Three Cheers for Molly Dewson." *Democratic Digest* 14 (Feb. 1937): 4, 26.
"She has made [Democratic women] educate themselves." Excerpts remarks made at Molly Dewson Round-up, Washington, 21 Jan.

D74   "Trialog on Office Holders." *Independent Woman* 17 (Jan. 1938): 17-18, 31.
Women have deeper feelings and can interject the human element into politics. Women need to study their communities, and they should remember that in public life one does not work for one's self but for the good of all. Condensation of 16 Dec. radio broadcast of a discussion between ER, Eleanor Medill Patterson, and Earlene White about women in public office.

D75   "Young Democrats Gather." *Democratic Digest* 14 (Sept. 1937): 28-29.
Through family discussions encourage children to engage in public service. Excerpts address to convention of the Young Democratic Clubs of America, Indianapolis, Ind., 20 June.

1938

D76   Aldrich, Bernice. "Mrs. Franklin D. Roosevelt's Message to Omaha Delphian Assembly--2,000 Attend." *Delphian Quarterly* (Jan. 1939): 57-58.
The nation's obligation as a democracy begins with individual citizens in local communities throughout the country. Excerpts address, 23 Oct.

D77   "Christmas Greetings." "An Analytical Study of Selected Radio Speeches of Eleanor Roosevelt." By Geneva Kretsinger. Thesis (M.A.) Univ. of Okla., 1941. 161-62.
A greeting to the nation. Text of radio broadcast, 20 Dec.

D78   "Mrs. Roosevelt's Speech to New York State Model Youth Legislature at Opening Session." *Proceedings of New York State Model Legislature of Youth, January 28-30, 1938 Held at College of the City of New York.* N.p.: n.p., 1938. cols. 11-14.
Youth want a peaceful world. To help ensure peace we must be concerned about conditions which peoples of all nations face. Happy and content people are less likely to go to war. Text of address, 28 Jan.

D79   "News from the States: New York Women Democrats Hear Stirring Speeches."
Democratic Digest 15 (July 1938): 30-31.
  Remember the importance of the individual citizen and the need to know about
conditions in one's community.   Excerpts address at annual conference of the
Women's Division of the Democratic State Committee, Utica, N.Y., 1 June.

D80   "The Role of Women in the Modern States." "The Philosophy of Social Reform
in the Speeches of Eleanor Roosevelt." By Eleanor Janice Bilsborrow. Diss. Univ. of
Denver, 1957. 192.
  World peace begins in our own country and homes. Working women still require
special protection under the law. Text of radio address to Federation of Business
Women.

D80a "Federation of Business Women Address." "An Analytical Study of Selected
Radio Speeches of Eleanor Roosevelt." By Geneva Kretsinger. Thesis (M.A.) Univ.
of Okla., 1941. 160-61.
  Text of "The Role of Women in the Modern States."

D81 "Seeking a Place in a Community." *Southern Workman* 67 (June 1938): 165-71.
  Being a citizen in this democracy is a demanding task.   Get involved in your
community, but remember that as a minority you will have to work harder.
Excerpts address at 70th anniversary of Hampton Institute, Hampton, Va., 21 Apr.
1938.

D82 Southern Conference for Human Welfare. *Report of Proceedings, Birmingham,
Alabama, November 20-23, 1938.* N.p.: n.p., n.d. 32p.
  All citizens must be allowed to contribute to our efforts as a nation to make
democracy work. The rest of the world is watching. Excerpts address, 22 Nov. (p.
29).

D83   "The WTUL's Radio Debut." *League Bulletin* (New York Women's Trade
Union League) (Nov. 1938): 3.
  Praise for the league and its role in educating working women.

D84 "Youth Peace Agents." *Democratic Digest* 15 (Sept. 1938): 19.
  Youth should recognize and practice the beliefs behind the Good Neighbor Policy.
Excerpts address at Second World Youth Congress, Vassar College.   Cordell Hull
calls for "peace by reason" in a companion address under the common title "Two
Paths to Peace."

D85 "Youth's Contribution." *"America Facing Tomorrow's World:" Report of the
Eighth Annual New York Herald Tribune Forum on Current Problems, the
Waldorf-Astoria, October 25 and 26, 1938, the New York World's Fair, October 27,
1938.* New York: New York Herald Tribune, 1938. 5-7.
  Share your wisdom with our young people but also listen to what they have to say.
Accept that youth have a greater appreciation for the need to cooperate at home and
abroad in a more complex world in which individuals and nations can no longer
attempt to be self-sufficient. Text of address, 25 Oct.

1939

D86 *Address by Mrs. Eleanor Roosevelt at the American Youth Congress Dinner.* New York: n.p., n.d. 4p. Typescript.
When youth are without jobs, citizens of all ages suffer. Government alone cannot solve the problem. Text of address, New York, 21 Feb.

D87 "Challenge." *The Guardian: A Bulletin of News and Suggestions for Leaders of Camp Fire Girls* 19 (Dec. 1939): 1-2.
Our country will need courage and heroism from its women, so prepare for the challenge. Text of radio address to conference of Camp Fire Girls leaders. Also includes discussion of the conference.

D88 "Children and the Future." Conference on Children in a Democracy. *Papers and Discussions at the 1939 Initial Session, Held in Washington, D.C., April 26, 1939.* Washington: GPO, 1939. 20-23.
What happens to children in any section of the country should concern all of us. Text of address, 26 Apr. ER served as honorary chair and gave the closing address.

D88a Perkins, Frances. "The White House Conference on Children in a Democracy." *Democratic Digest* 16 (May 1939): 4-5, 34.
Excerpts.

D88b "White House Conference on 'Children in a Democracy.'" *Youth Leaders Digest* 2 (Oct. 1939): 92.
Excerpts.

D89 "The Churchman Award Presented." *Churchman* 153 (15 Dec. 1939): 16-21.
The First Lady should make herself accessible, and all citizens should feel free to write to her and ask questions (pp. 20-21). Article describes the presentation of the award for promoting understanding among all peoples and includes the text of her remarks.

D90 "Democratic Women's Day in Washington." *Democratic Digest* 16 (Oct. 1939): 22.
We must look forward to the day when we can bring about a permanent peace. Urges women to work for the party at all levels. Text of radio address at Women's National Democratic Club, Washington, 16 Sept.

D91 Holmes, Mrs. George Sanford (Kathleen Sexton Holmes). "At the Women's National Democratic Club: Women Can Help Make America Example to World." *Democratic Digest* 16 (Nov. 1939): 15.
Since in our domestic affairs we set an example to the rest of the world, we should learn more about conditions in our communities and what is being done to help the less fortunate. Excerpts ER's address at Women's National Democratic Club banquet, 12 Oct.

D92 "Humanistic Democracy--The American Ideal." *"The Challenge to Civilization": Report of the Ninth Annual New York Herald Tribune Forum on Current Problems.* New York: New York Herald Tribune, 1939. 38-40.

Much of what is considered part of the "American Ideal" is not available to all citizens today. Also told audience that with a strong belief in democracy one has no need to fear Communists. Text of address.

D93   "Mrs. F.D.R. Supports Anti-Lynch Bill." *Crisis* 46 (Feb. 1939): 54.
The anti-lynching bill should be passed. Also endorsed "protest and agitation" by minorities when their rights are being denied. Excerpts address at Negro Youth Conference, Washington, 12 Jan.

D94   "Mrs. Roosevelt Awards Medal." *Crisis* 46 (Sept. 1939): 265, 285.
We should work together to create an environment which will enable all citizens to enjoy the benefits of education and citizenship. Text of address at 30th annual conference of the NAACP, Richmond, Va., 2 July when Spingarn Medal was presented to Marian Anderson.

D95   "Mrs. Roosevelt Counsels Women." *Democratic Digest* 16 (Jan. 1939): 11.
Women are interested in the human side of government, and their particular role is to educate men and women about party affairs and national concerns. Includes text of address at Jackson Day Tea, Washington, 7 Jan.

D96   "Remarks of Mrs. Roosevelt." *Journal of Social Hygiene* 25 (Mar. 1939): 138-40.
Praise for the work of head of the Public Health Service's fight to combat syphilis. Text of address at 26th annual conference of the American Social Hygiene Assoc., Washington, 1 Feb. Forms part of article "The Snow Medal Is Presented to Doctor Parran."

D97   Welshimer, Helen. "Marriage in the Making." *Good Housekeeping* 109 (Dec. 1939): 26-27, 154-55.
The fortunate bride is the one who learns what it means to love someone and who realizes that she must be herself, not what others want her to be. Excerpts ER's remarks to brides at the Good Housekeeping Institute, New York. Sometimes cited as "Talk to Brides" (pp. 27, 154-55).

D98   "Women in Politics." *Democratic Digest* 16 (July 1939): 13, 34.
Work with a political party because of what you can offer to it and your community. Calls for a national fund-raising day which became the annual Democratic Women's Day. Text of address at New York Regional Conference of the Women's Division of the Democratic National Committee, New York, 15 June.

1940

D99   "Address of Mrs. Franklin Delano Roosevelt." *Official Report of the Proceedings of the Democratic National Convention Held at Chicago, Illinois, July 15th to July 18th, Inclusive, 1940.* Washington: Democratic National Committee, n.d. 238-39.
The problems which the President faces today are too grave for one person to handle. Since he can neither campaign nor lead the nation alone, the selection of the vice presidential candidate is critical. Text of address, 18 July.

D99a McLaughlin, Kathleen. "No Campaigning, First Lady States." *New York Times* 19 July 1940: 1, 5.
The text of her address is included in an article about her appearance before the convention.

D99b "Democratic National Convention." *Congressional Record Appendix* (22 July 1940): A4496-97.
Text of address.

D99c "Chicago-1940." *Democratic Digest* 17 (Aug. 1940): 21-25, 48.
The text of her speech is contained in this account of activities of women at the 1940 Democratic National Convention (pp. 25, 48).

D100 "The American Home and Present Day Conditions." *What's New in Home Economics* 4 (Apr. 1940): 1, 11.
We need increased awareness of the interrelationship between farm and city and more consumer education. Text of address to Assoc. of Land-Grant Colleges and Universities, Washington.

D101 "Art and Our Warring World: A University of Chicago Round Table Broadcast in Celebration of National Art Week." *Round Table* (24 Nov. 1940): 1-27.
As chair of National Art Week ER participated with Clifton Fadiman, Archibald MacLeish, and Louis Wirth in a celebration of all forms of art and the value of artistic freedom. Text of radio discussion, 24 Nov.

D102 "As Seen by a Citizen." *Transcripts and Records of National Conventions, 1919-1944, and of General Councils, 1927-1943*. Papers of the League of Women Voters, 1918-1974, Pt. II, Ser. A. Research Collections in Women's Studies. Frederick: University Publications of America, 1985. reel 19, pp. 19-25.
Opportunities for our citizens will expand in the coming years, and how we utilize those opportunities will be a great adventure and challenge. The opportunity to expand spiritually as a nation will also present itself. Text of address at National League of Women Voters Convention, New York, 30 Apr.

D103 "The Backlog of Preparedness." *America's Second Fight for Freedom: Report of the New York Herald Tribune Tenth Annual Forum on Current Problems at the Waldorf-Astoria, New York City, October 22, 23 and 24, 1940*. New York: New York Herald Tribune, 1940. 7-10.
Behind any defense effort must be a belief in our democratic principles and a desire to see life improved for all citizens. Text of address, 22 Oct.

D104 *Civil Liberties-The Individual and the Community*. Chicago: Chicago Civil Liberties Committee, 1940. 8p.
Defends the right to liberties provided by the Bill of Rights and claims that some black citizens do not always enjoy those rights. Applauds the support of civil liberties by youth, warns against religion as an issue in politics, and asks for better relations between the races. Text of address at Chicago Civil Liberties Union, 14 Mar.

D104a "Civil Liberties-The Individual and the Community." *Representative American Speeches: 1939-1940*. Reference Shelf, 14:1. Introduction and comments by A. Craig Baird. New York: Wilson, 1940. 173-82.

D105 "Defense and the Minority Groups." *Opportunity* 18 (Dec. 1940): 356-58.
All citizens should be able to feel that their way of life is worth defending. Excerpts address at 30th anniversary dinner of the National Urban League.

D106 "First Lady Sets Precedent at House Inquiry; Criticizes Welfare Agencies of Washington." *New York Times* 10 Feb. 1940: 6.
Calls for improvement of welfare institutions in the District of Columbia in testimony before a congressional committee, 9 Feb. Reported as the first time a First Lady has testified before Congress. Excerpts.

D107 "Greetings by Mrs. Roosevelt." American Red Cross. National Convention. *Summary of Proceedings*. N.p.: American Red Cross, 1940. 49.
Throughout the world today the Red Cross is being challenged to relieve suffering. Text of remarks, Washington, 7 May.

D108 "Keeping the Record Straight on the Art." *Democratic Digest* 17 (May 1940): 29.
ER and congressional wives presented a 15 minute radio broadcast on misunderstandings about the 1940 census. She discussed the historical background of the census.

D109 "League of Women Voters Biennial Convention." *Transcripts and Records of National Conventions, 1919-1944, and of General Councils, 1927-1943*. Papers of the League of Women Voters, 1918-1974, Pt. II, Ser. A. Research Collections in Women's Studies. Frederick: University Publications of America, 1985. reel 18, document 53, pp. 1-5.
As a league member there are many opportunities to learn about the issues which face voters, and this can be more important than affiliating with a political party. Text of address, New York, 1 May.

D110 "The Meaning of Democracy." *Congressional Record Appendix* (15 May 1940): A2959-60.
What democracy means and how we can work to promote it. Text of address at National Institute of Government, Washington, 4 May.

D111 "Mrs. Roosevelt." *Congressional Record* (21 May 1940): 6538-39.
In praise of WPA workers and what they are doing to improve the lives of others. Text of radio address, 20 May.

D112 "Mrs. Roosevelt's Advice on Public Speaking: Have Something to Say, Be Honest, and Know How to Stop." *Democratic Digest* 17 (Feb. 1940): 33.
Excerpts remarks at School for Practical Platform Speaking, Washington, 11 Jan.

D113 *Norway* (1941): 42.
A untitled Christmas message to the women of Norway in which she extends them greetings of the season and the hope for a better new year. Text of radio broadcast, Dec. 1940?

D114 "Realities Which Woman Must Face about Themselves and about the World as It Is Now and as It Might Be: A Conversation among Experts." *Aframerican* [sic] *Woman's Journal* 1 (1941): 14-28, 37.

Text of round table discussion held as part of The Woman's Centennial Congress, New York, 25-30 Nov. ER presided, and other participants included Pearl Buck and Margaret Mead.   In her summation (pp. 28, 37) ER states that women must understand the needs of labor and of rural and urban America.   Women need to get out of the home and serve their communities, she said.

D115 "The Responsibility of the Individual and the Community." *Proceedings of the White House Conference on Children in a Democracy, Washington, D.C., January 18-20, 1940.* Children's Bureau Publication, 266, Washington: GPO, 1940. 83-84.

Each of us must learn more about the needs of our communities and be willing as a nation to provide the assistance required to improve economic conditions and opportunities for children in all areas of the country.   Text of address, 20 Jan.

D115a Lenroot, Katharine F.   "Protection for Democracy's Children." *Democratic Digest* 17 (Feb. 1940): 4-5, 38.

Excerpts (p. 38).

D116 "Sixty Years Constructive ORT Work." *ORT Economic Bulletin* 1 (Nov./Dec. 1940): 1-2.

ORT's present work in Europe is of particular note.   But all people, not just Jews, should help Europeans by working together for a democratic world.   Text of address at Chicago Organization for Rehabilitation through Training Council dinner, 16 Nov.

D117   "Statements by Prominent Writers Favoring President Roosevelt." *Congressional Record Appendix* (14 Oct. 1940): A6348-51.

The entire text of the pamphlet *Radio Program Presented Under the Auspices of the Women's Division Democratic National Committee, National Broadcasting Co., Blue Network, Friday, September 27, 1940* is reprinted.   ER interviews Thorton Wilder, Edna Ferber, Hendrik van Loon, Rex Stout, and others about why they support FDR's re-election.

D117a "Voices for Roosevelt on Democratic Women's Day." *Democratic Digest* 17 (Oct./Nov. 1940): 18-19.

A condensation of the discussion.

D118 "Testimony of Mrs. Franklin D. Roosevelt." *Interstate Migration: Hearings before the Select Committee to Investigate the Interstate Migration of Destitute Citizens, House of Representatives, Seventh-sixth Congress, Third Session.* Pt. 9. Washington, GPO, 1941. 3742-56.

She shares her knowledge of conditions in camps for migrant workers and her belief that the plight of the workers and their families is a national problem.   Text of statement, 9 Dec.   Responses to questions from committee members follows testimony.

D119 "What Can We Do for Youth?" *Occupations* 19 (Oct. 1940): 9-10.
Youth represent our future, and we should make them feel that they are needed. Text of address at 50th anniversary celebration of the Vocational Service for Juniors of New York City.

D120 *Youth Today.* Philadelphia: n.p., 1940. 25p.
Our young people want to work and improve themselves, but too often others do not take their problems seriously. Text of address, Democratic Women's Luncheon Club of Philadelphia, 17 Apr.

1941

D121 "Attitudes of Youth and Morale." *The Family in a World at War.* Ed. Sidonie Matsner Gruenberg. New York: Harper, 1942. 230-36.
Since they influence the attitudes of the young, older people must keep morale high during wartime. Text of address at Child Study Assoc. Institute on Family Morale in a World at War, 1941.

D121a "Youth Attitudes and Family Morale." *Child Study* 19 (Winter 1941-1942): 41-42.
Abbreviated version.

D122 *"Civil Liberties and the Crisis": An Address by Mrs. Franklin D. Roosevelt.* N.p.: n.p., 1941. 3p. Typescript.
"The best defense of our civil liberties is the exercise of responsible citizenship." She discusses at length the meaning of the Bill of Rights and FDR's Four Freedoms emphasizing the need to ensure that all citizens can benefit from both. Text of address on the anniversary of the Statue of Liberty, Chicago, 28 Oct.

D123 "The Community and Morale." *Educational Record Supplement* 15 (Jan. 1942): 63-68.
Since democracy and morale begin in the local community, one should know one's community well. Text of address at 10th Educational Conference, 30 Oct.

D124 *An Easter Message to the Children in Great Britain.* New York: Friends of Children, 1941. 6p. Typescript.
Her wishes for the children to have a better life after the war and her appreciation for the efforts of the Friends of Children to improve life for British children during the war. Text of radio, address, 10 Apr. Available in ER Papers, Box 3041, FDRL.

D125 "Every Worker Should Belong to a Trade Union Says Mrs. Roosevelt." *American Federationist* 48 (Mar. 1941): 14-15.
Employers and employees must work together to improve conditions and preserve our democratic way of life. Text of address to striking members of the International Brotherhood of Electrical Workers, New York.

D126 "Friendship Bridge." "An Analytical Study of Selected Radio Speeches of Eleanor Roosevelt." By Geneva Kretsinger. Thesis (M.A.) Univ. of Okla., 1941. 163-64.
Like the American West, South Africa is a country which is still developing. Condensation of radio address, 19 Feb. 1941.

D127 "Mrs. FDR Urges United Effort." *Weekly Review* (Young Communist League) 6 (16 Dec. 1941): 6.
What we had hoped was only the unthinkable has now happened, and we must face it. We must go about our daily affairs as best we can, help others, and build morale. Our young people will face a greater challenge.
Text of radio address, 7 Dec.

D128 "Mrs. Roosevelt Assails Bigots in Peace Camp." *New York Times* 29 Sept. 1941: 13.
Those leaders who advocate isolationism think that our country can live apart from the rest of the world. Others advocate religious and social prejudice, something which goes against the very basis of our democracy. Paraphrasing Thomas Wolfe she declares that "a wind is rising and the rivers flow" and men everywhere will be free. Excerpts radio address, 28 Sept., the first in the Pan American Coffee Bureau series.

D129 "Mrs. Roosevelt Calls on Youth to Find Its Part in Emergency." *Defense* 2 (7 Oct. 1941): 22.
To be ready to fulfill their obligations as citizens after conditions improve, youth must play a part now in the public life of the nation. In her concluding remarks she emphasized that the young will not have a promising future unless we work to preserve basic freedoms at home and elsewhere. Text of opening remarks in a radio discussion entitled "College Students and Civilian Defense", 2 Oct.

D129a "Mrs. Roosevelt Calls on Youth to Find Its Part in Emergency." *Victory* 2 (7 Oct. 1941): 22.

D130 "Mrs. Roosevelt Pays Tribute to Negroes on NBC Broadcast." *Opportunity* 19 (June 1941): 184.
Blacks have given our country many fine artists of every kind. Excerpts remarks for radio broadcast in observance of National Music Week, 11 May.

D131 "Over the Air on Democratic Women's Day." *Democratic Digest* 18 (Nov. 1941): 12.
Women in our democracy must work to improve conditions in their communities and the world. Text of radio address for Democratic Women's Day, 27 Sept. Read by Gladys Tillett.

D132 "Social Gains & Defense." *Common Sense* 10 (Mar. 1941): 71-72.
Social gains must continue while the country is at war, since we must know that a better future is being fought for. Based on an address in honor of *Common Sense*, New York.

D133 "Speech Training for the Youth." *Quarterly Journal of Speech* 27 (Oct. 1941): 369-71.
Training in public speaking and debating should begin early. Text of address opening series of classes on public speaking, Washington, 9 Jan.

D134 Tuller, Carol. "The Tie That Must Bind...Friendship!" *Secretary* [Hollywood] 2 (May 1941): 16-17.

An article based on a speech in Los Angeles in which ER emphasized the importance of a strong relationship with the nations of Central and South America and the need for North Americans to learn to speak Spanish.

D135 "What Is the Situation in the World Today, and What Is Our Relationship to That Situation?" *Congressional Record Appendix* (9 July 1941): A3297-3330.
   Since our country is not at war, it is our responsibility to help secure peace for the rest of the world. Text of address, St. Paul, Minn., 7 June.

D135a "Know What We Defend." *Democratic Digest* 18 (June 1941): 14.
   Excerpts.

D136 "What Must We Do to Improve the Health and Well-Being of the American People?" *Town Meeting* 7 (8 Dec. 1941): 3-23.
   Since the draft has revealed that many young men have medical problems, government needs to provide better health services. Text of radio address by ER and others, 4 Dec. ER's statement (pp. 13-15) and her response to questions (pp. 17, 19, 21-22).

1942

D137 "Civilian Defense." *Democratic Digest* 19 (Jan. 1942): 17.
   If we do not volunteer for civilian defense work, we will be sending a message to Hitler that we do not care about defending our country. Excerpts radio address, 16 Nov.

D138 "Mrs. Roosevelt." *Council on Candy as Food in the War Effort Presents Mrs. Franklin D. Roosevelt and Major General Edmund B. Gregory, Quartermaster General of the United States Army in a Coast-to-Coast Broadcast from Washington, D.C., December 9, 1942.* Chicago: The Council, 1942. 5-12.
   Observations of conditions in England and how gifts of candy would be appreciated by the British. Predicts that special candies developed for use by U.S. troops will become available in the U.S. after the war. Text of address.

D139 "Mrs. Roosevelt Attends New York Tea." *Democratic Digest* 19 (Oct. 1942): 14.
   Work toward winning the war and building a better world. Excerpts address to Democratic women, 24 Sept.

D140 "The People's Century." *Proceedings of the International Student Assembly Held at the American University, Washington, D.C., 2-5 September 1942.* Ed. William Allen Neilson. New York: Oxford Univ. Pr., 1944. 57-59.
   Individuals, communities, and nations must do all that they can to achieve the people's century when all peoples will be able to realize their dreams. The hopes for the people's century rests with the young who must learn the value of working together to win the war and bring dignity to all. Text of address at Fourth Plenary Session.

D141 "Salisbury Entertains." *Time* 40 (24 Aug. 1942): 11-12.
A call for equal opportunity in the workplace for all races. Excerpts address at African Methodist Episcopal Zion Church of America convention, Salisbury, N.C., Aug.

D142 "Sugar Hoarding." *Democratic Digest* 19 (Feb. 1942): 2.
Women should set an example by not buying more food than they need. Excerpts 25 Jan. radio broadcast.

D143 "Testimony of Mrs. Franklin D. Roosevelt, Assistant Director, Office of Civilian Defense." *National Defense Migration: Hearings before the Select Committee Investigating National Defense Migration, House of Representatives, Seventy-seventh Congress, First Session.* Washington: GPO, 1942. 9766-74.
Discrimination and poor standards in housing, health, and education affect war production, because when citizens do not feel secure in their daily lives our defense effort is jeopardized. Text of statement, 14 Jan. Responses to questions from committee members follows her statement.

D144 "War Work Is Not Enough." *Democratic Digest* 19 (Oct. 1942): 10, 14.
While the nation is at war women must continue to pursue Democratic Party principles, continue to work toward improving the education and health of children, and better prepare themselves for maintaining the peace which will come. Text of address on Democratic Women's Day, Washington, 26 Sept.

D145 "Your New World." *Life Story* 7 (Feb. 1943): 33.
Women in Great Britain are working along with men to win the war. Excerpts radio address, BBC, London, Oct.

1943

D146   "Democratic Women's Day in Washington. Eleanor Roosevelt Said:" *Democratic Digest* 20 (Oct. 1943): 10-11.
It was a rewarding experience to see what a wonderful job our young men are doing in the South Pacific. Excerpts from radio address on Democratic Women's Day, 27 Sept.

D147 "First Lady Makes Strong Plea for Racial Freedom, Unity." *People's Voice* 21 Aug. 1943: 3.
In her 15 Aug. radio address ER called for equality for all races in access to public transportation and facilities. Banner headline on p. 1 reads "Mrs. F.D.R. Blasts Jim Crow."

D148 "The First Lady on Home Safety." *Home Safety Review* 1 (May/June 1943): 10, 15.
We should try to prevent accidents in the home. Condensation of National Radio Forum address, 5 May.

D149 "A Free World after Victory." *Free World* 5 (Jan. 1943): 9.
We must work to convince the non-believers that there are certain basic needs for a free world: freedom from fear and want, freedom of religion, and freedom to be

different from others. Text of address at Conference of the World Confederation of International Groupments, New York, 5 Dec. ER presided.

D150 "Mrs. Franklin D. Roosevelt." *Visit to Australia of Mrs. Franklin D. Roosevelt, Official Luncheon by Commonwealth Government, Parliament House, Canberra, Saturday, 4th September 1943, Record of Speeches.* Canberra: Commonwealth Government Printer, n.d. 5-7.

We will win the war, and then it will be the peace which we have to win. As our youth are sacrificing today, we must all learn to think of the needs of others in the future. Otherwise, democracy will not prevail. Text of remarks.

D151 "Mrs. Roosevelt Addressed Largest NAACP Student Annual Conference." *Postal Alliance* (Dec. 1943): 6.

True democracy will never be achieved until equal education and job training are provided for all races. We must plan now how to cooperate with other nations in the post-war world. Excerpts address at NAACP annual student conference, Lincoln Univ., 29 Oct.

D152 "Mrs. Roosevelt Thrilled by Progress at Linden." *Eastern Craftsman* 2 (Mar. 1943): 1-2.

Be as productive and committed as your British counterparts. Excerpts remarks at General Motors aircraft plant, Linden, N.J., 25 Feb.

D153 "Responsibility to Our Men and Women in the Services." *Pioneering for a Civilized World: Report of the New York Herald Tribune Forum on Current Problems at the Waldorf-Astoria, New York City, November 16 and 17, 1943.* New York: New York Herald Tribune, 1943. 65-68.

Instead of thinking about our own problems, those of us at home must be as courageous as our young people in uniform and work to guarantee that they will have a secure economic future. Text of address, 16 Nov.

1944

D154 "Advice for War Hostesses: Mrs. Roosevelt Gives Hints to Government Girls on How to Meet and Talk with Men Returning from Fighting in Europe." *Science News Letter* 45 (17 June 1944): 397.

Women who volunteer in hospitals should be prepared to deal with the questions and bitterness which the wounded men have. Report of address to PAW-ETS, Washington, 1944.

D155 "The American Spirit." *Congress Bi-weekly* 11 (9 June 1944): 10-11.

The American spirit includes the recognition that people everywhere must enjoy liberties. Excerpts address to Women's Division of the American Jewish Congress, 1 June.

D156 "Building Rural Schools and Communities to Cope with the Problems of Tomorrow: Panel Discussion." *The White House Conference on Rural Education, October 3, 4, and 5, 1944.* Washington: National Education Assoc. of the United States, n.d. 98-114.

Text of discussion in which ER and others pursue the theme that good health is necessary for learning. All citizens must have access to health care even if it means socialized medicine, ER said.

D156a "Adult Education Required." *Youth Leaders Digest* 7 (Apr. 1945): 25 7.

Includes her remarks. Issued as part of "What a Few Speakers Said at the White House Conference on Rural Education" (pp. 257-58).

D157 "Closing the Conference." *The White House Conference on Rural Education, October 3, 4, and 5, 1944.* Washington: National Education Assoc. of the United States, n.d. 227-28.

A plea for improved education in rural areas.

D158 "Conference at the White House." *Independent Woman* 23 (July 1944): 225.

Heads of government agencies need lists of women qualified for positions. Excerpts opening address at a conference on women in the post-war world, Washington, 14 June.

D159 "Eleanor Roosevelt: A Leader in Practicing Democracy." *Childhood Education* 39 (Jan. 1963): 210-212.

Children of today must be taught to face the problems of citizenship in a more complicated world. Excerpts remarks to Assoc. for Childhood Education as reported in Mar./Apr. 1944 issue of *Branch Exchange*.

D160 Goodwin, Betty. "New York State Women Open '44 Campaign." *Democratic Digest* 21 (June/July 1944): 28-29.

The world is becoming smaller, and American women must work to promote friendship among all peoples while encouraging our own citizens to be full participants in the democratic process. Excerpts address "Women's Responsibility Now and in the Post-War World," to meeting of Democratic women, Syracuse, N.Y., 22 June.

D161 "Mrs. Eleanor Roosevelt." *Final Proceedings of the Seventh Constitutional Convention of the Congress of Industrial Organizations.* N.p.: Congress of Industrial Organizations, n.d. 110-13.

Look ahead to the end of the war and the responsibility which we will have as a nation to meet the challenges of peace and make our country an example for the rest of the world. Text of address, Chicago, 20 Nov.

D162 "Opening the Conference." *The White House Conference on Rural Education, October 3, 4, and 5, 1944.* Washington: National Education Assoc. of the United States, n.d. 21.

Residents of all areas of the country should be concerned that some children in rural areas are not receiving an adequate education.

D163 "Our Homes in the Post-War World." *National Parent-Teacher* 38 (June 1944): 22-23.

Young men who come back from the war will expect educational and employment opportunities. Recollections of her trip to the South Pacific. Based on address to National Conference of Parents and Teachers, New York, 22 May.

D164   "Psychological Gap." *Science News Letter* 45 (4 Mar. 1944): 149.

In an address to the Anthropological Society of Washington, she said that during her trip to the South Pacific she learned that soldiers felt a "psychological gap" between themselves and family at home.

D165   "The Refugee's Place in American Life." *Talks* 10 (Jan. 1945): 28-29.

Welcomes refugees and the skills which they bring.   Urges them to show appreciation for the freedoms available in this country and to accept the responsibilities of living in a democracy.   Text of radio address.

D166   "The Role of the Educator." *Journal of the National Education Association* 33 (Mar. 1944): 59-60.

Looking forward to the post-war years she emphasizes the role of the teacher, the value of education, and the need for federal aid to education. Based on an address to the National Education Assoc. headquarters staff, Washington, 21 Jan.

D166a "The Role of the Educator." *Youth Leaders Digest* 6 Apr. 1944): 253-55.

1945

D167   "At Unity House." *Out of the Sweatshop: The Struggle for Industrial Democracy*. Ed. Leon Stein. New York: Quadrangle/The New York Times Book Co., 1977. 254-55.

During her visit to the vacation resort of the International Ladies' Garment Workers' Union she was impressed with the eagerness of the union members to purchase war bonds.   Text of remarks.   Reprinted from the *New York World Telegram*, 21 June 1945.

D168   *Democracy in Education*. N.p.: n.p., 1945. 26p. Typescript.

A plea, with humor and personal recollections, for schools which will teach children how to live in a democracy.   Text of lecture at Workshop for Democracy of the Downtown Community School, New York, 26 Nov. Includes question and answer session.   Available in ER Papers, Box 3051, FDRL.

D169   *Housing and Community Planning: One Approach to Intercultural Relations*. N.p.: n.p., 1945. 36p. Typescript.

All citizens need to be concerned with the condition of the nation's housing. We need more and better housing and the jobs which home construction brings.   Text of lecture at Workshop for Democracy of the Downtown Community School, New York, 12 Nov. Includes question and answer session. Available in ER Papers, Box 3051, FDRL.

D170   "A 'Milestone' in Human Relations." *Council Woman* (National Council of Jewish Women) 7 (May-June 1945): 4-5, 16.

Since we are entering a time when we need the skills of all citizens, we must think of people as individuals not groups. This is a concept which should be remembered at organizational meetings of the UN, because it will succeed only if member nations are recognized as individual countries with a voice in what the UN does. Text of address at National Council of Jewish Women's presentation to an interracial commission, New York, 27 Mar.

D171 "Mrs. Roosevelt Urges Educators to See that Veterans Get the Best Education Has to Offer." *Education for Victory* 3 (20 Apr. 1945): 1-3.

The education of returning veterans will require special skills of the educator in order to satisfy the needs of the students and employers. Text of address at opening session of the Conference on Educational Progress for Veterans, Washington.

D172 "To the Women of the U.S.S.R." *Partners for Peace: A Selection of the Leading Addresses Delivered at the American-Soviet Friendship Rally in Madison Square Garden, the Red Army Day Celebration and International Women's Day Broadcast, 1944-1945, U.S.A.-USSR, Nations United for Victory, Peace and Prosperity.* New York: National Council of American-Soviet Friendship, 1945. 46-47.

"You are to be congratulated for your efforts during the war. I hope that as our countries worked together in wartime, we as women can work together to preserve a lasting peace." Text of radio address, 7 Mar.

D173 "Women Gathering for Paris Parley." *New York Times* 24 Nov. 1945: 14.

Includes the text of a message in which she expresses hope that European nations will soon be strong enough to contribute to the cause of peace.

1946

D174 "Eleanor Roosevelt Said...." *Oakwood Alumni News* (Dec. 1946): 2, 13.

We must continue to work toward achieving equality for all of our citizens, because through the UN we promote equality for all peoples of the world. Excerpts address.

D175 *The Home of Franklin D. Roosevelt, National Historic Site.* Publication, 1. Hyde Park: Hyde Park Historical Assoc., 1946.

FDR's home is turned over to the people with the pleasure of knowing that his spirit will continue to live there and in our minds and hearts. Text of remarks, Hyde Park, N.Y., 12 Apr.

D175a "Addresses at the Roosevelt Shrine Dedication." *New York Times* 13 Apr. 1946: 2.

D175b "Address by Mrs. Eleanor Roosevelt." *Congressional Record Appendix* (13 Apr. 1946): A2136.

D176 "Human Rights and Human Freedom: An American View by Mrs. Roosevelt. A Russian View by Mr. Vishinsky." *New York Times Magazine* 24 Mar. 1946: 21.

ER states that only weak nations fear freedom of speech. Text of 12 Feb. remarks made by ER and Andrei Vishinsky in the UN General Assembly.

D176a "What Are Human Rights? An American View by Mrs. Eleanor Roosevelt. A Russian View by Mr. Andrei Y. Vishinsky." *Negro* 4 (Sept. 1946): 81-83.
Adaptation.

D177 "Importance of Background Knowledge in Building for the Future." *Annals of the American Academy of Political and Social Science* 246 (July 1946): 9-12.

It is important to know the circumstances which caused the two world wars, and that background knowledge should enable the UN to succeed where the League of

Nations failed. Text of address at annual meeting of the American Academy of Political and Social Science, Philadelphia, 5 Apr.

D178 "Mrs. Franklin D. Roosevelt." *Proceedings at Dinner in Honor of Mrs. Franklin Delano Roosevelt.* Washington: GPO, 1946. 9-15.
As a nation we must take greater interest in the UN, and as individuals we must realize that we have to work to maintain the peace. Text of address to Women's Joint Congressional Committee, Washington, 14 Mar. Includes introduction by Tom Connally (pp. 7-9). Available in Clara Beyer Papers, Box 21, Folder 323, Schlesinger Library, Radcliffe College.

D178a "Mrs. Roosevelt Says That We Must Work for Peace." *Democratic Digest* 23 (Apr. 1946): 14.
Reports on two speeches made in Washington on 14 Mar.: at Women's National Press Club and at the Women's Joint Congressional Committee dinner. Excerpts dinner address.

D178b "Mrs. Franklin D. Roosevelt." *Congressional Record Appendix* (9 May 1946): A2549-51.
Text of address.

D179 "Mrs. Roosevelt." *Dinner in Honour of Mrs. Eleanor Roosevelt.* London: The Pilgrims, 1946. 4-8.
FDR's early life was a preparation for the responsibilities which he had to assume later. We are fortunate that he and Winston Churchill were the leaders of our two countries during the war years, and I wish that FDR were here today telling you of his hopes for the post-war world. Text of address to the Pilgrims, London, 4 Feb.

D179a "London Roosevelt Memorial Pilgrims' Aim; Society Breaks Custom in Dinner to Widow." *New York Times* 5 Feb. 1946: 5.
Excerpts.

D179b "Mrs. Roosevelt at Pilgrims' Dinner." *Times* [London] 5 Feb. 1946: 2.
Excerpts.

D180 "Mrs. Roosevelt Joins Board of African Culture Group." *Negro* 4 (Aug. 1946): 2-3 of cover.
After accepting membership on the board of the African Academy of Arts and Research ER addressed the press and academy members in her New York apartment. She praised the work of the academy and its interest in African students who can be of assistance to under-staffed UN representatives from African nations. Excerpts.
Also in *Twice a Year* 14-15. Copy not examined.

D181 "New York State Women Stage First Rally." *Democratic Digest* 23 (Nov. 1946): 14-15.
A call for voter registration in order to return the Democrats and progress to the state. Excerpts address, New York Democratic Women's rally, New York, 7 Oct. 1946.

D182 *Proceedings of the Democratic State Convention, Albany, New York, September 3rd and 4th, 1946.* N.p.: n.p., n.d. 176p. Typescript.

In an appeal to delegates to return home and work for the election of Democratic candidates she criticizes the current Republican policies in New York state in the areas of labor, housing, veterans' affairs, and education. Text of address, Albany, 3 Sept. Available at FDRL.

D182a "Text of Democratic Keynote Speech by Mrs. Roosevelt at Albany." *New York Times* 4 Sept. 1946: 12.

D183 "U.S. Women Send Greeting." *New York Times* 9 Mar. 1946: 16.
We join with women in those countries which suffered the most from the war. Text in English of message in *Izvestiia* sent by ER and others to International Women's Day meeting in Moscow on 8 Mar.

D184 "The United Nations and You." *Vital Speeches* 12 (1 May 1946): 444-45.
Nations must learn to live together just as all citizens must learn to live with one another. Stresses to a young audience the importance of making history come alive, dreaming the impossible, and emulating heroes. Text of address at New York Herald Tribune High School Forum, New York, 13 Apr.

1947

D185 Greenbaum, Lucy. "World Women Get Truman Greetings." *New York Times* 8 Sept. 1947: 18.
The cause of peace is furthered when women from around the world meet and exchange ideas. Text of brief statement sent to the International Council of Women conference, Philadelphia, 7 Sept.

D186 "Salutes Soviet Women." *New York Times* 21 Feb. 1947: 11.
Women of America and all other nations join you in your efforts to secure world peace. International Women's Day message to Soviet Women's Anti-Fascist Committee.

D187 "Women and the United Nations." *General Federation Clubwoman* 27 (Sept. 1947): 17-18.
The success of the UN begins with you the individual, the type of community you help create, and the type of people you elect to represent you. All citizens should be interested in the UN and urge the U.S. to lead the world to a lasting peace. Text of address at annual convention of the General Federation of Women's Clubs, New York, 22-28 June.

D188 "Women Protected in New Rights Bill." *New York Times* 18 Feb. 1947: 28.
In reaction to a bill on the legal status of women ER issued a statement supporting the removal of all barriers to women through legislative means while continuing her objections to the Equal Rights Amendment. Excerpts statement.

1948

D189 "Acceptance Address by Eleanor Roosevelt." *Bryn Mawr Alumnae Bulletin* 28 (Apr. 1948): 3-4.
Colleges have an obligation to train students for living in a democracy so that they can work to help achieve basic rights for all. Text of address upon acceptance of the

M. Carey Thomas Award, Bryn Mawr College. Issued as part of article "Fifth Presentation of the M. Carey Thomas Award," pp. 1-4, which includes presentation by Bryn Mawr president Katharine Elizabeth McBride.

D190   "Address Delivered by Mrs. Eleanor Roosevelt." *Congressional Record Appendix* (16 June 1948): A4370.
  What we are trying to do at the UN to guarantee basic rights to all is what Rep. Bloom is doing when he tries to help individuals with their problems.   Text of remarks at dinner in honor of Sol Bloom, New York, 10 June.

D191   *L'Amitie Franco-americaine.* Les Conference des Ambassadeurs: Grands Discours Francais et Internationaux, 30. Rennes: Les Grandes Editions de l'Hermine, 1949. 27p.
  Text of address, 6 Nov. 1948.   Copy not examined.

D192   "How ADA Has Grown." *ADA World* (2 Mar. 1948): 8.
  You are among those who believe that it is one's duty to be interested in government.   Excerpts address at Americans for Democratic Action convention, Philadelphia, 21 Feb.

D193   "Liberals in This Year of Decision." *Christian Register* 127 (June 1948): 26-28, 33.
  Liberals should work together to promote democracy as the best means of making the country stronger and ending racial discrimination.   Also discusses her experience in working with the Soviets in the UN.   Text of address at Middle Atlantic Laymen's Conference.

D194   "Mrs. Roosevelt Warns Germans on 'Sovietism.'" *New York Times* 24 Oct. 1948: 12.
  Sovietism cannot be allowed to replace nazism and fascism nor should any system of government be forced upon a nation.   Text of address delivered in German at meeting sponsored by League of Women Physicians, Stuttgart, 23 Oct.

D195   "Our Next Hundred Years." *Independent Woman* 27 (July 1948): 194-98.
  Women must decide what kind of world they want and then work for it.   Excerpts address on "Women in World Affairs" presented at a meeting of women's organizations, New York, 19 Mar.

D196   "The Rights of Assembly." *United Nations Bulletin* 6 (1 Jan. 1949): 5
  Reports on progress toward acceptance of the Universal Declaration of Human Rights by the UN General Assembly.   Part 1 of two-part series entitled "Universal Declaration of Human Rights."   Text of address to UN General Assembly.

D197   "The Struggle for Human Rights." *Department of State Bulletin* 19 (10 Oct. 1948): 457-60, 466.
  The UN is the proper forum for discussing human rights.   Describes how articles of the UN charter promote human rights and freedom.   Text of address, the Sorbonne, Paris, 28 Sept.

D197a "The Struggle for Human Rights." *Human Rights and Genocide: Selected Statements, United Nations Resolutions, Declaration and Conventions.* Dept. of State

Publication, 3643; International Organization and Conference Series III, 39. Washington, Dept. of State, 1949. 1-12.

D197b "The Struggle for Human Rights." *Human Rights and Genocide: Selected United Nations Resolutions, September 21-December 12, 1948.* Dept. of State Publication, 3416; International Organization and Conference Series III, 25. Washington: Dept. of State, 1949. 1-12.

D198 Stuart, Campbell. *Britain's Tribute to Franklin Roosevelt: The Story of the Memorial in Grosvenor Square.* London: n.p., n.d.
  We have to care about others as FDR did. He wanted all nations to work together for peace. Text of remarks, London, 12 Apr.

D199 "We Need the Kind of Strength That Some Nations Understand." *ADA World* 2 (2 Mar. 1948): 2.
  We can have universal military training if we trust ourselves as a nation to continue our devotion to peace. The best way to deal with the Russians is to demonstrate strength. Excerpts remarks in favor of resolution supporting universal military training made at Americans for Democratic Action annual convention, Philadelphia, 21 Feb. Preceded by editorial statement about the defeat of the resolution and how ER is the symbol of the ADA.

1949

D200 "Address." *Summary of Proceedings, The American National Red Cross National Convention, Atlantic City, New Jersey, June 27-30, 1949.* Washington: The American National Red Cross, 1949. 65-74.
  In the post-war world the U.S. must give economic aid but give it humbly. We are the leader of democratic countries, and we must try to preserve democracies throughout the world while also accepting the role as the world's spiritual leader. Text of address, 28 June.

D201 "'FDR Day' Celebrated at Dinner." *ADA World* 3 (16 Feb. 1949): 1, 3.
  In a hundred years it will matter little who our greatest President was. What is more important is the leadership which citizens exercise. Excerpts remarks, New York, 27 Jan.

D202 "For Better World Understanding." *Pi Lambda Theta Journal* 27 (May 1949): 196-203.
  An interpretation of the Universal Declaration of Human Rights. Text of address at Pi Lambda Theta initiation dinner, New York, 30 Mar.

D202a "For Better World Understanding." *Phi Delta Kappan* 31 (Sept. 1949): 28-33.
  Excerpts.

D203 "Freedom and Human Rights." *Columbia College Forum on Democracy, February 10-12, 1949.* N.p.: n.p., 1949. 38-44. Typescript.
  Text of address. Copy not examined.

D204 "The Human Factor in the Development of International Understanding." *Colgate Lectures in Human Relations, 1949.* Hamilton: Colgate Univ., 1949. 3-17.

The drafting of the Universal Declaration of Human Rights illustrates the extent to which language, religion, and customs complicate international understanding. Concludes with a plea for achieving democracy in every American community. Text of address, 21 Mar.

D205 "Making Human Rights Come Alive." *Phi Delta Kappan* 31 (Sept. 1949): 23-28.
A detailed discussion of the development of the Universal Declaration of Human Rights. Text of address at National Conference on UNESCO, Cleveland, 1 Apr.

D205a "Mrs. Roosevelt Describes Declaration as Forerunner of Bill of Rights." *Second National Conference, United States National Commission for UNESCO Journal* (2 Apr. 1949): 3.
Abridgment of her address.

D205b *Second National Conference, United States National Commission for UNESCO, Cleveland, Ohio, 1949.* Washington: GPO, 1949. 23p.
Text of address. Copy not examined.

D206 "Universal Declaration of Human Rights." *Cultural Groups & Human Relations: Twelve Lectures before the Conference on Educational Problems of Special Cultural Groups, Held at Teachers College, Columbia University, August 18 to September 7, 1949.* New York: Bureau of Publications, Teachers College, Columbia Univ., 1951; Freeport: Books for Libraries, 1970. 191-208.
The American people must accept the responsibility which comes with being a powerful nation and lead the world into democracy. Outlines the work of the Commission on Human Rights and the development of the Universal Declaration of Human Rights and the covenant. Text of address.

D207 "Winnipeg Speech (February 28, 1949)." "A Study of Selected Speeches by Mrs. Franklin D. Roosevelt on Human Rights." By Gloria Virginia Ranck. Thesis (M.A.) Univ. of Wash., 1952. 146.
The UN has had its successes and failures, and it will not be able to live up to the expectation of maintaining the peace unless those of us in democracies believe as strongly in our way of life as the Communists believe in theirs. Outline of address, 28 Feb.

D208 Introduction. *Your Human Rights: The Universal Declaration of Human Rights Proclaimed by the United Nations, December 10, 1948.* New York: Ellner, 1950. [i-ii].
Citizens can promote human rights in their local communities, and with the declaration nations can work together to improve the rights of all. Taken from a speech in commemoration of the first anniversary of the Universal Declaration of Human Rights, 1949.

1950

D209 "Address by Mrs. Eleanor Roosevelt to Americans for Democratic Action." *Congressional Record Appendix* (19 Apr. 1950): A2801-2.
Our record with race relations is watched around the world, but in a democracy we are able to have the courage and freedom to recognize our shortcomings and correct them. Text of address at Americans for Democratic Action convention, Washington, 31 Mar.

D209a "Convention Speeches Urge Democratic Plans." *ADA World* 4 (Apr. 1950): 1, 3.
   Excerpts.

D210   "Human Rights and Individual Responsibility." *Education-Dynamic of Democracy: Official Report, America Association of School Administrators, 76th Annual Convention, Atlantic City, N.J., February 25-March 2, 1950.* Washington: American Assoc. of School Administrators, 1950. 903-6.
   Work of the Commission on Human Rights and development of the Universal Declaration of Human Rights and the covenant. Text of address, 28 Feb.

D211 "Korean Problem Illustrates Great Decisions To Be Made by United Nations." *Department of State Bulletin* 23 (9 Oct. 1950): 582.
   ER asks Secretary of State Dean Acheson questions about UN activities during the Korean conflict. Text of 1 Oct. NBC televison program.

D212 "Mrs. Roosevelt's Centenary Visit." *Centenary Junior College Bulletin* 33 (Mar. 1950): 7.
   The world is watching how we practice democracy in our local communities. Excerpts address, 9 Feb.

D213 "Responsible Citizenship." *A Search for Peace.* N.p.: n.p., 1950. n.pag.
   The rest of the world will embrace a democratic way of life if they are convinced that citizens of the U.S. believe in and practice democracy. Text of brief radio address as part of series *Crusade in Europe.*

D214 "Rochester University Speech (February 11, 1950) 'The Universal Declaration of Human Rights and the United Nations.'" "A Study of Selected Speeches of Mrs. Franklin D. Roosevelt on Human Rights." By Gloria Virginia Ranck. Thesis (M.A.) Univ. of Wash., 1952. 149.
   Everyone should know why and how the declaration was conceived and written. Partial outline of address, Rochester, N.Y., 11 Feb.

D215 "Views on U.N. Affairs...Human Rights and Freedoms." *American Association for the United Nations-United Nations Reporter* 23 (Jan. 1951): 2.
   The observance of Human Rights Day in this country is an occasion to assess our progress in providing basic rights and freedoms to all our citizens. Abbreviated version of address, New York, 10 Dec.

1951

D216   "Messages to the Conference." *American Association for the United Nations-United Nations Reporter* 23 (25 Mar. 1951): 14.
   She regrets that she is unable to attend and help establish ways in which the work of the UN can be supported through activities of the AAUN in local communities. One of several messages sent to the AAUN conference, 25-27 Feb.

D217 "Mrs. Roosevelt Says M'Carthy [sic] Is Menace." *New York Times* 21 Sept. 1951: 12.
   Sen. Joseph McCarthy is a menace to the freedoms which we enjoy, and our democracy is in jeopardy because of him and his followers. Remarks at a question

and answer session after she made address "Our Place in the World Today" to students at the City College of New York, 20 Sept.

D218 "Restlessness of Youth: An Asset of Free Societies." *Department of State Bulletin* 26 (21 Jan. 1952): 94-96.
The restlessness of youth regenerates society. Warns that youth must help preserve freedom and calls for UN control of the uranium needed for peace and war-related activities. Text of address to Les Jeunes Amis de la Liberte, Paris, 18 Dec.

D219 "The United Nations and Youth." *National Association of Secondary-School Principals Bulletin* 35 (Apr. 1951): 265-59.
Young people need to know more about the UN and become aware of the emphasis which communism places on social and economic rights at the expense of civil and political liberties. Text of address at convention of the National Association of Secondary-School Principals, New York, 14 Feb.

D220 "A World for Peace." *International House Quarterly* 15 (Summer 1951): 136-40.
Tensions and misunderstandings in the UN make it difficult to reach agreements. Other countries are distrustful us when they do not see us providing to all of our own citizens the rights which we pursue for others. Text of address at New York International House, 5 Apr.

1952

D221 "ADA New Deal Heir." *ADA World* 7 (Oct. 1952): 1, 3.
The ADA is helping to carry out FDR's ideas, in particular supporting what is good for the country as a whole rather than what will help special groups. In reference to the candidacy of Adlai Stevenson, she states that he keeps to the issues and his work at the UN is good preparation for being a world leader. Excerpts 11 Oct. radio discussion with Jinx Falkenberg McCrary.

D222 "Address of Mrs. Franklin D. Roosevelt, United States Delegate to the United Nations." *Official Report of the Proceedings of the Democratic National Convention, Chicago, Illinois, July 21 to July 26 Inclusive, 1952....* N.p.: Democratic National Committee, n.d. 119-25.
The UN and its related organizations have their shortcomings, but in our changing world they represent the best hope for lasting peace. Text of address, 22 July.

D222a "Text of Convention Address by Mrs. Roosevelt Urging Support of United Nations' Program." *New York Times* 23 July 1952: 14.

D222b "Without the United Nations Our Country Would Walk Alone, Ruled by Fear, Instead of Confidence and Hope." *A Treasury of Great American Speeches: Our Country's Life and History in the Words of Its Great Men.* By Charles Hurd. New York: Hawthorn, 1959. 298-302.
Text of her address at the 1952 Democratic National Convention.

D223 "America Must Convince Nehru or Lose Asia to Communists." *ADA World* 7 (Apr. 1952): 1.
We must work hard to make Asians want our type of government. India, in particular, is watching to see if we really practice democracy in areas such as the

treatment of our minorities.   Excerpts address at Americans for Democratic Action convention.

D224   "First Need: Resettlement." *Nation* 174 (7 June 1952): 556-57.
After the Arabs are resettled the Israelis should help in the development of Arab countries.   Prefaced by a statement reaffirming her belief in America's freedoms and how they must be preserved.   Text of address at conference of the Nation Associates on Freedom's Stake in North Africa and the Middle East, New York, 25 May.

D225   "Messages to the Conference." *American Association for the United Nations-United Nations Reporter* 24 (25 Mar. 1952): 3-4, 14.
We need greater understanding of the potential of the UN to help all nations and in particular smaller ones (p. 4).   One of several messages to the AAUN conference.

D226   *Why the United Nations Is Unpopular and What We Can Do about It.* N.p.: n.p., n.d. 2, 11, 7p. Typescript.
The UN is "machinery" to be used by the member nations, and the people of the U.S. are not giving the UN the proper support.   Text of address at Citizens Conference on International Economic Union, New York, 19 Nov.   Issued with separately paged introduction (2p.) and remarks by H. Kohn (7p.).

1953

D227   "Citizens' Role in Public Opinion." *American Association of the United Nations-United Nations Reporter* 25 (25 Mar. 1953): 12-13.
Since the U.S. is a symbol of democracy, how we as citizens practice democracy is critical.   Text of address at AAUN conference, 2 Mar.

D228   "Judges for Children." *Record of the Association of the Bar of the City of New York* 9 (Jan. 1954): 8-19.
ER, John Warren Hill, Walter Gelhorn, and Alfred J. Kahn were panelists at a symposium sponsored by a City of New York Commission on the Domestic Relations Court.   ER stated her belief that children in trouble are not at fault.   Conditions in our society are to blame, and judges need to realize this.   Text of remarks, 29 Apr. (pp. 13-14).

D229   "Mrs. Roosevelt Elected ADA National Honorary Chairman." *ADA World* 8 (June 1953): 1, 3.
At the sixth annual Americans for Democratic Action convention ER was elected National Honorary Chairman.   She sent a message of acceptance to the convention stating that while she would be an active participant in ADA affairs she would also be relying on younger members to play a leading role.   She also urged the organization to attract a broader range of members who are "willing to fight for the traditional freedom and justice under which we have grown to be a great and powerful nation" (p. 1).

D230   "National Dinner Honors Mrs. Roosevelt; Humphrey Sees Liberal Job in the Suburbs." *ADA World* 8 (Feb. 1953): 1-2.
Our young people need to join political organizations and take chances.   By doing so they will preserve our country's spirit of adventure while also learning how to

recognize communist tactics. Excerpts remarks at Roosevelt Day dinner, New York, 6 Feb.

D231 "Our Responsibility to the United Nations." *Edward R. Embree Memorial Lectures, 1952-1953.* New Orleans: Dillard Univ., n.d.
Copy not examined.

D232 "Report on India and the East." *Town Meeting* 19 (8 Sept. 1953): 1-11.
ER made a brief statement about her trip before responding to questions from Sirdar Singh, James Michener, and members of the audience about current conditions in India and the East and U.S. relations with countries in the area. Transcript of ABC radio broadcast narrated by John MacVane, 8 Sept.

D233 "Teachers and the United Nations." "The Philosophy of Social Reform in the Speeches of Eleanor Roosevelt." By Eleanor Janice Bilsborrow. Diss. Univ. of Denver, 1957. 264-68.
The U.S. is expected to be the leader of the democratic world, and, like the UN, teachers can work to improve our understanding of other countries and customs and prepare our young people to be leaders. Text of address to Illinois Congress of Parents and Teachers, June.

D233a "The U.N. and the Welfare of the World." *National Parent-Teacher* 47 (June 1953): 14-16, 35.
Based on address to Illinois Congress of Parents and Teachers.

1954

D234 "The Fears of Free Americans." *Student Council Bicentennial Conference on the Rights of Free Americans.* Ed. Martin Howard Proyect. New York: Columbia Univ. Student Council, 1955. 3-5.
We cannot be afraid to speak out and rid ourselves of fear of association. Condensation of address, New York, Mar. 1954.

D235 "Mrs. Roosevelt Joins in Tribute to Elmer Davis." *ADA World* 9 (Feb. 1954): 2.
Many of our young people fear that they will be stigmatized if they join some organizations. "When I was young you could join the Socialists" and then change your mind with no fear. Excerpts address at Washington tribute to Elmer Davis, radio commentator and former Head of the Office of War Information.

D236 "Mrs. Roosevelt Praises ADA Stand on McCarthy." *ADA World* 9 (Apr. 1954): 3.
Members of both parties should work together to fight McCarthyism. Excerpts address at Roosevelt Day Dinner, Detroit, Jan.

D237 "UN and Public Opinion." *American Association for the United Nations-United Nations Reporter* 26 (25 Mar. 1954): 6-7, 20.
Our citizens need to develop a better understanding of the value of the UN. Although unlike many other nations our country does not need the direct assistance of UN specialized agencies, in the end our economy and world peace depend upon them. Text of address at AAUN conference on U.S. Responsibility for World

Leadership, Washington, 3 Mar. (pp. 7, 20). Also includes introduction by Gardner Cowles.

D238 "The United Nations as a Bridge." *The World's Greatest Speeches*. Ed. Lewis Copeland. New York: Dover, 1958. 640-41.

The UN was established to help maintain the peace, not to make the peace. But we have yet to enjoy a peaceful world since the UN was established. As the young organization learns from its failures it can continue to build bridges between nations. Abbreviated version of address at Brandeis Univ., 17 Dec.

1955

D239 "In the Service of Truth." *Nation* 181 (9 July 1955): 37.

These are frustrating times because of the fear of nuclear war and the unknowns about peaceful uses of atomic energy. Text of address at forum "Atoms for Peace," New York, 19 June.

D240 "Mrs. Franklin Delano Roosevelt." American Federation of Labor and Congress of Industrial Organizations. *Report of the 1st Constitutional Convention: Proceedings, New York, N.Y., December 5-8, 1955*. N.p., AFL-CIO, n.d. 143-45.

As two great labor organizations come together their members must use this new power to improve conditions for all of our citizens and to help our country lead the rest of the world. Organized labor has improved life for you as union members. Now you must work to improve life for others. Text of address, 8 Dec.

D240a "Mrs. Roosevelt Applauds Labor's Strength and Unity." *Railway Clerk* 55 (1 Jan. 1956): 7.

Excerpts.

D241 "Mrs. Roosevelt Speaks at State Convention." *ADA World* 10 (Nov. 1955): 3.

The current administration's foreign policy is based on the belief that peace will come all by itself. If a Democrat is elected in 1956, we will see some new ideas. In the meantime liberals must stand firm and not worry about attacks from the right. Excerpts address at Massachusetts Americans for Democratic Action convention.

D242 "'Patience, Persistence, Vision' and Work: We Can Create a Better World for All-If Everyone Works Together to Achieve It." *Christian Register* 134 (July 1955): 17-19.

Peace and a better world are possible if we understand and support the work of the UN. Text of address at annual dinner of the Unitarian Service Committee, May 1955.

D243 "Promise Fulfilled." *Hadassah Newsletter* 36 (Nov. 1955): 5.

Youth Aliyah is the hope for Israel's future, but the hopes of Israel and other nations to build a better world will take years to realize. Condensation of address at convention of Women's Zionist Organization, Chicago, 31 Oct.

D244 "Statement of Mrs. Eleanor Roosevelt, Former United States Representative to the Commission on Human Rights, United Nations Economic and Social Council; Former United States Representative to the United Nations General Assembly." *Review of the United Nations Charter: Hearings before a Subcommittee of the*

Committee on Foreign Relations, United States Senate, Eighty-fourth Congress, First Session. Pt. 12. Washington: GPO, 1955. 1799-1821.

A committee should be formed to study the charter, but the charter should not be revised now if it means the exclusion of the Soviet Union from the UN. She was questioned extensively about the organization of the UN and the role of the specialized agencies. Text of testimony and responses to questions from committee members, 22 Apr.

D244a "Charter Review: Some Opinions." *AAUN News* 27 (June 1955): 3-6.

Excerpts from the statements of ER, Herbert Hoover, and HST.

D244b "Is a U.N. Charter Review Conference Advisable Now? Con." *Congressional Digest* 34 (Nov. 1955): 275, 277.

Her testimony. John Bricker presents opposite viewpoint (pp. 274, 276, 278).

1956

D245 "Address of Mrs. Franklin Delano Roosevelt". *Official Report of the Proceedings of the Democratic National Convention, Chicago, Illinois, August 13 through August 17, 1956...* N.p.: Democratic National Committee, n.d. 66-68.

Asks for party unity and the selection of a candidate who can lead the country in overcoming poverty at home and improving the condition of all peoples of the world. Text of address at Democratic National Convention, 13 Aug.

D245a "Before the Democratic National Convention." *Representative American Speeches: 1956-1957.* Reference Shelf, 29:3. Ed. A. Craig Baird. New York: Wilson, 1957. 109-13.

D246 "Arms for Israel." "The Philosophy of Social Reform in the Speeches of Eleanor Roosevelt." By Eleanor Janice Bilsborrow. Diss. Univ. of Denver, 1957. 269-71.

The threat of Soviet intervention in the Middle East risks world peace, because the problems of refugees and borders require careful negotiation, not armed force. The U.S. should provide Israel with the arms needed for defending itself. Text of address, House of Representatives, June.

D246a "Arms for Israel." *Congressional Record Appendix* (19 June 1956): A925.

D247 "'Compromise' Democratic Nominee Would Risk Defeat, Convention Warns." *ADA World* 11 (June 1956): 1, 4.

President Eisenhower is not educating the country about foreign affairs. Excerpts address at Americans for Democratic Action annual convention, Washington, May.

D248 "Statement of Mrs. Franklin D. Roosevelt, Chairman of the Board of Governors of the American Association for the United Nations." *International Organizations and Movements: Hearings before the Subcommittee on International Organizations and Movements of the Committee on Foreign Affairs, House of Representatives, Eighty-fourth Congress, Second Session.* Washington: GPO, 1956. 123-39.

The work of the specialized organizations of the UN is critical to improving conditions for peoples throughout the world and helping to maintain a peaceful world. Text of statement, 24 Feb. Responses to questions from committee members follows testimony.

D249 "What We Can Do." *AAUN News* 28 (Apr. 1956): 8.

As citizens we should take interest in matters which are before the UN and in activities of the AAUN. Excerpts address at Conference of National Organizations, Washington, 28 Dec.

D250 "Winter Meetings." *Off the Agenda* (Women's City Club of New York) 13 (Apr. 1956): 4.

The club teaches the role of education in developing "informed citizens." Excerpts remarks at 40th anniversary meeting of the Women's City Club of New York, Apr.

1958

D251 Phillips, Ethel C. *You in Human Rights: A Community Action Guide for International Human Rights Year.* New York: American Jewish Committee, Publications Service, 1967.

Human rights begin in the home, the neigborhood, the school, and the place of work (p. [2]). Excerpts 27 Mar. remarks at the UN when presenting the pamphlet *In Your Hands: A Guide for Community Action* (New York: Church Peace Union, 1958). Address known as "The Great Question."

D251a "Mrs. Franklin D. Roosevelt." *Human Rights…Unfolding the American Tradition.* Washington: GPO, 1968. 81.

The same excerpt.

D252 "The Universal Declaration of Human Rights…." *United Nations Review* 5 (Jan. 1959): 16-17.

The 10th anniversary of the adoption of the Universal Declaration of Human Rights is an occasion to celebrate what has been accomplished and to dedicate ourselves during the next 10 years to promote improved human rights as the means for the UN to create "an atmosphere in which peace can grow in the world." Excerpts address at the UN, New York, 10 Dec. (p. 16).

D253 "We Can Meet Soviet Challenge by Educating All Those with Ability." *New Lincoln School Conference News* 1 (Spring 1958): 2.

We must teach students to pursue their lives without fear and like the Soviets, we should put more money into education. Excerpts address, New York.

1959

D254 "Is America Facing World Leadership?" *Journal of the American Association of University Women* 53 (Oct. 1959): 7-11.

Discusses economic and political problems here and elsewhere in the world and concludes that America must face its role as world leader or turn that responsibility over to the Communists. Excerpts address to American Assoc. of University Women, Kansas City, Mo., June 1959.

D255 Lovell, P.M. "Our Contribution Toward Peace." *W.V.S. Bulletin* (May 1959): 6-8.

If peace comes to the world, it will come because people want it. Those of us in the West must consider democracy as spiritual and want to share it with others. Excerpts address at Women's Voluntary Service 25th Anniversary meeting, London, 8 Apr. (pp. 6-7).

D256   "Russia-The Country and the People: As I Saw Them." *Journal of Home Economics* 51 (Sept. 1959): 555-60.
Detailed description of her observations of life in Russia. Adapted from address to American Home Economics Assoc., Milwaukee, 24 June.

D257 "Statement by Mrs. Eleanor Roosevelt." *Congressional Record* (26 May 1959): 9082.
The treatment of cancer and efforts to find a cure can be helped by the work of hospitals such as this. Text of remarks at founding dinner of the Eleanor Roosevelt Institute for Cancer Research, New York, 23 May.

D258   "Statement by Mrs. Franklin D. Roosevelt, on Behalf of the National Consumers League." *To Amend the Fair Labor Standards Act: Hearings before the Subcommittee on Labor of the Committee on Labor and Public Welfare, United States Senate, Eighty-sixth Congress, First Session.* Washington: GPO, 1959. 713-19.
The minimum wage should be increased and broadened to include more workers including those who work in agriculture. Text of testimony, 14 May. Responds to questions asked by members of the committee after making statement.

1960

D259 "Mrs. Franklin D. Roosevelt." *Adele Rosenwald Levy, July 19, 1892-March 12, 1960.* San Francisco: Grabhorn, n.d. 39-41.
She was a woman of courage who stood firm for what she believed. We are stronger and wiser because of her. Text of statement at funeral service, 15 Mar.

D260 "Mrs. Roosevelt Addresses Convention." *AAUN News* 32 (Mar. 1960): 1.
In her address entitled "The Role of Governments in the UN" she explains that while UN member nations have sovereign rights they also realize that the UN is the only forum for promoting better world understanding. Excerpts address at annual Conference of National Organizations. Washington, Mar.

D261 "Prospects of Mankind." *Listener* 64 (6 Oct. 1960): 543-48.
ER interviews Bertrand Russell, Hugh Gaitskell, and others about British defense policy, the threat of nuclear war, and the need for disarament agreements. A discussion recorded in London for her television series *Prospects of Mankind*. Text of discussion.

D262 "Remarks of the Honorable Eleanor Roosevelt Endorsing the Nomination of the Honorable Adlai Stevenson." *Official Report of the Proceedings of the Democratic National Convention and Committee.* John F. Kennedy Memorial ed. Washington: National Democratic Publishers, 1964. 146-47.
Stevenson is the best choice for a candidate who will build a better country and lead the world.

D263 "Women Air Views at 1960 Campaign Conference." *Democratic Digest* 7 (June 1960): 23-24.

Our women are doing the best they can to participate in the political process and hold office while also having to bear traditional family responsibilities.   Excerpts address at Campaign Conference for Democratic Women, Washington, 10 May.

1961

D264   "Mrs. Eleanor Roosevelt." *Proceedings of the Fourth Convention of the AFL-CIO, Miami Beach, Florida, December 7-13, 1961.* N.p.: AFL-CIO, n.d. 138-40.

Labor unions need to remember that they were founded to help improve living conditions and that they can play a part in demonstrating to the world that democracy has more to offer than communism.   Text of address, 8 Dec.

D264a Jamison, R.H.   "An Illustrious Woman." *Railway Carmen's Journal* 69 (May 1963): 15.

Excerpts.

D265   "Mrs. Roosevelt Addresses Midwest Group on Farm Surpluses and USSR Education." *AAUN News* 33 (June 1961): 3.

People in other countries ask me why the U.S. pays farmers not to plant crops and how we treat our minorities.   Excerpts address at regional AAUN conference, Racine, Wisc.

D266   "Practice Democracy, Mrs. FDR Urges." *AAUN News* 33 (Apr. 1961): 5.

We must demonstrate to the rest of the world what can be accomplished in a democracy.   Excerpts address at annual Conference of National Organizations, Washington.

D267 Sankey, Alice.   "First Lady of the World." *Elementary English* 38 (May 1961): 346-47.

Children need to learn to enjoy reading and to appreciate fine binding and printing at an early age.   Excerpts remarks upon receiving Constance Lindsay Skinner Award from the Women's National Book Association, New York, 24 Feb. 1961.

D267a "WNBA Skinner Medal Given to Eleanor Roosevelt." *Publishers Weekly* 179 (6 Mar. 1961): 27-28.

Excerpts.

D268   "Secretary of State Rusk Interviewed on Prospects of Mankind." *Department of State Bulletin* 45 (30 Oct. 1961): 708-9.

ER questions Dean Rusk about U.S.-Soviet Relations.   Text of television program of 14 Oct.

1962

D269   "Mrs. Eleanor Roosevelt." *Congressional Record* (12 June 1962): 10295-96.

Text of presentation of World Peace through World Health Award to Lyndon B. Johnson, Washington, 22 May.

D270 "Statement of Mrs. Eleanor Roosevelt, Chairman, President's Commission on the Status of Women, Accompanied by Mrs. Esther Peterson, Assistant Secretary of Labor, U.S. Department of Labor." *Equal Pay for Equal Work: Hearings before the Select Subcommittee on Labor of the Committee on Education and Labor, House of Representatives, Eighty-seventh Congress, Second Session*. Pt. 2. Washington: GPO, 1962. 224-27.

Testimony in support of legislation which would guarantee women the same rate of pay as men when they perform comparable work. Text of statement, 27 Apr.

D271 "Statement of Mrs. Eleanor Roosevelt, New York, N.Y." *Prices of Hearing Aids: Hearings before the Subcommittee on Antitrust and Monopoly of the Committee on the Judiciary, United States Senate, Eight-seventh Congress, Second Session*. Washington: GPO, 1962. 4-10.

Anyone with a hearing problem should seek medical advice before purchasing a hearing aid. Then if a hearing aid is appropriate, get one and wear it. Testimony followed by answers to questions from committee members. Text of testimony, 18 Apr.

D271a "Results of Hearing Aid Investigation Await Careful Study of Findings." *Hearing News* 30 (May 1962): 1, 5-6.

Excerpts from her testimony (pp. 5-6).

D272 "The Teaching Challenge of the Future." *Graduate Comment* 6 (Oct. 1962): 12-15, 23.

Text of ER's address, Detroit, 29 Mar. She received Education Day Award which goes to "an individual who has made noteworthy contributions to the principles, purposes and progress of education" (p.1).

D273 "Transcript of Interview with Mrs. Eleanor Roosevelt Recorded for National Educational Television." *Public Papers of the Presidents of the United States: John F. Kennedy, Containing the Public Messages, Speeches, and Statements of the President, January 1 to December 31, 1962*. Washington: GPO, 1963. 341-43.

ER asks JFK questions about the status of women. Why did you create the Commission on the Status of Women, why are there so few women in high posts in this country, are women making the most of their education, and what do you think about women holding jobs when men are unemployed? Recorded 18 Apr. at the White House for the 22 Apr. broadcast of *Prospects of Mankind*.

D274 "What Can I Do about Peace and People?" *Bookshelf* (YMCA) 45 (Summer 1962): 1, 10.

First, rid oneself of indifference. Then realize that slowly your efforts can help others. Excerpts address at YWCA/National Council of Jewish Women program making 50 years of public affairs programs.

D274a "What Can I Do about Peace and People?" *YMCA Magazine* (1962).
Copy not examined.

E

Reviews of the Writings of Eleanor Roosevelt

HUNTING BIG GAME IN THE EIGHTIES: THE LETTERS OF ELLIOTT ROOSEVELT, SPORTSMAN. Ed. Eleanor Roosevelt. 1932.

E1   *America* 49 (29 Apr. 1933): 89.
A human interest account which demonstrates the Roosevelt family bond. Review signed "J.M.P."

E2   *New York Times Book Review* 12 Nov. 1933: 10.
ER has published her father's letters because she wants him to be remembered.

WHEN YOU GROW UP TO VOTE. 1932.

E3   Eaton, Anne T. *New York Times Book Review* 12 Feb. 1933: 13.
The book is uneven and the style too lively. The author has a tendency to talk down to her potential audience.

E4   McLaughlin, Isabel. *Library Journal* 58 (1 Oct. 1933): 803.
An attractive and informative account of how our government works.

E5   *New York Herald Tribune Books* 26 Feb. 1933: 7.
Children will be left with a lasting impression from a book which is distinguished less by what it says than by how the information is presented.

IT'S UP TO THE WOMEN. 1933.

E6   Beard, Mary R. "Mrs. Roosevelt as Guide and Philosopher." *New York Herald Tribune Books* 5 Nov. 1933: 7.
Already accustomed to having a Great White Father in the White House we now have the Great White Mother, an appellation suitable to ER. Broad social reform is suggested by some of her statements in the book.

E7   *Booklist* 30 (Dec. 1933): 110.
She "sounds a challenge to the acceptance of new obligations to the social order in which women must play a larger part."

E8   Brickell, Herschel. "About President Roosevelt." *North American Review* 237 (Jan. 1934): 89.

Reviews of two books about FDR are concluded with a few statements about *It's Up to the Women* describing it as a common sense approach to the role of women in the recovery effort.

E9   Feld, Rose C. "Mrs. Roosevelt Speaks to Women." *New York Times Book Review* 12 Nov. 1933: 4.

ER urges other women to create the kind of world they want for their children and grandchildren. Feld considers the better chapters to be those on women in industry, women in politics, and women's role in preserving the peace.

E10   *Forum and Century* 91 (Jan. 1934): vii.

Common sense advice to women about how to care for their families.

E11   Jeffreys, Susan Fort. *Junior League Magazine* 20 (Jan. 1934): 64-65.

An "appeal to all women to meet the issues of the day."

E12   La Follette, Suzanne. "To the Ladies." *Saturday Review of Literature* 10 (11 Nov. 1933): 253-54.

Naive treatment, full of platitudes, of today's problems aimed at the middle class while ignoring the needs of working people.

E13   Meredith, Ellis. *Democratic Digest* 8 (Dec. 1933): 13.

Only ER could have written about how women today must go about the tasks of feeding and clothing their families.

THIS IS MY STORY. **1937.**

E14   Alsop, Joseph W., Jr. "Daughter of the Squirearchy." *Saturday Review of Literature* 17 (27 Nov. 1937): 5-6.

In a simple and direct manner she portrays herself and the era in which she grew up. Her concern for the less fortunate was apparent early in her life, and that has helped her to adjust to their present needs with calls for more substantial assistance. As a source of insight into FDR the book is a disappointment.

E15   Amidon, Beulah. "First Lady." *New Republic* 93 (8 Dec. 1937): 139-40.

The story of one American woman, not the wife of the President. She underestimates her own intelligence and sincerity. Written in good taste but not a great literary work.

E16   "Author of 'My Day' Writes 365 Pages and Sticks to the Story." *Newsweek* 10 (22 Nov. 1937): 32-33.

The book reveals little about the famous, but it tells us much about ER's own development from the little girl born into society and wealth to the person of great inner worth.

E17   Blair, Emily Newell. "Two Books of the Year." *Democratic Digest* 15 (Jan. 1938): 12.

It is an honest and objective account of her life which should make all women proud. Its greatest strength is the story of how she rose above class prejudices.

E18   Brogan, D.W.   "Lady into Woman." *Spectator* 160 (11 Feb. 1938): 236, 238.
An honest presentation of her childhood and life as First Lady.   The book is for women, and they should be pleased that she has managed to be herself after being thrust on the public scene.

E19   Converse, Florence.   *Atlantic Monthly* 161 (Jan. 1938): n.pag.
A book written for women who are interested in social, economic, and political issues.   In spite of the undistinguished writing style, the reader should succeed in gaining a true picture of the writer's personality and accomplishments.

E20   Elting, M.L.   *Forum and Century* 99 (Jan. 1938): vii.
The most important aspect of this truthful account of a shy young woman who became a world figure is how she learned to see humor in herself.

E21   *Independent Woman* 17 (Jan. 1938): 14.
It is an honest portrayal which women should read.

E22   Keyes, Frances Parkinson.   *National Historical Magazine* (National Society of the Daughters of the American Revolution) 72 (Jan. 1938): 72-73.
Her kindliness comes through as she "describes" and "interprets" the period covered.

E23   Morris, Lloyd.   "An Education for Life." *North American Review* 245 (Mar. 1938): 202-6.
This account of one woman's education is also a description of the emergence of a sense of social awareness in America during the years since her birth.

E24   "Mrs. Roosevelt's Story." *Christian Science Monitor* 15 Nov. 1937, Atlantic ed.: 18.
An "honest exposition" of her successes, failures, and shortcomings and her attempts to improve herself.   Review signed "M.S."

E25   Ross, Mary.   "The Girl Who Married Franklin Roosevelt." *New York Herald Tribune Books* 21 Nov. 1937: 1.
A personal and objective account of how she developed into a woman and a concerned citizen.

E26   Tarbell, Ida M.   "Eleanor Roosevelt's Story." *Survey Graphic* 27 (Jan. 1938): 48-49.
The story of how she overcame the "regimentation" of her class and realized the freedom to chart her own course.   A sequel describing how she used that freedom is hoped for.

E27   *Time* 30 (13 Dec. 1937): 80.
She reveals how on her own she was able to break away from the society to which she was born.   Better written than her columns.

E28   Woods, Katherine.   "Mrs. Roosevelt's Own Story." *New York Times Book Review* 21 Nov. 1937: 1, 30.
She succeeds in providing a look at the kind of world to which she was born and how it has changed.

E29   Wyatt, Euphemia Van Rensselaer.   "Will Power." *Commonweal* 27 (31 Dec. 1937): 275.
This story of an outstanding woman is about will power and inner strength. Reviewer recalls a childhood luncheon with an equally young ER.

MY DAYS.   1938.

E30   *Booklist* 35 (15 Sept. 1938): 23.
ER reveals how sympathetic a person she is.

E31   Graham, Gladys.   "The First Lady's Book of Days." *Saturday Review of Literature* 18 (27 Aug. 1938): 14.
These selections from "My Day" confirm how democratic ER is.   In her concern for people and their problems she values all opinions.   The book gives the reader a clear picture of the independent thinking First Lady's opinions on major issues.

E32   Hornaday, Mary.   "Mrs. Roosevelt's Days." *Christian Science Monitor* 27 Aug. 1938, Atlantic ed.: 18.
Although excised of the unnecessary what is left from some of her "My Day" columns may still appear trivial.   But her reporting of the daily lives of the Roosevelts appeals to today's reader and will be of historic value.

E33   Woods, Katherine.   "Culled from Mrs. Roosevelt's Column." *New York Times Book Review* 21 Aug. 1938: 5.
The book is a tribute to an amazing woman who shares her philosophy of life and her belief in democracy.

THIS TROUBLED WORLD.   1938.

E34   *Booklist* 34 (15 Jan. 1938): 188-89.
Uses "a simple, conversational style."

E35   *Commonweal* 27 (7 Jan. 1938): 307.
She makes suggestions on how to achieve peace.

E36   Cousins, Norman B.   "Price of Peace." *Current History* 48 (Feb. 1938): 80.
A call for people everywhere to join together and make a peaceful world.   Briefly and without "affectation" she makes her feelings known about some of the problems facing the world today.

E37   Davis, Elmer.   "What to Do?" *Saturday Review of Literature* 17 (1 Jan. 1938): 12.
The surest way to achieve a peaceful world is through a fundamental change in human nature.   Beyond that she proposes an international body to hear disputes among nations, impose economic boycotts, and oversee any military action required to stop the aggressor.

E38   Holmes, John Haynes.   "Planning a Road to Peace." *New York Herald Tribune Books* 9 Jan. 1938: 8.
She addresses war and peace with "modesty, simplicity, and quiet candor."

E39   Schain, Josephine.   "Two Books of the Month."   *Democratic Digest* 15 (Apr. 1938): 17.
American women should be indebted to ER for promoting international under-standing through a book which presents world problems in terms which can be understood by a lay person.

E40   Woods, Katherine.   "Mrs. Roosevelt's Views on Peace."   *New York Times Book Review* 2 Jan. 1938: 3.
Although much of what the author says has already been said by others, the book is useful because it addresses the relationship between peace and the individual's desire for it.

Introduction. *WASHINGTON, NERVE CENTER*. 1939.

E41   Herrick, Genevieve Forbes.   "A Good Guide to Government."   *Democratic Digest* 16 (Oct. 1939): 30.
Praises ER for her wise conclusion that democracy exists only because of the lives of individual democrats.

CHRISTMAS: A STORY. 1940.

E42   Scherman, Katharine.   "Virginibus Puerisque."   *Saturday Review of Literature* 23 (16 Nov. 1940): 22.
A sentimental story suitable for 9-11 year-olds.   One of several children's books reviewed.

THE MORAL BASIS OF DEMOCRACY. 1940.

E43   Barzun, Jacques.   *Saturday Review of Literature* 22 (12 Oct. 1940): 43.
The author is correct in assigning a moral value to democracy and in challenging youth to live up to the demands and obligations of a democratic life.

E44   Benet, Stephen Vincent.   "Reasoned Faith in Democracy."   *New York Herald Tribune Books* 29 Sept. 1940: 3.
To her democracy and the principle of loving "thy neighbor as thyself" are synonymous.   Different types of extremists will find fault with her conclusions, but most Americans will not.

E45   Bloch, Leon Bryce.   "Speaking of Books."   *Living Age* 359 (Nov. 1940): 286-88.
While her style is naive, she is correct in what she says.   It could have been a great book had she developed some of the themes.   Reviewed with Louis M. Hacker's *The Triumph of American Capitalism*.

E46   Broughton, Nick.   "Books in a World at War."   *Peace Action of the National Council for Prevention of War* 7 (Dec. 1940): 7.
She believes that it is not democracy that can fail us, it is our failure to follow democratic principles.   This book is better than the "banalities and trivia" of "My Day."   One of several books reviewed.

E47   *Christian Century* 57 (2 Oct. 1940): 1217.
Democracy will work if we love our neighbors.   A brief review.

E48 *Contemporary Jewish Record* 4 (June 1941): 325-26.

This sermon can be the basis for a broader examination of the citizen's moral obligation to participate in democracy.

E49 *Junior League Magazine* 27 (Dec. 1940): 66-67.

In our struggle against totalitarianism we should accept as a nation the example of Christ's life as a standard of what is possible. ER's philosophy has lasting significance. Review signed "S.F.S."

E50 Marshall, Margaret. "Notes by the Way." *Nation* 151 (12 Oct. 1940): 335-36.

Calls for every citizen to give time and energy to the democratic process. A brief descriptive review included with reviews of other publications.

E51 Tead, Ordway. "The Democratic Offensive." *Survey Graphic* 29 (Dec. 1940): 637.

Reviewed with *Shall Not Perish from this Earth* by Ralph Barton Perry. To both authors democracy is equated to Christianity as a standard to live by. ER's book, aimed at the ordinary citizen, reflects the high standards which she sets for herself.

E52 Young, G. Aubrey. "Democracy's Base." *Current History and Forum* 52 (26 Nov. 1940): 32.

This is intended as a book by a citizen who through her own example challenges other citizens to lead their lives in a democratic manner and be more concerned about the welfare of others.

THIS IS AMERICA. 1942.

E53 Becker, May Lamberton. "Hingham, Mass., U.S.A." *New York Herald Tribune Books* 13 Dec. 1942: 5.

This book succeeds in portraying both the unity and diversity of the country. It deserves the right to bear such a proud title.

E54 Borland, Hal. "The Wide American Scene." *New York Times Book Review* 27 Dec. 1942: 4.

Text and photographs capture many parts of the country and American life, but there are important aspects of our agricultural and industrial society which are lacking.

E55 *New Yorker* 18 (14 Nov. 1942): 71.

"Helpful commentary" by ER for the photographs.

IF YOU ASK ME. 1946.

E56 *Booklist* 42 (15 Apr. 1946): 263-64.

A brief descriptive review which lists some of the questions which she answers.

E57 Greenbaum, Lucy. "The Opinions of Eleanor Roosevelt." *New York Times Book Review* 28 Apr. 1946: 40.

The answers reveal her honesty, courage, and intelligence. She succeeds in making the reader "examine his own philosophy and prejudice."

E58 Hall, Helen. *Survey Graphic* 35 (May 1946): 173-74.
She has a gift for answering questions with "sympathy, common sense, good humor, and understanding."

E59 "They Asked Her." *New York Herald Tribune Weekly Book Review* 28 Apr. 1946: 30.
The questions which she answers do not require a probing mind, but the answers do reveal the author's candor and unaffected manner.

E60 White, W.L. "A Great Lady: Self Portrait." *Saturday Review of Literature* 29 (23 Mar. 1946): 25.
This collection of ER's responses to questions posed to her by *Ladies' Home Journal* readers and others is important for what it reveals about her: ER the politician and the caring person who can dispense wisdom from the heart. Highlights her responses to questions about blacks and Jews.

THIS I REMEMBER. 1949.

E61 Amidon, Beulah. *Survey* 85 (Dec. 1949): 686.
Public events and the private side of the Roosevelts are covered in this account of a life which has been one committed to duty. Offers insight into some of the personalities of the New Deal.

E62 *Booklist* 46 (1 Sept. 1949): 2.
"Simply written" and "candid." A brief review.

E63 *Canadian Forum* 29 (Feb. 1950): 259.
In an account full of anecdotes ER reveals herself as "a true democrat" who decided early in life to serve others. Signed "JLH."

E64 Gosnell, Harold F. *American Political Science Review* 44 (June 1950): 496-97.
Modesty and frankness characterize this account of the public lives of ER and FDR and includes her "shrewd observations" of many public figures.

E65 Hornaday, Mary. "A Wife and Stateswoman Looks Back." *Christian Science Monitor* 7 Nov. 1949, Atlantic ed.: 14.
"Absorbing reading" for what it reveals about life in the White House at the time when U.S. relations with the rest of the world changed forever. But we must wait for someone else to provide an account of ER's transformation to stateswoman.

E66 Janeway, Elizabeth. "Franklin and Eleanor Roosevelt." *New York Times Book Review* 6 Nov. 1949: 1, 30.
Only ER could have provided this look at FDR and the White House years of the Roosevelt family. The book is valuable for its vignettes of public figures and what it reveals about its author. She dedicated "herself to his work" and, thus, was one of FDR's greatest assets.

E67 *New Yorker* 25 (5 Nov. 1949): 133.
Other accounts of the Roosevelts' White House years may be better written, but this one provides more insight.

E68   Nichols, Jeannette P. *Annals of the American Academy of Political and Social Science* 268 (Mar. 1950): 212-13.
A straightforward account for which historians will be indebted.

E69   "One of Those Who Served." *Time* 54 (21 Nov. 1949): 108, 110.
A casual description of the period and of life in the White House.

E70   Read, Mary Dodge. *Library Journal* 75 (15 Feb. 1950): 331.
Everyone should find ER's recollections of interest. Reviewed for the young reader.

E71   Rosenau, James N. "Mrs. Roosevelt Recollects." *Nation* 169 (19 Nov. 1949): 496-97.
The book is exactly what the title suggests: her remembrances of family problems, life in the White House, and FDR as President. It is clear to Rosenau that ER was the greatest influence on FDR's life and activities.

E72   Schlesinger, Arthur M., Jr. "A First Lady's Memories." *Saturday Review of Literature* 32 (5 Nov. 1949): 12-13.
Although it is not very informative about the New Deal, the book fulfills the needs of both historian and general reader. The self-discipline which she has exhibited throughout her life is evident as is her ability to make realistic assessments about others.

E73   Sheean, Vincent. "A Very Human Document by the Wife of a President." *New York Herald Tribune Book Review* 6 Nov. 1949: 1, 29.
A discreet, but highly informative, account. The book's greatness comes not from advanced vocabulary or highly developed style, both of which are lacking, but instead from a sense of the character of the author which is readily apparent to the reader.

E74   Short, Clarice. *Western Humanities Review* 4 (Spring 1950): 175-77.
Because of what is revealed about ER's character and how she viewed her life as First Lady there is benefit for today's reader. The real value of the book will not be realized until many years hence when we can take an objective look at the Roosevelts and their era.

E75   Taylor, Helene Scherff. *Library Journal* 74 (1 Nov. 1949): 1674.
This memoir will find its place as one of the important accounts of our time.

E76   Weeks, Edward. "The Lady Who Traveled Far." *Atlantic Monthly* 185 (Jan. 1950): 82-83.
There are interesting accounts of how little she or anyone else influenced FDR, the difficulties encountered by her children, and her role as White House hostess, but the book's greatest strength is in the portrait which it presents of ER the worrier: worries about her family, the needs of the less fortunate, and disappointments such as Arthurdale and the American Youth Congress.

PARTNERS: THE UNITED NATIONS AND YOUTH. 1950.

E77   Baker, Augusta. *Library Journal* 76 (15 Feb. 1951): 341.
"Superb job" with particular praise for the chapter on human relations.

E78 *Booklist* 47 (1 Jan. 1951): 176.
This "exceptional" description of what the UN is doing for youth and what youth are doing for themselves is of value to readers of all ages.

E79 *Bulletin from Virginia Kirkus' Bookshop Service* 18 (1 Nov. 1950): 669.
ER and Helen Ferris have collaborated well in a book which restores faith in children and youth. It is a Junior Literary Guild selection, but it should also be read by adults.

E80 Davis, Mary Gould. *Saturday Review of Literature* 34 (20 Jan. 1951): 38.
A fine description of the UN and how it can help resolve the problems of the young. It should be made available in other languages for the benefit of all young people.

E81 "Good Reading for the Older Set." *Christian Science Monitor* 13 Nov. 1950, Atlantic ed.: 10.
One of several reviews. "A splendid book" which will increase the awareness of the UN among American youth.

E82 Hamilton, Thomas J. "Help for Youth." *New York Times Book Review* 19 Nov. 1950: 42.
An "admirable" explanation of UN-related organizations and their partnership with youth in solving the problems of the post-war world.

E83 *United Nations Bulletin* 9 (1 Dec. 1950): 651.
A "simply written" account of the mutual relationship between children and the UN.

INDIA AND THE AWAKENING EAST. 1953.

E84 Bogardus, Emory S. *Sociology and Social Research* 38 (1953): 124.
ER's experience at the UN prepared her for visiting India and the East and describing problems faced by the area.

E85 Bokhari, Ahmed S. "The Orbits of Mrs. Universe." *Saturday Review of Literature* 36 (8 Aug. 1953): 13-14.
She was well prepared to undertake the trip reported here in an account which brings perspective to the area. However, there are some aspects of the book which she may be asked to explain.

E86 *Bulletin from Virginia Kirkus' Bookshop Service* 21 (15 June 1953): 373.
The book is intended to inform those readers who have little understanding of the regions which she visited.

E87 Burnham, James. "A Too Sentimental Journey." *Freeman* 3 (24 Aug. 1953): 855-56.
The East provided her with a vast slum in which to practice her form of philanthropy. Like everything else she writes, her approach is simplistic. A "silly book" full of sentimentality. A Dutch translation issued as "Eleanor Roosevelt: Gedachtenloos Sentiment." *Elseviers Weekblad* [Amsterdam] 3 Oct. 1953.

E88 *Current History* 25 (Nov. 1953): 320.
The layman can benefit from this book. A brief review.

E89 Hornaday, Mary. "Good-Will Ambassador to India." *Christian Science Monitor* 24 July 1953, Atlantic ed.: 9.
This book is both a look at the culture of the area and the problems which are being faced and an interesting account for the traveler. She is to be commended for her diplomatic treatment of many sensitive issues.

E90 Kane, Albert E. *Annals of the American Academy of Political and Social Science* 291 (Jan. 1954): 191.
Its strength is the author's account of her exchange with students at Allahabad Univ. She provides no new insights into the countries visited.

E91 Le Maistre. Ian. "Books on the Far East." *Eastern World* 8 (July 1954): 28-29.
The book is simplistic enough to be a "My Day" column and appeal to American clubwomen. Le Maistre criticizes her for tying American generosity in helping Indonesia with the need to combat the potential spread of communism there.

E92 *New Yorker* 29 (29 Aug. 1953): 71.
As pleasant as it is to "travel" with her, her account of the East does not add much to our understanding of the area.

E93 Prescott, Orville. "Books of the Times." *New York Times* 22 July 1953: 25.
A good introduction to the region. The information is "elementary" and the writing is "artless."

E94 Rogers, Joseph W. *Library Journal* 78 (Aug. 1953): 1330.
Since she is not an expert on the history and affairs of India and the East, her book is more suitable for the average reader.

E95 Rolo, Charles J. "From Beirut to Nepal." *Atlantic Monthly* 192 (Sept. 1963): 76-77.
A "Girl Scoutish report" of her 1952 trip. The book's strengths are what she has to say about the efforts of Pakistan and India to solve their problems and why Asian nations do not trust the West.

E96 Roskolenko, Harry. "A Dedicated Lady." *New Republic* 129 (14 Sept. 1953): 18.
She succeeds in identifying the problems which the area faces. The review summarizes her trip.

E97 Steele, A.T. "Through Asia with Eleanor Roosevelt." *New York Herald Tribune Book Review* 26 July 1953: 6.
By taking a fresh look at some of the problems faced by India and the East she makes her account more than a travel book. The profound is not here, however.

E98 Trumbull, Robert. "Aspirations amid Stark Realities." *New York Times Book Review* 26 July 1953: 1, 12.
She captures most of the factors underlying the problems facing the people of the East and their leaders and which also challenge the rest of the world in its attempt

to work with and influence the area. The book "is an artful blend of treatise and travelogue."

UN: TODAY AND TOMORROW. 1953.

E99 *Booklist* 50 (1 Oct. 1953): 45.
A good account of the UN for the layperson.

E100 *Bulletin from Virginia Kirkus' Bookshop Service* 21 (1 Aug. 1953): 525.
An honest and informative account of the UN and its related agencies. Some anecdotes and information about UN leaders would have been appropriate.

E101 *Current History* 26 (Jan. 1954): 64.
This description of the UN is an attempt to improve the layperson's understanding of the organization.

E102 Douglas, William O. "United Nations at Work." *New Republic* 129 (2 Nov. 1953): 26.
An excellent account of the organization and purpose of the UN.

E103 Hamilton, Thomas J. "The Work's World Wide." *New York Times Book Review* 29 Nov. 1953: 16.
An informative account of how the UN and its related agencies work. The political sections of the book and ER's introduction contain many errors.

E104 *Sign* 33 (Dec. 1953): 70.
The book may be considered "inspirational."

IT SEEMS TO ME. 1954.

E105 *Booklist* 51 (1 Nov. 1954): 107.
This book of selections from her column "If You Ask Me" will appeal to women.

E106 *Bulletin from Virginia Kirkus' Bookshop Service* 22 (1 Oct. 1954): 690-91.
Her responses to questions presented in the book are "trite and obvious." The book was published simply because of who she is.

E107 Feld, Rose. "Wise Woman." *New York Herald Tribune Book Review* 5 Dec. 1954: 26.
It provides insight into the types of questions answered in her column "If You Ask Me." It also tells us a great deal about the author. For the most benefit read it over time, not all at once.

E108 Freeman, Lucy. "Personal Questions." *New York Times Book Review* 10 Oct. 1954: 12.
It is difficult to fault her opinions about education, religion, prejudice, and maturity.

LADIES OF COURAGE. 1954.

E109 Engle, Paul. "While the Stew Bubbles." *New Republic* 130 (14 June 1954): 23-24.
The authors ignore the fact that duties as wife and mother make it difficult for women to enter politics and that motherhood will never permit women to be men's political equal. A flawed book hindered by poor writing style.

E110 Hornaday, Mary. "Ladies Who Rule the World and Who Rocked the Cradle." *Christian Science Monitor* 27 May 1954, Atlantic ed.: 13.
Lorena Hickok's political profile of ER is the best part. The book should inspire other women to enlist for political duty. Reviewed with *Mothers of America* by Elizabeth Logan Davis.

E111 MacDonald, Bernice. *Library Journal* 79 (15 May 1954): 980.
The authors succeed in describing American women who have had successful political experience and in providing inspiration for others to participate in politics.

ON MY OWN. **1958.**

E112 *Booklist and Subscription Books Bulletin* 55 (1 Sept. 1958): 8.
The book is distinguished not for its style but for the portrait it provides of an active and committed woman.

E113 *Bulletin from Virginia Kirkus' Bookshop Service* 26 (1 Aug. 1958): 583.
In her "random, always personal, and usually buoyant manner" she tells the story of her life since 1945.

E114 Byrne, Thomas R. *America* 100 (15 Nov. 1958): 219-20.
We can better understand our times through this account of her activities. The book provides insight into the UN and about world leaders while making no claim as a work of scholarship.

E115 Coit, Margaret L. "Keeping Up with Mrs. Roosevelt." *New York Times Book Review* 14 Sept. 1958: 1, 22.
ER's latest autobiographical work is a sincere and genuine account of her activities after FDR's death. Reading the book is like visiting with this remarkable woman.

E116 "First Lady." *Times Literary Supplement* 2977 (20 Mar. 1959): 155.
"She has written a book just like herself--simple, straightforward, helpful, encouraging."

E117 Furman, Bess. "Thirteen Years by Herself." *Saturday Review* 41 (8 Nov. 1958): 18-19, 36.
For now ER does a better job than others in describing her own life and activities. She will continue to be the subject of historical study both as FDR's wife and an independent figure. Reviewed with Alfred Steinberg's *Mrs. R.* and *Eleanor Roosevelt: Her Life in Pictures* by Richard Harrity and Ralph G. Martin.

E118 *Horn Book Magazine* 35 (Feb. 1959): 72-73.
"A compound of humanity, shrewd perception, and salty wisdom."

E119 Howard, Jean. "Words to the Heathen." *Spectator* 202 (10 Apr. 1959): 517.
In her later years ER has traveled the world with two messages: the value of democracy and that not all Americans are militaristic.

E120 Marshall, John David. *Library Journal* 83 (1 Sept. 1958): 2312.
Her account of life after FDR helps explain why she is so admired.

E121 Meyer, Donald. "Eleanor Roosevelt's Life." *New Republic* 139 (6 Oct. 1958): 17-18.
In praise of her mind and how it is the result of a search for her own identity. Reissued as "Eleanor Roosevelt" in *Five Decades: Selections from Fifty Years of the New Republic, 1914-1965*, pp. 391-93 (New York: Simon & Schuster, 1964). Excerpts issued as "Eleanor Roosevelt--1884-1962." *New Republic* 147 (17 Nov. 1962): 8.

E122 Osborn, George C. *Annals of the American Academy of Political and Social Science* 322 (Mar. 1959): 183-84.
She is her best biographer, and the present effort together with her earlier autobiographical works make a "notable contribution" to the genre.

E123 Peterson, Virgilia. "A Remarkable Lady Who Never Thought of Resting on Her Laurels." *New York Herald Tribune Book Review* 14 Sept. 1958: 3.
Of all her autobiographical writings this one is the "freest" and "pithiest." By presenting the best view of her genuine concern for the well being of all human beings it allows the reader to enter her mind and heart.

E124 Powell, V. *Punch* 236 (1 Apr. 1959): 464.
She is candid about American politics but less so about the Roosevelt family.

E125 Ripley, Josephine, "Mrs. Roosevelt's Story since the White House." *Christian Science Monitor* 18 Sept. 1958, Atlantic ed.: 7.
Her account is that of a great reporter, not a literary figure. Like the author, the book deals with numerous issues and, except for the coverage of the UN, may leave many readers unsatisfied.

GROWING TOWARD PEACE. **1960.**

E126 Buell, Ellen Lewis. "Founded in Hope." *New York Times Book Review* 26 Feb. 1961: 44.
A "moving" account of the UN, a place for negotiation and a source of hope for the future. Reviewed with Jim Breetveld's *Getting to Know United Nations Crusaders*.

E127 Mathes, Miriam S. *Library Journal* 85 (15 Dec. 1960): 4571.
The same information is available in encyclopedias. Also paged as 67 of "Junior Libraries" section.

E128 Murphy, Aileen O' B., and Ann Beebe. *Library Journal* 85 (15 Dec. 1960): 4571.
"Interesting" and "attractive" with "expressive photographs." Also paged as 67 of "Junior Libraries" section.

E129 "Words and Deeds." *Christian Science Monitor* 3 Nov. 1960, Eastern ed.: 40.
The work of the UN is presented "thoroughly, simply, and inspiringly." One of two brief reviews.

YOU LEARN BY LIVING. 1960.

E130 Barrett, Mary L. *Library Journal* 85 (Aug. 1960): 2777.
ER's character is evident in this helpful guide to living a more rewarding life.

E131 *Booklist and Subscription Books Bulletin* 57 (15 Sept. 1960): 42.
"Seasoned counsel" on dealing with the challenges of living.

E132 Janeway, Elizabeth. "America's First Modern Woman." *New York Times Book Review* 21 Aug. 1960: 3
"What she has learned from living" including many platitudes is presented as advice to others by one who realizes that a successful life for her cannot be one in which "tragedy and exaltation" are commonplace. What has worked for her--"a child of her time, the first modern American woman"--has also worked for other women of her generation.

E133 Peterson, Virgilia. "The Day-to-Day Credo of a Former First Lady." *New York Herald Tribune Book Review* 21 Aug. 1960: 1.
She blends "humility and assurance" as she shares what she has learned during the various stages of her life. Gently, but convincingly, she informs us of our need to continue learning.

E134 Taylor, Millicent. "Mrs. Roosevelt Replies." *Christian Science Monitor* 25 Aug. 1960, Atlantic ed.: 11.
Advice from a loving "Big Sister." Girls will benefit from the advice of one who had to overcome shyness, and all readers will profit from still another look at her life.

THE AUTOBIOGRAPHY OF ELEANOR ROOSEVELT. 1961.

E135 Brogan, D.W. "First Lady." *Spectator* 209 (5 Oct. 1962): 524, 526.
She became a great figure after FDR's death. Her emergence in the world of "serious politics" preceded FDR's, and she has been criticized for her actions and for "My Day." Unfortunately, she does not write as well as she talks.

E136 Crossman, R.H.S. "Mrs. President." *New Statesman* 64 (3 Aug. 1962): 149.
The humane individual, the true ER, is not revealed in the condensed versions of her autobiographical writings. Crossman concludes that FDR would have been a greater President if he had been influenced more by ER's "liberal integrity."

E137 Deuss, Jean. *Library Journal* 86 (15 Sept. 1961): 2932-33.
Those parts which have been condensed are not as satisfying as the original publications.

E138 Knox, E.V. "Founding Aunt." *Punch* 243 (29 Aug. 1962): 320-21.
ER is America's respected "aunt" who describes her accomplishments with modesty.

E139 "Lady of the White House." *Times Literary Supplement* 3154 (10 Aug. 1962): 576.

The four parts of the book are "frank, direct, human, urbane, modest and imbued with common sense."

E140 Rusher, William A. "We Surrender, Dear." *National Review* 11 (4 Nov. 1961): 308-9.

It will take the historians to provide the balanced account of ER. The present work provides a new opportunity to read about her childhood and the New Deal and UN years plus a chance to learn of her recent activities. Her influence and popularity result from her long life, not from the correctness of her actions nor the soundness of her thinking.

E141 Ward, Barbara. "First Lady, First Person." *Saturday Review* 44 (30 Sept. 1961): 23.

ER's life has been one of duty, commitment, and a zeal for living. She is respected throughout the world and continues to work at extending the social gains of the New Deal to people everywhere.

YOUR TEENS AND MINE. **1961.**

E142 *Booklist and Subscription Books Bulletin* 58 (1 Jan. 1962): 284.
"Sincere, kindly, and helpful counsel."

E143 Brown, Margaret Warren. *Horn Book Magazine* 37 (Dec. 1961): 563.

Reading the book is like talking to one who has experienced the same problems which face girls today. A dose of wisdom, not preaching.

E144 Buell, Ellen Lewis. "Learning to Live." *New York Times Book Review* 24 Sept. 1961: 40.

A helpful guide for young girls by a modest woman who shares her own experiences as a young woman.

E145 Dalgliesh, Alice. "Gifts to Have and to Hold." *Saturday Review* 44 (16 Dec. 1961): 22-23.

She addresses the younger teen who needs help in gaining self-confidence.

E146 Jackson, Charlotte. "For Teen-Agers." *Atlantic Monthly* 208 (Dec. 1961): 121-22.

Young girls of today will profit from learning that this great woman overcame the shyness and fears of her youth.

E147 Sister Mary Hugh, S.M. *Library Journal* 86 (15 Oct. 1961): 3682.

"Interesting reading without being preachy." Also paged as 174 of "School Library Journal" section.

E148 "Widening Horizons." *Christian Science Monitor* 16 Nov. 1961, Atlantic ed.: 12b.

Since young people have confidence in ER and co-author Helen Ferris, this book of advice on how to deal with the problems which our youth face should be well received. Signed "W.J.T."

ELEANOR ROOSEVELT'S BOOK OF COMMON SENSE ETIQUETTE. 1962.

E149 Carson, Gerald. "Manners for Moderns." *New York Times Book Review* 4 Nov. 1962: 44.

Mrs. Roosevelt says that kindness is the basis of good manners. It is because she is responsible for the book that it is a valuable guide for modern etiquette.

E150 Trent, Nan. "Kindness, Key." *Christian Science Monitor* 12 Dec. 1962, Eastern ed.: 14.

She writes from the heart about making others feel at ease.

TOMORROW IS NOW. 1963.

E151 Barrett, Patricia. *America* 109 (9 Nov. 1963): 587-88.

A "superficial" consideration of what needs to be done to provide basic rights to all and create world order. She is too optimistic about the role of the UN.

E152 Burns, Helen. *Library Journal* 88 (15 Oct. 1963): 3839.

Like ER's life, this is a book of hope.

E153 Greene, Thomas F. *Sign* 43 (Nov. 1963): 71-72.

She urges her fellow citizens to live up to the demands of the complex world in which they are living. Her unselfish example will inspire us in the difficult years ahead.

E154 Hornaday, Mary. "Mrs. Roosevelt's Testament." *Christian Science Monitor* 19 Sept. 1963, Atlantic ed.: 13.

She has left us the worthy message that at both the domestic and international levels our ability to succeed and prosper as a nation rests with the courage and actions of the individual citizen.

E155 Johnson, Gerald W. "A Summing Up by Mrs. FDR." *New York Herald Tribune Books* 8 Sept. 1963: 6.

While not literary, intellectual, nor original this book is powerful. Her philosophy is presented more clearly here that in any of her other books.

E156 *Library Journal Children's Section* 88 (15 Nov. 1963): 4494.

Important suggestions for meeting the problems of today's world.

E157 Parton, Margaret. "Why Fear the Future?" *New York Times Book Review* 8 Sept. 1963: 12, 14.

She makes the difficult problems of the modern world appear simple to resolve and challenges the young to do so. A rich legacy for the future.

E158 Smith, Lillian. "Thoughts on Her Travels Ended." *Saturday Review* 46 (7 Sept. 1963):19-20.

Praise for the view which she has provided of the future and the problems which the country must face. The book is of particular value for young Americans. In part the review may be Smith's attempt to rebut some of the comments made by William F. Buckley, Jr. in "Mrs. Roosevelt, R.I.P." *National Review* 14 (29 Jan. 1963): 58.

F

Writings about
Eleanor Roosevelt

MAJOR BIOGRAPHICAL WORKS

F1   Berger, Jason. *A New Deal for the World: Eleanor Roosevelt and American Foreign Policy*. Atlantic Studies. New York: Social Science Monographs, 1981. xii + 177p. Index. Bibliography. Notes.
ER's role in foreign policy from 1920 until her death. Relies on the papers of ER and FDR. Based on his dissertation "A New Deal for the World: Eleanor Roosevelt and American Foreign Policy, 1920-1962" (City Univ. of N.Y., 1979).

F2   Black, Ruby. *Eleanor Roosevelt: A Biography*. New York: Duell, Sloan and Pearce, 1940. x + 331p. Index.
The first biography of ER. She concludes with the prediction that ER will be a significant figure for many years.

F3   Cook, Blanche Wiesen. *Eleanor Roosevelt, 1884-1933*. Vol.1. of *Eleanor Roosevelt*. New York: Viking, 1992. xviii + 587p. Index. Bibliography. Notes.
A comprehensive work up to the first inauguration of FDR. A second volume is planned. Prior to publication title announced as *Eleanor Roosevelt, 1884-1933, A Life: Mysteries of the Heart*. Excerpted in *Mirabella* 3 (Mar. 1992).

F4   Cooke, Robert John. "The Political Career of Anna Eleanor Roosevelt: A Study in the Public Conscience." Diss. Syracuse Univ., 1965. v + 305p. Bibliography. Notes.
The development of her political life and the role which she played for four decades.

F5   Davis, Kenneth S. *Invincible Summer: An Intimate Portrait of the Roosevelts, Based on the Recollections of Marion Dickerman*. New York: Atheneum, 1974. ix + 176p. Index.
Davis utilizes recorded interviews with Dickerman to tell the story of ER's relationship with Nancy Cook and Dickerman. Covers the development and decline of their friendship and business relationships with the Todhunter School and Val-Kill industries. Addresses the emergence of ER, FDR's rise to prominence, the role of Louis Howe, and the immediate Roosevelt family.

F6   Douglas, Helen Gahagan. *The Eleanor Roosevelt We Remember*. New York: Hill and Wang, 1963. 173p.
A tribute in words and photographs including Douglas' personal recollections. Some of her recollections of ER can also be found in her *A Full Life*, pp. 148-56 (Garden City: Doubleday, 1982).

F7   *Eleanor Roosevelt: An American Journey*. Ed. Jess Flemion and Colleen M. O'Connor. San Diego: San Diego State Univ. Pr., 1987. xix + 392p. Index. Further Readings.
Contributions to the Eleanor Roosevelt centennial observance held at San Diego State Univ., 26-27 Oct. 1984 and photographic essays on her life and career. Each part of the book is listed separately in this bibliography.
An extensive bibliography of works by and about ER was prepared, but it is not included in the publication.

F8   Gibber, Frances. "Eleanor Roosevelt, A Public Figure." Diss., i.e., Thesis (M.A.) St. John's Univ., 1959. vi + 125p. Bibliography. Notes.
A thorough examination of her public life derived from works by and about her. Includes texts of letters which FDR received in praise and criticism of her.

F9   Gurewitsch, A. David. *Eleanor Roosevelt: Her Day, A Personal Album*. New York: Interchange Foundation, 1973; New York: Quadrangle, 1974. 160p.
ER in her later years through words and photographs by her friend and physician.

F10   Hareven, Tamara K. *Eleanor Roosevelt: An American Conscience*. Chicago: Quadrangle, 1968. xx + 326p. Index. Notes.
The public life of ER with emphasis on her social thought. Based on her dissertation "The Social Thought of Eleanor Roosevelt" (Ohio State Univ., 1965). The dissertation contains an appendix based on the author's interview with psychologist Abraham Maslow about his perception of ER as a self-actualizing person (pp. 371-77).
Reissued in 1975 with a new introduction (New York: Da Capo) in which Hareven states that ER has become only an historical figure and along with the New Deal was criticized in the late 1960s for having brought about inadequate change. Hareven sees the need for studies of the political partnership between the Roosevelts and for a psychological biography of ER (pp. vii-xi).

F11   Harrity, Richard, and Ralph G. Martin. *Eleanor Roosevelt: Her Life in Pictures*. New York: Duell, Sloan and Pearce, 1958. 255p.
Her life through 1958. Divided into six parts each with text and many illustrations. Based on the film of the same title. Condensations issued in *McCall's* 86 (Oct. 1958): 51-56, 58, 60, 62-63 and *American Weekly* (16 Dec. 1962): 2, 14-15.

F12   Hershan, Stella K. *The Candles She Lit: The Legacy of Eleanor Roosevelt*. Westport: Praeger, 1993. xii + 160p. Index. Bibliography. Notes.
A tribute consisting of a biography (pp. 3-61), the perceptions of some who knew her well or only casually, a chronology, quotations from ER's writings, and brief tributes.
An expanded version of the account of ER's role in orchestrating the escape of German writer Lion Feuchtwanger from a French concentration camp and the escape from France of Feuchtwanger and his wife Marta (pp. 94-97) appeared as "Eleanor

Roosevelt and Emigre Writers." *Confrontation: A Literary Journal of Long Island University* 27-28 (1984): 127-30.

F13 ---. *A Woman of Quality*. New York: Crown, 1970. 256p. Index.
  Recollections by persons from all walks of life tell the story of ER's life and career.

F14 Hickok, Lorena A. *Reluctant First Lady*. New York: Dodd, Mead, 1962. ix + 176p.
  ER as governor's wife, First Lady, Hickok's traveling companion, and topic of her newspaper writing. Reissued in 1980 as *Eleanor Roosevelt: Reluctant First Lady* with an introduction by Allen Klots describing the writing of the book and Hickok's final years (New York: Dodd, Mead).

F15 Johnson, George. *Eleanor Roosevelt: The Compelling Life Story of One of the Most Famous Women of Our Time*. A Monarch Books Original Biography. Derby: Monarch, 1962. 142p.
  A laudatory biography published not long before her death.

F16 Kearney, James R. *Anna Eleanor Roosevelt: The Evolution of a Reformer*. Boston: Houghton Mifflin, 1968. xvi + 322p. Index. Bibliography. Notes.
  Intended to be the first comprehensive and documented account of ER's public life prior to 1941. Arranged around broad aspects of her career with little general biographical data included.   The chapter "Friend to a Neglected Promise" incorporates many of the findings of his master's thesis "Mrs. Eleanor Roosevelt and the American Negro" (Washington Univ., 1962). The introduction includes a critique of selected works about ER. Based on his dissertation "Anna Eleanor Roosevelt: Years of Experiment, 1884-1940" (Univ. of Wisc., 1967).

F17 Lash, Joseph P. *Eleanor and Franklin: The Story of Their Relationship, Based on Eleanor Roosevelt's Private Papers*. New York: Norton, 1971. xviii + 765p. Index. Notes.
  The detailed biography which ends with the death of FDR. Lash states that his work is the first to be based on ER's private papers at FDRL.   Continued by *Eleanor: The Years Alone*.
  Excerpts issued as "Eleanor: How Our Most Admired and Reviled First Lady Dealt with the Other Women in Her Husband's Life." *McCall's* 99 (Oct. 1971): 92-93, 124, 126, 128, 132, 134, 136, 138, 140, 142. An introduction to, and the text of, her childhood composition "The Flowers Discussion" from pp. 62-66 issued in Tuli Kupferberg and Sylvia Topp, *First Glance: Childhood Creations of the Famous*, pp. 134-35 (Maplewood: Hammond, 1978). An adaptation of pp. 393-417 issued as "The Roosevelts and Arthurdale." *Washington Monthly* 3 (Nov. 1971): 22-37. "Eleanor Roosevelt in Action" in *Women Leaders in American Politics*, pp. 292-305 (Englewood Cliffs: Prentice Hall, 1986) reprints pp. 452-69, 472.
  For background on the writing of the book and for the initial reaction to its publication, see Eileen Lottman, "Eleanor and Franklin." *Publishers Weekly* 201 (17 Apr. 1972): 48-49.
  At the time of the adapation for television there was "Eleanor and Franklin: The White House Years." *Media & Methods* 13 (Feb. 1977): 1-11 a separately paged insert consisting of "The White House Years: An Insider's Perspective" by Lash which provides an overview of the public and private lives of the Roosevelts during the White House years (pp. 1-4) and "The White House Years: A Teacher and Student

Guide." (pp. 1, 5-11). Excerpts from the adaptation issued as James Costigan, "Eleanor and Franklin: The White House Years." *Senior Scholastic* (Teachers' ed.) 109 (10 Mar. 1977): 14-17.

In addition to reviews listed separately in this bibliography there is Frank Freidel's in the *New York Times Book Review* 17 Oct. 1971: 1, 26, 28 which emphasizes the Roosevelts' political partnership.

F18 ---. *Eleanor Roosevelt: A Friend's Memoir.* Garden City: Doubleday, 1964. ix + 374p. Index.

His first work on ER. Provides insight into ER's involvement in the student movement during 1939-42.

F19 ---. *Eleanor: The Years Alone.* New York: Norton, 1972. 368p. Index. Notes.

Comprehensive biographical study beginning after FDR's death. Continues his *Eleanor and Franklin.* Excerpts issued as "Eleanor Roosevelt's Final Triumph." *McCall's* 99 (July 1972): 76-77, 113-15.

F20 ---. *"Life Was Meant to Be Lived": A Centenary Portrait of Eleanor Roosevelt.* New York: Norton, 1984. 197p.

Profusely illustrated remembrance of ER.

F21 MacLeish, Archibald. *The Eleanor Roosevelt Story.* Boston: Houghton Mifflin, 1965. 101p.

Text and selected illustrations from the motion picture of the same title. In an introductory letter MacLeish discusses ER's awakening to the needs of human suffering after 30 years of provincialism. Excerpts from the motion picture in script form issued as "Eleanor Roosevelt." *McCall's* 92 (May 1965): 98-101, 172. Condensations in *Reader's Digest Family Treasury of Great Biographies*, Vol. IV, pp. 7-56 (Pleasantville: Reader's Digest Assoc., 1970) and *Reader's Digest Great Biographies,* Vol. 8, pp. 411-60 (Pleasantville: Reader's Digest Assoc., 1989).

F22 Race, Edward Nathan. "Marie Antoinette and Eleanor Roosevelt: A Study of Countries, Periods, Personalities." Thesis (M.A.) Univ. of Colo., 1942. 91p + viii. Bibliography. Notes.

Compares their private and public lives and their attitudes toward social reform and their respective public roles. Relies on Black's *Eleanor Roosevelt*, ER's *This Is My Story*, and major articles by and about ER.

F23 Roosevelt, Elliott, and James Brough. *Mother R: Eleanor Roosevelt's Untold Story.* New York: Putnam's, 1977. 288p. Index.

The account of her activities from 1945 until her death. Excerpts issued as "How Eleanor Roosevelt Forgave the 'Other Woman.'" *Ladies' Home Journal* 94 (Apr. 1977): 84, 86, 88, 90, 92, 212, 214 and "The Last Days of Eleanor Roosevelt." *Ladies' Home Journal* 94 (Oct. 1977): 113, 221-22, 224-26.

F24 ---. *A Rendezvous with Destiny: The Roosevelts of the White House.* New York: Putnam's, 1975. 446p. Index.

His parents during the presidential years. Condensation issued in *Book Digest* 2 (Nov. 1975): 34-53.

F25   ---. *An Untold Story: The Roosevelts of Hyde Park*. New York: Putnam's, 1973. 318p. Index.

A son's attempt to present candid portraits of his parents during the period 1916-32. Excerpts issued as "Franklin and Eleanor: The Untold Story of My Mother and Father." *Ladies' Home Journal* 90 (Apr. 1973): 91-93, 137-44, 146-50, 156 and "Franklin and Missy: The Untold Story." *Ladies' Home Journal* 90 (May 1973): 90-91, 133-38, 140, 142-46, 150. "Missy and Franklin" in *Newsweek* 81 (26 Mar. 1973): 20-21 is about the latter excerpt and includes the reactions of the other Roosevelt children to Elliott's revelation about FDR and Missy LeHand.

For an account of his defense of the book and excerpts from the statement by the other children challenging the veracity of some of the book's claims, see "A Roosevelt Son Defends His Book." *New York Times* 19 Mar. 1973: 40.

F26   Roosevelt, James. *My Parents: A Differing View*. By James Roosevelt with Bill Libby. Chicago: Playboy, 1976. xi + 369p. Index.

The story of growing up a Roosevelt and being the child of famous parents. Written to correct perceived errors and misconceptions in recent books about FDR and ER. Excerpts issued as "My Parents: Franklin and Eleanor." *Good Housekeeping* 183 (Nov. 1976): 288, 290, 299, 306, 308, 312, 314. Condensation issued in *Book Digest* 4 (Jan. 1977): 66-94. Review by Stephen Birmingham in *New York Times* 2 Jan. 1977: 4.

F27   Sakanishi, Shio. *Amerika no Ryoshin*. Tokyo: Nihon Hyoron Sha, 1950. 215p.

A biography of ER with emphasis on her public life. In Japanese.

F28   Sandifer, Irene Reiterman. *Mrs. Roosevelt as We Knew Her*. Silver Spring: Sandifer, 1975. 134p.

The wife of Durward V. Sandifer, State Dept. official assigned to the U.S. delegation to the UN, provides an account of the relationship which the Sandifers had with ER from 1946 until 1962.

F29   Scharf, Lois. *Eleanor Roosevelt: First Lady of American Liberalism*. Twayne's Twentieth-Century American Biography Series. Boston: Twayne, 1987. x + 202p. Index. Bibliographical Essay. Notes.

Her life and career. Scharf considers ER's philosophy to be based on liberalism as it developed in the 1930s with a concern for what government can do.

An attempt to put ER's life and career in perspective is Sharon Hartman Strom's review of Scharf's work and Susan Ware's *Partner and I: Molly Dewson, Feminism, and the New Deal*, "'Practical Idealists': Women's Politics and Culture in the New Deal Years," *Reviews in American History* 16 (Dec. 1988): 604-11.

F30   Snowman, Daniel. *Eleanor Roosevelt*. Women Who Made History. Geneva: Elito Service, 1970. xi + 337p. Index.

He pursues several themes: many of ER's actions contributed to her search for self-esteem, her greatest contribution was to make many believe that the world was a better place because she had lived, and that overcoming the effects of a painful childhood was more remarkable than her accomplishments as an adult.

F31   Steinberg, Alfred. *Eleanor Roosevelt*. Lives to Remember. New York: Putnam's, 1959. 127p.

A thorough biographical study. The text is reproduced in Alan Shapiro, *American Literature: Four Representative Types*, pp. 381-488 (New York: Globe, 1964) and is accompanied by sections "About the Author" (p. 378), "About the Biography" which is really a biographical sketch of ER (pp. 378-80), "Editor's Epilogue to Eleanor Roosevelt" which carries Steinberg's biography through ER's death (pp. 489-91), and a series of student activities (pp. 492-500).

F32   ---. *Mrs. R.: The Life of Eleanor Roosevelt*. New York: Putnam's, 1958. 384p. Index. Bibliography.
Her life and work. Steinberg claims that this is the first biography written with access to ER's private papers.

F33   Ward, Geoffrey C. *Before the Trumpet: Young Franklin Roosevelt, 1882-1905*. New York: Harper & Row, 1985. viii + 390p. Index. Bibliography. Notes.
It is equally a study of the young ER with extensive attention to her parents and early life leading up to her marriage. The first of a two-part study based on manuscript sources. Continued by *A First Class Temperament*.

F34   ---. *A First-Class Temperament: The Emergence of Franklin Roosevelt*. New York: Harper & Row, 1989. xvii + 889p. Index. Bibliography. Notes.
Continues the account of FDR and ER up to his election as Gov. of N.Y. An excerpt issued as "The Wonderful Husband." *American Heritage* 40 (Sept./Oct. 1989): 57-58, 60, 62, 64, 66, 68, 70, 72, 74.

F35   *Without Precedent: The Life and Career of Eleanor Roosevelt*. Everywoman: Studies in History, Literature, and Culture. Ed. Joan Hoff-Wilson and Marjorie Lightman. Bloomington: Indiana Univ. Pr., 1984. xix + 266p. Index.
A collection of scholarly essays about her life and work published in recognition of her centenary. Individual contributions are listed separately in this bibliography.

F36   Youngs, J. William T. *Eleanor Roosevelt: A Personal and Public Life*. Library of American Biography. Boston: Little, Brown, 1985. xi + 246p. Index. Note on Sources.
An account of her public and private life.

BIOGRAPHICAL SKETCHES

Major Biographical Sketches

F37   Anderson, Alice E., and Hadley V. Baxendale. "Anna Eleanor Roosevelt Roosevelt." *Behind Every Successful President: The Hidden Power and Influence of America's First Ladies*. By Alice E. Anderson and Hadley V. Baxendale. New York: Shapolsky, 1992. 258-84.
Her life through 1945.

F38   Arocena, Berta. "Eleanor Roosevelt." *Bohemia* (Dec. 1940): 38-41, 52-53.
Her childhhood, early married life, emergence, and activities as First Lady. In Spanish.

F39   Atwell, Mary Welek. "Roosevelt, Anna Eleanor." *Biographical Dictionary of Internationalists*. Westport: Greenwood, 1983. 626-28. Bibliography.

A synopsis of her activities after the death of FDR. Her work with the U.N., opinions on foreign policy, and belief in the role which human rights can play in maintaining peace.

F40   Baker, Harry J. "Eleanor Roosevelt." *Biographical Sagas of Will Power*. By Harry J. Baker. New York: Vantage, 1970. 296-300.

F41   Barzman, Sol. "Eleanor Roosevelt." *The First Lady*. By Sol Barzman. New York: Cowles, 1970. 295-305. Bibliography.
An account of her life with emphasis on her relationship with FDR. Derived from numerous sources.

F42   Berger, Jason. "Roosevelt, (Anna) Eleanor." *Political Profiles: The Eisenhower Years*. New York: Facts on File, 1977. 523-24.
Activities with the American Association for the United Nations, her criticism of the foreign policy of the Eisenhower administration, her support for Adlai Stevenson in the 1952, 1956, and 1960 presidential campaigns, and her world travels. Also includes brief descriptions of her activities before and after the Eisenhower years.

F43   ---. "Roosevelt, (Anna) Eleanor." *Political Profiles: The Truman Years*. New York: Facts on File, 1978. 472-74.
Her activities at the UN, dissatisfaction with HST's foreign policy, break with Henry Wallace, the founding of the Americans for Democratic Action, and her support of Adlai Stevenson for the presidency in 1952. Also provides brief coverage of her activities before and after the Truman administration.

F44   Boller, Paul F., Jr. "Eleanor Roosevelt." *Presidential Wives*. By Paul F. Boller, Jr. New York: Oxford Univ. Pr., 1988. 284-311. Notes.
Derivative account of her life and activities with only brief coverage of the period after FDR's death.

F45   Bowie, Walter Russell. "Eleanor Roosevelt." *Women of Light*. By Walter Russell Bowie. New York: Harper & Row, 1963. 176-98. Notes.
ER's life derived from her autobiographical writings.

F46   Bugbee, Emma. "A Lady Who Never Stopped." *Reader's Digest Great Lives, Great Deeds*. Pleasantville: Reader's Digest, 1964. 187-93.

F47   Bussey, Charles J. "Eleanor Roosevelt." *Great Lives from History, American Series*. Vol. 4. Pasadena: Salem, 1987. 1951-54. Bibliography.
Separate sections on her early life and her career.

F48   Butterfield, Roger. "Eleanor." *FDR*. By Robert D. Graff and Robert Emmett Ginna. New York: Harper & Row, 1963. 174-93.
Includes previously unpublished photographs. Concludes with quotations from interviews conducted by Ben Feiner, Jr. near the end of ER's life.

F49   Caroli, Betty Boyd. "Eleanor Roosevelt." *Research Guide to American Historical Biography*. Vol. 3. Washington: Beacham, 1989. 1311-17.
Organized around several sections including chronology, activities, and overview and evaluation of biographical sources and works by ER.

F50   Chafe, William H.   "Biographical Sketch." *Without Precedent: The Life and Career of Eleanor Roosevelt*. Everywoman: Studies in History, Literature, and Culture. Ed. Joan Hoff-Wilson and Marjorie Lightman. Bloomington: Indiana Univ. Pr., 1984. 3-27. Sources.

Chafe utilizes the papers of ER and others plus published works in this sketch which emphasizes the period from 1917 onward. Based in part on his treatment of her in *Notable American Women*.

F51   ---.   "Roosevelt, Anna Eleanor." *Notable American Women, The Modern Period: A Biographical Dictionary*. Cambridge: Belknap-Harvard Univ. Pr., 1980. 595-601. Sources.

Comprehensive coverage of her public and private life with quotations from her autobiographical writings and writings about her.   Revised versions issued in *American Reformers: An H.W. Wilson Biographical Dictionary*, pp. 697-701 (New York: Wilson, 1985) and as "Eleanor Roosevelt" in *Portraits of American Women, from Settlement to the Present*, pp. 485-507 (New York: St. Martin's, 1991).

F52   Clark, Judith Freeman.   "Eleanor Roosevelt, 1884-1962." *Almanac of American Women in the 20th Century*. By Judith Freeman Clark. New York: Prentice Hall, 1987. 73-75.

Her public activities and the influence which she had on important events of the 20th century.

F53   Corrado, Anthony J.   "Eleanor Roosevelt." *Political Parties and Elections in the United States: An Encyclopedia*. Vol. 2. New York: Garland, 1991. 975-77. Bibliography.

Her activities in Democratic Party politics with emphasis on her efforts to promote the role of women.

F54   Darling, Edward.   "Anna Eleanor Roosevelt." *They Cast Long Shadows*. By Edward Darling. Boston: Beacon, 1969. 38-51. Bibliography.

ER is the subject of one of eight sketches of independent thinkers who dared to set a different course.   Reissued as "Eleanor Roosevelt" in his *When Sparks Fly Upward*, pp. 5-22 (New York Washburn, 1970).

F55   Diller, Daniel C., and Stephen L. Robertson.   "Eleanor Roosevelt." *The Presidents, First Ladies, and Vice Presidents: White House Biographies, 1789-1989*. By Daniel C. Diller and Stephen L. Robertson. Washington: Congressional Quarterly, 1989. 105-6.

Emphasis is on her years as First Lady.   Also issued in *Congressional Quarterly's Guide to the Presidency*, pp. 888-89 (Washington: Congressional Quarterly, 1989).

F56   Dos Passos, John.   "Rover: The Code of Mrs. Roosevelt, or Uplife Goes Global." *Esquire* 54 (Dec. 1960): 292.

Entitled "Rover" after ER's Secret Service code name.   Reissued as "Rover" in his *Mid-Century*, pp. 182-90 (Boston: Houghton Mifflin Riverside, 1961).

F57   Douglas, Emily Taft.   "Autumn Harvest: The Story of Eleanor Roosevelt." *Remember the Ladies: The Story of Great Women Who Helped Shape America*. New York: Putnam's, 1966. 211-33. Bibliography.

A detailed look at her life and work through 1945 with less attention given to the post-war years.

F58 Downs, Robert B. "Eleanor Roosevelt." *Memorable Americans, 1750-1959*. By Robert B. Downs, et al. Littleton: Libraries Unlimited, 1983. 272-73.
ER is the only First Lady and one of only a few women included.

F59 "Eleanor Roosevelt" [romanized]. *Amerika* [romanized] (1985):3-9.
Her life and work. In Russian. Updated version of the sketch which appeared in *Amerika* in 1961.

F60 "Eleanor Roosevelt." *Peace on Earth*. New York: Hermitage House, 1949. 238-39.

F61 "Eleanor Roosevelt's Birthday." *American Book of Days*. 3rd ed. Comp. and ed. Jane M. Hatch. New York: Wilson, 1978. 914-17.
Summary biography and posthumous tributes.

F62 "Eleonor Roosevelt." *De Vrouw en Haarhuis* (Sept. 1946): 132-36.
A comprehensive look at her life and career. In Dutch.

F63 Evans, Ernestine. "Anna Eleanor Roosevelt." *Urd* 50 (26 Okt. 1946): 677-679, 701-2.
Her life and career. In Norwegian.

F64 "Franklin D. Roosevelt." *The American Presidents*. Vol. 3. Ed. Frank N. Magill and John L. Loos. Pasadena: Salem, 1986. 572-624. Bibliographical References.
ER's childhood, early married life, and role as aide to FDR. While FDR may have married her because she was a member of the Oyster Bay branch of the Roosevelt family, ER's own accomplishments benefited his career more (pp. 579-81, 595).

F65 Halamandaris, Val J. "First Lady of the World." *Caring People* 4 (Fall 1991): 58-77.
Her life, career, character, and impact.

F66 Hareven, Tamara K. "Roosevelt, Anna Eleanor." *Encylopedia of American Biography*. New York: Harper & Row, 1974. 924-26.

F67 ---. "Roosevelt, Anna Eleanor." *Franklin D. Roosevelt, His Life and Times: An Encyclopedic View*. The G.K. Hall Presidential Encyclopedia Series. Ed. Otis L. Graham, Jr. and Meghan Robinson Wander. Boston: Hall, 1985. 360-67.
A comprehensive look at all aspects of her life and career analyzing her philosophy and activities as First Lady and later. More than the precedents which she set, the most important aspect of ER the First Lady was that she considered herself to be first a citizen.

F68 Hayward, Tamerin Mitchell, and Barbara Hope Klein. "Roosevelt, Eleanor." *Handbook of American Women's History*. Garland Reference Library of the Humanities, 696. New York: Garland, 1990. 520-22. References.
Emphasizes her association with feminists and her beliefs about the role of women as expressed in her *It's Up to the Women*.

F69   Healy, Diana Dixon. "Anna Eleanor Roosevelt Roosevelt." *America's First Ladies: Private Lives of the Presidential Wives.* By Diana Dixon Healy. New York: Atheneum, 1988. 181-90.
A sketch which concludes that ER and FDR were a good partnership for the country.

F70   Hickok, Lorena A. "A Political Profile of Mrs. Eleanor Roosevelt." *Ladies of Courage.* By Eleanor Roosevelt and Lorena A. Hickok. New York: Putnam's, 1954. 253-89.
A portrait of the public ER, a look at her political activities, those who helped educate her to the ways of politics, and her own view of public life. For a discussion, see Mary Hornaday's "Ladies Who Rule the World and Who Rocked the Cradle." Rev. of *Ladies of Courage* and *Mothers of America* by Elizabeth Logan Davis. *Christian Science Monitor* 27 May 1954, Atlantic ed.: 13. Hornaday thinks that since ER was only one of a number of women who decided that politics was not too dirty an undertaking for them, Hickok is too defensive about her.

F71   Lash, Joseph P. "Roosevelt, (Anna) Eleanor." *Dictionary of American Biography.* Suppl. 7, 1961-1965. New York: Scribner's, 1981. 658-62. [Additional sources].
A comprehensive, analytical sketch by her principal biographer.

F72   ---. "Roosevelt, Eleanor." *The Encyclopedia Americana.* Int'l. ed., 1989, v. 23, p. 762. Further Reading.

F73   Lindsay, Rae. "Anna Eleanor Roosevelt." *The Presidents' First Ladies.* By Rae Lindsay. New York: Franklin Watts, 1989. 234-44.

F74   Manchester, William. "Portrait of an American: Eleanor." *The Glory and the Dream: A Narrative of History in America, 1932-1972.* Boston: Little, Brown, 1974. 91-93.
A look at her life and career with considerable attention given to FDR's relationship with Lucy Mercer.

F75   Marlow, Joan. "Eleanor Roosevelt." *The Great Women.* A Hart Book. By Joan Marlow. New York: A & W, 1979. 245-52.
Her life and activities with brief quotations from tributes to her.

F76   McConnell, Jane, and Burt McConnell. "Anna Eleanor Roosevelt: Internationally Famous First Lady." *Our First Ladies, from Martha Washington to Lady Bird Johnson.* By Jane McConnell and Burt McConnell. New York: Crowell, 1964. 305-17.
Her life and career through 1945 with brief attention to the remainder of her life. Based primarily on her autobiographical writings. Subtitles of different eds. of *Our First Ladies* vary depending on date of publication.

F77   Means, Marianne. "Anna Eleanor Roosevelt." *The Woman in the White House: The Lives, Times and Influence of Twelve Notable First Ladies.* By Marianne Means. New York: Random House, 1963. 189-214.
The *Autobiography of Eleanor Roosevelt* and her son James' *Affectionately, FDR* were used to create this sketch.

F78   Milburn, Frank H.   "Roosevelt, (Anna) Eleanor." *Political Profiles: The Kennedy Years*. New York: Facts on File, 1976. 442-43.
   Her involvement with the Kennedy administration as chair of the President's Commission on the Status of Women, UN delegate, member of Advisory Council of the Peace Corps, and member of the Tractors for Freedom Committee.   Milburn concludes that her suggestions about foreign policy were rejected and that she had little influence on policy.   Also includes a discussion of her activities before 1961.

F79   Mueller, Jean, and Edward Miller.   "Tribute to Eleanor." *The Franklin Delano Roosevelt Library and Home*. A Halls of Greatness Book. By Jean Mueller and Edward Miller. New York: Meredith, 1966. 104-8.

F80   Northcroft, Dora.   "First Lady: Eleanor Roosevelt." *American Girls of Adventure*. By Dora Northcroft. London: F. Muller, 1947. 114-26.

F81   Pace, Dixie Ann.   "Eleanor Roosevelt." *Valiant Women*. By Dixie Ann Pace. New York: Vantage, 1972. 90-93.

F82   Paletta, Lu Ann.   "Anna Eleanor Roosevelt." *The World Almanac of First Ladies*. By Lu Ann Paletta. New York: World Almanac, 1990. 101-8.

F83   Pierce, Bessie Louise.   "Eleanor Roosevelt." *Famous Americans*. Second Series. Los Angeles: Webb, 1941. 463-70. Notes. Selected References.
   A thorough examination of her activities in political and humanitarian arenas and a sketch of her private life.

F84   Prindiville, Kathleen.   "Eleanor Roosevelt." *First Ladies*. 2nd ed. By Katherine Prindiville. New York: Macmillan, 1964. 263-77.
   Her life and work through the death of FDR.

F85   Reifert, Gail, and Eugene M. Dermody.   "Eleanor Roosevelt." *Women Who Fought: An American History*. By Gail Reifert and Eugene M. Dermody. Norwalk: Dermody, 1978. 203-12.
   A sketch of her life in this work about courageous women who met challenges in their lives.

F86   Robinson, Donald.   "Eleanor Roosevelt." *The 100 Most Important People in the World Today*. By Donald Robinson. Boston: Little, Brown, 1952. 63-66.

F87   "Roosevelt, (Anna) Eleanor." *Current Biography: Who's News and Why, 1949*. New York: Wilson, 1950. 528-32. References.
   Her life, activities, and writings as well as awards received.   Updates and expands the entry in *Current Biography: Who's News and Why, 1940*, pp. 691-93 (New York: Wilson, 1940).

F88   "Roosevelt, Anna Eleanor." *Something about the Author: Facts and Pictures about Authors and Illustrators of Books for Young People*. Vol. 50. Detroit: Gale, 1988. 167-82. "For More Information See."
   Arranged according to headings: personal, career, memberships and awards, writings, and sidelights.   The final one is a lengthy chronology of her life and career relying primarily on her own words.

F89   "Roosevelt, [Anna] Eleanor (Mrs. Franklin Delano Roosevelt)." *The National Cyclopedia of American Biography*. Vol. 57. Clifton: White, 1977. 601-4.
   A detailed description of her life and activities. A shorter account appeared in Current Vol. F, 1939-42 of *The National Cyclopaedia of American Biography, Being the History of the United States*, pp. 12-13 (New York: White, 1942). In the earlier account some aspects of her life, e.g., her association with the Todhunter School, are given more detailed treatment.

F90   "Roosevelt, Eleanor." *International Celebrity Register*. U.S. ed. New York: Celebrity Register, 1959. 644-45.
   Presented with generous quotations from her writings.

F91   "Roosevelt, Eleanor." *The Presidency A to Z: A Ready Reference Encyclopedia*. CQ's Encyclopedia of American Government, v. 2. Ed. Michael Nelson. Washington: Congressional Quarterly, 1992. 370-72.
   Emphasizes years as First Lady.

F92   Sadler, Christine. "Eleanor Roosevelt." *America's First Ladies: Women of the Century*. By Christine Sadler. New York: Macfadden, 1963. 211-23.
   Derivative account with no sources provided.

F93   Scharf, Lois. "Roosevelt, Anna Eleanor." *Historical Dictionary of the New Deal, from Inauguration to Preparation for War*. Westport: Greenwood, 1985. 427-30. Sources.
   The life and work of ER up to 1940 with emphasis on her involvement with New Deal programs.

F94   Schriftgiesser, Karl. *The Amazing Roosevelt Family, 1613-1942*. New York: Funk, 1942. xii + 367p. Index. Bibliography.
   An undocumented account of ER's life and activities (pp. 265-92).

F95   Schroeder, Eileen E. "Anna Eleanor Roosevelt, 1884-1962." *Read More about It*. Vol. 3. Ann Arbor: Pierian, 1989. 598-601. Bibliography.
   Her life and work followed by an annotated list of a few works by or about her, sources for additional information, and a list of major dates in her life.

F96   Shivvers, Martha E. "Eleanor Roosevelt: Champion of Human Rights and Peace." *Iowa Woman* 4 (Summer 1983): 4-7.
   She was an inspiration and fought for peace and the rights of others in everything which she did. Outlines her public and private life.

F97   Smith, Don. "Mrs. Eleanor Roosevelt." *Peculiarities of the Presidents: Strange and Intimate Facts Not Found in History*. Rev. ed. By Don Smith. Van Wert: Smith, 1946. 171-79.
   Anecdotal.

F98   Stoddard, Hope. "Eleanor Roosevelt." *Famous American Women*. By Hope Stoddard. New York: Crowell, 1970. 347-60. Bibliography.
   ER's life and career emphasizing achievements as First Lady, humanitarian, and as a woman respected throughout the world.

F99 Stone, Kirk. "E.R. Portrayed in Words and Photographs." *Social Education* 48 (Nov./Dec. 1984): 522-27.

F100 Waldrup, Carole Chandler. "Anna Eleanor Roosevelt Roosevelt." *Presidents' Wives: The Lives of 44 American Women of Strength*. By Carole Chandler Waldrup. Jefferson: McFarland, 1989. 277-88.

F101 Wandersee, Winifred D. "Roosevelt, Anna Eleanor." *Biographical Dictionary of Social Welfare in America*. New York: Greenwood, 1986. 639-43.
Traces her involvement in social welfare. Discusses sources for the study of ER's life and career.

F102 Whitehead, James L. *Eleanor Roosevelt in Pictures: A Few Highlights of Her Life*. Hyde Park: Franklin D. Roosevelt Library and Museum, 1975. 16p.
Her life as presented through photographs and limited text.

Brief Overviews of Her Life and Work

F103 Alexander, Charles. "Eleanor Roosevelt." *The McGraw-Hill Encyclopedia of World Biography*. Vol. 9. New York: McGraw-Hill, 1973. 265-67. Further Reading.

F104 *The Almanac of American History*. A Bison Book. New York: Putnam's, 1983. 466.

F105 *American Women: The Official Who's Who Among the Women of the Nation*. Los Angeles: American Publications, 1939. 772.

F106 *The Americana Annual, 1963: An Encyclopedia of the Events of 1962*. New York: Americana, 1963. 578-79.

F107 Benet, William Rose. *The Reader's Encyclopedia*. 2nd ed. New York: Crowell, 1965. 875.

F108 *Britannica Book of the Year, 1963: A Record of the Main Events of 1962*. Chicago: Encyclopaedia Britannica, 1963. 876.

F109 Brooks, Gertrude Zeth. "Eleanor Roosevelt: A Political Power in Her Own Right." *First Ladies of the White House*. By Gertrude Zeth Brooks. Chicago: Hallberg, 1969. 93-95.
Emphasis is on her political activities.

F110 Cassin, Rene. "Eleanor Roosevelt." *La Pensee et l'Action*. By Rene Cassin. [Boulogne-sur-Seine]: Ed. F. Lalou, 1972. 80-83.
In French.

F111 *Chambers Biographical Dictionary*. Rev. ed. Cambridge: Cambridge Univ. Pr., 1984. 1147-48.

F112 *Concise Dictionary of American Biography*. 4th ed. New York: Scribner's, 1990. 976-77.

F113 *Contemporary Authors*. Vol. 89/92. Detroit: Gale, 1980. 436.

F114   Cook, Blanche Wiesen.   *Eleanor Roosevelt: Woman of Conscience and Conviction*. Aids for Ending Sexism in Schools. Brooklyn: TABS, 1984. 2p. + poster.
  Succinct biography written to accompany poster "Eleanor Roosevelt, Champion of Social Change, Human Rights, International Cooperation."

F115 DeGregorio, William A. *The Complete Book of U.S. Presidents*. New York: Dembner, 1984. 484-85. Notes.

F116 Dickerson, Robert B., Jr. *Final Placement: A Guide to the Deaths, Funerals and Burials of Notable Americans*. Algonac: Reference Publications, 1982. 204-5.
  Basic facts about her life and career followed by limited information on her final illness and her death.

F117 *Eleanor Roosevelt*. Washington: National Park Service, U.S. Dept. of the Interior [1984]. 1 folded sheet. 2 sides.
  Issued as a handout for visitors to the Eleanor Roosevelt National Historic Site.

F118 "Eleanor Roosevelt." *Esquire* 100 (Dec. 1983): 547.
  Significant aspects of her personal and private life.   Follows John Kenneth Galbraith's account of her career entitled "Eleanor the Good." Reissued in *Fifty Who Made the Difference*, pp. 474-75 (New York: Villard, 1984).

F119 "Eleanor Roosevelt." *Woman of the Month Display Kits*. Set. I. Windsor: National Women's History Project, n.d. 24.8" x 10" captioned photograph.
  An overview of her life is included.

F120 *Encyclopedia of American History*. 6th ed. New York: Harper & Row, 1982. 1141.

F121 *Faces and Phases of Women*. Ed. Carol N. Stallone. Seneca Falls: National Women's Hall of Fame, 1983. 76p. (31 posters in portfolio).
  Brief biographies of 31 women including one of ER.

F122 *Famous American Women: A Biographical Dictionary from Colonial Times to the Present*. Ed. Robert McHenry. New York: Dover, 1980. 354.
  About her public activities, not her personal life. Originally published in 1980 as *Liberty's Women* (Springfield: Merriam) and reissued in 1983 as *Famous American Women* (New York: Dover) and in 1985 with the same title (New York: Merriam).

F123 Findling, John E. *Dictionary of American Diplomatic History*. Westport: Greenwood, 1979. 415-16. Sources.
  Includes a discussion of the positions which she took on issues which came before the UN, 1949-1953.

F124 *Four Hundred Notable Americans*. New York: Harper Perennial Library, 1965. 215-16.

F125 Fuentes, Jodi. *Historical Dictionary of the United States: Practical, Factual & Biographical*. Los Angeles: Alfa, 1978. 302.

F126 Garraty, John A. *1,001 Things Everyone Should Know about American History*. New York: Doubleday, 1989. 81.

F127 Gerlinger, Irene Hazard. *Mistresses of the White House: Narrator's Tale of a Pageant of First Ladies*. New York: French, 1950. 101-2.
  The conclusion of this sketch is that ER's energy and ideas make plausible the possibility of a woman as President.

F128 *The Good Housekeeping Woman's Almanac*. New York: Newspaper Enterprise Assoc., 1977. 491-92.
  Activities as First Lady and UN delegate.

F129 Hart, James D. *The Oxford Companion to American Literature*. 5th ed. New York: Oxford Univ. Pr., 1983. 651.

F130 Heath, Monroe. *Great American Women at a Glance*. The Great Americans Series, v. 4. Menlo Park: Pacific Coast, 1957. 27.
  Emphasizes her humanitarian activities.

F131 Herzberg, Max J., et al. *The Readers Encyclopedia of American Literature*. New York: Crowell, 1962. 974-75.

F132 *Historical Notes of Saint James' Parish, Hyde Park-on-Hudson, New York*. N.p.: n.p., 1961. 86.

F133 Horneman, Mary Ann. *The First Ladies of the White House (in Miniature)*. 2nd ed. Beloit: Call, 1944. 72-73.

F134 Hurwitz, Howard L. *An Encyclopedic Dictionary of American History*. New York: Washington Square, 1968. 579.

F135 *In Our Time: 20th Century Greats Selected by the Associated Press*. New York: Gallery, 1986. 60-61.

F136 *The International Dictionary of Women's Biography*. New York: Continuum, 1982. 399.
  Reissued in 1989 ed., pp. 463-64 (New York: Continuum). Also issued as *The Macmillan Dictionary of Women's Biography* (London: Macmillan, 1982; 2nd ed., London: Macmillan, 1989).

F137 *The International Who's Who*. 26th ed., 1962-63. London: Europa, 1962. 849.

F138 Jones, Barry O. *The Rutledge Dictionary of People*. New York: Rutledge, 1981. 675.

F139 Kane, Joseph Nathan. *Facts about the Presidents: A Compilation of Biographical and Historical Information*. 5th ed. New York: Wilson, 1989. 194, 205.
  Some earlier eds. published as *Know Your Presidents and Their Wives*.

F140 Klapthor, Margaret Brown. *First Ladies*. Washington: White House Historical Assoc., 1983. 72-73.

Her early life, preparation for role as First Lady, and activities while in the White House.

F141   Koykku, Arthur S. *Project Remember: A National Index of Gravesites of Notable Americans.* Algonac: Reference Publications, 1986. 251.

F142   *The Lincoln Library of Social Studies.* Buffalo: Frontier, 1968. 1137.

F143   Logan, Logna B. *Ladies of the White House.* New York: Vantage, 1962. 193.

F144   Macksey, Joan, and Kenneth Macksey. *The Book of Women's Achievements.* New York: Stein & Day, 1976. 42-43.
A sketch with emphasis on the period after 1945.

F145   *Men in the News 2. Biographical Sketches from The New York Times: Men and Women Who Made Headlines in 1959.* Philadelphia: Lippincott, 1960. 242-44.

F146   Morris, Dan, and Inez Morris. *Who Was Who in American Politics.* New York: Hawthorn, 1974. 497-98.
Her career and the criticism which she received.

F147   *Mothers of Achievement in American History, 1776-1976.* Rutland: Tuttle, 1976. 394-95.

F148   *The New Encyclopaedia Britannica.* 1989 ed., vol. 10, p. 172.
Her life and prestige plus the controversial aspects of her activities.

F149   O'Brien, Steven G. *American Political Leaders: From Colonial Times to the Present.* Santa Barbara: ABC-CLIO, 1991. 343-44. Bibliography.

F150   Olsen, Kirstin. *Remember the Ladies: A Woman's Book of Days.* Pittstown: Main Street Pr., 1988. 171-72.
Emphasizes her success in developing an independent life and career for herself.

F151   Palmer, Alan. *Who's Who in Modern History, 1860-1980.* London: Weidenfeld and Nicolson, 1980. 277.

F152   Pederson, Kern. "Eleanor Roosevelt: American Writer and Humanitarian." *Leaders of America: Capsule Biographies of Over 260 Famous Personalities.* Waukesha: Country Beautiful, 1967. 212.
Presented in cartoon format.

F153   *The Presidents and Their Wives from George Washington to James Earl Carter Jr.* Washington: National Souvenir Center, 1977. 60-61.

F154   Raven, Susan, and Alison Wier. *Woman of Achievement: Thirty-five Centuries of History.* New York: Harmony, 1981. 49-50.

F155   *The Reader's Digest Family Encyclopedia of American History.* Pleasantville: Reader's Digest, 1975. 967.

F156 Siegel, Mary-Ellen. *Her Way: A Guide to Biographies of Women for Young People*. 2nd ed. Chicago: American Library Assoc., 1984. 201-3. Bibliography.
   The first ed. was as Mary-Ellen Kulkin, *Her Way: Biographies of Women for Young People*, pp. 243-45 (Chicago: American Library Assoc., 1976).

F157 *The Simon and Schuster Encyclopedia of World War II*. A Cord Communications Book. New York: Simon and Schuster, 1978. 533.

F158 Snyder, Louis L. *Louis L. Snyder's Historical Guide to World War II*. Westport: Greenwood, 1982. 590. Bibliography.

F159 Steinberg, Alfred. *Collier's Encyclopedia*. 1988 ed., vol. 20, pp. 204-5.

F160 *10 Eventful Years: A Record of Events of the Years Preceding Including and Following World War II, 1937 through 1946*. Vol. 3. Chicago: Encyclopaedia Britannica, 1947. 810.

F161 *The Twentieth Century: An Almanac*. Rev. ed. A Bison Book. New York: World Almanac, 1985. 320.

F162 Vernoff, Edward, and Rima Shore. *The International Dictionary of 20th Century Biography*. New York: New American Library, 1987. 607.

F163 Ward, A.C. *Longman Companion to Twentieth Century Literature*. 3rd ed. Harlow, Essex: Longman, 1981. 457.

F164 *Webster's American Biographies*. Springfield: Merriam, 1979. 890-91.

F165 *Webster's Guide to American History: A Chronological, Geographical, and Biographical Survey and Compendium*. Springfield: Merriman, 1971. 1201.

F166 *Who Was Who. Vol. 6, 1961-70*. London: Adam & C. Black, 1972. 975.
   A few facts about her life and work. Basically the same sketch which appeared in *Who's Who* from 1948 through 1963.

F167 *Who Was Who in America with World Notables. Vol. 4, 1961-1968*. Chicago: Marquis-Who's Who, 1968. 809.
   Basically the same entry which appeared in *Who's Who in America* beginning with the 1930-1931 ed. Also appeared in 1958-1959 and 1961-1962 eds. of *Who's Who of American Women* (Chicago: Marquis-Who's Who).

F168 *Who's Who in New York (City and State), 1947*. New York: Lewis Historical Publishing, 1947. 891.
   Includes a list of memberships which she maintained.

F169 *Who's Who in the Nation's Capital, 1938-1939*. Washington: Ransdell, 1938. 721.

F170 Wilson, Vincent J. *The Book of Distinguished American Women*. Brookeville: American History Research Assocs., 1983. 82-83.
   Accompanied by a brief chronology.

F171 *Women of Achievement*. New York: House of Field, 1940. 23.
Her early life, publications and honors, and current association and club affiliations.

F172 *The Women's Book of World Records and Achievements*. Information House Book. Garden City: Anchor-Doubleday, 1979. 738.
Emphasis is on the acclaim which she received.

F173 *Workers and Allies: Female Participation in the American Trade Union Movement, 1824-1976*. Exhibition organized by Judith O'Sullivan. Catalog by Judith O'Sullivan and Rosemary Gallick. Washington: Smithsonian Institution Pr., 1975. 78. Bibliography.

PRIVATE LIFE

F174 Adams, David. "The Place Which Gave FDR His Values." *Listener* 109 (2 Mar. 1983): 9-10.
After FDR's death the author visited ER in Hyde Park. He recalls those visits with the "grand lady" who helped him to learn more about the character of FDR (p. 10).

F175 Alsop, Joseph. *FDR, 1882-1945: A Centenary Remembrance*. New York: Viking, 1982. 256p.
Relationship between ER and FDR (p. 9), early married life (pp. 27-42 passim, 65-67), FDR's affair with Lucy Mercer (pp. 67-73), and ER's friendship with other women (pp. 109-10).

F176 Alsop, Joseph, and Robert Kintner. "The Roosevelt Family Album." *Life* 9 (9 Sept. 1940): 62-64, 66-67.
An historical look at the Roosevelt family. Attention to ER is limited to captions to photographs.

F177 *The American Heritage Pictorial History of the Presidents of the United States*. 2 vols. (1023p.). New York: American Heritage-Simon and Schuster, 1968. Index.
Her childhood and early married life (v. 2, pp. 789-90, 815).

F178 Anthony, Carl Sferrazza. *First Ladies: The Saga of the Presidents' Wives and Their Power, 1789-1961*. Vol.[1] of *First Ladies*. New York: Morrow, 1990. 685p. Index. Notes.
Her early life (pp. 280, 286, 308-9), married life (pp. 310-12, 315-16, 348, 358, 361), FDR's affair with Lucy Mercer (pp. 348, 358, 364), and her later life (pp. 520, 568-69, 578).

F179 ---. *First Ladies: The Saga of the Presidents' Wives and Their Power, 1961-1990*. Vol. 2 of *First Ladies*. New York: Morrow, 1990. 511p. Index. Bibliography. Notes.
The death and funeral of ER, an account derived from other sources (pp. 80-82).

F180 ---. "Like Father, Like First Lady." *Washington Post* 16 June 1985, sect. G: 1, 10-11.
Father Elliott Roosevelt's concern for the less fortunate had a tremendous impact on ER. An article about the influence of fathers on first ladies.

F181   Asbell, Bernard. *The F.D.R. Memoirs*. *As Written by Bernard Asbell*. New York: Doubleday, 1973. xvii + 461p. Index. Bibliography. Notes.

Asbell provides FDR's memoirs as he thinks FDR would have written them. Included are background memoranda which accompany each section. Writings by and about ER play a major role. Her private life (pp. 205-56 passim). FDR's affair with Lucy Mercer (pp. 228-33).

F182   Asbury, Edith Evans. "Drive to Save Mrs. Roosevelt's Val-Kill Pressed." *New York Times* 16 May 1977: 48.

Hyde Park residents remember ER and Val-Kill as they work to see her home made a National Historic Site.

F183   Barber, James David. *The Presidential Character: Predicting Performance in the White House*. 2nd ed. Englewood Cliffs: Prentice-Hall, 1977. xi + 576p. Index. Notes.

Succinct account of the Roosevelts' early married life, the influence of Sara Roosevelt, and the subservient position of ER (pp. 190-92).

F184   Beard, Timothy, and Henry B. Hoff. "The Roosevelt Family." *New York Genealogical and Biographical Record* 118 (Oct. 1987): 193-202; 119 (Jan. 1988): 19-34.

The pre-19th century American ancestors of ER and FDR.

F185   Bergquist, Laura. "Eleanor Roosevelt Today." *Look* 20 (17 Apr. 1956): 92-98, 100.

About her life and activities at age 71. Profusely illustrated.

F186   Birmingham, Stephen. *America's Secret Aristocracy*. Boston: Little, Brown, 1987. 334p. Index.

Popular treatment of the private lives of America's famous families. ER's Roosevelt, Livingston, and Hall forbearers are treated briefly. Limited treatment of ER as a child (pp. 123-24, 126-28).

F187   Blodgett, Bonnie, and D.J. Tice. *At Home with the Presidents*. Woodstock: Overlook, 1988. 256p. Index.

A discussion of the homes of FDR and ER and what they meant to them (pp. 190-95).

F188   Boettiger, John R. *A Love in Shadow*. New York: Norton, 1978. 279p.

ER's grandson uses many of his mother Anna Roosevelt's own words to tell the story of his parents' marriage. Attention is given to ER, FDR, and other family members.

F189   Bowen, Croswell. "An Afternoon at Hyde Park." *PM's Sunday Picture News* 16 Dec. 1945: 8-9.

Bowen has lunch with ER and FDR, Jr. and inspects the latter's Christmas tree farm.

F190   Brough, James. *Princess Alice: A Biography of Alice Roosevelt Longworth*. Boston: Little, Brown, 1975. 335p. Index.

FDR's affair with Lucy Mercer (pp. 243-44, 304). Includes a general discussion of ER's childhood (pp. 60-64).

F191   Bugbee, Emma. "Happy Days at Campobello." *New York Herald Tribune* 7 July 1963, sect. 2: 5.
Bugbee recalls a 1935 trip to Campobello when a day was spent sailing with ER at the helm.

F192   *Burke's Presidential Families of the United States of America.* London: Burke's Peerage, 1975. xix + 676p. Index.
Her lineage is documented in chapters "Theodore Roosevelt" (pp. 411-24) and "Franklin Delano Roosevelt" (pp. 489-506).

F193   Burns, James MacGregor. *Roosevelt: The Lion and the Fox.* New York: Harcourt, Brace, 1956. xvi + 553p. Index. Bibliography.
Burns' political biography of FDR treats the Roosevelts' early married life superficially. Similar coverage is in his *The Crosswinds of Freedom*, pp. 8-9 (New York: Knopf, 1989).

F194   Burt, Nathaniel. *First Families: The Making of an American Aristocracy.* Boston: Little, Brown, 1970. xiii + 503p. Index.
As one who had to struggle against domination by other women in her own family, ER helped FDR to escape from his mother's domination (pp. 361-69).

F195   Carmody, Deirdre. "Letters by Eleanor Roosevelt Detail Friendship with Lorena Hickok." *New York Times* 21 Oct. 1979: 34.
About the correspondence between ER and Hickok used in Doris Faber's *The Life of Lorena Hickok.* Contains biographical data on Hickok and extensive quotations from the letters.

F196   Churchill, Allen. *The Roosevelts: American Aristocrats.* New York: Harper & Row, 1965. v + 294p. Index. Bibliography.
A popular treatment of both branches of the family. ER's childhood, early married life, and children (pp. 192-99, 202-3, 211, 216-18, 235, 237-40).

F197   "Clan Roosevelt." *Fortune* 4 (Oct. 1931): 61-65.
The Roosevelt men. ER is mentioned only as FDR's wife, Theodore Roosevelt's niece, and Hall Roosevelt's sister.

F198   Clapper, Olive Ewing. *Washington Tapestry.* New York: Whittlesey House, 1946. 303p.
The relationship between ER and FDR including ER's acceptance of criticism (pp. 236-39). Believed to contain the first published reference to FDR's affair with Lucy Mercer.

F199   Clayton, Frederick. "Eleanor Roosevelt: Pt. I- Humanitarian." *Wisdom* 2 (Jan. 1958): 4-19.
A sympathetic picture of ER as a child, young wife and mother, and helpmate to FDR.

F200 Collier, Fred. "The First Lady of the World." *Yale Review* 77 (Summer 1988): 492-500.

In 1945 as a Yale medical student Collier sought and received financial aid from ER. He describes his subsequent personal association with her. An abridged version issued as "The Intern and the President's Wife." *American Way* (American Airlines) (1 Oct. 1988): 84-86, 122.

F201 Conrad, Peter. "Roosevelt." *Great American Families*. New York: Times Books, 1977. 124-67.

A study of both branches of the family. ER is both the link and the central character with her emergence as the world's conscience being the family's most outstanding accomplishment. When contrasting FDR to Theodore Roosevelt, ER is always a central figure (pp. 124-67).

F202 Cook, Blanche Wiesen. Rev. of *The Life of Lorena Hickok: ER's Friend* by Doris Faber. *Feminist Studies* 6 (Fall 1980): 511-16.

Faber employs stereotypes (Hickok as having the physical characteristics of a lesbian) and denial (lesbianism cannot be a meaningful experience). For now Cook considers a better look at ER to be Dorothy Strachey Bussy's autobiographical novel *Olivia* (London: Hogarth, 1949) in which she believes a young ER at Allenswood is portrayed. An abbreviated version of the review issued as "Exploitative Book Distorts Relationship." *New Directions for Women* (May/Apr. 1980): 12-13.

F203 Corr, Maureen. "The Eleanor Roosevelt I Knew." *Eleanor Roosevelt: An American Journey*. Ed. Jess Flemion and Colleen M. O'Connor. San Diego: San Diego State Univ. Pr., 1987. 47-50.

Her last secretary recalls the personal side of ER.

F204 Costopoulos, Liz. "ER: First Lady of the Hudson Valley." *Hudson Valley* (Oct. 1984): 30-34.

Mainly about her life in Hyde Park.

F205 "Critics Answered by Mrs. Roosevelt." *New York Times* 16 Jan. 1933: 17.

In a letter which will appear in today's *Chicago Tribune* ER defends her decision to continue her association with the Todhunter School since schools provide employment opportunities for teachers.

F206 Dall, Anna Roosevelt. "Thoughts about My Mother." *Liberty* 11 (19 May 1934): 34-35.

Daughter Anna pays tribute to ER and tells how when she was a child her mother gave her companionship and a sense of equality.

F207 Dall, Curtis B. *F.D.R.: My Exploited Father-in-Law*. Rev. ed. Washington: Liberty Lobby, 1970. iii + 192p. Index. Notes.

Recollections of ER by the first husband of Anna Roosevelt (pp. 41-60).

F208 Daly, Macdonald. "Mrs. Roosevelt Keeps Up a Tradition." *Illustrated* (22 Jan. 1955): 50.

Her Scottish Terrier successors to Fala.

F209 Daniels, Jonathan. *The End of Innocence.* Philadelphia: Lippincott, 1954; New York: Da Capo, 1972. 351p. Index.

Daniels relies heavily on the unpublished diary of his father Josephus Daniels, newspaper accounts, and FDR's letters in this description of World War I Washington with his father and FDR as central figures. The numerous brief references to ER provide insight into the relationship between the Roosevelts at the time.

F210 ---. *The Time between the Wars: Armistice to Pearl Harbor.* Garden City: Doubleday, 1966; New York: Garland, 1979. viii + 372p. Index. Bibliography.

ER's relationship with FDR at the time when she believed that he had ended his relationship with Lucy Mercer (pp. 208-10). "In New Book: Story of an FDR Romance." *U.S. News & World Report* 61 (22 Aug. 1966): 13 is an account of a UPI report that Mercer's daughter does not believe that there was an affair. In his column for 16 Aug. 1966 Drew Pearson speculates on the impact which knowledge of the affair had on ER. He claims that it was the stimulus for her travels, writings, and intense interest in New Deal programs, all undertaken to overcome loneliness. Title and date of Pearson's column vary.

F211 ---. *Washington Quadrille: The Dance beside the Documents.* New York: Doubleday, 1968. 370p. Index. Notes.

A social history of Washington, from the time of Henry Adams' arrival in 1877 until the death of FDR, which attempts to establish the social context of the relationship between FDR and Lucy Mercer. Detailed description of ER from childhood to 1945 derived from published sources.

F212 Davis, Kenneth S. *FDR, into the Storm, 1937-1940: A History.* New York: Random House, 1993. 691p. Index. Notes.

Davis on the dissolving of Val-Kill Industries, ER's resignation from the Todhunter School, and the break-up of her close relationship with Nancy Cook and Marion Dickerman (pp. 297-99, 301-6).

F213 ---. *FDR, the Beckoning of Destiny: A History, 1882-1928.* New York: Putnam's, 1972. 936p. Index. Notes.

The chapter "Enter, Eleanor" extends up to her marriage (pp. 171-93). Abridged version issued earlier as "Miss Eleanor Roosevelt." *American Heritage* 22 (Oct. 1971): 48-59.

F214 ---. *FDR, the New Deal Years, 1933-1937: A History.* New York: Random House, 1986. x + 756p. Index. Notes.

Attempts to explain ER by describing her relationship with Lorena Hickok (pp. 175-82, 339-54, 375-77, 707) and through a psychological analysis of her character (pp. 165-74).

F215 ---. *FDR, the New York Years, 1928-1933.* New York: Random House, 1985. 512p. Index. Notes.

ER's activities for the period including her relationships with Earl Miller, Nancy Cook, and Marion Dickerman. Her 1929 European trip. Excerpts of several sections, in particular the one about her European trip, issued as "Symbolic Journey." *Antioch Review* 37 (Summer 1979): 259-76.

F216 Dawe, Nancy Anne. "Sooner or Later, Everyone Who's Anyone Sits for the Bachrachs." *Yankee* 45 (June 1981): 70-75.
ER's photograph is captioned with the information that Louis F. Bachrach approached her about having her photograph taken.

F217 Delano, Daniel W., Jr. *Franklin Roosevelt and the Delano Influence.* Pittsburgh: Nudi, 1946. 368p. Index.
Courtship and marriage (p. 176). "My Day" tribute to Sara Roosevelt (pp. 192, 195). Her letter from the auction catalog of FDR's stamp collection is reproduced (p. 270). ER and the death and burial of FDR (pp. 280, 285, 290, 300-302, 307). ER presents the Hyde Park home to the nation (pp. 315-16).

F218 Donaldson, Norman, and Betty Donaldson. "Roosevelt, Eleanor." *How Did They Die?* By Norman Donaldson and Betty Donaldson. New York: St. Martin's, 1980. 318-19.
Details of her final illness.

F219 Dows, Olin. *Franklin Roosevelt at Hyde Park.* New York: American Artists Group, 1949. 181p.
Illustrated study of the life of FDR with a generous number of quotations from the writings of ER (*This Is My Story* and "My Day") which provide insight into their relationship.

F220 Duffill, Alma. "Coincidence at Mount Vernon." *Alexandrian Magazine* 5 (Summer 1979): 24-25.
Vignette about a dress ER wore.

F221 "E. & E. Roosevelt, Props." *Time* 51 (19 Apr. 1948): 82.
ER and son Elliott plan to open the Val-Kill Inn.

F222 Eastman, John. *Who Lived Where: A Biographical Guide to Homes and Museums.* New York: Facts on File, 1983. xxii + 513p. Index.
Descriptions of ER's residences. Chronological listing (p. 496). Selected residences (pp. 20, 114, 153, 200-201, 203).

F223 "Eleanor Roosevelt and the Styles of Friendship." *Washington Post* 23 Oct. 1979, sect. C: 1-2, 4.
Consists of two articles. Henry Mitchell and Megan Rosenfeld in the more lengthy article discuss reactions to Doris Faber's *The Life of Lorena Hickok.* FDR, Jr. and ER's granddaughter Eleanor Seagraves claim that she used a loving style in her letters to most people. Rhoda Lerman thinks that while it is possible that ER had a physical relationship with other women she preferred men (pp. 1, 4). In the second article Arthur M. Schlesinger, Jr. states that ER followed a 19th century style of letter writing which seems strange in the 20th century. Even if she had been a lesbian Schlesinger does not think that one should let that diminish what she achieved (pp. 1-2). Schlesinger continues with this theme in "Interesting Women." Rev. of *The Life of Lorena Hickok* by Doris Faber and *Eleanor Roosevelt* by Lorena A. Hickok. *New York Times Book Review* 17 Feb. 1980: 3, 25.
See Kenneth C. Lynn, "The First Lady's Lady-Friend." *Times Literary Supplement* 4033 (11 July 1980): 787-88. Lynn, who thinks that Faber misses the significance of ER's gaining self-confidence, also criticizes Schlesinger's reaction to the book.

Lynn's article reissued in his *The Air-line to Seattle: Studies in Literary and Historical Writing about America*, pp. 152-62 (Chicago: Univ. of Chicago Pr., 1983).

Christopher Lehmann-Haupt in his review of the Faber and Hickok books ("Books of the Times." *New York Times* 5 Feb. 1980, sect. C: 9) believes that there are doubts about the nature of the relationship between the two women, but that ER may have been more conscious about her feelings than Faber and others want to admit.

F224 *Eleanor Roosevelt on Her Own: Personal Papers and Objects of Mrs. Roosevelt, Photographs by Dr. A. David Gurewitsch.* N.p.: Eleanor Roosevelt Memorial Foundation, 1963. [4]p.

The program for an exhibition held 22 Oct.-7 Nov. 1963 in New York at Lincoln Center. Lists items exhibited. Reproduced on fiche 004,370 of the New York Public Library's *Schomburg Center Clipping File, 1925-1974.*

F225 "Eleanor Roosevelt's Val-Kill." *Women New York* 1 (Sept./Oct. 1976): 1, 4-7.

Interviews with Nancy Dubner and Joyce Ghee, co-chairs of a committee formed to reclaim Val-Kill as a memorial to ER, (pp. 4-5) and with ER's grandson Curtis Roosevelt. Roosevelt attempts to establish the significance of ER's life and career and the extent of FDR's influence on his wife's accomplishments (pp. 6-7). Includes an introductory statement about her life (p. 1).

F226 Elwood, Ann. "The Elusive Extrovert: Franklin Delano Roosevelt." *The Intimate Sex Lives of Famous People.* Ed. Irving Wallace, et al. New York: Delacorte, 1981. 326-28.

The Roosevelts' marital relations, FDR's affair with Lucy Mercer, and suspicions about other affairs. A separate section on ER raises suspicions about her relationship with Lorena Hickok (p. 328).

F227 Erikson, Joan M. "Nothing to Fear: Notes on the Life of Eleanor Roosevelt." *Daedalus* 93 (Spring 1964): 781-801.

ER's autobiographical writings and what they reveal about her as a child and young woman explain ER's success in becoming a strong and disciplined person with her own agenda who overcame the unhappiness and fear which plagued her early life. As an adult she was driven to be her father's daughter, and FDR became a substitute for him when with her help he overcame handicap and despair. Describes her relationships with her mother, Grandmother Hall, and Marie Souvestre. Reissued in *The Woman in America*, pp. 267-87 (Boston: Houghton-Mifflin, 1967) and in *Our Selves/Our Past*, pp. 307-24 (Baltimore: Johns Hopkins Univ. Pr., 1981).

F228 Faber, Doris. *The Life of Lorena Hickok: ER's Friend.* New York: Morrow, 1980. 384p. Index. Note on Sources.

Relying heavily on letters from the 1930s between ER and Hickok, Faber traces the life of Hickok with ER as an inevitable central character. Also makes much use of Hickok's *Reluctant First Lady* as a supplement to the letters. The article "The Life of Lorena Hickok: ER's Friend." *Publishers Weekly* 217 (1 Feb. 1980): 61, 64 is a discussion, mainly in Faber's words, of the discovery of the letters and of the writing of the book. Excerpts from the letters are in the brief "First Lady a Lesbian?" *Lesbian Tide* (Nov./Dec. 1979): 25. For Helen Gahagan Douglas' reaction to Faber's book, see Douglas' *A Full Life*, pp. 367-69 (Garden City: Doubleday, 1982).

F229 ---. *The Presidents' Mothers.* New York: St. Martin's, 1978. xv + 316p. Index. Bibliography. Notes.

Derivative account of the relationship between ER and Sara Roosevelt (pp. 97-113). Earlier ed. issued as *The Mothers of American Presidents* (New York: New American Library, 1968).

F230 Faber, Harold. "Where Mrs. Roosevelt Got Away from It All." *New York Times* (16 Nov. 1984).

He explains how ER found relaxation and renewal in Val-Kill. Date from photocopy at FDRL. Not located in the *New York Times Index*.

F231 "A Famous Furniture Factory." *Inter-State Milk Producers Review* [West Chester and Philadelphia, Pa.] 14 (Apr. 1934): 9.

ER started her factory to provide employment to youth in the Hyde Park area. Today some of the products of that factory can be found in the White House.

F232 Felsenthal, Carol. *Alice Roosevelt Longworth.* New York: Putnam's, 1988. 320p. Index. Bibliography. Notes.

Although Mrs. Longworth promoted the relationship between FDR and Lucy Mercer and always made ER the subject of ridicule, Felsenthal suggests that she was proud that ER was her cousin (pp. 48-269 passim).

F233 Filler, Martin. "At Home with Sally, Franklin, & Babs." *House & Garden* 154 (Jan. 1982): 106-11, 132-33.

Springwood, the residence in Hyde Park, was always Sara Roosevelt's home. FDR was forever the son and ER always the uncomfortable daughter-in-law.

F234 "First Lady's Protegees." *New Yorker* 16 (10 Aug. 1940): 12-13.

ER befriended and continues to support two small businesswomen in Manhattan: a painter of decorative screens and a woman who runs a small bakery.

F235 Flemion, Jess. "Childhood and Early Married Life." *Eleanor Roosevelt: An American Journey.* Ed. Jess Flemion and Colleen M. O'Connor. San Diego: San Diego State Univ. Pr., 1987. 13-15.

Brief account of the life of ER up to 1920. Serves as an introduction to 24 photographs.

F236 ---. "I Suppose I Must Slow Down." *Eleanor Roosevelt: An American Journey.* Ed. Jess Flemion and Colleen M. O'Connor. San Diego: San Diego State Univ. Pr., 1987. 313-16.

ER did not slow down until the very end. Introduction to 21 photographs.

F237 Fogel, Nancy A. "Change in Hyde Park." Senior thesis. Vassar College, 1979. 52 + [20]p. Bibliography. Notes.

Based primarily on interviews. ER is the subject of several of them, in particular that of the Rev. Gordon Kidd.

F238 Fox, J. DeWitt. "Eleanor Roosevelt's Health Secrets." *Life & Health* 72 (Jan. 1957):18-19, 32-34.

She remains healthy by keeping active, disciplining herself, and doing her best while leaving the rest to God. Includes description of her current activities.

F239 "Franklin and Eleanor Roosevelt's Fortune." *Fortune* 6 (Oct. 1932): 40-45, 105.
   Sources and amounts of their income and financial resources.   Reissued in *The Roosevelt Omnibus*, pp. 136-47 (New York: Knopf, 1934).

F240 *Franklin D. Roosevelt, His Life and Times: An Encyclopedic View*. The G.K. Hall Presidential Encyclopedia Series. Ed. Otis L. Graham, Jr. and Meghan Robinson Wander. Boston: Hall, 1985. 483p. Selected Critical Bibliographies.
   Her married life, family, relationship with Sara Roosevelt, and other aspects of her private life (pp. 52, 136, 172-73, 256-57, 361, 373-74, 380-81).

F241 Freidel, Frank. *Franklin D. Roosevelt: A Rendezvous with Destiny*.   Boston: Little, Brown, 1990. viii + 710p. Index. Notes.
   This one volume study of FDR treats ER's early years (pp. 11-12), marriage and relationship with FDR (pp. 12-14, 43-44, 508-12), and FDR's affair with Lucy Mercer (pp. 33-36, 509, 511).   For a discussion of ER and FDR as a team, see pp. 12-13.

F242 Furman, Bess.   "Home Is Where Hyde Park Is." *Democratic Digest* 15 (July 1938): 10-11.
   Description of the Roosevelts' life at the Hyde Park home and the Val-Kill cottages.

F243 Furnas, J.C. *Stormy Weather: Crosslights on the Nineteen Thirties, An Informal Social History of the United States, 1929-1941*. New York: Putnam's, 1977. 669p. Index. Bibliography, Notes.
   The settlement house worker and the teacher were always to be found in ER's actions and writings.   Her marriage and FDR's rise to prominence prevented her from achieving what she probably wanted most--the opportunity to run a school for girls and lead a life similar to that of Marie Souvestre.   Although ER was accomplished in public relations, Furnas cites examples of how she failed (pp. 173-81, 534-37).

F244 Garrison, Webb. *A Treasury of White House Tales*. Nashville: Rutledge Hill, 1989. 254p. Index.
   A discussion of ER's relationship with Sara Roosevelt (pp. 127-28).   There are numerous other references to ER in this undocumented collection of tidbits about presidents and their families.

F245 Gies, Joseph. *Franklin D. Roosevelt: Portrait of a President*. Garden City: Doubleday, 1971. 233p. Index. Suggested Reading.
   ER's childhood and married life (pp. 11-61 passim.).

F246 Gill, Brendan.   "Stern Daughter of the Voice of God." Rev. of *Eleanor and Franklin* by Joseph P. Lash. *New Yorker* 47 (16 Oct. 1971): 177-81.
   ER is that "stern daughter" who was committed to doing good for others but struggled against her own lack of self respect.   An appreciation of the reasons ER's marriage was a private failure is essential for an understanding of the years which the Roosevelts spent together.

F247 Goodman, Elizabeth B. "A Home of Her Own." *National Parks* 56 (July/Aug. 1982): 4-8.
   ER considered the house at Campobello as her home prior to the Roosevelts' rise to political prominence.

F248 Grafton, David. *The Sisters: Babe Mortimer Paley, Betsey Roosevelt Whitney, Minnie Astor Fosburgh: The Lives and Times of the Fabulous Cushing Sisters.* New York: Villard, 1992. xiv + 316p. Index.

ER and the first wife of son James clashed when Betsey Roosevelt tried to play a role in the running of the White House. When FDR showed his daughter-in-law too much attention and she tried to cater to him, her relationship with ER became more strained. Also discusses ER and her female friends and White House guests (pp. 42-46, 51-52, 98). Less explicit is E.J. Kahn's biography of Betsey's second husband, *Jock: The Life and Times of John Hay Whitney,* pp. 140-41 (Garden City: Doubleday, 1981).

F249 Graham, Hugh Davis. "The Paradox of Eleanor Roosevelt: Alcoholism's Child." *Virginia Quarterly Review* 63 (Spring 1987): 210-30.

Graham provides a clinical explanation to the paradoxes in ER's life and career. As the daughter of the alcoholic Elliott Roosevelt she became the "Lost Child" while also trying to play the role of "Hero." She tried to over achieve in order to make the life of her father meaningful. A comprehensive treatment of this theme with significant attention given to her parents, children, and brother Hall.

F250 "Grandmother Eleanor Roosevelt's Magic Carpet." *Look* (10 Oct. 1950): 77-78, 81-84, 86, 88-89.

Pictorial account of ER's European trip taken with Malvina Thompson and son Elliott and two of his children.

F251 Greenbie, Sydney. "Whither, Eleanor Roosevelt? A Refugee from Speed and Monotony--Val-Kill." *Leisure* (May 1934): 6-9.

ER wants to support craftsmanship, the making of things slowly and carefully. In spite of what she says, modern techniques are used in the making of her furniture. Modern tools and speed are not undesirable in constructing something which lasts since it provides more leisure time for those who construct it, she contends.

F252 Greenblatt, Robert B. "Eleanor Roosevelt (1884-1962): 'The First Lady of the World!'" *Sexualmedizin* 5 (1983): 222-24.

ER's reactions to FDR's relationships with Lucy Mercer and Missy LeHand plus her relationships with Lorena Hickok and Earl Miller. To the end ER wanted to reconcile with FDR, but did not know how to do so. In German.

F253 Gulick, Dorothy. "Mrs. Roosevelt and the Sleeping Bags." *Yankee* 6 (June 1940): 23.

Mrs. Gulick and her husband were shopping for sleeping bags at L.L. Bean's in Freeport, Me. when normal activity in the store was disrupted by the unexpected arrival of ER. The Gulicks do not have fond memories of the experience.

F254 Gunther, John. *Roosevelt in Retrospect: A Profile in History.* New York: Harper, 1950. xii + 410p. Index Bibliography. Notes.

ER's relationship with FDR, her children, and Sara Roosevelt (pp. 178-86, 195-99).

F255 Gurewitsch, A. David. "The Busiest Great-Grandmother of Our Time." *Family Weekly* (11 Oct. 1959): 14-16.

Her private and public life.

F256 Gurewitsch, Edna P. "Remembering Mrs. Roosevelt: An Intimate Memoir."
American Heritage 33 (Dec. 1981): 10-19.
   Gurewitsch and her husband David had a close association with ER during the
final years of ER's life, and this article consists of her answers to questions about ER
and her private life.   Preceded by the author's statement about the loving
relationship which her husband had with ER.   An abbreviated version issued as
"Mrs. Roosevelt: An Intimate Memoir" in *Eleanor Roosevelt: An American Journey*,
pp. 345-50 (San Diego: San Diego State Univ. Pr., 1987)

F257 Hacker, Jeffrey H. *Franklin D. Roosevelt*. An Impact Biography. New York:
Watts, 1983. 119p. Index.
   Many brief references to ER with the emphasis on her private life.

F258 Halsted, Anna Roosevelt. *The Reminiscences of Anna Roosevelt Halsted*. New
York Times Oral History Program. Columbia University Oral History Collection, pt.
4, no. 93. Sanford: Microfilming Corp. of America, 1979. 1 microfiche.
   Daughter Anna talks about ER as a mother and public figure.   This look at the
personal life of ER and FDR is interwoven with views of ER's public career.   Also
discusses other Roosevelt family members.

F259 Hammer, Armand. *Hammer*. By Armand Hammer with Neil Lyndon. New
York: Putnam's, 1987. 544p. Index.
   On ER as character witness for Hammer in 1958 tax case (p. 268).   Hammer's
purchase in 1952 of the Roosevelt cottage at Campobello, ER's restoration of the
cottage with Victor Hammer, and her visits to the island after Hammer purchased
the cottage (pp. 275-76).

F260 Hammer Galleries. *Books from the Library of Mrs. Eleanor Roosevelt,
Exhibition and Sale, September 18 to October 3, 1964*. New York: Hammer Galleries,
1964. 108p.

F261 ---. *Exhibition and Sale of the Collection of the Late President Franklin D.
Roosevelt and Mrs. Eleanor Roosevelt, November 12 to December 3, 1951*. New York:
Hammer Galleries, 1951.

F262 ---. *Exhibition and Sale: Personal Possessions from the Estate of Eleanor
Roosevelt, September 18 to October 3, 1964*. New York: Hammer Galleries, 1964. 51p.
   On cover: "Catalog proceeds for the benefit of the Eleanor Roosevelt Foundation."

F263 Hatch, Alden. *Franklin D. Roosevelt: An Informal Biography*. New York: Holt,
1947. 413p. Index.
   Childhood, courtship, and early married life (pp. 14, 29, 37-47, 49-53, 57-121
passim.

F264 Hay, Peter. *All the Presidents' Ladies: Anecdotes of the Women behind the Men
in the White House*. New York: Viking, 1988. xix + 343p. Index. Bibliography.
   In a topical arrangement there are numerous anecdotes about ER as wife, mother,
and First Lady.   Derived from published sources.

F265 Heath, Mary. "Marriages: Zelda & Scott, Eleanor & Franklin." Rev. of *Exiles from Paradise: Zelda & Scott Fitzgerald* by Sara Mayfield and *Eleanor and Franklin* by Joseph P. Lash. *Massachusetts Review* 13 (Winter/Spring 1972): 281-88.

Through marriage the Roosevelts and the Fitzgeralds sought purpose for their lives. The men's greatest accomplishments were possible because of their wives while the women sought with different degrees of success to emerge as independent figures. An analysis of the two marriages and the relationships which ensued in the public lives of the four figures.

F266 Hennefrund, Bill. "The Last Campobello Survivor." *Yankee* 46 (Sept. 1982): 222-23, 200-204, 207.

Linnea Calder, the last surviving member of the Roosevelt household at Campobello, thinks that the strained relationship between ER and Sara Roosevelt has been exaggerated. Recalls ER as Campobello hostess and during her final visit in 1962.

F267 Herbert, Elizabeth Sweeney. "This Is How I Keep House." *McCall's* 77 (Mar. 1950): 88-90, 93-94.

About entertaining and housekeeping at ER's Val-Kill cottage by one who helps her do it.

F268 Heseltine, Guy. "The Roosevelts at Home: Some Personal Impressions." *Windsor* 77 (Mar. 1933): 421-27.

The friends and personal interests of ER and FDR as they enter the White House. Heseltine claims that ER's assistance to FDR has been on the personal level rather than on the public scene. It is predicted that she will now be able to devote more time to writing including the sharing of her insights as a teacher.

F269 Hess, Stephen. *America's Political Dynasties: From Adams to Kennedy*. Garden City: Doubleday, 1966. 736p. Index. Bibliography. Notes.

In this social history the emphasis is on her personal life (pp. 178-79, 188-92, 195-202, 209-10, 212).

F270 Hill, C.P. *Franklin Roosevelt*. Clarendon Biographies. London: Oxford Univ. Pr., 1966. 62p. Index.

Her married life. Hill makes a case for the influence which ER had on the development of FDR's social consciousness (pp. 9-11).

F271 Hodges, Margaret. *Making a Difference: The Story of an American Family*. New York: Scribner's, 1989. xii + 196p. Index.

ER's 40-year association with a Cornwall, N.Y. family, Mary Sherwood and her five children. One of Mary's daughters worked as a tutor for the Roosevelts, and Anna was engaged to Mary's son.

F272 Holland, Bobby. "'Me and Mrs. Roosevelt': When I Was at Warm Springs." *Psychology* (Aug. 1934): 18-20.

A young polio victim tells how ER made it possible for him to go to Warm Springs.

F273 *Horn* (Todhunter School for Girls).

The school's yearbooks contain dedicatory statements and other references to ER as well as photographs of her. Vols. for 1928 and later are in the Marion Dickerman Papers, FDRL.

F274 Hunt, Irma. "Lucy Mercer." *Dearest Madame: The Presidents' Mistresses.* By Irma Hunt. New York: McGraw-Hill, 1978. 151-79. Notes.

Both ER and Lucy Mercer are central figures. Hunt's popular treatment derived from published sources puts the blame for FDR's affair on ER. ER's childhood, early married years, and her discovery of the affair.

F275 "Hyde Park Comes Alive Again." *TV Guide* 24 (3 Jan. 1976): 8-9.

The ABC television program based on Lash's *Eleanor and Franklin* will give viewers a look at the Roosevelt home.

F276 Jackson, Ronald Vern, et al. *Franklin Delano Roosevelt and Anna Eleanor Roosevelt Ancestry.* Bountiful: Accelerated Indexing Systems, 1980. [37] + 275 + R10p.

Copy not examined.

F277 Jaffe, Eli. "Eleanor Roosevelt--Young at 75!" *Journal of Lifetime Living* 25 (Oct. 1959): 26-28.

She credits her youthful outlook to self-discipline, a brief rest during the day, realizing the value of change and relaxation, and maintaining an interest in life.

F278 Johnson, Gerald W. *Franklin D. Roosevelt: Portrait of a Great Man.* New York: Morrow, 1967. 192p. Index.

The chapter devoted to ER traces her childhood and describes at length the period immediately before her marriage. Johnson makes much of his belief that FDR's most important decision as a young man was to marry ER (pp. 42-49). Johnson made the same claim earlier in *Roosevelt: Dictator or Democrat,* pp. 67-68 (New York: Harper, 1941).

F279 Kahn, E.J. "The Years Alone." *New Yorker* 24 (12 June 1948): 30-34, 36, 39-41; 24 (19 June 1948): 30-34, 36, 39-41.

Her private life in the years immediately after the death of FDR. Also includes a discussion of Westbrook Pegler's attacks on her and her reactions to them.

F280 Karsh, Yousuf. "Anna Eleanor Roosevelt." *Faces of Destiny: Portraits by Karsh.* Chicago: Ziff-Davis; London: Harrap, 1946. 126-27.

Accompaning his photograph of ER is a statement about her charm and the eloquence of her hands.

F281 Kelly, Rita Mae, and Mary Boutilier. *The Making of Political Women: A Study of Socialization and Role Conflict.* Chicago, Nelson-Hall, 1978. x + 368p. Index. Notes.

An examination of the lives of 36 women who played a political role. Being orphaned at an early age and her relationship to family and FDR are assessed for their impact on ER's public life (pp. 107-9, 219-20, 280).

F282 Kiernan, R.H. *President Roosevelt*. London: Harrap, 1948. 240p. Index. Bibliography.
The discussion of the Roosevelts' early married life contains an overview of her strengths and priorities which did not emerge until later (pp. 22-25).

F283 Kleeman, Rita Halle. *Gracious Lady: The Life of Sara Delano Roosevelt*. New York: Appleton-Century, 1935. xvi + 333p. Index.
ER's childhood (pp. 233-35) and her courtship and wedding (pp. 242-44). Leaves the impression that Sara Roosevelt gladly accepted ER as her daughter-in-law and reveals none of the conflicts between the two. Most of the book written with the cooperation of Sara Roosevelt.

F284 Kohn, George C. "Roosevelt-Mercer Affair." *Encyclopedia of American Scandal*. By George C. Kohn. New York: Facts on File, 1989. 287-88.
A good synopsis of the relationship between FDR and Lucy Mercer from 1916 until his death. ER's reaction to that relationship.

F285 Lash, Joseph P. Preface. *Campobello: Roosevelt's "Beloved Island"*. By Stephen O. Muskie. Camden: Down East Books, 1982. xiii-[xvi].
ER shared FDR's love for Campobello. Quotations from her writings are used to describe their visits including her last one in 1962.

F286 ---. *Eleanor Roosevelt on Campobello*. N.p.: n.p., n.d. 12p.
A more extensive account of time spent at Campobello.

F287 ---. *Helen and Teacher: The Story of Helen Keller and Anne Sullivan Macy*. Radcliffe Biography Series. New York: Delacorte, Lawrence, 1988. xiv + 811p. Index. Bibliography.
Brief references to correspondence between Keller and ER and to Keller's meetings with her.

F288 Lewis, Jack. *The Hudson River*. N.p.: n.p., 1964. 272p.
Artist Jack Lewis' account of a visit with ER at Val-Kill near the end of her life (pp. 220-22). The book is dedicated to her.

F289 Lilienthal, David E. *The Journals of David E. Lilienthal*. 7 vols. Vol. 7 Ed. Helen M. Lilienthal. New York: Harper & Row, 1964-1983. Index.
ER is the subject of numerous entries in these 1939-1981 journals of the TVA pioneer and first chair of the Atomic Energy Commission. Topics range from ER trying to learn to smoke and her recollections about what FDR told her about the Yalta Conference.

F290 Lippman, Theo, Jr. *The Squire of Warm Springs: F.D.R. in Georgia, 1924-1945*. Chicago: Playboy, 1977. 248p. Index. Notes on Sources.
The author's interviews with Warm Springs residents reveal that she was not well-liked (pp. 91, 221).

F291 Littell, Norman M. *My Roosevelt Years*. Ed. Jonathan Dembo. Seattle: Univ. of Wash. Pr., 1987. xxi + 422p. Index. Notes.
Littell's diary entries on the death and funeral of ER's brother Hall (pp. 21-22).

F292 Ludwig, Emil. *Roosevelt: A Study in Fortune and Power.* New York: Viking, 1938. xii + 350p. Index.
Includes an account of ER's childhood (pp. 32-46). Translated from the German ed. *Roosevelt, Studie uber Gluck und Macht* (Amsterdam: Querido, 1938).

F293 Maine, Basil. *Franklin Roosevelt: His Life and Achievement.* London: Murray, 1938. vii + 286p.
ER's youth, early association with FDR, engagement, and marriage (pp. 38-45), influence of Marie Souvestre (pp. 45-47), early interest in humanitarianism (pp. 48-50), and early married life (pp. 52-62). Based in part on ER's *This Is My Story*.

F294 "Malvina Thompson Dies in Hospital, 61." *New York Times* 13 Apr. 1953: 27.
The obituary of her long-time secretary recalls their working relationship.

F295 Maney, Patrick J. *The Roosevelt Presence: A Biography of Franklin Delano Roosevelt.* Twayne's Twentieth-Century American Biography Series. New York: Twayne, 1992. xv + 255p. Index. Bibliographic Essay. Notes.
Childhood, courtship, early married life, and FDR's affair with Lucy Mercer (pp. 8-9, 20-23, 83).

F296 Maslow, Abraham H. *Motivation and Personality.* New York: Harper, 1954. xiv + 411p. Index. Bibliography.
Maslow studied ER as a self-actualizing personality. She is listed in the chapter on "self-actualizing people" as one of Maslow's subjects (p. 202). Although not mentioned, she is believed to be one of the subjects discussed in his "Lessons from Peak Experiences." *Journal of Humanistic Psychology* 2 (1962): 9-13 and *The Farther Reaches of Human Nature*, pp. 41-52 (New York: Viking, 1971).

F297 Matson, Howard. Letter. *World* 2 (Nov./Dec. 1988): 47.
As a young Unitarian minister in the l930s Matson spent time with the same New England farm family ER had visited in 1932. He believes that the human kindness associated with her visit is worth remembering.

F298 McClure, Ruth. *Eleanor Roosevelt: Patron, Practitioner and Promoter of the Arts.* Hyde Park: The Eleanor Roosevelt Center at Val-Kill, 1987. [14]p. Notes.
ER developed an appreciation for the arts early in her life. She practiced the art of writing and promoted a broad range of the arts as First Lady and in her private life.

F299 McElvaine, Robert S. *The Great Depression: America, 1929-1941.* New York: Times Books, 1984. xiv + 402p. Index. Notes.
The basic facts of ER's personal life and a discussion of her learning of FDR's affair with Lucy Mercer. While ER and Lorena Hickok had a close relationship, he doubts that there was any physical involvement (pp. 106-10).

F300 Meehan, Lina di Nogarole, Countess. "The Roosevelt Family." *Empire* 1 (Xmas 1932): 409.
A visit to Hyde Park. Most of the article is devoted to ER--her early life and avocations and the graceful hostess which the author found her to be.

F301 Mehling, Harold. "Living Legends." *Today's Health* 37 (Mar. 1959): 6, 57.
Without identifying her, facts are presented about ER's childhood and adult life. Readers are then asked to guess the identity of this shy and unselfish woman.

F302 Miller, Hope Ridings. *Scandals in the Highest Office: Facts and Fictions in the Private Lives of Our Presidents*. New York: Random House, 1973. 280p. Index. Bibliography.
ER's reaction to FDR's relationship with Lucy Mercer and others. Based on an unidentified interview and published works including ER's autobiographical writings (pp. 33-44).

F303 Miller, Nathan. *FDR: An Intimate History*. Garden City: Doubleday, 1983. viii + 563p. Index. Bibliography. Notes.
Frequent glimpses into ER's private life. Chapter "Call It Loving" describes her courtship and early married life (pp. 41-54).

F304 ---. *The Roosevelt Chronicles*. Garden City: Doubleday, 1979. vi + 377p. Index. Bibliography.
ER's early life, marriage, children, and death. The FDR-Lucy Mercer affair (pp. 231-37, 244-48, 266-71, 282-84, 287-89, 302-6, 336-38, 341-42).

F305 Mitchell, Jack. *Executive Privilege: Two Centuries of White House Scandals*. New York: Hippocrene, 1992. 430p. Index. Bibliography.
A chatty account with few details of the relationships between FDR and Lucy Mercer and ER and Lorena Hickok (pp. 167-68, 181-83, 172-74).

F306 Mitgang, Herbert. "Letters Show Strain in Roosevelts' Domestic Life." *New York Times* 2 May 1982: 66.
Highlights from the letters of ER and Anna published as *Mother & Daughter* illustrate both the strain between ER and FDR and how dependent they were on one another.

F307 Morris, Sylvia Jukes. *Edith Kermit Roosevelt: Portrait of a First Lady*. New York: Coward, McCann & Geoghegan, 1980. 581p. Index. Bibliography. Notes.
ER declined Edith Roosevelt's invitation to hold her wedding in the White House. The Roosevelts' gift to the couple (pp. 288-89).

F308 Moses, Belle. *Franklin Delano Roosevelt: The Minute Man of '33*. New York: Appleton-Century, 1933. ix + 202p.
Undocumented account of ER's childhood association with FDR and a description of ER as a young woman (pp. 53-66).

F309 "Motorist." *Time* 48 (26 Aug. 1946): 38.
A brief account of the automobile accident which broke ER's front teeth. Based on a "My Day" column. See also "Crash." *Newsweek* 28 (26 Aug. 1946): 50 and "Picture of the Week." *Life* 21 (9 Sept. 1946): 36-37.

F310 Mouckley, Florence. "Eleanor Roosevelt's Controversial Friendship." *Christian Science Monitor* 9 Apr. 1980, Eastern ed.: 17.
ER looked to Lorena Hickok for companionship. Hickok was obsessed with her, and it destroyed her career.

F311 "Mrs. Roosevelt and Her Val-Kill Partners Give Their Furniture Shop to an Employee." *New York Times* 14 May 1936: 22.

The furniture portion of Val-Kill Industries has been given to an employee and will be moved from the Roosevelt estate. The pewter and iron craft portion has been given to another employee. Nancy Cook will continue to advise on all aspects of the operation.

F312 "Mrs. Roosevelt in Quadruplicate." *Life* 30 (18 June 1951): 101.

Reproduction of Douglas Chandler's montage with a palmist interpretation.

F313 "Mrs. Roosevelt Joins Faculty at Brandeis." *New York Times* 4 Oct. 1959: 1, 41.

The announcement that she will lecture in the area of international relations includes a description of the courses that she will help teach, information on her own education, and how she has used travel to enhance her limited formal schooling. John H. Fenton, "Mrs. Roosevelt Begins Teaching." *New York Times* 6 Oct. 1959: 22 discusses her first day in a Brandeis classroom. Her appointment was hailed in "Professor Roosevelt." Editorial. *New York Times* 5 Oct. 1959: 30.

F314 "Mrs. Roosevelt on Connubial Bliss." *Argonaut* 123 (18 Feb. 1944): 1-2.

In a "My Day" column she makes the interesting conclusion that she has known "few happy marriages." She probably considers her own a happy one since as wife of the President she is provided with the means of giving "instructions for the salvation of the world."

F315 "Mrs. Roosevelt: She Laughs over 'Terrible Hats.'" *Newsweek* 1 (17 Feb. 1933): 16.

The woman who will soon become First Lady has many interests and enjoys a joke on herself such as one about her hats.

F316 "Mrs. Roosevelt's Christmas Sampler: Best-Loved Christmas Words and Customs of a Much-Loved Lady." *McCall's* 90 (Dec. 1962): 20.

Her favorites about Christmas.

F317 "...Mrs. Roosevelt's Hands Make Interesting Studies." *Life* 17 (11 Dec. 1944): 14-15.

Yousuf Karsh's photograph of ER plus those of her hands, a feature which Karsh found to be fascinating.

F318 "Mrs. Roosevelt's Story of Val-Kill Furniture." *Delineator* 123 (Nov. 1933): 22-23, plus unidentified page number.

The style of furniture manufactured and the skill required to make it.

F319 Nowlan, Alden. *Campobello: The Outer Island*. Toronto: Clarke, Irwin, 1975. 132p.

Three chapters on the history of the island deal with the Roosevelts and the time they spent there (pp. 101-19).

F320 O'Day, Mrs. Daniel (Caroline). "Copying Old Furniture." *Quarterly* (Women's City Club of New York) (Oct. 1928): 17-19.

The type of furniture which is being produced and how it is made. Nancy Cook, not ER, is credited with being the force behind the endeavor. Also issued in a slightly expanded form as "Bringing Back Artistic Furniture of the 17th Century." *Motordom* (March 1929): 8-9 and "The Art of Creating Heirlooms." *Alumni News* (Syracuse University) (Sept. 1930): 5-6, 36.

F321 Parsons, Frances Theodora. *Perchance Some Day*. N.p.: Parsons, 1951. xv + 360p.
Parsons claims to have known her from birth, and this memoir provides brief glances of ER: as a child (p. 64), in 1911 (pp. 249, 280), in a 1924 political debate with the author (p. 328), and in 1925 (p. 330). Parsons' dislike of ER is evident.

F322 Patton, Lillian, and Thomas Patton. "Eleanor Roosevelt's 'Education for Citizenship.'" *Social Studies* 75 (Nov./Dec. 1984): 236-39. Notes.
ER felt that a primary role of education is to produce informed citizens capable of promoting democracy, and she taught through her speeches and writings as well as in the classroom. Her Todhunter School notebooks are used to describe the classes which she taught and the methods which she employed.

F323 "The People Concerned." *Newsweek* 51 (10 Feb. 1958): 69.
Following a review of the Broadway opening of *Sunrise at Campobello* are ER's reactions. She read the play and liked it, but she does not think that it has much to do with her. For similar comments by ER, see Fern Maria, "I Told Them to Make It a Good Play and They Did." *New York Post* 31 Jan. 1958: 2, 63.
Also about the play is "A Time of Courage for Young F.D.R.: Eleanor Roosevelt Helps Actor Prepare New Play." *Life* 44 (10 Feb. 1958): 91-94 which describes how ER helped Ralph Bellamy learn FDR's mannerisms. Mostly photographs.

F324 Perkins, Frances. *The Roosevelt I Knew*. New York: Viking, 1946. viii + 408p. Index.
FDR's family including FDR and ER as parents (pp. 61-68).

F325 Perney, Linda M. "FDR's Hyde Park." *Travel Holiday* 174 (Feb. 1991): 106-9.
An overview of the Roosevelt estate and the lives which FDR, ER, and Sara Roosevelt lived there. Aimed at the casual tourist.

F326 Pickard, M. Fortescue. *The Roosevelts in America*. London: Joseph, 1941. 288p.
ER and other women in the family receive little attention in this history of 300 years of Roosevelts.

F327 Pierce, Eleanor G. "Mrs. Franklin D. Roosevelt, Attending the White Top Music Festival Rode the Trails Her Father Covered 40 Years Ago." *Norfolk and Western Magazine* 11 (Sept. 1933): 313-17.
On 12 Aug. ER traveled by train through Va. on the Norfolk and Western to the White Top Music Festival which she attended as the daughter of Elliott Roosevelt. While there she listened to the music of Frank Blevins and awarded him the ribbons which he won that day. The following year he wrote seeking a public endorsement from her. She sent a reply, but no endorsement. For an account of Blevins' encounter with ER, see Marshall Wyatt, "Frank & Eleanor." *Old-Time Herald* 2 (Feb./Apr. 1991): 18-19.

F328 Potter, Jeffrey. *Men, Money & Magic: The Story of Dorothy Schiff*. New York: Coward, McCann & Geoghegan, 1976. 352p. Index.

This biography of *New York Post* owner Dorothy Schiff includes reminiscences of ER from the 1920s through the 1950s. Reports Nancy Cook's claim that ER and FDR would have divorced because of Lucy Mercer had FDR not contracted polio (p. 144). A memo from Schiff describes a dinner in the 1950s with ER and is the book's most substantial assessment of her: shy and fearful of emotional involvement but capable of strong feelings about matters of interest to her (pp. 255-56).

F329 "President Gives Bride Away." *New York Times* 18 Mar. 1905: 2.

The marriage ceremony of FDR and ER is described, members of the wedding party are identified, and selected guests named.

F330 "Profits Are Denied by Mrs. Roosevelt." *New York Times* 24 Apr. 1934: 6.

Her rebuttal to a 22 Apr. claim in the U.S. Senate contends that she is not making a profit from Val-Kill Industries and is not using her position as First Lady to promote the furniture.

F331 *Public Auction...Mr. & Mrs. John A. Roosevelt...March 7, 1970....* Garrison-on-Hudson: O. Rundle Gilbert, Auctioneer, 1970. 30p.

Included among the items to be sold are 75 pieces of Val-Kill furniture. The foreword contains a brief description of the furniture factory and ER's involvement with it (p. 1).

F332 Reyes, Karen C. "Eleanor's Christmas." *Modern Maturity* 29 (Dec. 1986/Jan. 1987): unnumbered regional page.

Descriptions of how ER planned for Christmas and how the National Park Service recreates an ER Christmas at Val-Kill.

F333 Rixey, Lilian. *Bamie: Theodore Roosevelt's Remarkable Sister*. New York: McKay, 1963. xi + 308p.

Anna Roosevelt Cowles ("Bamie"), ER's aunt, was an influential figure to the young ER (pp. 230, 288). ER made summer visits to her home and lived with her in Washington during the winters of 1903 and 1904 (pp. 167, 181-82, 227-30, 257). ER's memories of her in her own later years (p. 294).

F334 Roberts, Gary Boyd. "Franklin Delano Roosevelt." *Ancestors of American Presidents*. Prelim. ed. Comp. Gary Boyd Roberts. Santa Clarita: Carl Boyer, 3rd, 1989. 65-71.

FDR's ancestors and, therefore, in part ER's ancestors. "Published in cooperation with the New England Historic Genealogical Society."

F335 Rollyson, Carl. *Nothing Ever Happens to the Brave: The Story of Martha Gellhorn*. New York: St. Martin's, 1990. xvii + 398p. Index. Notes.

A description of the closeness of ER's relationship with David Gurewitsch, how she and Gellhorn both sought his affections, and the advice which ER gave Gurewitsch about his wife and Gellhorn. The situation strained relations between ER and Gellhorn (pp. 240-46, 253, 274). Based on ER's letters published as *A World of Love*.

F336 Roosevelt, Elliott. "My Mother." *Eleanor Roosevelt: An American Journey.* Ed. Jess Flemion and Colleen M. O'Connor. San Diego: San Diego State Univ. Pr., 1987. 43-46.
ER as a devoted mother.

F337 Roosevelt, Felicia Warburg. *Doers & Dowagers.* Garden City: Doubleday, 1975. ix + 228p.
In the sketch of Alice Roosevelt Longworth is her candid opinion that ER was not very interesting (pp. 219-25).

F338 Roosevelt, Franklin D. *F.D.R.: His Personal Letters, Early Years.* Ed. Elliott Roosevelt. New York: Duell, Sloan and Pearce, 1947. xvi + 543p. Index.
ER is mentioned in letters written to and by FDR during their early association and engagement. There are also letters from ER to Sara Roosevelt.

F339 ---. *F.D.R.: His Personal Letters, 1905-1928.* Ed. Elliott Roosevelt and James N. Rosenau. New York: Duell, Sloan and Pearce, 1948. xix + 674p. Index.
Letters written from ER and FDR to Sara Roosevelt during their honeymoon in Europe. Many letters about ER, to her, and from her to recipients other than FDR, but ER is not named in the index. Excerpts issued as "Letters from Our Honeymoon." *Ladies' Home Journal* 65 (Dec. 1948): 42-43, 95-97, 99, 102, 104-5. An analysis issued as "My Dear Franklin." *Time* 52 (13 Dec. 1948): 28.

F340 ---. *F.D.R.: His Personal Letters, 1928-1945.* 2 vols. (xvii + 1615p.) Ed. Elliott Roosevelt and Joseph P. Lash. New York: Duell, Sloan and Pearce, 1950. Index.
Letters about ER and to her. Memoranda exchanged between ER and FDR. Some letters from ER to recipients other than FDR.

F341 ---. *The Roosevelt Reader: Selected Speeches, Messages, Press Conferences, and Letters of Franklin D. Roosevelt.* Ed. Basil Rauch. New York: Holt, Rinehart and Winston, 1957. xii + 391p. Bibliography.
For the period 1914-34 there are six letters to ER which blend personal matters with a discussion of public issues. A detailed table of contents is provided.
All correspondence to ER contained in this work is reprinted from the four volumes of FDR's personal letters issued 1947-1950.

F342 Roosevelt, James, and Sidney Shalett. *Affectionately, F.D.R.: A Son's Story of a Lonely Man.* New York: Harcourt, Brace, 1959; Westport: Greenwood, 1975. 394p. Index. Bibliography.
Drawn from the author's recollections and from letters, this intimate biography by FDR's oldest son is also a study of ER. The author discusses at length ER as a parent (pp. 5-12, 23-25, 35-43, 81-86, 91-92, 96-98, 112-13, 172-74, 219-20). Appears to be excerpted as "My Mother, Eleanor Roosevelt." *Good Housekeeping* 150 (May 1960): 62-63, 134, 136, 138, 141 and as "My Mother, Eleanor Roosevelt." *Congressional Record* (3 May 1960): 9340-42.

F343 Roosevelt, Patricia Peabody. *I Love a Roosevelt.* Garden City: Doubleday, 1967. xii + 387p.
Married to ER's son Elliott only a few years before ER died, the author describes the few occasions when she was with her (pp. 103-11, 149-61, 163-66, 185-90, 197-202) and provides an insider's account of ER's death and funeral (pp. 1-4,

209-31). Excerpts issued as "Eleanor Roosevelt: A Great Lady's Last Brave Days." *Good Housekeeping* 164 (June 1967): 80-83, 142, 144, 146, 148.

F344 Roosevelt, Sara D. *My Boy Franklin*. By Sara D. Roosevelt as told to Isabel Leighton and Gabrielle Forbush. New York: Long & Smith, 1933. viii + 115p.
   In this mother's story of her son ER is presented as a perfect young wife, mother, and daughter-in-law (pp. 62-68).

F345 "Roosevelt for Bryn Mawr?" *Time* 35 (1 Jan. 1940): 42.
   Her qualifications are listed, but serious consideration of ER as president of Bryn Mawr will depend on FDR's future.

F346 "Roosevelt Home to Show Furniture." *New York Times* 15 Nov. 1931: sect. 2: 4.
   About an exhibition of Val-Kill furniture to be shown at her New York home. Includes a lengthy description of why ER started Val-Kill Industries and the type of furniture which is being made.

F347 Rosenman, Samuel I. *The Reminiscences of Samuel I. Rosenman*. New York Times Oral History Program, Columbia University Collection, pt. 2, no. 163. Sanford: Microfilming Corp. of America, 1975. 3 microfiche. Index.
   ER liked to "mother" her children and others too much. Since she considered it a great handicap to be the child of a President, she condoned more than most mothers would have done. Recollections of ER during FDR's years as Gov. of N.Y. and as President (pp. 99-104).

F348 Ross, Leland M., and Allen N. Grobin. *This Democratic Roosevelt: The Life Story of "F.D.": An Authentic Biography*. New York: Dutton, 1932. 312p. Index.
   The first meeting of ER and FDR and their early married life (pp. 161-62).

F349 Ross, Shelley. *Fall from Grace: Sex, Scandal, and Corruption in American Politics from 1702 to the Present*. New York: Ballantine, 1988. xxi + 327p. Index. References.
   A tale of FDR's relationships with Lucy Mercer and Missy LeHand and what ER knew about them. ER's relationship with Lorena Hickok. Relies on writings of Elliott Roosevelt (pp. 172-79).

F350 Schlesinger, Arthur M., Jr. *The Crisis of the Old Order, 1919-1933*. The Age of Roosevelt [1]. Boston: Houghton Mifflin, 1956. xiv + 557p. Index. Notes.
   The childhood of ER and her engagement and marriage (pp. 325-29). Reissued in 1988 with a new foreword (Boston: Houghton Mifflin).

F351 ---. "F.D.R.'s Secret Romance." *Ladies' Home Journal* 83 (Nov. 1966): 66, 68, 71.
   In the summer of 1917 FDR may have had an emotional involvement with Lucy Mercer, but the press is now making too much of it. He doubts that ER and FDR avoided divorce because of any possible harm to his political career nor that she remained bitter about the relationship. Written on the occasion of the publication of Jonathan Daniels' *The Time between the Wars* (Garden City: Doubleday, 1966). For a reaction, see Kenneth S. Lynn's "The First Lady's Lady-Friend." *Times Literary Supplement* 4033 (11 July 1980): 787-88 and reissued in his *The Air-Line to*

Seattle: Studies in Literary and Historical Writing about America, pp. 152-62 (Chicago: Univ. of Chicago Pr., 1983).

F352 ---. "Historic Houses: Campobello." *Architectural Digest* 42 (Mar. 1985): 220-28.
The cottage at Campobello and the style of life the Roosevelts enjoyed on the island.

F353 Schorr, Daniel L. "Mrs. Roosevelt Pays an Ancestral Call." *Christian Science Monitor Magazine* 22 July 1950: 13.
ER and son Elliott visit the van Roosevelts in Oud Vossemeer, Holland. However, no one can be certain that these are distant relations of the Roosevelts.

F354 Seagraves, Eleanor. "Memories of Grandmere." *Eleanor Roosevelt: An American Journey*. Ed. Jess Flemion and Colleen M. O'Connor. San Diego: San Diego State Univ. Pr., 1987. 337-43.
In her recollections of ER, Anna Roosevelt's daughter discusses her mother, FDR, Lucy Mercer, Malvina Thompson, and Lorena Hickok.

F355 Sears, John F. "Eleanor Roosevelt and the Uses of Time." *Directions* (IBM) (Sept. 1984): 19-22.
She followed a daily routine, maintained self control, and was at peace with herself. But the greatest source of her energy and the need to make the most of her time was the interest she had in what she was doing.

F356 Sherman, E. David. "Geriatric Profile of Eleanor Roosevelt (1884-1962)." *Journal of the American Geriatric Society* 31 (Jan. 1983): 28-33. Notes.
She had what is required for a productive life. An analysis of the mental and physical state of ER as she aged and a clinical view of her final illness.

F357 Sibley, John. "Mrs. Roosevelt Left Mementos to Many." *New York Times* 16 Nov. 1962: 1, 21.
The details of her will. Highlights provided in "Grandmother's Pink China." *Newsweek* 60 (26 Nov. 1962): 44.

F358 "Sister's Tribute." *Time* 38 (6 Oct. 1941): 17-18.
Reports on the life and death of ER's brother Hall and reprints her tribute to him from "My Day" of 26 Sept. 1941.

F359 Stevenson, Adlai E. *The Papers of Adlai E. Stevenson*. Ed. Walter Johnson, et al. 8 Vols. Boston: Little, Brown, 1972-1979. Index. Notes.
Letters to ER in 1949 and 1951 in which he discusses personal matters and tries to arrange for them to see one another during her domestic travels (v. 6, pp. 130, 357, 377, 484).
Letters to her about personal matters, e.g., visits, casual opportunities to see her, and the death of her granddaughter in 1960 (v. 7, pp. 92, 141, 148, 313, 356, 558-59). A 1958 letter about the value of educational films (v. 7, p. 179) and one about her planned appearance on the Chicago television program *V.I.P.* on 14 Dec. 1958 (v. 7, p. 303).
Messages from Stevenson to ER during her final illness (v. 8, pp. 286, 294-95) and other personal communication (v. 8, p. 126, 170, 173).

F360 Stidger, William L. *These Amazing Roosevelts*. New York: Macfadden, 1938. 89p.

While more attention is devoted to FDR than to the other family members, there is coverage of ER: domineering role of Sara Roosevelt (p. 15), ER's engagement and marriage (pp. 15-17), and ER as a grandmother (pp. 43-45).

F361 Storey, Walter Rendell. "The Home Crafts Movement Grows." *New York Times Magazine* 15 Apr. 1934: 17.

An article about the Mrs. F.D. Roosevelt Home Crafts Project, an effort named in honor of ER's support of the crafts movement.

F362 Storm, Carson. *The Roosevelt Christmases, 1933-1945*. Arlington: Storm, 1983. 133p. Bibliography. Typescript.

Extensive coverage of Roosevelt family Christmas celebrations.   Available at FDRL.

F363 "Styled by Mrs. F.D.R." *New York Times Magazine* 15 Oct. 1950: 70-71.

Six photographs illustrating ER's changing hair styles from 1905 to the present.

F364 Sullivan, Michael John. *Affairs of State: The True, Untold Stories of the Illicit Love Lives of the Presidents of the United States*. New York: Hampton House, 1987. 242p.

In the chapter "Mistress 'Hers'" Sullivan concludes that ER was homosexual and Lorena Hickok was her lover. He tries to refute arguments put forward by others that there was no sexual relationship between the two women (pp. 189-96). The chapter "Mistress 'His'" discusses ER's reactions to FDR's relationships with Lucy Mercer, Missy LeHand, and Princess Martha of Norway (pp. 173-85). Reissued as *Presidential Passions: The Love Affairs of America's Presidents--from Washington and Jefferson to Kennedy and Johnson* (New York: Shapolsky, 1991). "Mistress 'Hers'" appears on pp. 145-51; "Mistress 'His'" on pp. 133-43.

F365 *Tax Evasion and Avoidance: Hearings before the Joint Committee on Tax Evasion and Avoidance, Seventy-fifth Congress, First Session. Pt. 4, July 28, 1937*. Washington: GPO, 1937. iii + pp. 425-40.

Transcript of the testimony of Robert H. Jackson, Assistant Attorney General, who claims that ER's practice of donating what she is paid for her radio broadcasts directly to charity does not constitute tax evasion. Also includes his response to questions from members of the committee.

Earlier Rep. Hamilton Fish queried Treasury Secretary Henry Morgenthau, Jr. about Jackson's ruling. Fish's letter to Morgenthau and his statement on ER's approach to reporting her income are available as "Urging the Treasury Department to Issue an Official Ruling Regarding Contributions to Charity." *Congressional Record Appendix* (19 July 1937): A1823-24.

Reported in the *New York Times* as "Fish Lays Evasion to Mrs. Roosevelt." 10 July 1937: 4 and "Drops Tax Inquiry of Mrs. Roosevelt." 29 July 1937: 21.

F366 Teague, Michael. *Mrs. L: Conversations with Alice Roosevelt Longworth*. Garden City: Doubleday, 1981. xviii + 203p. Notes.

Mrs. Longworth admired her cousin ER for her accomplishments as First Lady but found her tedious and boring. Covers childhood to ER's death (pp. 151-63). Similar information is in Henry Brandon, "A Talk with an 83-Year-Old Enfant

Terrible." *New York Times Magazine* 6 Aug. 1967: 8-9, 69-70, 72-74 and Jean Vanden Heuvel, "The Sharpest Wit in Washington." *Saturday Evening Post* 238 (4 Dec. 1965): 30-33.

F367 Teichmann, Howard. *Alice: The Life and Times of Alice Roosevelt Longworth.* Englewood Cliffs: Prentice-Hall, 1977. xvi + 286p. Index. Bibliography. Notes.
Her mimicking of ER began at an early age (pp. 49-51). Comparison of ER and Alice as young women (pp. 160-61) and as newspaper columnists (pp. 182-83).

F368 "These Are the Distinguished Editors of the Junior Literary Guild." *Young Wings* (undated): [10-11].
A brief description of her activities as educator and writer. Undated copy available at FDRL.

F369 Thompson, Darryl. "Eleanor Roosevelt: The Shakers and the Meaning of Craftsmanship." *Shaker Messenger* 13 (1991): 13-15, 19-21. Notes.
Examination of ER's association with the Shakers and its relationship to her interest in furniture and crafts at Val-Kill. Relies heavily on coverage of Val-Kill Industries in the *New York Times*.

F370 "3,360 Intimate Letters Raise Questions about Lorena Hickok, the Woman Eleanor Roosevelt Called 'Darling.'" *People Weekly* 12 (12 Nov. 1979): 42-43.
Faber's *The Life of Lorena Hickok*, based on these letters, suggests an intimate relationship between ER and Hickok. The truth may never be known.

F371 Tinling, Marion. *Women Remembered: A Guide to Landmarks of Women's History in the United States.* New York: Greenwood, 1986. xiv + 796p. Index. Notes.
ER is the subject of three entries which describe her activities at the time she resided at Campobello, Val-Kill, and in the New York townhouse built by Sara Roosevelt (pp. 26, 375-76, 404).

F372 *To Enrich Young Life: Ten Years with the Junior Literary Guild in the Schools of Our Country.* Garden City: Junior Literary Guild, 1939. vi + 144p.
ER served on the screening board. Her experience as a mother and an educator, her belief in the value of reading, and the opportunity to talk with parents and children during her travels give her insight into the types of books which are suitable for today's young people (p. 16-17).

F373 "Too Busy to Be Sick." *Time* 80 (16 Nov. 1962): 67.
A detailed account of her final illness.

F374 Torres, Louis. *Eleanor Roosevelt National Historic Site (Val-Kill), Hyde Park, New York. Historic Resource Study.* Denver: Denver Service Center, Mid-Atlantic/North Atlantic Team, Branch of Historic Preservation, National Park Service, Dept. of the Interior, 1980. vii + 221p. Bibliography. Notes.
The life of ER, why Val-Kill structures were erected, their construction and renovation, Val-Kill Industries, and Val-Kill as ER's home.

F375 ---. *Eleanor Roosevelt National Historic Site (Val-Kill), Hyde Park, New York. Historic Structure Report. Historical Data.* Denver: Denver Service Center, Mid-Atlantic/North Atlantic Team, Branch of Historic Preservation, National Park

Service, Dept. of the Interior, 1980. viii + 121p. + 16 appendices. Bibliography. Notes.

The initial construction of Val-Kill structures and their renovation. Uses made of structures by ER. A list of the historical and archeological studies conducted by the National Park Service at Val-Kill is in Dwight T. Pitcaithley, *The National Park Service in the Northeast: A Cultural Resource Management Bibliography*, pp. 63-64 (Boston: Dept. of the Interior, National Park Service, North Atlantic Regional Office, Division of Cultural Resources, 1984).

F376 Trohan, Walter. *Political Animals: Memoirs of a Sentimental Cynic*. Garden City: Doubleday, 1975. xiii + 411p.

In these memoirs of a Washington reporter attention is given to the suspected affairs of FDR and ER's knowledge of them. Also included is information on FDR's relationship with Princess Martha of Norway and ER's relationship with Earl Miller (pp. 134-38).

F377 Tugwell, Rexford G. *FDR: Architect of an Era*. New York: Macmillan, 1967. xvii + 270p. Index. Additional Readings.

ER's early life and marriage (pp. 28-30) and death (p. 260).

F378 Tyska, Cynthia Ann. "A Comparative Case Study of Self-Actualization in Eleanor Roosevelt and Antoine de Saint-Exupery." Thesis (M.A.) Univ. of Ill. at Urbana-Champaign, 1980. iv + 101p. Bibliography.

ER was used as the subject to test Abraham Maslow's theory of self-actualization. Statements by and about her from Lash's *Eleanor: The Years Alone* were rated and compared to the results from an earlier study about Antoine de Saint-Exupery. Tyska concludes that ER was a non-transcending, self-actualizing person.

Based on the Tyska study is Michael M. Piechowski and Cynthia Tyska, "Self-Actualization Profile of Eleanor Roosevelt, a Presumed Nontranscender." *Genetic Psychology Monographs* 105 (1982): 95-153. Bibliography. Notes.

F379 *The Val-Kill Cookbook*. Comp. and ed. Eleanor R. Seagraves. Hyde Park: Eleanor Roosevelt Center at Val-Kill, 1984. 150p.

In the introduction Seagraves explains that this collection of recipes is intended to convey ER's love of entertaining family and friends. Also describes the establishment and activities of the Eleanor Roosevelt Historic Site and the Eleanor Roosevelt Center at Val-Kill (pp. [1-4]). The book includes sketches and photographs of ER at Val-Kill.

F380 "Val-Kill-Cottage Waar de Koningin Logeerde." *Vrouw en Haar Huis* (1952): 210-12.

In Dutch. Copy not examined.

F381 Walker, Turnley. *Roosevelt and the Warm Springs Story*. New York: Wyn, 1953. 311p.

This popular and undocumented account includes a description of the Roosevelts' first visit to Warm Springs and ER's concern about living conditions in the area (pp. 19-35). Her visit with a young polio patient (pp. 191-93).

F382 Ward, Geoffrey C. "Eleanor Roosevelt Drew Her Strength from a Sanctuary Called Val-Kill." *Smithsonian* 15 (Oct. 1984): 62-66, 68, 70-73.
She cherished the life which she made for herself at Val-Kill.

F383 ---. "First among First Ladies." Rev. of *Love, Eleanor* by Joseph P. Lash and *Mother & Daughter* ed. Bernard Asbell. *New York Times Book Review* 13 June 1982: 11, 28-29.
These books provide insight into ER's personality and help to put Doris Faber's *The Life of Lorena Hickok* in perspective. ER wrote letters to maintain bonds and friendships, and many of those letters were affectionate but less so than her early ones to Hickok. Toward the end of her life she should have found satisfaction in knowing that she was a beloved figure, but she did not.

F384 ---. "The House at Hyde Park." *American Heritage* 38 (Apr. 1987): 41-46, 48-50.
Sara Roosevelt devoted her life to her son and her home. ER always felt like a visitor and retreated to Val-Kill.

F385 ---. "Mrs. Roosevelt Faces Fear." *American Heritage* 35 (Oct./Nov. 1984): 18, 20.
Unlike FDR, self-confidence did not come naturally to ER. She had to overcome fears beginning with childhood. An informal review of Lash's *A World of Love* and *Life Was Meant to Be Lived*, plus Joan Hoff-Wilson and Marjorie Lightman, eds., *Without Precedent* and *Eleanor Roosevelt, an Eager Spirit* by Dorothy Dow Butturff.

F386 ---. "Outing Mrs. Roosevelt." Rev. of *Eleanor Roosevelt, 1884-1933* by Blanche Wiesen Cook. *New York Review of Books* 39 (24 Sept. 1992): 49-52, 54-56.
Cook's use of sources in her analysis of ER's personal life is criticized in this thorough review. A different look at how Cook used sources is David M. Kennedy, "Up from Hyde Park." *New York Times Book Review* 19 Apr. 1992: 1, 19, 21. See also Florence King, "In Bed with Mrs. Roosevelt." *National Review* 44 (22 June 1992): 51-53; Christine Stansell, "Wonder Woman." *New Republic* 206 (25 May 1992): 36-39; Brenda Maddox, "The Perfect Wife." *Book Review* (Los Angeles Times) 19 Apr. 1992: 1, 8; and Merle Rubin, "A Feminist Portrait of Eleanor Roosevelt." *Christian Science Monitor* 19 May 1992, Eastern ed.: 13. There is also Joyce Antler, "A Purposeful Journey." *Nation* 255 (13 July 1992): 58-60 and Kenneth S. Lynn's critical review in *American Spectator* 25 (Oct. 1992): 58-60. Other reviews which emphasize Cook's treatment of ER's private life are Elizabeth Fox-Genovese, "First Ladylike Behaviour." *Times Literary Supplement* 4703 (21 May 1993): 13-14 and Cynthia Harrison's review in *American Historical Review* 98 (Feb. 1993): 123-25.

F387 Watson, Lee Rae. "Revival of Hand Craft: New York Governor's Wife and Associates Reproducing Furniture of Early Periods." *Modern Home* (ca. 1930).
Copy not examined.

F388 "White House: Just a Parent at Groton." *Newsweek* 1 (27 May 1933): 12.
ER visits sons FDR, Jr. and John at Groton.

F389 Whiting, Frances. "The Most Unforgettable Character I've Met." *Reader's Digest* 57 (Aug. 1950): 19-22.

Whiting recalls a 1936 meeting with ER at Val-Kill. The day was a constant interruption with the unpretentious ER doing thoughtful and kind things for others.

F390 "Who's a Rascal?" *Time* 55 (13 Mar. 1950): 43.
Last week in his column Westbrook Pegler tried to prove that ER is descended from Rufus King Bullock, a thief and worse. But Pegler is confused about ER's southern ancestry. She is descended from the Bulloch family of Georgia, not the relocated New York Bullocks.

F391 Williams, Dennis A. "Letters of Mrs. FDR." By Dennis A. Williams with Eric Gelman. *Newsweek* 94 (5 Nov. 1979): 50.
While letters in Doris Faber's *The Life of Lorena Hickok* hint at a lesbian relationship between ER and Hickok, scholars interviewed for this article feel that the relationship was only a loving one.

F392 "Woman of Valor." *Congress Bi-weekly* 26 (19 Oct. 1959): 3-4.
Because of her "strength and dignity" ER meets the Biblical test of a "woman of valor." Congratulations to her on her 75th birthday and to Brandeis Univ. for adding her to its faculty.

F393 Woodbury, Clarence. "Will There Always be a Roosevelt?" *American Magazine* 155 (Jan. 1953): 15-19, 112, 114-21.
Woodbury talked to ER in New York and at Val-Kill, and his report of those discussions is a description of ER's busy and unpretenious lifestyle. Written by a self-proclaimed Roosevelt neutral who draws no conclusions about the family's continued presence in politics.

F394 [Wotkyns], Eleanor Roosevelt. "Val-Kill Remembered." *Barrytown Explorer* [Barrytown, N.Y.] 22-24 (1980-1982).
In a series of articles ER's neice recalls life in Hyde Park with her famous aunt. These personal accounts also describe the public life which ER led there. Annotation based on examination of incomplete file of the series at the New York State Library.

F395 Wright, Emily L. "Eleanor Roosevelt and the Val-Kill Industries, 1927-1938." Thesis (M.A.) State Univ. of N.Y. College at Oneonta. Cooperstown Graduate Program, 1982. xiii + 71p. Bibliography. Notes.
An account of the Val-Kill Industries experiment and ER's role in it. Includes descriptions of ER's early association with partners Nancy Cook and Marion Dickerman, Val-Kill furniture making, metal works and weaving, and the design and distribution of Val-Kill products. As a proponent of the American crafts movement ER provided financial support and promoted the value of craftsmanship through her writing and public speaking.

F396 ---. "Val-Kill." *American Craft* 44 (Dec. 1984/Jan. 1985): 53-55.
ER's involvement with Marion Dickerman and Nancy Cook in furniture making and other crafts plus her later use of Val-Kill as her home.

F397 Wright, Emily, and Katherine B. Menz. *Val-Kill: Eleanor Roosevelt National Historic Site, Hyde Park, New York. Historic Furnishings Report.* Harpers Ferry: Harpers Ferry Center, National Park Service, U.S. Dept. of the Interior, 1986 [i.e., 1987]. iii + 637p. Bibliography.

ER's occupancy of Val-Kill cottage, famous guests, observance of holidays, and her typical schedule. Based on ER's writings and writings about her including the series of articles by her niece Eleanor Wotkyns which appeared in the *Barrytown Explorer* (pp. 5-34). Extensive photographs of the cottage while occupied by ER (pp. 35-250).

Her will (pp. 261-69), appraisal of contents of cottage (pp. 270-300), and inventory of present furnishings (pp. 418-595). The transcription of Irene Roosevelt's Oct. 1979 oral history in which Val-Kill furnishings are discussed.

Contains reproductions of Hammer Galleries catalog for sale of her personal possessions (pp. 302-48), catalog of 1970 sale of items belonging to son John (pp. 350-64), 25 July 1966 *New York Times* article "Mementos of Mrs. Roosevelt to be Auctioned Here" by Nancy J. Adler (p. 367), "Roosevelt Memorabilia Finds Its Way into Area Homes" from the *Poughkeepsie Journal* [Poughkeepsie, N.Y.] of 15 Nov. 1970 (pp. 368-69), and the undated "An Era Ends in Hyde Park" by Bert Burns most likely from the *Poughkeepsie Journal* (p. 370).

EMERGENCE AS A PUBLIC FIGURE

F398 Alsop, Joseph. *FDR, 1882-1945: A Centenary Remembrance*. New York: Viking, 1982. 256p.
Emergence of ER as aide to FDR and as independent figure (pp. 109-10).

F399 Anthony, Carl Sferrazza. *First Ladies: The Saga of the Presidents' Wives and Their Power, 1789-1961*. Vol. [1] of *First Ladies*. New York: Morrow, 1990. 685p. Index. Notes.
ER's association with Louis Howe and her early Democratic Party activities (pp. 334-36, 358, 381-82, 389-91, 403, 429-31, 450).

F400 Barnard, Eunice Fuller. "Madame Arrives in Politics." *North American Review* 226 (Nov. 1928): 551-56.
The only mention of ER is as chair of the Democratic Party Women's Division. The same reference is repeated in her "Women in the Campaign." *Woman's Journal* n.s. 12 (Dec. 1928): 7-9, 44-45.

F401 Barron, Gloria J. "Molly Dewson: The Roosevelts' 'Aid to the End.'" *Franklin D. Roosevelt: The Man, the Myth, the Era, 1882-1945*. Contributions in Political Science, 189. Ed. Herbert D. Rosenbaum and Elizabeth Bartelme. New York: Greenwood, 1987. 269-85. Notes.
From 1924 until 1940 Dewson assisted the Roosevelts and in the process furthered social causes shared by the three. Provides insight into ER's role in the 1932 campaign and the Women's Division of the Democratic Party through 1940. Paper presented at Hofstra Univ. Conference, 4-6 Mar. 1982.

F402 Blair, Emily Newell. "Are Women a Failure in Politics?" *Harper's Magazine* 151 (Oct. 1925): 513-22.
In this lengthy article by the vice-chair of the Democratic National Committee ER is not mentioned by name, but her role is addressed when Blair discusses the work of women to promote social welfare legislation (p. 519) and the role of women at the 1924 Democratic National Convention (p. 521). Some of Blair's themes about what women must do to become more effective participants in the political process can be found in ER's 1928 article "Women Must Learn to Play the Game as Men Do."

F403 "Both Old Parties Woo Women Voters." *New York Times* 10 Oct. 1924: 5.
ER has attacked the Republicans for not developing a foreign policy or promoting an association of nations and for failing to recognize the adverse impact of the current tariffs on the American housewife.

F404 Brown, Christine M. "Historical Study of First Ladies in Communication Roles: Eleanor Roosevelt to Betty Ford." Project (M.A.) Fairfield Univ., 1975. 150p. Bibliography. Notes.
Includes a discussion of how her years as the wife of the Gov. of N.Y. prepared her for life as the wife of the President (pp. 16-21). Derived in large part from Lash's *Eleanor and Franklin*.

F405 Burns, James MacGregor. "Private Lives of Two Public People." Rev. of *Eleanor and Franklin* by Joseph P. Lash. *Life* 71 (15 Oct. 1971): 10.
Emphasizes Lash's treatment of ER's emergence and the development of self-confidence in her private and public life.

F406 ---. *Roosevelt: The Lion and the Fox*. New York: Harcourt, Brace, 1956. xvi + 553p. Index. Bibliography.
ER's emergence as a political figure (pp. 91, 99, 107, 118). For a description of how ER strengthened her commitment to party politics and social work while FDR attempted to succeed on the national level, see his *The Crosswinds of Freedom*, pp. 9-10 (New York: Knopf, 1989).

F407 Churchill, Allen. *The Roosevelts: American Aristocrats*. New York: Harper & Row, 1965. v + 294p. Index. Bibliography.
ER's emergence (pp. 210, 213-14, 236, 243-47).

F408 Cook, Blanche Wiesen. "Eleanor Roosevelt, Power and Politics: A Feminist Perspective." *Eleanor Roosevelt: An American Journey*. Ed. Jess Flemion and Colleen M. O'Connor. San Diego: San Diego State Univ. Pr., 1987. 209-21.
ER's 1928 article "Women Must Learn to Play the Game as Men Do" is used to demonstrate the feminist and political activist which ER had become. Cook explores why the ER of power and politics who was part of a network of feminists disappeared from writings about her. Also ER's relationship with Earl Miller and her stance on the Equal Rights Amendment.

F409 Culligan, Glendy. Rev. of *Eleanor and Franklin* by Joseph P. Lash. *Saturday Review* 54 (16 Oct. 1971): 44-47.
ER's emergence as a public figure began with the discovery of FDR's affair with Lucy Mercer and reached fruition when FDR contracted polio. The benefit which each provided to the other became apparent during the period when the Roosevelts were emerging as public figures.

F410 Davis, Clare Ogden. "Politicians, Female." *North American Review* 229 (June 1930): 749-56.
Ogden compares her list of the top 10 female political figures with others. Sarah Schuyler Butler's list includes ER, a woman considered as capable a politician as FDR (p. 753).

F411 Davis, Kenneth S. *FDR, the Beckoning of Destiny: A History, 1882-1928*. New York: Putnam's, 1972. 936p. Index. Notes and Sources.
Study of FDR up to his nomination for Gov. of N.Y. ER's emergence as an independent figure (pp. 673-75, 833-38).

F412 Davis, Maxine. "Candidates for the White House." *Ladies' Home Journal* 49 (Nov. 1932): 23.
ER now maintains her silence on political matters, and she predicts that official duties will not keep her from pursing other activities. While not imposing her ideas on FDR, ER is a woman with personal ambition who has used his political rise as a means of realizing her own agenda. Glimpses of ER, Lou Hoover, and the wives of the vice presidential candidates.

F413 DeBenedetti, Charles. "The $100,000 American Peace Award of 1924." *Pennsylvania Magazine of History and Biography* 98 (Apr. 1974): 224-49. Notes.
A comprehensive examination of the competition for the Bok prize. Includes ER's role as a member of the competition's Policy Committee.

F414 "Democratic Women to Help on Platform." *New York Times* 31 Mar. 1924: 2.
ER is named as chair of advisory group asked to suggest social welfare planks for the 1924 Democratic national platform. In the subsequent "Many Women Named to Aid Convention." *New York Times* 18 May 1924: 2 ER names others who will help her.

F415 "Democrats with Acclaim Name Smith; Governor Responds in Fighting Speech, Declaring 'Myth' and 'Name' Can't Win." *New York Times* 27 Sept. 1924: 1-2.
Reports on ER's speech seconding Al Smith's nomination. ER campaigned for Smith and debated the merits of his candidacy on 1 Nov. For excerpts of the debate, see "Women Debate Campaign Issues." *New York Times* 2 Nov. 1924: 7.

F416 "The Distaff Side of the Ticket." *Modern Priscilla* 35 (Nov. 1920): 1.
ER is described as a busy woman who is content as wife and mother in this article about the wives of the 1920 Democratic candidates for President and Vice President.

F417 Driscoll, Kate. "Mrs. Roosevelt, Apostle of Enduring Americanism." *Knickerbocker Press* [Albany, N.Y.] 29 Dec. 1929, society and magazine sect.: 5, 14.
Her public and private interests as the Gov.'s wife.

F418 Ekirch, Arthur A., Jr. *Ideologies and Utopias: The Impact of the New Deal on American Thought*. Chicago: Quadrangle, 1969. ix + 307p. Index. Notes.
Cites Maxwell Perkins' 1932 prediction that if FDR is elected we will have ER as President (p. 86).

F419 Elshtain, Jean Bethke. *Women and War*. New York: Basic Books, 1987. xvi + 288. Index. Bibliography. Notes.
ER is one of the women discussed in the section on noncombatants. Utilizing ER's own words, Elshtain claims that World War I transformed ER into a person with her own identity (pp. 187-89).

F420 Flemion, Jess. "A Public Figure Emerges." *Eleanor Roosevelt: An American Journey*. Ed. Jess Flemion and Colleen M. O'Connor. San Diego: San Diego State Univ. Pr., 1987. 53-55.

FDR's affair with Lucy Mercer changed ER's life. She developed new interests and friends. By the time of the 1932 election she had more political experience than any other First Lady. Introduces 25 photographs.

F421 *Franklin D. Roosevelt, His Life and Times: An Encyclopedic View*. The G.K. Hall Presidential Encyclopedia Series. Ed. Otis L. Graham, Jr. and Meghan Robinson Wander. Boston: Hall, 1985. 483p. Selected Critical Bibliographies.

Her early political and humanitarian activities, the influence of Louis Howe, and the impetus which the FDR-Lucy Mercer relationship gave to her emergence (pp. 102-3, 268, 362-63, 380-81).

F422 Freidel, Frank. *Franklin D. Roosevelt: A Rendezvous with Destiny*. Boston: Little, Brown, 1990. viii + 710p. Index. Notes.

The emergence of ER as adviser to FDR and as a public figure in her own right (pp. 36-37, 49-50). Attention to ER in his earlier works on FDR, *The Ordeal* (Boston: Little, Brown, 1954) and *The Triumph* (Boston: Little, Brown, 1956), is slight.

F423 Galbraith, John Kenneth. "Eleanor and Franklin Revisited." Rev. of *Eleanor and Franklin* by Joseph P. Lash. *New York Times Book Review* 19 Mar. 1972: 2.

Galbraith rejects Lash's theory that ER's emergence was a result of her unhappy childhood and FDR's affair with Lucy Mercer. She would have become the same person because she was never "cast for a subordinate role."

F424 Gallagher, Hugh Gregory. *FDR's Splendid Deception*. New York: Dodd, Mead, 1985; Atlanta: Cherokee, 1992. xiv + 250p. Index. Bibliography. Notes.

The political partnership between ER and FDR and her influential role in keeping FDR's name before the public during the early years of his illness (pp. 11-18, 20-22, 59, 62-63, 68-69).

F425 George, Elsie L. "The Women Appointees of the Roosevelt and Truman Administrations: A Study of Their Impact and Effectiveness." Diss. American Univ., 1972. v + 317p. Bibliography. Notes.

ER's political activities in the 1920s made the Roosevelts close to women involved in Democratic Party politics. These associations helped bring about New Deal appointments for women. Utilizes papers of Molly Dewson, Hilda Smith, and Ellen Woodward to establish ER's involvement in the work of these three.

F426 Goldberg, Richard Thayer. *The Making of Franklin D. Roosevelt: Triumph Over Disability*. Cambridge: Abt Books, 1981. xiv + 242p. Index. Bibliography. Notes.

The effect of polio on FDR's career. Coverage of ER includes her relationship with FDR and Sara Roosevelt, her role in FDR's struggle to overcome the effects of his illness, and her own emergence. Relies heavily on unpublished material.

F427 Gosnell, Harold F. *Champion Campaigner: Franklin D. Roosevelt*. New York: Macmillan, 1952. 235p. Index. Notes.

He emphasizes the importance of ER's role in FDR's campaigns (pp. 20-26). Derived from published works, ER's autobiographical writings in particular.

F428   Gould, Jean. *A Good Fight: The Story of F.D.R.'s Conquest of Polio*. New York: Dodd, Mead, 1960. 308p.
ER's role in FDR's struggle. Based in part on interviews with her (pp. 68-89).

F429   Hager, Alice Rogers. "Candidates for the Post of First Lady." *New York Times Magazine* 2 Oct. 1932: 5, 16.
ER and Lou Hoover are compared in this look at the private and public lives of the two women.

F430   Hartman, Violet. "Mrs. Franklin D. Roosevelt's Political Development, 1920-1940." Thesis (M.A.) N.Y. Univ., 1955.
No known extant copy.

F431   Hatch, Alden. "Franklin D. Roosevelt." *Heroes of Our Times*. Ed. Will Yolen and Kenneth Seeman Giniger. Harrisburg: Giniger-Stackpole, 1968. 25-50.
ER's determination that FDR would overcome the effects of polio. Louis Howe's role in her emergence (pp. 27-30).

F432   "Knifing the Happy Warrior." *Ave Maria* 70 (17 Dec. 1949): 772-73.
It appears that in spite of her close association with him, ER considered Al Smith's educational and cultural background to be lacking. Her revelations in *This I Remember* are a slur on Smith, but his background and beliefs are to be preferred over hers.

F433   Lape, Esther Everett. *Ways to Peace: Twenty Plans Selected from the Most Representative of Those Submitted to the American Peace Award....* New York: Scribner's, 1924. xviii + 465p. Index.
Lape, ER, and Mrs. Frank Vanderlip were the original members of the Policy Committee for the award. ER's role is outlined by Lash in *Eleanor and Franklin*, pp. 282-85.
For an announcement and rules of the competition, see "The American Peace Award." *World Peace Foundation Pamphlets* 6 (1923): 77-80.

F434   Lewis, Grace Hegger. "The Democrats." *Delineator* 121 (Oct. 1932): 23, 71.
A pre-election look at the candidates describes the preparation which ER has had for becoming First Lady and how she has been responsible for keeping FDR's name before the public while he tried to overcome a crippling illness.

F435   Lindley, Ernest K. *Franklin D. Roosevelt: A Career in Progressive Democracy.* New York: Blue Ribbon, 1931. 379p.
ER as the busy wife of the Gov. of N.Y. (pp. 337-38). Belle Moses in *Franklin Delano Roosevelt: The Minute Man of '33*, pp. 135-40 (New York: Appleton-Century, 1933) quotes Lindley in his description of ER.

F436   Looker, Earle. *This Man Roosevelt*. New York: Brewer, Warren & Putnam, 1932. vii + 233p. Index.
A popular book written during the 1932 campaign which includes an early sketch of the public ER. The author's enthusiasm about her is boundless (pp. 39-48).

F437   Ludwig, Emil. *Roosevelt: A Study in Fortune and Power*. New York: Viking, 1938; New York: Garden City, 1941. xii + 350p. Index.

FDR was attracted to ER because their relationship made it easier for him to confirm his social consciousness, and as niece of Theodore Roosevelt she provided a desirable link. The emergence of ER (pp. 115-16). Translated from the German ed. *Roosevelt, Studie uber Gluck und Macht* (Amsterdam: Querido, 1938).

F438 MacKaye, Milton. "The Governor." *New Yorker* 7 (15 Aug. 1931): 18-22; 7 (22 Aug. 1931): 24-26, 28-29.
Includes a recognition of the role which ER played in FDR's return to the political scene and of the influence she has exerted on him to think more about social issues.

F439 MacKenzie, Compton. *Mr. Roosevelt*. London: Harrap, 1943. 256p. Index.
While MacKenzie covers the period through 1943, his treatment of ER centers on the pre-White House years. Derived largely from *This Is My Story*.

F440 MacLeish, Archibald. "Eleanor Roosevelt: The Awakening." *New York Times* 7 Nov. 1965, sect. 2: 11.
After rejecting other events, he concludes that it was the horror of World War I that awoke in ER the humanitarian role which she was destined to fill. Adapted from a letter to Sidney Glazier, producer of *The Eleanor Roosevelt Story*.

F441 Maine, Basil. *Franklin D. Roosevelt: His Life and Achievement*. London: Murray, 1938. vii + 286p. Index.
Louis Howe used his development of ER as a public figure to aid FDR's political comeback, and by 1928 ER had become a political figure in her own right (pp. 80, 106-7, 116-18, 129-30). ER's detachment from politics during FDR's campaign for the N.Y. Senate and during 1912 Democratic National Convention (pp. 65-66, 76-77). Based in part on *This Is My Story*

F442 Marbury, Elizabeth. "Women in Politics." *Saturday Evening Post* 198 (12 Sept. 1925): 21, 53.
ER and others at the 1924 Democratic National Convention.

F443 McElvaine, Robert S. *The Great Depression: America, 1929-1941*. New York: Times Books, 1984. xiv + 402p. Index. Notes.
The importance of ER's support and advice in FDR's political development. McElvaine questions if FDR would have achieved the presidency if it had not been for ER (pp. 104-5, 109).

F444 Meyer, Donald. "A Separate Glory." Rev. of *Eleanor and Franklin* by Joseph P. Lash. *New Republic* 165 (16 Oct. 1971): 19-23.
Her discovery of FDR's relationship with Lucy Mercer allowed ER to become an independent figure. From then on their reconciliation was limited to promoting the other's agenda.

F445 Miller, Nathan. *FDR: An Intimate History*. Garden City: Doubleday, 1983. viii + 563p. Index. Bibliography. Notes.
Brief references to ER's emergence as a public figure.

F446 Morgenthau, Henry, III. *Mostly Morgenthaus: A Family History*. Boston: Ticknor & Fields, 1991. xxi + 501p. Index. Notes. Sources.

The son of ER's friend and associate Elinor Morgenthau recalls the women's N.Y.
2Democratic Party activities during FDR's gubernatorial years (pp. 248-50, 254-60,
262).

F447 "Mrs. F.D. Roosevelt a Civic Worker." *New York Times* 9 Nov. 1932: 9.
A thorough look at her emergence as a public figure written at the time of FDR's
election to the presidency.

F448 "Mrs. Roosevelt." *Observer Profiles*. London: Observer, 1948; Freeport: Books
for Libraries, 1970. 112-15.
Unidentified quotations by ER describe her emergence and role as aide to FDR.

F449 "Mrs. Roosevelt to Keep on Filling Many Jobs Besides Being the 'First Lady'
at Albany." *New York Times* 10 Nov. 1928: 1.
The wife of the newly-elected Gov. of N.Y. is outlining a busy schedule for herself.

F450 "Mrs. Shaver Assails Democratic Chiefs." *New York Times* 7 July 1928: 14.
The wife of the chair of the Democratic National Committee attacked presidential
nominee Al Smith for his wet plank and duplicity. ER fights back with the charge
that Mrs. Shaver and her associates are more concerned with the enforcement of
prohibition than with telling the truth.   For editorial reaction, see "When Greek
Meets Greek." *New York Times* 9 July 1928: 18.   With the right to vote came
women's right to debate the political issues. A good example of this is Mrs. Clem
Shaver's attack on Al Smith and how ER has proven to be a capable opponent.

F451 "News of Democrats and Their Activities." *Bulletin* (Women's National
Democratic Club) 3 (Dec. 1928): 18-19.
ER's activities during the 1928 campaign as head of the Women's Activities and
Advisory Committee.

F452 Perkins, Frances. *The Reminiscences of Frances Perkins*. New York Times
Oral History Program. Columbia University Oral History Collection pt. 3, no. 182.
Glen Rock: Microfilming Corp. of America, 1976. 9 books (61 microfiche).
ER's personal appearance at the time FDR became Gov. of N.Y. (bk. 3, p. 2).
Perkins' candid recollections of ER's opposition to Belle Moskowitz as possible
secretary to FDR (bk. 3, pp. 13-15, 18, 20-24, 28, 30, 37). ER as wife of the Gov.
(bk. 3, pp. 3-5, 289-93). ER told Perkins her life story (bk. 3, pp. 529-43).

F453 Perry, Elisabeth Israels. *Belle Moskowitz: Feminine Politics and the Exercise
of Power in the Age of Alfred E. Smith*. New York: Oxford Univ. Pr., 1987. xv +
280p. Index. Bibliography. Notes.
In the capacity as an adviser Moskowitz promoted social reform by working
through Smith at the time ER was emerging as a public figure (pp. 146-47, 165-66).
ER worked under her during the 1928 campaign (pp. 195-97). ER on Moskowitz as
possible secretary to Gov. Roosevelt (pp. 206-7).

F454 ---. "The Political Apprenticeship of Eleanor Roosevelt." *Eleanor Roosevelt:
An American Journey*. Ed. Jess Flemion and Colleen M. O'Connor. San Diego: San
Diego State Univ. Pr., 1987. 81-85. Note on Sources.

ER's career was not totally dependent on FDR as evidenced by her leadership roles in the early 1920s with the New York Women's City Club and the Women's Division of the New York State Democratic Committee.

F455 ---. "Training for Public Life: ER and Women's Political Networks in the 1920s." *Without Precedent: The Life and Career of Eleanor Roosevelt.* Everywoman: Studies in History, Literature, and Culture. Ed. Joan Hoff-Wilson and Marjorie Lightman. Bloomington: Indiana Univ. Pr., 1984. 28-45.
During the years 1924-1928 ER was an active participant in the New York Women's City Club. She made friendships with important women of the era, developed her leadership ability, expanded her knowledge of the legislative process, and extended her awareness of social issues of the time. Excerpted as "Eleanor Roosevelt's Career Began with Women's Political Networks of the Early 1920s." *Media Report to Women* 12 (July/Aug. 1984): 15.

F456 "Political Debate by Women Radioed." *New York Times* 3 Nov. 1927: 29.
ER and Republican Mrs. Charles H. Sabin debate whether the term of N.Y. Gov. should be extended to four years and elections held in the same year as presidential elections. ER spoke against both. Article excerpts debate.

F457 "Poor Find Champion in Mrs. Roosevelt." *New York Times* 2 July 1932: 7.
The wife of the Democratic presidential candidate has found the time to teach school, start her own business, and become deeply involved in social and political causes. A comprehensive look at her accomplishments.

F458 "Prepares to Unite Democratic Women." *New York Times* 4 Aug. 1928: 4.
As head of the Women's Division ER has named the members of a national advisory committee. She predicts that women will join in the campaign and support the candidacy of Al Smith when they learn more about his record.

F459 Prideaux, Tom. "A Sleeping Beauty and Hercules." *Life* 59 (3 Dec. 1965): 10.
In his *The Eleanor Roosevelt Story* Archibald MacLeish compares ER's emergence to Sleeping Beauty. Her experiences during World War I instilled in her the realization that she was a human being first and a public figure second. Review of MacLeish's motion picture and an unrelated play.

F460 Ralph, J.P. "Do You Remember the Nation's Most Glamorous Career Girl?" *Yankee* 41 (June 1977): 74-79, 167-68, 171-72, 174. Bibliography.
The life and career of Missy LeHand. During FDR's struggle to return to public life it was FDR's secretary LeHand, more than ER, who was there to help.

F461 *Records of the Women's City Club of New York, 1916-1980.* Research Collections on Women's Studies. Grassroots Women's Organizations. Ed. Elisabeth Israels Perry. Frederick: University Publications of America, 1989. 24 reels of microfilm.
As reported in the club records ER was an active participant in activities from 1923 until her resignation at the end of 1928. In 1924 she was named chair of the City Planning Dept. of the Committee on Transit (reel 3). In 1925 she was acting chair of the Committee on Transit, served on the Women's Committee for the International Congress on Town, City, and Regional Planning held 20-25 Apr. in New York, and was on the Political Committee (reel 3). At a 2 Mar. 1925 meeting

she responded to questions on what the club was doing about transit problems (reel 1) and on 15 Jan. 1925 chaired the program "Regional Plan of New York and Its Environs" (reel 15). In 1926 she was the representative to the New York Council for International Cooperation to Prevent War and was named chair of the club's Legislation Committee in Dec. of that year (reel 3). In 1928 she was asked to represent the club on the Committee of Twenty to work on the clean streets campaign (reel 3).

She was elected first vice president in 1926 and a member of the Board of Directors in 1928 (reel 1). Ballots for 1926-1928 list her past and present activities (reel 23).

She spoke on numerous occasions. On 22 Jan. 1924 she addressed members about "The Referendum on the Bok Peace Prize" (reel 15). Records about that speech indicate that she demonstrated "a lively interest in her topic and an ability to arouse a similar interest in her hearers" (reel 17). On 6 Apr. 1925 she participated in a radio broadcast (reel 15) in which she described the club's purpose (a discussion of her remarks is included in "She Finds Sheiks Far from Alluring." *New York Times* 7 Apr. 1925: 14). In Oct. 1926 she was in a debate about candidates for the U.S. Senate speaking on behalf of Robert Wagner (reel 3). Excerpts and discussion issued as "Women in Debate on Race for Senate." *New York Times* 19 Oct. 1926: 14. In another debate on 10 Oct. 1927 she argued against the topic "Four-Year Term for Governor with Election in the Presidential Year" (reels 15, 17). For excerpts and discussion, see "Term of Governor Debated by Women." *New York Times* 11 Oct. 1927: 5. On 8 Oct. 1928 she debated on behalf of presidential candidate Al Smith in the program "Who Next in the White House?" (reels 1, 15).

Although she resigned at the end of 1928 (reel 3), she continued to speak at club functions. In Jan. 1929 she spoke on "Women in Politics" (reel 1) and on the same topic in an 8 Nov. 1929 radio broadcast as part of "The March of Events Series" (reels 3, 15, 17). A report on the 8 Nov. broadcast is "Mrs. F.D. Roosevelt Urges Peace Work." *New York Times* 9 Nov. 1929: 25. At a dinner on 13 Jan. 1930 she once again discussed "Women in Politics" (reels 3, 15, 17). The role of women in public life was her topic at a 10 Jan. 1934 dinner (reels 4, 15). On 23 Oct. 1939 she spoke about "the function of a non-partisan civic organization" (reel 16). Records indicate that she was scheduled to speak about the UN on 10 Mar. 1953 (reel 16).

She was honored on several occasions: dinners and luncheons on 9 Jan. 1929, 13 Jan. 1930, 7 Dec. 1932, and 10 Jan. 1934 (reels 1, 3, 4, 15) and at other events held on 23 Oct. 1939, 26 Nov. 1946, and in Apr. 1956 (reels 1, 4, 5, 16, 17). For a report on 9 Jan. 1929 dinner including brief excerpts of her remarks, see "Mrs. Pratt Advises Watch on Officials." *New York Times* 10 Jan. 1929: 3.

F462 Richardson, Anna Steese. "Women in the Campaign." *Harper's Magazine* 158 (Apr. 1929): 585-92.

The author expresses her disappointment with the way in which women participated in the 1928 presidential campaign and concludes that women are no better citizens than men. ER is characterized as the type whose participation was well organized but highly partisan.

F463 Richardson, Eudora Ramsay. "The Ladies of the Lobby." *North American Review* 227 (June 1929): 648-55.

Richardson does not think much of what women have done with the vote. ER's prominent role in women's affairs of the Democratic Party is attributed to name appeal, not leadership ability (p. 649).

F464 Rollins, Alfred B. *Roosevelt and Howe*. New York: Knopf, 1962. x + 479p. + xviii. Index. Bibliographical Essay. Notes.

Letters, ER's published works, and interviews which the author conducted with her document this account of the fruitful relationship between ER and Louis Howe (pp. 56-454 passim).

F465 Roosevelt, Elliott. "The Most Unforgettable Character I've Met." *Reader's Digest* 62 (Feb. 1953): 26-30.

It was Louis Howe. His influence on ER's character and personality was immense, and the impact which he had on the lives of ER and FDR has impacted us all.

F466 ---. "My Mother." *Eleanor Roosevelt: An American Journey*. Ed. Jess Flemion and Colleen M. O'Connor. San Diego: San Diego State Univ. Pr., 1987. 43-46.

Her entry into political affairs was at the insistence of Louis Howe who hoped that her involvement would encourage FDR to return to public life.

F467 Roosevelt, James, and Sidney Shalett. *Affectionately, F.D.R.: A Son's Story of a Lonely Man*. New York: Harcourt, Brace, 1959. 394p. Index. Bibliography.

Includes an account of the emergence of ER as a public figure (pp. 149-53).

F468 Ross, Leland M., and Allen N. Grobin. *This Democratic Roosevelt: The Life Story of "F.D.": An Authentic Biography*. New York: Dutton, 1932. 312p. Index.

FDR's early political career and the emergence of ER. Brief references about her emergence (p. 182).

F469 Russell, Francis. *The President Makers: From Mark Hanna to Joseph P. Kennedy*. Boston: Little, Brown, 1976. vi + 407p. Index. Bibliography. Notes.

Analyzes the role which Louis Howe played in FDR's political career and traces the evolution of ER's relationship with Howe (pp. 267-323).

F470 Schlesinger, Arthur M., Jr. *The Crisis of the Old Order, 1919-1933*. The Age of Roosevelt [1]. Boston: Houghton Mifflin, 1956. 557p. Index. Notes.

Relationship with Louis Howe and her emergence (pp. 369-70). Reissued in 1988 with a new foreword (Boston: Houghton Mifflin).

F471 Scott, Janet. "Covering Mrs. Franklin D. Roosevelt." *Junior League Magazine* 17 (Mar. 1931): 48-49.

As the wife of the Gov. of N.Y. ER has maintained an incredible schedule of official and personal duties. Includes an unidentified quotation by ER on the role of a good teacher and an account of her first ride in an airplane. The reflections of a reporter who covered ER for the *Albany Evening News* [Albany, N.Y.] and the *Knickerbocker News* [Albany, N.Y.]. Another report of the flight is "Mrs. Roosevelt Names Plane 'Governor,' Starts Here by Air, Forced Down at Poughkeepsie." *New York Times* 6 June 1929: 1.

F472 Smith, Helena Huntington. "Noblesse Oblige." *New Yorker* 6 (5 Apr. 1930): 23-25.

The political education and emergence of ER is outlined in a thorough portrait of her as the reform-minded wife of the Gov. of N.Y. Reissued in *The Roosevelt Omnibus*, pp. 125-35 (New York: Knopf, 1934).

F473 "Smith for President Will Be Demanded by State Convention." *New York Times* 15 Apr. 1924: 1, 13.

Women under ER's leadership revolt about not having the right to select their own delegates to the Democratic National Convention. Includes text of ER's lengthy remarks about the status of women in the Democratic Party. The women got most of what they wanted as reported in "Democratic Women Win." *New York Times* 16 Apr. 1924: 2.

F474 Stidger, William L. *These Amazing Roosevelts*. New York: Macfadden, 1938. 89p.

ER's emergence (pp. 18-20).

F475 Stiles, Lela. *The Man behind Roosevelt: The Story of Louis McHenry Howe*. Cleveland: World, 1954. 311p. Index. Notes.

Stiles, journalist and assistant to Howe, relies heavily on personal recollections, published works, and interviews including one with ER. An account full of anecdotes about the role Howe played in ER's emergence.

F476 Taylor, Paul C. "The Entrance of Women into Party Politics: The 1920's [sic]." Diss. Harvard Univ., 1966. 551p. Bibliography. Notes.

At the time of the 1932 election ER was the leader of Democratic women in upstate New York, the only group which could still be considered "progressive reform feminism." While FDR's election allowed the group to assume the leadership of the women's movement, it forced ER behind the scenes (pp. 500-520).

F477 "To Develop Washington." *New York Times* 5 Feb. 1925: 2.

Announcement that ER will head the American Civic Association's New York Committee on the Federal City which has as its goal the continued development of the nation's capital.

F478 "Trooping for Democracy." *Women's Democratic News*.

Appeared as occasional feature and described the political activities of Nancy Cook, Marion Dickerman, and Caroline O'Day. Frequent references to ER's activities. Sometimes appeared under a different title, e.g., "Our Tireless Troopers Start Afield" by Caroline O'Day (Aug. 1929): 3-4.

F479 Tugwell, Rexford G. "The Fallow Years of Franklin D. Roosevelt." *Ethics* 66 (Jan. 1956): 98-116. Notes.

While considered fallow years for FDR, it was in 1921-1928 when ER emerged with the help of Louis Howe. By 1929 the Roosevelts had separate, but interdependent, careers and identities. Reissued as "Fallow Years" in his *Search for Roosevelt*, pp. 34-59 (Cambridge: Harvard Univ. Pr., 1972).

F480 "Wants Owen Young to Run with Smith." *New York Times* 4 Aug. 1926: 21.

ER urges the nomination of Owen Young for U.S. senator and the renomination of Gov. Al Smith. Includes lengthy excerpts of her remarks about the interests of the two men in issues of concern to women voters. Her support for Smith is repeated in *New York Times* accounts "Women to Work for Smith." 3 Oct. 1926: 3 and "Says Women Want Smith." 2 Nov. 1926: 2.

F481 Ware, Susan. "ER and Democratic Politics: Women in the Postsuffrage Era." *Without Precedent: The Life and Career of Eleanor Roosevelt.* Everywoman: Studies in History, Literature, and Culture. Ed. Joan Hoff-Wilson and Marjorie Lightman. Bloomington: Indiana Univ. Pr., 1984. 46-60. Sources.

The activities of ER, Molly Dewson, and others in the Democratic Party during the 1920s and 1930s.

F482 ---. *Partner and I: Molly Dewson, Feminism, and New Deal Politics.* New Haven: Yale Univ. Pr., 1987. xix + 327p. Index. Notes.

A biography of Dewson--political activist and associate of ER and FDR--and companion Mary Gurley (Polly) Porter. Extensive use is made of ER's papers to document the early relationship between ER and Dewson in Democratic Party activities.

F483 Watrous, Hilda R. *In League with Eleanor: Eleanor Roosevelt and the League of Women Voters, 1921-1962.* New York: Foundation for Citizen Education, League of Women Voters of New York State, 1984. 25p.

A chronology of the league and ER's role in it. Portions related to the 1920s excerpted as "LWV Work Provided ER Experience and New Contacts." *Media Report to Women* 12 (July/Aug. 1984): 15.

F484 "Women Debate Issues." *New York Times* 5 Apr. 1928: 29.

At a district League of Women Voters meeting ER debated a Republican counter-part on the issue of water power. ER spoke in favor of government assuming the responsibility.

F485 "Women Democrats Split on Dry Issue." *New York Times* 30 Jan. 1928: 4.

Excerpts of correspondence between ER and Mrs. Jesse W. Nicholson of the National Woman's Democratic Law Enforcement League. ER criticizes the league for not supporting the enforcement of the 14th and 15th amendments as enthu-siastically as the 18th.

F486 [Editorial]. *Women's Democratic News* 4 [new style 5] (Nov. 1928): 6.

"Courageous, unselfish, untiring" are words used to describe ER upon her resignation as editor. ER is also praised as a moving force in the Women's Division of the New York State Democratic Party.

FIRST LADY, CONTEMPORARY WRITINGS

F487 Abell, George, and Evelyn Gordon. *Let Them Eat Caviar.* New York: Dodge, 1936. xiv + 304p. Index.

A humorous look at Washington society including anecdotes about ER as First Lady (pp. 55-68).

F488 "According to Timothy Turner." *Democratic Digest* 9 (Jan. 1934): 10.

The First Lady can put all types of people at ease and, as the hostess for the Gridiron Widows dinner, she distinguishes herself as a warm and amazing person.

F489 "According to Timothy Turner." *Democratic Digest* 12 (Feb. 1935): 10.
ER has accepted the invitation of the Women's National Press Club to be guest of honor at its annual stunt party on 5 Mar. The second of these brief statements is a description of White House dogs Jack and Jill, two Irish Setters, who intrude into her weekly press conferences.

F490 Aguiar, Jose. *Hacia la Comunidad Democratica Americana = Towards the American Democratic Commonwealth. Homenaje a Franklin D. y Eleanor Roosevelt, Primer Ciudadano y Primera Dama de America.* Monteviedo: Ed. "Comini," 1943. 46p.
Copy not examined. In Spanish and English.

F491 Allen, Frederick Lewis. *Since Yesterday: The Nineteen-thirties in America.* New York: Harper, 1940. xiv + 362p. Index.
Allen describes the visit of the British Royal couple and how ER entertained them at the White House and Hyde Park and reported the daily events in "My Day" (pp. 341-43).

F492 *Amidst Crowded Days: Diary in Clippings of Mrs. Franklin D. Roosevelt.* 2 vols. Comp. A. Cypen Lubitsh. New York: Lubitsh, 1943.
Copies of editorials and newspaper articles about her plus selected "My Day" columns. Includes detailed table of contents. A unique resource on the White House years available in ER Papers, FDRL.

F493 "Anna Eleanor Roosevelt." *Vida* (Oct. 1940): 8.
As a wife of an elected official her influence is unequaled, and her influence over public opinion is not matched by any other woman. In Portuguese.

F494 Barnett, Lester. "What the Roosevelts Like in Swing Music." *Senator* (17 June 1939): 23-24.
She enjoys waltzes and old American dances such as the Virginia Reel. An interview with band leader Ruby Newman.

F495 Barry, Judy. "Making a Home For That MAN!" *Ladies' Home Journal* 61 (Nov. 1944): 152-53, 160.
ER and Frances Dewey as homemakers in their respective executive mansions.

F496 Bealle, Morris A. *Washington Squirrel Cage.* Washington: Bealle, 1944. 64p.
ER is criticized for everything from Arthurdale to the rapid rise of her sons in the military. Her current activities are calculated to promote FDR's fourth term candidacy. It is as "Madame Gadabout" wasting fuel with needless and silly trips to military installations and war zones that she receives the most criticism (pp. 19-22). Similar to his *Fugitives from a Brain Gang* (Washington: Columbia, 1940).

F497 Benjamin, Louise Paine. "How to Meet People." *Ladies' Home Journal* 61 (Nov. 1944): 150.
Brief accounts of how ER and Frances Dewey go about meeting people.

F498 Benson, George A. "Making Up the President's Mind." *Review of Reviews* 93 (June 1936): 66-67.

ER is an idealist and knows little about economics, but she is among those who advise FDR. Her influence includes support for the ideas of Rexford Tugwell. Reprinted from *Farm Journal*.

F499 Berger, V. *President Franklin D. Roosevelt Svenska Harstamning*. New York: Bonniers, 193-. 14p.
FDR and the Roosevelt family. In Swedish. Copy not examined.

F500 Black, Ruby. "Can Eleanor Roosevelt Stop Willkie?" *Look* 4 (8 Oct. 1940): 12-15.
On the eve of the 1940 election Black discusses the reasons why Wendell Willkie must defeat ER if he is to win the presidency. These are her immense popularity, the pivotal role which she has played in involving women in politics, her involvement with youth, and the "political strategist" which she has become.

F501 ---. "Covering Mrs. Roosevelt." *Matrix for Women in Journalism* 18 (Apr. 1933): 3-4, 6, 16.
A look at ER's first week in the White House and the early press conferences.

F502 ---. "How and Why Eleanor Roosevelt Does It." *Democratic Digest* 17 (Oct./Nov. 1940): 16-17, 51.
"She works with her government because she knows that democracy survives only if it works for the people." She is a "a living, working example of true democracy."

F503 ---. "Ladies of the White House Secretariat." *Democratic Digest* 15 (Feb. 1938): 10-11, 43.
ER credits Malvina Thompson for making her daily activities possible. Traces the relationship of the two back to 1927 and provides anecdotes about the conditions under which Thompson must often work.

F504 ---. "'New Deal' for News Women in Capital." *Editor & Publisher* 66 (10 Feb. 1934): 11, 31.
A thorough examination of ER's weekly press conferences by a regular participant. Details the content of some of the early press conferences.

F505 Blair, Emily Newell. "Society 'Off the Record': Washington's Matrons on Strike." *Today* 1 (21 Apr. 1934): 9.
The Roosevelts have changed Washington society, and women are following ER's lead by inviting guests because of what they can offer rather than simply to fulfill social obligations. Less extensive coverage is in her "If You Were Gadding about Washington--A Personal and Intimate Article." *Good Housekeeping* 98 (Mar. 1934): 26-27, 110.

F506 Bliven, Bruce. "Pre-Election Flash." *New Republic* 89 (4 Nov. 1936): 10-13.
Bliven thinks that the appeal of "My Day" to a broad segment of the population has been a positive factor in the 1936 campaign.

F507 Bloom, Vera. *There's No Place Like Washington*. New York: Putnam's, 1944. 296p.

ER's energy, busy schedule, sense of humor, and lack of vanity make her an admirable figure. Bloom wonders what long-term impact she will have on the women of America (pp. 85-88).

F508 Brogan, D.W. "Mrs. Roosevelt as a Political Force." *Spectator* 169 (30 Oct. 1942): 403-4.
She is a political force, not a politician, and sees political action as a means of helping those in need, not as a means of benefiting herself. It is unlikely that she will succeed FDR, but it is an interesting prospect.

F509 Broun, Heywood. "The First Traveler of the Land." *It Seems to Me.* By Heywood Broun. New York: Harcourt, Brace, 1935. 299-302.
Broun and ER board the same train in New York. Throughout the trip he observed that she requested no special treatment and none was offered. From the *New York Herald Tribune.*

F510 "Buffalo '400' in Schism over Skit 'My Day,' Mrs. Mack Gains Backing in War on Satire." *New York Times* 14 Oct. 1944: 8.
Mrs. Norman E. Mack, widow of state Democratic leader and friend of ER, resigns from the Twentieth Century Club of Buffalo after an uncomplimentary skit about ER is presented. Local coverage as "Irked by Skit Aimed at First Lady, Mrs. Mack Offers Club Resignation." *Courier-Express* [Buffalo, N.Y.] 12 Oct. 1944: 17.

F511 Bugbee, Emma. "America's Most Traveled First Lady." *Literary Digest* 117 (28 Apr. 1934): 9, 39.
Her trip to Puerto Rico, hectic schedule upon her return, and frequent use of air travel. Anecdotal. Bugbee concludes by calling her a "Right-Wing" feminist "who looks forward to a kindlier social order."

F512 ---. "First Lady Begins 7th Year Active as Ever." *Washington Post* 15 Jan. 1939, sect. C: 1, 5.
It has been another active year for the First Lady. She made 85 speeches, received 96,423 pieces of mail, and her travels took her 42,000 miles. Since the public is now accustomed to her activities, not every speech and trip are reported in the press.

F513 ---. "Keeping Up with Mrs. Roosevelt a Joy, Not a Job, Secretary Says." *New York Herald Tribune* 18 Dec. 1939: 20.
An interview with Malvina Thompson who as ER's secretary travels with her, types from her dictation, and handles her mail. Thompson provides insight into how the large quantity of mail is handled and claims that ER writes everything which appears under her name.

F514 ---. "Mrs. Roosevelt Never Falters during Burial." *Varied Harvest: A Miscellany of Writing by Barnard College Women.* New York: Putnam's, 1953. 51-56.
Poignant account of ER at FDR's burial. From the *New York Herald Tribune,* 16 Apr. 1945.

F515 ---. "'Mrs. Roosevelt' of Press Skit Stages White House Sit-Down." *New York Herald Tribune* 2 Mar. 1937: 21.
An account of 1 Mar. Women's National Press Club stunt party. The skit imagined ER on strike from her duties.

F516 ---. "New Interpretation of the 'First Lady's' Role." *Literary Digest* 116 (16 Sept. 1933): 22.

Without fear of physical harm or criticism ER has become a different kind of First Lady. She has continued to pursue her own interests while also fulfilling her official duties.

F517 ---. "Not Strictly Political." *Today* 1 (7 Apr. 1934): 11.

Although she vowed in her first year as First Lady to avoid issues which are "strictly political," she has through her travels, speeches, and press conferences pursued many causes.

F518 "Campaigner: First Lady 'From Hyde Park' Helps a Kindred Spirit." *Newsweek* 4 (3 Nov. 1934): 8.

How in only two days the First Lady made campaign speeches for congressional candidate Caroline O'Day in cities across N.Y.

F519 [Carter, John Franklin]. *The New Dealers*. By The Unofficial Observer. New York: Simon and Schuster, 1934; New York: Da Capo, 1975. ix + 414p. Index.

Beginning with the 1920 vice presidential campaign FDR relied on a small group--ER, Louis Howe, Missy LeHand, Stephen Early and Marvin McIntyre--and in this early account of the New Deal there is a discussion of that group. Ten aspects of ER's personality are discussed, and the conclusion is that future society can be seen in the Roosevelts (pp. 203-33). A lengthy estimate of ER is excerpted in "Roosevelts: President Hopes Home State Bill Will Pass." *Newsweek* 3 (24 Mar. 1934): 12.

F520 Childs, Marquis W. "Mr. Roosevelt." *Survey Graphic* 29 (May 1940): 283-85.

This election year look at FDR includes a glimpse of ER who is described as being of equal stature with her husband and the one who has made life in the White House more interesting and educational for the President (pp. 283-84).

F521 Clapper, Raymond. "Mrs. Roosevelt Sees No Evil." *Liberty* 19 (4 Apr. 1942): 10-11, 38.

An anecdotal account of ER as First Lady and White House hostess highlighting worthwhile activities as well as some blunders.

F522 ---. "The Ten Most Powerful People in Washington." *Look* 5 (28 Jan. 1941): 22-27.

ER and nine men. She is credited for numerous New Deal programs and is considered indispensable to FDR. Abridged version appeared in *Reader's Digest* 38 (May 1941): 45-48.

F523 Clark, Delbert. *Washington Dateline*. New York: Stokes, 1941. 322p. Index.

Contemporary account of Washington reporters and their beat. Clark questions if ER's women only news conferences result in any worthwhile news, are of any benefit to the careers of the women who participate, and if ER herself wants to continue them (pp. 205-6, 210-19).

F524 Clark, William Lloyd. *From Belshazzar to Roosevelt*. Milan, Ill.: Rail Splitter Pr., 1935. 207p.

In this expose of corruption and immorality in the Roosevelt White House is the lengthy "An Open Letter to Mrs. Franklin D. Roosevelt" in which Clark accuses ER of being a frequent smoker and condoning the use of alcohol by young women. Through her example and words she is affecting the morality of young women who will bear deformed children if they use tobacco and alcohol. The letter reprints numerous editorials, letters to editors, and other accounts critical of ER's radio discussion about the need for young girls to learn how much alcohol they can tolerate (pp. 29-44). In another section it is claimed that the type of entertaining that ER supports in the White House does not set the proper moral example (pp. 130-31).

F525 "The Coat." *Newsweek* 25 (19 Mar. 1945): 44, 47-48.
At a public ceremony promoting Canadian-U.S. trade ER accepts a $8,000 fur coat on behalf of American women and agrees to keep it for her own use. In "Gifts from Near & Far." *Time* 45 (19 Mar. 1945): 16 it is revealed that she has accepted other gifts: a silk harem gown, a gold bracelet, and a jeweled crown.

F526 "Constitution Safe, Cummings Asserts." *New York Times* 26 Feb. 1934: 2.
An article about the "Rollins Antimated Magazine" presented at Rollins College. The "issue" contained a tribute to ER by Fannie Hurst entitled "Here Comes Mrs. Roosevelt," the First Lady who is an inspiration to other women.

F527 Culbertson, Mary Haeseter. "Our Hospitable and Homeloving First Family, and Favorite White House Recipes." *Better Homes & Gardens* 12 (May 1934): 22-23, 73-75.
A luncheon with the Roosevelts at Hyde Park plus a visit to the White House and a discussion with housekeeper Henrietta Nesbitt. The life style and food enjoyed by the Roosevelts are simple and unaffected.

F528 Dall, Anna Roosevelt. "Twelve Months in the White House." *Liberty* 11 (3 Mar. 1934): 28-31.
An intimate account of the Roosevelts' first year in the White House by ER's daughter.

F529 ---. "When the White House Gives a Party." *Cosmopolitan* (Mar. 1935).
Copy not examined.

F530 Davis, Maxine. "The New Deal Hits Washington Society." *Liberty* 11 (9 June 1934): 20-22.
The White House is now more like a home where the Roosevelts' guests are expected to enjoy themselves. The Roosevelts' informality has filtered down through Washington society.

F531 "Democratic Women's Day in Birmingham." *Democratic Digest* 15 (Dec. 1938): 21.
On 26 Oct. 1938 ER visited Birmingham, Ala. on a lecture tour. She made brief greetings to Democratic women at a luncheon and presented a lecture that evening.

F532 "Democratic Women's Day on the Radio." *Democratic Digest* 16 (Oct. 1939): 33.
On 16 Sept. ER moderated a discussion with women executives in the federal government about the work of their agencies.

F533 Dilling, Elizabeth. *The Red Network: A "Who's Who" and Handbook of Radicalism for Patriots.* Kenilworth: Dilling, 1934. 352p. Index.

The entry for ER in "Who Is Who in Radicalism" lists the radical and pacifist organizations with which she is associated (p. 317). An elaboration on these associations is contained in the section "The New Deal and Roosevelt Appointees" (p. 86).

F534 ---. *The Roosevelt Red Record and Its Background.* Kenilworth: Dilling, 1936. 439p. Index.

Various sections discuss ER's associates and organizational affiliations describing all of them as communistic. Cites from many newspaper accounts of ER's activities. Index is not complete.

F535 Diogenes. "News and Comment from the National Capital." *Literary Digest* 116 (23 Sept. 1933): 10.

Washingtonians are no longer skeptical about ER's sincerity. Predictions that she would say or do something to embarrass FDR have not come true.

F536 ---. "News and Comment from the National Capital." *Literary Digest* 117 (12 May 1934): 12.

Controversy about ER's activities has reached the floor of the U.S. Senate. She claims that she has never received a return on her investment in the Val-Kill furniture factory, that her obligations to the Todhunter School are slight, and that her publishing activities are not time-consuming. In spite of her critics she plans to continue these activities as well as her travels on behalf of FDR.

F537 ---. "News and Comment from the National Capital." *Literary Digest* 119 (26 Jan. 1935): 13.

Is ER the "assistant president"? Federal agencies take action when she speaks. The distribution of surplus food was her idea. Subsistence homesteads and other programs have resulted from her involvement and interest. Many find her activities acceptable because of her genuine concern for human welfare. Others think that she oversteps the bounds of someone who has not been elected to public office.

F538 "Discussing Mrs. Roosevelt." *Argonaut* (19 May 1944): 1, 5.

Because of her travels she neglects her duties at the White House. Disputes columnist Dorothy Thompson's claim that ER is a "decorous woman."

F539 Donahue, Elizabeth. "Mrs. FDR Says Farewell to Ladies of the Press." *PM* 20 Apr. 1945: 9.

Before leaving the White House ER gave a farewell party for the women who had attended her press conferences. With no intention of running for office or being in the public eye she plans to write, not to be written about. A similar account is the "The Story Is Over." *Newsweek* 25 (30 Apr. 1945): 44, 46.

F540 ---. "Mrs. Roosevelt Turns to a New Role in Nation's Life." *PM* 16 Apr. 1945: 10.

By the day following FDR's burial there are ample speculations about ER's future. While she could be named a delegate to the UN conference in San Francisco, it is more likely that she will retain her independence and succeed Henry Wallace as the spokesperson for liberals.

F541 "Driftwood--A Column about Noteworthy People Published by a Noted South Dakota Columnist." *Congressional Record Appendix* (12 Nov. 1943): A4811.

Marie Christopherson's column "As Mrs. Roosevelt Views the Elections" is reprinted from the *Daily Argus Leader* [Sioux Falls, S.D.]. ER believes that tradition is upheld by re-electing candidates. She never hesitates to speak out, right or wrong, but in the end she has little influence over the thinking of other women.

F542 Ducas, Dorothy. "Ladies in Waiting in the White House." *Who* 1 (May 1941): 2-6, 58-59.

The backgrounds and daily activities of the three secretaries: Malvina Thompson, Edith Helm, and Missy LeHand.

F543 "Eleanor Everywhere." *Time* 22 (20 Nov. 1933): 12-14.

A look at the many and varied activities of the First Lady.

F544 "Eleanor Roosevelt." *Congressional Record Appendix* (19 Apr. 1945): A1818.

Includes Josephine Ripley's "Eleanor Roosevelt, Private Citizen" from the *Christian Science Monitor* which is a tribute to her accomplishments as First Lady.

F545 "Eleanor Roosevelt: First Lady Has Her 50th Birthday." *Newsweek* 4 (13 Oct. 1934): 17.

She accomplishes so much because she follows a daily routine, has endless energy, is comfortable with all types of people, and enjoys jokes which others make about her.

F546 Essary, Helen. "First Secretary." *Democratic Digest* 14 (June 1937): 13.

Anecdotal account of the working day of Malvina Thompson, personal secretary to ER and supervisor of other secretaries.

F547 ---. "Gay Luncheon at White House Follows Rain-Drenched Inauguration." *Democratic Digest* 14 (Feb. 1937): 17.

Anecdotes about ER, FDR, and Sara Roosevelt on the day of FDR's second inauguration.

F548 ---. "Royalty Picnics at Hyde Park." *Democratic Digest* 16 (June 1939): 8-9.

Guests, including the royalty of Britain and Europe, do not forget the Hyde Park picnics prepared by ER.

F549 ---. "So You're Going to the White House." *Democratic Digest* 16 (Feb. 1939): 8-9, 30.

Descriptions of receptions hosted by ER and an account of a White House dinner attended by the author.

F550 Evans, Ernestine. "Chief Woman-Elect." *New Outlook* 161 (Dec. 1932): 26-27.

Like the Apaches who selected a chief woman in addition to a chief, FDR will need a chief woman who can alert him to problem areas. ER has had the right experience to fill that role.

F551 Fairfax, Beatrice. *Ladies Now and Then.* New York: Dutton, 1944. 254p. Index.

The memoirs of a seasoned Washington newspaperwomen who attended ER's press conferences. Her recollections are centered on ER's kindness and the lack of decorum exhibited by some of Fairfax's reporter colleagues (pp. 199, 206-9). White House visits by British and Dutch royalty (pp. 215-17).

F552 Farley, James A. *Behind the Ballots: The Personal History of a Politician.* New York: Harcourt, Brace, 1938; Westport: Greenwood, 1972; New York: Da Capo, 1973. 392p. Index.

After discussing the likelihood of FDR seeking a third term, Farley praises ER's influential role in improving the status of women and the Democratic Party in New York politics and describes ways in which she has been an asset as First Lady (pp. 353-55).

F553 "A Feminine Complement to the Gridiron Club?" *Democratic Digest* 9 (Jan. 1934): 4.

Comment on how the first of what were to be known as the Gridiron Widows Club dinners is another example of ER's "genius for 'taking occasion by the hand.'"

F554 Finney, Ruth. "First Lady." *New York World-Telegram* 7 June-12 June 1937.

A series syndicated by Scripps-Howard. An excerpt which explains that by her example she has done much to promote democracy and that her travels and speeches have helped the American people regain confidence issued as "A Portrait of a Modern Woman." *Democratic Digest* 14 (July 1937): 25.

F554a Pt. 1. "She Now Is Beloved All over America, but Mrs. Roosevelt Had a Hard Fight." 7 June 1937.

The American people now accept her precedent-setting ways as First Lady. Through her daily activities she personifies democratic principles, and she is at her best when she goes directly to the people to learn more about their daily lives.

F554b Pt. 2. "Varied Activities of Mrs. Roosevelt, Once a Sensation, Taken Calmly." 8 June 1937.

When FDR assumed the presidency ER was determined to be herself, but it took a while for her activities to be accepted. Finney then works her way through a long list of travels, speeches, and other activities which ER has undertaken in 1937 concluding that ER is setting a new standard for public life.

F554c Pt. 3. "President's Wife Has Visited 47 States to Study Conditions for Husband's Guidance." 9 June 1937.

She is modest about her accomplishments as First Lady, but to her must go the credit for the unemployed receiving surplued food and for Arthurdale and some WPA programs. Her extensive travels have provided FDR with valuable information. She has never missed an important White House function nor neglected the needs of her family, however.

F554d Pt. 4. "Earlier Antipathy to Mrs. Roosevelt Changed Gradually to Wide Popularity." 10 June 1937.

The American people support her efforts to improve living conditions, and they have made her a popular figure.

F554e Pt. 5. "Born a Roosevelt, She Soon Learned to Win Admiration by Being Useful." 11 June 1937.

The Eleanor Roosevelt of today is a very different person from the young girl who grew up in comfortable surroundings. Her skill in making others feel at ease makes her an endearing figure.

F554f Pt. 6. "Future Candidates for Her Job Will Find It Difficult to Emulate Mrs. Roosevelt in Poise, Tact and Thinking." 12 June 1937.

Her successors will not be able to be "figureheads." A concluding look at some of the reasons she is admired as a public and private figure.

F555 "First Lady." *Newsweek* 11 (9 May 1933): 13-14.

ER's words and activities continue to invoke controversy, but there are few who do not respect her right to speak out or the sincerity of her concerns. Her defense of divorce and the White House screening of the documentary *The Birth of a Baby* have brought her criticism.

F556 "First Lady Impressed by Inaugural Ceremony." *Newsweek* 1 (11 Mar. 1933): 10.

Her activities on inauguration day.

F557 "First Lady in Milwaukee." *Life* 1 (7 Dec. 1936): 18-19.

A montage of candid photographs are reproduced along with a description of her busy schedule during a recent visit.

F558 "First Lady: Press Conferences Help Pet Projects and F.D.R." *Newsweek* 9 (17 Apr. 1937): 24.

After three years her press conferences are still important sources of news for women reporters. A discussion of the format of the conferences and some of the issues which have been addressed.

F559 "First Lady's Week." *Time* 35 (15 Apr. 1940): 17.

A busy one. While in California on a lecture tour she visited squatters' camps.

F560 Flynn, Elizabeth Gurley. *Women Have a Date with Destiny*. New York: Workers Library, 1944. 31p.

Women's strength in numbers can help re-elect FDR. Since the Roosevelts are a modern couple, FDR allows ER to have her own life and opinions. She is an invaluable partner to him, a source of strength to many, and a symbol of defiance to the Nazis' low opinion of women (pp. 27-28).

F561 Flynn, John T. *Country Squire in the White House*. New York: Doubleday, Doran, 1940; New York: Da Capo, 1972. vii + 131p.

The earnings of ER and other family members (pp. 111-12).

F562 "The Fortune Survey." *Fortune* 21 (May 1940): 76-77, 160, 168-171.

Sect. III, "ER's Career," reports that more that 44 percent of those responding feel that she should continue in public life if FDR is not in the White House after 1940 (pp. 77, 160).

F563 Franken, Rose. "Second Thoughts on the First Lady." *Redbook* 81 (June 1943): 16-19, 79-80.
Her 1943 White House visit with ER, FDR, and Malvina Thompson made her realize that ER's greatness is in her simplicity.

F564 Franklin, Jay. "American vs. European Women in Politics." *Vanity Fair* 43 (Oct. 1935): 21-22.
ER is a "political hostess" who uses the power of White House entertaining to help further New Deal programs.

F565 ---. "First, Second and Third Lady--Mrs. Roosevelt." *Vanity Fair* 45 (Jan. 1936): 37-38, 64.
She is a political force in her own right with an interest in changing policy. Determined to improve the social and economic conditions of all citizens, she realizes that it cannot be done through laws and money alone. Paraphrased as "Mrs. Roosevelt." *Democratic Digest* 8 (Feb. 1936): 3-4.

F566 Franklin, P.L. "The First Lady of the Land." *National Republic* 24 (Nov. 1936): 4-5.
A comparison of ER and Theo Landon, the wives of the 1936 presidential candidates. ER has proven herself fit to be First Lady.

F567 Furman, Bess. "The Lady of the Fireside Forum." *Democratic Digest* 14 (Dec. 1937): 10, 40.
When she holds fireside forums at her Val-Kill cottage ER asks questions and gathers information to report to FDR.

F568 ---. "Mrs. Roosevelt Retains Her Calm." *New York Times* 15 Apr. 1945: 3.
ER controls her grief during Washington ceremonies for her late husband. In the lead article about FDR's burial Frank L. Kluckhohn describes ER during the service (16 Apr. 1945: 1, 3).

F569 ---. "Public Man's Wife--Her Work Is Never Done." *New York Times Magazine* 14 May 1939: 9, 20.
Furman looks at the way a number of women try to be all things to their families and the public. She includes ER's advice: do what is expected of you as quickly as possible and then get out of the way.

F570 ---. "Royal Way through the U.S.A. and Two Who'll Help to Smooth It." *Democratic Digest* 16 (May 1939): 8-9, 35.
Edith Helm and Henrietta Nesbitt will assist ER with the details of the White House visit of the British royal couple. Includes lengthy description of the working relationship between ER and Nesbitt.

F571 Furnas, Helen. "White Housekeeping." *Coronet* 15 (Dec. 1943): 17-21.
With minimal involvement from ER, Henrietta Nesbitt is in charge of food and housekeeping. Condensation issued as "She Runs the White House." *Reader's Digest* 44 (Apr. 1944): 71-72.

F572 Gallup, George H. *The Gallup Poll: Public Opinion, 1935-1971.* 3 vols. (xliv + 2388p.). New York: Random House, 1972. Index.

Jan. 1938 poll on ER as First Lady (v. 1, p. 135). Her resignation from the Daughters of the American Revolution, Mar. 1938 poll (v. 1, p. 142).

ER as First Lady, 1940 poll (v. 1, p. 214). 1942 poll asked what was liked and disliked about ER. Those polled were almost equally divided. While some thought that she should stay at home more, others liked the fact that she did not. While some thought that her actions aroused racial prejudices, an almost equal number praised her social consciousness (v. 1, pp. 356-57). Her trips as First Lady, 1944 poll (v. 1, p. 445).

F573 ---.   "Mrs. Roosevelt More Popular Than President, Survey Finds." *Washington Post* 15 Jan. 1939, sect. 3: 1.

ER has an approval rating of 67 percent compared to FDR's 58 percent. The American people like how she has changed the perception of the role of First Lady and sets a good example. On specific issues such as her business activities, her approval is less.

F574 Gardner, Mona. "Meet the Roosevelts." *Ladies' Home Journal* 61 (Nov. 1944): 141-44, 166.

The Roosevelts' family life in the White House and ER's activities as First Lady in a pre-election story preceding one about the Deweys.

F575 Garrett, Evelyn. *The Four Queens.* London: MacDonald, 1944. xi + 224p.

Includes a detailed, but undocumented, view of ER as First Lady (pp. 109-22, 169-77). Visit of the British royal couple (pp. 181-86).

F576 Goode, Bill. "The First Lady." *Current History* 51 (Mar. 1940): 47-48.

Goode talks to a friend about ER the humble and genuine woman whose sincerity about the problems faced by ordinary people gives hope and encouragement. Condensed from a column in the *Washington Post.* Issued following an article about FDR entitled "Mr. and Mrs. Roosevelt: Recent Pen Portraits."

F577 Gordon, Keith V. *North America Sees Our King and Queen.* London: Hutchinson, 1939. 227p.

The royal couple's visit to Washington and Hyde Park and ER's role as hostess (pp. 181-99, 216-24).

F578 "A Great Day for Pennsylvania Women: Mrs. Roosevelt Visits Enthusiastic Women." *Democratic Digest* 13 (June 1936): 28.

On 8 May 1936 ER addressed Democratic women. By the time she departed she had been dubbed the "eighth wonder of the world."

F579 Griffin, Isabel Kinnear. "Mrs. Roosevelt's Press Conferences." *Democratic Bulletin* 8 (May 1933): 8-9.

There is substantive content to ER's weekly press conferences which means that she speaks out on important issues.

F580 ---. "Your White House." *Democratic Digest* 13 (July 1936): 31.

ER's tours for young people, her use of the White House for conferences on social issues, and the entertaining of all types of citizens have made the American people identify more closely with the White House.

F581 Haber, Paul. *The House of Roosevelt*. Rev. ed. Brooklyn: Author's, 1936. 123p.
He finds ER meddlesome and ingratiating (pp. 109-10).

F582 Halle, Rita S. "That First Lady of Ours." *Good Housekeeping* 97 (Dec. 1933): 20-21, 195-96.
Halle admits that she was tired of hearing about ER, but after a first-hand look she developed respect for the First Lady and her activities. While not neglecting traditional duties as hostess of the White House, ER has undertaken activities unlike any ever tried by her predecessors.

F583 Hazen, Davis W. *Interviewing Sinners & Saints*. Portland: Binfords & Mort, 1942. 431p.
Hazen, a writer for the *Oregonian* [Portland, Ore.] excerpts discussions with ER in the 1930s about FDR and a third term, women in politics, and possibilities of her own candidacy for public office (pp. 153-54).

F584 Hellman, Geoffrey T. "Mrs. Roosevelt." *Life* 8 (5 Feb. 1940): 70-76, 78.
A map of her travels is featured is this comprehensive examination of her activities as First Lady. Her mail and speaking engagements and her typical annual schedule. ER as a columnist and examples of how the United Feature Syndicate has edited some "My Day" columns.

F585 Herrick, Genevieve Forbes. "Eleanor Roosevelt's Patriotic Penny." *Democratic Digest* 8 (Nov. 1933): 7, 12.
ER has told women that the nation's industrial recovery will depend largely on how they spend their pennies.

F586 Hildebrandt, Fred H. "The Nation's First Lady." *Congressional Record* (7 June 1935): 8862.
In a tribute to the role of women in public life is a salute to ER for her travels, the public role which she has created for herself, and the concern which she has for her fellow citizens.

F587 Holmes, Mrs. George Sanford (Kathleen Sexton Holmes). "At the Woman's National Democratic Club: Democratic Women's Day." *Democratic Digest* 16 (Oct. 1939): 25.
Appreciation for ER's participation and her laudatory remarks about the Woman's National Democratic Club and the need for women in all areas of the country to support it.

F588 Hoover, Irwin Hood (Ike). *Forty-two Years in the White House*. Boston: Houghton Mifflin, 1934; Westport: Greenwood, 1974. xii + 332p. Index.
ER's pre-inauguration visit to the White House and her plans for entertaining on inauguration day (pp. 224-27).

F589 Hornaday, Mary. "At Home in the White House." *Christian Science Monitor Magazine* 27 July 1938, Atlantic ed.: 8-9, 13.
The Roosevelts' changes in the decoration of the White House.

F590 ---. "Eleanor Roosevelt the Woman Nobody Understands." *Look* 7 (28 Dec. 1943): 41-42, 44.

After an early life full of many frustrations she has become an unusual First Lady. A description of her life as First Lady including a comparison with Mme. Chiang Kai-shek.

F591 ---. "Intimate Message from Washington." *Christian Science Monitor* 28 May 1938, Atlantic ed.: 1.

ER's press conferences are informal, and a complete record of their content is not being preserved. The reporters and her secretary Malvina Thompson try to protect her, but ER is not concerned about making embarrassing comments.

F592 ---. "Mrs. Roosevelt--A Campaign Issue." *Christian Science Monitor Magazine* 24 June 1936, Atlantic ed.: 5.

Although ER is modest about the influence which she exerts, Hornaday credits her with many New Deal accomplishments. In the 1936 campaign she will be criticized, but her efforts for the less fortunate and the assistance which she provides FDR will bring her praise.

F593 ---. "The President and Mrs. Roosevelt Request the Pleasure of Your Company." *Christian Science Monitor Magazine* 25 Nov. 1939, Atlantic ed.: 5.

Reproductions of invitations are used in this description of White House entertaining.

F594 ---. "White House Traveler." *Christian Science Monitor Magazine* 31 May 1941, Atlantic ed.: 4.

A collection of anecdotes about ER's travels and legendary energy.

F595 "Housekeeper's Week." *Time* 34 (11 Dec. 1939): 16-17.

A lengthy report of a particularly busy week for the First Lady. Speeches, awards, her travel with youth on the way to testify before the Dies Committee, and, most significantly, her appearances at meetings of the committee.

F596 Howe, Louis McHenry. "Women's Ways in Politics." *Woman's Home Companion* 62 (June 1935): 9-10.

Howe examines the role of women in politics and concludes that within 10 years the election of a woman as President will be both possible and advisable since the types of issues promoted by the New Deal are better understood by women. Howe's prediction can be taken as part of his efforts to promote ER for the presidency.

F597 Hurd, Charles. *The White House, a Biography: The Story of the House, Its Occupants, Its Place in American History.* New York: Harper, 1940. xiv + 339. Index.

Entertaining in the Roosevelt White House (pp. 310-11).

F598 Hurst, Fannie. "A First First Lady." *Democratic Digest* 12 (Mar. 1935): 7.

ER is the only First Lady who has refused to accept the established mold. She has shaped her life around the time, one in which there has been improved status for women.

F599 Hynes, Betty. "Fashions Respond to Cheerful Democracy: Public Women Feminine Though Capable." *Democratic Digest* 8 (Oct. 1933): 11, 15.

FDR and ER have helped the country regain its sense of humor while ER leads in bringing "fashion out of the doldrums."

F600 "If Mrs. Roosevelt Were a Railroad Woman." *Baltimore and Ohio Magazine* (May 1935): 9, 11.
The energy which she exhibits as First Lady and the perception that she is committed to seeing that her husband is well fed, that he has a social life, and that his interests and hobbies are also hers would make her a good wife of a railroad man.

F601 "Inaugural Blues." *New Yorker* 9 (18 Feb. 1933): 10.
ER and daughter Anna shop for inaugural gowns. A witty report.

F602 "It Pays to Fly." *Time* 34 (9 Oct. 1939): 49.
Her photograph while on board, a few words by her in support of commercial aviation, and the balance of an advertisement by the Air Transport Assoc.

F603 Johnson, Gerald W. *Roosevelt: Dictator or Democrat*. New York: Harper, 1941. 303p. Index.
ER's name is "anathema" to many, and she has been subjected to vicious attacks. She is disliked because she has been so effective in aiding FDR's career (pp. 67-68).

F604 Jones, Edward Stafford. "Mrs. Roosevelt No Dilletante [sic] According to U. of B. Psychologist; Wide Range of Her Capabilities Revealed in Times 'My Day' Column." *Buffalo Times* 29 Mar. 1936, sect. C: 7.
She has a wide range of interests, with home life and education given the most importance, and does not suppress her feelings and opinions. She is modest and restrained. She has sympathy for others, and she would score high in intelligence tests. No matter how she will be judged by historians, no one will deny that her objective is to help others.

F605 Kamp, Jospeh P. *The Fifth Column in the South*. New Haven: Constitutional Education League, 1940. 42p.
Kamp presents evidence of ER's involvement with Communist organizations in the South. She associated with faculty and supported Commonwealth College in Mena, Ark. and the Highlander Folk School in Monteagle, Tenn. (pp. 12, 14, 18-20) and participated in the Southern Conference for Human Welfare (pp. 26, 29-31).

F606 Kent, George. "Mrs. President." *Radio Stars* (Oct. 1934): 20-21, 99-100.
As First Lady she has broken precedents and continued her efforts to see conditions in the country for herself.

F607 Keyes, Frances Parkinson. *Capital Kaleidoscope: The Story of a Washington Hostess*. New York: Harper, 1937. 358p.
ER is a woman of great intellect with a pleasing personality, but her actions are often misunderstood (pp. 321-33). Gridiron Widows parties are described in detail (pp. 303-9). There is also a biographical sketch of White House reporter Ruby Black, ER's first biographer (pp. 295-97).

F608 ---. "Washington Looks at the Roosevelts: An Exciting Glimpse of What the Capital Thinks of the President and His Wife." *Delineator* 123 (July 1933): 15, 41-42.

Early in the first term Keyes provides an intimate and complimentary look at ER as First Lady and White House hostess.

F609 Kiplinger, W.M. *Washington Is Like That.* New York: Harper, 1942. vi + 506p. Index.

ER continues to be among the most influential persons in Washington. She has influence over government policy, is liked by a broad segment of official Washington, and keeps herself before the public eye. She deserves the credit for the public role which women have now achieved (pp. 299-301).

F610 Knox, Paul. "White House Reception." *Life* 103 (Apr. 1936): 8-9, 11.

What it is like to attend a reception hosted by the Roosevelts. Condensation issued in *Reader's Digest* 28 (May 1936): 48-50.

F611 Krock, Arthur. "'My Day' Anticipates and Echoes Press Conferences." *New York Times* 10 Aug. 1939: 18.

Her "My Day" columns for 8 and 9 Aug. 1939 marked a departure from their usual bland content. At an 8 Aug. press conference ER was at FDR's side when he borrowed from her column already in print. On 9 Aug. her column displayed political acumen in connection with the press conference, and, since she did not credit FDR for her remarks, it is concluded that the thinking was her own. "My Day" is now required reading. The press conference was reported as "Mrs. Roosevelt Joins In." *New York Times* 9 Aug. 1939: 4. For an article about Krock's column, see "My Day." *Saturday Evening Post* 212 (9 Sept. 1939): 24.

F612 ---. "Offensive Action Begun on the Hyde Park Front." *New York Times* 13 Aug. 1939, sect. 4: 3.

FDR is joined by ER when he vows to send back to Congress what they rejected in the last session. She serves "as prologue and epilogue" to his actions.

F613 Kutner, Nanette. If You Worked at the White House." *Good Housekeeping* 118 (May 1944): 4, 163.

Activities of Edith Helm, social secretary to ER.

F614 "Ladies of Washington's Working Press: They Get Their Copy--and Their Rights." *Newsweek* 21 (1 Mar. 1943): 64.

ER arranged for members of her Press Conference Assoc. to be invited to a press conference held by Mme. Chiang Kai-shek. About the women journalists in Washington during the Roosevelt years.

F615 Lawrence, William H. "Mrs. Roosevelt Breaks Still More Traditions." *New York Times* 25 Oct. 1942, sect. 4: 7.

Flying across the Atlantic, a visit abroad without the President, and being placed in physical danger are all firsts for the wife of a President. Both friends and foes recognize the influence which she has on FDR and, through "My Day," on public opinion. There is great impact when she fights discrimination, and who can deny the importance of her appearance before the 1940 Democratic convention.

F616 Lazell, Louise T. "7,000 Farmers Give Mrs. Roosevelt a Picnic." *Democratic Digest* 13 (Aug. 1936): 21.

Edith Helm arranged for ER to be entertained by farm families in Ill.   A description of her visit.

F617 Lindley, Ernest K. *The Roosevelt Revolution, First Phase.* New York: Viking, 1933; New York: Da Capo, 1974. viii + 328p.
Journalist Lindley's account of the early days of the New Deal includes an analysis of ER's character, activities, and influence.   She is a woman with traditional values who has taken her place in a new world for women (pp. 281-83).

F618 Longworth, Alice Roosevelt. "The Ideal Qualifications for a President's Wife." *Ladies' Home Journal* 53 (Feb. 1936): 8-9.
After describing how first ladies from Ida McKinley to Grace Coolidge approached the role, she characterizes ER as the most active and the first to have a public career. No longer will we have to expect the First Lady to cease those activities which she engaged in before her husband was elected.   Mrs. Longworth doubts that wife and children should campaign, however.

F619 ---. "Lion Hunting in the New Deal." *Ladies' Home Journal* 51 (Dec. 1934): 27, 79.
The Roosevelts appear to be the happiest when entertaining, and their casual approach has influenced hostesses throughout Washington.   ER makes every effort to see that her guests are enjoying themselves.

F620 MacKenzie, Catherine. "Simple Fare for the White House." *New York Times Magazine* 9 Dec. 1934: 16.
ER prefers meals to be informal gatherings.

F621 Maine, Basil. *Franklin Roosevelt: His Life and Achievement.* London: Murray, 1938. vii + 286p. Index.
ER uses her time wisely, accomplishes much, and makes life at the White House manageable for FDR.   She goes about her activities with enthusiasm and genuine concern, not just for appearance (pp. 241-42).

F622 Mallon, Paul. "Roosevelt Gets His Story Over." *New York Times Magazine* 19 Nov. 1933: 1, 2, 15.
The new First Lady is helping by encouraging women to write to her about their concerns and hardships.   Her mail is already heavy, and it is predicted that before FDR has to face the voters again she will have consoled countless numbers of women voters (p. 2).

F623 Manning, Marjorie. "Keeping Up with Mrs. Roosevelt." *Delineator* 126 (Mar. 1935): 10, 27.
A regular at ER's weekly press conference reports on her travels with the First Lady.   Unlike the press who accompany her, ER never seems to tire.

F624 Marston, William Moulton. "Who Influences the President More...His Wife or His Mother?" *Look* 3 (14 Mar. 1939): 6-7.
A psychologist examines the personalities and activities of the two Mrs. Roosevelts and concludes that ER, not Sara, exercises more influence over FDR.

F625 Martin, George W. "Preface to the President's Autobiography." *Harper's Magazine* 188 (Feb. 1944): 193-98.

Contains a lengthy assessment of ER. To her goes the credit for FDR's return to public life. She is a lady of social standing, and like others has become complacent. She has become lazy with her public speaking, and "My Day" is "plain balderdash." She has harmed the cause of blacks (pp. 194-95).

F626 McAllister, Dorothy S. "News for the States!" *Democratic Digest* 16 (July 1939): 30.

Quotes from 23 May "My Day" in which ER calls for a national Democratic Women's Day for fund-raising and announces that the first will be on 16 Sept.

F627 McCarten, John. "Pegler: Tough-Guy Columnist." *American Mercury* 60 (Feb. 1945): 174-82.

Pegler now considers ER to be a "cunning" politician who is ready to forfeit our rights as Americans (p. 175).

F628 McLaughlin, Kathleen. "Mrs. Roosevelt Goes Her Way." *New York Times Magazine* 5 July 1936: 7, 15.

Not since Dolley Madison has there been so visible and active a First Lady. The way in which she has shaped her role will be a factor when the voters decide if FDR should have a second term.   She has traveled extensively, made speeches, held regular press conferences, and promoted causes aimed at improving the welfare of all citizens. But not everyone approves.

F629 ---. "The Next First Lady?" *New York Times Magazine* 27 Oct. 1940: 6-7, 22.

After comparing the abilities and styles of the two women, McLauglin concludes that Edith Willkie, like ER, would be a democratic White House hostess with little formality.

F630 Mejia, Aimee S.B. de Ramos. "Un Almuerzo en la Casa Blanca." *Saber Vivir* (Aug. 1941): 22-23.

Admiration for ER as an intellectual and literary figure. In Spanish.

F631 Meredith, Ellis. "At the Woman's National Democratic Club: Mrs. Roosevelt Launches Our Summer Class." *Democratic Digest* 20 (May 1943): 13.

ER has agreed to be the first speaker for the Woman's National Democratic Club's summer program.

F632 Moorstern, Betty. "The First Lady Had a Fitting." *PM* 23 Jan. 1945: 17.

A detailed account of how at the New York firm of Arnold Constable ER tried on her fourth inauguration wardrobe.

F633 "Mr. Roosevelt's New Deal for Women." *Literary Digest* 115 (15 Apr. 1933): 22, 24.

In this early look at the roles being played by women in the New Deal ER's existence is acknowledged, but there is no discussion of her activities as First Lady or her efforts on behalf of women.

F634 "Mrs. Franklin D. (Anna Eleanor) Roosevelt." *Public Opinion* 7 (Sept. 1937): 17-18.

It will be women who bring about a better world, and ER is doing more than anyone else to see that they do. She and FDR have done much to improve life for all citizens.

F635 "Mrs. Franklin D. Roosevelt." *Democratic Digest* 14 (Jan. 1937): 20.
A brief statement on her life and activities on the occasion of FDR's second inauguration.

F636 "Mrs. Roosevelt Calls Year in White House an Experience of Absorbing Interest." *New York Times* 27 Feb. 1934: 21.
Her first year in the White House taught her much about the American people and their strength.

F637 "Mrs. Roosevelt Chooses Inaugural Gown; Picks 'Eleanor Blue' Dress in 30 Minutes." *New York Times* 11 Feb. 1933: 1.
This and "Wrap of 'Anna Blue' for Mrs. Roosevelt." *New York Times* 25 Feb. 1933: 7 detail her inaugural wardrobe.

F638 "Mrs. Roosevelt Counsels Jews: Did the President's Wife Warn or Defend or Do Both." *Frauds and Answers* (May 1942): 22-23.
In her "If You Ask Me" columns for Dec. 1941 and Feb. 1942 ER responded to questions about anti-Semitism. Her answers raise other questions. Should Jews be less concerned about anti-Semitism? Are they wrong to place "Jewishness on a parity with Americanism?" Are other religious groups also guilty of this? In any event, she should continue to make statements like these.

F639 "Mrs. Roosevelt Flies to Georgia; Was at Benefit When News Came." *New York Times* 13 Apr. 1945: 4.
Only minutes after HST was sworn in as President ER left by plane for Warm Springs, Ga. Reports on her departure from the White House, her other activities on the day of FDR's death, and what she had scheduled for the next week.

F640 "Mrs. Roosevelt Keeps to Routine." *New York Times* 17 Feb. 1933: 5.
After the 16 Feb. assassination attempt on FDR, ER issued a statement that she could not imagine living in fear of physical harm. While rejecting the idea of protection for herself she also expressed doubt that even the President can be protected at all times.

F641 "Mrs. Roosevelt Lends a Helping Hand." *Democratic Digest* 15 (Apr. 1938): 42.
Brief statement about the assistance which ER gave White House maid Elizabeth McDuffie in making a movie screen test.

F642 "Mrs. Roosevelt Returns for Visit." *New York Times* 15 Mar. 1933: 19.
Upon arriving in New York she reported that there has been no increase in her mail, that there is nothing tiring about living in the White House, and that she will not comment about political matters.

F643 "Mrs. Roosevelt--Snappy Dresser." *Democratic Digest* 12 (May 1935): 10.
Admiration for her clothes and the frequency with which she must change for different engagements.

F644 "Mrs. Roosevelt Tells the Truth." *Christian Century* 61 (26 July 1944): 868.
While it may not have been a wise move in this election year, ER was correct in a speech at Antioch College to call for an independent body to watch over the actions of all countries.

F645 "Mrs. Roosevelt Tries on Her Inauguration Frocks." *Life* 10 (13 Jan. 1941): 26-27.
Gowns and coats for the first three inaugurations are illustrated in this brief article about how she is not overly concerned with her wardrobe.

F646 "Mrs. Roosevelt's New Kitchen." *Delineator* 127 (Nov. 1935): 70.
The old kitchen, the new one, and the White House kitchen staff.

F647 "Mrs. Roosevelt's Red Roses." *Democratic Digest* 13 (May 1936): 34.
When she was presented red roses, she decided to carry them instead of wearing them on her wine-colored dress.

F648 "Mrs. Roosevelt's Role as White House Adviser." *United States News* 9 (20 Dec. 1940): 10-11.
FDR's attention must now be directed to the war effort, but ER will not let New Deal programs be forgotten. She is FDR's adviser on social problems and next to him the country's most influential person. Since the causes which she has pursued are those which have been emphasized by the New Deal, her influence is obvious.

F649 Nesbitt, Henrietta. "At Home in the White House." *Ladies' Home Journal* 61 (Nov. 1944): 158.
Captioned photographs containing quotations by ER describe how the Roosevelts have decorated their White House living quarters.

F650 "New Mistress of White House Plans Conferences with Press." *Christian Science Monitor* 4 Mar. 1933, Eastern ed.: 3.
ER's press conferences and the activities of her family will give women reporters much to write about. Provides insight into the Roosevelt family and ER's wardrobe, activities, and preparation for her new duties.

F651 "Okay, Eleanor." *Collier's* 105 (23 Mar. 1940): 86.
No more jokes about her. Since she and her actions are taken seriously, criticism should be on political grounds only.

F652 "Open House: Hospitality on Tap When the President and First Lady Entertain." *Literary Digest* 124 (3 July 1937): 4-5.
How the Roosevelts greet visitors to the White House.

F653 "Oracle." *Time* 33 (17 Apr. 1939): 21-23.
ER is "the world's foremost political force" and through her impact on public opinion she is "a woman of unequaled influence in the world." When she became First Lady her activities brought jokes, but now she is taken seriously. Examples are cited of how she is less hesitant in public statements and is an "oracle" to women regarding issues such as the U.S.'s role in the current world situation.

F654 "Our President's Wife." *Adult School Messenger* 7 (29 Nov. 1934): 3, 8.
Her energy, enthusiasm, and genuine interest in people make her our most remarkable First Lady.

F655 "Our Tireless Traveler." *New York Times* 17 Jan. 1938: 18.
She has been almost everywhere but the moon, although she has traveled nearly that far by train, plane, and car. In the editorial column "Topics of the Times."

F656 Parker, Maude. "The New Social Deal." *Saturday Evening Post* 206 (28 Apr. 1934): 10-11, 97-98.
The Roosevelts entertain with simplicity and grace.

F657 Partridge, Bellamy. *The Roosevelt Family in America: An Imperial Saga.* New York: Hillman-Curl, 1936. xvi + 325p. Bibliography.
There is some attention to her private life and early political activities, but the emphasis is on ER as First Lady. Her travels, radio broadcasts, public speaking, and relations with the Oyster Bay branch of the family are addressed (pp. 283-92).

F658 Pasley, Virginia. "First Lady to the Common Man." *American Mercury* 58 (Mar. 1944): 275-83.
The sophisticated cannot understand how one of their own is so appealing to the common people. It is because this woman, who is neither a good writer nor speaker, is more like the common people than one would expect and therefore they feel comfortable with her and her philosophy. Concludes that she has little or no influence on FDR. In two subsequent issues readers criticize ER's activities and motives: 58 (May 1944): 635-36; 58 (June 1944): 762, 766.

F659 Pearson, Drew, and Robert S. Allen. "Eleanor Roosevelt: Home Maker." *Look* 3 (14 Mar. 1939): 8-9.
She is an effective First Lady who values her success as a wife, mother, and grandmother.

F660 ---. "The First Secretary of the Land." *Redbook* (Mar. 1937): 19, 105-7.
It is as much about ER's secretaries Malvina Thompson and Edith Helm as it is about Missy LeHand. Their daily working relationship with ER.

F661 ---. "How the President Works." *Harper's Magazine* 173 (June 1936): 1-14.
In spite of some of the "half-baked" information which she gives FDR, ER is his best avenue for maintaining contact with the rest of the nation. It is apparent that they discuss national issues (pp. 11-12).

F662 Peck, Mary Gray. *Carrie Chapman Catt: A Biography.* New York: Wilson, 1944; New York: Octagon, 1975; Westport: Hyperion, 1976. 495p. Index. Notes.
Catt on ER as White House hostess (pp. 450-52) and Catt's admiration for her (p. 446).

F663 Pegler, Westbrook. "Fair Enough." *New York World-Telegram* 17 Mar. 1938.
Pegler's highly complimentary look at ER in his syndicated column. He describes her as "the greatest American woman," one who has no interest in partisan politics or profiting from her position. "Mrs. Roosevelt Is Hailed as 'The Greatest American Woman.'" *Life* 4 (11 Apr. 1938): 31 excerpts the column. The text which accom-

panies Paul Calvert's photograph also discusses the extent of her travels during Mar. 1938.

F664 ---. "Trying on a Shoe." *The Dissenting Opinions of Mister Westbrook Pegler.* New York: Scribner's, 1938. 78-81.

In a "My Day" column ER maligns a fellow columnist, and Pegler defends himself by tracing the roots of his cynicism to FDR.

F665 Perkins, Frances. "Eleanor Roosevelt's Talent." *Democratic Digest* 13 (Aug. 1936): 21.

The extent of her love for the human race is a special talent. Tribute made at the Democratic National Convention Breakfast for Women, Philadelphia, 24 June 1936.

F666 "Power behind Throne." *New York Times* 14 Mar. 1939: 20.

ER says that she does not advise FDR because she seldom sees him. But she is too modest. She sees him often and advises him too. In the editorial column "Topics of the Times."

F667 "President's Wife Off to Haiti Today." *New York Times* 6 Mar. 1934: 12.

A report written on the train ER took to Miami before her flight to Haiti and then Puerto Rico. About the preparations she was making for her mission and how she entertained herself while traveling. "Virgin Islanders Cheer First Lady." *New York Times* 8 Mar. 1934: 3 discusses her arrival in St. Thomas and San Juan. Harwood Hull's "Island Is Inspired by Mrs. Roosevelt." *New York Times* 18 Mar. 1934, sect. 4: 8 describes how her visit has provided hope for a better life.

F668 "President's Wife Raising O'Day Fund." *New York Times* 16 Oct. 1934: 1, 3.

She will chair the fund-raising effort and campaign for friend and congressional candidate Caroline O'Day. The Young Republicans have rallied behind O'Day's opponent as reported in "Women to Oppose Mrs. Roosevelt." *New York Times* 17 Oct. 1934: 17.

F669 "Press Women Give Annual Frolic." *New York Times* 21 Mar. 1933: 14.

Parodies of ER's activities are presented at 20 Mar. Women's National Press Club dinner.

F670 Pringle, Henry F. "The President." *New Yorker* 10 (16 June 1934): 20-25; 10 (23 June 1934): 20-24; 10 (30 June 1934): 20-24.

In this study of FDR's first year in office there are descriptions of ER as First Lady and White House hostess in the parts dated 16 and 23 June.

F671 Putnam, George Palmer. *Soaring Wings: A Biography of Amelia Earhart.* New York: Harcourt, Brace, 1939. x + 294p.

Earhart's husband describes visits to the White House, ER and Earhart flying over Washington at night, and a late night drive in ER's new Dymaxion automobile (pp. 128-36).

F672 Rand, Clayton. *The New Deal & the New Slavery.* Gulfport: Dixie, 1944. [16]p.

Bureaucracy is the new slavery which FDR is practicing. References to ER as his helpmate and instigator of racial unrest (pp. [4, 6, 9]).

F673 Randolph, Mary. *Presidents and First Ladies*. New York: Appleton-Century, 1936. 257p. Index.

The secretary to Grace Coolidge and a frequent White House visitor discusses ER as White House hostess (pp. 233-49). Excerpts issued in pt. 4 of "Presidents and First Ladies." *Ladies' Home Journal* 53 (Aug. 1936): 14, 55-58.

F674 Rondon, Alberto. "Interesantes Declaraciones de la Sra. de Roosevelt." *Cinelandia* 15 (Dic. 1941): 10, 45.

ER understands why Latin Americans can be resentful of the U.S., but all citizens of the Americas should work together for their mutual benefit and for the good of the rest of the world. In Spanish.

F675 "Roosevelt Goes West to Say 'Howdy' and 'Meet the Wife.'" *Newsweek* 10 (4 Oct. 1937): 14-15.

During their trip to the West FDR made every effort to showcase ER, and she was well received by the crowds which gathered when the train made stops.

F676 Ross, Ishbel. *Ladies of the Press: The Story of Women in Journalism by an Insider*. New York: Harper, 1936; New York: Arno, 1974. xii + 622p. Index.

First ladies and the press with particular emphasis on ER's associations with newspaperwomen who attended her White House press conferences (pp. 309-22).

F677 "Sees Mrs. Roosevelt as Tradition Breaker." *New York Times* 26 June 1936: 12.

Fannie Hurst has said that in the face of criticism ER is dispensing with the traditional role of First Lady and that her actions mean advancement for all women.

F678 "Seventieth Anniversary of Hampton Institute." *Southern Workman* 67 (June 1938): 173-77.

ER's unassuming arrival and her activities while there.

F679 Shaw, Albert. "Talking Sense." *Review of Reviews* 93 (May 1936): 21.

ER is the New Deal's leading spokesperson for social welfare policies and she is courageous in her discussion of world affairs in "My Day." In the editorial column "Progress of the World."

F680 "Sixty Girls Enjoy White House Fete." *New York Times* 17 May 1936: 25.

At the White House ER entertains black girls from the National Training School.

F681 "Smart New York Democratic Women Stage Non-Partisan Meeting." *Democratic Digest* 16 (Dec. 1939): 28.

Brief announcement of conference sponsored by Dutchess County, N.Y. Federation of Democratic Women's Club. ER attended the Vassar College meeting.

F682 Smith, Gerald L.K. *Too Much Roosevelt*. Detroit: Committee of 1,000,000, 1940. 100p.

There are several sections critical of ER: her involvement with Communists in the youth movement, examples of how she uses her position as First Lady to earn huge sums of money, her presence at the 1940 Democratic National Convention, and her belief that young girls should learn to drink (pp. 40-41, 43, 46, 62-63, 70).

F683 Smith, Helena Huntington. "The First Lady." *McCall's* 62 (Sept. 1935): 4, 33, 61, 65, 68.

A perceptive look at ER as First Lady, her official role and her influence on New Deal programs. Smith predicts that someday the historical signifance of the Roosevelt team will be recognized. For a discussion of the article, see "The Vitality of Mrs. Roosevelt." *Democratic Digest* 12 (Sept. 1935): 28. ER "dominates the feminine side of her husband's party organization, and she decides most of the appointments of women." Many have forgotten that she had an earlier career in Democratic Party affairs.

F684 ---. "The President Never Rings Twice." *Delineator* 126 (May 1935): 4-5, 73.

White House secretaries including Malvina Thompson and Edith Helm and the roles which they play in ER's activities as First Lady.

F685 Smith, Rembert Gilman. *Eleanor Roosevelt: First in Travels, First in Writings, First in the Hearts of the Communists*. Tulsa: Smith, 1941. 14p.

ER and Smith exchanged letters about her financial assistance of Communist Party members in Okla. Reissued in his *Mourning Becomes Columbia!*, pp. 116-31 (Tulsa: Columbia, 1943). Her involvement with the "Communists" had been reported as "Mrs. F.D. Roosevelt Sends \$25 to Defend 'Reds.'" *Fiery Cross* (Knights of the Ku Klux Klan) 1 (Nov. 1940): 1-2.

F686 "Speaking of Mrs. Roosevelt." *Democratic Digest* 15 (Mar. 1938): 27.

Selections from recent newspaper editorials in praise of ER as First Lady.

F687 Stern, Elizabeth Gertrude. "Exacting Role of the First Lady." *New York Times Magazine* 17 Mar. 1937: 10, 21.

In an article mainly about her predecessors ER is described as the first to break tradition and pursue outside interests.

F688 "Story Over." *Time* 45 (30 Apr. 1945): 24.

ER packs family possessions, tries to cope with an avalanche of mail, and leaves the White House. She tells reporters in New York that the story is over.

F689 Strayer, Martha. "Last Press Conference of Eleanor Roosevelt." *Guild Reporter* (May 1945).

Copy not examined. Also cited as 20 Apr. 1945.

F690 "That 'Foreign Agent' Gag." Editorial. *Daily Worker* 24 Nov. 1939: 6.

ER has called Communists "foreign agents" and has won praise for doing so, but she is as mistaken as those who want to deny basic rights to the accused. In another editorial published 15 Dec. (p. 6), "Mrs. Roosevelt Finds a New Way," it is claimed that the Justice Dept. is as bad as the Dies Committee by thinking that the Bill of Rights applies to everyone but Communists. As the unofficial spokeswoman of the administration ER opposes the Dies Committee but does not speak out against Justice's tactics.

F691 "They Stood Out from the Crowd in 1934." *Literary Digest* 118 (29 Dec. 1934): 7, 39.

ER ranked seventh in a vote by the American press for the year's outstanding personalities. Brief statements about the top 10.

F692 Thompson, Dorothy. "In Defense of Mrs. Roosevelt." *New York Herald Tribune* 29 Apr. 1938: 21.

Catholic organizations are wrong to try to deny ER her right to express opinions about divorce and the film *The Birth of a Baby*. We should be proud that as First Lady she does not hesitate to share her views.

F693 "Throngs Pay Honor to New First Lady." *New York Times* 5 Mar. 1933: 4.

ER and Lou Hoover at FDR's first inauguration. The serious look on ER's face changed, and she responded to the crowd as the ceremony concluded.

F694 "Tireless Lady: Eleanor Roosevelt Charms as Public Precedent Breaker." *Literary Digest* 123 (23 Jan. 1937): 4-5.

Without her FDR might never achieved the presidency. Praise for her energy and her 15 firsts as First Lady.

F695 "To a Great Lady." *Congressional Record Appendix* (24 Apr. 1945): A1894.

With her departure from Washington, the city has lost a great friend. Reprint of 21 Apr. editorial from the *Washington News*.

F696 "To Paint Mrs. F.D.R." *Art Digest* 15 (15 Mar. 1941): 16.

Darrel E. Brown is to produce a portrait of ER in her inaugural gown, but there are those in the art world who disagree with the selection of Brown.

F697 Tyndale, Hall. "The White House: President and Mrs. Roosevelt at Home." *Windsor* 88 (July 1938): 195-204.

ER's activities as First Lady and how she ignores her critics. "She directs her energies to doing everything she can to help her man."

F698 "Valiant Lady." *Newsweek* 25 (23 Apr. 1945): 39-40.

With the death of FDR we have also lost "a great lady."

F699 Van Deman, Ruth. "U.S. Kitchen No. 1." *Journal of Home Economics* 28 (Feb. 1936): 93-94.

During her 16 Dec. 1935 press conference ER conducted a tour of the remodeled White House kitchen and staff areas.

F700 Villard, Oswald Garrison. "Issues and Men." *Nation* 142 (15 Apr. 1936): 482.

Since ER's dedication to peace does not equal that of Jane Addams' she is not her successor as the country's foremost woman. Although there is praise for ER's approach to the position of First Lady, he is critical of "My Day" and her too frequent speeches and radio broadcasts.

F701 ---. "Issues and Men." *Nation* 148 (31 Dec. 1938): 15.

ER deserves praise for her approach to the role of First Lady and her desire to see presidents' families lead normal lives.

F702 Villareal, Maximiano Marmito. "Mrs. Roosevelt and the World Peace." *Congressional Record Appendix* (16 June 1938): A2894-95.

She is right to advocate a common language as a way of securing a lasting peace in all areas of the world. Reprinted in the *Congressional Record*. Original publication not known.

F703 "Washington's Social Calendar Calls for Gay Garden Parties." *Christian Science Monitor* 15 June 1934, Eastern ed.: 7.
Garden parties are a favorite of the First Lady, and recently she has given several of them.

F704 "Watch Mrs. Roosevelt." *Time* 37 (3 Mar. 1941): 13-14.
We have observed her concern over economic ills and her exit from communistic groups. Westbrook Pegler has concluded that our freedoms are at risk in her hands. Now the *Wall Street Journal* is advising its readers to listen to her for hints about possible new government policies.

F705 Weiss, Katherine Sigler. "The First Junior League First Lady." *Junior League Magazine* 20 (Nov. 1933): 9-10.
She is untiring and unselfish and loves all peoples. Writing from Los Angeles, the author relates numerous examples of ER's kindness during a recent trip.

F706 Wells. H.G. *Experiment in Autobiography: Discoveries and Conclusions of a Very Ordinary Brain (Since 1866).* New York: Macmillan, 1934. x + 718p.
Brief account of a 1934 visit to the White House where he found ER to be neither the anticipated "school marm" nor one overcome by her own self-importance (pp. 679-80).

F707 Whipple, Wayne. *The Story of the White House and Its Home Life.* By Wayne Whipple and completed by Alice Roosevelt Longworth. Boston: Dwinell-Wright, 1937. 62p.
The Roosevelts fill the White House with children and grandchildren and bring informality to White House entertaining (pp. 60-61).

F708 "White House: Bars Let Down by Roosevelts." *Newsweek* 1 (18 Mar. 1933): 10-11.
The Roosevelts have brought new life to the White House and Washington. She is a whirlwind of activity.

F709 Whitehurst, Ben. "Dear Mister President--." *Saturday Evening Post* 209 (20 Mar. 1937): 12-13, 52, 54, 56.
In an article about FDR's mail selections of letters received by ER are included (p. 56).

F710 "Wives of Candidates." Editorial. *Equal Rights* 2 (1 Aug. 1936): 170.
The Republicans are trying to portray Theo Landon as the opposite to ER. As much as some men might prefer a First Lady who restricts her interests to being a wife, mother, and White House hostess, Mrs. Landon is really not that different from ER. While Mrs. Landon's interests in philanthropic and human welfare issues have been limited to Kan., Mrs. Roosevelt has operated in a larger arena. During the campaign both wives have tried to stay in the background.

F711 Wolf, Ann M. *No Fourth Term.* N.p.: Blackwell Printing, 1944. 118p.
Argues against a fourth term for both FDR and ER. ER is mentioned frequently with substantive attention to her earnings from speaking and writing (pp. 31-32) and her use of the poor, youth, and blacks to build support for the New Deal (pp. 28-29,

62-67). She is presented as a cunning politician and the real power in the administration (pp. 61-67).

F712 "A Woman at the Desk." Editorial. *New York Times* 23 Feb. 1933: 16.
   When ER becomes the First Lady she will also serve as housekeeper for the White House. Like other women who run households she will see that economy is introduced in her new home.

F713 Woodruff, Caroline S. "A Visit to the White House by the President of the National Education Association, Caroline S. Woodruff." *Journal of the National Education Association of the United States* 27 (May 1938): 131-32.
   A busy ER was the perfect hostess during her stay at the White House.

F714 Wright, James L. "Trouping with the Roosevelts." *Democratic Digest* 14 (Nov. 1937): 23, 34.
   During a trip to the West with the Roosevelts he was impressed with ER's busy schedule. An amusing account.

F715 Young, G. Gordon. *Voyage of State*. London: Hodder and Stoughton, 1939. 319 + 4p.
   A comprehensive treatment of the British royal visit of June 1939 to Washington and Hyde Park (pp. 222-42, 253-61).

FIRST LADY, LATER WRITINGS

F716 Aikman, Lonnelle. *The Living White House*. 3rd ed. Washington: White House Historical Assoc., 1976. 147p. Index.
   Anecdotes about ER as First Lady (pp. 64, 73, 96, 101-2, 140).

F717 Alexander, Will W. *The Reminiscences of Will W. Alexander*. New York Times Oral History Program. Columbia University Oral History Collection, pt. 1, no. 185. Glen Rock: Microfilming Corp. of America, 1972. 8 microfiche. Index.
   Alexander's casual recollections about political and social issues of interest to ER as First Lady; visit of the British royal family (pp. 508-12, 578-81, 621, 674).

F718 Alsop, Joseph. *FDR, 1884-1945: A Centenary Remembrance*. New York: Viking, 1982. 256p.
   ER as First Lady (pp. 128-29, 156-58, and 166-67).

F719 "America Loved the Roosevelts." *Life* 21 (25 Nov. 1946): 110-11.
   An informal photograph of ER and FDR taken at Hyde Park in 1941 with accompanying text about how they went about their duties during the White House years.

F720 *The American Heritage Pictorial History of the Presidents of the United States*. 2 vols. (1023p.) New York: American Heritage-Simon and Schuster, 1968. Index.
   Sections on ER as First Lady and aide to FDR (v. 2, pp. 844-45, 854).

F721 Anthony, Carl Sferrazza. *First Ladies: The Saga of the Presidents' Wives and Their Power, 1789-1961*. Vol. [1] of *First Ladies*. New York: Morrow, 1990. 685p. Index. Notes.

Her activities as First Lady (pp. 449-513). ER and Bess Truman compared (p. 513). Based on manuscript sources, interviews, and derivations from published works.

F722 ---. *First Ladies: The Saga of the Presidents' Wives and Their Power, 1961-1990.* Vol. 2 of *First Ladies.* New York: Morrow, 1991. 511p. Index. Bibliography. Notes.
Correspondence with Jacqueline Kennedy, comparison with Lady Bird Johnson, and Mrs. Johnson's admiration of ER (pp. 59-61, 113-14, 125, 127, 140, 142).

F723 ---. "The First Ladies: They've Come a Long Way, Martha." *Smithsonian* 23 (Oct. 1992): 135-36, 138-52, 154-58.
ER and other modern first ladies as campaigners.

F724 Asbell, Bernard. *The F.D.R. Memoirs*. *As Written by Bernard Asbell.* New York: Doubleday, 1973. xvii + 461p. Index. Bibliography. Notes.
ER as First Lady in memoirs which rely heavily on writings by and about her (pp. 22-146 passim, 256-335 passim, and 349-416 passim).

F725 Ayres, B. Drummond Jr. "The Importance of Being Rosalynn." *New York Times Magazine* 3 June 1979: 39-40, 42, 44.
While Rosalynn Carter claims that she has never tried to emulate ER, others think that she plays a role similar to that of her predecessor because of the input which she has (p. 44).

F726 Beasley, Maurine. "Bess Truman and the Press: A Case Study of a First Lady as Political Communicator." *Harry S. Truman: The Man from Independence.* Contributions in Political Science, 145. Ed. William F. Levantrosser. New York: Greenwood, 1986. 208-16.
Beasley's paper includes the inevitable comparison of Bess Truman's relationship with the press with that of her predecessor (pp. 208, 210-14). Paper presented at a Hofstra Univ. conference, 1983.

F727 ---. "Eleanor Roosevelt's Press Conferences: Symbolic Importance of a Pseudo-Event." *Journalism Quarterly* 61 (Summer 1984): 274-79, 338.
She establishes the symbolic values of ER's White House press conferences: as a "means of influencing women," as a "forum for [discussing] political ideas," and as a way of institutionalizing "the First Lady as a news source."

F728 ---. "Lorena A. Hickok: Journalistic Influence on Eleanor Roosevelt." *Journalism Quarterly* 57 (Summer 1980): 281-86.
Hickok is credited with facilitating ER's early relationship with women reporters who covered the White House. ER came to realize that her activities as First Lady were newsworthy, that she provided an opportunity for women reporters by encouraging them to cover her activities, and that press coverage helped promote her image.

F729 ---. "Mrs. Bush, Meet Mrs. Roosevelt." *Washington Journalism Review* 1 (Jan./Feb. 1989): 39-41.
No other First Lady has equaled ER's close involvement with Washington journalists, but Barbara Bush might consider trying to match ER's successful use of

the press. The origins of ER's press conferences, some of the reporters who participated, and the issues which were discussed.

F730 Belford, Barbara. "Emma Bugbee." *Brilliant Bylines: A Biographical Anthology of Notable Newspaperwomen in America*. New York: Columbia Univ. Pr., 1986. 173-82. Bibliography.

New York Herald Tribune reporter Bugbee was one of the inner circle of reporters who covered the First Lady, and it was that opportunity which boosted her career.

F731 Bishop, Jim. *FDR's Last Year, April 1944-April 1945*. New York: Morrow, 1974. xiv + 690p. Index. Bibliography.

Lengthy references to ER related to FDR's health, death, and burial. Based in part on interviews conducted by Bishop through which he encountered many ER devotees and distractors.

F732 Bloom, Sol. *The Autobiography of Sol Bloom*. New York: Putnam's, 1948. 345p. Index.

Rep. Bloom provides a moving tribute to ER. To him no one has given more of herself. "I am her devoted servant" (p. 326).

F733 Blum, John Morton. *From the Morgenthau Diaries, Years of Crisis, 1928-1938*. Boston: Houghton Mifflin, 1959. 583p. Index. Notes.

In an introductory statement Henry Morgenthau, Jr. expresses his admiration for ER, and throughout the volume there are significant references to her which reveal her presence as a major force in FDR's governorship and presidency.

F734 ---. *From the Morgenthau Diaries, Years of Urgency, 1938-1941*. Boston: Houghton Mifflin, 1965. 443p. Index. Notes.

There is a lengthy entry from the diaries which outlines Morgenthau's reliance upon the advice and direction of ER in dealing with FDR (pp. 26-29).

F735 Boller, Paul F., Jr. *Presidential Wives*. New York: Oxford Univ. Pr., 1988. viii + 533p. Index. Notes.

ER and Rosalynn Carter are compared. As first ladies they both had a keen interest in politics and served as reporters for their husbands. ER developed her own identity which was foremost to her, but Mrs. Carter had no such identity and viewed herself first as a wife (p. 434).

F736 Brown, Christine M. "Historical Study of First Ladies in Communication Roles: Eleanor Roosevelt to Betty Ford." Project (M.A.) Fairfield Univ. 1975. 150p. Bibliography. Notes.

How ER used the media and was viewed by the press. Includes biographical information (pp. 11-43). Derived in large part from Lash's *Eleanor and Franklin*.

F737 Bugbee, Emma. "Eleanor Roosevelt: My Most Unforgettable Character." *Reader's Digest* 83 (Oct. 1963): 91-97.

As First Lady and as a person ER was genuine and humble.

F738 Burns, James MacGregor. *The Crosswinds of Freedom*. The American Experiment, 3. New York: Knopf, 1989. xi + 864p. Index. Notes.

ER's influence on FDR (pp. 29, 83, 113, 133). For less extensive coverage, see his *The Lion and the Fox* (New York: Harcourt, Brace, 1956).

F739 ---. *Roosevelt: The Soldier of Freedom*. New York: Harcourt Brace Jovanovich, 1970. xiv + 722p. Index. Bibliography. Notes.
  Burns portrays ER on election night 1940 as a First Lady whose efforts for the less fortunate had come to be generally accepted. Although she had developed into a strong personality, she was still the caring woman who aided FDR by being his conscience. Her public life--causes, activities, and travels--had become a substitute for the passion which was no longer part of her private life (pp. 7-8, 59-60). An excerpt about ER at the time of FDR's death and burial issued as "F.D.R.: The Last Journey." *American Heritage* 21 (Aug. 1970): 9-11, 78-85.

F740 Butturff, Dorothy Dow. *Eleanor Roosevelt, an Eager Spirit: The Letters of Dorothy Dow, 1933-1945*. Ed. Ruth K. McClure. New York: Norton, 1984. 252p.
  Dow, assistant to ER's secretary Malvina Thompson, wrote to family and friends about ER's activities at the White House and Val-Kill.

F741 Cannon, Poppy, and Patricia Brooks. *The Presidents' Cookbook: Practical Recipes from George Washington to the Present*. New York: Bonanza, 1968. x + 561p. Index.
  Private and official dining during the Roosevelt years. ER as White House homemaker and hostess (pp. 430-48). Dedicated to ER.

F742 Caroli, Betty Boyd. "America's First Ladies." *American History Illustrated* 24 (May 1989): 26-31, 48, 50.
  As First Lady ER broke many precedents. Her press conferences, her efforts on behalf of women, youth, and minorities, and her travels brought her admiration and criticism (p. 31).

F743 ---. *First Ladies*. New York: Oxford Univ. Pr., 1987. xxii + 398p. Index. Notes.
  Activities and accomplishments of ER as First Lady (pp. 184-202).   She is compared to her successors (pp. 202-78 passim). Includes various rankings of first ladies (pp. 383-90).

F744 Chamberlain, John. "FDR's Missus." Rev. of *Eleanor and Franklin* by Joseph P. Lash. National Review 23 (3 Dec. 1971): 1357-58.
  Lash's account of the White House years demonstrates how naive the Roosevelts were about economics, communism, and the post-war world. Any advice ER may have given FDR was probably wrong.

F745 Churchill, Allen. *The Roosevelts: American Aristocrats*. New York: Harper & Row, 1965. v + 294p. Index. Bibliography.
  ER as First Lady (pp. 259-60, 262-63, 268, 270).

F746 Clark, Electra. *Leading Ladies: An Affectionate Look at American Women of the Twentieth Century*. New York: Stein and Day, 1976. 252p. Index.
  ER the active, precedent-breaking First Lady. Mainly anecdotal (pp. 131-34).

F747 Cohen, Meg. "First Ladies." *Harper's Bazaar* 3373 (Jan. 1993): 133.
A brief article about how some modern first ladies, including ER, approached their roles.

F748 Collins, Jean E. "Eleanor Roosevelt and Her Press Group." *She Was There: Stories of Pioneering Women Journalists*. By Jean E. Collins. New York: Messner, 1980. 34-51.
Kathleen McLaughlin, Emma Bugbee, and Dorothy Ducas recall ER when they were reporters covering the White House.

F749 Cook, Blanche Wiesen. "Before Hillary, There Was Eleanor." *Los Angeles Times* 17 Jan. 1993, sect. M: 1, 3.
Hillary Rodham Clinton is the type of well-educated articulate woman ER hoped would enter the public scene. If Mrs. Clinton puts herself forward and speaks out, she will simply be doing what ER did before her.

F750 Cooper, Ethel A. *That Wicked Woman with Her Organized Crime in the White House and Other Literary Selections*. Dallas: Cooper, 1977. 45p.
Cooper claims that ER had hired killers at her disposal and that she had been an intended victim.

F751 Craig, Barbara. "The Day Bob Fogg Flew under the Bridge with His Friend Eleanor Roosevelt." *Yankee* 27 (Nov. 1973): 115, 192, 195, 197, 202, 204.
Robert Fogg reminiscences about a seaplane flight with ER when she took over the controls. Issued as part of article "A Roosevelt Trilogy."

F752 Daniels, Jonathan. *White House Witness, 1942-1945*. Garden City: Doubleday, 1975. xii + 299p. Index.
Daniels was FDR's last press secretary, and his diary gives brief glimpses into the activities of ER and some of her acquaintances.

F753 Davis, Kenneth S. *FDR, into the Storm, 1937-1940: A History*. New York: Random House, 1993. 691p. Index. Notes.
"My Day" and ER's lecture tours served as trial balloons for FDR's ideas (pp. 289-90). ER and the death of Louis Howe (pp. 5-6). Writing of *This Is My Story* (pp. 160-62). ER and the 1940 Democratic National Convention (pp. 594-96).

F754 ---. *FDR, the New Deal Years, 1933-1937: A History*. New York: Random House, 1986. 756p. Index. Notes.
ER's activities as First Lady during FDR's first term (pp. 165, 168-75). ER's first 100 days (p. 165).

F755 Diller, Daniel C., and Stephen L. Robertson. *The Presidents, First Ladies, and Vice Presidents: White House Biographies, 1789-1989*. Washington: Congressional Quarterly, 1989. ix + 147p. Index. Notes.
ER's activities as First Lady and how she changed the role (pp. 10, 12-13). In balance, her style proved to be more of an asset than a liability. Also issued in *Congressional Quarterly's Guide to the Presidency*, pp. 868, 870 (Washington: Congressional Quarterly, 1989). Similar, but less extensive, is *The Presidency A to Z: A Ready Reference Encyclopedia*, p. 180 (Washington: Congressional Quarterly, 1992).

F756 Duffy, Martha. "The Spur." Rev. of *Eleanor and Franklin* by Joseph P. Lash. *Time* 98 (29 Nov. 1971): 86-87.
The book's strength is in bringing "all of [ER] alive." The private side of her life reveals that she was FDR's conscience, a "spur."

F757 "Eleanor Roosevelt: A Moralist in Politics." *Columbia Law Alumni Observer* (Columbia University) 13 (Apr./May 1984): 1, 8.
She helped to increase FDR's social consciousness, and they became a strong team. About Joseph Lash's lecture at Columbia Law Symposium, 31 Mar. 1984.

F758 "Eleanor Roosevelt: Humanitarian First Lady of the World." *Life* 13 (Fall 1990): 8-9.
She demonstrated what women can do, and she broadened the range of issues of interest to first ladies and all women. One of 100 Americans who most influenced the 20th century. The only First Lady and one of 12 women included.

F759 "Eleanor Roosevelt Portfolio." *Wisdom* 2 (Jan. 1958): 20-25.
Captioned photographs of ER when First Lady and later.

F760 Erskine, Helen Worden. "The Riddle of Mrs. Truman." *Collier's* 129 (9 Feb. 1952): 11-13, 59-61.
Comparison of Bess Truman and ER as White House hostesses.

F761 Farley, James A. *Jim Farley's Story: The Roosevelt Years.* New York: Whittlesey House-McGraw-Hill, 1948; Westport: Greenwood, 1984. x + 388p. Index.
Farley, Democratic National Committee chair, broke with FDR over the third term. He recalls a July 1940 conversation when ER pleaded that he head FDR's campaign (pp. 313-17).

F762 Farmer, Susan J. "Anna Eleanor Roosevelt: Mirror, Mirror on the Wall--Was She the Fairest First Lady of Them All?" Thesis (Honors) St. Lawrence Univ., 1986. 152 + 16p. Bibliography. Notes.
Utilizing published works by and about ER, Farmer presents the contradictions between the public and private aspects of ER's life. Annotation based on examination of introduction and notes.

F763 Fields, Alonzo. *My 21 Years in the White House.* New York: Coward-McCann, 1961. 223p.
Chief Usher Fields provides an informal account of ER as White House hostess (pp. 38-118). Earlier version is in *Ladies' Home Journal* 77 (May 1960): 50-51, 149-51, 153-56, 158; (June 1960): 68-69, 84, 86, 88-91.

F764 Fields, W.C. *W.C. Fields by Himself: His Intended Autobiography.* Commentary by Ronald J. Fields. Englewood Cliffs: Prentice-Hall, 1973. xiv + 510p.
Refers to ER as "Tornpocket" and includes brief, humorous accounts of her as the incessant traveler (pp. 182-83, 195-97, 425).

F765 "The First Lady: The LHJ Roper Poll of the American Women." *Ladies' Home Journal* 105 (Sept. 1988): 90.
A poll of American women ranked ER as the most admired First Lady since 1933.

F766 "A First Lady with Her Own Agenda." *Life* 9 (Fall 1986): 367.
    In an survey of the first 50 years of photography in *Life* ER is shown in her 1941 inaugural gown posing for Edward Steichen.

F767 Fischer, Louis. *Men and Politics: An Autobiography, with an Appendix of Letters from Mrs. Eleanor Roosevelt Added to the Reprint Edition.* Westport: Greenwood, 1970. ix + 672p. Index.
    Concluding unnumbered pages consist of entries from Fischer's diary and letters from ER which he felt could not be published earlier. In Feb. 1938 they discussed the effect of the U.S. arms embargo on the Spanish republic. Diary entries and letters relate to this and ER's role in efforts to secure the release of Fischer's wife and sons from Russia. The appendix appeared earlier in a different form as "Letters from Mrs. Roosevelt." *Journal of Historical Studies* 1 (1967): 24-30.

F768 Flemion, Jess. "First Lady of the Land." *Eleanor Roosevelt: An American Journey.* Ed. Jess Flemion and Colleen M. O'Connor. San Diego: San Diego State Univ. Pr., 1987. 99-104.
    Summary of her activities as First Lady demonstrating her precedent-breaking role. Introduction to 48 photographs.

F769 ---. "The Unorthodox First Lady Meets the Political Cartoonists." *Eleanor Roosevelt: An American Journey.* Ed. Jess Flemion and Colleen M. O'Connor. San Diego: San Diego State Univ. Pr., 1987. 175-79.
    During the White House years ER was the frequent subject of cartoonists with many of the cartoons illustrating changing opinions about American women. Introduction to 30 pages of cartoons.

F770 Flynn, Edward J. *You're the Boss.* New York: Viking, 1947; Westport: Greenwood, 1983. x + 244p. Index.
    The autobiography of this Bronx politician deals with FDR as a political leader. There are many personal recollections of ER, and he concludes that she was not a strong influence on FDR (pp. 214-15).

F771 Flynn, John T. *The Roosevelt Myth.* Rev. ed. New York: Devin-Adair, 1956. 465p. Index. Bibliography. Notes.
    An unfavorable picture of ER as First Lady. Flynn considers her radio broadcasts, writing, and speaking as inappropriate, because they satisfied her compelling desire for attention and money. Discusses at length ER's association with Communists (pp. 244-57).

F772 Frank, Sid, and Arden Davis Melick. *The Presidents: Tidbits & Trivia.* New York: Greenwich House, 1982. Index. Bibliography. 160p.
    A limited number are about ER as First Lady (pp. 24, 33, 97, 130, 151). Her 1917 interview about household economy is incorrectly attributed to the World War II period (p. 45). Includes the undated "Ethics of Parents" attributed to ER in which she lists seven rules for parents (p. 126).

F773 Free, Ann Cottrell. "Eleanor Roosevelt and the Female White House Press Corps." *Modern Maturity* 27 (Oct./Nov. 1984): 98-101.
    A member of the press corps remembers ER and her press conferences.

F774 Freidel, Frank. *Franklin D. Roosevelt: A Rendezvous with Destiny.* Boston: Little, Brown, 1990. viii + 710p. Index. Notes.

There are numerous brief descriptions of ER as First Lady and adviser to FDR (pp. 123-25, 246, 426-27, 578 in particular). ER and FDR as a team (pp. 12-13) and his conclusion that the Roosevelts viewed the nation's problems from a moral viewpoint rather than an economic one (p. 94).

F775 ---. "Her Place in History." *Boston Sunday Globe Magazine* 27 May 1962: 23.

In his comparison of Jacqueline Kennedy with other first ladies ER is described as one who was frightened by the burdens which she faced.

F776 ---. *Launching the New Deal.* Franklin D. Roosevelt, 4. Boston: Little, Brown, 1973. 574p. Index. Bibliographical Note. Notes.

From the 1932 election through the first year of the New Deal. The personal and non-political aspects of the first year in the White House (pp. 267-88). The beginnings of ER's activities as First Lady (pp. 289-98).

F777 Frooks, Dorothy. *Lady Lawyer.* New York: Speller, 1975. iv + 201p. Index.

In her autobiography Frooks reflects on ER's career and concludes that in spite of her frequent pronouncements she did not support the ideals for which the U.S. was founded (pp. 132-33). Frooks' dislike of ER extended back to two incidents in the 1930s: ER's desire to launch "My Day" caused her to lose her own column (pp. 67-68) and she lost her congressional race with Caroline O'Day because of ER's active campaigning (pp. 127-28).

F778 Furman, Bess. "Independent Lady from Independence." *New York Times Magazine* 9 June 1946: 20, 47-48.

A portrait of Bess Truman which includes a comparison of her style as First Lady with that of her predecessor.

F779 ---. *Washington By-Line: The Personal History of a Newspaperwoman.* New York: Knopf, 1949. x + 348p. Index.

The 1928-1948 memoir of a Washington reporter. Extensive and mainly anecdotal account of ER as First Lady.

F780 ---. *White House Profile: A Social History of the White House, Its Occupants and Its Festivities.* Indianapolis: Bobbs-Merrill, 1951. 368p. Index. Bibliography.

Traces the history of the White House with attention to ER as White House hostess (pp. 320-22, 328-29).

F781 Garrison, Webb. *A Treasury of White House Tales.* Nashville: Rutledge Hill, 1989. 254p. Index.

An undocumented work which presents random comments about White House occupants. ER's press conferences and "My Day" (p. 113). ER and the Secret Service and her travels (p. 117).

F782 Gies, Joseph. *Franklin D. Roosevelt: Portrait of a President.* Garden City: Doubleday, 1971. 233p. Index. Suggested Readings.

ER's activities as First Lady (pp. 101, 124-28, 157, 187, 194, 201, 205, 211, 214).

F783 Gladstone, Valerie. "Putting a Former First Lady in Perspective." *New York Times* 7 June 1992, sect. LI: 8.

In the research for her biography of ER, Blanche Wiesen Cook discovered that ER did have a personal life other than that of FDR's wife. These revelations and her claim that furthering women's rights was a priority for ER have been criticized. Cook claims that ER was a woman of great vision who put forward a substantive social agenda in the 1930s and in the end never realized her own greatness. A discussion with Cook.

F784 Goldman, Harry Merton. "Pins and Needles: A White House Command Performance." *Educational Theatre Journal* 30 (Mar. 1978): 90-101. Notes.

Pins and Needles, the longest running musical of the 1930s, was a satirical look at current events produced by and for garment workers. ER saw the play in New York several times before and after the White House performance of 3 Mar. 1938 (a lengthy description of the play is in "My Day" of 17 Feb. 1938). This article is about ER as hostess for the White House performance and her attendance at a later presentation for the Dept. of Labor.

F785 Goodwin, Doris Kearns. "Hillary & Eleanor." *Mother Jones* 18 (Jan./Feb. 1993): 48-50.

A letter to Hillary Rodham Clinton advising her to create a role for herself and to profit from ER's successes and mistakes. Reissued as "Advice to Hillary" in the *Arkansas Times* 25 Feb. 1993: 23.

F786 Gould, Lewis L. "First Ladies." *American Scholar* 55 (Autumn 1986): 528-35.

First ladies since 1900 have been considered as celebrities, and this has inhibited meaningful accomplishments. ER affected little social change because she was too much the celebrity. Her approach to the First Lady's role changed forever what was to be expected of her successors, however.

F787 ---. "The Historical Legacy of Modern First Ladies." Afterword. *Modern First Ladies: Their Documentary Legacy*. Comp. and ed. Nancy Kegan Smith and Mary C. Ryan. Washington: National Archives and Records Admin., 1989. 167-75.

In his attempt to provide historical perspective to the role and activities of 20th century first ladies Gould concludes that ER's approach to the role encouraged curiosity about her. She made news and took advantage of opportunities to publicize her activities and views. However, she did not channel her energy and attention so as to make a lasting impact on national programs (p. 172).

F788 ---. *Lady Bird Johnson and the Environment*. Lawrence: Univ. Pr. of Kan., 1988. xv + 312p. Index. Bibliographical Essay. Notes.

Mrs. Johnson's empathy for ER began in 1937, but unlike ER her focus as First Lady was more carefully directed (pp. 33-34).

F789 ---. "Modern First Ladies: An Institutional Perspective." Introduction. *Modern First Ladies: Their Documentary Legacy*. Comp. and ed. Nancy Kegan Smith and Mary C. Ryan. Washington: National Archives and Records Admin., 1989. 1-18. Notes.

ER's activities required additional staff: the quantity of mail required more secretarial assistance, Edith Helm was hired to help fulfill social obligations, and friends were drafted to help. All of this meant that future first ladies were going to need more staff (p. 8). Except for a expansion of the coverage of Betty Ford and Rosalynn Carter this is the same as "Modern First Ladies: An Institutional Perspective." *Prologue* 19 (Summer 1987): 71-83.

Russell Bourne, "When the First Lady Speaks Her Mind." *American Heritage* 38 (Sept./Oct. 1987): 108-9 discusses the growing body of papers related to first ladies and Gould's use of papers on ER in particular.

F790 ---. "Modern First Ladies in Historical Perspective." *Presidential Studies Quarterly* 15 (Summer 1985): 532-40. Notes.

Historians are still trying to assess ER's role.

F791 Graff, Robert D., and Robert Emmett Ginna. *FDR*. Text by Roger Butterfield. Butterfield. New York: Harper & Row, 1963. 255p. Index.

With emphasis on FDR as President the book is based on the ABC television series for which Ben Feiner, Jr. interviewed ER about her recollections of FDR.

F792 Green, Jerald R. "Mrs. Roosevelt's Etchings." *Print Collector's Newsletter* 17 (Sept./Oct. 1986): 123-25. Notes.

On 9 Feb. 1939 ER accepted from Luis Qunitanilla the controversial gift of a limited edition of Goya etchings from the Loyalist government of Spain. The events leading up to the presentation and the disposition of the prints and another set which was brought into the country at the same time. To be a chapter in a planned biography of Qunitanilla.

In her *Eleanor Roosevelt* Ruby Black cites European press reaction to the event: the Fascist *Il Tevere* claimed on 14 Feb. 1939 that she had been given stolen original works, and on 28 Feb. 1939 *Popolo di Roma* accused her of writing too much and being a bad influence on FDR (p. 268).

For coverage by the *New York Times,* see "Loyalists to Offer Mrs. Roosevelt Gift." 29 Nov. 1938: 17, "Bringing Goya Etchings." 22 Dec. 1938: 10, and "Displays Goya Etchings." 14 Feb. 1939: 21.

F793 Gunther, John. *Roosevelt in Retrospect: A Profile in History*. New York: Harper, 1950; New York: Pyramid, 1962. xii + 410p. Index. Bibliography. Notes.

Using ER's autobiographical writings and other sources Gunther establishes the significant role which ER played in FDR's career. Overview of ER's life and activities up to 1950 (pp. 178-99). While Gunther makes much of the ER and FDR team, he also states that in retrospect their relationship may appear closer than it was. (p. 191).

F794 Gup, Ted. "Eleanor and Edgar: 'Hoot Owl' vs. the 'Gestapo.'" *Washington Post* 6 June 1982, sect. C: 1-2.

The FBI's file on ER reveals a strained relationship between J. Edgar Hoover and ER which began during the White House years and continued until her death.

F795 Gutin, Myra G. "Political Surrogates and Independent Advocates: Eleanor Roosevelt." *The President's Partner: The First Lady in the Twentieth Century.* Contributions in Women's Studies, 105. By Myra G. Gutin. New York: Greenwood, 1989. 81-107. Index. Bibliography. Notes.

An examination of ER as First Lady, White House hostess, and political figure follows an overview of her life. Based on the more detailed chapter "Political Surrogates and Independent Advocates: Anna Eleanor Roosevelt." in Gutin's dissertation "The President's Partner: The First Lady as Public Communicator, 1920-1976," pp. 259-400 (Univ. of Mich., 1983).

F796 Hailey, Foster. "50 Who Made It Relive History." *New York Times* 28 Apr. 1960: 24.

ER was one of the Americans honored for their roles in important national and international events. The visual presentation "The Living History of the Critical Years, 1935-1960" written by Allen Nevins was presented 27 Apr. in New York. ER received the most enthusiastic welcome from the audience.

F797 Harris, Theodore F. *Pearl S. Buck: A Biography*. 2 vols. By Theodore F. Harris in consultation with Pearl S. Buck. New York: Day, 1969-1971. Index. Bibliography.

Buck corresponded with ER in an effort to better educate the First Lady about Far Eastern customs, political conditions, and beliefs about the West (v. 2, pp. 315-29). Her recollections of ER visiting Cornell while Buck was a student, when ER hosted Mme. Chiang Kai-shek at the White House, and later in life (v. 1, pp. 289-94). A brief account of their relationship is in Nora Stirling, *Pearl Buck: A Woman in Conflict*, pp. 72, 202, 280 (New York: New Century, 1983).

F798 Hassett, William D. *Off the Record with F.D.R., 1942-1945*. New Brunswick: Rutgers Univ. Pr., 1958; Westport: Greenwood, 1980. xviii + 366p. Index.

White House and Hyde Park entertaining and other activities place ER in many of these diary entries of an FDR aide.

F799 Hatch, Alden. *Franklin D. Roosevelt: An Informal Biography*. New York: Holt, 1947. 413p. Index.

The role ER played in the Roosevelt administration and some aspects of her private life. A derivative account lacking analysis.

F800 Helm, Edith Benham. *The Captains and the Kings*. New York: Putnam's, 1954. 307p. Index.

The social secretary in the Wilson, Roosevelt, and Truman administrations provides an account of ER as White House hostess and public figure.

F801 Hickok, Lorena. "Eleanor Roosevelt...First Lady." *Democratic Digest* 22 (June 1945): 7, 35.

A tribute to her character and accomplishments as First Lady and a prediction that she will continue trying to win battles and overcome injustice.

F802 Hicks, Granville. "The Remarkable Life of Eleanor Roosevelt." Rev. of *Eleanor and Franklin* by Joseph P. Lash. *Business Week* 2198 (16 Oct. 1971): 8, 12.

He had underestimated ER's contributions during the Roosevelt presidency when she was driven by her conscience and unbelievable stamina.

F803 Hofstadter, Bernice K. "How to Be First Lady." *American Heritage* 34 (Aug./Sept. 1983): 98-100.

When a man runs for the presidency his wife is running too, but all the wives run against ER. In this broad discussion of the nature of the First Lady's position ER's precedent-breaking style emerges as the gauge against which her successors continue to be measured.

F804 Humphrey, Kelly N. "Fascinating First Ladies." *Good Housekeeping* 209 (July 1989): 176.
One of the questions in this quiz is about ER.

F805 Hurd, Charles. *When the New Deal Was Young and Gay*. New York: Hawthorn, 1965. 288p. Index.
Recollections and anecdotes about the early years of the New Deal. An informal portrait of ER at the time (pp. 207-14).

F806 ---. The White House Story. New York: Hawthorn, 1966. 240p. Index.
The variety of ER's activities as First Lady (pp. 160-61, 218-19).

F807 Hurst, Fannie. *Anatomy of Me: A Wonderer in Search of Herself*. New York: Doubleday, 1958; New York: Arno, 1980. 367p.
Hurst's autobiography contains amusing accounts of election night 1932 and a luncheon at the White House with the Roosevelts (pp. 306-9, 319-22).

F808 Jeffries, Ona Griffin. "New Deal in the White House: Franklin and Eleanor Roosevelt." *In and out of the White House...from Washington to Eisenhowers*. By Ona Griffin Jeffries. New York: Funk, 1960. 341-60.
ER as White House hostess. Includes account of visit of the British royal couple.

F809 Jensen, Amy La Follette. "Franklin D. Roosevelt, 1933-1945: A Four-Term Lease." *The White House and Its Thirty-four Families*. New, enlarged ed. By Amy La Follette Jensen. New York: McGraw-Hill, 1965. 235-47.
The Roosevelts at home in the White House. Titles of different eds. vary depending on date of publication.

F810 ---. "The President's Lady." *American Heritage* 15 (Aug. 1964): 54-61.
Through portraits and text the White House years of several first ladies are described. ER's activities (pp. 60-61).

F811 Johnson, Marilyn. "Ladies of the House." *Life* 4 15 (30 Oct. 1992): 80-85.
The roles of first ladies including the activities of ER.

F812 Johnson, Walter. *1600 Pennsylvania Avenue: Presidents and the People, 1929-1959*. Boston: Little, Brown, 1960. x + 390p. Index. Bibliography. Notes.
Includes a brief look at ER's activities as First Lady and the reactions which they caused (pp. 191-92).

F813 Josephson, Emanuel M. *The Strange Death of Franklin D. Roosevelt: History of the Roosevelt-Delano Dynasty, America's Royal Family*. New York: Chendey, 1948. 333p. Index.
ER exploited the presidency through her money making efforts, and she gave her earnings to Communist causes. Her close relationship with Harry Hopkins is considered suspicious (pp. 205-11). Rev. ed. issued in 1959.

F814 Kemp, Barbara H., and Shirley Cherkasky. *Eleanor Roosevelt's Washington: A Place of Personal Growth and Public Service*. Washington: Smithsonian Institution, 1984. 31p. Bibliography. Notes.

Intended as a self-guided tour of the buildings and sites of Washington which played a part in ER's life in the city. Extensive use is made of accounts published in Washington newspapers. Jack Eisen, "An Involved First Lady." *Washington Post* 19 Oct. 1984 discusses the publication and the interest which ER took in the city. Photocopy of Eisen article from FDRL. Page no. lacking.

F815 King, Florence. "She." *National Review* 45 (26 Apr. 1993): 64.
"She" was how King's grandmother referred to ER when her daily reading of "My Day" would almost be fatal to the older woman. Hillary Rodham Clinton will never be another ER. Mrs. Clinton, like ER, has "repulsive" friends though ER's friends were more cultivated than the women we see surrounding Mrs. Clinton.

F816 Kingdon, Frank. *As FDR Said: A Treasury of His Speeches, Conversations, and Writings*. New York: Duell, Sloan and Pearce, 1950. 256p. Index.
He draws from *This I Remember* to illustrate the humorous side of FDR (pp. 57-59, 64-67).

F817 Kirk, Elise K. *Music at the White House*. Music in American Life. Urbana: Univ. of Ill. Pr., 1986. xviii + 457p. Index. Bibliographical Essay.
ER took interest in selecting the musicians, dancers, and actors who performed at the White House. Relies on ER's papers and on interviews conducted by the author (pp. 221-52). Includes "White House Decorative Interlude," an imaginary exchange between ER and FDR about a new White House piano, published in the *Philadelphia Inquirer*, 15 Feb. 1937: 238-39.

F818 Kirkendall, Richard S. "ER and the Issue of FDR's Successor." *Without Precedent: The Life and Career of Eleanor Roosevelt*. Everywoman: Studies in History, Literature, and Culture. Ed. Joan Hoff-Wilson and Marjorie Lightman. Bloomington: Indiana Univ. Pr., 1984. 176-97. Sources.
In spite of her appearance before the 1940 Democratic National Convention relations between ER and Henry Wallace continued to be strained until he assumed the vice presidency. Kirkendall speculates that Wallace might have been on the 1944 ticket if the relationship between ER and FDR had been stronger at the time.

F819 Klapthor, Margaret Brown. "Franklin D. Roosevelt." *The First Ladies Cook Book: Favorite Recipes of All of the Presidents of the United States*. By Margaret Brown Klapthor. New York: Parents' Magazine Pr., 1969. 191-96.
ER as White House hostess. The type of entertaining and meals enjoyed by the Roosevelts. A rev. ed. issued in 1982 (New York: GMG Publishing-Parents Magazine Enterprises).

F820 Klehr, Harvey. "The Strange Case of Roosevelt's 'Secret Agent.'" *Encounter* 59 (Dec. 1982): 84-91.
Josephine Truslow Adams began writing to ER in 1941, and in time her letters became the vehicle for Earl Browder's "communication" with ER and, ultimately, FDR. Adams tried to present herself as a Nazi hunter, but always doubtful of her ER responded to the letters briefly if at all.

F821 Kleinerman, Lois B. "Eleanor Roosevelt: First Modern First Lady." Thesis (M.A.) Columbia Univ., 1966. 162p.

An analysis of "the ways in which Mrs. Roosevelt as First Lady used her resources to provide precedent-making services for the President in his relationships with different constituencies" (pp. 6-7). Relies heavily on "My Day" columns.

F822 Klemesrud, Judy. "The 42 First Ladies: Their Place in History." *New York Times* 6 Dec. 1982, sect. B: 14.
ER ranks ahead of all others, but what she did as First Lady would shock and outrage some people even today. Excerpts papers presented at Hunter College conference, New York, 4 Dec. There is also "First Ladies." *Hunter Magazine* 2 (Mar. 1983): 9-12 which includes brief comments by some participants on ER's role as First Lady and a report of a survey on first ladies.

F823 Koenig, Louis W. *The Invisible Presidency*. New York: Rinehart, 1960. 438p. Index. Bibliography.
Interviews with ER used in this study of presidential aides reveal that her relationship with Harry Hopkins became so strained that in the final years of the New Deal they avoided one another (pp. 304-6, 317-19).

F824 Kohlhoff, Dean. "Eleanor Roosevelt: The New Deal's First Lady." *Cresset* 41 (Nov./Dec. 1977): 3-5.
FDR and ER shared the same ideology, and together they pursued a liberal agenda. She as his conscience; he with the restrictions of an elected official. She was more the humanitarian whose activities for the less fortunate and those excluded from the political process demonstrated that humanitarian principles are never enough.

F825 Krock, Arthur. *Memoirs: Sixty Years on the Firing Line*. New York: Funk & Wagnalls, 1968. xii + 508p. Index.
ER felt more strongly about social issues and wanted a career of her own through which she could influence FDR. She was a great woman in spite of her lack of a sense of humor (pp. 149-50).

F826 Lait, Jack, and Lee Mortimer. *Washington Confidential*. New York: Crown, 1951. x + 310p. Index.
In this expose of Washington ER is given harsh treatment. How she "killed" Washington society (pp. 134-35) and resentment of her support of civil rights (pp. 9-10, 16, 38-41, 43).

F827 Lash, Joseph P. *Dealers and Dreamers: A New Look at the New Deal*. New York: Doubleday, 1988. x + 510p. Index. Notes.
Numerous references place ER in the midst of his description of New Deal accomplishments and dilemmas, but only with the question of the third term is coverage of her extensive (pp. 363, 365, 368, 397, 405-6).

F828 ---. "Nancy Reagan, Meet Eleanor Roosevelt." *Los Angeles Times* 8 Mar. 1987, pt. 5: 5.
As First Lady Mrs. Reagan might avoid some of the criticism of her perceived interference if she were to follow ER's example and conceal the extent of her influence. ER had a deeper social conscience than FDR, considered FDR's first responsibility to be to the duties which he had been elected to fulfill, and never ceased to expose him to the needs of the less fortunate. FDR and the country benefited from her ideas and actions.

F829 ---. "Would Eleanor Have Made a Good President?" *Family Weekly* (17 Dec. 1972): 4.
Yes, because she could lead, liked people, was knowledgeable about politics, and was a tough manager.

F830 Leonard, Thomas M. *Day by Day: The Forties*. New York: Facts on File, 1977. xviii + 1051p. Index.
A daily account of the 1940s arranged by ten topics. ER's actions and statements are covered by numerous entries.

F831 Letts de Espil, Courtney. *La Esposa del Embajador: Diez Anos en la Embajada Argentina en Washington--1933-1943*. Coleccion Como Nos Ven. Buenos Aires: Ed. Alvarez, 1967. 166p.
ER is recalled in these memoirs of the wife of the former Ambassador from Argentina. She is remembered as being energetic and constantly on the go speaking and listening on FDR's behalf (pp. 20-23, 44-55, 59-60, 65-72, 125, 134-136, 138, 158). In Spanish.

F832 Leuchtenburg, William E. *In the Shadow of FDR: From Harry Truman to Ronald Reagan*. Ithaca: Cornell Univ. Pr., 1983. xii + 346p. Index. Bibliography. Notes.
Presidents since FDR have been compared to him, and Democratic presidents have attempted to be his successor. While all later first ladies have been compared to ER, her presence or the memory of her were critical to the aspirations of those Democratic presidents. Updated eds. issued through 1993 (Ithaca: Cornell Univ. Pr.).

F833 Lewis, Dorothy Roe. "What F.D.R. Told Hoover March 3, '33." *New York Times* 13 Mar. 1981: 31.
ER overheard a private pre-inauguration conversation between FDR and Herbert Hoover. When she shared the story that FDR had rejected Hoover's request that the two of them issue a joint proclamation closing the banks, Lewis and other female journalists who were offered the story used better judgment and rejected it.

F834 Littell, Norman M. *My Roosevelt Years*. Ed. Jonathan Dembo. Seattle: Univ. of Wash. Pr., 1987. xxi + 422p. Index. Notes.
In this collection of diaries and letters his 1944 assessment of ER is mixed (she is a great woman but is too self-important and has become the type of woman who can be repelling to men), and he reserves judgment on the wisdom of her approach to race relations because he thinks that she wanted to move too quickly (pp. 227-28). His involvement with her in the government's negotiations to purchase the Breakers Hotel (pp. 224-35 passim) and Harry Hopkins and strained relations between ER and FDR (pp. 126-29).

F835 Loots, Barbara Kunz. "The President's Eyes and Ears, April 1938." *Fascinating First Ladies: Memorable Moments in the Lives of Fifteen Presidents' Wives*. Written and edited by Barbara Kunz Loots. Kansas City: Hallmark, 1977. 35-37.
A brief account of ER's preparations for another trip to meet and talk with the American people.

F836 Lovell, Mary S. *The Sound of Wings: The Life of Amelia Earhart*. New York: St. Martin's, 1989. xxv + 420p. Index. Selected Reading. Notes.

Earhart and ER were casual acquaintances, and she and her husband George P. Putnam were occasional White House guests (pp. 199, 216-17). Letters and telegrams reveal ER's assistance in Earhart's plans for her final flight (pp. 233-38). Less documented is Doris Rich, *Amelia Earhart: A Biography* (Washington: Smithsonian Institution, 1989).

F837 Manchester, William. *The Glory and the Dream: A Narrative of America, 1932-1972*. Boston: Little, Brown, 1974. x + 1397p. Index. Bibliography. Notes.

A detailed account of ER's activities at the time of FDR's death and burial (pp. 350-54, 356-62).

F838 Martin, George. *Madam Secretary, Frances Perkins*. Boston: Houghton Mifflin, 1976. xv + 589p. Index. Bibliography. Notes.

Utilizing Perkins' papers and oral history interview plus works by ER and others, Martin claims that ER and Perkins were never close and that ER was resentful of her (pp. 234-35, 364-65, 461-62).

F839 Matthews, J.B. "Communists and the New Deal." *American Mercury* 76 (June 1953): 33-40.

Matthews lists the many "Communist" organizations with which he says ER was associated and cites from her writings about the value of Communist Party leaders (pp. 37-38).

F840 Mayer, Allan J. "America's First Ladies." *Newsweek* 94 (5 Nov. 1979): 49.

It has been through ER's example that subsequent first ladies have been able to assume a political role and promote causes.

F841 Mayo, Edith P. "The Influence and Power of First Ladies." *Chronicle of Higher Education* 40 (15 Sept. 1993): A52.

ER and others first ladies were their husbands' closest political advisers. Hillary Rodham Clinton is not the first to serve that role. Attention to ER is restricted to a discussion of how she is considered to be the only politically active First Lady since her role has been described so often through scholarship about her.

F842 McCarthy, Abigail Q. "Eleanor Roosevelt as First Lady." *Hunter Magazine* 2 (Mar. 1983): 11.

ER broke precedents and created controversy because she created a role for herself. Abbreviated text of address at Hunter College conference, New York, 4 Dec. 1982.

F843 ---. "ER as First Lady." *Without Precedent: The Life and Career of Eleanor Roosevelt*. Everywoman: Studies in History, Literature, and Culture. Ed. Joan Hoff-Wilson and Marjorie Lightman. Bloomington: Indiana Univ. Pr., 1984. 214-25. Sources.

She was well prepared for the job, and her role and activities as First Lady forever changed the nature of all "political" wives. A comparison with other first ladies, mainly her successors. ER and her mutually beneficial relationship with the press.

F844 ---. "First Helpmate: Influence in the White House." *Commonweal* 114 (24 Apr. 1987): 230-31.
   The only match for the current attacks on Nancy Reagan are those which ER suffered. Voters need to realize that when a man is elected they also get his wife. ER was the first First Lady to campaign and make speeches, and thereafter the First Lady's role has been what each First Lady wants and her husband will allow.

F845 McJimsey, George. *Harry Hopkins: Ally of the Poor and Defender of Democracy.* Cambridge: Harvard Univ. Pr., 1987. xiv + 474p. Index. Bibliography.
   Hopkins' relationship with ER flourished when he was able to implement some of her ideas. When ER and FDR developed their separate agendas--continuation of the New Deal vs. waging the war effort--Hopkins' relationship with her became strained. Based on published sources and oral history of his daughter Diana Hopkins Halsted (pp. 69, 109, 330-32).

F846 Medved, Michael. *The Shadow Presidents: The Secret History of the Chief Executives and Their Top Aides.* New York: Times Books, 1979. xi + 401p. Index. Sources.
   ER's relationship with Harry Hopkins--her success in bringing him to the forefront of the Roosevelt administration and her eventual breach with him (pp. 198-216). Derived in large part from *This I Remember*.

F847 Menendez, Albert J. *Christmas in the White House.* Philadelphia: Westminster, 1983. 127p. Bibliography.
   How the Roosevelts celebrated (pp. 16-19, 26, 41, 44-45, 64, 71-72, 76, 78, 102).

F848 Mesta, Perle. "First Ladies I Have Known." *McCall's* 90 (Mar. 1963): 36, 162-65.
   ER was a loving and energetic First Lady, and to Mesta she was also a good friend and ally.

F849 Miller, Nathan. *FDR: An Intimate History.* Garden City: Doubleday, 1983. viii + 563p. Index. Bibliography. Notes.
   Brief accounts of ER as First Lady (pp. 306-508 passim). For the most detailed discussion of her activities and social thought, see pp. 358-60.

F850 ---. *The Roosevelt Chronicles.* Garden City: Doubleday, 1979. vi + 377p. Index. Bibliography.
   ER's activities as First Lady and hostess of the White House (pp. 313, 316-19, 321-31, 334).

F851 Miller, William M. *Fishbait: The Memoirs of the Congressional Doorkeeper.* By William "Fishbait" Miller as told to Frances Spatz Leighton. Englewood Cliffs: Prentice-Hall, 1977. ix + 389p. Index.
   Miller claims that while FDR slept ER approved the selection of HST as the 1944 running mate (pp. 285-86).

F852 Mohr, Lillian. *Frances Perkins: "That Woman in FDR's Cabinet!"* N.p.: North River, 1979. viii + 328p. Index. Bibliography. Notes.
   Coverage of ER consists of many quotations from *Ladies of Courage* and *This I Remember*.

F853 Moley, Raymond. *The First New Deal*. By Raymond Moley with the assistance of Elliot A. Rosen. New York: Harcourt, Brace & World, 1966. xxiii + 577p. Index. Notes.

Moley published this account 27 years after his *After Seven Years* (New York: Harper, 1939), a candid account of the first seven years of the Roosevelt administration.   In both this and the earlier work there are only a few minor references to ER. Moley states that ER rarely tried to influence policy (p. 10).

F854 ---. *27 Masters of Politics in a Personal Perspective*. New York: Funk and Wagnalls, 1949; Westport: Greenwood, 1972. xii + 276p. Index.

FDR did not consult ER about political matters because he did not rely on her judgment.   Her ideas about economic and social matters were never given much attention (pp. 38-39).

F855 Montgomery, Ruth. *Hail to the Chiefs: My Life and Times with Six Presidents*. New York: Coward-McCann, 1970. 320p. Index.

Although a newcomer to Washington, Montgomery was president of ER's Press Conference Assoc. at the time of FDR's death. Her recollections of ER at that time (pp. 19-23) and an irreverent look at the press conferences (pp. 16-17)

F856 Morgenthau, Henry, III. *Mostly Morgenthaus: A Family History*. Boston: Ticknor & Fields, 1991. xxi + 501p. Index. Sources. Notes.

The political and social relationship between Henry Morgenthau, Jr.'s wife Elinor and ER. White House entertaining (pp. 273-74, 284-85, 293-96, 304-5).

F857 Moscow, Warren. *Roosevelt and Willkie*. Englewood Cliffs: Prentice-Hall, 1968. xi + 210p.

Events leading up to ER's address at the 1940 Democratic National Convention, excerpts from the address, and reactions to it (pp. 123-25).

F858 Nesbitt, Henrietta. "My 13 Years in the White House." *Woman's Home Companion* 73 (Oct. 1946): 22-23, 39-40.

The White House housekeeper during the Roosevelt years remembers ER as First Lady and White House hostess and the arrangements made for famous guests, most notably the British royal couple. In a subsequent article "Parties and Polishing for Presidents." 73 (Dec. 1946): 4, 164 Mrs. Nesbitt responds to questions about family life and entertaining in the White House.

F859 ---. *The Presidential Cookbook: Feeding the Roosevelts and Their Guests*. Garden City: Doubleday, 1951. 246p. Index.

A cookbook with introductory sections which reveal the Roosevelts' culinary likes and dislikes. Coverage of ER (pp. 8, 24, 92-93, 104, 124-25).

F860 ---. *White House Diary*. Garden City: Doubleday, 1948. 314p.

In this behind the scenes account the White House housekeeper portrays the Roosevelts as a happy family. Recollections of Anna Roosevelt, Harry Hopkins, Louis Howe, Mme. Chiang Kai-shek, and the British royal couple. A lengthy review issued as "Secretary of the Interior." *Time* 52 (2 Aug. 1948): 76-77.

F861 "The New Deal and the First Lady." Rev. of *The Failure of Independent Liberalism, 1930-1941* by R. Alan Lawson and *Eleanor and Franklin* by Joseph P. Lash. *Times Literary Supplement* 3678 (25 Aug. 1972): 995-96.

Lash succeeds in portraying ER as a strong figure independent of FDR who did much to get the American people to accept a big and helping government.

F862 Nixon, Robert G. "From the Record." *The Real F.D.R.* Ed. Clark Kinnaird. New York: Citadel, 1945. 97-122.

A White House correspondent's sketch of FDR supports the idea that ER played a significant role in FDR's political career.

F863 Ostromecki, Walter A., Jr. "Anna Eleanor Roosevelt Roosevelt." *The First Ladies of the United States: An Historical Look at Each and Their Autograph Materials, 1789-1989*. Rev. and updated ed. By Walter A. Ostromecki, Jr. Encino: Ostromecki, 1991. 189-99.

A summary of ER's activities as First Lady followed by examples of autograph material.

F864 Oursler, Fulton. *Behold the Dreamer!: An Autobiography*. Ed. and with commentary by Fulton Oursler, Jr. Boston: Little, Brown, 1964. x + 501p. Index.

The senior Oursler, editor of *Liberty*, began his association with the Roosevelts in 1931. Their public and private sides are revealed in his descriptions of White House visits through 1940 (pp. 364-443).

F865 Papanek, Hanna. "Men, Women, and Work: Reflections on the Two-Person Career." *American Journal of Sociology* 98 (Jan. 1973): 852-72. References.

ER is an example of the type of woman whose public career is based on that of a prominent husband and, therefore, the wife is subject to both adoration and criticism. But she is the rare example of the wife who achieves an independent stature (p. 863). Reissued in *Changing Women in a Changing Society*, pp. 90-110 (Chicago: Univ. of Chicago Pr, 1973).

F866 Park, Edwards. "Around the Mall and Beyond." *Smithsonian* 22 (Mar. 1992): 22-24, 26.

The National Museum of American History has mounted a major exhibit on first ladies and how they viewed their role. Briefer coverage is given in Jo Ann Tooley, "The Last Word on First Ladies." *U.S. News & World Report* 112 (30 Mar. 1992): 16-17.

There is also Gayle Turim, "First Ladies Restored to Prominence." *Americana* 20 (Apr. 1992): 54-57 which gives primary attention to ER.

F867 Parks, Lillian Rogers. *My Thirty Years Backstairs at the White House*. By Lillian Rogers Parks in collaboration with Frances Spatz Leighton. New York: Fleet, 1961. x + 346p.

A White House maid recalls White House families. "...There Can Be Only One Mrs. 'R'" (pp. 235-51) and "With Mrs. 'R' in Peace and War" (pp. 252-74) are accounts of ER and FDR. Comparison of ER with Lou Hoover, Bess Truman, and Mamie Eisenhower (pp. 19-58 passim).

F868 ---. "Problems of a President's Wife." By Lillian Rogers Parks as told to Frances Spatz Leighton. *Good Housekeeping* 152 (Jan. 1961): 62-64, 160-63, 169-70.

Parks gives advice to the incoming First Lady and reminiscences about those she worked under. Anecdotes about ER as White House hostess.

F869 ---. *The Roosevelts: A Family in Turmoil*. By Lillian Rogers Parks in collaboration with Frances Spatz Leighton. Englewood Cliffs: Prentice-Hall, 1981. xiv + 285p. Index.

Anecdotal treatment of the Roosevelts in the White House and ER as First Lady.

F870 Parmet, Herbert S., and Marie B. Hecht. *Never Again: A President Runs for a Third Term*. New York: Macmillan, 1968. xii + 306p. Index. Notes on Sources.

A study of the 1940 election including ER's role in securing the nomination of Henry Wallace for Vice President (pp. 191-93) and her attitude about a third term for FDR (pp. 18-19, 27, 176, 186).

F871 Parten, Ailese. "An Evening with Eleanor Roosevelt." *Mature Living* 3 (Oct. 1978): 12-13.

A retired journalism teacher recalls an eventful evening spent with ER at the home of Ruby Black.

F872 Peebes, Jacqueline Neel. "Eleanor Roosevelt and the Washington Press, 1933-1945." Thesis (M.A.) Georgetown Univ., 1991. vi + 132p. Bibliography. Notes.

Peebles investigates how ER's actions, particularly those aimed at helping women and blacks, were viewed during the time she was First Lady. Transcripts of her press conferences, *This I Remember*, and accounts from numerous Washington newspapers are used as sources.

F873 Pegler, Westbrook. "Zangara Missed!" *American Opinion* 6 (June 1963): 9-16.

Among what would have been different with the nation and the world if FDR had been assassinated in Feb. 1933 is ER. She would have been nothing more than an eccentric quack with no power base.

F874 Pepper, Claude D. "Eleanor Roosevelt." *The Making of the New Deal: The Insiders Speak*. Ed. Katie Louchheim. Cambridge: Harvard Univ. Pr., 1983. 305-11.

Praise for her humanitarian activities, the way in which she carried out her duties as White House hostess, and how she helped FDR personally and politically. Follows a biographical sketch.

F875 Perkins, Frances. *The Reminiscences of Frances Perkins*. New York Times Oral History Program. Columbia University Oral History Collection, pt. 3, no. 182. Glen Rock: Microfilming Corp. of America, 1976. 9 bks, 61 microfiche. Index.

The origins of ER's press conferences and how she never intended to be politically active (bk. 4, pp. 335-38). Perkins' role in ER's decision to speak at the 1940 Democratic National Convention and about the speech (bk. 7, pp. 460-61, 464, 466-69, 471-76). ER's association with Harry Hopkins and Aubrey Williams (bk. 7, pp. 541-48). At the beginning of World War II when she advised ER to spend more time at the White House, ER felt that FDR did not need her presence (bk. 7, pp. 550-55). Bess Truman worried about succeeding ER (bk. 7, pp. 745-58). ER is recalled at the time of FDR's death and burial (bk. 8, pp. 774-77, 779, 791-92, 794-96, 799, 802, 804, 809, 811-18).

F876 ---. *The Roosevelt I Knew*. New York: Viking, 1946. viii + 408p. Index.
ER as aide to FDR, but no case is made for ER being an independent figure with influence (pp. 61-70).

F877 Pilat, Oliver. *Pegler: Angry Man of the Press*. Boston: Beacon, 1963; Westport: Greenwood, 1973. vii + 288p. Index. Bibliography.
Pegler's attacks in his column and his other public statements against ER during and after the White House years (pp. 11-13, 150-51, 184-85).

F878 Pruden, Edward Hughes. *A Window on Washington*. New York: Vantage, 1976. 136p.
Pruden, longtime minister at the Washington's First Baptist Church, recalls ER as First Lady. An anecdotal account of a "gracious lady" (pp. 16-17).

F879 Rabinowitz, Dorothy. "Madam President." Rev. of *Eleanor and Franklin* by Joseph P. Lash. *Commentary* 53 (Feb. 1972): 86, 88, 90.
We still know little about ER's innermost self. His theme is that ER was critical to the Roosevelt presidency, a claim which she never made. ER may have changed the role of First Lady, but she had less influence on FDR than Lash claims.

F880 Radcliffe, Donnie. "First Ladies, Second to None." *Washington Post* 8 Dec. 1992, sect. D: 1, 4.
Speaking at a 7 Dec. dinner in honor of Rosalynn Carter, Hillary Rodham Clinton names ER as a woman she has always admired and notes that ER was also criticized for speaking out.

F881 Reilly, Michael F. *Reilly of the White House*. By Michael F. Reilly as told to William J. Slocum. New York: Simon and Schuster, 1947. vi + 248p.
The chief of the White House Secret Service detail reveals that he was fond of ER but found some of her guests troublesome. Also confirms that she disliked being accompanied by the Secret Service (pp. 80-85).

F882 Robertson, E. Guy. *Ladies of the White House: Martha to Mamie*. N.p.: n.p., n.d., 16, 14, 20p.
Copy not examined.

F883 Rollyson, Carl. *Nothing Ever Happens to the Brave: The Story of Martha Gellhorn*. New York: St. Martin's, 1990. xvii + 398p. Index. Notes.
Gellhorn's first encounter with ER at the N.Y. governor's mansion was uneventful (p. 41). But during her service as a field representative for the Federal Emergency Relief Admin. (pp. 74-80), her association with Ernest Hemingway, and while she reported on the Spanish Civil War and war in Europe (pp. 92-93, 95, 109-12, 120, 122, 129-30, 135-36, 144, 147, 157-58, 168-69) she and ER became close friends and Gellhorn was a frequent White House visitor. She developed an "emotional tie" to ER and came to regard her as a mother figure (p. 78) who was dedicated to helping others (p. 169). Based on letters between ER, Gellhorn, and Gellhorn's mother Edna Gellhorn.

F884 Roosevelt, Anna. "White House Vignettes: My Life with FDR, pt. 5." *Woman* 23 (Oct. 1949): 42-47, 115.

Glimpses of the Roosevelts' life in the White House and ER as White House hostess. Other parts of "My Life with FDR" not examined.

F885 *Roosevelt and Daniels: A Friendship in Politics.* Ed. Carroll Kilpatrick. Chapel Hill: Univ. of N.C. Pr., 1952. xvi + 226p. Index.
Numerous references to ER in this selection of correspondence between FDR and Daniels with the final entry that of Josephus Daniels' telegram to her on the day of FDR's death.

F886 *Roosevelt and Frankfurter: Their Correspondence, 1928-1945.* Annotated by Max Freedman. Boston: Little, Brown, 1967. xiv + 772p. Index.
Contains a limited amount of correspondence between ER and Felix Frankfurter which includes public reaction to her position on race relations, exchange of speeches between the two, and comments about each other's speeches.

F887 Rosen, Ruth. "Untraditional First Lady." *Christian Science Monitor* 4 Sept. 1992, Eastern ed.: 19.
Like ER, Hillary Rodham Clinton is the target of the right wing. ER personified a new generation of women; so does Mrs. Clinton. Also issued in *View from Hyde Park: The Newsletter of the Roosevelt Institute and Library* 7 (Spring 1993): [6].

F888 Rosenman, Samuel I. *Working with Roosevelt.* New York: Harper, 1952; New York: Da Capo, 1972. 551p.
Rosenman, New York jurist and FDR adviser and speechwriter, makes frequent mention of the significant role which ER played in his account of FDR from 1928 until 1945 (in particular, pp. 346-48 where he describes how ER assisted in making FDR's speeches more appealing to the average citizen). Anecdotes about ER's relationship with FDR (pp. 152-53).

F889 Ross, Ishbel. *Sons of Adam, Daughters of Eve.* New York: Harper, 1969. viii + 340p. Index. Bibliography. Notes.
A popular study of female public figures and wives of office holders with emphasis on first ladies. ER's activities and influence are described (pp. 81-87). Numerous other references to her are only informal comparisons with other first ladies.

F890 Sabath, Adolph J. "Eleanor Roosevelt." *Congressional Record Appendix* (19 Apr. 1945): A1818.
Sabath plans to ask HST to name her to some major post in the government now that she is no longer First Lady.

F891 Schlesinger, Arthur M., Jr. *The Politics of Upheaval.* The Age of Roosevelt [v.3]. Boston: Houghton Mifflin, 1960. 749p. Index. Notes.
A lengthy quotation from ER's memorandum of July 1936 to James Farley about the lack of organization in the 1936 campaign (pp. 587-89). Reissued in 1988 with a new preface (Boston: Houghton Mifflin).

F892 Schorr, Daniel. "What Hillary Problem?" Editorial. *New Leader* 76 (8-22 Feb. 1993): 4-5.
Hillary Rodham Clinton has a long way to go before she is object of the type of criticism which was leveled against ER.

F893 Schuck, Joyce. *Political Wives, Veiled Lives*. Madison: Lanham, 1991. xx + 224p. Index. Notes.
   ER as First Lady (pp. 120-22, 137). ER on being a political wife (pp. 142, 188).

F894 Scobie, Ingrid Winther. "Helen Gahagan Douglas and the Roosevelt Connection." *Without Precedent: The Life and Career of Eleanor Roosevelt*. Everywoman: Studies in History, Literature, and Culture. Ed. Joan Hoff-Wilson and Marjorie Lightman. Bloomington: Indiana Univ. Pr., 1984. 153-75. Sources.
   In her political activities during the New Deal Douglas tried to emulate ER in style and approach. There is also Scobie's *Center Stage: Helen Gahagan Douglas, a Life* (New York: Oxford Univ. Pr., 1992).

F895 Seale, William. *The President's House: A History*. 2 vols. (xx + 1224p.) Washington: White House Historical Assoc., 1986. Index. Bibliography. Notes.
   Three chapters document the Roosevelts' stay in the White House and ER's activities as First Lady (v. 2, pp. 915-1001).

F896 Severen, Bill. *Frances Perkins: A Member of the Cabinet*. New York: Hawthorn, 1976. 256p. Index. Suggested Reading.
   Includes an undocumented description of the role which Perkins played in convincing ER to address the Democratic National Convention in 1940 (pp. 207-10).

F897 Shaffer, Ellen. "Glimpses of Five First Ladies." *Manuscripts* 22 (Spring 1970): 88-95.
   In early 1937 ER began a correspondence with a young girl in an attempt to build the child's self-confidence.

F898 Sherwood, Robert E. *Roosevelt and Hopkins: An Intimate History*. rev. ed. New York: Harper, 1950. xix + 1002p. Index. Notes.
   Since Sherwood decided against interviewing ER, there is less about her that might have been the case. Her life in the White House (pp. 203-5), ER and Hopkins' daughter Diana (pp. 106-7, 117-18), a discussion of Hopkins' memorandum of 28 May 1939 which describes a talk with ER in which she states that the New Deal was greater than any one individual and that it could continue without FDR (p. 933).

F899 Smith, A. Merriman. *Thank You, Mr. President*. New York: Harper, 1946. x + 304p.
   When the secret presidential retreat Shangri-la, later Camp David, was being planned ER unwittingly violated security by breaking the story with the press. According to Smith, this was not the only example of this. For similar anecdotes about ER as First Lady, see *Merriman Smith's Book of Presidents*, pp. 119-20 (New York: Norton, 1972). His account of the death and burial of FDR including ER's activities at the time from *Thank You, Mr. President* is reprinted in *Coronet* 27 (Apr. 1950): 58-61 and in *Fabulous Yesterday: Coronet's 25th Anniversary Album*, pp. 58-60 (New York: Harper, 1961).

F900 [Smith, Gerald L. K.]. *The Roosevelt Death: A Super Mystery. Suicide? Assassination? Natural Death? Still Alive?* [St. Louis: Christian Nationalist Crusade], 1947. 30p.
   The world is waiting for ER to explain why FDR's casket was never opened (p. 3). A recitation of unpleasant causes addressed by ER in her columns and how she

forced son John into the military when he preferred to be a conscientious objector (pp. 9-10).

F901 Smith, Marie. "The Entertaining Roosevelts." *Entertaining in the White House*. By Marie Smith. Washington: Acropolis, 1967; New York: Macfadden-Bartell, 1970. 190-204.

Describes various luncheons, dinners, and receptions during the Roosevelt years. The White House portion of the 1939 visit of the British royal couple is described in detail.

F902 Tabouis, Genevieve. "Eleanor Chez Elle." *Notre Europe* (Mar. 1951): 7-13.

French journalist Tabouis recalls a wartime visit to Val-Kill and some of the questions which ER answered at a White House press conference. She recalls that ER opposed interracial marriages and expressed her wish that black domestic workers would apply themselves more rather than form Eleanor Clubs. ER was firm in her belief in the right of all citizens to have equal access to education, to enjoy the right to participate in public functions, and to vote Tabouis recalls. In French.

F903 "Too Old, Too Bold, Too Pushy, Too Plastic--First Ladies Hear It All, but Never 'She's Perfect!'" *People Weekly* 27 (18 May 1987): 93-94, 99-100.

Lou Hoover made radio speeches and promoted the role of women in government, and ER built on that. ER knew that someone would criticize everything about her. From an interview with Betty Boyd Caroli.

F904 "Tribute." *Time* 51 (19 Apr. 1948): 45.

When ER unveiled a London statue to FDR, Winston Churchill credited her for making it possible for a crippled FDR to serve his country during such difficult times.

F905 Trohan, Walter. *Political Animals: Memoirs of a Sentimental Cynic*. Garden City: Doubleday, 1975. xiii + 411p.

Journalist Trohan writes off ER's women only press conferences as not very newsworthy while stating that ER may have exceeded FDR in understanding politics (pp. 101-2) as well as recognizing the danger posed by Hitler (pp. 61).

F906 Truett, Randle Bond. "Eleanor Roosevelt." *The First Ladies in Fashion*. By Randle Bond Truett. New York: Hastings House, 1954. 76-77.

Brief account of ER as First Lady.

F907 Truman, Harry S. *Memoirs*. 2 vols. Garden City: Doubleday, 1955-1956. Index.

His recollections of ER at the death of FDR (v. 1, pp. 5-7).

F908 ---. *Where the Buck Stops: The Personal and Private Writings of Harry S. Truman*. Ed. Margaret Truman. New York: Warner, 1989. x + 388pp. Index.

HST had a high regard for the memory of Dolley Madison, and he thought that ER compared favorably with her. He claims that FDR always consulted ER on matters of policy.

F909 Truman, Margaret. *Bess W. Truman*. New York: Macmillan, 1986. 445p. Index.

Bess Truman first met ER in 1935 and always marveled at her energy and interest in women's rights. While she approved of ER's approach to the duties of First Lady, she could not accept them as her own (pp. 139-40, 198, 256-57, 331).

F910 ---. *Souvenir: Margaret Truman's Own Story*. By Margaret Truman with Margaret Cousins. New York: McGraw-Hill, 1956. 365p.
Her recollections of ER on the death of FDR (pp. 86, 91).

F911 Tugwell, Rexford G. *The Democratic Roosevelt: A Biography of Franklin D. Roosevelt*. Garden City: Doubleday, 1957. 712p. Index. Bibliography. Notes.
His extensive portrayal of ER's role in FDR's career and the New Deal is laudatory and affectionate. Tugwell believes that an understanding of ER is a prerequisite to an understanding of FDR.

F912 ---. *FDR: Architect of an Era*. New York: Macmillan, 1967. xvii + 270p. Index. Additional Readings.
As First Lady ER played an active role in the development of New Deal policies (pp. 93-94, 133, 182-83). ER and the death of FDR (pp. 258-59).
He concludes with a joint tribute to the Roosevelts. They overcame personal ordeals and realized their duty, and in the process left the country and democracy stronger since they worked to see that modern technology can benefit all, not just the privileged (pp. 260-64).

F913 Tully, Grace. *F.D.R., My Boss*. New York: Scribner's, 1949. xiii + 391p. Index.
FDR's last secretary had joined ER's staff in 1928. From an insider's perspective she provides an anecdotal look at ER as First Lady. Many references to her with some sections continuing for several pages. Index entry for ER is not arranged by topic.

F914 Wallace, Henry A. *The Price of Vision: The Diary of Henry A. Wallace, 1942-1946*. Ed. John Morton Blum. Boston: Houghton Mifflin, 1973. x + 707p. Index. Notes.
Numerous entries from Wallace's diary provide insight into ER's opinions about many public figures, the political and social philosophies of Democratic Party leaders, and her fears about FDR seeking a fourth term.

F915 Walton, Richard J. *Henry Wallace, Harry Truman, and the Cold War*. New York: Viking, 1976. x + 388p. Index. Bibliography. Notes.
ER's role in Wallace's nomination for Vice President in 1940 and her efforts to see him renominated in 1944 (pp. 7-8, 20-21, 30).

F916 Ware, Susan. *Holding Their Own: American Women in the 1930s*. American Women in the Twentieth Century. Boston: Twayne, 1982. xxii + 223p. Index. Bibliography. Notes.
ER's press conferences (pp. 75-78). As First Lady (pp. 171-72). Ware considers *It's Up to the Women* an attempt to convince women that they could play a crucial role in bringing the country through its economic crisis (pp. 1-3, 8, 14).

F917 Waterhouse, Helen. "A 'First Lady' Interview." *Christian Science Monitor* 14 Nov. 1962, Eastern ed.: editorial page.

An Akron, Ohio reporter recalls her Mar. 1933 interview conducted at the time she accompanied ER into a coal mine.

F918 Weiser, Marjorie P.K., and Jean S. Arbeiter. "Powers behind the President." *Womanlist*. By Marjorie P.K. Weiser and Jean S. Arbeiter. New York: Atheneum, 1981. 364.
A brief summary of ER's activities as First Lady which support the belief that she was a power behind FDR.

F919 Welter, Barbara. "First Ladies before Mrs. Roosevelt." *Hunter Magazine* 2 (Mar. 1983): 10.
A legacy to her successors is the fact that since her time as First Lady we have come to expect more of the President's wife. Text of address at Hunter College conference, New York, 4 Dec. 1982.

F920 West, J.B. *Upstairs at the White House: My Life with the First Ladies*. By J.B. West with Mary Lynn Katz. New York: Coward, McCann & Geoghegan, 1973. 381p. Index. Bibliography.
Toward the end of the Roosevelt administration West was assistant to the White House Chief Usher. His coverage of ER is mainly anecdotal (pp. 13-57).

F921 Westin, Jean. *Making Do: How Women Survived the '30s*. Chicago: Follett, 1976. xi + 331p. Index.
Brief interviews with women about life in the 1930s provide vignettes of ER's activities and significance of her role as First Lady (pp. 205, 244-46, 276, 294-95, 298, 300, 303).

F922 White, Betty. "The White House Years." *Saturday Evening Post* 249 (Mar. 1977): 16, 18.
Written at the time of the broadcast of the White House years portion of the dramatization of Lash's *Eleanor and Franklin* it is a discussion of the Roosevelts' relationship and how their children have written about it. Quotes from James Roosevelt's *My Parents*.

F923 White, William S. "Eisler Plea Made by Mrs. Roosevelt to Sumner Welles." *New York Times* 25 Sept. 1947: 1, 19.
Testimony before the House Committee on Un-American Activities claims that as First Lady ER intervened to help Hans Eisler, a former German Communist, enter the country. Continued, and with reactions from ER, on 26 Sept.: 1, 18 and 27 Sept.: 1, 13.

F924 ---. *Majesty & Mischief: A Mixed Tribute to F.D.R.* New York: McGraw-Hill, 1961. 221p. Index.
Contains a succinct account of ER's activities during the days following FDR's death (pp. 18-20, 99, 100, 102).

F925 *The White House Press Conferences of Eleanor Roosevelt*. Modern American History. Ed. Maurine Beasley. New York: Garland, 1983. xi + 354p. Index.
Reconstructed transcripts of ER's press conferences from 6 Mar. 1933-12 Apr. 1945. The papers of Martha Strayer and Bess Furman Armstrong serve as primary sources. Excerpts issued as "Dr. Maurine Beasley Locates 87 of Eleanor Roosevelt's

1933-1945 All-Women Press Conferences." *Media Report to Women* 11 (Nov./Dec. 1983): 15. For a discussion of Beasley's preparation of the book and what it reveals about ER's daily schedule and her range of interests, see Henry Mitchell's column "Any Day" entitled "Eleanor Roosevelt: Her New Deal for Women in the Press." *Washington Post* 23 Mar. 1984, sect. C: 1-2.

F926 Winfield, Betty Houchin. "Anna Eleanor Roosevelt's White House Legacy: The Public First Lady." *Presidential Studies Quarterly* 18 (Spring 1988): 331-45. Notes.
   Winfield compares the public ER with other first ladies of this century. In addition to the independent activities which she pursued, ER was the first to be so public with her roles as wife and mother, White House hostess, and aide to the President. After ER first ladies have traveled alone and publicly, been visible, pursued good works, and done things "in [their] own right." ER gave a new meaning to the "public woman."

F927 ---. "The Legacy of Eleanor Roosevelt." *Presidential Studies Quarterly* 20 (Fall 1990): 699-706. Notes.
   Among first ladies ER was the first to have a public life of her own, and those who have followed her have been expected to have one as well. Her career also resulted in new expectations for all women, for she was the embodiment of the new woman capable of a life and career separate from that of her husband.

F928 ---. "Mrs. Roosevelt's Press Conference Association: The First Lady Shines a Light." *Journalism History* 8 (Summer 1981): 54-55, 63-70. Notes.
   The origin of the press conferences, their organization, and the journalists who attended. Just as the press conferences were beneficial to ER, they also helped to keep her and her activities before the public.

F929 Wolf, Ann M. *The Long Shadow of Franklin D. Roosevelt*. Philadelphia: Dorrance, 1974. 81p.
   An extreme critic of FDR, HST, and military conscription, Wolf levels criticism toward ER too for her social engineering ideas and support of a military economy. She contends that ER was always in step with FDR and that he approved of her actions (pp. 22, 29-30, 32-33, 34, 36, 55).

ELEANOR ROOSEVELT AND WORLD WAR II

F930 Adamic, Louis. *Dinner at the White House*. New York: Harper, 1946. 276p.
   The author of *Two-Way Passage* uses an early 1942 dinner with the Roosevelts and Winston Churchill to discuss the relevance of his book to the post-war world. Coverage of ER (pp. 3-111, 140, 245-49).

F931 Aglion, Raoul. *Roosevelt and de Gaulle, Allies in Conflict: A Personal Memoir*. New York: Free Press, 1988. x + 237p. Index. Bibliography. Notes.
   Aglion, who served as a representative of Charles de Gaulle, recalls his first meeting with ER in 1941 and describes her work for the Free French (pp. 80-81).

F932 "America's First Lady Speaks at Federation Dinner." *Independent Woman* 22 (Dec. 1943): 359, 374.

At a Nov. 1943 National Federation of Business and Professional Women's Clubs dinner in New York ER responded to several questions. There must be changes in economic thinking if there is to be enough employment for women in the post-war world. Our servicemen in Australia and New Zealand asked questions about conditions at home. When they get home will they be able to finish their education?

F933 "Antipodes Day." *Newsweek* 22 (13 Sept. 1943): 56.
Her trip to the South Pacific, visits with troops in New Zealand and Australia, and meetings with women's groups in Australia.

F934 Beaton, Cecil. *The Years Between: Diaries, 1939-44.* New York: Holt, Rinehart and Winston, 1965. 352p.
During ER's wartime trip to England Beaton was summoned to Buckingham Palace to photograph the royal family and their famous visitor. He provides a humorous description of the difficulties which he had posing ER (pp. 207-9).

F935 "Blueprint for Civilian Defense." *Independent Woman* 20 (Oct. 1941): 292-94, 316.
In this article about the civilian defense effort the appointment of ER as assistant director of the Office of Civilian Defense is hailed as the best thing which has happened (p. 293).

F936 Blum, John Morton. *From the Morgenthau Diaries, Years of War, 1941-1945.* Boston: Houghton Mifflin, 1967. xi + 526p. Index. Notes.
There are numerous brief sections about ER during the war years concerning her opinions about wartime efforts and FDR's possible successors.

F937 Breitman, Richard, and Alan M. Kraut. *American Refugee Policy and European Jewry, 1933-1945.* Bloomington: Indiana Univ. Pr., 1987. viii + 310p. Index. Bibliographical Note. Notes.
Several brief references to ER's efforts on behalf of Jewish refugees (pp. 129, 131-33).

F938 Burns, James MacGregor. *Roosevelt: The Soldier of Freedom.* New York: Harcourt Brace Jovanovich, 1970. xiv + 722p. Index. Bibliography. Notes.
This study of FDR as war leader includes numerous references to ER's activities during the period.

F939 "Children of the World." *MD: Medical Newsmagazine* 9 (June 1965): 266-71.
Founded in 1937 the Foster Parents' Plan has had many famous participants. During the war ER sponsored several children.

F940 Childs, Marquis W. *I Write from Washington.* New York: Harper, 1942. ix + 331p. Index.
A reporter's recollections about Washington from the beginning of the New Deal to the early days of U.S. involvement in the war. Describes the activities of ER and Fiorello La Guardia in the Office of Civilian Defense as amateurish (pp. 260-65).

F941 *Churchill & Roosevelt: The Complete Correspondence.* 3 vols. Ed. Warren F. Kimball. Princeton: Princeton Univ. Pr., 1984. Index.

Their wives are mentioned frequently. ER is the subject of some of Kimball's commentaries, and her 1942 trip to England is covered by numerous communications (v. 1, pp. 541, 633, 636, 639, 642-43, 654-56).

F942 Clapper, Olive Ewing. "Biography." *Watching the World*. By Raymond Clapper. New York: Whittlesey House-McGraw-Hill, 1944. 3-33.
Contains an account of Clapper's outrage with the way in which ER went about her duties at the Office of Civilian Defense (p. 17).

F943 *Congressional Record Appendix*. 1941.
Before U.S. entry into the war two episodes enraged some members of Congress. After ER reported on FDR's 1941 State of the Union address in "My Day" of 7 Jan. expressing regret that only Democrats appeared to support his plan to develop an arsenal, editorials critical of her conclusion were reprinted ("Cause for Regret." 10 Jan. 1941: A83 and "In Reply to Mrs. Roosevelt." 13 Jan. 1941: A92). More editorials appeared when she tried to rationalize FDR's 1940 campaign pledge to stay out of a European war with his 1941 actions ("Mrs. Roosevelt Mistaken." 12 May 1941: A2253, "Eleanor Roosevelt Fails to Explain Why the President Broke His Promise." 5 Nov. 1941: A4998-99, and "Mrs. Roosevelt." 18 Nov. 1941: A5180-81).

F944 *Congressional Record Appendix*. 1942.
ER's actions as assistant director of the Office of Civilian Defense, particularly that of hiring her friend the dancer Mayris Chaney, brought criticism. Editorials were reprinted ("Fan Dancers in Our War Effort." 16 Feb. 1942: A558-59 and "Note to Mrs. Roosevelt." 16 Feb. 1942: A561).

F945 *Congressional Record Appendix*. 1943.
Her trip to the South Pacific prompted criticism and praise. In "The First Lady's Contribution to the Winning of the War." 7 Oct. 1943: A4187-88 Rep. Clare E. Hoffman condemns ER for her lack of awareness of the realities of the war and introduces Westbrook Pegler's 4 Oct. column highly critical of her trip as "political propaganda." On the positive side an article by former newsman Capt. Robert M. White, II and an editorial in praise of the White article were reprinted ("Anna Eleanor Roosevelt." 25 Oct. 1943: A4494-95 and "Public Energy No. 1." 18 Dec. 1943: A5586). "A Mother at the Front." *Christian Advocate* 1636 (30 Dec. 1943): 4 is about what White wrote to his wife concerning ER's visit.

F946 "Don't Draft Girls." Editorial. *Review* (Young Communist League) 6 (23 June 1943): [16].
ER has proposed that young women be conscripted for forced labor. This would help destroy American life as we know it, not prepare girls for marriage as ER claims. "It is Mrs. Roosevelt and the class she represents which is hourly and daily breaking up the American family."

F947 Eichelberger, Robert L. *Our Jungle Road to Tokyo*. By Robert L. Eichelberger in collaboration with Milton Mackaye. New York: Viking, 1950; Washington: Zenger, 1982. xxvi + 306p. Index.
He was placed in charge of ER's 1943 trip to Australia. Praise for the purpose and benefits of her visit (pp. 78-88).

F948 "Eleanor in England." *Newsweek* 20 (2 Nov. 1942): 48, 51.
Her arrival in London and the warm reception which she received.

F949 "Eleanor Roosevelt Visits South Pacific: As Others View the Trip." *Democratic Digest* 20 (Sept. 1943): 8-9.
She wore a Red Cross uniform and paid her own way when she went to the South Pacific. Excerpts from *Time* and *Newsweek*, United Press dispatches, and a letter written by a soldier applaud her energy and enthusiasm.

F950 "Eleanor's Playmates." *Time* 39 (16 Feb. 1942): 49-50.
Dubbed "OCDiva" *Time* wonders if ER has gone too far by putting actor Melvyn Douglas and dancer Mayris Chaney on the payroll. Is it time for her to resign her post as assistant director of the Office of Civilian Defense? For a similar account, see Scott Hart, *Washington at War: 1941-1945* (Englewood Cliffs: Prentice-Hall, 1970).

F951 Fay, Bernard. "Roosevelt et l'Europe." *Ecrits de Paris* 211 (1963): 60-71.
Influenced by the Soviets, FDR caused the war through his diplomatic and political miscalculations and schemes, and ER promoted and encouraged what he was doing. In French.

F952 Feingold, Henry L. *The Politics of Rescue: The Roosevelt Administration and the Holocaust, 1938-1945.* [Expanded and updated ed.]. New York: Holocaust Library, 1980. xvi + 416p. Index. Bibliography. Notes.
A source for references to ER's attempt to direct FDR toward a more liberal refugee policy.

F953 "First Lady Here." *Tattler and Bystander* (28 Oct. 1942): 98.
Her visit to Britain is another example of how ER has often gone where FDR could not during their long and remarkable relationship. Issued as a section of the column "Way of War." Additional statements of appreciation are "Active Guest." (4 Nov.): 131 and "Palace Visitor." (11 Nov.): 162.

F954 "First Lady Named to Defense Post." *New York Times* 14 Sept. 1941: 2.
Fiorello La Guardia announces that ER will become his assistant director at the Office of Civilian Defense. "OCD Job Assumed by Mrs. Roosevelt." *New York Times* 30 Sept. 1941: 28 reports on her first day on the job, a task which she describes as facilitating the efforts of every citizen who wishes to volunteer his or her services.

F955 "First Lady Takes 'A' Card for 'Gas.'" *New York Times* 15 May 1942: 16.
She will take a day train coach and not drive, and she is using a bicycle at Hyde Park. "First Lady Cuts Her Travel Plans." *New York Times* 21 May 1942: 23 announces that she is doing so because of the war effort. The editorial "Gasoline Codes of Honor." *New York Times* 23 May 1942: 12 praises her actions.

F956 "First Lady Through with Federal Posts." *New York Times* 28 Feb. 1942: 1.
After her brief stint at the Office of Civilian Defense, ER says that she will not be taking a position with the Women's Auxiliary Army Corps or any other federal agency.

F957 "First Lady's South Pacific Tour." *Life* 15 (11 Oct. 1943): 27-31.
Report of her recent tour. Consists mainly of photographs.

F958 Fishman, Jack. *My Darling Clementine: The Story of Lady Churchill.* New York: McKay, 1963. 384p. Index. Bibliography.
Account of ER's 1942 visit to England (pp. 139-43) and other occasions which brought ER and the Churchills together. Based on ER's autobiographical writings and conversations between the author and ER.

F959 *Foreign Relations of the United States, 1941. Vol. 2. Europe.* 77th Congress, 2d Session. House Document, 916. Dept. of State Publication, 6788. Washington: GPO, 1959. vii + 1011p. Index.
ER tried to involve herself in Dept. of State matters during the war years (p. 601). For similar information, see 1942, v. 3, pp. 151-52, 161-63, 177-78; 1944, v. 1, pp. 977-78, and 1945, v. 8, pp. 690-91.

F960 *Foreign Relations of the United States, The Conference at Quebec, 1944.* 92d Congress, 2d Session. House Document, 92-315. Dept. of State Publication, 8627. Washington: GPO, 1972. 1 + 527p. Index.
ER's role in the Second Quebec Conference (11-16 Sept.) and discussions following at Hyde Park (18-19 Sept.) was primarily a social one.

F961 Frazer, Heather T., and John O'Sullivan. "Forgotten Women of World War II: Wives of Conscientious Objectors in Civilian Public Service." *Peace & Change* 5 (Fall 1978): 46-51. Notes.
ER entered the debate about lack of compensation for men who were performing civilian public service and allotments for their dependents when she responded to a question in her "If You Ask Me" column of June 1944 and continued to express in "My Day" her view that neither were entitled to compensation because the men were "not performing any service for the country."

F962 Friedman, Saul S. *No Haven for the Oppressed: United States Policy toward Jewish Refugees, 1938-1945.* Detroit: Wayne State Univ. Pr., 1973. 315p. Index. Notes.
Several references to ER's attempt to direct FDR toward a more liberal refugee policy. Includes discussion and partial text of a 1941 letter to ER from Albert Einstein urging a liberalization of the policy (p. 124). A fuller text of the letter with discussion can be found in Arthur D. Morse, *While Six Million Died: A Chronicle of American Apathy,* pp. 303-4 (New York: Random House, 1968; Woodstock: Overlook, 1983).

F963 Garrett, Evelyn. *The Four Queens.* London: MacDonald, 1944. xi + 224p.
The story of ER and three contemporary women--Queen Elizabeth, Queen Wilhelmina, and Mme. Chiang Kai-shek--who influenced events in the 1930s and 1940s and the extent to which World War II brought them together. Detailed, but undocumented, coverage of significant periods in ER's life with a foreigner's view of her emergence and role as First Lady of particular note. Concludes with an informative account of ER's 1942 trip to England (pp. 29-50, 60-70, 109-22, 169-86, 202-24).

F964   Gitlitz, Susan. "Eleanor Roosevelt's Visit at Antioch, 1944." Class paper. Antioch College, 1957. 24p. Bibliography. Notes.

ER spoke twice at the Institute on Conditions for an Enduring Peace, 11 July 1944, Yellow Springs, Ohio and stated that the challenges of the post-war world would require all citizens to participate in the democratic process. She called for a world "police force" to keep all nations in check.

F965   Goodman, Charles. "Eleanor Roosevelt Visits Island." *Pacific Times* (undated): 1-2.

A stop during her South Pacific trip reassured those who saw her that there was someone who cared about them. From a publication written and produced by enlisted men.

F966   Gruber, Ruth. *Haven: The Unknown Story of 1,000 World War II Refugees.* New York: Coward-McCann, 1983. 335p. Index.

Records of the refugee camps and recollections of some of the refugees are sources for this study of the sheltering European refugees in Oswego, N.Y. ER visited the camp in 1944, and Gruber recalls that visit with the help of "My Day" columns (pp. 208-11).

F967   Gutin, Myra G. "Political Surrogates and Independent Advocates: Eleanor Roosevelt." *The President's Partner: The First Lady in the Twentieth Century.* Contributions in Women's Studies, 105. By Myra G. Gutin. New York: Greenwood, 1983. 81-107. Index. Bibliography. Notes.

ER's role with the Office of Civilian Defense and her trips to the South Pacific and the Caribbean (pp. 90-92). Based on a more lengthy section, which also describes ER's efforts on behalf of Jewish refugees, in her dissertation "The President's Partner: The First Lady as Public Communicator, 1920-1976," pp. 300-315 (Univ. of Mich., 1983).

F968   Halsey, William F., and Joseph Bryan, III. *Admiral Halsey's Story.* New York: McGraw-Hill, 1947. xvii + 310p. Index.

Halsey thought ER's visit to the South Pacific would be a nuisance, but he concluded that it benefited his men and was the most effective trip to the area by any civilian (pp. 166-68). Halsey's account is also presented in E.B. Potter, *Bill Halsey*, pp. 236-37 (Annapolis: Naval Institute, 1985). This portion of Halsey's auto-biography is also issued as "Admiral Halsey Tells His Story, Pt. 6." *Saturday Evening Post* 220 (19 July 1947): 34-35, 71-76.

F969   Harriman, Kathleen. "Mrs. Roosevelt and the Blinkin' Heroes." *Newsweek* 20 (2 Nov. 1942): 48.

When ER tries to call them heroes, Londoners respond that they are only doing their duty for the war effort.

F970   Harriman, Kathleen, and Merrill Mueller. "With the First Lady and the First WAAC." *Newsweek* 20 (9 Nov. 1942): 45.

Harriman reports that demonstrations occur at every stop which ER makes in England.

F971 Heckscher, August. *When LaGuardia Was Mayor: New York's Legendary Years*. By August Heckscher with Phyllis Robinson. New York: Norton, 1978. 448p. Index. Bibliography. Notes.

ER and Fiorello La Guardia working together in the Office of Civilian Defense (pp. 301-2, 314-15, 321-22, 324-25).

F972 Howard, James T. "Males Squirm at First Lady's Parley." *PM* 28 Sept. 1943: 5.

When she returned from the Pacific men were allowed to attend her press conference for the first time because she considered the discussion of her trip of such importance. A brief account appeared as "Coed Conference." *Newsweek* 22 (11 Oct. 1943): 88, 90.

F973 "I Shall Tell My Husband." *Time* 40 (9 Nov. 1942): 20.

During her wartime trip to England ER's many activities including seeing a piglet named Franklin about which she plans to tell her husband.

F974 Jackson, Alice. "She's an Awfully Nice Lady!" *Australian Women's Weekly* (18 Sept. 1943): 12-13.

Words and numerous photographs trace one of ER's days during her trip to the South Pacific. Everywhere she went those who saw or spoke with her were impressed with her "charm and friendliness."

F975 Keil, Sally Van Wegenen. *Those Wonderful Women in Their Flying Machines*. New York: Rawson, Wade, 1978. x + 334p. Index.

ER was a proponent of women's role in aviation. ER and Amelia Earhart (p. 26), Jacqueline Cochran (p. 44), and support of Cochran's efforts to see a place for female pilots in the Army Air Corps (pp. 47-48, 51).

F976 Land, Emory Scott. *Winning the War with Ships: Land, Sea and Air--Mostly Land*. New York: McBride, 1958. 310p. Index.

Adm. Land, chair of the Maritime Commission and head of the War Shipping Admin., credited ER with much interference. A Christmas luncheon exchange between the two marked his last invitation to the White House (pp. 214-15).

F977 Lash, Joseph P. *Roosevelt and Churchill, 1939-1941: The Partnership That Saved the West*. New York: Norton, 1976. 528p. Index. Notes.

Lash, who was at the White House on New Year's Day 1942, recalls the visit of Churchill and dinner conversation about the war with the Roosevelts and Churchill (pp. 15-19).

F978 "Legion Head Asks Quiet by First Lady." *New York Times* 17 Apr. 1942: 19.

The commander of the New York State American Legion takes issue with ER's view that those who fought in the last war came home and joined the American Legion rather than worked to improve their communities and country. If the American people had followed the lead of the American Legion rather than listening to unrealistic persons like ER, he says, we might not be in this war. Her rebuttal appears in "First Lady Intends to Continue Her Speeches; She Denies She Made Attack on Legion." *New York Times* 18 Apr. 1942: 17.

F979 Lingeman, Richard R. *"Don't You Know There's a War On?" The American Home Front, 1941-1945.* New York: Putnam's, 1970. 415p. Index. Bibliography.

ER's involvement with the Office of Civilian Defense and public and congressional criticism of her actions (pp. 34-38).

F980 Lombard, Helen. *While They Fought: Behind the Scenes in Washington, 1941-1946.* New York: Scribner's, 1947. 322p. Index.

Her friendship with Melvyn and Helen Douglas, Joseph Lash and others considered by some to be too liberal made ER the topic of Washington conversation. Her 1942 trip to England and the harm which she was doing to the Democratic Party (pp. 283-99). Her work with the Office of Civilian Defense (pp. 32-40). See pp. 138-39 for her relations with Churchill and pp. 218-19 for those with Constaine Oumansky.

F981 Long, Tania. "Mrs. Roosevelt in London; Greeted by King and Queen." *New York Times* 24 Oct. 1942: 1-2.

The first in a series of daily stories about her visit. In the editorial "Unofficial Ambassadress." 24 Oct. 1942: 14 it is predicted that the trip will be a clear success. A series of photographs summarized the visit: "'My Days' in England." *New York Times Magazine* 8 Nov. 1942: 8-9.

F982 Maga, Timothy P. "Humanism and Peace: Eleanor Roosevelt's Mission to the Pacific, August-September, 1943." *Maryland Historian* 19 (Winter 1988): 33-47. Notes.

The trip was a success because she helped to improve critical wartime relations between Australia and the U.S., she focused attention on the need to change and enlarge upon the efforts of the Red Cross in the region, and her reports helped to improve the flow of essential provisions to the Pacific theater. A comprehensive study of her efforts to promote a speedy peace and to improve humanitarian conditions for American and allied forces. Based mainly on her papers and other archival sources.

F983 Martin, Ralph. "Mrs. Roosevelt Visits Orphans, Lauds Stars and Stripes Plan." *Stars and Stripes* 4 Nov. 1942: 1, 4.

During her trip to England ER visits war orphans.

F984 McLaughlin, Kathleen. "'No Sam Browne Belts,' Says Mrs. Roosevelt." *New York Times Magazine* 27 July 1941: 6, 18.

ER thinks that women in the volunteer defense effort deserve an appropriate uniform.

F985 Meredith, Ellis. "At the Women's National Democratic Club: First Lady Speaks." *Democratic Digest* 21 (Apr. 1944): 18.

She discussed her Caribbean trip.

F986 "Mrs. FDR Endorses Dies." *In Fact* 2 (17 Mar. 1941): 4.

Now that there is tension throughout the world ER has endorsed Rep. Martin Dies and his congressional committee in their investigation of anti-war groups. Quite a change from her earlier position when Dies was investigating American youth groups. In a follow-up entitled "The Roosevelts and Dies." *In Fact* 2 (31 Mar. 1941): 3 there is further elaboration of her past and present positions.

F987 "Mrs. FDR Quits Finns." *In Fact* 3 (15 Sept. 1941): 1.
After she was asked to explain her support for an organization which is behind Fascists in Finland, she resigned from For Finland, Inc.

F988 "Mrs. F.D. Roosevelt Is in New Zealand." *New York Times* 27 Aug. 1943: 1.
A brief report of her surprise arrival lacking any information as to why she had made the journey.

F989 "Mrs. Roosevelt." *Sphere* (7 Nov. 1942): 162.
ER is to be commended for her "pluck" in making a wartime trip here. Her sense of duty symbolizes the help which her country is giving to England. Issued as a section of the column "A War Newsletter."

F990 "Mrs. Roosevelt." Editorial. *Times* [London] 24 Oct. 1942: 5.
We welcome the American First Lady who has distinguished herself through her words and deeds, and we look forward to her input on our war effort.

F991 "Mrs. Roosevelt as a Nuisance." *Argonaut* 122 (22 Oct. 1943): 1, 4.
ER is the type who never seems to know her proper place. During the war she should stay at the White House and let those who have a job to do get on with it.

F992 "Mrs. Roosevelt in England." *Life* 13 (16 Nov. 1942): 44-46.
Photographs reporting her visit to defense sites in England.

F993 "Mrs. Roosevelt in London." *Times* [London] 24 Oct. 1942: 4.
Extensive coverage of her visit to England, Scotland, and Ireland begins with the account of her arrival on 23 Oct. and a dinner in her honor at Buckingham Palace. Articles, photographs, and entries in the daily "Court Circular" through 11 Nov. trace her activities.

F994 "Mrs. Roosevelt Nails McClure Syndicate Lie." *In Fact* 8 (8 Nov. 1943): 2.
Upon her return from England it was reported that ER brought back the news that soldiers are disturbed by U.S. civilian workers striking for higher wages. In a letter included in this article she stated that the soldiers want to know more about why the strikes are occurring.

F995 "Mrs. Roosevelt Named 'No. 1 Volunteer.'" *Victory* 2 (16 Sept. 1941): 22.
In the announcement that she will become assistant director of the Office of Civilian Defense ER is referred to as "America's No. 1 Volunteer."

F996 "Mrs. Roosevelt Should Resign." Editorial. *New York Herald Tribune* 8 Feb. 1942, sect. 2: 8.
ER is to blame for Congress' failure to provide adequate funding for civilian defense. Her interest in expanding the scope of the Office of Civilian Defense works against its real purpose. The article "Smearing Mrs. F.D.R." *In Fact* 4 (23 Feb. 1942): 1, 2. criticizes the paper for following the editorial with a letter from a reader who pledges to organize an effort against the purchase of war bonds if more jobs are created like the civilian defense one held by ER's friend dancer Mayris Chaney.

F997 "Mrs. Roosevelt's Anti-Americanism." *Argonaut* 123 (10 Mar. 1944): 1-2.
Her repeated call for national service for all young men and women is the occasion for labeling ER a near-Fascist and a nuisance.

F998 "Mrs. Roosevelt's Plan." *Time* 37 (23 June 1941): 18.
Not opposed to the idea, *Time* reports on ER's continuing efforts to see a year of compulsory service for women. She tried without success to get FDR to include women in the legislation that enables men to be drafted.

F999 "Mrs. Roosevelt's Postscript." Editorial. *Times* [London] 9 Nov. 1942: 5.
While in our country she has endeared herself to the mighty and the humble. She will help other Americans to better understand what the war really means to us. The post-war world will also be a time of sacrifice, she warns, as we work to maintain the peace.

F1000 "'My Day' in the Caribbean." *Time* 43 (27 Mar. 1944): 19.
An amusing map of her trip to the Caribbean accompanied by text describing how she is trying to make servicemen think of home.

F1001 "My Day in the South Pacific." *Time* 42 (13 Sept. 1943): 20.
ER has conquered the South Pacific with her combined fact finding and good will trip.

F1002 "Nation's Libraries Asked to Establish Departments for Defense Information; OCD Assistant Detailed to Help." *Victory* 3 (13 Jan. 1942): 30.
ER has asked that libraries enter the defense effort by making civilian defense literature available.

F1003 "Nazis Ask Mrs. Roosevelt to End Public Comment." *New York Times* 5 Feb. 1939: 38.
In a 4 Feb. editorial *Lokal-Anzeiger* [Berlin] attacked ER for defending the sale of U.S. planes to France when she should be concerning herself with social problems in her own country. Her response that it appears that women's views do not matter appeared in the *New York Times* 8 Feb. on p. 17 as "First Lady Scorns Nazi Press Advice." For her call for a repeal of the embargo, see "First Lady Urges Repeal of Arms Embargo: Holds Neutrality and Third Term Unrelated." *New York Times* 28 Sep. 1939: 11. She continued to be criticized by the European press: *Boerson Zeitung* accused her on 3 Nov. 1939 of promoting fear of a German attack on the U.S. Excerpts in "Nazi Paper Accuses Mrs. F.D. Roosevelt." *New York Times* 4 Nov. 1939: 5. On 7 Nov. *Popolo d'Italia* [Milan] said that to keep out of the war the U.S. might embargo ER. Excerpts in "Embargo Mrs. Roosevelt, Mussolini's Paper Urges." *New York Times* 8 Nov. 1939: 3.
These attacks in the foreign press are discussed in Ruby Black, *Eleanor Roosevelt*, pp. 267, 269.

F1004 Parrish, Thomas. *Roosevelt and Marshall: Partners in Politics and War.* New York: Morrow, 1989. 608p. Index. Bibliography. Notes.
Army Chief of Staff George Marshall instructed his staff to give inquiries from ER prompt attention when she wrote about the quality of the entertainment and recreational facilities afforded enlisted men or when she questioned the treatment of

black soldiers. Includes a description of her travels during the war. Based in part on letters from ER to Marshall (pp. 375-77).

F1005 "Peace and Mrs. Roosevelt." *New Yorker* 21 (25 Aug. 1945): 16-17.

After her radio broadcast on the national day of thanksgiving at the end of hostilities ER discussed FDR and the war. He feared that Germany would develop the atomic bomb first and that Russia would enter the war against Japan soon after the defeat of Germany.

F1006 Penkower, Monty N. "Eleanor Roosevelt and the Plight of World Jewry." *Jewish Social Studies* 49 (Spring 1987): 125-36. Notes.

Comprehensive examination of ER's involvement in efforts to aid Jews during the war and to influence U.S. policy on Jewish refugees.

F1007 "Policy in Offering Defense Substitutes Wins Salesgirl Prize, First Lady's Praise." *Defense* 2 (28 Oct. 1941): 23.

ER has praised a Philadelphia salesgirl's essay describing how she explained to customers the need to accept substitutes for goods needed in the defense effort.

F1008 "Report to Mothers." *Time* 42 (4 Oct. 1943): 25.

ER has reported to FDR and the nation's mothers that the commitment of young men in the South Pacific and their concern about conditions at home impressed her.

F1009 "Return Visit." *Time* 40 (2 Nov. 1942): 20.

ER's wartime arrival in London, a press conference, and her promises to American servicemen about socks and mail.

F1010 Ritchie, Donald A. *James M. Landis: Dean of the Regulators*. Cambridge: Harvard Univ. Pr., 1980. ix + 267p. Index. Notes.

ER's position as assistant director of the Office of Civilian Defense, the appointment of Landis as Fiorello La Guardia's successor at the OCD, and ER's efforts to see volunteer operations continue after the war (pp. 105-6, 108, 111-12, 115).

F1011 Robey, Ralph. "Mrs. Roosevelt on Conscription of Wealth." *Newsweek* 16 (19 Aug. 1940): 38.

In "My Day" for 6 Aug. she proposed the need for conscription to support the war effort. She is confused since wealth is already going to the defense effort through income taxes.

F1012 Roosevelt, Elliott. *As He Saw It*. New York: Duell, Sloan and Pearce, 1946. xviii + 270p. Index.

Son Elliott was in London at the time and recalls a portion of ER's 1942 trip to England (pp. 57-59).

F1013 "Rover Girl." *Newsweek* 20 (30 Nov. 1942): 38, 40.

After traveling in England for three weeks under the code name "Rover," ER tells of her travels in a radio broadcast and advises parents not to complain about conditions at home when writing to their sons.

F1014 "She Came, She Smiled--and She Conquered." *New Zealand Free Lance* (8 Sept. 1943): 5.
During her wartime trip her pleasing personality and genuine concern for all whom she met made her a big success in Auckland.

F1015 "Sidelights of the Week." *New York Times* 23 Aug. 1942, sect. 4: 2.
ER is in trouble with the war censor who has decreed that no weather maps may be published, because she is using "My Day" to report on the weather wherever she travels.

F1016 Soames, Mary. *Clementine Churchill*. London: Cassell, 1979. xix + 556p. Index. Bibliography. Notes.
An account of ER's 1942 visit to England derived from Lash's *Eleanor and Franklin* (pp. 318-19). Letters from Clementine Churchill plus the author's diary are used to describe the activities of the two wives during the Second Quebec Conference and the Churchills' visit to Hyde Park, Sept. 1944 (pp. 358-60).

F1017 "Sons and War." *Time* 34 (9 Oct. 1939): 12-13.
As Europe becomes more embroiled in war ER's views as reported through her press conferences and "My Day" reveal her transition from one who considered war to be obsolete to a mother who accepts the likelihood of U.S. involvement.

F1018 Spence, Benjamin A. "Mrs. Eleanor Roosevelt and Refugee Problems, 1938-1952." Thesis (M.S.) Univ. of Wisc., 1962. iii + 129p. Bibliographic Essay. Notes.
Her efforts on behalf of refugees during World War II, as a private citizen working on behalf of legislation aimed at liberalizing refugee policy, and as a UN delegate.

F1019 Spencer, Gwen Morton. "A Visit and Its Value." *Australia* (Dec. 1943): 11-12.
During her visit she praised the role of the British in the war effort. This charming woman represented her country well.

F1020 Strong, Tracy B., and Helene Keyssar. *Right in Her Soul: The Life of Anna Louise Strong*. New York: Random House, 1983. xiii + 399p. Index. Bibliography. Notes.
Letters are used to illustrate the friendship between ER and Anna Louise Strong, but those same letters reveal that ER was not responsive to Strong's petitions in support of causes such as a U.S.-Chinese alliance (p. 182) and the Nazi-Soviet Non-Aggression Pact (pp. 189-90). In 1939-40 she toured the U.S. at ER's suggestion and reported her findings to ER (pp. 184, 186-88) and to the public in *My Native Land* (New York: Viking, 1940).

F1021 Thomas, Bert. "The Famous and the Infamous as a Child Might See Them." *New York Times Magazine* 2 Aug. 1943: 10-11.
Drawings of wartime personalities from a British viewpoint. ER is described a one who writes a lot and is jolly and broad-minded.

F1022 *Visit to Australia of Mrs. Franklin D. Roosevelt, Official Luncheon...Record of Speeches*. Canberra: Commonwealth Government Printer, n.d. 1-5.
Speeches in her honor made at a luncheon, Canberra, 4 Sept. 1943.

F1023 Waldrop, Frank. "Quit Kiddin' Lady." *Congressional Record Appendix* (18 Aug. 1944): A3644-45.

What ER fails to tell us about her pleasure with the change in regulations which will allow troops to receive magazines once again is that the restrictions had been imposed to curb the flow of government propaganda about the accomplishments of FDR in promotion of a fourth term bid. From the *Washington Times-Herald*, 18 Aug. 1944.

F1024 Weil, Martin. *A Pretty Good Club: The Founding Fathers of the U.S. Foreign Service*. New York: Norton, 1978. 313p. Index. Bibliography. Notes.

Weil claims that ER lacked respect for the foreign service and that her views on foreign policy were dictated by her attitudes as a social reformer (p. 88). Before and during the war she tried to interfere in affairs of the State Dept. (pp. 95, 123, 131, 135-36, 184-86).

F1025 "Woman Bomb Aide Sees Future Good." *New York Times* 10 Aug. 1945: 6.

In a radio interview conducted by ER, German nuclear scientist Lise Meitner called on other women to help prevent another war. ER called for the atomic bomb to be used to end the war and then to aid humanity through peaceful means.

F1026 Wyman, David S. *The Abandonment of the Jews: America and the Holocaust, 1941-1945*. New York: Pantheon, 1984. xix + 444p. Index. Bibliography. Notes.

ER was sympathetic to the plight of the Jews; however, she was reluctant to call for American action or to participate in events such as the Emergency Conference to Save the Jewish People of Europe, preferring instead to make no statements nor take any actions which would jeopardize efforts to win the war (pp. 91-92, 145-46, 148-49, 315). Her efforts to rescue Jewish children detained in Europe (pp. 37, 133-34) and her sympathy for refugees detained in Oswego, N.Y. (pp. 271-73).

F1027 ---. *Paper Walls: America and the Refugee Crisis, 1938-1941*. Amherst: Univ. of Mass. Pr., 1968. ix + 306. Index. Bibliography. Notes.

ER figures in this account of "America's response to the plight of Jewish refugees in the years 1938-1941." ER and the Non-Sectarian Foundation for Refugee Children and the United States Committee for the Care of European Children (p. 94). How she deferred to official channels and was reluctant to advocate the admittance of Jewish children from Europe (pp. 95, 117, 142, 145, 147). Reissued in 1985 with a new preface (New York: Pantheon).

SOCIAL REFORMER

General

F1028 Abels, Margaret D. "Frances Perkins and Eleanor Roosevelt: Two Women in Reform America." Thesis (M.A.) State Univ. College of N.Y. at Buffalo, 1974. ii + 100p. Bibliography. Notes.

Events in her private life were crucial to her emergence as a social reformer. As a reformer her interests encompassed women, blacks, and children as well as living conditions for all Americans (pp. 1-3, 55-80, 95-96).

F1029 Anderson, Mary. *Woman at Work: The Autobiography of Mary Anderson*. By Mary Anderson as told to Mary N. Winslow. Minneapolis: Univ. of Minn. Pr., 1951; Westport: Greenwood, 1973. 266p. Index.

Long-time head of the U.S. Women's Bureau recalls how ER promoted the rights of women, blacks, and labor (pp. 177-78, 218-20, 239, 241-43, 245).

F1030 Asbell, Bernard. *The FDR Memoirs*. *As Written by Bernard Asbell*. New York: Doubleday, 1973. xvii + 461p. Index. Bibliography. Notes.

Writings by and about ER address her social reform activities (pp. 147-204 passim).

F1031 Biles, Roger. *A New Deal for the American People*. DeKalb: Northern Ill. Univ. Pr., 1991. ix + 274p. Index. Bibliography. Notes.

A derivative account from other works about ER as a social reformer (civil rights, pp. 181-82; women's rights, pp. 195-97, 204-5).

F1032 Buckley, William F., Jr. *Up from Liberalism*. New York: McDowell, Obolensky, 1959. xvi + 205p. Index. Notes.

In this analysis of the ideology and influence of liberals and liberalism ER is the first person named (p. 4). It is assumed that the ensuing discussion of beliefs of liberals (belief in the perfectibility of man, chief among them) is meant to apply to ER (pp. 5-7). Examples of what he considers to be her fuzzy thinking and her "lack of intellectual vigor" (pp. 8-11, 32, 88, 99).

F1033 Chafe, William H. *The Paradox of Change: American Women in the 20th Century*. New York: Oxford Univ. Pr., 1991. xvi + 256p. Index. Bibliographical Essay.

ER and a network of other women pursued a social reform agenda before and during the New Deal years (pp. 33-44). For particular attention to ER, see pp. 36-39. An expansion of his *The American Woman: Her Changing Social, Economic, and Political Roles, 1920-1970*, pp. 39-44, 188 (New York: Oxford Univ. Pr., 1972).

For similar treatment, see Glenna Matthews, *The Rise of Public Woman: Woman's Power and Woman's Place in the United States, 1630-1970*, pp. 181, 184-86 (New York: Oxford Univ. Pr., 1992).

F1034 "The Churchman Award Presented." *Churchman* 153 (15 Dec. 1939): 16-21.

ER was the first recipient of the award given for promoting understanding among all peoples. It was presented in New York on 29 Nov. 1939. Article includes text of remarks by participants.

George Gordon Battle spoke about ER's activities for mankind and how she and FDR are leading the nation (p. 16). In his remarks Frank Kingdon compares ER to the biblical Deborah since like Deborah she leads, but ER does so on a grander scale. She has managed to preserve her own personality and not be overshadowed by the position which she holds, the White House, or FDR. ER demonstrates that a woman can be a public figure (pp. 17-18). Dorothy Thompson compares ER's zeal for equality for all to that of Thompson's father (pp. 19-20).

F1035 Clapper, Raymond. *Watching the World*. Ed. and with a biographical sketch by Mrs. Raymond Clapper. New York: Whittlesey House-McGraw-Hill, 1944. x + 372p.

In a reprinted column dated 4 Apr. 1942 Clapper uses an amusing account of dancing at the White House to illustrate ER's stamina and determination. For all the good which she does and all the important social causes which she promotes her judgment and her kind heart can cause trouble. But her place in history is secure because of her early championing of causes which will become more acceptable in the future (pp. 121-25).

F1036 Conrad, Peter. "Teddy and Franklin and Eleanor." *Sunday Times Magazine* [London] 30 Nov. 1975: 44-53, 55-56, 58-59, 61, 63, 65-66.
ER's sense of duty and social consciousness were neither profound nor sincere, just American politics.

F1037 Cox, Carolyn. "President's Wife Makes History about as Much as President." *Saturday Night* 60 (25 Nov. 1944): 2.
This Canadian finds ER to be a popular figure who has strong opinions about the role which women can play in public life. Although she has made family her first obligation, ER has managed to involve herself in public affairs and as First Lady has made a lasting impact on her fellow citizens by getting out among them and learning of the effects of the depression.

F1038 Cox, James M. *Journey through My Years.* New York: Simon and Schuster, 1946. xi + 463p. Index.
In defense of ER's humanitarian, but often impractical, projects (pp. 417-18) in a book by the 1920 Democratic presidential nominee.

F1039 Des Marteau, Genie Lynn. "Eleanor Roosevelt: Portrait of a Leader." Thesis (M.A.) Kansas State Univ., 1979. 77p + ii. Bibliography. Notes.
ER succeeded as a humanitarian because it did not require the intimacy with others which she was never able to achieve. Derived from a limited number of published sources but not Lash's *Eleanor and Franklin* and *Eleanor: The Years Alone.*

F1040 Dykeman, Wilma, and James Stokely. *Seeds of Southern Change: The Life of Will Alexander.* Chicago: Univ. of Chicago Pr., 1962. xvi + 343p. Index. Bibliography.
The authors use correspondence and interviews with numerous individuals including ER in this loosely structured biography. Coverage of ER is restricted to the methods which she employed in pursuing social and economic concerns (pp. 243-45, 251-52).

F1041 "Eleanor Roosevelt." *Sisters United II* 25 (Winter 1986): 28.
She will be remembered for her work for social justice. Includes numerous unidentified quotations from her writings and speeches.

F1042 Elshtain, Jean Bethke. "Eleanor Roosevelt as Activist and Thinker: 'The Lady' and the Life of Duty." *Power Trips and Other Journeys: Essays in Feminism As Civic Discourse.* By Jean Bethke Elshtain. Madison: Univ. of Wisc. Pr., 1990. 24-41. Notes.
ER "remained a lady" throughout her career while she tried to revolt from the then current perception of ladyhood and struggled to find a sense of herself which she considered to be the duties which she saw herself pursuing. Elshtain also claims that ER's devout Christian thinking was central to her career. Concludes by tracing

the connections between ER's life and work with that of Jane Addams. "Written originally to be delivered at Vassar College for its centenary celebration of Roosevelt's birth."

F1043 Ernst, Morris L. *The Best Is Yet....* New York: Harper, 1945. xiii + 291p.
The chapter "The Roosevelts" is a tribute to FDR and, to a lesser extent, ER. Ernst sees them as inspirations for believing that the human lot can be made better for all. In addition to her own contributions ER has been of assistance to FDR by going where he cannot go and seeing what he cannot see. She stands up to him, and he respects her strength and convictions (pp. 283-89). Also issued in *Saturday Review of Literature* 28 (21 Apr. 1945): 14-15.

F1044 *Franklin D. Roosevelt, His Life and Times: An Encyclopedic View.* The G.K. Hall Presidential Encyclopedia Series. Ed. Otis L. Graham, Jr. and Meghan Robinson Wander. Boston: Hall, 1985. 483p. Selected Critical Bibliographies.
ER's activities as First Lady on behalf of blacks and the downtrodden (pp. 39, 187, 393, 407, 459).

F1045 "From the Bill of Fare." *Nation* 150 (18 May 1940): 623-27.
ER was honored at a 1 May dinner as the first recipient of an award sponsored by the *Nation* for "distinguished service in the cause of American social progress." Excerpted remarks by William Allen White, John Gunther, Melvyn Douglas, Ferdinand Pecora, and Frank Kingdon praise her as one whose liberalism and commitment to democratic principles are part of her daily life as a citizen who works to improve life for others while not seeking recognition for herself. Dorothy Canfield Fisher stated that ER has set an example of how a woman can lead a full life as homemaker and still be an active citizen.

F1046 Gordon, Linda. "Black and White Visions of Welfare: Women's Welfare Activism, 1890-1945." *Journal of American History* 78 (Sept. 1991): 559-90. Notes.
The characteristics and activities of black and white female social reformers are compared. ER is one of those studied. Gordon concludes that ER failed to integrate the black and white networks and to bring white support behind the anti-lynching bill.

F1047 Gutin, Myra G. "Political Surrogates and Independent Advocates: Eleanor Roosevelt." *The President's Partner: The First Lady in the Twentieth Century.* Contributions in Women's Studies, 105. By Myra G. Gutin. New York: Greenwood, 1989. 81-107. Index. Bibliography. Notes.
ER as an advocate for racial equality and subsistence homesteads (pp. 87-90). Based on the more lengthy section, which also describes ER's efforts to resolve the problems of youth, in her dissertation "The President's Partner: The First Lady as Public Communicator, 1920-1976," pp. 280-300 (Univ. of Mich., 1983).

F1048 Hareven, Tamara K. "ER and Reform." *Without Precedent: The Life and Career of Eleanor Roosevelt.* Everywoman: Studies in History, Literature, and Culture. Ed. Joan Hoff-Wilson and Marjorie Lightman. Bloomington: Indiana Univ. Pr., 1984. 210-13. Sources.
As a pragmatist ER used circumstances and conditions to further social reform.

F1049 Johnson, Gerald W. *Incredible Tale: The Odyssey of the Average American in the Last Half Century*. New York: Harper, 1950. viii + 301p. Index.

ER's example proves that the aristocrat is not by definition uninterested in the concerns and needs of the common man (pp. 198-204).

F1050 Johnson, Lyndon B. "Remarks upon Presenting the First Eleanor Roosevelt Award to Judge Anna M. Kross." *Public Papers of the Presidents of the United States: Lyndon B. Johnson, Containing the Public Messages, Speeches, and Statements of the President, 1963-64, Book 1--November 22, 1963 to June 30, 1964*. Washington: GPO, 1965. 334-37.

Includes a lengthy and moving tribute to ER, "the First Lady and the Best Lady." She never stopped speaking for the weak and the less fortunate, and her words and action personified what F. Scott Fitzgerald considered as this nation's defining principle--"a willingness of the heart." Text of address, Washington, 4 Mar. 1964.

F1051 Kunin, Madeleine M. "She Touched Our Lives." *Eleanor Roosevelt and the Universal Declaration of Human Rights: An Agenda for Action in 1988*. Hyde Park: The Franklin and Eleanor Roosevelt Institute, 1988. 9-13.

She was compelled to work to improve the rights of others, and her example encourages us still. Were she alive today, she would be speaking out against the social injustices in our country. Text of address, 7 Nov. 1987, Hyde Park, N.Y.

F1052 Mannes, Marya. "A Woman for the People." Rev. of *Eleanor and Franklin* by Joseph P. Lash. *Atlantic Monthly* 228 (Nov. 1971): 136-39.

ER set the stage for a society where women play an equal role with men in governing. The Roosevelts dedicated their lives to public service, and their union aided them in pursuing that goal. But Lash makes it clear that ER was the one more dedicated to change, and Mannes questions whether the New Deal would have brought as much social change had it not been for ER.

F1053 "Mrs. Roosevelt Accepts $1,000 Gimbel Award as 'Outstanding' Woman, Gives It to Cripple." *New York Times* 13 Dec. 1934: 3.

ER receives the Gimbel Award in Philadelphia as "'the outstanding American woman' for 1934" and donates the prize money to a child with polio. A similar account is "Aids Paralysis Victims." *Literary Digest* 118 (22 Dec. 1934): 8.

F1054 "Mrs. Roosevelt Outlines Causes for Which She Will Work." *Democratic Digest* 14 (Feb. 1937): 20.

Quotes from a press conference in which ER indicates that her priorities during FDR's second term will include housing, youth, working conditions for women, and peace.

F1055 "On Bought Time." *Time* 33 (6 Mar. 1939): 11.

Last week ER spoke in New York in support of government pensions for the elderly and programs for youth such as the National Youth Admin. But these programs only buy time, she thinks, for our underlying economic problems to be solved.

F1056 Parrish, Michael E. *Anxious Decades: America in Prosperity and Depression, 1920-1941.* New York: Norton, 1992. xiv + 529p. Index. Bibliographic Essay.
A broad view of ER as social reformer (pp. 398-403).

F1057 Rothchild, Florence. "The Mistress of the White House: A Portrait of America's Brilliant and Energetic First Lady." *Wisconsin Jewish Chronicle* (9 Mar. 1934): 7.
Rothchild provides examples of ER's public and private efforts to improve the daily lives of the less fortunate as evidence of her concern with social reform.

F1058 Salmond, John. *Southern Rebel: The Life and Times of Aubrey Willis Williams, 1909-1965.* The Fred W. Morrison Series in Southern Studies. Chapel Hill: Univ. of N.C. Pr., 1983. xii + 337p. Index. Bibliography. Notes.
Involvement with the National Youth Admin. was the original basis of ER's friendship with Williams. Salmond also addresses ER and Williams' work with the Southern Conference for Human Welfare, the American Youth Congress, the March on Washington, and the Southern Conference Educational Fund. Relies heavily on the papers of Williams, ER, and others (pp. 70-287 passim). For Salmond's use of Williams' papers to describe ER's role in the establishment of the Fair Employment Practices Commission, see his "'Aubrey Williams Remembers': A Note on Franklin D. Roosevelt's Attitude toward Negro Rights." *Alabama Review* 25 (Jan. 1972): 62-77. Notes.

F1059 Stevenson, Adlai E. "Eleanor Roosevelt: A Lady for All Seasons." *Saturday Review* 47 (10 Oct. 1964): 26-27.
She was our social conscience, and if she were here today she would be at the forefront of the effort to provide equality of opportunity to all citizens.

F1060 Swing, Raymond. *Good Evening!: A Professional Memoir.* New York: Harcourt, Brace & World, 1964. 311p.
Newspaperman and radio commentator Swing concludes that ER, as a social reformer rather than a feminist, deserves with Harry Hopkins much of the credit for the social reforms of the New Deal (pp. 232-34).

F1061 Tufty, Esther Van Wagoner. "A Journalist Remembers Eleanor Roosevelt." *Eleanor Roosevelt: An American Journey.* Ed. Jess Flemion and Colleen M. O'Connor. San Diego: San Diego State Univ. Pr., 1987. 153-54.
A newspaperwoman who attended ER's press conferences remembers what ER did for women and blacks. Claims that during the White House years ER became a proponent of the Equal Rights Amendment.

F1062 "A Warm Springs Donkey to Mrs. Roosevelt." *Democratic Digest* 15 (June 1938): 34.
ER was awarded a "Bronze Donkey of Achievement" by the Georgia Woman's Democratic Club. The presentation applauded her success as wife and mother and praised her work for charity as an example to other women.

F1063 Warren, Ruth. *A Pictorial History of Women in America.* New York: Crown, 1975. 228p. Bibliography. Index.
ER's role as humanitarian during the New Deal (pp. 190, 195).

F1064 "Wife Acclaims Roosevelt's Deeds in First Two Years as President." *New York Times* 3 Mar. 1935: 1, 31.

In a press conference she hails accomplishments of the New Deal such as the Tennessee Valley Authority, the Civilian Conservation Corps, and subsistence homesteads. She also expresses hope that more can be done for the nation's youth, that health care can be improved, and a program of old age insurance can be established.

F1065 *Women: Their Changing Roles.* The Great Contemporary Issues. Ed. Elizabeth Janeway. New York: Arno, 1973. x + 556p. Index.

Numerous articles about ER from the period 1925-1961 are included in this collection of articles from the *New York Times.* Most are about her role as a social reformer.

F1066 Woodruff, Caroline S. "Presentation of Life Membership Key to Mrs. Roosevelt." National Education Association of the United States. *Proceedings of the Seventh-sixth Annual Meeting, New York, 26-30 June 1938.* Washington: National Education Association of the United States, 1938. 122.

Presented to ER as humanitarian, advocate of peace, and supporter of the role of women, 30 June 1938. Also reported in the *Journal of the National Education Association of the United States* 27 (Sept. 1938): 167.

F1067 *Words of Wisdom.* Kansas City: Hallmark, n.d. n.pag.

ER had those qualities which all persons have, but few utilize, to make the world a better place for all. A portrait by Donald Edward Dubowski is accompanied by an unidentified quotation.

Human Welfare

F1068 American Federation of Labor-Congress of Industrial Organizations. *Proceedings of the Fourth Constitutional Convention of the AFL-CIO, Miami Beach, Florida, December 7-13, 1961.* Vol. 1. N.p.: American Federation of Labor and Congress of Industrial Organizations, n.d. 140-42.

ER, referred to as "Sister Roosevelt," is presented a gold pin in recognition of her efforts on behalf of organized labor and the 25th anniversary of her membership in the American Newspaper Guild. Text of 8 Dec. remarks.

F1069 "Answers Attack on Reedsville Plan." *New York Times* 4 Oct. 1934: 25.

Reports on her 3 Oct. press conference when she responded to attacks on subsistence homesteads which have appeared in recent publications.

F1070 Barclay, Sarah. "Seeing Is Believing." *Horizons: An Anthology of Prose and Verse* (East High School, Cleveland, Ohio) (1941): 5-6.
ER visits Arthurdale.

F1071 Baruch, Bernard M. *Baruch: The Public Years.* New York: Holt, Rinehart and Winston, 1960. xii + 431p. Index.

In his discussion of Arthurdale there is a tribute to ER's role (pp. 254-55). Baruch came to the defense of the project in a letter which ER made public. For text of letter and her own defense of the Arthurdale project, see "Baruch Defends Reedsville Cost." *New York Times* 29 Jan. 1935: 23.

F1072 Bauman, John F., and Thomas H. Coode. *In the Eye of the Great Depression: New Deal Reporters and the Agony of the American People*. DeKalb: Northern Ill. Univ. Pr., 1988. x + 230p. Index. Sources. Notes.

Limited coverage of the public relationship between ER and Lorena Hickok and Martha Gellhorn in their capacities as reporters on the depression (pp. 23-24, 27-28).

F1073 Beezer, Bruce G. "Arthurdale: An Experiment in Community Education." *West Virginia History* 36 (1974): 17-36. Notes.

ER had a particular interest in Arthurdale's community school. Beezer outlines the role which she played and concludes that her association with the project was a detriment because of the negative publicity which resulted.

F1074 Bolles, Blair. "Resettling America: Dr. Tugwell's Dream Cities of Utopia." *American Mercury* 39 (Nov. 1936): 337-45.

The present subsistence homesteads effort is as futile as the failed Cottage-Holding System of 18th century England. Arthurdale is close to ER's heart, and we can thank her for a program which is producing young people with useless skills and eager for a hand-out.

F1075 Burlingham, Lloyd. "So Mrs. Roosevelt Said to Us." *Mexico Magazine* (Apr. 1938): 10-11.

She has an understanding of human conditions today but objects to labels such as "socialized medicine" or "social revolution" to describe any New Deal programs. Parallel text in Spanish.

F1076 Bye, George T. "Keeping Up with Mrs. Roosevelt." *Connecticut Nutmeg* 1 (9 June 1938): 2.

When Bye accompanied the Roosevelts to Arthurdale ER gave him a tour of the project. ER drove her own car to W.Va., and Bye was astonished by her non-stop activities.

F1077 Carskadon, T.R. "Hull House in the Hills." *New Republic* 79 (1 Aug. 1934): 312-14.

ER is so determined to see the Arthurdale experiment succeed that she has involved herself with many details: the style of houses, the furniture factory, and the schools.

F1078 "Child Labor: Mrs. Roosevelt and Her Son Totally at Odds." *Newsweek* 2 (3 Mar. 1934): 12.

ER and son James disagree over the Child Labor Amendment.

F1079 Clapp, Elsie Ripley. *Community Schools in Action*. New York: Viking, 1939; New York: Arno, 1971. xviii + 429p. Index. Notes.

ER's role in the founding of the Arthurdale School and the development of Arthurdale (pp. 70, 72, 245). In 1934 the local women organized themselves as a club known as "The Eleanor Roosevelt Farm Women's Association" (p. 121).

F1080 ---. *The Use of Resources in Education*. New York: Harper, 1952. 159p., 174p. Index. Notes.

Consists of two separately paged parts. Pt. 2, "Educational Use of Resources in West Virginia, at Arthurdale," contains brief, informative recollections of ER (pp. 5-6, 8, 11, 12, 79, 139, 159).

F1081 Coit, Margaret L. *Mr. Baruch.* Cambridge: Houghton Mifflin, 1957; Westport: Greenwood, 1975. xiv + 784p. Index. Bibliography. Notes.

Coit claims that as much as anyone in the New Deal ER appreciated the value of Baruch's influence. Relying heavily on letters between the two, ER's auto-biographical writings and her own correspondence with ER, Coit develops the relationship between ER and Baruch throughout the New Deal and later. The fullest treatment is given to Baruch's financial support of Arthurdale, a project in which Coit claims that he had little confidence. Limited attention is in James Grant, *Bernard M. Baruch: The Adventures of a Wall Street Legend,* pp. 273-74 (New York: Simon and Schuster, 1983).

F1082 "Confer at Capital on Aid to Women." *New York Times* 13 May 1940: 15.

ER helped organize the 12 May gathering of the "Daughters of the American Depression" made up of representatives of women's groups and women or wives of men on WPA assistance. They discussed the problems with living on public relief and what a proposed cut in wages for women WPA workers would mean. The women shared a five cent meal with ER.

F1083 Conkin, Paul K. *Tomorrow a New World: The New Deal Community Program.* Ithaca: Cornell Univ. Pr. for the American Historical Assoc., 1959; New York: Da Capo, 1976. ix + 350p. Index. Notes.

Conkin establishes ER's influence on the activities of the subsistence homesteads program with emphasis on Arthurdale (pp. 36, 103-5, 108, 114-15, 122, 193, 200, 237-49, 251, 253, 255).

F1084 Coode, Thomas H., and Dennis E. Fabbri. "The New Deal's Arthurdale Project in West Virginia." *West Virginia History* 36 (1975) 291-308. Notes.

Traces the roles played by ER and Louis Howe and documents how their good intentions proved in the end to be detrimental.

F1085 Cowan, Holly. "Arthurdale." Thesis (M.A.). Columbia Univ., 1968. 58p. Bibliography. Notes.

Derivative account about ER and Arthurdale (pp. 19-52).

F1086 Daniels, Roger. *The Bonus March: An Episode of the Great Depression.* Contributions in American History, 14. Westport: Greenwood, 1971. xiii + 370p. Index. Bibliography. Notes.

Corrections to earlier accounts of ER's 1933 visit to the Bonus March camp (pp. 223-25). Exchange between ER and Herbert Hoover's Secretary of War Patrick Hurley about accounts of the 1932 Bonus March (pp. 257-61, 264). Daniels cites a 1 Nov. 1949 *Washington Times-Herald* editorial "Eleanor Set Right" in support of Hurley (p. 344).

F1087 De Hart-Mathews, Jane. *The Federal Theatre, 1935-1939: Plays, Relief, and Politics.* Princeton: Princeton Univ. Pr., 1967; New York: Octagon, 1980. xii + 342p. Index. Bibliography. Notes.

Brief references to ER's support of the Federal Theatre Project with particular attention given to her efforts to ensure artistic freedom (pp. 13, 64-65, 67, 170, 212, 286).

F1088 De Kruif, Paul. "Notes on Life or Death." *Ken* 1 (21 Apr. 1938): 31.
The author recalls a 1936 discussion with ER. When she visited a WPA whooping cough research facility in Grand Rapids, Mich. she questioned the value of saving the lives of young children if economic conditions will not allow them to lead decent lives as adults.

F1089 *Down & Out in the Great Depression: Letters from the "Forgotten Man"*. Ed. Robert S. McElvaine. Chapel Hill: Univ. of N.C. Pr., 1983. xvii + 251p. Index. Notes.
Letters to ER, FDR, and others describe the conditions which confronted many Americans. While some who wrote considered her a mother figure (p. 221) or likened her to a saint (pp. 218-19), many were critical of her (e.g., pp. 147, 177-79).

F1090 "Drive Is Inspired by Mrs. Roosevelt." *New York Times* 10 Feb. 1935: 20.
She has convinced several hundred Hyde Park residents to work together in an attempt to end unemployment. She has also suggested the establishment of a not-for-profit corporation to support local industries, a concept which she hopes will be adopted in other communities.

F1091 "Eden Liquidated." *Business Week* (27 July 1946): 22, 24, 26, 29.
As Arthurdale is being sold off at a lost ER's close involvement with the project and the controversy which ensued are remembered. She is described as the community's "fairy godmother."

F1092 "Eleanor Roosevelt: A First Lady, Unionist, Fighter for Peace." *Labor Today* 29 (Spring/Summer 1990): 14.
A tribute to an active union member who was regarded as a saint by her contemporaries. The present generation seems to have forgotten her, however. Published originally in *Labor Press*.

F1093 *The Fiftieth Anniversary of the Homesteading of Arthurdale, W.Va.* N.p.: n.p., [1984?]. 20p.
The commemmorative program contains "'The First Lady': Eleanor Roosevelt" describing her work with homesteaders as evidence of her social consciousness (pp. 4-7).
Also issued in conjunction with the anniversary celebration were Colleen Anderson, "Eleanor and Arthurdale: A Community Celebrates 50 Years." *Goldenseal* (Fall 1984): 5-8, "Eleanor Roosevelt, She Guided Arthurdale with a Loving Hand." *Panorama* 17 June 1984: 7, and "Eleanor Roosevelt's Secret Visit to Arnettsville." *Panorama* 19 Aug. 1984: 7.
All are available in Subject Files Relating to the Eleanor Roosevelt Centennial Commission, Box 3, New York State Archives.

F1094 "The 'First Lady' Co-operates." *Friends Intelligencer* (26 May 1934): 328-29.
Appreciation from the Quakers for ER's interest in subsistence homesteads and the contributions to the American Friends Service Committee from income from her radio broadcasts.

F1095 "First Lady Sees WPA at Work." *Work* (District of Columbia Works Progress Administration) (1 Sept. 1936): 2.

Recently ER went to the WPA sewing rooms to see the progress which is being made in putting women to work.

F1096 Flanagan, Hallie. *Arena*. New York: Duell, Sloan and Pearce, 1940; New York: Bloom, 1965; New York: Arno, 1980; New York: Limelight, 1985. ix + 475p. Index. Bibliography.
Contains numerous undocumented statements by ER about the Federal Theatre Project in this work by its director.

F1097 Franklin, P.L. "The First Lady of the Land." *National Republic* 24 (Nov. 1936): 4-5.
An examination of the activities of the wives of the 1936 presidential candidates. ER's involvement with subsistence homesteads projects is emphasized.

F1098 Furman, Bess, and Lucile Furman. "Discover Your Home Town: First Lady in Third of Series Limelights Capital Institutions." *Democratic Digest* 17 (Mar. 1940): 18-19, 37.
ER visits health and welfare institutions in Washington and urges that wives of members of Congress do the same.

F1099 ---. "Discover Your Home Town: First Lady Inspects Schools and Play-grounds." *Democratic Digest* 17 (Apr. 1940): 12-13, 37.
Washington schools and playgrounds visited by ER.

F1100 ---. "Discover Your Home Town: First Lady Says in Second of Series to Test Your City's Health." *Democratic Digest* 17 (Feb. 1940): 20-21, 37, 39.
ER makes a health inspection of Washington.

F1101 ---. "Discover Your Home Town: Mrs. Roosevelt Asks about Labor Laws in Capital City." *Democratic Digest* 17 (May 1940): 10, 38.
ER learns of poor working conditions and encourages women who invest in businesses to exercise their influence to improve wages and working conditions.

F1102 ---. "Mrs. Roosevelt and Housing: Discovering Your Home Town." *Democratic Digest* 17 (Jan. 1940): 7, 33.
She began her advocacy for better housing before becoming First Lady.

F1103 Gladwin, Lee A. "Arthurdale: Adventure into Utopia." *West Virginia History* 28 (July 1967): 305-17. Notes.
While ER is not blamed for the failure of Arthurdale, her interest brought ill-conceived federal involvement. A detailed account, based on official sources, critical of the attempt to create a utopia when continued support of the Quakers' efforts would have been more fruitful.

F1104 Haid, Stephen Edward. "Arthurdale: An Experiment in Community Planning, 1933-1947." Diss. W.Va. Univ., 1975. vi + 345p. Bibliography. Notes.
Detailed account of involvement of ER, Louis Howe, Bernard Baruch, and Elsie Clapp with Arthurdale. Relies on manuscript sources, primarily ER's papers (pp. 65-343 passim).

F1105 Hauptman, Laurence M. *The Iroquois and the New Deal*. Syracuse: Syracuse Univ. Pr., 1981. xvi + 256p. Index. Bibliography. Notes.

The assistance which ER provided Namee Henricks was essential for building the WPA-sponsored Tonawanda Indian Community House in western New York. Based in part on letters to ER (pp. 129-30, 132, 134).

F1106 Hickok, Lorena A. *One Third of a Nation: Lorena Hickok Reports on the Great Depression*. Ed. Richard Lowitt and Maurine Beasley. Urbana: Univ. of Ill. Pr., 1981. xxxv + 378p. Index. Notes.

Reports and letters from Hickok to Harry Hopkins when she traveled as chief investigator for Hopkins in his capacity as head of the Federal Emergency Relief Admin. Included are 13 letters to ER from the period 31 Oct. 1933-21 Nov. 1934 which describe Hickok's travels, conditions in the country, and ER's concerns about those conditions. The introduction includes a discussion of the Hickok-ER relationship (pp. xxx-xxxv).

F1107 "Homesteader's Wife." *Liberty* 14 (2 Jan. 1937): 12-13.

In these selections from the diary of an Arthurdale resident are 4 Dec. 1935, ER visits; 6 Apr. 1936, ER attends a dance and she dances with her; and 21 May 1936, her husband goes to the White House at the invitation of ER.

F1108 "Homesteading, 1934." *Architectural Forum* 61 (Dec. 1934): 400-407.

With her emphasis on the Arthurdale project, ER is the real force behind the subsistence homesteads program.

F1109 Ickes, Harold L. *The Secret Diary of Harold L. Ickes*. 3 vols. New York: Simon and Schuster, 1953-1954; New York: Da Capo, 1974. Index.

The opinions of FDR's Secretary of the Interior about ER ranged from praise to disdain (v. 2, p. 64). The most extensive attention is given to his dealings with ER and Harry Hopkins in the affairs of the Subsistence Homesteads Corp. (v. 1).

F1110 "Is Reedsville Communistic? Mrs. Roosevelt Says 'No.'" *Literary Digest* 117 (21 Apr. 1934): 45.

William A. Wirt considers Arthurdale to be communistic because families will move to fine houses and no longer pay rent. ER rebutted by pointing out that the families were on relief and not paying much if any rent. To her it is not communistic to help people get on their feet, and she thinks that what the government is doing could serve as an example for the private sector. A related article about her rebuttal, which also includes photographs of her at Reedsville building sites, is "A Mistake at Reedsville." *Architectural Forum* 60 (May 1934): 398. "Wirt Challenged by Mrs. Roosevelt." *New York Times* 12 Apr. 1934: 8 reports on her 11 Apr. press conference when she refuted charges by Wirt that the homestead projects are "communistic." For additional information on her response to Wirt, see *Congressional Record* (23 Apr. 1934): 7185-86.

F1111 Kornbluh, Joyce L. *A New Deal for Workers' Education: The Workers' Service Program, 1933-1942*. Urbana: Univ. of Ill. Pr., 1987. xii + 175p. Index. Bibliography. Notes.

ER's belief that workers' education was the key to solving economic and political problems made her a willing ally to Hilda Smith's efforts under the Federal Emergency Relief Admin. and the Works Progress Admin. (pp. 13-127 passim).

Based on her dissertation "A New Deal for Workers' Education: The Workers' Service Program under the Federal Emergency Relief Administration and the Works Progress Administration, 1933-1942" (Univ. of Mich., 1983).

F1112 Laning, Edward. "The New Deal Mural Projects." *The New Deal Art Projects: An Anthology of Memoirs.* Ed. Francis V. O'Connor. Washington: Smithsonian Institution Pr., 1972. 79-113. Notes.

Laning disputes the idea that government sponsorship resulted from the Roosevelts' interest in the arts. It was because of their humanitarinism (p. 90).

F1113 "The Letter of an Unknown Woman to Mrs. Herbert Hoover and Mrs. Franklin D. Roosevelt." *Women Are Here to Stay: The Durable Sex in Its Infinite Variety through Half a Century of American Life.* By Agnes Rogers. New York: Harper, 1949. 167.

A victim of the depression who still manages to help those less fortunate asks ER and Lou Hoover if as women they have answers to the problems which all women are facing. Reissued from *McCall's*, Oct. 1932.

F1114 Lisio, Donald J. *The President and Protest: Hoover, Conspiracy, and the Bonus Riot.* Columbia: Univ. of Mo. Pr., 1974. viii + 346p. Index. Bibliographical Essay. Notes.

Herbert Hoover's reaction to ER's allegation in *This I Remember* that he had ordered troops to fire on the Bonus Marchers. Hoover encouraged the publication of a rebuttal, Patrick J. Hurley, "The Facts about the Bonus March." *McCall's* 77 (Nov. 1949): 2, 142-43. ER issued an apology in the same issue (pp. 301-3). For Hurley's rebuttal, see also Don Lohbeck, *Patrick J. Hurley*, pp. 487-88 (Chicago: Regnery, 1956).

F1115 Mangione, Jerre. *The Dream and the Deal: The Federal Writers' Project, 1935-1943.* Boston: Little, Brown, 1972. xvi + 416p. Index. Bibliography. Notes.

Mangione, a Federal Writers' Project staff member, remembers a 1939 White House dinner when he tried to promote continued federal funding for the project (pp. 8-13).

F1116 Mason, Lucy Randolph. *To Win These Rights: A Personal Story of the CIO in the South.* New York: Harper, 1952; Westport: Greenwood, 1970. xvi + 206p. Index.

Mason recalls meeting ER in Birmingham, Ala. at the 1938 Southern Conference for Human Welfare and at other times when ER was involved in southern labor problems (pp. 57-59).

F1117 Mathews, Thomas. *Puerto Rican Politics and the New Deal.* Gainesville: Univ. of Fla. Pr., 1960. xii + 345p. Index. Bibliography. Notes.

ER developed an interest in Puerto Rico's economic and social problems, and Ruby Black was a witness to ER's discussions about those problems (pp. 104-5). Black accompanied ER to Puerto Rico in 1934 (pp. 154-58), and the account of the trip includes a discussion of the "Round Table Conference on Possible Permanent Plans Relating to Relief and Civil Works Administration" held 10 Mar. 1934. Sources include Black's writings in the newspaper *La Democracia*. Based on Mathews' dissertation (Columbia Univ., 1957).

F1118 McDonald, William F. *Federal Relief Administration and the Arts*. Columbus: Ohio State Univ. Pr., 1969. xiv + 869p. Index. Notes.

ER's participation in the 1933 Conference on Emergency Needs of Women signified the role which she was to play in relief efforts (pp. 44-46). Ellen Woodward and ER (pp. 167-78, 210). Hallie Flanagan and ER (p. 50l). ER and the Federal Art Project (pp. 360-63).

F1119 McGarvey, G.A. "Home-Made and Hand-Made: Fireside Occupations in a Machine Age." *School Life* 19 (Feb. 1934): 120-21, 131.

ER provided funding for N.Y. to survey craft work in the state.

F1120 McKinzie, Richard D. *The New Deal for Artists*. Princeton,: Princeton Univ. Pr., 1973. xii + 203p. Index. Note on Sources. Notes.

Includes numerous references to ER's role in the New Deal's support of the arts.

F1121 Meursinge-Warnsinck, Catherina. "De 'Homestead and Hope' Beweging in Amerika." *Het Landhuis* (23 Oct. 1935): 693-95.

ER's trip into a coal mine and her involvement with Arthurdale. In Dutch.

F1122 Myhra, David. "Rexford Guy Tugwell: Initiator of America's Greenbelt New Towns, 1935 to 1936." *Journal of the American Institute of Planners* 40 (May 1974): 176-88. Bibliography. Notes.

Myhra derives from Lash's *Eleanor and Franklin* to illustrate ER's support of resettlement projects in the face of public and congressional opposition (p. 185).

F1123 Palmer, Charles F. *Adventures of a Slum Fighter*. Atlanta: Tupper and Love, 1955. 272p. Index.

Palmer provides an account of ER's 1937 visit to an Atlanta housing project (pp. 212-15). The chapter "White House--Via Mrs. Roosevelt" is a description of how ER acted as an intermediary between FDR and Palmer who was seeking federal funding for housing projects (pp. 212-27).

F1124 Patterson, James T. "Mary Dewson and the American Minimum Wage Movement." *Labor History* 5 (Spring 1964): 134-52. Notes.

There is limited attention to ER's association with Dewson; however, the author cites his Mar. 1961 interview with ER in which she credits Dewson's impact on the minimum wage concept in N.Y. and at the national level (pp. 149-50).

F1125 Penkower, Monty Noam. *Federal Writers' Project: A Study in Government Patronage of the Arts*. Urbana: Univ. of Ill. Pr., 1977. ix + 266p. Index. Bibliography. Notes.

Coverage of ER's involvement with the Federal Writers' Project (pp. 37, 48, 166, 208).

F1126 Pickett, Clarence E. *For More Than Bread: An Autobiographical Account of Twenty-two Years' Work with the American Friends Service Committee*. Boston: Little, Brown, 1953. 433p. Index.

ER's introduction to the coal mining region of W.Va. and her involvement in federal assistance to the area as remembered by the Executive Secretary of the American Friends Service Committee (pp. 45-60).

F1127 Pope, Linda Karen Gunter. "Return to Eden: Three Models of Community Planning in the Early Twentieth Century." Thesis (M.A.) Tex. A & M Univ., 1978. ix + 123p. Bibliography. Notes.

Derivative account of ER, Frank Lloyd Wright, and Charlotte Perkins Gilman as community planners. ER and Arthurdale (pp. 41-80, 110-15).

F1128 "Praises Mrs. Roosevelt." *New York Times* 13 May 1934: 25.

Because of her personification of motherhood and her efforts on behalf of subsistence homesteads Frenchman Marcel Olivier promotes the nomination of ER for the Nobel Peace Prize.

F1129 Rice, Millard Milburn. "Footnote on Arthurdale." *Harper's* 180 (Mar. 1940): 411-19.

Arthurdale today and what was learned from the experiment. Attention to ER's initial role is of a factual nature (p. 413).

F1130 Richardson, G. Dexter. "Eleanor Roosevelt Investigates." *Republicanism: Authentic Review of Suppressed History.* By G. Dexter Richardson. N.p.: n.p., 1955. n.pag.

It is time to praise ER for her efforts in helping mining families in W.Va. whose plight had been ignored by successive Republican administrations.

F1131 Robey, Ralph. "What Mrs. Roosevelt 'Knows,' or Does She?" *Newsweek* 26 (1 Oct. 1945): 71.

He dissects, almost line by line, a "My Day" column on current economic conditions, labor, wages, and income. In the end, he claims, ER is simply asking that workers be given "more pay for less work."

F1132 Robinson, Felix G. "The Arthurdale Story." *Tableland Trails* 1 (Summer 1954): 98-105.

Successes and failures at Arthurdale. ER's interest and involvement were a result of unselfish interest in the plight of the local citizens, and they in turn developed a great admiration for her (pp. 99-100).

F1133 Schlesinger, Arthur M., Jr. *The Coming of the New Deal.* The Age of Roosevelt, [Vol. 2]. Boston: Houghton Mifflin, 1959. xii + 669p. Index. Notes.

ER and Arthurdale (pp. 364-66). Reissued in 1988 with a new foreword (Boston: Houghton Mifflin).

F1134 Schneiderman, Rose. "1700 Strong." *Life and Labor Bulletin* 2nd ser., 21 (Apr. 1941): 1-2.

When she addressed strikers in Mar. 1941 ER credited the Women's Trade Union League for educating her about the labor movement (p. 1).

F1135 Schwarz, Jordan A. *The Speculator: Bernard M. Baruch in Washington, 1917-1965.* Chapel Hill: Univ. of N.C. Pr., 1981. xvii + 679p. Index. Bibliography. Notes.

During their long association ER and Baruch used one another, and it was primarily through Arthurdale that this happened. She needed his clout and support of the project, and he needed a vehicle to get closer to FDR and the center of power. Contains the most informative account to date of their relationship (pp. 308-12, 569).

F1136 Stout, Wesley. "The New Homesteaders." *Saturday Evening Post* 207 (Aug. 4, 1934): 5-7, 61-62, 64-65.

An examination of the Arthurdale project. ER is featured significantly in a chronology of events between 29 Sept. 1933 and 8 June 1934 (pp. 64-65).

F1137 "Surveyors Are Swarming over a West Virginia Farm Which the Government Has Selected as a \$250,000 Homestead Laboratory." *Architectural Forum* 59 (Nov. 1933): 430-31.

In this early account of the Arthurdale project ER's interest in subsistence homesteads is recognized. Reports on her recent visit to the area and predicts that her interest will not be limited to this one project. Another account of her visit is "Mrs. Roosevelt Sees Graves of 200 Slaves." *New York Times* 23 Nov. 1933: 7.

F1138 "Veterans: Most of Bonus Men Join Reforestation Army." *Newsweek* 1 (27 May 1933): 12-13.

An account of ER's visit to the camp of the Bonus Army containing quotations from her remarks in which she recalls her work as a volunteer during World War I. A similar account is "Bonus Camp Visited by Mrs. Roosevelt." *New York Times* 17 May 1933: 10.

F1139 "Vetoing Mrs. Roosevelt's Pet Project." *Christian Century* 51 (14 Mar. 1934): 348.

Arthurdale was dealt a blow with Congress' refusal to approve a factory which would have made postal equipment. For a discussion of her efforts to locate the plant, see *Congressional Record* (28 Feb. 1934): 3417.

F1140 White, Graham, and John Maze. *Harold Ickes of the New Deal: His Private Life and Public Career.* Cambridge: Harvard Univ. Pr., 1985. vi + 263p. Index. Notes.

Based on Ickes' published autobiography and diary as well as his unpublished memoirs and papers, there is an analysis of his relationship with ER relevant to the activities of the Subsistence Homesteads Corp. (pp. 129-34). There is also T.H. Watkins, *Righteous Pilgrim: The Life and Times of Harold L. Ickes, 1874-1952*, pp. 387-88 (New York: Holt, 1990).

F1141 *The White House Conference on Rural Education, October 3, 4, and 5, 1944.* Washington: National Education Assoc. of the United States, n.d. 272p. Index.

Without ER's interest and involvement the conference would never have been held (pp. 26-28).

F1142 Whitman, John Pratt. "Reedsville: One Year Later." *Today* 3 (24 Nov. 1934): 10-11, 24.

The president of the homesteaders recognizes ER's interest in the project.

F1143 Zinsser, Caroline. "The Best Day Care There Ever Was." *Working Mother* (Oct. 1984): 76-80.

In 1943 Edgar Kaiser wanted to offer day care to women working in his Portland, Ore. shipyards and sought the help of ER. The "Kaiser Centers" would not have been possible without her.

Race Relations

F1144 "'Aid to the South Is Aid to the Nation' Mrs. Roosevelt Tells the North." *Southern Patriot* 3 (Mar. 1945): 8.
The Southern Conference for Human Welfare honored her on 6 Mar. 1945. About her remarks, but no excerpts are included.

F1145 Alexander, Will W. "The Negro and the Nation." *Survey Graphic* 36 (Jan. 1947): 92-96.
ER's gracious 1935 reception of a black sharecropper is used as an example of the status of blacks. The portion about ER was reissued as "Sharecroppers and the White House Door" in *Eyewitness: The Negro in America*, pp. 438-39 (New York: Putnam's, 1967).

F1146 Anderson, Jervis. *A. Philip Randolph: A Biographical Portrait*. New York: Harcourt Brace Jovanovich, 1973. xiv + 398p. Index. Notes.
In an account which is primarily a derivation from Lash's *Eleanor and Franklin* ER is credited with FDR's support of equal wartime employment for blacks (pp. 242-44, 251-52, 255, 260).

F1147 Anthony, Carl S. "Skirting the Issue: First Ladies and African Americans." *American Visions* 7 (Oct./Nov. 1992): 28-32.
The attitudes of first ladies about racial equality and what some of them did to improve race relations. ER did more than any other by raising "public conscientiousness" through "symbolic acts."

F1148 Badger, Anthony J. *The New Deal: The Depression Years, 1933-40*. London: Macmillan, 1989. x + 392p. Index. Bibliographical Essay.
ER had to learn that blacks had a special need for government assistance (pp. 208, 254, 305).

F1149 Berman, William C. *The Politics of Civil Rights in the Truman Administration*. Columbus: Ohio State Univ. Pr., 1970. xi + 261p. Index. Bibliography. Notes.
After a 1946 racial incident in Columbia, Tenn., ER and others formed what became the National Emergency Committee Against Mob Violence (pp. 45-46). Based on his dissertation (Ohio State Univ., 1963).

F1150 Bethune, Mary McLeod. "My Secret Talks with FDR." *Ebony* 4 (Apr. 1949): 42-51.
Talks with FDR convinced her of his sincerity about race relations. Bethune establishes the breadth of her friendship with ER and concludes by stating that ER is the one woman who has done most to improve race relations. Reissued in *The Negro in Depression and War: Prelude to Revolution, 1930-1945*, pp. 54-65 (Chicago: Quadrangle, 1969).

F1151 Bickerstaff, Joyce, and Wilbur C. Rich. "Mrs. Roosevelt and Mrs. Bethune: Collaborators for Racial Justice." *Social Education* 48 (Nov./Dec. 1984): 532-34. Notes.
Their friendship was genuine and mutually advantageous. Comparison of their backgrounds and a discussion of the assistance which each provided the other in working toward their common goal of improved social justice for blacks.

F1152 Black, Allida M. "Championing a Champion: Eleanor Roosevelt and the Marian Anderson 'Freedom Concert.'" *Presidential Studies Quarterly* 20 (Fall 1990): 719-36. Notes.

ER's decision to resign from the Daughters of the American Revolution after they refused to allow Anderson to perform at Constitution Hall was neither easy nor immediate. As First Lady ER had already promoted racial equality through her speaking and writing as well as through actions such as opening the White House to blacks. Since the Anderson episode provided her with an opportunity to influence the thinking of the American people, she aimed her objections at the DAR, not at local laws or practices in Washington. She kept the issue before the American people through "My Day" and her subsequent presentation of the Spingarn Medal to Anderson. As a result of her actions ER gained the trust of black leaders and increased her own political power.

F1153 ---. "A Reluctant but Persistent Warrior: Eleanor Roosevelt and the Early Civil Rights Movement." *Women in the Civil Rights Movement: Trailblazers and Torchbearers, 1941-1965.* Ed. Vicki L. Crawford, et al. Brooklyn: Carlson, 1990. 233-49. Notes.

In her time ER spoke out more about racial discrimination than other white Americans. Her resignation from the Daughters of the American Revolution for their refusal to allow Marian Anderson to sing at Constitution Hall and her efforts to prevent the execution of black sharecropper Odell Waller are used to illustrate her efforts during the White House years and the limitations under which she was forced to proceed.

F1154 *The Black Women Oral History Project: From the Arthur and Elizabeth Schlesinger Library on the History of Women in America, Radcliffe College.* 10 vols. Ed. Ruth Edmonds Hill. Westport: Meckler, 1991.

These transcripts of interviews include references to ER. Their significance varies. Margaret Walker Alexander, author and college professor, 1977 (v. 2, p. 57); Etta Moten Barnett, singer and actress, 1985 (v. 2, pp. 176-77); and Dorothy Boulding Ferebee, physician and Howard Univ. professor, 1979 (v. 3, p. 471). The interview with Dorothy L. Height, black youth leader and community and national black leader, 1974-76 includes references to ER and the youth movement of the 1930s (v. 5, pp. 63-65), her comparison of ER and Mary McLeod Bethune and the relationship which the two had (v. 5, pp. 66-68, 73-74), and Height's association with ER (v. 5, pp. 111-12, 223, 277-78). There is also Maida Springer Kemp, labor unionist, 1971 (v. 7, pp. 60, 70, 83) and Constance Allen Thomas, Seattle black leader, 1977 (v. 9, pp. 386-87).

F1155 Blum, John Morton. *V Was for Victory: Politics and American Culture during World War II.* New York: Harcourt Brace Jovanovich, 1976. xii + 372p. Index.

The role which ER played to promote better race relations and the adverse public reaction to that role (pp. 182-99).

F1156 Brown, Claude. *Manchild in the Promised Land.* New York: Macmillan, 1965. 415p.

Dedicated "to the late Eleanor Roosevelt, who founded the Wiltwyck School for Boys." In this autobiographical work Brown describes a visit to Hyde Park for one of ER's (that "crazy old white lady") hot dog meals for Wiltwyck boys.

F1157 Brown, Earl. "American Negroes and the War." *Harper's* 184 (Apr. 1942): 545-52.

In this black journalist's assessment of the apathy which other blacks have about the war there are references to ER's position on the March on Washington and her public statements about how she can understand why blacks feel apathetic toward the war. Cites her address of 8 Jan., Rector's Aid Society of St. Thomas' Episcopal Church, Washington (pp. 546-49).

F1158 Bunche, Ralph J. *The Political Status of the Negro in the Age of FDR*. Ed. and with an introduction by Dewey W. Grantham. Chicago: Univ. of Chicago Pr., 1973. xxxiii + 682p. Index. Bibliography.

ER did not hesitate to be photographed with blacks, and such occurrences added to the fear which many had about the role of black citizens (pp. 33, 97, 390). Prepared as a report during the New Deal years. For a discussion of Bunche's meetings with ER and the preparation of the report, see Brian Urquhart, *Ralph Bunche: An American Life*, pp. 96-97 (New York: Norton, 1993).

F1159 Burnham, Louis. "We Are Tired of Waiting, Mrs. Roosevelt." *Student Advocate* 1 (Mar. 1936): 16-17, 29.

At a meeting of the American Youth Congress National Council in Jan. 1935 ER responded to a question about how to "fight against Negro discrimination." She told them that the most important weapon was education and that "the rest will follow." Above all have patience, she said. A year later at the National Negro Congress the youth sent a message to ER that patience was not enough. It is time for militancy (p. 16).

F1160 Calvin, Floyd G. "The First Lady of Our Land." Editorial. *Sunday School Messenger* (July 1939): 3.

A black columnist praises ER for having the courage to criticize racial policy and to support the needs of the less fortunate of all races.

F1161 Cannon, Poppy. *A Gentle Knight: My Husband, Walter White*. New York: Rinehart, 1956. 309p. Index.

The long association between White and ER is referred to in several brief passages (pp. 9, 161-62, 230-31, 289, 296). She claims that it was ER who convinced a majority of the other directors of the NAACP not to remove White as Executive Secretary after his marriage to Cannon (p. 178).

F1162 Carter, Elmer F. "The Ladies of the D.A.R." Editorial. *Opportunity* 17 (Mar. 1939): 67.

"A true daughter of the American Revolution," ER has resigned from the Daughters of the American Revolution in protest over the DAR's decision to bar Marian Anderson from performing at Constitution Hall.

F1163 "Celebrities Pick Favorite Heroes." *Ebony* 8 (Feb. 1953): 90-91.

Lena Horne, Mary McLeod Bethune, Arthur Lee Simpkins, Ralph Metcalfe, and Frank Yerby honor ER with brief tributes.

F1164 Current, Gloster B. "Mrs. Eleanor Roosevelt and the NAACP." *Crisis* 70 (Apr. 1963): 197-203.

ER was on the Board of Directors of the NAACP from 1948 until her death, and many of the actions which endeared her to the NAACP and its causes are described: she was one of the first prominent citizens to speak out for equal rights for all, her resignation from the Daughters of the American Revolution, her speech when presenting the Spingarn Medal to Marian Anderson in 1939, her work to ban discrimination in World War II defense plants, and her efforts to educate the American people about the effect which racial inequality can have on the country's foreign relations. Excerpts her 2 July 1939 Spingarn Medal address, 1 Dec. 1953 address to Amityville, L.I. branch of the NAACP, and 3 June 1958 address to Spring Valley, N.Y. branch.

F1165 Dalfiume, Richard M. *Desegregation of the U.S. Armed Forces: Fighting on Two Fronts, 1939-1953*. Columbia: Univ. of Mo. Pr., 1969. viii + 252p. Index. Bibliography. Notes.

Communications between ER and Henry Stimson and John McCloy taken from the papers of the Secretary and Assistant Secretary of War demonstrate her involvement during World War II with efforts to integrate the armed services (pp. 48, 76, 87, 93). Based on his dissertation "Desegregation of the United States Armed Forces, 1939-1953" (Univ. of Mo., 1966).

F1166 Davis, Lenwood G. *A Paul Robeson Research Guide: A Selected, Annotated Bibliography*. Westport: Greenwood, 1982. xxv + 879p. Index.

Newspaper accounts of NBC's cancellation of ER's 19 Mar. 1950 television program on which Robeson was to have been a participant in the discussion "The Negro's Position in Politics Today" (entries 1105-6, 1485-98). Robeson's Constitution Hall concert for which ER and Cornelia Pinchot withdrew their support (entries 758, 1241). Account of 17 Sept. 1949 editorial, "Mrs. FDR Acts Like the President" in the *Afro-American* about ER's comments on Peekskill, N.Y. riots (entry 1161). The cancellation of Robeson's appearance on *Today with Mrs. Roosevelt* as reported in "My Day" columns is in Martin Bauml Duberman, *Paul Robeson*, pp. 384-85 (New York: Knopf, 1988).

F1167 Debnam, W.E. *Weep No More, My Lady*. Raleigh: Debnam, 1950. 68p.

On 8 and 9 May 1950 there were broadcasts over the Smith-Douglas radio network rebutting ER's comments in "My Day" about the South. This publication expands on those broadcasts. Several eds. issued in 1950 with slight variations in pagination. Also issued in 1955.

F1168 Eagles, Charles W. *Jonathan Daniels and Race Relations: The Evolution of a Southern Liberal*. Knoxville: Univ. of Tenn. Pr., 1982. xviii + 254p. Index. Bibliography. Notes.

In spite of the attempts of FDR's aides to undercut her efforts to improve race relations (pp. 87-88) ER continued to pursue that agenda and in the process support for New Deal programs among southerners suffered (pp. 52, 95). Her efforts to find a position for Mary McLeod Bethune after the National Youth Admin. was dissolved (p. 112).

F1169 "Eleanor Roosevelt Resigns from the DAR: A Study in Conscience." *Social Education* 48 (Nov./Dec. 1984): 536-41.

Background of the Daughters of the American Revolution's 1939 decision to deny Marian Anderson use of Constitution Hall. Reaction to ER's resignation was mixed, but it is claimed that the political repercussions included shattering John Nance Garner's hopes for the 1940 nomination and sealing white liberal and black support behind FDR. Includes classroom exercises about the incident.

F1170 "Eleanor Roosevelt's Warm Springs Myth." Letter. *American Mercury* 86 (Feb. 1958): 87-88.
   Members of a Dalton, Ga. law firm dispute ER's claim in her Nov. 1957 "If You Ask Me" column that FDR was required by Ga. law to have a clause in his Warm Springs deed forbidding resale to blacks. Her all black White House domestic staff is seen as further evidence of her own prejudice. The same charge is repeated by Rep. E.L. Forrester in his attack on ER's column on Southern juries, "Southern Juries Will Ignore Negro Rights." *Congressional Record* (8 Aug. 1957): 14148. Forrester continued to attack ER, e.g., see "Representative Walter Is Prejudiced." *Congressional Record* (29 Apr. 1958): 7667-68.

F1171 *Facts on Film*. Reel 9. Nashville: Southern Education Reporting Service, 1958.
   A group of newspaper clippings, including some "My Day" columns, which address her position on race relations and school integration with particular reference to the 1957 integration crisis in Little Rock, Ark. (items I9:2543-46). Also includes two 1957 columns by Westbrook Pegler in which he questions her reasoning and revels in the dislike which he claims others now have for her (item I9:2546).

F1172 "First Lady." *Opportunity* 14 (Jan. 1936): [5].
   ER is the "first lady" among those fighting to better the lives of blacks.

F1173 Fishel, Leslie H. "The Negro in Depression and War." *Wisconsin Magazine of History* 48 (Winter 1964): 111-26. Notes.
   In the area of race relations ER was the conscience for FDR and the New Deal. She spoke and acted and was criticized for doing so. Reissued in *The Negro in Depression and War: Prelude to Revolution, 1930-1945*, pp. 7-28 (Chicago: Quadrangle, 1969) and as "The Negro in the New Deal Era" in *Twentieth-Century America: Recent Interpretations*, pp. 288-301 (New York: Harcourt, Brace & World, 1969) and in an abbreviated form in *The Negro American: A Documentary History*, pp. 446-53 (Glenview: Scott, Foresman, 1967) and *The Black American: A Documentary History*, pp. 446-53 (New York: Morrow, 1970).

F1174 Foreman, Clark. "The Decade of Hope." *Phylon* 12 (June 1951): 137-50. Notes.
   ER's role in establishing the Southern Conference for Human Welfare. Presented from the perspective of a review of the progress toward racial equality in the period 1938-1948. Reissued in *The Negro in Depression and War: Prelude to Revolution, 1930-1945*, pp. 150-65 (Chicago: Quadrangle, 1969).

F1175 Garson, Robert A. *The Democratic Party and the Politics of Sectionalism, 1941-1948*. Baton Rouge: La. State Univ. Pr., 1974. xiii + 353p. Index. Bibliography. Notes.
   Eleanor Clubs and other attacks on ER for her views on racial equality as reported by *Alabama* (10 Mar. 1944) and the Glenville, Ga. *Sentinel* (pp. 83-84).

F1176 Gibbs, Margaret. *The DAR*. New York: Holt, Rinehart and Winston, 1969. 244p. Index.

The reaction of the Daughters of the American Revolution to ER's resignation (162-63, 165-66). There is also Peggy Anderson, *The Daughters: An Unconventional Look at America's Fan Club--The DAR*, pp. 133, 141, 143-44, 146-48 (New York: St. Martin's, 1974).

F1177 Gilliam, Dorothy. "A Powerful Friendship." *Washington Post* 19 Nov. 1984, sect. B: 3.
ER and Mary McLeod Bethune were collaborators. ER worked to eliminate racism, and Bethune knew that the efforts of a powerful person like ER were required. Bethune repaid the Roosevelts by representing them with other blacks. Gilliam thinks that ER's efforts in the 1930s were truly significant when not judged against today's standards. Based on address by Bettye Collier-Thomas to the American Political Science Assoc.

F1178 Golden, Harry. *The Right Time: An Autobiography.* New York: Putnam's, 1969. 450p. Index.
Golden recalls a young ER volunteering at the Unity Settlement House in New York, the two days which they spent as lecturers at the integrated Highlander Folk School in 1957, and at a civil rights seminar convened by JFK. To Golden, being in her presence was to sense greatness (pp. 313-17).

F1179 "Grand Lady: Mrs. Roosevelt Has Birthday." *Negro History Bulletin* 19 (Dec. 1955): 60-61.
She has been a source of hope for many. May she enjoy many more birthdays.

F1180 Green, Thomas Lee. "Black Cabinet Members in the Franklin Delano Roosevelt Administration." Diss. Univ. of Colo., 1981. v + 270p. Bibliography. Notes.
The extent of ER's involvement in many aspects of the Roosevelt administration enhanced her ability to serve as an advocate for racial equality. Her efforts were often blocked by key aides to FDR and rarely promoted by Roosevelt himself because of his reluctance to antagonize powerful southern Democrats in Congress (pp. 225-32).

F1181 Greenbaum, Fred. "The Anti-Lynching Bill of 1935: The Irony of 'Equal Justice-Under Law.'" *Journal of Human Relations* 15 (1967): 72-85. Notes.
Comprehensive account of the unsuccessful Costigan-Wagner Bill. Cites ER's letters to Walter White regarding FDR's belief that the bill was of limited value.

F1182 Hine, Darlene Clark. "Mabel K. Staupers and the Integration of Black Nurses into the Armed Forces." *Black Leaders of the Twentieth Century.* Blacks in the World. Ed. John Hope Franklin and August Meier. Urbana: Univ. of Ill. Pr., 1982. 241-57. Note on Sources.
Staupers sought ER's assistance in working for acceptance of black nurses in the World War II military (pp. 252-53).

F1183 Kearney, James R. "Mrs. Eleanor Roosevelt and the American Negro." Thesis (M.A.), Washington Univ., 1962. 120p. Bibliography. Notes.
Her efforts on behalf of racial equality as First Lady and later. Portions related to her years as First Lady form the basis of the chapter "Friend to a Neglected Promise" in his *Anna Eleanor Roosevelt: The Evolution of a Reformer.*

F1184 Kifer, Allen Francis.   "The Negro under the New Deal, 1933-1941." Diss. Univ. of Wisc., 1961. 289p. Bibliography. Notes.

Establishes, but does not develop fully, ER's role as a link between FDR and blacks (pp. 273-74).

F1185 Kirby, John B. *Black Americans in the Roosevelt Era: Liberalism and Race.* Twentieth Century America Series. Knoxville: Univ. of Tenn. Pr., 1980. xvii + 254p. Index. Bibliography. Notes.

Central to his belief that the relationship between race reform and New Deal programs was the dominant theme during the Roosevelt era is the attention given to ER.   In the chapter "Eleanor Roosevelt and the Evolution of Race Liberalism" he traces her association with white liberals and black leaders and concludes that more than anyone else she represented the promise of the New Deal to minorities (pp. 76-96).   Relies heavily on ER's speeches and published writings.   Based on his dissertation "The New Deal Era and Blacks: A Study of Black and White Race Thought, 1933-1945" (Univ. of Ill., 1971).   For a discussion of ER's role, see the chapter based on his dissertation "The Roosevelt Administration and Blacks: An Ambivalent Legacy" in *Twentieth-Century America: Recent Interpretations*, 2nd ed., pp. 265-88 (New York: Harcourt Brace Jovanovich, 1972).

F1186 Krueger, Thomas A. *And Promises to Keep: The Southern Conference for Human Welfare, 1938-1948.* Nashville: Vanderbilt Univ. Pr., 1967. xi + 218p. Index. Bibliographical Essay. Notes.

From 1938 until 1945 ER was active in this organization which had as its mission the promotion of the New Deal in the South.   Although there is no lengthy treatment of her, there are numerous references to the role which she played with quotations from her speeches.   Based on his dissertation "The Southern Conference for Human Welfare" (Univ. of Minn., 1965).

F1187 "A Letter from the D.A.R." *McCall's* 81 (Nov. 1953): 8.

The fact that Marian Anderson has sung at Constitution Hall twice is used to dispute ER's charge in her Sept. 1953 "If You Ask Me" column that the DAR is not forward thinking.

F1188 Maney, Patrick J. *The Roosevelt Presence: A Biography of Franklin Delano Roosevelt.* Twayne's Twentieth Century American Biography Series. New York: Twayne, 1992. xv + 255p. Index. Bibliographic Essay. Notes.

An overview of ER's efforts as First Lady to further civil rights (pp. 62, 82-83, 159-60).

F1189 Martin, Louis.   "The Negro in the Political Picture." *Opportunity* 21 (July 1943): 104-7, 137-39.

More than New Deal programs, it has been ER's actions on behalf of blacks which have upset southerners (p. 104).

F1190 McGuire, Phillip. *Taps for a Jim Crow Army: Letters from Black Soldiers in World War II.* Santa Barbara: ABC-Clio, 1983. li + 278p. Index. Notes.

A sympathetic account of ER's involvement with the March on Washington movement (pp. 125-29).   A 1943 letter to ER from a black soldier asking for help in securing duties commensurate with his qualifications (p. 133).

F1191 Melton, Harve L. *Hate-Roosevelt: An Emotional Orgy, a Wartime Nightmare.* Oklahoma City: n.p., [1944?]. 53p.

Intense hatred was directed at ER after 1940 because of her association with blacks and Jews (pp. 10-14, 25-27, 41).

F1192 Morrison, Allan. "The Secret Papers of FDR." *Negro Digest* 9 (Jan. 1951): 3-13.

While Morrison questions the extent to which FDR helped blacks, he did allow ER the freedom to speak and act. In conversations with the author ER defends FDR's actions and the political reasons why he had to be cautious. Reissued in *The Negro in Depression and War: Prelude to Revolution, 1930-1945*, pp. 66-77 (Chicago: Quadrangle, 1969).

F1193 "Mrs. F.D.R. Lauds 'Untouchables.'" *Southern Patriot* 10 (Dec. 1952): 1.

In "My Day" for 17 Oct. 1952 she discussed the Southern Conference Educational Fund pamphlet *The Untouchables* and asked her white readers to imagine what their reactions would be if they were to experience the type of prejudice described in the pamphlet.

F1194 "Mrs. Roosevelt Assists SCEF." *Southern Patriot* 16 (Apr. 1958): 1, 4.

ER hosted a reception honoring Aubrey Williams with proceeds going to the Southern Conference Educational Fund. She told her guests that the efforts of blacks and progressive whites in the South should be praised.

F1195 "Mrs. Roosevelt Quits D.A.R., Protesting Anderson Ban." *Washington Post* 28 Feb. 1939: 1, 6.

ER's resignation followed the DAR's refusal to allow Marian Anderson to sing at Constitution Hall.

F1196 "Mrs. Roosevelt's Letter Called Bid for Southern Vote." *Afro-American* [Baltimore, Md.] 16 Sept. 1944: 4.

After a letter from ER to a white southern woman was made public black leaders reacted with disbelief to her denial of being an advocate of "social equality" and to her proposal that blacks should be relocated in order to avoid a black voting majority in one area.

F1197 "Mrs. Roosevelt's Speech." *Crisis* 46 (Aug. 1939): 243.

When she presented the Spingarn Medal to Marian Anderson at the NAACP convention she spoke to the audience not as blacks but as fellow citizens who must accept along with equal opportunity the responsibilities of citizenship in a democracy. Reprinted from the *Defender* [Chicago].

F1198 Murray, Pauli. "Challenging Mrs. R." *Hunter Magazine* 3 (Sept. 1983): 21-23.

Murray began her correspondence with ER in 1940 accusing the Roosevelts of moving too slowly on improving race relations. She challenged ER to do more. Text of address at Hunter College conference on first ladies, Dec. 1982.

F1199 ---. *Song in a Weary Throat: An American Pilgrimage.* New York: Harper, 1987. xii + 451p. Index.

These memoirs of a civil rights activist and feminist contain many references to ER outlining the long, but sometimes difficult, relationship between the two women.

Exchange of letters on race relations in wartime (pp. 189-97). Murray's participation in ER's public life and poignant glimpses of the private ER during the early 1950s (pp. 289-93). ER on Adlai Stevenson's position on civil rights (pp. 308-10). Reissued in 1989 as *Pauli Murray: The Autobiography of a Black Activist, Feminist, Lawyer, Priest, and Poet* (Knoxville: Univ. of Tenn. Pr.).

F1200 Odum, Howard W. *Race and Rumors of Race: Challenge to American Crisis.* Chapel Hill: Univ. of N.C. Pr., 1943; New York: Negro Univ. Pr., 1969. x + 245p. Bibliography.

An account of rumors about the emergence and dominance of the Negro race during the period 1942-1943. "The Romance of the Eleanor Clubs" and "The First Lady's Heritage to the Folk Story" describe the emergence of Eleanor Clubs and the rumors about ER's association with blacks (pp. 73-89). "The Romance of the Eleanor Clubs" reissued in *The Burden of Race: A Documentary History of Negro-White Relations in America*, pp. 402-8 (New York: Harper, 1966).

The text of a file maintained by J. Edgar Hoover on the clubs is in *From the Secret Files of J. Edgar Hoover*, pp. 92-94 (Chicago: Dee, 1991).

F1201 Osur, Alan M. *Blacks in the Army Air Forces during World War II: The Problem of Race Relations.* Washington: GPO, 1977; New York: Arno, 1980. xiii + 227p. Index. Bibliography. Notes.

Limited attention to ER's efforts to desegregate the armed forces (pp. 13, 98-99, 110). Discusses 25-26 Nov. 1940 conference at Hampton Institute convened by ER and others to discuss the black's role in the war effort (pp. 15-17). ER and the March on Washington (p. 18). Based on his dissertation "Negroes in the Army Air Forces during World War II: The Problem of Race Relations" (Univ. of Denver, 1974).

F1202 Parker, Albert. "Pressure from the White House." *Fighting Racism in World War II.* Ed. C.L.R. James, et al. New York: Monad, 1980. 110-13.

ER wrote A. Philip Randolph urging him to cancel the March on Washington planned for 1 July 1941, and George Breitman writing under the name of Albert Parker uses that letter in an attempt to discredit ER as a friend of blacks. Reprinted from *Militant*, 28 June 1941.

F1203 Pfeffer, Paula F. *A. Philip Randolph: Pioneer of the Civil Rights Movement.* Baton Rouge: La. State Univ. Pr., 1990. xiv + 336p. Index. Bibliography. Notes.

Brief references about the March on Washington and civil rights groups and events with which ER worked with Randolph (pp. 48-49, 94, 102, 110, 192).

F1204 *Racial Distinction Abolished: President Roosevelt Permits Wife to Dine with Negro Porters to Obtain Votes for New Deal.* N.p.: n.p., n.d. [4]p.

Contains "My Day" of 20 Sept. 1940 in which ER describes her dinner with members of the Brotherhood of Sleeping Car Porters and with accompanying text claiming that "higher type Negroes" resent the familiarity which the Roosevelts show them. "Published by a southern Democrat who is voting for Willkie." Available in House Papers, Container 9, Lyndon Baines Johnson Library.

F1205 "Redd Foxx: 'Auntie Eleanor' Film Tells How President's Wife Proved Blacks Could Fly U.S. Planes." *Jet* 66 (2 Apr. 1984): 58-61.

Foxx will star in a motion picture about ER's success in having a flying school for blacks established in Tuskegee, Ala. and how she flew with a black instructor to prove that blacks should be allowed to fly U.S. military planes. 'Auntie Eleanor' originated from an unrelated friendship which she had with a young black delinquent who later became a Calif. assemblyman. Confirmation of ER's flight is in Thomas D. Boettcher, "The Hard-Won Successes of Black Pilots." *Christian Science Monitor* 30 Sept. 1982, Eastern ed.: 15.

F1206 "Routine for Mrs. F.D." Editorial. *Afro-American* 23 May 1936: 4.
ER's response to criticism of her public appearances with blacks is to be seen with them so often that it becomes routine.

F1207 Ruchames, Louis. *Race, Jobs, & Politics: The Story of FEPC.* New York: Columbia Univ. Pr., 1953. x + 255p. Index. Notes.
Excerpts 10 June 1941 letter from ER to A. Philip Randolph urging that the March on Washington be cancelled. A few days later she participated in a conference with Fiorello La Guardia, Aubrey Williams, and black leaders at which time she renewed her plea (pp. 17-18).

F1208 "Salisbury Entertains." *Time* 40 (24 Aug. 1942): 11-12.
Despite protests from city leaders ER spoke at a convention of the African Methodist Episcopal Zion Church in Salisbury, N.C. *Time* claims that southern blacks have organized "Eleanor Clubs" or called themselves "Daughters of Eleanor." "Find No 'Eleanor Clubs.'" *New York Times* 23 Sept. 1942: 13 states that ER has reported that in spite of the letters and calls which she has received about the clubs, the FBI has failed to find that any exist.

F1209 Salmond, John A. *Miss Lucy of the CIO: The Life and Times of Lucy Randolph Mason, 1882-1959.* Athens: Univ. of Ga. Pr., 1988. xiii + 227p. Index. Bibliography. Notes.
During the New Deal and later Mason conducted an extensive correspondence with ER seeking advice and help with civil rights and labor matters. Salmond quotes from many of Mason's letters to ER (pp. 83-167 passim).

F1210 Schlesinger, Arthur M., Jr. *The Politics of Upheaval.* The Age of Roosevelt, [Vol. 3]. Boston: Houghton Mifflin, 1960. 749p. Index. Notes.
ER's role with civil rights policies during FDR's first term (pp. 435, 442, 522). Reissued with a new foreword in 1988 (Boston: Houghton Mifflin)

F1211 Schneiderman, Rose. *All for One.* By Rose Schneiderman with Lucy Goldthwaite. New York: Erickson: 1967. viii + 264p.
This autobiographical work by the president of the New York Women's Trade Union League contains reminiscences of ER and FDR during the gubernatorial and presidential years (pp. 175-209). Her tribute to ER as a proponent of trade unions in this work dedicated to her (p. 251).

F1212 Shapiro, Herbert. *White Violence and Black Response: From Reconstruction to Montgomery.* Amherst: Univ. of Mass., Pr., 1988. xvi + 565p. Index. Bibliography. Notes.

Three notes elaborate on ER's position on the 1948 UN petition about the rights of blacks in the U.S., describe Communist front allegations about her, and explain her intervention on behalf of two young black boys (pp. 509, 522-23).

F1213 Shelton, Isabelle. "No Peace Without Equality--Mrs. Roosevelt Launches New Group." *Congressional Record* (27 Feb. 1960): 3696.
The 18 Feb. 1960 article from the *Washington Star* is entered into the record by Sen. Richard B. Russell who introduces it with an attack on ER and others in the new group, the National Organization of Women for Equality in Education which she will head, who view the South as the only villain when it comes to segregation.

F1214 Sitkoff, Harvard. "The Emergence of Civil Rights as a National Issue: The New Deal Era." Diss. Columbia Univ., 1975. 418p. Bibliography. Notes.
In the early years of the New Deal ER's relations with black leaders was attacked by Stephen Early and other FDR advisers (pp. 53-54). The chapter "The Start of a New Deal" concentrates on ER's role in improving race relations (pp. 75-105). Letters to ER from Mary McLeod Bethune (pp. 106-21) and from Walter White (pp. 325-57). ER and Marian Anderson (pp. 394-95).

F1215 ---. "The New Deal and Race Relations." *Fifty Years Later: The New Deal Evaluated*. Ed. Harvard Sitkoff. Philadelphia: Temple Univ. Pr., 1985. 93-112. Suggested Readings.
A separate section devoted to ER provides a succinct discussion of her activities aimed at furthering the rights of blacks during the New Deal (pp. 105-6). Based on a paper presented at a symposium, Univ. of N.H., 17-18 Mar. 1983.

F1216 ---. *A New Deal for Blacks: The Emergence of Civil Rights as a National Issue.* Vol. 1. New York: Oxford Univ. Pr., 1978. xi + 397p. Index. Notes.
The New Deal and ER in particular are credited for bringing about more participation by blacks in society (pp. 59-65, 128-32). The first of a projected three volume work.

F1217 Smith, Elaine M. "Mary MacLeod [sic] Bethune and the National Youth Administration." *Clio Was a Womam: Studies in the History of American Women.* National Archives Conferences, 16. Ed. Mabel E. Deutrich and Virginia C. Purdy. Washington: Howard Univ. Pr., 1980. 148-77. Notes.
The association between ER and Bethune involved the National Youth Admin. and numerous other projects aimed at improving the condition of blacks as evidenced by NYA documents and Bethune's papers (pp. 151-52, 157, 161-63). Paper presented at Conference on Women's History, 22-23 Apr. 1976.

F1218 Sosna, Morton. *In Search of the Silent South: Southern Liberals and the Race Issue.* New York: Columbia Univ. Pr., 1977. xvi + 275p. Index. Bibliography, Notes.
ER at the Southern Conference for Human Welfare (pp. 94-96) and Virginius Dabney's belief that ER and others are agitating southern blacks (pp. 131, 137-38). Based on his dissertation "In Search of the Silent South: White Southern Racial Liberalism, 1920-1950" (Univ. of Wisc., 1972).

F1219 Stokes, Anson Phelps. *Art and the Color Line: An Appeal Made May 31, 1939 to the President General and Other Officers of the Daughters of the American*

Revolution to Modify Their Rules so as to Permit Distinguished Negro Artists Such as Miss Marian Anderson to Be Heard in Constitution Hall. Washington: n.p., 1939. 26p.
Reaction to ER's resignation from the DAR (pp. 14, 16).

F1220 Strayer, Martha. *The D.A.R.: An Informal History.* Washington: Public Affairs, 1958; Westport: Greenwood, 1973. vi + 262p. Index.
An unauthorized account by a Washington reporter. Included is a discussion of ER's membership and resignation (pp. 170-72).

F1221 "Unfortunate Ambiguity." *Newsweek* 23 (6 Mar. 1944): 44, 46.
When a Memphis, Tenn. resident sent ER clippings from the Memphis *Commercial Appeal* about racial incidents in Ripley, Tenn., he told her that he was certain that she would be satisfied with the violence. Her ambiguous response leaves the impression that she did not find the accounts bad.

F1222 Weaver, Robert C. "Eleanor and L.B.J. and Black America." Rev. of *Eleanor and Franklin* by Joseph P. Lash and *The Vantage Point* by Lyndon B. Johnson. *Crisis* 79 (June/July 1972): 186-93.
Both ER and Johnson changed their attitudes about minorities. Lash portrays ER as the only sincere advocate of racial equality in FDR's White House and describes her relationships with Walter White, Mary McLeod Bethune, and Pauli Murray.

F1223 Weiss, Nancy J. *Farewell to the Party of Lincoln: Black Politics in the Age of FDR.* Princeton: Princeton Univ. Pr., 1983. xx + 333p. Index. Note on Sources.
Blacks joined the Democratic Party ranks because of the economic benefits which the New Deal provided. Unlike most others in the New Deal ER made the fight for racial equality a high priority. The chapter "Eleanor Roosevelt" describes the extent of her efforts toward providing equal opportunity, reactions of others to those efforts, and her relationship with Walter White (pp. 120-35). ER and White's unsuccessful efforts to achieve passage of anti-lynching legislation (pp. 104-19, 245, 248) and her appearance at the Southern Conference for Human Welfare (pp. 255-56). An earlier discussion of ER's efforts is in Weiss' *The National Urban League, 1910-1940*, pp. 265-66, 270-71 (New York: Oxford Univ. Pr., 1974).

F1224 "What Interests Negroes." *New York Times* 2 Apr. 1946: 26.
At the risk of appearing self-serving black audiences refrain from asking ER about the poll-tax and fair employment legislation. They leave those issues to white audiences. Issued as a section of the editorial column "Topics of the Times."

F1225 White, Walter. *How Far the Promised Land?* New York: Viking, 1955; New York: AMS, 1973. xii + 144p. Index.
In this his last work White discusses the progress of racial equality in the 20th century and the September 1950 conference devoted to considering action which could be taken to eliminate racial inequality. ER was a participant (pp. 22-24).

F1226 ---. *A Man Called White: The Autobiography of Walter White.* New York: Viking, 1948; New York: Arno, 1969; New York: Negro Univ. Pr., 1971. viii + 382p. Index.
NAACP leader White recalls his contact with ER in numerous brief segments.

F1227 ---. *A Rising Wind.* Garden City: Doubleday, Doran, 1945; New York: Negro Univ. Pr., 1971. 155p.

The title of White's work about blacks in World War II is a paraphrase of Thomas Wolfe's "a wind is rising" as used by ER. Her words, as reprinted from the *New York Herald Tribune* of 29 Sept. 1941, appear on p. [7].

F1228 Wilkins, Roy. *Standing Fast: The Autobiography of Roy Wilkins.* By Roy Wilkins with Tom Mathews. New York: Viking, 1982. viii + 361p. Index.

In the early years of the New Deal Wilkins and Walter White sought ER's acknowledgment of the need to improve the civil rights of blacks and her assistance in trying to convince FDR to support anti-lynching legislation (pp. 128-31). ER's wish to resign from the NAACP in 1956 (p. 233).

F1229 ---. "Watchtower." *New York Amsterdam Star-News* 5 July 1941: 14.

In his column Wilkins expresses gratitude that FDR has issued an executive order banning discriminatory employment practices in the defense industry, but he states that it is ER who deserves the credit for any advances which blacks have realized. Her desire to see our race recognized seems genuine, and as the one who has "run interference" for FDR in this area "she has done a good job."

F1230 Wolters, Raymond. *The New Deal and the Negro.* Vol. 1 of *The New Deal.* Modern America, 4. Ed. John Braeman, et al. Columbus: Ohio State Univ. Pr., 1975. 170-217. Notes.

ER, more than FDR, championed the rights of blacks during the New Deal years (pp. 208-9).

F1231 Zangrando, Joanna Schneider, and Robert L. Zangrando. "ER and Black Civil Rights." *Without Precedent: The Life and Career of Eleanor Roosevelt.* Everywoman: Studies in History, Literature, and Culture. Ed. Joan Hoff-Wilson and Marjorie Lightman. Bloomington: Indiana Univ. Pr., 1984. 88-107. Sources.

To erase racial inequality ER advocated slow and steady progress through equal opportunity.

F1232 Zangrando, Robert L. *The NAACP Crusade against Lynching, 1909-1950.* Philadelphia: Temple Univ. Pr., 1980. ix + 309p. Index. Bibliography. Notes.

Walter White's efforts through ER to secure passage of anti-lynching legislation. Based on ER's papers and those of the NAACP at the Library of Congress (pp. 113, 118-20, 123-24, 133-35, 138). Also see his "The NAACP and a Federal Antilynching Bill, 1934-1940." *Journal of Negro History* 50 (Apr. 1965): 106-17 and as reprinted in *The Era of Integration and Civil Rights, 1930-1990*, pp. 612-23 (New York: Garland, 1992).

Women's Rights

F1233 *American Women: The Report of the President's Commission on the Status of Women and Other Publications of the Commission.* Ed. Margaret Mead and Frances Bagley Kaplan. New York: Scribner's, 1965. xi + 274p. Index.

In the introduction Mead praises the choice of ER as chair of the commission (p. 4). Esther Peterson and Richard A. Lester's 11 Oct. 1963 "Letter of Transmittal" to JFK recognizes ER for her role as chair and for what she did for the status of women throughout the world (p. 9). Quotations from statements by ER emphasizing the necessity of economic stability for improving the status of women (15 June 1962 statement is on p. 15, and an excerpt from a commission progress report of Aug. 1962 is on p. 17). The report was originally published as *American Women: The Report of the President's Commission on the Status of Women* (Washington: GPO, 1963). On p. 448 of Peterson's summarization of the report issued as "The Status of Women in the United States." *International Labour Review* 89 (May 1964): 447-60 there is the statement that ER believed that opportunity, not special treatment, was the way in which women can realize equality.

F1234 Anthony, Susan B., II. "Woman's Next Step, as Women See It." *New York Times Magazine* 12 Jan. 1941: 11, 20.
ER's views on the current status of women are included. She personifies today's independent woman and considers the freedom from many of the drudgeries of housework to be what has given today's woman the ability to pursue a career. In the home women will always be looked upon as a woman, but outside the home the time will come when a woman will be viewed only as a person.

F1235 Badger, Anthony J. *The New Deal: The Depression Years, 1933-40.* London: Macmillan, 1989. x + 392p. Index. Bibliographical Essay.
The friendships which she made while she emerged as a public figure and her highly visible activities as First Lady made it possible for her to promote the potential of women (pp. 256-58).

F1236 Banner, Lois W. *Women in Modern America: A Brief History.* Harbrace History of the United States. New York: Harcourt Brace Jovanovich, 1974. xii + 276p. Index. Bibliography. Notes.
ER is the subject of two sections: "Eleanor Roosevelt: Exemplar of Her Era" (pp. 174-83) and "Changes for the Working Woman: The New Deal, Unemployment, New Union Strengths" (pp. 184-91). After a brief sketch of ER's early years Banner characterizes her as a "social feminist" who encouraged women to seek a place on the public scene. Also discusses how she encouraged the appointment of women to federal posts and, working with a network of other women, pursued humanitarian causes during the New Deal years. A 2nd rev. ed. issued in 1984 abbreviates the coverage of ER in "Eleanor Roosevelt: Exemplar of Her Era" (pp. 185-98) while expanding it in the section "The Women's Networks and New Deal Programs" (pp. 192-98).

F1237 Becker, Susan D. *The Origins of the Equal Rights Amendment: American Feminism between the Wars.* Contributions in Women's Studies, 23. Westport: Greenwood, 1981. viii + 300p. Index. Bibliography. Notes.
ER's failure to support the Equal Rights Amendment was significant (pp. 79, 149, 183-84, 216-17).

F1238 Bird, Caroline, and Sara Welles Briller. *Born Female: The High Cost of Keeping Women Down.* Rev. ed. New York: McKay, 1970. xiv + 302p. Notes.
While ER was chairing the President's Commission on the Status of Women Attorney General Robert Kennedy ruled that the President was able to require that women be considered equally with men for civil service promotions, something she had been working for since 1941 (pp. 43-44).

F1239 Black, Ruby A. "Is Mrs. Roosevelt a Feminist?" *Equal Rights* 1 (27 July 1935): 163-64.

Although she is opposed to the Equal Rights Amendment ER is a feminist. Her many statements about women's rights, her actions as First Lady on behalf of programs to benefit women, her White House press conferences for women reporters, and her public life as writer, speaker, and political activist demonstrate that she is indeed a feminist.

F1240 Burns, James MacGregor. *The Crosswinds of Freedom*. The American Experiment, 3. New York: Knopf, 1989. xi + 864p. Index. Notes.

During her life ER observed great progress in the role of women, and just as the "social refomer" died women were truly emerging (pp. 433-34).

F1241 Carney, Anne E. "The Nature and Significance of the Role of Mrs. Eleanor Roosevelt in the Field of Women's Rights during the Years 1933-1936." Thesis (M.A.) San Jose State College, 1970. 96p. Bibliography. Notes.

Through her energy, compassion, and pragmatism she improved life for American women. She deserves credit for making women more politically active and for improving conditions for the working woman.

F1242 Clark, Electra. *Leading Ladies: An Affectionate Look at American Women of the Twentieth Century*. New York: Stein and Day, 1976. 252p. Index.

As wife of the Gov. of N.Y. and as First Lady ER broke traditions. She worked to support the rights of women when she made direct appeals to New Deal officials (pp. 131-34.)

F1243 Clark, Judith Freeman. *Almanac of American Women in the 20th Century*. New York: Prentice Hall, 1987. xii + 274p. Index.

During the New Deal years ER was the leading advocate for the rights of women. Her friendships with women who held public positions were vital to the influence which she exerted to secure funding for women's programs (p. 57).

F1244 Cohen, Miriam. "New Deal (1933-1941)." *History, Philosophy, and Religion*. Vol. 3 of *Women's Studies Encyclopedia*. Ed. Helen Tierney. New York: Greenwood, 1989. 335-37. Further References.

ER and the other women around her considered it more important during the New Deal years to promote social reforms which could benefit women and children than to increase the political involvement of women.

F1245 Cook, Blanche Wiesen. "The Real Eleanor Roosevelt." *Ms* 13 (Sept. 1984): 86-88, 90, 91, 132-33.

In this tribute to her life and accomplishments Cook claims that ER was more a feminist than many current day feminists acknowledge. The publication of Doris Faber's *Lorena Hickok* revealed that ER may have had a secret life, and this revelation has prompted a closer look at her role as a feminist.

F1246 Danker, Anita. "Government Policy and Women in the Workplace through Depression and War." *New England Journal of History* 45 (1988): 16-38. Notes.

Another source for the activities on behalf of women by ER, Frances Perkins, Ellen Woodward, and Rose Schneiderman. Derivative.

F1247 Davis, Ann. "The Character of Social Feminism in the Thirties: Eleanor Roosevelt and Her Associates in the New Deal." *Franklin D. Roosevelt: The Man, the Myth, the Era, 1882-1945.* Contributions in Political Science, 189. Ed. Herbert D. Rosenbaum and Elizabeth Bartelme. New York: Greenwood, 1987. 287-306. Bibliography. Notes.

As social feminists ER and her associates worked for an expanded role for women in politics and government and, unlike hard-core feminists, they did not pursue changes in the role of the family. Based on correspondence between ER and Mary Dewson, Frances Perkins, Rose Schneiderman, and Ellen Woodward. Paper presented at Hofstra Univ. Conference, 4-6 Mar. 1982.

F1248 "Democrats Hailed for Aid to Women." *New York Times* 17 June 1937: 8.

Speaking in New London, Conn. about advances for women in the Roosevelt administration, Emma Guffey Miller praised ER. We "will never see another woman as great as Mrs. Eleanor Roosevelt."

F1249 Ellickson, Katherine P. "Eleanor Roosevelt and the Commission on the Status of Women." *Eleanor Roosevelt: An American Journey.* Ed. Jess Flemion and Colleen M. O'Connor. San Diego: San Diego State Univ. Pr., 1987. 93-96.

ER's leadership and influence made the work of the commission a success, and its report paved the way for protective legislation. ER on the Equal Rights Amendment.

F1250 Evans, Sara M. *Born for Liberty: A History of Women in America.* New York: Free Press-Collier Macmillan, 1989. xii + 386p. Index. Notes.

A brief look at how ER used her position as First Lady and her speaking and writing activities to promote women's issues (pp. 205-7).

F1251 "First Lady Scores Housing in Capital." *New York Times* 10 May 1942: 30.

She and the wives of the heads of federal agencies have issued a statement about the status of public housing in Washington for female government workers which calls for the construction of dormitories with cafeterias and medical facilities.

F1252 Fisher, Dorothy Canfield. "Eleanor Roosevelt." *American Portraits.* By Dorothy Canfield Fisher. New York: Holt, 1946. 191-94.

A tribute to the modern American women as personified by ER.

F1253 Foner, Philip S. *Women and the American Labor Movement: From World War I to the Present.* New York: Free, 1980. vi + 682p. Index. Bibliography. Notes.

ER promoted the status of working women through her active participation in the Women's Trade Union League (p. 276) and as First Lady through her promotion of women's issues under the Works Progress Admin. (pp. 292-93).

F1254 Fowler, Robert Booth. *Carrie Catt: Feminist Politician.* Boston: Northeastern Univ. Pr., 1986. xx + 226p. Index. Bibliography. Notes.

Catt considered ER the personification of the modern "independent person" and a loyal supporter of women's rights. Catt's efforts on behalf of world peace won ER's respect. Based on speeches by Catt (pp. 97-98).

F1255 George, Elsie L. "The Women Appointees of the Roosevelt and Truman Administrations: A Study of Their Impact and Effectiveness." Diss. American Univ., 1972. v + 317p. Bibliography. Notes.

Throughout the Roosevelt administration ER employed various means to promote the role of women in government (pp. 4, 23, 43-45, 87-88).

F1256 Harrison, Cynthia. *On Account of Sex: The Politics of Women's Issues, 1945-1968.* Berkeley: Univ. of Calif. Pr., 1988. xxii + 337p. Index. Bibliography. Notes.
ER's position on the Equal Rights Amendment, 1941-1962 (pp. 19, 22, 26, 32, 277-78). JFK and his naming of ER as chair of the President's Commission on the Status of Women (pp. 111-12). A note reports on ER's address to the Lucy Stone League in support of the Equal Rights Amendment (pp. 277-78).

F1257 Hartmann, Susan M. "Eleanor Roosevelt and Women's Rights." *Eleanor Roosevelt: An American Journey.* Ed. Jess Flemion and Colleen M. O'Connor. San Diego: San Diego State Univ. Pr., 1987. 87-92. Note on Sources.
ER considered herself a feminist. Many of the women's issues which she promoted were carried on by others, and her role as chair of the President's Commission on the Status of Women was a bridge between the earlier women's movement and that of the 1960s.

F1258 "He May Be More Attentive." Editorial. *Equal Rights* 2 (7 Mar. 1936): 2.
Women are distressed that FDR has done nothing to secure passage of legislation which would repeal the restrictive law against federal employment for some women. Because of this his political future and his integrity are at risk. Since she too has done nothing about the resolution, ER's integrity is also in jeopardy.

F1259 Hoff-Wilson, Joan. Introduction. "Significance of the Defeat of the ERA." *Rights of Passage: The Past and Future of the ERA.* Ed. Joan Hoff-Wilson. Bloomington: Indiana Univ. Pr., 1986. 93-96.
By the 1940s the only woman who could have united other women behind the Equal Rights Amendment was ER, but instead she was still leading the forces which favored protective legislation for women. An example of her efforts in oppositon to the ERA is reported in "80 Sign to Oppose Rights Amendment." *New York Times* 19 Aug. 1943: 16 which includes the text of a statement signed by ER and others in the National Consumers League.

F1260 Humphries, Jane. "Women: Scapegoats and Safety Valves in the Great Depression." *Review of Radical Political Economics* 8 (Spring 1976): 98-121. Notes.
An attempt to show that depression fosters a continuation of male dominance and impedes liberation of the sexes. ER, also associated with government programs of the 1930s upon which women were dependent, was a symbol for the new type of woman who emerged in that period.

F1261 Hymowitz, Carol, and Michaele Weissman. *A History of Women in America.* New York: Bantam, 1978. xii + 400p. Index. Notes.
As a political and social activist and as a First Lady who continued her own career, ER had perhaps the most significant impact on the successes which women have realized in defining a role in public and political life (pp. 310-11).

F1262 Kenneally, James J. *Women and American Trade Unions.* Monographs in Women's Studies. St. Albans: Eden, 1978. ii + 240p. Index. Notes.

A summary of her activities with the Women's Trade Union League and its leaders during the pre-White House years (p. 153). Highlights of her efforts as First Lady to support the women's labor movement (p. 158-59).

F1263 Kennedy, John F. "Statement by the President on the Establishment of the President's Commission on the Status of Women." *Public Papers of the Presidents of the United States: John F. Kennedy, Containing the Public Messages, Speeches, and Statements of the President, January 20 to December 31, 1961.* Washington: GPO, 1962. 799-800.

When this statement was released on 14 Dec. 1961 ER was named as chair of the commission. Included in the volume for 1962 (Washington: GPO, 1963) are "Remarks to the Members of the President's Commission on the Status of Women" dated 12 Feb. 1962 in which JFK recognizes ER for her willingness to "serve the country" once again (p. 130) and the 26 Aug. 1962 "Letter to Mrs. Eleanor Roosevelt on Receiving Report by the Commission on the Status of Women" in which he highlights the work of commission and thanks ER for her participation (p. 644).

The volume for 1963 (Washington: GPO, 1964) contains "Remarks at Presentation of the Final Report of the President's Commission on the Status of Women." At the 11 Oct. 1963 ceremony JFK refers to the report as "a legacy of hers [ER's] in a very real sense" (pp. 780-81).

F1264 Krock, Arthur. "Mrs. Roosevelt's Conversion to Joint Tax Returns." *New York Times* 9 June 1942: 22.

She supports mandatory joint tax returns for married couples, because she feels that the requirement will strengthen the wife's position and will bring in more revenue from couples with higher incomes. But leaders of women's groups and others claim that couples with lower incomes would be affected most, thus hurting women. See also "Mrs. Roosevelt Backs Joint Income Return." *New York Times* 9 June 1942: 18.

F1265 Lash, Joseph P. "Eleanor Roosevelt's Role in Women's History." *Clio Was a Woman: Studies in the History of American Women.* National Archives Conferences, 16. Ed. Mabel E. Deutrich and Virginia C. Purdy. Washington: Howard Univ. Pr., 1980. 242-53. Notes.

Relying on his *Eleanor and Franklin* Lash provides a poignant overview of ER's contributions to women's rights and the influence which other women had on her. Paper presented at Conference on Women's History, 22-23 Apr. 1976.

F1266 Miringoff, Marque-Luisa. *Eleanor Roosevelt, Women and Work: Considerations for the 1980's* [sic]. Hyde Park: Eleanor Roosevelt's Val-Kill, 1981. 47p. Bibliography. Notes.

ER's speeches and writings are used to illustrate her view on work: how work can enable one to make a contribution, work can be in the home as well, and everyone should have the right to enjoy the value and benefits of work.

F1267 "Mrs. Roosevelt Counsels Women." *Equal Rights* 1 (22 June 1935): 128.

ER believes that while women today face more challenges than ever before, they should also realize the many opportunities which they have. Reissue of article about a White House press conference from the *New York Herald Tribune*, 5 June 1935.

F1268 "New Deal in Women's Reading." Editorial. *Christian Science Monitor*, Eastern ed., 4 June 1934: 24.

When she spoke to the American Newspaper Publishers' Assoc., ER expressed her view that today women are more interested in reading about world problems than about household matters.

F1269 Paterson, Judith. *Be Somebody: A Biography of Marguerite Rawalt*. Austin: Eakin, 1986. xxii + 274p.

ER and the Commission on the Status of Women (pp. 124-25, 130, 133-40). Rawalt was a member of the commission.

F1270 Peterson, Esther. "The Kennedy Commission." *Women in Washington: Advocates for Public Policy*. Sage Yearbooks in Women's Policy Studies, 70. Ed. Irene Tinker. Beverly Hills: Sage, 1983. 21-34.

Peterson cites ER's influence on the work and outcome of the commission.

F1271 ---. "Mrs. Roosevelt's Legacy." *McCall's* 91 (Oct. 1963): 84, 227.

The report of the President's Commission on the Status of Women will be presented to JFK on 11 Oct., the 79th anniversary of ER's birth. ER is credited for providing the structure for the commission's work and securing the involvement of many distinguished citizens. The concept of "full partnership" advocated by ER is a vital part of the report. An account of the report "as a living memorial" to ER is Dorothy McCardle, "Report to JFK: Women Settle for Second Class Status." *Washington Post* 12 Oct. 1963, sect. 3: 8-10.

F1272 "Roosevelt and Women's Rights." *Equal Rights* 1 (6 July 1935): 143.

Speaking at a regional conference of the National Woman's Party in Atlantic City, N.J. Harriot Stanton Blatch recalled as evidence of FDR's lack of commitment to women's issues how he missed an important vote in the N.Y. Senate because he was "looking after the babies while Mrs. Roosevelt was moving into their summer home." Blatch is now amused by the incident since she has learned that ER has the "ability to lead an army over mountain tops." Reissue of an editorial in the *Philadelphia Inquirer*, 23 June 1935.

F1273 Scharf, Lois. "The Employment of Married Women during the Depression, 1929-1941." Diss. Case Western Reserve Univ. 1977. v + 462p. Bibliography. Notes.

By late 1933 ER was sharing with federal officials her concern about the plight of women on relief. She was troubled by lack of jobs and pay differentials between men and women (pp. 325-26, 353). But Scharf points out that in *It's Up to the Women* ER advocated more traditional roles: women should enter those professions which have always been considered appropriate for them, wives should not work if there are men who need jobs, and women need protective labor laws (pp. 354-55).

F1274 ---. "ER and Feminism." *Without Precedent: The Life and Career of Eleanor Roosevelt*. Everywoman: Studies in History, Literature, and Culture. Ed. Joan Hoff-Wilson and Marjorie Lightman. Bloomington: Indiana Univ. Pr., 1984. 226-53. Sources.

Although biographer Ruby Black labeled her a feminist, ER's commitment to feminist issues was rooted in a broader liberal agenda. ER's role in feminist and social reform causes.

F1275 ---. *To Work and to Wed: Female Employment, Feminism, and the Great Depression*. Contributions in Women's Studies, 15. Westport: Greenwood, 1980. xiii + 240p. Index. Essay on Sources. Notes.

ER worked against Mass. restrictions placed on married women who work (pp. 56, 59).

F1276 Scime, Joy A. "Government Policy, Working Women and Feminism in the Great Depression: Section 213 of the 1932 Economy Act." Diss. State Univ. of N.Y. at Buffalo, 1987. vi + 283p. Bibliography. Notes.

Limited attention to the pressure directed at ER to influence the repeal of Sect. 213 which caused women to lose their federal jobs so that more positions would be available to men (pp. 127, 130, 185, 188-89). Her acceptance of the law (p. 128).

F1277 Seder, Florence M. "The Women's Crusade." *Junior League Magazine* 20 (Oct. 1933): 42-43.

ER served as chair of the National Women's Committee of the 1933 Mobilization for Human Needs. In this article about the campaign is a lengthy quotation in which ER states that since women know how to live on a budget they can help mold public opinion in favor of support for human welfare services and in the realization that government aid alone is not enough. In an editorial, "The 'Ususal' Needs," the *New York Times* praises ER's willingness to serve as chair and urges all other women to help make the effort a success (5 Aug. 1933: 10).

F1278 Seeber, Frances M. "Eleanor Roosevelt and Women in the New Deal: A Network of Friends." *Presidential Studies Quarterly* 20 (Fall 1990): 707-17. Notes.

Through their association with ER, Molly Dewson, Frances Perkins, and Ellen Woodward promoted the role of women in the New Deal. ER used her women-only press conferences to help female journalists, and she provided women an equal opportunity with men to attend White House functions. "My Day" and writings by and about her in the *Democratic Digest* also helped to promote what women were capable of achieving.

F1279 Smith, Hilda W. "New Schools for Unemployed Women." *Women's Democratic News* 10 (Sept. 1934): 2.

Recognition of ER's role in promoting relief camps for women.

F1280 Sochen, June. "Eleanor Roosevelt: A Heroine for All Times." *Herstory: A Woman's View of American History*. By June Sochen. New York: Alfred, 1974. 326-30.

Sochen echoes the notion that ER was a "Right-Wing feminist" while still believing that as First Lady she was an effective advocate for women's rights. ER believed that a woman could have a career while still being a homemaker. To her it could be done without changing the system or society.

F1281 ---. "Eleanor Roosevelt: A Living Symbol of Feminism." *Movers and Shakers: American Women Thinkers and Activists, 1900-1970*. By June Sochen. New York: Quadrangle, 1973. 151-61.

Writings by and about ER are used to illustrate her actions on behalf of women in the 1920s and 1930s. Considers her the only First Lady to achieve an identity completely separate from that of her husband.

F1282 Swain, Martha H. "ER and Ellen Woodward: A Partnership for Women's Work Relief and Security." *Without Precedent: The Life and Career of Eleanor Roosevelt*. Everywoman: Studies in History, Literature, and Culture. Ed. Joan Hoff-Wilson and Marjorie Lightman. Bloomington: Indiana Univ. Pr., 1984. 135-52. Sources.

Throughout the Roosevelt administration ER and Woodward collaborated to secure economic and social benefits for women.

F1283 ---. "The 'Forgotten Woman': Ellen S. Woodward and Women's Relief in the New Deal." *Prologue* 15 (Winter 1983): 200-213. Notes.

ER's role in promoting women's relief activities which came under attack by organized labor and Congress. Documented by ER's correspondence.

F1284 Tuve, Jeanette E. *First Lady of the Law: Florence Ellinwood Allen*. Lanham: Univ. Pr. of America, 1984. vi + 220p. Index. Bibliography. Notes.

Appointed by FDR in 1934, Allen was the first woman to serve on a federal court of appeals. She and ER were acquaintances, and ER promoted Allen for a seat on the Supreme Court. Contains numerous brief sections based on Allen's letters to ER.

F1285 Ware, Susan. *Beyond Suffrage: Women in the New Deal*. Cambridge: Harvard Univ. Pr., 1981. 204p. Index. Notes.

Ware contends that the emergence of a network between those women who played significant roles in the New Deal was their greatest accomplishment. ER was the network's "foremost member." Relies heavily on correspondence received by ER and provides an account of her activities between 1933 and 1945. Based on Ware's dissertation "Political Sisterhood in the New Deal: Women in Politics and Government, 1933-1940." (Harvard Univ., 1978).

F1286 ---. "Women and the New Deal." *Fifty Years Later: The New Deal Evaluated*. Ed. Harvard Sitkoff. Philadelphia: Temple Univ. Pr., 1985. 113-32. Suggested Readings.

A study of the historiography of women's history during the New Deal. ER's emphasis on women's issues is recognized, and she is credited for bringing attention to the need for relief efforts for women and for the progress which women realized under the New Deal. Based on a paper presented at a symposium, Univ. of N.H., 17-18 Mar. 1983.

F1287 Williams, Barbara. "Esther Eggertsen Peterson, Presidential Appointee." *Breakthrough: Women in Politics*. By Barbara Williams. New York: Walker, 1979. 131-52.

Contains Peterson's recollections of ER when the two of them served on the President's Commission on the Status of Women (pp. 141-43).

F1288 Williams, Charl Ormond. "Women's Work Recognized." *The Democratic Book, 1936*. N.p.: Democratic Party, 1936. 319-20.

Includes praise for ER and what she has done for women. More than any other First Lady her inspiration and influence have "done more for the woman who works" (p. 319).

F1289 Woloch, Nancy. *Women and the American Experience*. New York: Knopf, 1984. xi + 567p. Index. Bibliography.

A discussion of ER's efforts to promote opportunities for women under the New Deal appears in the chapter "Humanizing the New Deal, 1933" (pp. 419-37) and in the section "Women's New Deal" (pp. 452-57).

F1290 "Women at Odds on 48-Hour Bill." *New York Times* 26 Feb. 1925: 23.
On 25 Feb. ER spoke at a N.Y. State Assembly hearing in support of limiting the work week to 48 hours. She called for the need for protective legislation and urged all working women to support reducing the work week from 54 to 48 hours. "Democratic Women to Aid 48-Hour Bill." *New York Times* 22 Mar. 1926: 8 reports on support for the legislation from Republican women and includes the text of a letter from ER proposing that work for the bill's passage become a bipartisan effort. Republican women declined as reported in "Mrs. Vanamee Spurns Democratic Offer." *New York Times* 23 Mar. 1926: 6.

F1291 *Women's Trade Union League Publications.* Papers of the Women's Trade Union League and Its Principal Leaders, Collection IX. Ed. Edward T. James, et al. Woodbridge: Research Publications for Schlesinger Library, Radcliffe College, 1981.
Her activities during the 1930s and 1940s in the New York Women's Trade Union League including "Eleanor Roosevelt Club for Unemployed Women," a report of a 24 Jan. 1941 testimonial dinner, and references to occasions when she spoke at league functions or led discussions (reels 7-9).

F1292 Wood, Wilma H. "Eleanor Roosevelt: Gentlewoman and Feminist." Thesis (M.A.). Wayne Univ., 1937. iv + 76p. Bibliography. Notes.
A study of ER's social consciousness is used to approach the present "age through a woman" (p. ii). To ER life is "a series of social problems awaiting solution" (p. 20). Wood considers ER's philosophy about four issues--home, education, work, and international relations--in an analysis of her beliefs about the relationship of contemporary woman to society.

F1293 Woolley, Mary E. "Introducing Mrs. Franklin D. Roosevelt." *Public Speaking for Women.* By J.V. Garland. New York: Harper, 1938. 12-13.
A tribute to ER, one who has done much to unify women and their causes. Text of statement by the president of Mount Holyoke College at the 11th Conference on the Cause and Cure of War, Washington. Date lacking.

F1294 Zelman, Patricia G. *Women, Work, and National Policy: The Kennedy-Johnson Years.* Studies in American History and Culture, 33. Ann Arbor: UMI Research Pr., 1982. x + 160p. Index. Bibliography. Notes.
In this revision of her dissertation (Ohio State Univ., 1980) Zelman emphasizes the place of Esther Peterson in the Kennedy administration. The author's interview with Peterson describes JFK's reluctance to name ER as chair of the Commission on the Status of Women and then ER's reluctance to accept (p. 26).

Young Americans and Their Problems

F1295 Abramowitz, Mildred. "Eleanor Roosevelt and Federal Responsibility and Responsiveness to Youth, the Negro, and Others in Time of Depression." Diss. N.Y. Univ., 1970. 255p. Bibliography. Notes.

Examines how ER brought New Deal attention to the problems of youth and helped create the National Youth Admin. Significant attention given to Aubrey Williams and Mary McLeod Bethune. Based on ER's articles, speeches, and "My Day" columns and on the papers of Williams and others.

F1296 ---. "Eleanor Roosevelt and the National Youth Administration, 1935-1943--An Extension of the Presidency." *Presidential Studies Quarterly* 14 (1984): 569-80. Notes.

Her involvement in the NYA as one of its originators, staunch proponents, and active participants in its efforts to promote democracy and a better future for youth allowed her to fill a role which would have been difficult for FDR. Based on ER's correspondence with Aubrey Williams and Charles W. Taussig and on "My Day" columns.

F1297 Adams, Frank S. "Youth Advancing on Capital Meets General Attack." *New York Times* 9 Feb. 1940: 1, 10.

The extensive coverage given to the American Youth Congress when it convened the Citizenship Institute in Washington includes accounts of ER's activities and the criticism which ensued. Additional articles by Adams are "Anti-Reds Balked in Floor Scuffles at Youth Session." 10 Feb. 1940: 1, 7 and "First Lady Balks at Advising Youth to Uphold Finland." 12 Feb. 1940: 1, 11.

Prior to the institute she spoke out against charges that the AYC was dominated by Communists. Her remarks are excerpted in "Hamilton Chided by Mrs. Roosevelt." *New York Times* 6 Feb. 1940: 1, 3.

F1298 Cadden, Joseph. "AYC Leader Explains Mrs. FDR's 'Goodbye.'" *Review* (Young Communist League) 6 (17 Feb. 1941): 4.

The American Youth Congress is still interested in working with ER to improve conditions for youth. But her support of compulsory public service for young people and her backing of measures such as Lend-lease will lead the country to war and make cooperation difficult.

F1299 Cook, Blanche Wiesen. "Biographer and Subject: A Critical Connection." *Between Women*. Ed. Carol Ascher, et al. Boston: Beacon, 1984. 396-411. Notes.

Writing about the subjects of her biographical research Cook provides a tribute to one of them--ER. In her final years ER continued to inspire youth, including Cook, to work on behalf of social reform. Cook describes how ER's social and political perceptions evolved over a long period of time (pp. 398, 407-10).

F1300 Davis, Maxine. *The Lost Generation: A Portrait of American Youth Today*. New York: Macmillan, 1936. xii + 385p. Index.

An early acknowledgment of ER's interest in the problems of youth and the symbolic importance of her actions (p. 318).

F1301 Dies, Martin. *Martin Dies' Story*. New York: Bookmailer, 1963. 283p. Index. Notes.

Dies considered the writing of this book an obligation in order to share with the American people the truths which he learned as chair of the House Committee on Un-American Activities. In a chapter devoted to her he concentrates on ER's relationship with Joseph Lash, Lash's testimony to the committee in 1939 and 1942, and an exchange of letters with ER which followed a 1954 interview with Dies (pp. 149-55). Text of letters (pp. 260-64).

F1302 "Dies vs. Mrs. Roosevelt." *Current History* 51 (Jan. 1940): 8.
Her concern for youth has resulted in brushes with the Dies Committee, and she has stated publicly that the committee acts in an undemocratic manner.

F1303 "Eleanor Roosevelt on Discipline in the School." Editorial. *Journal of Business Education* 22 (Feb. 1947): 7.
Praise for her call for better teaching methods before adopting the ideas of progressive education.

F1304 Flynn, John T. "Youth as Cat's-Paw." *New Republic* 102 (26 Feb. 1940): 278.
ER's behavior at the Citizenship Institute is worthy of praise. Courageous and frank, she stood by those she had befriended earlier.

F1305 Gellermann, William. *Martin Dies*. New York: Day, 1944. 310p. Index. Notes.
Includes statements Dies made about the activities and beliefs of ER (pp. 93, 108, 227, 229, 261). Gellermann considers Dies to be misguided.

F1306 Goodman, Walter. *The Committee: The Extraordinary Career of the House Committee on Un-American Activities*. New York: Farrar, Straus and Giroux, 1968. xviii + 564p. Index. Bibliography. Notes.
ER and her problems with the committee. In particular, the 1939 investigation of the American Youth Congress under chair Martin Dies (pp. 77-80) and the 1939 and later investigations of German alien Hanns Eisler (pp. 204-6).

F1307 Gould, Leslie A. *American Youth Today*. New York: Random House, 1940. xii + 307p. Index. Notes.
The author's laudatory description of ER's contributions to the 1940 Citizenship Institute and the answers which she provided to questions put to her during one of the sessions (pp. 23-28). American Youth Congress testimonial dinner for ER (pp. 97-98). Her attendance at the 1939 Congress of Youth and excerpts from her speech (pp. 105-7).

F1308 "Hall of Fame Citizenship Builders." *Jr.* (Apr. 1955): [2-3].
For her efforts on behalf of children worldwide ER is honored as the first Hall of Fame Youth Citizenship Builder by the Junior Americans of the United States.

F1309 Hoffman, Clare E. "Who Is the Present Boss?" *Congressional Record Appendix* (12 Apr. 1940): 705-6.
Is it FDR, ER, or John L. Lewis? Rep. Hoffman attacks ER for the fees which she commands when touring the country is search of what is wrong and in need of correction. His most severe criticism is leveled at her actions in support of the obvious Communists in the American Youth Congress.

F1310 Huie, William Bradford. "How Eleanor Roosevelt Let Our Generation Down." *Today's Woman* 28 (July 1953): 26-27, 40, 42.
She has failed us because of her lack of wisdom. Her advice on childrearing has been poor as evidenced by her own children, during the 1930s she failed to give proper direction to American youth, and in her pre-UN years she failed to recognize the dangers of communism and appeared to serve as Stalin's mouthpiece.

F1311 Kornbluh, Joyce L. "The She-She-She Camps: An Experiment in Living and Learning, 1934-1937." *Sisterhood and Solidarity: Workers' Education for Women, 1914-1984.* Ed. Joyce L. Kornbluh and Mary Frederickson. Philadelphia: Temple Univ. Pr., 1984. 253-83. Bibliography. Notes.

ER's work with Hilda Smith and Ellen Woodward to further relief efforts for young women (pp. 257-61, 270-72).

F1312 Laski, Harold J. "London Diary." *New Statesman and Nation* 24 (28 Nov. 1942): 353-54.

One of several editorial comments. ER's concern for youth and their ability to lead the post-war world is worthy of praise. Urges Americans to be proud of this great woman. Written after her 1942 trip to England (p. 353).

F1313 Lewis, Fulton, Jr. "Has the Youth Congress Washed Itself Out?" *Liberty* 17 (6 Apr. 1940): 9-10.

Fulton indicts the American Youth Congress for its actions during the recent Citizenship Institute, and he reports on ER's role in making arrangements and providing housing as well as her current disillusionment with the organization.

F1314 Lindley, Betty. "American Youth Look with Hope and Confidence to Eleanor Roosevelt, the First Lady Who Wants Youth to Have a Chance." *Click* 3 (Apr. 1940): 4-7.

ER has gained her knowledge of today's youth by traveling around the country, and now they know that she is interested in them and their problems.

F1315 Lindley, Betty, and Ernest K. Lindley. *A New Deal for Youth: The Story of the National Youth Administration.* New York: Viking, 1938. xvi + 309p. Index.

While this early history of the NYA makes no mention of ER, the dedication recognizes her influence on American youth [v].

F1316 Lyons, Eugene. "Mrs. Roosevelt's Youth Congress." *American Mercury* 49 (Apr. 1940): 481-84.

Criticizes ER for supporting the American Youth Congress' Citizenship Institute. It is irresponsible to let herself be used by such a group says Lyons. Reprinted with a lengthy attack by Rep. Karl E. Mundt on the Roosevelts' misguided efforts on behalf of America's youth as "Mrs. Roosevelt's Youth Congress--What Is Its Portent for America?" *Congressional Record Appendix* (9 Apr. 1940): 1952-54.

F1317 ---. *The Red Decade: The Stalinist Penetration of America.* Indianapolis: Bobbs-Merrill, 1941. 423p. Index.

ER is criticized for associating with organizations which he considers to be communistic, but his major criticism is that she has supported the American Youth Congress for too long (pp. 209-15). Reissued in 1970 as *The Red Decade: The Classic Work on Communism in America during the Thirties* (New Rochelle: Arlington House). Also see "Anti-Red Resolution Voted Down in Youth Congress; 14 Groups Bolt." *New York Times* 4 July 1939: 1, 11 which includes an account of the 1 July meeting of the Youth Congress and excerpts her remarks calling for the young to learn more about their local communities and to devote themselves to the principles of "faith" and "courage."

F1318 Martin, Prestonia Mann. *Prohibiting Poverty: Suggestions for a Method of Obtaining Economic Security.* New York: Farrar & Rinehart, 1932. x + 115p.

Martin's book with its idea of a camp for young workers is believed to have had significant impact on ER's thinking. For a discussion of ER's reaction to the book, see Lash's *Eleanor and Franklin,* pp. 385-86, 536.

F1319 Minton, Bruce. "The Plot against the Youth." *New Masses* 38 (31 Dec. 1940): 9-10.

ER and ally Joseph Lash want to revive the International Student Service as the organization for youth work camps. In the subsequent article Milton Meltzer and Ralph Forrest, "The Students Say 'Twaddle.'" *New Masses* 38 (14 Jan. 1941): 10-11 it is reported that Lash failed to produce youth's support for the war in Europe because the youth leaders saw that support tied to labor camps at home.

F1320 "The Nation's Honor Role for 1939." *Nation* 150 (6 Jan. 1940): 6.

ER tops the list and is recognized for her support of youth.

F1321 "New Deal Assailed before First Lady." *New York Times* 28 Feb. 1936: 1, 3.

Mrs. Eugene Meyer attacks New Deal programs for youth at New York Town Hall meeting on 27 Feb. presided over by ER.

F1322 Oakes, John B. "Mrs. Roosevelt Hears Witness Sing Dies Song." *Washington Post* 2 Dec. 1939: 2.

ER turned her back to the cameras and refused to make any public statement, but she said that she would testify at congressional hearings on the American Student Union if asked to do so. Other accounts of her attendance at hearings on 30 Nov. and 1 Dec. include Charles W. Hurd, "First Lady Visits Dies Committee to Hear Youth Congress Defended." *New York Times* 1 Dec. 1939: 1, 25 and "Denies Red Sway in Student Union." *New York Times* 2 Dec. 1939: 1, 6. Both include her terse responses to reporters' questions.

F1323 Ogden, August Raymond. *The Dies Committee: A Study of the Special House Committee for the Investigation of Un-American Activities, 1938-1944.* 2nd. ed., rev. Washington: Catholic Univ. of America Pr., 1945; Westport: Greenwood, 1984. vi + 318p. Index. Bibliography. Notes.

Report of ER's attendance at 30 Nov. 1939 committee hearing and conjecture as to whether her presence had any bearing on the unbiased treatment given members of the American Youth Congress. Her discussions of the hearings in "My Day" (pp. 169-71). Based on his dissertation (Catholic Univ. of America, 1944).

F1324 O'Reilly, Kenneth. *Hoover and the Un-Americans: The FBI, HUAC, and the Red Menace.* Philadelphia: Temple Univ. Pr., 1983. xiii + 411p. Index. Bibliography. Notes.

Relying on works of Joseph Lash and letters of ER and J. Edgar Hoover, O'Reilly provides an analysis of ER's involvement with Lash and the American Youth Congress and her relationship with Hoover (pp. 51-53). Appeared originally in part as "New Deal for the FBI." *Journal of American History* 69 (Dec. 1982): 638-58.

F1325 Pitt, David E. "Joseph P. Lash, Pulitzer-Winning Biographer, Dies." *New York Times* 23 Aug. 1987: 40.

Includes a synopsis of ER's association with youth organizations during the 1930s.

F1326 "President's Wife Interviews Girl, 16." *New York Times* 7 Nov 1935: 21.

A Camp Fire Girl tells ER that teachers are not sufficiently informed to provide vocational guidance. ER agrees and discusses the problem in more detail.

F1327 "Radicals at Vassar." *America* 59 (6 Aug. 1938): 420.

By agreeing to participate at the 16 Aug. World's Youth Congress at Vassar ER sends the wrong signal to the rest of the world, because it will appear that the U.S. is condoning a group which is neither Christian nor dedicated to basic American principles.

F1328 Rawick, George Philip. "The New Deal and Youth: The Civilian Conservation Corps, the National Youth Administration, and the American Youth Congress." Diss. Univ. of Wisc., 1957. iv + 408p. Bibliography. Notes.

ER's address to the 1933 National Conference of Students in Politics was indicative of her thinking about the youth movement (p. 279). Her support of the American Youth Congress gave the group significance while she took too long to realize its Communist domination (pp. 342-76 passim).

F1329 Reiman, Richard A. *The New Deal & American Youth: Ideas & Ideals in a Depression Decade*. Athens: Univ. of Ga. Pr., 1992. viii + 253p. Index. Bibliography. Notes.

Reiman tries to establish the origin of the National Youth Admin. and to attribute credit to FDR. He takes a revisionist approach to the claims made in memoirs of some New Deal figures and biographers of ER who have given her almost all of the credit (pp. 118, 120, 183-84, 192-98).

F1330 Roosevelt, Archie, and Murray Plavner. "Why We Know the Youth Congress Is Pro-Stalin." *Liberty* 17 (27 Apr. 1940): 12-14.

Two participants in the Feb. 1940 National Youth Citizenship Institute say that it is time that ER learns the truth about the American Youth Congress. In Feb. 1940 major newspapers carried numerous letters from readers who expressed concern about ER's involvement with the Youth Congress, e.g., the *New York Herald Tribune* 14 Feb. 1940: 20 and 16 Feb. 1940: 22.

F1331 "Roosevelt Names Used by Red Chiefs, Says Dies Witness." *New York Times* 10 Oct. 1939: 1, 15.

In 8 Oct. testimony a witness claims that ER and FDR are being used by Communists. Whether she knows it or not, she has entertained Communists in Hyde Park.

F1332 Salmond, John A. "Aubrey Williams: Atypical New Dealer?" *The New Deal*. Vol. 1. Modern America, 4. Ed. John Braeman, et al. Columbus: Ohio State Univ. Pr., 1975. 218-45. Notes.

Relationship between National Youth Admin. director Williams and ER.

F1333 Springer, Gertrude, and Kathryn Close. "Children in a Democracy." *Survey Midmonthly* 76 (Feb. 1940): 37-49.

ER opened the Jan. 1940 White House Conference on Children with a message from FDR, but since she was an hour early there were no delegates present. She opened the session on the third day with a plea for the delegates to apply the principles discussed at the local community level.

F1334 Straight, Michael. *After Long Silence*. New York: Norton, 1983. 351p. Index.

Straight's autobiography contains numerous references to ER in the 1930s and later. The chapter "Confrontation in Washington" describes the assistance ER provided in preparing for the American Youth Congress' Institute on Government (pp. 147-54).

F1335 "Students and Communism: Dies Inquiry Airs Charges; Mrs. Roosevelt Looks On." *Newsweek* 14 (11 Dec. 1939): 53-54.

Although ER let it be known that she was willing to face questions from the committee about the American Youth Congress, she was not given the chance. ER's association with leaders of the AYC and others suspected as being Communists had already been debated in Congress, e.g., *Congressional Record* (9 Oct. 1939): 218-19.

F1336 Theoharis, Athan G., and John Stuart Cox. *The Boss: J. Edgar Hoover and the Great American Inquisition*. Philadelphia: Temple Univ. Pr., 1988. xi + 489p. Index. Notes.

An extensive note describes Hoover's surveillance of ER via organizations and individuals: American Youth Congress, International Student Service, and Joseph Lash. In 1953 Hoover shared with the Eisenhower administration "proof" of ER's affair with Lash (pp. 191-93). The content of the note was discussed earlier in his "J. Edgar, Eleanor--and Herbert Too?" *Nation* 234 (20 Feb. 1982): 200-201. Partial texts of Hoover's files are contained in *From the Secret Files of J. Edgar Hoover*, pp. 59-65 (Chicago: Dee, 1991). There is also Curt Gentry, *J. Edgar Hoover: The Man and the Secrets*, pp. 289-307 (New York: Norton, 1991). Similar coverge is also in Richard Gid Powers, *Secrecy and Power: The Life of J. Edgar Hoover*, pp. 265-66 (New York: Free, 1987).

For a discussion of ER's file dating from 1924, see p. 472 of Blanche Wiesen Cook, "The Impact of Anti-Communism in American Life." *Science & Society* 53 (Winter 1989): 470-75.

F1337 "They Tried to Get Me, Too." *U.S. News & World Report* 37 (20 Aug. 1954): 56-61, 64-71.

This interview with Martin Dies includes his recollection of events surrounding Lash's congressional testimony and ER's involvement (p. 59). The subsequent "Mrs. Roosevelt, Mr. Dies Debate: Recollections of Early Congressional Inquiry into Communism." 37 (27 Aug. 1954): 94-95 contains the texts of ER's 17 Aug. letter to Dies disputing the comments made in his interview plus Dies' 19 Aug. reply.

F1338 "23 1/2-Cent Chicken Dinners for Beauties in Distress." *Literary Digest* 116 (8 July 1933): 22.

When ER paid a visit to Camp Tera, a youth camp for needy young women in N.Y. sponsored by her, she was pleased with the quality of the food but disappointed with the number of girls who are taking advantage of the facility. Her call for the establishment of the camp is reported as "Girl Camp Mapped by Mrs. Roosevelt." *New York Times* 2 June 1933: 21.

F1339 Wandersee, Winifred. "ER and American Youth: Politics and Personality in a Bureaucratic Age." *Without Precedent: The Life and Career of Eleanor Roosevelt*. Everywoman: Studies in History, Literature, and Culture. Ed. Joan Hoff-Wilson and Marjorie Lightman. Bloomington: Indiana Univ. Pr., 1984. 63-87. Sources.

Her involvement with the National Youth Admin. and the American Youth Congress.

F1340 Wechsler, James. *The Age of Suspicion*. New York: Random House, 1953; Westport: Greenwood, 1971; New York: Primus, 1985. 333p. Index.
In her controversial association with the youth movement ER had the final word because of the mutual support which she developed with youth who did not realize the ideological leanings of the American Youth Congress (p. 72).

F1341 Weiss, Max. "Reply to Mrs. Roosevelt." *Weekly Review* (Young Communist League) 8 (1 June 1943): 3, 14.
When ER attacks the Young Communist League in speeches to youth groups, she hinders the efforts of all youth groups to unite and work for victory in the war.

F1342 "What the Lady Said." *Ave Maria* 70 (24 Sept. 1949): 388.
In her "If You Ask Me" column for Aug. 1949 she claims that she continued her association with the American Youth Congress in an attempt to change its Communist direction. That explanation is hard to accept.

F1343 Williams, Aubrey. Foreword. *Final Report of the National Youth Administration, Fiscal Years 1936-1943*. Washington: GPO, 1944. v-viii.
Includes a tribute to ER, "one of the NYA's ablest and wisest friends" for "her deep and sympathetic understanding of the problems of youth" (pp. vi-vii).

F1344 Wreszin, Michael. "The Dies Committee, 1938." *Congress Investigates: A Documentary History, 1792-1974*. Vol. 4. Ed. Arthur M. Schlesinger, Jr. and Roger Bruns. New York: Chelsea House in association with Bowker, 1975. 2923-3112.
Discussion of Dies Committee with official sources reprinted.

F1345 "Youth." *Fortune* 21 (May 1940): 88-92, 99-100, 102.
In an article on youth, their problems, and the American Youth Congress ER is identified as the most valiant supporter of the AYC and as a public figure trusted by youth (p. 100).

F1346 "Youth Congress in Washington Hears President Roosevelt Tell Them They're All Wet." *Life* 8 (26 Feb. 1940): 17.
Related articles "Youthful Pacifists Parade against War But Lodge in Barricks as Army Guests" (pp. 18-19) and "First Lady Befriends Grim Young Delegates" (pp. 20-21) follow. Captioned photographs plus minimal text report on the 9-12 Feb. 1940 Citizenship Institute with most attention given to ER's activities: she helped to arrange housing, was one of few to attend the parade, and sat through speeches including those critical of FDR.

F1347 *Youth Demands a Peaceful World: Report of 2d World Youth Congress, Vassar College, Poughkeepsie, New York, August 16-23, 1938*. New York: World Youth Congress, n.d. 52p.
ER was in attendance. Although she is featured in two photographs, there is no text about her (pp. 27-28).

F1348 *Youth Today: Proceedings of the Hearing and Conference, October 29, 1934, New York City*. New York: Community Chests and Councils, Inc., 1934. 34p.

ER participated in the hearing conducted by Harry A. Overstreet on jobs, recreation, youth clubs, personal conduct, and social responsibility (pp. 8-25). In "'Youth Meets on Its Eternal Quest': The Younger Generation Pours Out Its Tragic Story at a Conference and Hears Good Advice from the Elders." *Literary Digest* 118 (10 Nov. 1934): 19 it is reported that after it was advocated that there be government subsidies for marriage, she argued that someone has to pay for such subsidies.

CARDINAL SPELLMAN AND PAROCHIAL SCHOOLS

Background and General Accounts

F1349 Boggs, Ronald James. "Culture of Liberty: History of Americans United for Separation of Church and State, 1947-1973." Diss. Ohio State Univ., 1978. 789p.

Background on the legislation which resulted in the public dispute and details of the controversy (pp. 249-60).

F1350 "The Cardinal and the Lady." *Newsweek* 34 (1 Aug. 1949): 18.

Quotes from ER's initial remarks and Spellman's reaction.

F1351 "Cardinal Is Guest of Mrs. Roosevelt." *New York Times* 25 Aug. 1949: 25.

Spellman pays ER a surprise visit. They may have reconciled their differences.

F1352 Cooney, John. *The American Pope: The Life and Times of Francis Cardinal Spellman.* New York: Times Books, 1984. xix + 364p. Index. Bibliography. Notes.

The public controversy over ER's support of the Barden Bill, the long-standing reasons for mutual dislike between the two, public reaction to the controversy, and the role of Ed Flynn in bringing the matter to a close (pp. 176-79, 181-85).

F1353 Crowell, Paul. "Mayor Seeks Peace of Mrs. Roosevelt and the Cardinal." *New York Times* 3 Aug. 1949: 1, 14.

N.Y. Mayor William O'Dwyer expresses hope that the dispute can be resolved, a controversy which he considers damaging to the city.

F1354 Dales, Douglas S. "Cardinal Gives School Ideas; 'Fair,' Says Mrs. Roosevelt." *New York Times* 6 Aug. 1949: 1, 10.

Spellman explains that he favors federal aid to parochial schools for only health services and transportation. ER considers his statement to be "clarifying." The texts of their respective statements (p 10). Support for providing some types of aid to all school children is expressed in the editorial "All America's Children." *New York Times* 7 Aug. 1949, sect. 4: 8. Her acknowledgment that certain types of aid could be acceptable is reported in "View Is Modified by Mrs. Roosevelt." *New York Times* 24 Aug. 1949: 20.

F1355 Dewey, Ralph Francis. "Federal Aid to Education: Equalization of Educational Opportunity." Thesis (M.S.E.) Southern Ill. Univ., 1950. 72p. Bibliography. Notes.

An abbreviated account of the controversy based on articles from the *New York Times.*

F1356 Gannon, Robert I. *The Cardinal Spellman Story.* Garden City: Doubleday, 1962. vi + 447p. Index. Notes.

Discusses the public controversy between ER and Spellman, reprints 1949 "My Day" columns for 23 June and 8 and 15 July and the subsequent exchange of letters between the two (pp. 314-21).

F1357 Grant, Philip A., Jr. "Catholic Congressmen, Cardinal Spellman, Eleanor Roosevelt, and the 1949-1950 Federal Aid to Education Controversy." *Records of the American Catholic Historical Society* 90 (Mar./Dec. 1979): 3-14. Notes.
Grant is critical of the actions of both ER and Spellman in his description based on congressional documents and newspaper accounts. Although he makes laudatory comments about ER, he regrets that she expressed her opinions about the issue in several "My Day" columns.

F1358 Lachman, Seymour P. "The Cardinal, the Congressmen,and the First Lady." *Journal of Church and State* 7 (Winter 1965): 35-66. Notes.
A detailed treatment of the controversy including the background of the Barden Bill and ensuing press coverage particularly that in the *New York Times*.

F1359 "The Lady Replies." *Newsweek* 34 (8 Aug. 1949): 14-15.
About ER's response to Spellman.

F1360 "A Letter from the United States. The Cardinal and Mrs. Roosevelt: Background to an Argument. From an American Correspondent." *Tablet* [London] 194 (20 Aug. 1949): 117-18.
The current status of financial support for education and highlights of the controversy.

F1361 "Mrs. Roosevelt Stands by Her Position on Schools." *Christian Century* 66 (7 Sept. 1949): 1028.
After Spellman made his conciliatory visit to Hyde Park it was reported that ER had changed her position. However, "My Day" for 24 Aug. reveals that she still opposes federal aid for the basic costs of parochial education.

F1362 "Mrs. Roosevelt Writes Cardinal." *New York Times* 27 July 1949: 21.
She responds to Spellman's letter. Support for her position is received from a variety of groups including the American Jewish Congress and the Association of Baptist Colleges and Schools.

F1363 "My Day in the Lion's Mouth." *Time* 54 (1 Aug. 1949): 11.
Report and analysis of the exchange between ER and Spellman. "Truce." *Time* 54 (15 Aug. 1949): 15-16 reports on subsequent conciliatory statements issued by them.

F1364 Parke, Richard H. "Cardinal Calls Mrs. Roosevelt Anti-Catholic on School Bill." *New York Times* 23 July 1949: 1, 26.
The public dispute between Spellman and ER begins. Accompanied by ER's 23 June "My Day" column and Spellman's 21 July letter (p. 26).

F1365 ---. "Clergymen Enter the Controversy of Spellman and Mrs. Roosevelt." *New York Times* 25 July 1949: 13.
Support for both ER and Spellman is reported.

F1366 ---. "Lehman Condemns Spellman Attack on Mrs. Roosevelt." *New York Times* 24 July 1949: 1, 36.

Former N.Y. Gov. Herbert Lehman denies any religious bias on ER's part and defends her right to state her opinion.

F1367 ---. "Mrs. Roosevelt Denies Bias, Citing Her Support of [Al] Smith." *New York Times* 26 July 1949: 1, 25.

On 25 July she uses "My Day" to reaffirm her position and her respect for all religions. Text of the column is included (p. 25).

F1368 "Pope Sees Dispute Resolved by Cardinal, Mrs. Roosevelt." *New York Times* 14 Aug. 1949: 1, 15.

Pope Pius XII tells American journalists that the statements issued by the two should end the matter.

F1369 Stevens, Austin. "Mrs. Roosevelt Tells Cardinal She Must Speak Out on Issues." *New York Times* 28 July 1949: 1, 16.

Discussion and text of her letter.

F1370 Stokes Anson Phelps. "Controversy between Cardinal Spellman and Mrs. Roosevelt." *Church and State in the United States*. Vol. 2. By Anson Phelps Stokes. New York, Harper, 1950. Notes. 744-58.

Detailed account of the controversy including full or partial text of relevant "My Day" columns and letters between Spellman and ER. Reissued in revised one volume ed., pp. 436-42 (New York: Harper & Row, 1964).

F1371 "What Is the Barden Bill?" *Churchman* 163 (1 Sept. 1949): 12-14.

Text of radio discussion between Rep. William Barden and a Washington commentator. The bill is discussed, but the public controversy is not mentioned.

Writings in Support of Spellman

F1372 *Ave Maria*.

During the controversy several editorials appeared in support of Spellman and attacking ER's position and those who came to her defense. General criticism of ER's earlier activities as First Lady is also included. Editorials include "Knights to Arms." 70 (6 Aug. 1949): 163 about defense by Herbert Lehman and others, and "Pegler Refutes Lehman." 70 (20 Aug. 1949): 228 about Westbrook Pegler's attack on Lehman and Pegler's review of criticism of ER's earlier activities.

In "Mrs. Roosevelt Misses Bus." 71 (1 Apr. 1950): 386 it is reported that she never expected anyone else to pay the cost of sending her children to private schools. She seems not to realize that Catholics do not expect that either. We have already paid the cost of school buses through our taxes it is stated.

F1373 Burnham, Philip. "The Separation of Cardinal Spellman and Mrs. Roosevelt." *Commonweal* 50 (5 Aug. 1949): 404-5.

Ideology is at the heart of the dispute. Our Catholic conceptions vs. her "ideological liberalism" and "secularism."

F1374 "The Cardinal States the Issue Clearly." *Catholic School Journal* 49 (Sept. 1949): 228.

The Cardinal has made his position clear: he opposes the Barden Bill, because it denies federal aid to parochial schools for auxiliary services. ER realizes that his statement is clear and fair, but she objects to any religion trying to pressure the government.

F1375 "Clarifying and Fair." *Commonweal* 50 (19 Aug. 1949): 452-53.
The Cardinal's contention that tax dollars paid by all could be used for auxiliary services in all schools deserves consideration.

F1376 "Freedom from Irresponsible Opinion." *Sign* 29 (Sept. 1949): 9-10.
Questions ER's qualifications for having an opinion on whether Catholic schools should receive federal support. Qualified or not, she is bigoted on the issue.

F1377 "Light on a Dormant Issue." *Social Justice Review* 42 (Nov. 1949): 231-32; 42 (Dec. 1949): 268-69.
A reprinting of Frederick J. Zwierlein's statement about ER's position with beginning and concluding editorial additions. Zwierlein traces the relationship of church, state, and education back to the early days of the republic in order to demonstrate how misinformed ER is.

F1378 "Mrs. F.D.R. Comments on America." *America* 84 (31 Mar. 1951): 739.
While she believes that parochial schools deserve the same auxiliary services as public school, she advocates fewer services. She should remember that all of these services are supported by tax dollars and that all types of schools deserve to receive them.

F1379 Sheerin, John B. "Church, State and Mrs. Roosevelt." *Catholic World* 169 (Sept. 1949): 401-5.
ER's objection to federal aid to parochial schools is based on her liberalism and her refusal to accept the power and guidance of "supernatural religion." Her reverence for democracy and reliance on the will of the people to determine what is right for the country is dangerous.

Writings in Support of Roosevelt

F1380 "Basic Church-State Issue." *Congressional Record Appendix* (28 July 1949): A4855-56.
Includes editorial from *Greenville News* [Greenville, S.C.] in support of separation of church and state as defended by ER.

F1381 "Cardinal Spellman Climbs Down." *Christian Century* 66 (17 Aug. 1949): 955.
Spellman now admits that ER was right to cite constitutional grounds in her objections to federal aid for parochial schools.

F1382 "Cardinal Spellman Overreaches." Editorial. *Christian Century* 66 (3 Aug. 1949): 907.
Spellman has been "reckless" and "arrogant" in his attacks on ER.

F1383 "The Cardinal's Blunder." Editorial. *Churchman* 163 (1 Sept. 1949): 4.
What a mistake it was to attack ER. We are unaware of any prejudice she might have toward Catholics, and we agree with her defense of the separation of church and state.

F1384 "Echoes." *Time* 54 (8 Aug. 1949): 54-55.
Reactions of non-Roman Catholic groups in support of ER's position.

F1385 Laughlin, Nancy Bartlett. "Christian Attitude." Letter. *Nation* 169 (13 Aug. 1949): 163-64.
A typical letter in defense of ER's position. For others, see the *New York Times* 27 July 1949: 22.

F1386 "Mrs. Roosevelt Replies to the Cardinal." *Christian Century* 66 (10 Aug. 1949): 931.
A comparison of the letters which ER and Spellman exchanged reveals Spellman's arrogance and the dangers of "clerical absolutism."

F1387 "Oxnam on School Aid." *Churchman* 163 (1 Sept. 1949): 11-12.
Text of 8 Aug. radio discussion between Bishop Oxnam and a Washington radio commentator (Spellman declined an invitation to participate). Oxnam claims that the church hierarchy has hurt Roman Catholics, and he regrets Spellman's attack on ER. For another report, see "Oxnam Denounces Catholics' 'Plan.'" *New York Times* 8 Aug. 1949: 13.

F1388 Pfeffer, Leo. *Church, State and Freedom*. Rev. ed. Boston: Beacon, 1967. xiii + 832p. Index. Bibliography. Notes.
Account of the 1949 controversy over federal aid to parochial schools. ER's position is defended (pp. 590-92).

F1389 "The Press Comments on the Roosevelt-Spellman Dispute." *Liberty: A Magazine of Religious Freedom* 44 (Fourth Quarter 1949): 13-28.
A statement signed "F.H.Y." introduces a series of editorials about the controversy. Most of them defend ER's position. Included are "The Romans Are Worried." *Churchman* (July 1949); "Helping the Red Fascist War on Religion." *Boston Daily Record* 6 July 1949; "Bigotry Is Not the Issue." *St. Louis Post Dispatch* 10 July 1949; "Cardinal Spellman Does Not Aid His Cause." *Courier-Journal* [Louisville, Ky.] 23 July 1949; "The Cardinal and Mrs. Roosevelt." *Milwaukee Journal* 23 July 1949; "More Heat Than Light." *Minneapolis Star* 23 July 1949; "Cardinal Spellman's Letter." *St.Louis Post Dispatch* 24 July 1949; "The Cardinal's Letter." *Washington Sunday Star* 24 July 1949; "Examining an Issue." *Minneapolis Morning Tribune* 25 July 1949; "Parochial School Issue." *Minneapolis Star* 25 July 1949; "Cardinal's Letter Doesn't Help." *Register and Tribune* [Des Moines, Iowa] 25 July 1949; "A Regrettable Incident." *Denver Post* 26 July 1949; "Only a Side Issue." *Arizona Daily Star* [Tucson, Ariz.] 27 July 1949; "Any Cause Is Hurt When Temper Rises." *Detroit News* 27 July 1949; "Church Schools." *Chicago Daily News* 29 July 1949; "We Take Our Stand." *Detroit Free Press* 29 July 1949; "Cardinal Spellman Overreaches." *Christian Century* (3 Aug. 1949); "Never Say Dead." *Washington Post* 4 Aug. 1949; "Mrs. Roosevelt Replies to the Cardinal." *Christian Century* (10 Aug. 1949); and "A Cardinal Error." *Pathfinder* (10 Aug. 1949).

F1390 "The Shape of Things." *Nation* 169 (30 July 1949): 97.
Spellman's attack on ER is an attempt to influence politics. Herbert Lehman, however, has defended her and most likely at a high political price.

F1391 "The Shape of Things." *Nation* 169 (13 Aug. 1949): 145-46.
The Cardinal's actions have hurt the chances for any federal aid to education.

F1392 "Spellman vs. Democracy." *Churchman* 163 (1 Sept. 1949): 20.
The text of the American Civil Liberties Union's resolution condemning Spellman's attack on ER and his confusing the separation of church and state with religious intolerance.

FIRST LADY OF THE WORLD

UN Delegate: As Reported in United Nations Publications

F1393 "Assembly Debate on Repatriation and Resettlement." *United Nations Bulletin* 6 (1 June 1949): 599-601.
A 12 May debate in the Third Committee about refugees was brought to an end by ER's argument that a Polish resolution under consideration presented nothing new.

F1394 "Convention on Freedom of Information: Committee Defers Action." *United Nations Bulletin* 7 (15 Oct. 1949): 473-74.
On 27 Sept. the Third Committee considered two proposals related to the Draft Convention on Freedom of Information. ER spoke in favor of the proposal to direct the Commission on Human Rights to address freedom of information in the covenant.

F1395 "Establishment of High Commissioner's Office: Assembly Approves Third Committee Recommendations on Refugees." *United Nations Bulletin* 7 (15 Dec. 1949): 721-23.
The Third Committee had approved a resolution to establish the Office of the High Commissioner for Refugees, but in the General Assembly discussion ER introduced four amendments which were subsequently adopted. Text of the amendments and ER's comments.

F1396 "Fund Appeal for Refugee Aid Recommended by Committee." *United Nations Bulletin* 12 (1 Feb. 1952): 133-39.
On 10 Jan. the Third Committee recommended authorization for the High Commissioner for Refugees to seek emergency funds for the neediest groups. In the debate ER responded to Byelorussian charges that refugees were being ill-treated by some of the democratic nations (pp. 137-38).

F1397 "A High Commissioner for Refugees: Committee Recommends Appointment." *United Nations Bulletin* 7 (1 Dec. 1949): 690-93.
On 15 Nov. the Third Committee recommended the position. The particulars of the appointment were forwarded by opposing U.S. and French resolutions. ER spoke on "the definition of refugees, who should appoint the High Commissioner, and the latter's authority to allocate funds" (p. 690). A joint U.S.-French resolution was accepted.

F1398 Katzin, Alfred. "Shall We Fail the Children?" *United Nations Bulletin* 6 (15 May 1949): 516-17.

Report on a Dec. 1948 debate on the continuation of the United Nations Appeal for Children includes a plea made by ER for continuing the program.

F1399 "Measures to Relieve Housing Shortage." *United Nations Bulletin* 11 (15 Dec. 1951): 538-39.

Third Committee debate on "a comprehensive plan of information, advice and assistance to governments to increase housing for low income groups." ER supported the original proposals made by Greece.

F1400 "New United Nations Gift Centre." *United Nations Bulletin* 13 (15 Oct. 1952): 347.

On 13 Oct. ER opened a display and sales area for arts and handicrafts of member nations.

F1401 "Personalities of the General Assembly." *United Nations Weekly Bulletin* 1 (17 Dec. 1946): 28-29.

ER is one of those featured. A few facts about her life plus a listing of her UN responsibilities (p. 29).

F1402 "Plan for Refugee Office Adopted." *United Nations Bulletin* 10 (1 Jan. 1951): 61-66.

On 14 Dec. 1950 the General Assembly approved the establishment of the High Commissioner's Office for Refugees. During the three days of debate which had taken place in the Third Committee ER stressed the importance of the debate, argued successfully against a Byelorussian amendment indicting the U.S., United Kingdom, and France of exploiting refugees, and pursued a definition of "refugee."

F1403 "Practical Action for Social Progress." *United Nations Bulletin* 11 (15 Dec. 1951): 535-37.

Report on resolution adopted by the Third Committee on 27 Nov. calling for the UN to review its social programs and develop a plan of action. ER succeeded in defeating USSR amendments critical of the Economic and Social Council's past actions in this area.

F1404 "Proposal to Continue Children's Fund for Three Years." *United Nations Bulletin* 9 (1 Nov. 1950): 489-94.

A report on ER's lengthy remarks constitutes a large portion of this announcement that the Third Committee has adopted a resolution to continue UNICEF for another three years. She argued for the need to realize "permanent improvements" of the problems affecting children, not just emergency measures.

F1405 "Self-Determination Recognized--Progress Reports Requested." *United Nations Bulletin* 14 (1 Jan. 1953): 32-33.

Includes ER's remarks in support of two U.S. amendments to resolutions related to self-determination. The General Assembly adopted the resolutions but without the U.S. amendments.

F1406 "Seminar on Teaching United Nations." *United Nations Bulletin* 5 (1 Sept. 1948): 682.

At Hyde Park ER hosts participants of an international seminar on the UN being held at Adelphi College.

F1407 "Soviet Wives of Foreign Citizens: Assembly Recommends Withdrawal of U.S.S.R. Measures." *United Nations Bulletin* 6 (15 May 1949): 522-25.

On 25 Apr. the General Assembly considered a complaint lodged by Chile that Soviet women married to citizens of the U.S., United Kingdom, Canada, and France were not being allowed to leave the Soviet Union. Lengthy excerpt from ER's statement about the problem and what the U.S. is doing to resolve it (p. 523).

F1408 "Stateless Persons: Governments Will Review Draft Protocol." *United Nations Bulletin* 13 (1 Nov. 1952): 417-18.

21 Oct. discussion and vote in the Third Committee on Draft Protocol on the Status of Stateless Persons which would extend to stateless persons those same benefits afforded refugees under the un-ratified Refugees Convention. ER states that she will vote for it, "although there was little likelihood that the United States would ever accede to the protocol."

F1409 Stones, Betty. "The First Ladies of the World." *United Nations World* 6 (Feb. 1952): 28-31.

Because of her humanitarianism ER is the best known American woman. The acceptance of the human rights covenant will be the "greatest achievement of any woman in history" (p. 30).

F1410 "Suppressing Traffic in Persons: Third Committee's Progress on Draft Convention." *United Nations Bulletin* 7 (1 Nov. 1949): 538-44.

On 30 Sept. the Third Committee began nine days of debate on a "Draft Convention for the Suppression of the Traffic in Persons and of the Exploitation of the Prostitution of Others." ER figured significantly in the debate with her most noteworthy contribution being a successful attempt to clarify the procedures for referring disputes to the International Court of Justice.

F1411 "Treatment of Immigrant Labor." *United Nations Bulletin* 7 (1 Nov. 1949): 553-54, 562.

On 17 Oct. the Third Committee considered a Polish request that the General Assembly acknowledge that many countries discriminate against immigrant labor. ER spoke in favor of the British proposal to apply the International Labor Office Convention to immigrants. In her statement she discussed the status of immigrants and displaced persons in the U.S. (p. 554). Her statements were summarized on p. 656 of "Discrimination against Immigrant Labor." *United Nations Bulletin* 7 (1 Dec. 1949): 655-57.

F1412 United Nations Official Records.

The UN issued the verbatim proceedings of the General Assembly, the Economic and Social Council, the Third Committee, and the Human Rights Commission and reports produced by the commission and ad-hoc committees. These records are also available as micropaque (*Mimeographed and Printed Documents*. New York: Readex Microprint).

For references to statements by and about ER, see *Index to the Official Records of the First Part of the First Session of the General Assembly (London, 1946)* (London:

United Nations, [1946?]); Millwood: Kraus Reprint, 1973). *Index to the Proceedings of the General Assembly, First Special Session-Second Session* (New York: United Nations, 1947; Millwood: Kraus Reprint, 1973). *Index to Proceedings of the General Assembly, Second Special Session-Ninth Session, 1948-54.* 4 vols. (New York: United Nations, 1948-54; Millwood: Kraus Reprint, 1973).

There is also *Checklist of United Nations Documents, Commission on Human Rights, 1947-1949.* Sales no. 1952.I.6 (New York, United Nations, 1952) and *Ten Years of United Nations Publications, 1945 to 1955: A Complete Catalog.* Sales no. 1955.I.8 (New York, United Nations, 1955).

United Nations Documents, 1946-1960: Checklist of the Readex Microprint Edition (New York: Readex, 1978) lists the contents of the Readex micropaque ed. of UN records.

F1413 "Women on the General Assembly Scene." *United Nations Bulletin* 13 (15 Nov. 1952): 452-54.

Photographs of women in the UN and summaries of their activities. ER has traveled extensively for the UN and has dedicated herself to the cause of human rights (p. 454). Praise for her courage and leadership.

F1414 "Women Representatives in the General Assembly." *United Nations Bulletin* 5 (1 Dec. 1948): 976-77.

Photographs and brief statements.

UN Delegate: As Reported in Department of State Publications

F1415 "Communist Charges against U.S. Territorial Policies." *Department of State Bulletin* 27 (29 Dec. 1952): 1032-33.

ER's 24 Nov. 1952 statement in the Third Committee countering Soviet claims about conditions in Puerto Rico. Also as "Statement to Committee III (Social, Humanitarian, and Cultural) of the UN General Assembly on Defense of American Territorial Policies." in *Annals of America*, v. 17, pp. 128-30 (Chicago: Encyclopaedia Britannica, 1968).

F1416 *Foreign Relations of the United States, 1946. Vol. I. General: The United Nations.* Dept. of State Publication, 8573. Washington: GPO, 1972. xiii + 1544p. Index.

Appointment of U.S. delegates, letter of appointment from HST, and initial committee assignments. At the first meeting of the delegation (17 Oct.) ER raised questions about the policy on voting in committee (pp. 44-45). She suggested locating UN headquarters in Hyde Park, N.Y. (p. 103). The minutes of all 1946 meetings of the delegation reveal how involved she became in the discussions and deliberations.

F1417 *Foreign Relations of the United States, 1947. Vol. I. General: The United Nations.* Dept. of State Publication, 8674. Washington: GPO, 1973. xxiii + 1096p. Index.
Minutes of meetings of the UN delegation.

F1418 *Foreign Relations of the United States, 1947. Vol. V. The Near East and Africa.* Dept. of State Publication, 8592. ix + 1377p. Index.
Actions of U.S. delegation regarding Palestine.

F1419 *Foreign Relations of the United States, 1948. Vol. I. General: The United Nations, Pt. 1.* Dept. of State Publication, 8805. Washington: GPO, 1975. xvi + 505p. + xv. Index.
Minutes of meetings of the U.S. delegation.

F1420 *Foreign Relations of the United States, 1948. Vol. IV. Eastern Europe: The Soviet Union.* Dept. of State Publication, 8743. Washington: GPO, 1974. xv + 1161p. Index.
Communications praising the tone of ER's 28 Sept. 1948 speech at the Sorbonne (pp. 379, 931).

F1421 *Foreign Relations of the United States. 1948. Vol. V. The Near East, South Asia, and Africa.* 2 vols. (xvi + 1730p. + xxxi). Dept. of State Publication, 8840. Washington: GPO, 1976. Index.
Communications about Palestine between ER as acting head of the U.S. delegation and Secretary of State George Marshall.

F1422 *Foreign Relations of the United States, 1949. Vol. I. National Security Affairs, Foreign Economic Policy.* Dept. of State Publication, 8850. Washington: GPO, 1976. xxv + 836p. Index.
Minutes of the U.S. delegation's discussions of arms control.

F1423 *Foreign Relations of the United States, 1949. Vol. II. The United Nations: The Western Hemisphere.* Dept. of State Publication, 8789. Washington: GPO, 1975. xii + 827p. Index.
Minutes of meetings of the U.S. delegation.

F1424 *Foreign Relations of the United States, 1949. Vol. IV. Western Europe.* 81st Congress, 2d Session. House Document 81-742, Vol. IV. Dept. of State Publication, 8791. Washington: GPO, 1975. x + 878p. Index.
Communication to Dept. of State concerning the U.S. delegation's discussion about change in U.S. position toward Spain (pp. 737-39).

F1425 *Foreign Relations of the United States, 1950. Vol. II. The United Nations: The Western Hemisphere.* Dept. of State Publication, 8853. Washington: GPO, 1976, xii + 1088p.
Minutes of meetings of the U.S. delegation.

F1426 *Foreign Relations of the United States, 1950. Vol. V. The Near East, South Asia, and Africa.* Dept. of State Publication, 8927. Washington: GPO, 1978. xvii + 1889p. Index.
Internal Dept. of State communication about request from ER on how to reply to a human rights inquiry regarding French action in Tunis (pp. 1767-77).

F1427 *Foreign Relations of the United States, 1950. Vol. VI. East Asia and the Pacific.* Dept. of State Publication, 8858. Washington: GPO, 1976. x + 1581p. Index.
Minutes of the U.S. delegation's discussions about Formosa.

F1428 *Foreign Relations of the United States, 1950. Vol. VII. Korea.* Dept. of State Publication, 8859. Washington: GPO, 1976. xiii + 1675p. Index.
Minutes of the U.S. delegation's discussions about the situation in Korea.

F1429 *Foreign Relations of the United States. 1951. Vol. I. National Security Affairs: Foreign Economic Policy.* Dept. of State Publication, 8975. Washington: GPO, 1979. xii + 1774p. Index.
Minutes of meetings of the U.S. delegation.

F1430 *Foreign Relations of the United States, 1951. Vol. II. The United Nations: The Western Hemisphere.* Dept. of State Publication, 8962. Washington: GPO, 1979. xviii + 1720p. Index.
Minutes of meetings of the U.S. delegation. Letters and other communications between ER and Secretary of State Dean Acheson.

F1431 *Foreign Relations of the United States, 1951. Vol. VI. Asia and the Pacific.* 2 vols. (xi + 2276p.) Dept. of State Publication, 8889, 8918. Washington: GPO, 1977. Index.
Communications between ER as acting head of the U.S. delegation and Secretary of State Dean Acheson about the Kashmir dispute (pt. 2, pp. 1917-21).

F1432 *Foreign Relations of the United States, 1952-1954. Vol. III. United Nations Affairs.* Dept. of State Publication, 8957. Washington: GPO, 1979. xxii + 1629p. Index.
Minutes of meetings the U.S. delegation. Contains "United States Policy Regarding the Draft United Nations Covenants on Human Rights: The 1953 Change" which includes minutes of 1952 discussions about the status of the covenants and the U.S. position (pp. 1536-81).

F1433 *Foreign Relations of the United States, 1952-1954. Vol. IX. The Near and Middle East.* 2 vols. Dept. of State Publication, 9447, 9448. Washington: GPO, 1986. Index.
Communication from ER as acting head of the U.S. delegation to the Dept. of State concerning Arab-Israeli conflict (pt. 1, pp. 283-84). Minutes of U.S. delegation include ER's report on her visit to Arab refugee camps (pt. 2, pp. 1072-76).

F1434 "General Assembly of UNO." *Department of State Bulletin* 14 (20 Jan. 1946): 62-65, 83.
ER has told representatives of international groups that they can help the UN succeed by promoting its goals and explaining the work of the UN-related organizations.

F1435 "The International Children's Emergency Fund." *Documentary Textbook on the United Nations: Humanity's March Towards Peace.* 2d. ed., rev. and enl. By J. Eugene Harley. Los Angeles: Center for International Understanding, 1950. 315-19.
In a detailed look at the nature and value of the work of UNICEF greater financial support from UN member nations is called for. Text of ER's remarks before the Third Committee, 2 Dec. 1948. Also in *Relief for Children: Selected Statements United Nations Resolutions, September 21-December 12, 1948*, pp. 1-8 (Washington: Dept. of State, 1948).
Excerpted as "Two Years' Activity of the International Children's Emergency Fund." *Department of State Bulletin* 19 (26 Dec. 1948): 802-3.

F1436 "Soviet Attacks on Social Conditions in U.S." *Department of State Bulletin* 28 (19 Jan. 1953): 116-17.

ER refutes the Soviet bloc charge that preparations for war are resulting in a decline in the U.S. standard of living but admits that it is not as high as desired. Text of her statement to the Third Committee, 9 Dec. 1952.

F1437 "Statement by the U.S. Representative to the General Assembly." *Department of State Bulletin* 17 (2 Nov. 1947): 874-77.
The Yugoslav resolution to prevent dissemination of statements which could be detrimental to other nations should be rejected. A plea for freedom of the press. Text of ER's statement in the Third Committee, 24 Oct. 1947. Issued with statement by Warren R. Austin under common title "U.S. Rejects Resolutions Limiting Free Flow of Information."
Also as "False or Distorted Reports." *The United States and the United Nations: Report by the President to the Congress for the Year 1947*, pp. 294-98 (Washington: GPO, 1948).

F1438 "U.N. Deliberations on Draft Convention on the Political Rights of Women." *Department of State Bulletin* 28 (5 Jan. 1953): 29-32.
Text of ER's 12 and 15 Dec. 1952 statements in the Third Committee. Discussion of articles of the draft elaborating on rights for women (12 Dec.); defends the American concept of family in response to Soviet delegates' charge of discrimination against women and describes the rights and accomplishments of women, including black women, in the U.S. (15 Dec.).

F1439 "United Appeal for Children." *Relief for Children: Selected Statements United Nations Resolutions, September 21-December 12, 1948*. Dept. of State Publication, 3415. International Organization and Conference Series III, 24. Washington: Dept. of State, 1949. 9-15.
A plea for private and public contributions to support the International Children's Emergency Fund. Text of statement in the Third Committee, 2 Dec. 1948.

F1440 "The United States in the United Nations." *Department of State Bulletin* 19 (7 Nov. 1948): 575-76.
Includes extensive excerpts from ER's proposal for a Palestine refugee aid program.

F1441 "The Universal Validity of Man's Right to Self-Determination." *Department of State Bulletin* 27 (8 Dec. 1952): 917-19.
ER outlines the history of the concept of "self-determination" and calls for it to be applied to all peoples not just those in colonial states. Excerpts her statement in the Third Committee, 18 Nov. 1952.

F1442 "U.S. Position on International Refugee Organization." *Department of State Bulletin* 15 (24 Nov. 1946): 935-38.
Explanation of U.S. support of the IRO and lengthy rebuttal of the Soviet view on the organization and rights of refugees. Text of ER's statement in the Third Committee, 8 Nov. 1946. Also in *Documents on American Foreign Relations, Vol. 8, July 1, 1945-December 31, 1946*, pp. 396-400 (Princeton: Princeton Univ. Pr. for the World Peace Foundation, 1948). Summarized in *The United States in World Affairs, 1945-1947*, p. 78 (New York: Harper for the Council on Foreign Relations, 1947).

UN Delegate: Other Accounts

F1443 Atwell, Mary Welek. "Eleanor Roosevelt and the Cold War Consensus." *Diplomatic History* 3 (Winter 1979): 99-113. Notes.
ER considered the Truman Doctrine to be in conflict with the U.S. commitment to the UN. She persisted in her belief that the UN should be more than a means of legitimizing U.S. policy, that economics is the preferred way to approach the cold war, and that to promote the value of democracy is more effective than to simply oppose communism.

F1444 Carter, Jimmy. "Eleanor Roosevelt National Historic Site." *Public Papers of the Presidents of the United States: Jimmy Carter, 1977, Book 1--January 20 to June 24, 1977*. Washington: GPO, 1977. 1028.
Her greatest contribution was to human rights. At the UN and through other activities she worked to remove "the barriers of prejudice, discrimination, and injustice." Text of 26 May 1977 statement designating Val-Kill as a national historic site.

F1445 "Defying the Future in North Africa." *Christian Century* 69 (30 Apr. 1952): 517.
Praise for ER as the one who had the courage to speak against U.S. efforts to block UN investigation of charges against the French for their governing of Tunisia.

F1446 *Dinner in Honour of Eleanor Roosevelt*. London: The Pilgrims, 1946. 20p.
ER was the first woman to be honored by the Pilgrims, but the occasion was more a tribute to the memory of FDR and a statement of confidence in the future of the UN. Held in London, 4 Feb. 1946.

F1447 Du Bois, W.E.B. *The Correspondence of W.E.B. Du Bois*. 3 vols. Ed. Herbert Aptheker. Amherst: Univ. of Mass. Pr., 1973-1978. Index. Notes.
Vols. 2 and 3 contain references to ER by Du Bois and others. Of note is correspondence of 17 July 1946 (v. 3, p. 149) transmitting to her a draft of a letter about plans for the NAACP to petition the UN to take steps to see that the views of African peoples can be heard and 1 July 1948 (v. 3, pp. 188-89) about the NAACP petition to the UN to improve the rights of American blacks.
For discussion of the correspondence and circumstances surrounding the NAACP petition there is Gerald Horne, *Black and Red: W.E.B. Du Bois and the Afro-American Response to the Cold War, 1944-1963*, pp. 81-82, 84, 100-103 (Albany: State Univ. of N.Y. Pr., 1986).
Also see Jane Bedell, "UN News: Paper Victory." *New Republic* 117 (17 Nov. 1947): 30 which includes a discussion of the NAACP's petition to the UN about the lack of rights enjoyed by American blacks. ER, chair of the commission and also a board member of the NAACP, is in a difficult position. Through "My Day" she presents herself as a liberal, but as a spokesperson of the State Dept. is less so.
Another black American and a member of the first U.S. delegation to UN, Ralph Bunche, had welcomed ER's appointment with enthusiasm. The previous year ER had urged the appointment of a black to the delegation to the San Francisco organizational meeting of the UN. For both, see Brian Urquhart, *Ralph Bunche: An American Life*, pp. 116, 130 (New York: Norton, 1993).

F1448 ---. "The Winds of Time." *Chicago Defender* 27 Mar. 1948, City ed.: 19.
    In his column Du Bois criticizes ER who, as chair of the Commission on Human Rights, is ignoring the NAACP's petition because she believes that the UN cannot act on petitions.

F1449 Edwards, India. "Tribute to Mrs. Franklin D. Roosevelt." *Official Report of the Proceedings of the Democratic National Convention, Chicago, Illinois, July 21 to July 26 Inclusive 1952....* N.p.: Democratic National Committee, n.d. 125.
    Praise for ER's work with the UN. Text of address, 22 July 1952.

F1450 Eichelberger, Clark M. *Organizing for Peace: A Personal History of the Founding of the United Nations.* New York: Harper, 1977. xiii + 317p. Index. Notes.
    ER's work with the UN and the American Association for the United Nations (pp. 294-96).

F1451 Fasulo, Linda M. *Representing America: Experiences of U.S. Diplomats at the UN.* New York: Praeger, 1984. xvii + 337p. Index. Bibliography.
    Recollections of ER at the UN by Francis Wilcox, Arthur Vandenberg, Marietta Tree, and Shirley Temple Black (pp. 52-53, 83-85, 154).

F1452 "First Lady." *Time* 52 (25 Oct. 1948): 25-26.
    As she reaches her 64th birthday ER is known and respected throughout the world. In her work with the Commission on Human Rights she appears to be achieving the difficult task of developing a declaration of human rights for the world while holding her own against Soviet attacks on the U.S.

F1453 Ganin, Zv. *Truman, American Jewry, and Israel, 1945-1948.* New York: Holmes & Meier, 1979. xvi + 238p. Index. Bibliography. Notes.
    Draws from correspondence between ER and HST about the Jewish vote in the election of 1948 (pp. 180-81). ER and the U.S. position in the UN on the question of the partition of Palestine (pp. 128-30).

F1454 Gardner, Richard N. "'First Lady' of the Voice of America." *New York Times Magazine* 3 Feb. 1952: 14.
    In 1951 the Voice of America asked ER to serve as a link between the U.S. delegation and the French people by presenting a weekly radio broadcast, *The United Nations Today,* explaining the work of the UN from an American perspective. Reprinted in *Congressional Record Appendix* (7 Feb. 1952): A775-76 and in an abbreviated form in *Congressional Record* (22 Feb. 1985): 3229.

F1455 ---. "Human Rights: Eleanor Roosevelt and the United Nations." *Vital Speeches of the Day* 51 (1 Feb. 1985): 249-53.
    An analysis of her tenure at the UN, the development of the Universal Declaration of Human Rights, and her negotiations with the Soviets. Text of address, Washington, 10 Dec. 1984. Reprinted in *Congressional Record* (22 Feb. 1985): 3225-28.

F1456 Hahn, Lorena B. "Women Leaders in the United Nations." *Delta Kappa Gamma Bulletin* 29 (Fall 1962): 11-18.
    ER is recognized for her work with the Commission on Human Rights, as a delegate to the General Assembly, and for her present role of adviser to the U.S. delegation (pp. 11-12).

F1457 Holborn, Louise W. *Refugees, a Problem of Our Time: The Work of the United Nations High Commissioner for Refugees, 1951-1972.* 2 vols. By Louise H. Holborn with the assistance of Philip and Rita Chartrand. Metuchen: Scarecrow, 1975. Index. Bibliography. Notes.

When the UN deliberated on the establishment of a successor to the International Refugee Organization ER presented the U.S. position that the UN is a deliberative body not a relief organization, and to maintain control over the relief activities fiscal control should be retained by the UN General Assembly (v. 1, pp. 70-73).

F1458 Janeway, Elizabeth. "First Lady of the U.N." *New York Times Magazine* 22 Oct. 1950: 12, 61-65.

As the U.S. representative to the Third Committee and as chair of the Commission on Human Rights ER has learned to deal with the Russian delegates, conduct meetings, and either live with the policies of her own government or try to change them. Her position on the drafting of the covenants is a realistic one: go slowly and gain acceptance for a covenant on civil and political rights before addressing the sensitive areas of economic and social rights. Also in *Women: Their Changing Roles*, pp. 303-5 (New York: Arno, 1973).

F1459 Jessup, Philip C. *The Birth of Nations.* New York: Columbia Univ. Pr., 1974. xiv + 361p. Index. Notes.

His account of ER's attitude about the UN's role in the creation of Israel (pp. 267-69, 286). Relies heavily on Lash's *Eleanor: The Years Alone.*

F1460 Kahn, E.J., Jr. "The Years Alone." *New Yorker* 24 (12 June 1948): 30-34, 36, 39-41; 24 (19 June 1948): 30-34, 36, 39-41.

ER as UN delegate and chair of the Commission on Human Rights in a comprehensive study of her activities since the death of FDR.

F1461 Kohn, Hans. "Remarks by Hans Kohn, College of the City of New York, following Speech by Eleanor Roosevelt on Why the United Nations Is Unpopular." *Why the United Nations Is Unpopular and What We Can Do About It.* By Eleanor Roosevelt. N.p.: n.p., [1952?]. 7p.

After praising ER's work with the UN, he takes issue with some of the points in her speech. But his remarks deal more with his views on the UN than with her speech.

F1462 Lamson, Peggy. *Roger Baldwin, Founder of the American Civil Liberties Union: A Portrait.* Boston: Houghton Mifflin, 1976. xii + 304p. Index.

ER was the subject of one of Lamson's interviews with Baldwin who respected ER's work with the UN while sharing her frustration with the organization (pp. 275-76).

F1463 Lima, Oscar de. "The UN's First Lady: Mrs. Eleanor Roosevelt." *UN 20 = The United Nations: Twenty Years.* New York: United Nations Association of the United States, 1965. 108-9, 162.

She inspired peoples of all nations as she tried to improve their lives by ensuring basic human rights. Her greatest contribution was the Universal Declaration of Human Rights.

F1464 Manly, Chesly. *The UN Record: Ten Fateful Years for America*. Chicago: Regnery, 1955. xi + 256p. Index. Notes.

Manly's review of the UN includes evidence of why ER is unfit to represent the U.S. Her proposal for the establishment of a Subcommission on Freedom of Information and of the Press played into the hands of the Communists (pp. 116-17). Her sordid record of support for Communist youth organizations (pp. 151-53). The insincerity of her statements about the effect the covenants would have on American rights and liberties (pp. 204-5). She calls for constraint in criticizing Communist countries (pp. 234).

F1465 Manzon, Jean, and Joao Gray. "A Falta de Roosevelt." *O Cruzeiro* (12 Julho 1947): 8-16.

A tribute to ER as UN delegate and member of the Commission on Human Rights. Some photographs are captioned with statements by her on human rights. Also addresses Fala. In Portuguese.

F1466 McDonough, Aloysius. "If You Ask Me." *Sign* 29 (Jan. 1950): 49-50.

In her Sept. 1949 column ER displays her agnosticism. Just like many of the other UN delegates who have the world's future in their hands, she is an agnostic and is indifferent to "man's immortality and eternal responsibility." Reprinted from *Indiana Catholic & Record*. Related articles on her beliefs about immortality and her fitness to represent the U.S. issued in *Ave Maria* are "Upside Down Thinking." 72 (18 Nov. 1950): 645, "Mrs. Roosevelt's Appraisal." 73 (24 Feb. 1951): 228, "Mrs. Roosevelt Speculates." 74 (29 Dec. 1951): 803, "Minister Off Course." 75 (5 Jan. 1952): 5, "More Confusion." 75 (26 Jan. 1952): 99, and "Mrs. F.D.R. Wrong Again." 75 (10 May 1952): 580-81.

F1467 Miller, Nathan. *The Roosevelt Chronicles*. Garden City: Doubleday, 1979. vi + 377p. Index. Bibliography.

ER as UN delegate (pp. 339-40).

F1468 "Mon Jour." *Newsweek* 32 (11 Oct. 1948): 40.

In Paris her responsibilities with the UN, speaking engagements, and her column make for busy days.

F1469 "Mrs. Roosevelt Is Elected Chairman of U.N. Human Rights Commission." *New York Times* 28 Jan. 1947: 13.

She is elected to chair the commission and predicts that the most difficult task will be to enforce a statement of human rights.

F1470 "Mrs. Roosevelt's Resignation." Editorial. *New York Times* 18 Jan. 1953: 12.

Praise for a job well done at the UN and hope that she will continue her public career in some way.

F1471 "The Mystery of Mrs. Roosevelt...Dodging the Fact of Soviet Genocide." *America* 86 (12 Jan. 1952): 385.

As acting head of the U.S. delegation ER does not have the right priorities. She considers disarmament the major issue while ignoring the more serious problem of Soviet genocide.

F1472 "No One Like Her." *Democratic Digest* 23 (Mar. 1946): 6.

Importance of ER's appointment to the UN delegation and the commitment which she has made to her duties.

F1473 "Nomination of Eleanor Roosevelt." *Nation* 161 (29 Dec. 1945): 722.

Praise for her nomination as a delegate to the UN. She will be an able spokesperson for the better world which U.S. citizens want.

F1474 O'Connor, Colleen M. "Eleanor Roosevelt and the United Nations." *Eleanor Roosevelt: An American Journey*. Ed. Jess Flemion and Colleen M. O'Connor. San Diego: San Diego State Univ. Pr., 1987. 253-62.

Published and manuscript sources are used to outline ER's role in the UN.

F1475 Ostromecki, Walter A., Jr. "Eleanor Roosevelt Speaks Out on Her U.N. Duties." *Manuscripts* 43 (Spring 1991): 155-58.

Reproduction and discussion of a 1950 letter from ER in which she urges support for the work of the UN and the adoption of the Universal Declaration of Human Rights.

F1476 "Proceedings at Dinner in Honor of Mrs. Franklin Delano Roosevelt." *Congressional Record Appendix* (9 May 1946): A2547-51.

Text of several statements made at 14 Mar. tribute to her as UN delegate. Mrs. Louis Ottenberg, Sen. Tom Connally, and Henry Wallace praise her efforts as an humanitarian and her early accomplishments at the UN. Her success will enhance opportunities for other women. Also issued as a pamphlet (Washington: GPO, 1946). Pamphlet is available in Box 21, Folder 323 of the Clara Beyer Papers, Schlesinger Library, Radcliffe College.

F1477 Reston, James B. "UNO Delegates Confirmed but Policy Is Challenged." *New York Times* 21 Dec. 1945: 1, 4.

On Dec. 20 the Senate confirmed HST's nominees to the UN. Consideration of the nomination of ER provoked Sen. Theodore G. Bilbo to criticize her support of racial equality while other senators rose to her defense. For these remarks, see *Congressional Record* (20 Dec. 1945): 12440, 12455-56. For editorial "People's Champion" by Thomas L. Stokes from the *Washington Daily News*, see *Congressional Record Appendix* (21 Dec. 1945): A5746.

F1478 *Review of the United Nations 33d Commission on Human Rights: Hearing before the Subcommittee on International Organizations of the Committee on International Relations, House of Representatives, Ninety-fifth Congress, First Session, May 19, 1977*. Washington: GPO, 1977. vi + 35p.

A tribute to ER's success in getting her fellow delegates to reach agreement on what is meant by "human rights" by Rep. Allard K. Lowenstein (p. 19).

F1479 Scharf, Lois. "Roosevelt, Anna Eleanor." *The Harry S. Truman Encyclopedia*. The G.K. Hall Presidential Encyclopedia Series. Ed. Richard S. Kirkendall. Boston: Hall, 1989. 309-10. Bibliography.

As a UN delegate ER's link to the new administration was not as strong as HST would have liked since the two were not always in agreement.

F1480 Schlesinger, Arthur M., Jr. "Two Years Later--The Roosevelt Family." *Life* 22 (7 Apr. 1947): 112-14, 116, 119-20, 122, 124, 126, 129.

An assessment of ER and her children two years after the death of FDR. The shy and insecure ER has developed into the confident world figure which she is today. The self-confidence which she had to develop in her private life serves her well today as a member of the UN delegation.

F1481 "The Shape of Things." *Nation* 161 (29 Dec. 1945): 721-24.

One of a series of brief editorial comments. The one related to ER praises her selection as a UN delegate and concludes that she is the only independent member of the U.S. delegation (p. 722).

F1482 Singer, Kurt. "Eleanor Roosevelt." *This Month* 2 (Apr. 1946): 82-85.

A tribute to her humanitarianism and to her present contributions as a UN delegate. Includes a brief account of her activities and the criticism which she receives. Also issued as "Eleanor Roosevelt...." *Negro* 4 (July 1946): 76-78.

F1483 Stevenson, Adlai E. *The Papers of Adlai E. Stevenson*. Ed. Walter Johnson, et al. 8 vols. Boston: Little, Brown, 1972-1979. Index. Notes.

Stevenson served as senior adviser to the first UN delegation. Entries document his developing friendship with ER and respect for her abilities at the UN (v. 2, pp. 339-40, 387-88, 390).

In 1961 JFK named ER as a special adviser to the U.S. delegation. On 15 Jan. 1962 Stevenson sent her a letter of appreciation for her services and in a letter of 30 Sept. 1962 he expresses regret that illness was preventing her from participating in the work of the delegation (v. 8, p. 196, 294-95).

F1484 Stoessinger, John George. *The Refugee and the World Community*. Minneapolis: Univ. of Minn. Pr., 1956. v + 239p. Index. Bibliography. Notes.

In the description of the discussion about refugees at the first session of the UN General Assembly numerous remarks by ER are cited (pp. 62, 69, 72-73, 77).

F1485 Teltsch, Kathleen. "Mrs. Roosevelt Says Ruled Press Is Like Egg: All Bad If Bad in Part." *New York Times* 7 Oct. 1947: 1, 17.

On 6 Oct. ER defended the U.S. press against Soviet charges that they are warmongering: we will not try to control our press. For editorial support for her position, see "The Egg and Mrs. Roosevelt." *New York Times* 8 Oct. 1947: 24.

F1486 "This Is Your Delegation: Here Are Your Representatives to the General Assembly." *American Association for the United Nations-United Nations Reporter* 22 (25 Sept. 1950): 6-7, 31-32.

Activities of the delegates. The entry for ER contains a lengthy and unidentified statement by her about the role of the UN (p. 32).

F1487 Tillett, Gladys Avery. "Mrs. Roosevelt Is Named UNO Delegate." *Democratic Digest* 23 (Jan. 1946): 3.

With ER's appointment to the UN delegation the country has a woman at the peace table at last. She has had good preparation, and she can be trusted to represent all citizens.

F1488 Truman, Harry S. "Remarks at the Opening Session of the Women's Bureau Conference." *Public Papers of the Presidents of the United States, Harry S. Truman, Containing the Public Messages, Speeches and Statements of the President, January 1, 1948 to December 31, 1948.* Washington: GPO, 1964. 142-44.

Includes praise for ER as a delegate to the UN (p. 143). In his "Address at the National Convention Banquet of the Americans for Democratic Action" there is a call to recognize the need to support equal rights for all and an acknowledgment of ER's efforts to make other countries realize that we are committed to doing so. His remarks are included in *Public Papers of the Presidents...January 1, 1952, to January 20, 1953,* p. 346 (Washington: GPO, 1966).

F1489 "U.N. Group Headed by Mrs. Roosevelt." *New York Times* 30 Apr. 1946: 9.

ER is elected to chair the Commission on Human Rights. The text of her brief remarks expressing optimism for the UN is included in a report of the commission's first meeting.

F1490 "U.N. Urged to Act on Women's Vote." *New York Times* 14 Nov. 1946: 11.

On 13 Nov. ER spoke in the Third Committee against the adoption of an "equal-rights-for-women resolution." She favored referring the matter to the Economic and Social Council in hopes of seeing a means adopted for enforcing the principle of equal rights. We should want action not just words, she said.

F1491 "US Must Face Challenges of Soviet Growth, Says Reuther." *ADA World* 14 (Feb./Mar. 1959): 1.

At the Roosevelt Day dinner in New York ER was given a citation in commemoration of the 10th anniversary of the Universal Declaration of Human Rights. It read that her "unflagging patience and energy" were critical to the adoption of the declaration.

F1492 Weil, Martin. *A Pretty Good Club: The Founding Fathers of the U.S. Foreign Service.* New York: Norton, 1978. 313p. Index. Bibliography. Notes.

Weil claims that while HST felt enmity toward ER he also realized that he needed her to help deliver the black vote and that is why he named her as a delegate to the UN (pp. 224-25).

F1493 Whitman, Alden. "Eleanor Roosevelt's Old Acquaintances Remember Her with Flowers." *New York Times* 25 Oct. 1975: 31.

For the 10th year old friends have gathered on the grounds of the UN to honor her with words and flowers.

F1494 "Women in This First Year of Peace." *Democratic Digest* 23 (Aug. 1946): 3-5, 20.

Women are playing a significant role with the most notable being that of ER as UN delegate.

F1495 Yorck, Ruth E. "Eleanor Roosevelt: 'la Femme la Plus Aimee des Etats-Unis.'" *Jardin des Modes* (Jan. 1952): 11-12.

An affectionate look at ER as she returns to Paris for meetings of the UN. In French.

Universal Declaration of Human Rights and the Covenants:
Chronology as Reported in UN Publications

F1496 "Opening of Human Rights Commission: Mrs. Roosevelt Elected Chairman." *United Nations Weekly Bulletin* 2 (4 Feb. 1947): 91-93.
On 27 Jan. Henri Laugier opened the first session of the Commission on Human Rights and outlined the duties and significance of the commission. After ER was elected chair she commented on the commission's role and the human rights appeals which she receives.

F1497 "Commission on Human Rights Meets: Groundwork Laid for an International Bill of Rights." *United Nations Weekly Bulletin* 2 (25 Feb. 1947): 169-72.
At the first meeting of the commission from 27 Jan. to 10 Feb. ER proposed that the initial step should be for the commission to draft a Declaration on Human Rights and Individual Freedoms, but instead it was decided that she, P.C. Chang, and Charles Malik should develop a Draft International Bill of Rights before the next meeting scheduled for 21 July.

F1498 "International Bill of Rights to Be Drafted." *United Nations Weekly Bulletin* 2 (17 June 1947): 639-42.
After the commission's first meeting the Economic and Social Council suggested the establishment of an expanded drafting committee. That committee first met on 6 June with ER as chair. Included is her description of the work to be performed and her call for the group to first define what human rights are.

F1499 "Fundamental Human Rights." *Yearbook of the United Nations, 1946-47*. Lake Success: United Nations, Dept. of Public Information, 1947. 523-32.
Establishment of the Commission on Human Rights and detailed account of meetings of the drafting committee for an International Bill of Human Rights. This and subsequent editions document ER's statements and provide references to UN reports of verbatim proceedings.

F1500 "First Drafts of Human Rights Bill Completed." *United Nations Bulletin* 4 (15 Jan. 1948): 74-78.
In Dec. 1947 the Commission on Human Rights issued for comment the Draft International Covenant on Human Rights and the Draft International Declaration on Human Rights.

F1501 "'...Free and Equal in Dignity and Rights...': Further Progress toward Universal Declaration" *United Nations Bulletin* 4 (15 June 1948): 487-88.
The commission has been working since 24 May on the revision of the declaration. It hopes to complete it and prepare a draft of the Covenant on Human Rights by July. The U.S. position on the approach which should be taken with the declaration is outlined.

F1502 Malik, Charles. "International Bill of Human Rights." *United Nations Bulletin* 5 (1 July 1948): 519-24.
Description of the completed draft and highlights of debate in the drafting committee and the Commission on Human Rights.

F1503 "Searching Study of Human Rights Declaration." *United Nations Bulletin* 5 (1 Nov. 1948): 858-61.
 Report on the debate of Articles 1-2.

F1504 "Progress on Human Rights Declaration." *United Nations Bulletin* 5 (15 Nov. 1948): 932-35.
 Committee debate of Articles 3-6.

F1505 "Shaping the Declaration of Human Rights." *United Nations Bulletin* 5 (1 Dec. 1948): 966-70.
 Articles 7-15 are debated.

F1506 "Universal Declaration of Human Rights." *United Nations Bulletin* 5 (15 Dec. 1948): 1003-8.
 Final wording of the proposed declaration with a summary of the committee's debate.

F1507 "Human Rights." *Yearbook of the United Nations, 1947-48.* Lake Success: United Nations, Dept. of Public Information, 1949. 572-86. Notes.
 Meetings of the Commission on Human Rights and consideration of work of Commission by the Economic and Social Council.

F1508 "Concluding Phases of Assembly Debate." *United Nations Bulletin* 6 (15 Jan. 1949): 94-99.
 Report of Third Committee debate on Articles 24-28 includes ER's participation (pp. 94, 96-97).

F1509 "Progress of Human Rights Commission." *United Nations Bulletin* 6 (15 June 1949): 642.
 When the commission convened on 9 May ER was re-elected as chair. Before turning their attention to the Draft Covenant on Human Rights, the members dealt with matters related to the Sub-Commission on the Prevention of Discrimination and the Protection of Minorities.

F1510 "Decisions of the Commission." *United Nations Bulletin* 7 (1 July 1949): 7-13, 63-64.
 ER stated that the purpose of the covenant was "to make governments answerable internationally for their misconduct toward the people whose lives they have sworn to protect" (p. 7). The commission recessed on 20 June after six weeks of deliberation over the draft which had been prepared during 1947-1948 by the drafting committee.

F1511 Malik, Charles. "The Covenant on Human Rights." *United Nations Bulletin* 7 (1 July 1949): 2-6.
 Initial work by the Commission on Human Rights to develop the covenant.

F1512 "Assembly Postpones Action on Convention." *United Nations Bulletin* 7 (1 Nov. 1949): 505-7.
 On 20 Oct. the General Assembly confirmed the 27 Sept. decision of the Third Committee to take no further action on the Draft Convention on Freedom of Information until the Commission on Human Rights submits the Draft Covenant on

Human Rights or a progress report. ER spoke at length in favor of the proposed action (pp. 505-6).

F1513 "Human Rights." *Yearbook of the United Nations, 1948-49.* New York: Columbia Univ. Pr. in co-operation with the United Nations, 1950. 524-53. Notes.

Work of the commission, development of the draft declaration and its adoption by the Third Committee, and discussion of the declaration by the General Assembly. The General Assembly's consideration of a draft covenant.

F1514 "Human Rights Session to Complete Covenant." *United Nations Bulletin* 8 (1 Apr. 1950): 327-29.

The commission convened on 27 Mar. to continue work on the drafts of the Covenant and Measures of Implementation. It was decided that a consideration of the reactions of member countries to the completed articles will be an essential part of the commission's work.

F1515 Malik, Charles. "How the Commission on Human Rights Forged Its Draft of a First Covenant." *United Nations Bulletin* 8 (1 June 1950): 471-73, 501.

Debate in the commission on the development of a covenant.

F1516 "Shaping First Covenant on Human Rights." *United Nations Bulletin* 9 (15 Nov. 1950): 525-27.

In the Third Committee's examination of the individual articles of the First Covenant on Human Rights ER presented the U.S. position that the articles were satisfactory subject to some minor editing changes.

F1517 "Assembly Approves Plan for Human Rights Covenant: Assembly Resolutions Lay Down General Policy." *United Nations Bulletin* 9 (15 Dec. 1950): 708-16.

On 4 Dec. the General Assembly directed the Third Committee to rewrite the covenant so as to make it applicable to colonial and other holdings of member nations which are not self-governing. Reported are the Third Committee's discussions of those issues including remarks made by ER (pp. 709, 711, 713, 715).

F1518 "Human Rights." *Yearbook of the United Nations, 1950.* New York: Columbia Univ. Pr. in co-operation with the United Nations, 1951. 519-43. Notes.

Development of the Draft Covenant on Human Rights and Measures of Implementation.

F1519 "Revising the Draft Covenant on Human Rights." *United Nations Bulletin* 10 (15 Mar. 1951): 292-95.

Progress of the commission in responding to the directive of the Economic and Social Council to revise the draft of the covenant.

F1520 "Main Tasks of Seventh Session of Human Rights Commission: Heavy Program for Geneva Meetings." *United Nations Bulletin* 10 (15 Apr. 1951): 387-88.

When the commission meets on 16 Apr. the main task will be to prepare in accordance with the directive of the General Assembly a new draft of the covenant and a draft of Measures of Implementation.

F1521 "Commission Begins Redrafting the Human Rights Covenant: New Proposals Submitted at Geneva Session." *United Nations Bulletin* 10 (1 May 1951): 429.
ER announced that she would be stepping down as chair.

F1522 "Provisions for Economic Rights: Commission Adopts New Articles for Human Rights Covenant." *United Nations Bulletin* 10 (15 May 1951): 481-82.
Since convening on 16 Apr. the commission has made provisional changes to the draft covenant.

F1523 Malik, Charles. "Progress of Covenant on Human Rights." *United Nations Bulletin* 10 (15 June 1951): 554-57.
More progress has been made in revising the draft of the covenant.

F1524 "Human Rights." *Yearbook of the United Nations, 1951.* New York: Columbia Univ. Pr. in co-operation with the United Nations, 1952. 477-508. Notes.
Consideration of the Draft Covenant on Human Rights and Measures of Implementation by the Economic and Social Council and the General Assembly.

F1525 "Basic Issues Relating to Human Rights Covenant." *United Nations Bulletin* 12 (1 Jan. 1952): 21.
The possibility of needing two covenants is raised.

F1526 "New Decisions on Human Rights Pact." *United Nations Bulletin* 12 (15 Feb. 1952): 204.
Two covenants have been called for. One is to address economic, social, and cultural rights and another civil and political rights. A similar article on pp. 347 of the same issue is "Human Rights Commission Given New Policy Directives on Pacts."

F1527 "Commission Begins Final Work on Draft Human Rights Pact." *United Nations Bulletin* 12 (15 Apr. 1952): 345-46.
The commission is attempting to complete both covenants.

F1528 "Human Rights Commission Gets Off to Quick Start." *United Nations Bulletin* 12 (1 May 1952): 374.
The commission convened on 14 Apr. and a week later completed a draft of an article on self-determination.

F1529 "Right of All to Self-Determination Defined in Two Covenants." *United Nations Bulletin* 12 (1 May 1952): 371-73.
Specifics of the commission debate on the article on self-determination. ER's remarks are on p. 371.

F1530 "Commission's Progress in Drafting Conventions on Human Rights." *United Nations Bulletin* 12 (15 May 1952): 411-14.
Report of the debate of 30 Apr.-9 May on four articles in the covenant on economic, cultural, and social rights. ER pursued the concept that it is each nation's obligation to provide these rights.

F1531 "Preamble, Sixteen Articles of Rights Covenant Drafted." *United Nations Bulletin* 12 (1 June 1952): 438-39.

The commission has completed a Draft Covenant on Economic, Social and Cultural Rights.

F1532 "'Progressively' Free Education Provided for in Draft Article." *United Nations Bulletin* 12 (15 June 1952): 468-69.
A report on the Commission on Human Rights debate on the right to education as contained in the draft covenant. ER argued in favor of "ensuring free primary education" with the method of doing so not prescribed. The article was accepted without her suggested deletion of an anti-discrimination clause which she felt should be mentioned only in respect to all articles, not individual ones.

F1533 "Commission Debates Rights: Life, Movement, Expression." *United Nations Bulletin* 13 (1 July 1952): 39-42.
Report of debate on Covenant on Civil and Political Rights articles includes the U.S. position as presented by ER.

F1534 Malik, Charles. "Human Rights in the United Nations." *United Nations Bulletin* 13 (1 Sept. 1952): 248-57.
Drafting of the covenants.

F1535 "The Principle of Self-Determination Recommended for Peoples and Nations." *United Nations Bulletin* 13 (15 Dec. 1952): 612-21.
The Third Committee debated two resolutions on 12 Nov. ER's amendments promoted "the universal nature of the right of self-determination."

F1536 "Human Rights." *Yearbook of the United Nations, 1952.* New York: Columbia Univ. Pr. in cooperation with the United Nations, 1953. 439-58. Notes.
Consideration of resolutions on the Right of Peoples and Nations to Self-Determination by the commission, the Economic and Social Council, and the General Assembly. Further consideration of Draft International Covenant on Human Rights and Measures of Implementation. Consideration of report on Prevention of Discrimination and Protection of Minorities.

Universal Declaration of Human Rights and the Covenants: Chronology as Reported in Department of State Publications

F1537 "Commission on Human Rights: U.S. Proposals Regarding an International Bill of Rights." *Department of State Bulletin* 16 (16 Feb. 1947): 277-78.
Proposals for how it should be drafted and what it should contain.

F1538 "Proposal for a Declaration of Human Rights." *Department of State Bulletin* 17 (7 Dec. 1947): 1075-77.
A U.S. draft of a declaration is presented by ER. "Principles for a World Bill of Rights." *World Affairs* [Toronto] 13 (Jan. 1948): 9 provides the U.S. draft and calls for all U.S. citizens to enjoy the rights and liberties which are being recommended for citizens of other nations. Article reprints editorial from *Daily Star* [Toronto] plus additional comment.

F1539 "Human Rights." *The United States and the United Nations: Report by the President to the Congress for the Year 1947.* Dept. of State Publication, 3024.

International Organization and Conference Series III, 1. Washington: GPO, 1948. 122-23.
Progress in drafting a bill of human rights.

F1540 Hendrick, James P. "An International Bill of Rights." *Department of State Bulletin* 18 (15 Feb. 1948): 195-208. Notes.
A detailed account of meetings of the Commission on Human Rights and the Human Rights Drafting Committee. Also issued as a pamphlet (Washington: Dept. of State, 1948).

F1541 ---. "Progress Report on Human Rights." *Department of State Bulletin* 19 (8 Aug. 1948): 159-73. Notes.
An expansion of his article of 15 Feb. 1948. Also issued as a pamphlet (Washington: GPO, 1948).

F1542 "The International Declaration of Human Rights." *Human Rights and Genocide: Selected Statements, United Nations Resolutions, September 21-December 12, 1948.* Dept. of State Publication, 3416. International Organization and Conference Series III, 25. Washington: Dept. of State, 1949. 13-16.
The declaration is a statement of basic principles, not a treaty or legal document. Many compromises were necessary in order to reach agreement among members of the commission. Text of ER's statement before the Third Committee, 30 Sept. 1948.
Also in *Human Rights and Genocide: Selected Statements, United Nations Resolutions, Declaration and Conventions.* Dept. of State Publication, 3643. International Organization and Conference Series III, 39, pp. 13-16 (Washington: Dept. of State, 1949).

F1543 "General Assembly Adopts Declaration of Human Rights." *Department of State Bulletin* 19 (19 Dec. 1948): 751-52.
Text of ER's 9 Dec. 1948 statement announcing the adoption of the declaration in which she states that it may become the Magna Carta for all people. Also as "Adoption of Declaration of Human Rights" in *Human Rights and Genocide: Selected Statements, United Nations Resolutions, Declaration and Conventions.* Dept. of State Publication, 3643. International Organization and Conference Series, III, 39, pp. 24-25. 28-29 (Washington: Dept. of State, 1949) and in *Human Rights and Genocide: Selected Statements, United Nations Resolutions, September 21-December 12, 1948.* Dept. of State Publication, 3416. International Organization and Conference Series III, 25, pp. 24-25, 28-29 (Washington: Dept. of State, 1949).

F1544 "Human Rights." *United States Participation in the United Nations: Report by the President to the Congress for the Year 1948....* Dept. of State Publication, 3437. International Organization and Conference Series III, 29. Washington: GPO, 1949. 129-32.
The activities of ER and others in securing the passage of the Universal Declaration of Human Rights and pursuing the draft of the covenant.

F1545 Simsarian, James. "United Nations Action on Human Rights in 1948." *Department of State Bulletin* 20 (2 Jan. 1949): 18-23.
Approval of the declaration by the General Assembly and work on the covenant. Written by adviser to ER at the UN.

F1546 Sandifer, Durward V. "New International Frontiers in Human Rights." *Department of State Bulletin* 20 (27 Feb. 1949): 258-63.

When the UN General Assembly adopted the Universal Declaration of Human Rights it made the protection of human rights an international concern. ER's remarks at the plenary session are quoted (pp. 258, 261-262). Text of Sandifer's address at National Citizens Conference on Civil Liberties, Washington, 27 Feb. 1949.

F1547 Simsarian, James. "Human Rights: Draft Covenant Revised at Fifth Session of Commission on Human Rights." *Department of State Bulletin* 21 (11 July 1949): 3-12.

Work on the covenant. Remarks and debate by ER. A less detailed account is his "Draft Covenant on Human Rights Revised at Fifth Session of the United Nations Commission on Human Rights." *American Journal of International Law* 43 (Oct. 1949): 779-86. Notes.

F1548 "International Covenant of Human Rights." *United States Participation in the United Nations: Report by the President to the Congress for the Year 1949....* Dept. of State Publication, 3765. International Organization and Conference Series III, 48. Washington: GPO, 1950. 138-39.

Activities of the Commission on Human Rights and the formulation of human rights instruments.

F1549 "The United States in the United Nations." *Department of State Bulletin* 22 (3 Apr. 1950): 538-39.

Work on a Draft International Covenant on Human Rights. Remarks by ER.

F1550 "International Covenant on Human Rights." *United States Participation in the United Nations: Report by the President to the Congress for the Year 1950.* Dept. of State Publication, 4178. International Organization and Conference Series III, 67. Washington: GPO, 1951. 185-87.

The debate in the Commission on Human Rights which led up to the completion of the draft of the covenant.

F1551 "The United States in the United Nations." *Department of State Bulletin* 24 (23 Apr. 1951): 672-73.

Work on the Draft Covenant on Human Rights and Measures of Implementation continues. ER plans to step down as chair of Commission on Human Rights.

F1552 Cates, John M., Jr. "Expanding Concept of Individual Liberties." *Department of State Bulletin* 25 (31 Dec. 1951): 1058-64.

The present status of the covenant and events in the UN which have brought us to this point. Argues that liberties enjoyed by U.S. citizens are not jeopardized by the covenant.

F1553 "Statement by Mrs. Franklin D. Roosevelt." *Department of State Bulletin* 25 (31 Dec. 1951): 1059, 1064-65.

ER defends the need for two covenants and describes how civil and political rights can be implemented quickly while it will take member nations longer to provide the desired economic, social, and cultural rights. Text of statement in the Third

Committee, 5 Dec. 1951. Issued as a separate section of John M. Cates, Jr., "Expanding Concept of Individual Liberties."

F1554 "Reply to Attacks on U.S. Attitude toward Human Rights Covenant." *Department of State Bulletin* 26 (14 Jan. 1952): 59-61.
    It is not the position of the U.S. government to condone discrimination of its black citizens. We favor two covenants because that is the practical way to proceed, not because we lack interest in promoting the economic and social rights of all of our citizens. Text of ER's statement in the Third Committee, 20 Dec. 1951.

F1555 "Draft Covenants on Human Rights." *United States Participation in the United Nations: Report by the President to the Congress for the Year 1951.* Department of State Publication, 4583. International Organization and Conference Series III, 80. Washington: GPO, 1952. 195-98.
    The covenant was expanded to include economic, social, and cultural rights.

F1556 "Progress toward Completion of Human Rights Covenants." *Department of State Bulletin* 26 (30 June 1952): 1024-28.
    Text of two statements made 13 June 1952. "Mrs. Roosevelt's Press Statement" (pp. 1024-26) describes recent work of the Commission on Human Rights in developing the covenants; "Statement to Committee Members" (pp. 1026-28) refutes attacks on the U.S. made by Soviet and Polish delegates during meetings of the commission. Excerpts in "The United States in the United Nations." *Department of State Bulletin* 26 (30 June 1952): 1041-42.

F1557 Simsarian, James. "Two Covenants on Human Rights Being Drafted." *Department of State Bulletin* 27 (7 July 1952): 20-31.
    Recent work on the covenants. Emphasizes ER's argument that the covenants will promote liberty in all nations, not reduce those which are already enjoyed. Similar to his "Progress in Drafting Two Covenants on Human Rights in the United Nations." *American Journal of International Law* 46 (Oct. 1952): 710-13. Notes.

F1558 "The United States in the United Nations." *Department of State Bulletin* 27 (1 Dec. 1952): 880-83.
    Debate including excerpted remarks by ER in the Third Committee on the right to self-determination. Continued in 27 (8 Dec. 1952): 924-27 and 27 (29 Dec. 1952): 1042-47.

F1559 "Draft Covenants on Human Rights." *United States Participation in the UN: Report by the President to the Congress for the Year 1952.* Department of State Publication, 5034. International Organization and Conference Series III, 90. Washington: GPO, 1953. 153-55.
    Work of the commission on creating two covenants.

Universal Declaration of Human Rights and the Covenants: Other Accounts

F1560 "The American Struggle against Human Rights." By A Special Correspondent. *Monthly Review* 2 (Jan. 1951): 409-18.
    The U.S. position on identifying and securing human rights was one of "maneuvering" to limit rights to those which would be accepted by the American people. Provides numerous examples of U.S. efforts, as pursued by ER, to qualify

the language of the Universal Declaration of Human Rights and control the scope of a covenant.

F1561 Burns, James MacGregor, and Stewart Burns. *A People's Charter: The Pursuit of Rights in America*. New York: Knopf, 1991. xi + 577p. Index. Notes.
The authors provide an overview of ER as chair of the Commission on Human Rights, the problems which were faced in drafting the Universal Declaration of Human Rights and the covenants, and her efforts to gain congressional approval of the covenants (pp. 419-24).

F1562 Cassin, Rene. "Looking Back on the Universal Declaration of Human Rights." *Review of Contemporary Law* 15 (1968): 13-26.
ER's contributions.

F1563 *Eleanor Roosevelt and the Universal Declaration of Human Rights: An Agenda for Action in 1988*. Hyde Park: The Franklin and Eleanor Roosevelt Institute, 1988. 46p.
Contains selected addresses presented as part of "Eleanor Roosevelt and the Universal Declaration of Human Rights: A Convocation for Remembrance and Rededication" held 7 Nov. 1987 at the Franklin D. Roosevelt Library on the occasion of the 25th anniversary of ER's death and the 40th anniversary of the Universal Declaration of Human Rights. The complete program of events and speakers is provided on pp. 41-44.

F1564 Fleming, William. "Danger to America: The Draft Covenant on Human Rights." *American Bar Association Journal* 37 (Oct. 1951): 739-42, 794-99; 37 (Nov. 1951): 816-20, 855-60.
Calls for a rejection of the document. Includes numerous quotations from ER's speeches and writings.

F1565 *For Fundamental Human Rights*. Lake Success: United Nations, Dept. of Public Information, n.d. 126p. Notes.
An account of events related to the Universal Declaration of Human Rights up to the opening of the third session of the General Assembly. ER is mentioned (pp. 11, 16, 21) and is the subject of a tribute "The Part Played by Mrs. Eleanor Roosevelt" (p. 75). Notes refer to verbatim reports of meetings relevant to human rights.

F1566 Gardner, Richard N. "Eleanor Roosevelt and the Universal Declaration of Human Rights." *Eleanor Roosevelt and the Universal Declaration of Human Rights: An Agenda for Action in 1988*. Hyde Park: The Franklin and Eleanor Roosevelt Institute, 1988. 15-17.
Had ER not insisted on a statement of human rights before the development of covenants there would have been no Universal Declaration of Human Rights. She would have mixed feelings about the condition of human rights today and would be saddened by the our continued failure to ratify the covenants and the present attitude in the country about the UN. Text of address, 7 Nov. 1987, Hyde Park, N.Y.

F1567 Grammatico, Angelina Carmela. "The United Nations and the Development of Human Rights." Diss. N.Y. Univ., 1956. 454p. Bibliography. Notes.
Based on UN publications, the chapters "The Commission on Human Rights" (pp. 54-62), "The Formulation and Adoption of the International Declaration of Human

Rights" (pp. 63-159) and "The Formulation of the Human Rights Covenants" (pp. 160-84) trace ER's role. There is also the dissertation by Leo John Moser, "The Human Rights Program of the United Nations" (Univ. of Southern Calif., 1957). Contents and first chapter examined.

F1568 Green, James Frederick. *The United Nations and Human Rights*. Washington: Brookings Institution, 1956. 194p. Notes.

The chapter "Attempt to Define Human Rights" traces the drafting of the Universal Declaration of Human Rights, the Draft Covenant on Civil and Political Rights, and the Draft Covenant on Economic, Social and Cultural Rights. Based, with no analysis, on official documents (pp. 24-67). Also in *The United Nations and the Promotion of the General Welfare*, pp. 664-707 (Washington: Brookings Institution, 1957).

F1569 Hicks, Donald R. "Eleanor Roosevelt and the Universal Declaration of Human Rights." Thesis (M.A.) Univ. of Akron, 1984. iii + 107p. Bibliography. Notes.

ER's role in drafting the document. The development of her social conscience is outlined through a description of her childhood, private life, emergence, and activities as First Lady. There is a chronology of the development of the Universal Declaration of Human Rights based on UN documents, an unpublished manuscript by John P. Humphrey, and ER's unpublished article "The Human Rights Commission" followed by an evaluation of the role which she played.

F1570 Holcombe, Arthur N. *Human Rights in the Modern World*. New York: N.Y. Univ. Pr.; London: Oxford Univ. Pr., 1948. viii + 162p. Index. Notes.

The Commission on Human Rights is at work "under the wise and inspiring leadership of Mrs. Franklin D. Roosevelt" (p. 120). She was right to have wanted a less extensive document, not one which tries to solve all the problems which can arise among nations (p. 124-25).

F1571 Holman, Frank E. "International Proposals Affecting So-Called Human Rights." *Law and Contemporary Problems* 14 (Summer 1949): 479-89.

The former American Bar Assoc. president sees the declaration and the covenants as threats to the rights of Americans. A critical look at the documents and at ER, a "social reformer" with no training in the law. For the same themes, see his "An 'International Bill of Rights': Proposals Have Dangerous Implications for the United States." *American Bar Association Journal* 34 (Nov. 1948): 984-86, 1078-81 and as "Human Rights on Pink Paper." *American Affairs* 11 (Jan. 1949): 18-24; "Giving America Away." *Vital Speeches* 16 (1 Oct. 1950): 748-53; and "The Constitution and the United Nations." *Vital Speeches* 18 (1 Sept. 1952): 678.

ER has tried "to bind the American people" to something which will result in a change in American government he states in "President Holman's Comments on Mr. Moskowitz's Reply." *American Bar Association Journal* 35 (19 Apr. 1949): 288-90, 360-62.

Holman discusses his opposition to the human rights documents in his autobiographical *The Life and Career of a Western Lawyer, 1886-1961*, pp. 361, 383, 394-97, 402-3 (N.p.: Holman, 1963). Several of his speeches, including some not cited above, are in his *Selected Speeches and Articles on American Education...*, pp. 101-73 (N.p.: Holman, 1964).

F1572 "Human Rights." *Documents on American Foreign Relations. Vol. 8, July 1, 1945-December 31, 1946.* Princeton: Princeton Univ. Pr. for the World Peace Foundation, 1950. 400-401. Notes.

Describes efforts to establish a commitment to human rights within the new UN organization. On 16 Feb. 1946 the Commission on Human Rights was established and met 29 Apr. to 20 May 1946 with ER as chair.

F1573 "Human Rights." *Documents on American Foreign Relations. Vol. 9, January 1-December 31, 1947.* Princeton: Princeton Univ. Pr. for the World Peace Foundation, 1949. 497-503. Notes.

The work of the first session of the Commission on Human Rights is documented. Includes the text of three proposals made by ER: about the organization of the Subcommission on Protection of Minorities and Prevention of Discrimination (29 Jan.), pertaining to the functions of the Subcommission on Freedom of Information and of the Press (29 Jan.), and how to proceed in the development of an International Bill of Rights (6 Feb.).

F1574 "Human Rights." *Documents on American Foreign Relations. Vol. 10, January 1-December 31, 1948.* Princeton: Princeton Univ. Pr. for World Peace Foundation, 1950. 428-30. Notes.

Further discussion of the drafting of the Universal Declaration of Human Rights.

F1575 "Human Rights." *Documents on American Foreign Relations. Vol. 11, January 1-December 31, 1949.* Princeton: Princeton Univ. Pr. for the World Peace Foundation, 1950. 457-59. Notes.

Discussion on the nature of the covenant is documented. Includes excerpts of ER's statement of 3 Jan. 1950 on the U.S. position on the Draft International Covenant on Human Rights.

F1576 "Human Rights." *Documents on American Foreign Relations. Vol. 12, January 1-December 31, 1950.* Princeton: Princeton Univ. Pr. for the World Peace Foundation, 1951. 351-55. Notes.

Reports on the work of the commission. ER pursued efforts to establish means of implementing human rights documents and supported the delay of provisions for social, cultural, and political rights. Includes text of her 18 May statement to the General Assembly on the draft of the first covenant.

F1577 "Human Rights." *Documents on American Foreign Relations. Vol. 13, January 1-December 31, 1951.* Princeton: Princeton Univ. Pr. for the World Peace Foundation, 1953. 365-66. Notes.

Describes the work of the commission to add economic, social, and cultural rights to human rights instruments. Documents ER's remarks in support of drafting the covenants.

F1578 Humphrey, John P. *Human Rights and the United Nations: A Great Adventure.* Dobbs Ferry: Transnational, 1984. 350p. Index.

The long-time director of the UN Division of Human Rights presents his recollections of the drafting of the Universal Declaration of Human Rights and the activities of the commission. His numerous references to ER present a balanced picture of the role which she played, and he contends that her shortcomings were a result of the direction which she received from State Dept. officials (pp. 60-61, 85-86,

88, 105). Chapters 3-7 and 11 also issued as "The Memoirs of John P. Humphrey, the First Director of the United Nations Division of Human Rights." *Human Rights Quarterly* 5 (Nov. 1983): 387-489.

F1579 ---. "International Protection of Human Rights." *Annals of the American Academy of Political and Social Science* 255 (Jan. 1948): 15-21.
    The early work of the UN on behalf of human rights. A recognition of ER's contribution (p.15).

F1580 Johnson, M. Glen. "The Contributions of Eleanor and Franklin Roosevelt to the Development of International Protection for Human Rights." *Human Rights Quarterly* 9 (Feb. 1987): 19-48. Notes.
    Johnson examines the possible reasons for the scant attention which has been given to ER's role (she was a woman, human rights was not always a high priority in the U.S. in the post-war era, and her own reluctance to bring attention to the significance of her role). He examines how her role has been treated by other scholars, how in her own writings she demonstrated a greater concern for both economic and social rights than was the official U.S. position, and the fears which surfaced in the U.S. that international treaties could be used to impose social change. Johnson concludes that the period of ER's leadership "was the high point of U.S. participation in multilateral efforts" to "promote the protection of human rights."

F1581 ---. "Historical Perspectives on Human Rights and U.S. Foreign Policy." *Universal Human Rights* 2 (July/Sept. 1980): 7-18. Notes.
    At the UN ER spoke in support of the U.S. position that economic objectives were not part of human rights policy, but Johnson claims that behind the scenes she argued against the policy.

F1582 Kaufman, Natalie Hevener. *Human Rights Treaties and the Senate: A History of Opposition.* Chapel Hill: Univ. of N.C. Pr., 1990. x + 256p. Index. Bibliography. Notes.
    A detailed examination of the development of the declaration and the covenants and of the opposition to them in the U.S. Senate. A valuable source on the origins of the proposed Bricker constitutional amendment and ER's role in the drafting of the human rights documents. Kaufman relies heavily on verbatim records of UN proceedings (pp. 64-93, 165-166, 170).

F1583 Korey, William. "Eleanor Roosevelt and the Universal Declaration of Human Rights." *Eleanor Roosevelt: Her Day, a Personal Album.* By A. David Gurewitsch. New York: Interchange Foundation, 1973; New York: Quadrangle, 1974. 13-24.
    A factual and interpretative description of ER's role.

F1584 "Magna Carta for the World?" *Freedom & Union* 4 (Feb. 1949): 23-27.
    Consists mainly of excerpted remarks by ER: debate with Andrei Vishinsky and her address in the General Assembly when presenting the Universal Declaration of Human Rights out of committee.

F1585 Malik, Charles. "Human Rights in the United Nations." *International Journal* 6 (Autumn 1951): 275-80.

A fellow member of the Human Rights Drafting Committee recalls the development of the Universal Declaration of Human Rights and the UN's subsequent efforts to further human rights.

F1586 Meyer, Peter. "The International Bill: A Brief History." *The International Bill of Human Rights*. Ed. Paul Williams. Glen Ellen: Entwhistle, 1981. xxiii-xlvii.
ER's role in the writing and passage of the Universal Declaration of Human Rights.

F1587 Mower, A. Glenn, Jr. *The United States, the United Nations, and Human Rights: The Eleanor Roosevelt and Jimmy Carter Eras*. Studies in Human Rights, 4. Westport: Greenwood, 1979. xii + 215p. Index. Bibliography. Notes.
The 1940s were the Eleanor Roosevelt era in the U.S.'s foreign human rights policy. The first part of this mostly derivative study is devoted to ER's emergence as a human rights leader and her career in the UN (pp. 3-85).

F1588 "Mrs. Roosevelt and Our Freedoms." Editorial. *America* 80 (4 Dec. 1948): 222-23.
ER's performance in the development of the Universal Declaration of Human Rights and her ability to distinguish between Marxist and democratic thinking is praiseworthy. So why can she not demonstrate such clear thinking when responding to readers' questions in the *Ladies' Home Journal?*

F1589 *Our Rights as Human Beings: A Discussion Guide on the Universal Declaration of Human Rights*. Sales no. 1955.1-13. New York: United Nations, 1955. 31p.
Unidentified quotations by ER about the development and importance of the declaration. Reissued as *Our Rights as Human Beings: A Discussion Guide*. Sales no. 1955.1-23. (New York: United Nations, 1955).

F1590 Pratt, Virginia Anne. "The Influence of Domestic Controversy on American Participation in the United Nations Commission on Human Rights, 1946-1953." Diss. Univ. of Minn., 1971. 298p. Bibliography. Notes.
Chapter "Drafting the U.N. Human Rights Covenants: The American Delegation on the Defensive" describes ER's role (pp. 135-69). Relies heavily on UN documents.

F1591 "Recollections of 1948." *UN Chronicle Perspective* 21 (Feb. 1984): ii-iv.
When the General Assembly adopted the declaration ER had mixed feelings. She was pleased with what had been accomplished, but she felt that the document suffered from compromise.

F1592 Robinson, Nehemiah. *The Universal Declaration of Human Rights: Its Origin, Significance, Application, and Interpretation*. New York: Institute of Jewish Affairs, World Jewish Congress, 1958. xxii + 173p. Bibliography. Notes.
Chapters on the drafting of the declaration and its significance provide a detailed description of the work of ER with excerpts from her statements. Contains references to verbatim reports of meetings of the Commission on Human Rights (pp. 25-30, 33-63).

F1593 Tananbaum, Duane. "The Death of the Dream: Eleanor Roosevelt, Human Rights and Domestic Politics." *Eleanor Roosevelt: An American Journey*. Ed. Jess

Flemion and Colleen M. O'Connor. San Diego: San Diego State Univ. Pr., 1987. 263-74. Note on Sources.

ER and the Truman administration worked for a covenant of human rights which would be acceptable to the Senate. Then the Eisenhower administration blocked the ratification of the covenant and eliminated the need to consider the Bricker amendment.

F1594 *These Rights and Freedoms*. Sales no. 1950.1-6. N.p.: United Nations, Dept. of Public Information, 1950. iii + 214p.

In a discussion of the deliberations about the declaration ER's statements from the time are included (pp. 21-86 passim).

F1595 Tolley, Howard. *The U.N. Commission on Human Rights*. Westview Special Studies in International Relations. Boulder: Westview, 1987. xv + 300p. Index. Bibliography. Notes.

ER's role in the UN and early activities of the Commission on Human Rights. Consists of basic factual information (pp. 9-29 passim, 46-47).

F1596 "U.N. Hails Mrs. Roosevelt's Rights Efforts." *Chronicle of America*. Ed. Clifton Daniel, et al. Mount Kisco: Chronicle, 1989. 743.

On 10 Dec. 1948 ER was praised at the UN and around the world for her role in developing the Universal Declaration of Human Rights.

F1597 "U.N. Orders Draft of Bill of Rights." *New York Times* 4 Feb. 1947: 3.

ER, P.C. Chang, and Charles Malik have been charged with developing the first draft of "an international bill of rights." It was reported that a lecture tour will take her away for a month.

F1598 *United Nations Action in the Field of Human Rights*. New York: United Nations, 1988. xviii + 359p.

The steps in the development of the declaration and the covenants (pp. 31-38). Others eds. published earlier.

F1599 "United Nations Work for Human Rights." *United Nations Review* 3 (Dec. 1956): 72-79, 93.

Includes a review of the work of the Commission on Human Rights in developing the declaration and the covenants.

F1600 Verdoodt, Albert. *Naissance et Signification de la Declaration Universelle des Droits de l'Homme*. Etudes Morales, Sociales et Juridiques. Louvain: Societe d'Etudes Morales, Sociales et Juridiques-Editions Nauvielaerts, 1964. xiv + 356p. Index. Notes.

Numerous references to ER related to statements which she made before the Commission on Human Rights. In French.

F1601 Whiteman, Marjorie M. "Mrs. Franklin D. Roosevelt and the Human Rights Commission." *American Journal of International Law* 62 (Oct. 1968): 918-21.

Whiteman was a State Dept. official who served as ER's adviser. ER's work with the commission was characterized by "courageous and intelligent leadership," but the declaration never became the document memorized by school children as she had wanted.

F1602 "World-wide Celebrations Mark Human Rights Day." *United Nations Bulletin* 13 (15 Dec. 1952): 588-89.

The 1952 observance included a radio broadcast narrated by ER in which UN representatives talked about the acceptance of the Universal Declaration of Human Rights in their countries.

American Association for the United Nations

F1603 "AAUN Conference." *American Association for the United Nations-United Nations Reporter* 25 (Mar. 1953): 8.

ER led the discussion about the field program at the Board of Governors meeting on 4 Mar. 1953.

F1604 Baillargeon, Patricia. "Eleanor Roosevelt and the American Association for the United Nations." *Eleanor Roosevelt: An American Journey.* Ed. Jess Flemion and Colleen M. O'Connor. San Diego: San Diego State Univ. Pr., 1987. 293-98.

ER's secretary at the AAUN remembers their association and travels from 1953 to 1960.

F1605 "Closed Circuit TV Program Acclaimed by UN Speakers." *AAUN News* 33 (Mar. 1961): 3-4.

ER spoke about the value of understanding other cultures and the need for public support of the UN on the 2 Mar. 1961 broadcast about issues before the current session of the General Assembly.

F1606 Daniell, Constance. "A Friend Remembers Mrs. Roosevelt." *Biography News* 1 (Dec. 1974): 1445.

Daniell interviews former AAUN staff member Estelle Linzer who traveled with ER. Linzer recalls the hatred which some had for ER. Reprinted from the *Milwaukee Journal*, 20 Oct. 1974.

F1607 Linzer, Estelle. "Eleanor Roosevelt Revisited." *Wingspread Journal* (Fall 1984): 4.

She recalls ER during the AAUN years.

F1608 McGill, Ralph. "Faith in Humanity Is Her Fountain of Youth: Mrs. Roosevelt Is Still on the Go." *Democratic Digest* 1 (Dec. 1953): 86-87.

Reports on his conversation with ER about her work in support of the UN. He concludes that the efforts of her critics are futile.

F1609 "United Nations Associations Discuss Education and Information Problems." *United Nations Review* 3 (Oct. 1956): 31-33.

In her capacity as chair of the Board of Governors of the American Association for the United Nations ER made remarks during the meeting of the World Federation of United Nations Associations on the theme of "the role played by public opinion."

World Figure

F1610 "Add Your Name to Hers in the Pioneer Women Graduate Library School in Israel." *Pioneer Woman* (Feb. 1963): 11.

ER supported the school, and others are encouraged to do so.

F1611 "Ambassador Roosevelt." *New Republic* 119 (29 Nov. 1948): 7-8.
   Since she would be able to relate to the French labor organization, it is predicted that ER will be named Ambassador to France.

F1612 Bealle, Morris A. *Red Rat Race: The Unexpurgated Bare-Knuckled, No-Punches-Pulled, Story of World Communism's Infiltration into American Public Life, Our Schools, Our Press, Our Books, Our Movies and Other Mediums of Public Information.* Washington: Columbia, 1953. 287p. Index.
   Undocumented account of alleged Communist infiltration. ER is given the labels of "Madam Gadabout" and "Long Nose." Bealle is critical of her senseless traveling and interference and with her involvement in the deportation hearings for Harry Bridges (pp. 77-81, 163-65).

F1613 "Belated Discovery." *Ave Maria* 69 (12 Feb. 1949): 197.
   ER has finally realized that she trusted Stalin too long. This is not being disloyal to FDR's memory since he put even more faith in the Soviet leader.

F1614 Breig, Joe. *Ave Maria* 78 (22 Aug. 1953): 7.
   ER "has never understood Communism" because she lacks spirituality. She is "a menace" to Catholics and their beliefs. Untitled.

F1615 Chamberlain, John. "Eleanor as Cold Warrior." Rev. of *Eleanor: The Years Alone* by Joseph P. Lash. *National Review* 24 (15 Sept. 1972): 1015.
   Despite ER's innocence and lack of intellectual vigor, Chamberlain has admiration for the woman who saw through the Soviets, took an anti-Communist stand, and approached the cold war with realism.

F1616 Clayton, Frederick. "Eleanor Roosevelt: Part II.--Citizen of the World." *Wisdom* 2 (Jan. 1958): 26-29.
   She is still idealistic and enthusiastic. Now her attention centers on world problems.

F1617 Cohen, Michael J. *Truman and Israel.* Berkeley: Univ. of Calif. Pr., 1990. xiii + 342p. Index. Bibliography. Notes.
   To ER solving the problems surrounding the establishment of a Jewish state was a test of the strength of the UN. Letters between ER and HST reveal the strain which the issue placed on their relationship (pp. 69, 125, 152-54, 180-81, 193-94, 211, 221, 248-49).

F1618 "The Continuing Education of Mrs. Roosevelt." *Christian Century* 68 (26 Dec. 1951): 1500-1501.
   We should be thankful for what ER does to inform others of efforts to achieve a better world, but a revelation in "My Day" is alarming. Only recently has she realized that there is doubt about a U.S. commitment to peace. With the current armaments build up why has it taken her so long?

F1619 Cook, Blanche Wiesen. "Eleanor Roosevelt and Human Rights: The Battle for Peace and Planetary Decency." *Women and American Foreign Policy: Lobbyists, Critics, and Insiders.* Contributions in Women's Studies, 76. Ed. Edward P. Crapol. New York: Greenwood, 1987. 91-118. Notes.

ER's international role and use of power through a chronology of her writings, speeches, and associations from 1923 until her death.

F1620 ---. "'Turn toward Peace': ER and Foreign Affairs." *Without Precedent: The Life and Career of Eleanor Roosevelt.* Everywoman: Studies in History, Literature, and Culture. Ed. Joan Hoff-Wilson and Marjorie Lightman. Bloomington: Indiana Univ. Pr., 1984. 108-21. Sources.

During the years before the White House she worked on behalf of the League of Nations and began her commitment to peace. Throughout her life she considered the need to ensure personal freedom and democracy more important than maintaining the peace.

F1621 De Bruin, Elizabeth. "Mevrouw Roosevelt." *Herfstlicht* (Apr. 1961): 116-18.
ER's activities on the world scene. In Dutch.

F1622 "Eleanor Roosevelt." *Voice of America World Program Schedule* (July/Aug. 1950): 19.
Cover story about her busy schedule.

F1623 "Eleanor Roosevelt Portfolio." *Wisdom* 2 (Jan. 1958): 20-25.
Captioned photographs of ER as First Lady and world figure.

F1624 "Eleanor Should Wait until She Has the Facts." *Our Sunday Visitor* 37 (13 Feb. 1949): 1, 9.
After defending Cardinal Mindszenty in a "My Day" column she backtracked when she received letters critical of her position. She has let herself be influenced by Communists.

F1625 "Enlightenment from Eleanor." *Catholic World* 165 (July 1947): 293-94.
Should the Russians no longer be feared since ER does not know why we should fear them? About her 6 June 1947 "My Day" column.

F1626 Feldman, Trude B. "Letters from Israel." *Jewish Press* 12 (30 Mar. 1962): 14; 12 (13 Apr. 1962): 22; 12 (27 Apr. 1962): 17.
A report on ER's activities during her Feb. 1962 visit to Israel. Also issued as "Mrs. Roosevelt's Last Trip: Five Days in Israel." *National Jewish Monthly* 77 (Dec. 1962): 8-9; 77 (Jan. 1963): 6-7, 33.

F1627 Flemion, Jess. "First Lady of the World." *Eleanor Roosevelt: An American Journey.* Ed. Jess Flemion and Colleen M. O'Connor. San Diego: San Diego State Univ. Pr., 1987. 225-27.
Her work with the UN and the American Association for the United Nations plus the regard which world leaders had for her earned her the title. Introduction to 23 photographs.

F1628 *Foreign Relations of the United States, 1948. Vol. VII. The Far East: China.* Dept. of State Publication, 8678. Washington: GPO, 1973. vi + 887p. Index.
Communication from Ambassador J. Leighton Stuart to the Dept. of State suggesting that ER be sent to China as a lecturer (p. 330).

F1629 *Foreign Relations of the United States, 1950. Vol. I. National Security Affairs, Foreign Economic Policy.* Dept. of State Publication, 8887. Washington: GPO, 1977. xi + 945p. Index.

A humble letter from ER to Secretary of State Dean Acheson regarding his remarks about U.S. relations with the Soviet Union and Acheson's reply (pp. 50, 54-56). A memorandum by ER concerning a conversation about the possibility of the use of nuclear weapons in Korea (p. 116).

F1630 *Foreign Relations of the United States, 1952-1954. Vol. XIV. China and Japan.* 2 vols. Dept. of State Publication, 9410, 9411. Washington: GPO, 1985. Index.

Dept. of State communications from New Delhi related to ER's trip to India (pt. 1, pp. 63-64).

F1631 "Ghost Thinker Needed." *Ave Maria* 75 (15 Mar. 1952): 523.

ER needs someone to do her thinking after she stated in Karachi that perhaps all nations, including the U.S., may have to give up some of their sovereignty if there is to be a peaceful world.

F1632 Gould, Jean, and Lorena Hickok. *Walter Reuther: Labor's Rugged Individualist.* New York: Dodd, Mead, 1972. xvi + 399p. Index. Bibliography.

Reuther's long association with ER included wartime planning and their efforts on behalf of Sane Nuclear Policy and the Tractors for Freedom Committee (pp. 204-5, 207, 210, 216-17). His last visit to Val-Kill and the death of ER (pp. 343-46).

F1633 Hanegbi, Yehuda. *The Eleanor Roosevelt Youth Centre in Beersheba.* Etudes Pedagogiques (Federation Interationale des Communautes d'Enfants-FICE), 11. Jerusalem: Jerusalem Post, 1967. 144p.

Includes a description of the 1960 ceremony attended by ER when the center was named in her honor (pp. 48-49). The book is dedicated to ER for her work with Youth Aliyah (p. [7]).

F1634 Hoff-Wilson, Joan. "Conclusion: Of Mice and Men." *Women and American Foreign Policy: Lobbyists, Critics, and Insiders.* Contributions in Women's Studies, 76. Ed. Edward P. Crapol. New York: Greenwood, 1987. 173-83. Notes.

Generalizations about the role of ER and others in developing American foreign policy are used to illustrate the marginal role which women have played.

F1635 Hurteau, Laure. "Un Hommage Canadien a la Grande Dame des Etats-Unis." *Actualite* 1 (July 1960): 9.

In a press conference in Montreal she refuses to predict the outcome of the 1960 presidential election but expresses her pleasure with the peaceful sit-ins which are taking place in the South. In French.

F1636 *Images of Peace: A Television Chronicle of a Turning Point in History.* New York: Columbia Broadcasting System, 1960. 113p.

Excerpts ER's informal comments made as she escorted the Khrushchevs at Hyde Park on 18 Sept. 1959 (pp. 79, 81-83, 85).

F1637 Josephson, Emanuel M. *Roosevelt's Communist Manifesto.* New York: Chendey, 1955. 128p. Index. Bibliography.

Considers ER's planned trip to Russia in 1954 as part of a larger scheme to secure the Communist vote for sons James and Franklin (p. 32). Uses her 1938 article in *Liberty* as evidence of her anti-Semitism. Cites article as 31 Dec. 1938; it is 25 Nov. (pp. 57-58).

F1638 Kurth, Peter. *American Cassandra: The Life of Dorothy Thompson*. Boston: Little, Brown, 1990. xv + 587p. Index. Notes.

At the time of the UN disarmament conference in Paris ER went public with her claims that Thompson's organization W.O.M.A.N. was a Communist tool and that the group was impeding the disarmament process. ER sent a letter to women's group about Thompson's mistaken ideas. Thompson reacted with her own public statements. The report of this Dec. 1951-Jan. 1952 exchange is based on letters (pp. 409-10).

F1639 Lash, Trude W. "Mrs. Roosevelt Revisits Israel." *Hadassah Newsletter* 35 (May 1955): 8-9.

ER was impressed with the country's development since her last visit and with the activities of the children. There is also Magda Cohen, "Eleanor Roosevelt Visits Jerusalem Home." *News Bulletin* (Jewish Telegraphic Agency) 12 (Apr./May 1955): 1-2. Copy not examined.

F1640 Lasky, Victor. "She Read It in the Papers." *Freeman* 3 (18 May 1953): 595-96.

After ER claimed in "My Day" of 10 Jan. 1953 that she had read that former Communist Louis Budenz had named Clarence Pickett and Earl Harrison as fellow Communists it took her until 24 Feb. to retract her statement. She must consider ex-Communists such as Budenz and Whittaker Chambers more dangerous than a traitor like Alger Hiss.

F1641 "Let the Ladies Do the Talking. *McCall's* 77 (Apr. 1950): 44-45, 115, 118-21.

ER and UN Indian delegate Vijaya Pandit discuss the advantages and disadvantages of being women who pursue public careers.

F1642 Luce, Clare Boothe. "Mrs. Roosevelt and Chinese Democracy." *Congressional Record Appendix* (7 Dec. 1945): A5348-49.

Rep. Luce criticizes a recent "My Day" column in which ER states that while Madame Chiang Kai-shek can talk about democracy while not knowing how to live it, it is the Chinese who live a democratic life. Includes 7 Dec. 1945 editorial from the *Washington Post* which takes issue with ER's position.

F1643 Matthews, Herbert L. "Mrs. Roosevelt Hailed at Oxford." *New York Times* 14 Nov. 1948: 29.

"A pillar of world affairs" and one to whom we are indebted for her efforts on behalf "of freedom, truth and social justice" were words used when ER received an honorary degree of Doctor of Civil Law on 13 Nov. In her address, excerpted here, she bemoaned the failure of the West and the Soviet Union to find common ground since they both want peace and freedom. The receipt of this honor will be welcomed by many including the American soldiers she visited in wartime hospitals, claims the editorial "Dr. Eleanor Roosevelt." *New York Times* 17 Nov. 1948: 26.

A different reaction questioning what she has done to receive such an honor is "D.C.L. from Oxford." *Ave Maria* 69 (23 Apr. 1949): 516.

F1644 "Medal." *United Nations Review* 1 (June 1955): 52.

Announcement that ER has been selected as the recipient of the 1954 Nansen Medal for "great services to the humanitarian cause of refugees and in commemoration of the outstanding initiatives taken by the late President Roosevelt." For accounts of her receipt of the medal, see "Mrs. Roosevelt Lauded." *New York Times* 16 Sept. 1955: 5 and "Refugees." *United Nations Review* 2 (Nov. 1955): 1.

F1645 Mesta, Perle. *Perle, My Story*. By Perle Mesta with Robert Cahn. New York: McGraw-Hill, 1960. viii + 251p. Index.

Recalls ER's visit to Luxembourg and Mesta's gratitude for the complimentary article in *Flair* which ER wrote about Mesta's appointment as ambassador. Reprints most of the article.

F1646 Morgenthau, Ruth S. "Eleanor Roosevelt and Jean Monnet: A Shared Vision." *Brandeis Review* 10 (Spring 1991): 42-45.

The author searches for every possible association between ER, the American UN delegate, and Monnet, the Frenchman who promoted the European Community. Both sought international cooperation among nations and the guarantee of the rights of individuals. She wishes that both were here to comment on the current status of international cooperation and human rights and to provide their assistance in securing peace in the Middle East.

F1647 "Mrs. R." *Time* 59 (7 Apr. 1952): 42-44, 47-50.

Her trip to India and the East was the occasion for this cover story assessing her life and activities. After years of incessant activity as First Lady she has become an influential figure who appears to thrive in the public eye. In the past she was too closely associated with persons and organizations considered Communistic. Now she is a symbol of human dignity to the world and an effective UN delegate. Reprinted in *Congressional Record Appendix* (10 Apr. 1952): A2352-54.

F1648 "Mrs. Roosevelt in India." *America* 86 (15 Mar. 1952): 630.

Here is something for which she can be praised. When ER made convincing comments about strides toward racial equality in the U.S. at her 1 Mar. news conference in New Delhi, she reassured "colored Asians" and improved U.S.-India relations.

F1649 "Mrs. Roosevelt Lives and Learns." Editorial. *Times Herald* (Washington) 16 Jan. 1948: 20.

We recall how she has told us that we must "love and understand" the Russians, but on 14 Jan. she stated that while living with the Russians we must demonstrate through words and deeds that we are stronger. Her experience at the UN has enlightened her.

F1650 "Mrs. Roosevelt on Tito." *Ave Maria* 78 (5 Sept. 1953): 6.

Why does she prefer this dictator, a "'good' communist" as she describes him, over Sen. Joseph McCarthy?

F1651 "Mrs. Roosevelt Scored." *New York Times* 25 Oct. 1948: 12.

According to the Russian *Literaturnaia Gazeta* her anti-Soviet views indicate that she has become feeble and is letting others control what she writes and says.

F1652 "Mrs. Roosevelt Visits India." *Congressional Record* (9 May 1952): 5000-5001.
Her visit to India. Includes her responses to questions she was asked while in India, excerpts of speeches she made, and portions of introductions given by Prime Minister Jawaharlal Nehru and President Rajendra Prasad. Reprinted from *India Today*.

F1653 "My Say." *Newsweek* 26 (12 Nov. 1945): 33.
ER, six months out of the White House, is still making news. In recent "My Day" columns she has spoken out about foreign policy, atomic weapons, military training in the post-war era, and conversion to a peacetime society.

F1654 *Order of Ceremony at the Unveiling of the Memorial to President Roosevelt by Mrs. Roosevelt in Grosvenor Square, London, Monday, April 12th, 1948.* London: The Times, 1948. 17p.
The text of remarks including tributes to ER.

F1655 "The Other Anna." *Newsweek* 41 (8 June 1953): 50.
Anna Rosenberg Fujikawa, who is sometimes confused with Anna M. Rosenberg, led an anti-war demonstration against ER.

F1656 Palmer, Gretta. "Can America Be Prosperous in a Sea of Human Misery? A Discussion between Mrs. Roosevelt and the Editors of Ladies' Home Journal." *Ladies' Home Journal* 63 (May 1946): 35, 131-32, 134.
In a conversation with Bruce and Beatrice Gould, ER challenges the free world to feed the world's hungry before the Soviets do so. Sees the UN as a means of bringing the U.S. and Soviet Union closer. A letter on p. 10 of the Aug. 1946 issue refutes ER's belief that American women do not understand the need for aid to Europe.

F1657 Penkower, Monty N. "Eleanor Roosevelt and the Plight of World Jewry." *Jewish Social Studies* 49 (Spring 1987): 125-36. Notes.
Her role in efforts to establish a Jewish state. Cites her writings and speeches and describes honors and tributes bestowed on her by the people of Israel.

F1658 Reddy, John. "Eleanor Roosevelt: First Lady of the World." *American Mercury* 68 (June 1949): 656-62.
A brief overview of her life plus a more detailed anecdotal account of her activities as a world figure. ER is committed to her work with the UN, and she reinforces this through her travels, writings, and speeches. Includes excerpts from editorial comments in the foreign press. For readers' reactions, see 69 (Aug. 1949): 249. Condensation issued as "The Evolution of Eleanor." *Reader's Digest* 54 (June 1949): 13-18.

F1659 Ross, Irwin. "Mrs. Roosevelt." *Liberty* (1 Mar. 1947): 20-21.
She is a world figure who devotes her energy to the UN, to her writing and speaking, and to responding to a heavy volume of mail. Reissued in *The Liberty Years, 1924-1950*, pp. 393-95 (Englewood Cliffs: Prentice-Hall, 1969).

F1660 "Se Non e Vero...e Ben Trovato." *America* 106 (6 June 1962): 430.
On 19 Dec. the *New York Times* printed most of a telegram from ER critical of Secretary of State Dean Rusk for praising Francisco Franco.

F1661 "Ein Tag mit Eleanor Roosevelt." *Zuricher Zeitung* [Zurich] Sept. 1946.
ER and a Swiss couple discuss political and social issues during at visit at Val-Kill.
From photocopy at FDRL. Page numbers lacking.

F1662 Tenney, Elizabeth Mackintosh, "Mrs. Roosevelt, the Russian Sniper, and
Me." *American Heritage* 43 (Apr. 1992): 28-31.
In a 1957 speech ER tells of her trip to Russia and her success in locating a World
War II heroine who had accompanied her on a 1942 tour of the U.S. and whom the
author had met during that tour.

F1663 Trotter, Zoe Pauline. "Mrs. Roosevelt Views the Future with Hope." *Echoes*
201 (Autumn 1951): 22, 30.
About ER on the occasion of her speech to the Canadian National Exhibition, 4
Sept. 1951.

F1664 Truman, Harry S. *Off the Record: The Private Papers of Harry S. Truman.*
Ed. Robert H. Ferrell. New York: Harper & Row, 1980. viii + 448p. Index.
Bibliography. Notes.
During his administration HST and ER corresponded, and this collection contains
letters from him about the end of the war, Winston Churchill, Soviet-American
relations, and conscientious objectors.

F1665 "U.S. Bars China Trip for Mrs. Roosevelt." *New York Times* 26 June 1957: 1,
8.
The State Dept. has told her that like all other journalists she cannot visit China.
She considers it essential that communication be maintained with Communist
countries but will not challenge the decision. "Mrs. Roosevelt's Whirl." *Newsweek*
50 (8 July 1957): 82-83 refers to the *New York Post*'s support for the trip. But James
Wechsler's supportive editorial in that paper does not appear to be shared by others,
states *Newsweek*.

F1666 "Wallace Pays Tribute to Mrs. Roosevelt." *Democratic Digest* 23 (Apr. 1946):
14.
Excerpts address made at the 14 Mar. 1946 Women's Joint Congressional Committee Dinner held in ER's honor. Henry Wallace calls her a great person who has won
the respect of the American people. "In this crusade for a peaceful world, no figure
is more important than that of Eleanor Roosevelt" and "Eleanor Roosevelt is no
longer the first lady of the land--she is now the first lady of the world."

F1667 Weart, William G. "His Adopted City Honors Franklin." *New York Times* 18
Jan. 1956: 17.
In Philadelphia ER is awarded the Franklin Medal for her efforts to promote
world understanding.

F1668 Weiser, Marjorie P.K., and Jean S. Arbeiter. "Sixteen International
Women." *Womanlist*. By Marjorie P.K. Weiser and Jean S. Arbeiter. New York:
Atheneum, 1981. 374-75.
A brief description of her activities as an "international" woman (p. 374).

F1669 Wise, Stephen S. *Stephen S. Wise: Servant of the People, Selected Letters*. Ed. Carl Hermann Voss. Philadelphia: Jewish Publication Society of America, 1970. xxi + 332p. Index.

Contains text of 1942 letter to ER about the possibilities for a Jewish homeland (pp. 246-48).

F1670 "Worldly Lesson from New Prof." *Life* 47 (7 Dec. 1959): 90-92.

As a Brandeis Univ. faculty member ER discusses world affairs and the UN in a seminar setting.

F1671 Zarina. "America's Great Lady." *Mysindia* 14 (30 Mar. 1952): 17, 20.

The places visited in India and the events held in her honor. Constitutes an issue of the column "Feminine Fancies."

F1672 "'Zindabad!' for Mrs. Roosevelt." *Life* 32 (17 Mar. 1952): 42-43.

She received a Hindu greeting wishing her long life as reported in this mainly photographic account her visit to India and Pakistan.

POLITICAL ACTIVITIES AFTER THE DEATH OF FDR

F1673 "ADA Opens National Sessions Here; Liberals Rally in Regional Groups." *ADA World* 1 (29 Mar. 1947): 1.

The Americans for Democratic Action becomes "a full-fledged national organization of independent progressives" as it meets today in Washington.

F1674 Anthony, Carl Sferrazza. *First Ladies: The Saga of the Presidents' Wives and Their Power, 1789-1961*. Vol. [1] of *First Ladies*. New York: Morrow, 1990. 685p. Index. Notes.

ER and the 1960 Democratic National Convention and presidential election (pp. 578-79, 589-90). At JFK's inauguration (pp. 600-601, 603).

F1675 "Assert Negro Vote Will Swing to GOP." *New York Times* 18 Oct. 1946: 13.

It is reported that since she is no longer a major force in the Democratic Party and because ER the private citizen and ER the First Lady are not at all the same, she will not prevent a large black turnout for Republican candidates.

F1676 *Ave Maria*.

The investigations undertaken by Sen. Joseph McCarthy were a part of the political scene in the years after the death of FDR, and ER was a frequent target in the Communist scare which was present in the U.S. In Merle Miller, *The Judges and the Judged* (Garden City: Doubleday, 1952) the omission of ER from *Red Channels: The Report of Communist Influence in Radio and Television* (New York: American Business Consultants, 1950) is discussed with its compilers Theodore Kirkpatrick and Kenneth Bierly who state that since her activities, including support of Communist organizations, are so well known nothing would have been gained by including her (pp. 124-25).

Examples of attacks on her in *Ave Maria* are "Mrs. Roosevelt Guiding." 68 (28 Aug. 1948): 260, "Mrs. Roosevelt's Logic." 74 (21 July 1951): 66, and "Strange Suggestion." 77 (10 Jan. 1953): 36-37. All criticize her for supporting suspected Communists. ER and others who have founded the National Issues Committee are afraid of McCarthy it is claimed in "National Issues Committee." 78 (21 Sept. 1953): 4.

Westbrook Pegler called for her to be put before the committee and revealed for what she really is. See his column "As Pegler Sees It" for 11 Nov. 1953 which appeared in the *New York Journal American*, p. 3 as "Discusses Mrs. F.D.R.'s Attitude on Communism."

F1677 Bell, Jack. *The Splendid Misery: The Story of the Presidency and Power Politics at Close Range*. Garden City: Doubleday, 1960. 474p. Index.

Poignant account of a 1956 California primary speech by ER for Adlai Stevenson (pp. 268, 270-71).

F1678 "Boy's Best Friend: Mother Spends 31 1/2 Hours Helping Jimmy Roosevelt." *Life* 29 (25 Sept. 1950): 40-41.

A report, mainly photographic, of ER's tour of Calif. on behalf of her son's candidacy for Gov. and Helen Gahagan Douglas' candidacy for the U.S. Senate. Most of her speechmaking was related to the UN, however. For similar coverage, see "Mamma Knows Best." *Time* 56 (25 Sept. 1950): 23-24.

F1679 Burns, James MacGregor. *The Crosswinds of Freedom*. The American Experiment, 3. New York: Knopf, 1989. xi + 864p. Index. Notes.

ER's involvement with presidential campaigns between 1948 and 1960 and with the Americans for Democratic Action (pp. 234-36, 238, 286-88, 325-26).

F1680 Butler, Paul M. "Dear Fellow Democrats:" *Democratic Digest* 6 (Oct. 1959): inside front cover.

Praise for the aid which she provided FDR, her accomplishments after his death, and the importance of her present contributions. An open letter from the chair of the Democratic National Committee on the occasion of ER's 75th birthday.

F1681 "Coffee & a New Role." *Time* 62 (24 Aug. 1953): 12-13.

ER has accepted an invitation to chair the National Issues Committee, a group concerned with explaining current issues on a non-partisan liberal basis and considered by the Republican Party to be left of the Americans for Democratic Action.

F1682 Collier, Peter, and David Horowitz. *The Kennedys: An American Drama*. New York: Summit, 1984. 576p. Index. Bibliographic Note. Notes.

ER's opposition to JFK was because she was jealous of the success of Joseph Kennedy's children (pp. 240-41).

F1683 Dales, Douglas. "Democratic Liberals Open Drive to Remove De Sapio." *New York Times* 23 Jan. 1959: 1, 12.

ER, Herbert Lehman, and Thomas Finletter have issued a statement about their wish to remove political leader Carmine De Sapio, eliminate "bossism" from N.Y. politics, and return power to the people. Text of statement is on p. 12.

F1684 "A Democratic Party of Youth and Unity." *Life* 41 (27 Aug. 1956): 20-35.

Although featured on the cover of this issue with includes lengthy coverage of the 1956 national convention, the only attention given to ER is a brief mention of her address.

F1685 Egan, Leo. "Mrs. Roosevelt Disputes Truman on Liberals' Role." *New York Times* 8 Dec. 1959: 1, 53.

When he introduced ER at her birthday celebration HST complained that the liberal cause is being hurt by the affluent who have decided to embrace liberalism. ER responded that all kinds of liberals are needed. Also reported as "Two Scrappy 75-Year-Old Democrats." *Life* 47 (21 Dec. 1959): 35-36

F1686 "La Esposa de Roosevelt, Candidata Presidencial de los Estados Unidos." *Republica* (Oct. 1949): 4.

Perhaps ER will will become a candidate for the presidency in 1952 and carry on FDR's programs. In Spanish.

F1687 "Forward Look Keynote of Tenth Anniversary Convention Mar. 29-31." *ADA World* 12 (Jan. 1957): 1.

Includes quotes from ER's invitation to members. She states that the Americans for Democratic Action came into existence to offset conservatism and Soviet aggression. Those needs are still appropriate today, and our meeting will "chart a course for liberals in the years ahead."

F1688 Fox, Victor J. "'Very Strange Bedfellows': In Politics 'Birds of a Feather Flock Together.'" *American Mercury* 91 (Aug. 1960): 91-93.

Democratic presidential candidates need ER's endorsement, but her activities on behalf of Communists and against those who try to protect the country could prove to be a negative with many voters. Fox refers to a pocket-size book about ER's affiliations, but no copy was located.

F1689 Fuchs, Lawrence H. "The Senator and the Lady." *American Heritage* 25 (Oct. 1974): 57-61, 81-83.

Background on the strained relations between ER and JFK over the 1956 and 1960 nominations. After their 1960 reconciliation JFK utilized ER, she communicated with him about matters of concern to her, and she developed an intense loyalty to him as President. Also addresses her frustrations with Adlai Stevenson over his reluctance to accept her advice to get closer to the average citizen. An abbreviated version appeared as "The Lady and the Senator." *Brandeis Review* 4 (Fall 1984): 6-10.

F1690 Galbraith, John Kenneth. *A Life in Our Times: Memoirs*. Boston: Houghton Mifflin, 1981. x + 563p. Index. Bibliography.

The relationship between ER and JFK prior to his nomination (pp. 375-76).

F1691 Hamby, Alonzo L. *Beyond the New Deal: Harry S. Truman and American Liberalism*. Contemporary American History Series. New York: Columbia Univ. Pr., 1973. xx + 635p. Index. Bibliography. Notes.

Hamby's study of liberalism in the period immediately following the New Deal attempts to establish HST's position in the liberal movement. There are brief references to ER's reactions to his policies (pp. 65, 68, 78, 177, 189, 191, 220, 255-56, 334, 406, 433).

F1692 "Hurt Feelings." *Ave Maria* 72 (2 Dec. 1950): 708.

Son James lost the election for Gov. of Calif. to Earl Warren, and ER should not place the blame on HST for failing to campaign for her son.

F1693 *Inside Politics: The National Conventions, 1960.* America's Politics Series, 2. Ed. Paul Tillett. Dobbs Ferry: Oceana, 1962. 281p.

ER's role in the selection of New York delegates (pp. 197-98) and her support of Adlai Stevenson at the Democratic National Convention (pp. 209, 249).

F1694 *John Fitzgerald Kennedy...As We Remember Him.* A Columbia Legacy Book. Ed. Joan Meyers. New York: Atheneum, 1965. ix + 241p. Index.

William Walton recalls ER during the 1960 presidential campaign. He accompanied JFK to Val-Kill to see ER and went with her when she made campaign speeches for JFK.

F1695 Kahn, E.J., Jr. "The Years Alone." *New Yorker* 24 (12 June 1948): 30-34, 36, 39-41; 24 (19 June 1948): 30-34, 36, 39-41.

The role which she has been playing in Democratic Party politics as described in a study of her activities since the death of FDR.

F1696 Kennedy, Edward M. "Eleanor Roosevelt and John F. Kennedy." *Eleanor Roosevelt: An American Journey.* Ed. Jess Flemion and Colleen M. O'Connor. San Diego: San Diego State Univ. Pr., 1987. 299-301.

After they made their peace during the 1960 campaign, President Kennedy utilized ER's abilities and influence.

F1697 Kraft, Joseph. "The Decline of the New York Democrats." *Commentary* 30 (July 1960): 17-21.

There are no young faces in a state party led by ER and veterans of the Roosevelt years. The 1958 state convention resulted in a split with ER and others bolting to form the New York Committee of Democratic Voters. Also discussed in James Q. Wilson, *The Amateur Democrat: Club Politics in Three Cities*, pp. 58-64 (Chicago: Univ. of Chicago Pr., 1962).

F1698 Lasky, Victor. *J.F.K.: The Man and the Myth.* New Rochelle: Arlington House, 1966. 653p. Index. Notes.

From the time of the 1956 Democratic Convention to JFK's nomination in 1960, Lasky makes frequent mention of ER's belief that JFK lacked courage because of his soft stand on McCarthyism (pp. 184, 229, 239-40, 243, 317-18). JFK's post-convention visit with ER (pp. 415-16).

F1699 Lavine, Harold. "Life with Eleanor." *Newsweek* 34 (22 Aug. 1949): 20-23.

Cover story. Her writings, speaking, and UN activities have kept her in the public eye, and she is highly regarded by the American people and many in the Truman administration. Lavine disputes the claim that she is at odds with HST and was an early opponent of his renomination.

F1700 Louchheim, Katie. *By the Political Sea.* Garden City: Doubleday, 1970. xii + 293p. Index.

ER and Adlai Stevenson's 1956 and 1960 campaigns (pp. 76, 78, 81, 85-87, 95-96).

F1701 MacDougall, Curtis D. *Gideon's Army.* 3 vols. New York: Marzani & Munsell, 1965.

A study of Henry Wallace's Progressive Party movement in the election of 1948 and Wallace as the heir to FDR. Suggests reasons why ER sided with FDR, Jr.

against Elliott in a 1947 public dispute. ER's disputes with Wallace (v. 1, pp. 181-82).

F1702 Martin, John Bartlow. *Adlai Stevenson and the World: The Life of Adlai E. Stevenson*. Garden City: Doubleday, 1977. 946p. Index. Notes.
Covering the period from Nov. 1952 until Stevenson's death and based primarily on Stevenson's speeches, letters, memoranda, and press conferences, the work contains numerous brief references to ER. The frequency of their personal contact and depth of friendship (pp. 26, 31, 176, 209, 213, 396, 397, 426, 446, 574, 611, 667). ER's role in the 1956 campaign (pp. 215-392 passim). ER's role in the 1960 campaign (pp. 459-530 passim). Stevenson on the death of ER (pp. 748-49, 757).

F1703 Martin, Ralph G. *Hero for Our Time: An Intimate Story of the Kennedy Years*. New York: Macmillan, 1983. ix + 596p. Index. Notes.
Since much of this work is based on interviews, including one with ER, it may be the best discussion of the relationship between JFK and ER. Their meeting during the 1960 Democratic National Convention (pp. 107-8). Their post-convention meeting at Val-Kill marked the beginning of the admiration which she had for him as President (pp. 220-21).

F1704 Massey, Michael J. "Relations between Harry S. Truman and Eleanor Roosevelt: A Constructive Friendship." Senior Honors Thesis, Ind. Univ., 1985. 74p. Bibliography. Notes.
Massey considers HST's relations with ER as symbolic of his relationship with the entire liberal movement. HST and ER and other liberals needed one another. Coverage is provided of the political events in 1945-1947 and the election of 1948. Available at FDRL.

F1705 McKeever, Porter. *Adlai Stevenson: His Life and Legacy*. New York: Morrow, 1989. 591p. Index. Bibliography.
ER's support of Stevenson for the Democratic nomination in 1956 and 1960 (pp. 367, 374-75, 457, 459, 463). Their friendship (pp. 104, 367, 398-99). The death of ER (pp. 516, 529-30).

F1706 Meyer, Robert S. "The National Committee for an Effective Congress." *Peace Organizations Past and Present: A Survey and Directory*. By Robert S. Meyer. Jefferson: McFarland, 1988. 92-93.
ER was one of the committee's founders in 1948. Consists of a description of the its founding and activities.

F1707 Miller, Nathan. *The Roosevelt Chronicles*. Garden City: Doubleday: 1979. vi + 377p. Index. Bibliography.
ER and Democratic Party politics after the death of FDR (pp. 338-41).

F1708 "Mrs. Roosevelt for Stevenson, with Kennedy as Running Mate." *New York Times* 10 June 1960: 14.
She believes that world conditions call for a more experienced leader. JFK should be prepared to accept the vice presidential nomination in the best interests of the country. For complete text of her statement, see "Endorsement by Mrs. Eleanor Roosevelt of Adlai Stevenson for President." *Congressional Record* (10 June 1960): 12362-63.

F1709 "Mrs. Roosevelt Speaks." *New Republic* 116 (3 Feb. 1947): 8.
   Reports on ER's appeal that progressive groups work together. Lengthy excerpts from a "My Day" column constitute both a denial of difficulties with Henry Wallace and a recognition that not all progressives are as concerned as she is about having Communists on their staffs.

F1710 "Mrs. Vice President?" *Newsweek* 32 (12 July 1948): 21.
   Republican Clare Boothe Luce suggests that only with ER on the ticket will HST have a chance of being re-elected, but Luce knows that as men the Democrats will never let it happen. ER rules it out first.

F1711 Muller, Herbert J. *Adlai Stevenson: A Study in Values.* New York: Harper and Row, 1967. xiii + 338p. Index.
   Brief references to ER illustrating the mutual respect which she and Stevenson had for one another. Favorable comparisons of Stevenson to ER.

F1712 Nevins, Allen. *Herbert H. Lehman and His Era.* New York: Scribner's, 1963. 456p. Index. Bibliography. Notes.
   Nevins' study of FDR's successor as Gov. of N.Y. contains a lengthy discussion of events in 1958-1961 which with ER's close involvement led to the ouster of New York City political boss Carmine De Sapio (pp. 372-89). Relies heavily on Lehman's papers and his oral history memoir.

F1713 Nichols, Lewis. "Mrs. R." *New York Times Book Review* 1 Oct. 1961: 8.
   In *The Autobiography of Eleanor Roosevelt* she states that her days of campaigning are over, but at a recent luncheon hosted for book people she left her guests with a different impression.

F1714 "130 Liberals Form a Group on Right." *New York Times* 5 Jan. 1947: 5.
   ER and others found the Americans for Democratic Action to espouse liberal ideals while rejecting sympathy to Communists.

F1715 Parmet, Herbert S. *The Democrats: The Years after FDR.* New York: Macmillan, 1976. xi + 371p. Index. Bibliography. Notes.
   Limited attention to ER's involvement with Democratic national politics from 1948 to 1960. Draws from her letters (pp. 34-181 passim).

F1716 ---. *JFK: The Presidency of John F. Kennedy.* New York: Dial, 1983. viii + 407p. Index. Notes.
   The post-1960 Democratic convention reconciliation of ER and JFK. Details his 14 Aug. visit to Val-Kill and how she did not promote Adlai Stevenson for Secretary of State. ER's efforts on JFK's behalf during the early part of the campaign (pp. 34-37).

F1717 Pearson, Drew. *Diaries, 1949-1959.* Ed. Tyler Abell. New York: Holt, Rinehart and Winston, 1974. xiv + 592p. Index.
   In Pearson's recollections of ER there are revelations about HST's feelings about ER and her private and public activities during the period.

F1718 *Proceedings of the Democratic State Convention, Albany, New York, September 3rd and 4th, 1946.* N.p.: n.p., n.d. 176p. Typescript.
ER as temporary chair of the convention (pp. 35-45). Available at FDRL.

F1719 Redding, Jack. *Inside the Democratic Party.* Indianapolis: Bobbs-Merrill, 1958. 319p. Index.
The presidential election of 1948. Democratic campaign publicity director Redding describes the successful effort to get ER to support HST in a radio broadcast (pp. 226-32).

F1720 Reeves, Thomas C. *A Question of Character: A Life of John F. Kennedy.* New York: Free, 1991. xv + 510p. Index. Notes.
ER and JFK at the 1956 Democratic National Convention and ER's refusal to support him for Vice President (pp. 132, 134). Her criticism for his weak stand on Sen. Joseph McCarthy (pp. 146, 150-52). Their 1960 post-convention meeting (p. 188).

F1721 Roche, John P. "Escape from Her Husband's Towering Shadow." Rev. of *Eleanor: The Years Alone* by Joseph P. Lash. *New York Times Book Review* 30 July 1972: 3.
Roche finds Lash's treatment of ER's role in Democratic Party politics disappointing. He provides his own interpretation of her continued attraction to the candidacy of Adlai Stevenson.

F1722 "Roosevelts Hit Tactics of 3rd Party." *ADA World* 2 (17 Apr. 1948): 4.
ER and children James and Anna have spoken out against the use of FDR's name in association with the third party movement in Ore. ER has said that Henry Wallace's progressive movement is dangerous.

F1723 Scharf, Lois. "Roosevelt, Anna Eleanor." *The Harry S. Truman Encyclopedia.* The G.K. Hall Presidential Encyclopedia Series. Ed. Richard S. Kirkendall. Boston: Hall, 1989. 309-10. Bibliography.
Highlights of the sometimes uneasy relationship between HST and ER in party politics after FDR's death.

F1724 Shelton, Willard. "The ADA's Dilemma: HST or GOP." *New Republic* 118 (1 Mar. 1948): 9.
At the first national convention of the Americans for Democratic Action ER was referred to as "the ADA's 'moving spirit.'"

F1725 Smith, Gerald L. K. *Too Much and Too Many Roosevelts.* St. Louis: Christian Nationalist Crusade, 1950. 74p.
Fearful that ER is trying to orchestrate a return of the Roosevelt dynasty to Washington, Smith attacks FDR's policies and intentions. Also, much criticism and ridicule are aimed at her in the section "An Open Letter to Eleanor Roosevelt" (pp. 67-74). This section was published separately as a pamphlet, *An Open Letter to Eleanor Roosevelt from Gerald L.K. Smith* (N.p.: n.p., 1949).

F1726 Steinberg, Alfred. *Sam Johnson's Boy: A Close-up of the President from Texas.* New York: Macmillan, 1968. 871p. Index. Bibliography.

Quotes from unidentified 1960 television program on which ER criticizes Lyndon Johnson for lacking an agenda and from conversations about her dislike for him (pp. 524-25).

F1727 Stevenson, Adlai E. *The Papers of Adlai E. Stevenson*. 8 vols. Ed. Walter Johnson, et al. Boston: Little, Brown, 1972-1979. Index. Notes.
Letters to ER about the 1952 presidential campaign (v. 4, pp. 23, 44, 198) and his letter about forthcoming announcement of candidacy for the 1956 nomination (v. 4, p. 582). A letter of 9 Apr. 1954 expressing regret that he could not attend the Americans for Democratic Action convention (v. 4, p. 350). Letters about miscellaneous political topics (v. 4, pp. 219-20, 299, 356).
During the 1956 presidential campaign ER spoke frequently on Stevenson's behalf. Correspondence to ER and others about those speeches and Stevenson's position on civil rights (v. 6, pp. 81, 83, 109, 132, 145-46, 151-52, 169, 177-78, 180, 182, 190-91, 230, 300).
Letters to ER and references to her concerning Stevenson's 1960 candidacy for the Democratic nomination and ER's subsequent support of JFK (v. 7, pp. 511-13, 515-17, 519, 522, 536-37, 546, 548-49, 561). Her 14 Feb. 1956 statement in defense of his civil rights record is excerpted (v. 7, p. 67).

F1728 Thompson, Charles A.H., and Frances M. Shattuck. *The 1956 Presidential Campaign*. Washington: Brookings Institution, 1968. xv + 382p. Index. Notes.
ER's efforts in support of Stevenson, her position on the issues, and her opposition to JFK's vice-presidential candidacy (pp. 25, 60, 69, 107, 141, 154). Her 12 Aug. press conference at the Democratic National Convention (pp. 135-36).

F1729 Vidal, Gore. "The Holy Family." *Esquire* 67 (Apr. 1967): 99-103, 201-4.
In his look at the Kennedys, Vidal recalls a 1960 conversation in which JFK denounced ER. Vidal concludes that JFK discounted those actions of his with which ER found fault and that neither ever understood the other.

F1730 "Wallace Bid: 'An Invitation to Disaster.'" *ADA World* 2 (8 Jan. 1948): 1, 3.
Henry Wallace's third party movement has alienated him with liberals. ER has made an analysis of the situation in a series of "My Day" columns in which she disputes Wallace's position.

F1731 Walton, Richard J. *Henry Wallace, Harry Truman, and the Cold War*. New York: Viking, 1976. x + 388p. Index. Bibliography. Notes.
ER and Wallace in the Union for Democratic Action (pp. 289-90). Her involvement with the Americans for Democratic Action and Wallace's with Progressive Citizens of America brought about the split between them and ER's decision to support HST in 1948 (pp. 190, 298).

F1732 "Washington's Ten Most Powerful Women." *McCall's* 78 (Jan. 1951): 26-29.
ER is still one of them.

F1733 "Woman Leader Calls for More Women Leaders." *Democratic Digest* 25 (June 1948): 16.
Excerpts "My Day" column in which she urges an expanded role for women. More should be appointed to positions and others should run for elective office.

F1734 Yarnell, Allen. *Democrats and Progressives: The 1948 Presidential Election as a Test of Postwar Liberalism*. Berkeley: Univ. of Calif. Pr., 1974. xii + 155p. Index. Bibliography. Notes.

ER's reaction to a Progressive victory in an early 1948 congressional primary differed from those of her fellow Democrats since she felt that the victory indicated the American people's concern over inflation and fear of war (pp. 54-55, 89).

WRITER, PUBLIC SPEAKER, AND MEDIA PERSONALITY

F1735 "Academic Freedom Absurd, Says Lawyer." *New York Times* 24 May 1940: 21.

In New York on 23 May the American Parents Committee on Education was told that ER advocates in her writings a type of tolerance which is "a sickly anemic thing which counsels us to have no convictions, to defend no principles and to condemn no abuses." The charge was made by an "A.E. Stevenson," but Adlai Stevenson established that he had not made the claim. See *The Papers of Adlai E. Stevenson*, v. 1, p. 449 (Boston: Little, Brown, 1972).

F1736 Adams, Val. "Mrs. Roosevelt Helped TV Series." *New York Times* 9 Nov. 1962: 71.

When the 26-part ABC television series *F.D.R.* appears in the Fall of 1963 it will benefit from advice provided by ER and about 100 hours of narration which she completed not long before her death.

F1737 ---. "Mrs. Roosevelt May Film TV Ads." *New York Times* 10 Feb. 1959: 66.

She is considering making a commercial for the Lever Bros. product Good Luck margarine. His "Mrs. Roosevelt to Appear in Ads." *New York Times* 16 Feb. 1959: 53 confirms that the commercial will be broadcast beginning 16 Feb. She agreed to do it in order to get an important message to the American people about the need to be concerned for the hungry in other nations. The text of her statement is included in a separate section of his "Godfrey Will Do Murrow Program." *New York Times* 18 Feb. 1959: 67.

Jack Gould in "TV: Dubious Judgment." *New York Times* 17 Feb. 1959: 63 states that it is sad that ER had the lapse of good judgment which has resulted in her appearance in a television commercial. Includes text of commercial in which she promotes the product while also reminding viewers that many people in other nations lack sufficient food.

F1738 ---. "Mrs. Roosevelt Plans TV Series." *New York Times* 9 June 1959: 75.

She will make a pilot for a television series in which she will discuss international affairs with a panel of college students. The article also recalls her 1950-1951 series *Mrs. Roosevelt Meets the Public*.

F1739 "And Mrs. F.D.R. Said--." *Guild Reporter* 4 (15 Jan. 1937): 2.

She joined the New York chapter of the American Newspaper Guild with the understanding that she would not be expected to strike, join picket lines, or attend guild meetings. Excerpts *New York Times*, *Editor & Publisher*, and Associated and United Press accounts of her remarks about guild membership.

F1740 Baird, A. Craig. "Before the Democratic National Convention: Eleanor Roosevelt." *Representative American Speeches: 1956-1957*. Reference Shelf 29, no. 3. New York: Wilson, 1957. 109. Notes.

Credits ER's success as a speaker to her direct approach and the personal nature of her remarks.

F1741 ---. "Civil Liberties--The Individual and the Community. Eleanor Anna (sic) Roosevelt Roosevelt." *Representative American Speeches: 1939-1940*. Reference Shelf 14, no. 1. New York: Wilson, 1940. 173. Notes.
Analysis of her speaking ability.

F1742 Beasley, Maurine. "Eleanor Roosevelt and 'My Day': The White House Years." *Franklin D. Roosevelt: The Man, the Myth, the Era, 1882-1945*. Contributions in Political Science, 189. Ed. Herbert D. Rosenbaum and Elizabeth Bartelme. New York: Greenwood, 1987. 257-68. Notes.
For its contribution to women's studies a reappraisal of "My Day" is needed. Members of her family attributed her decision to undertake the column to a desire to accomplish something on her own, gain influence and power, and aid FDR. During the White House years she used the column to explain her position on the Marian Anderson incident, provide support for youth organizations, and speak on behalf of the war effort and the type of post-war world which she envisioned. Through "My Day" women could see a middle aged woman start a new career, empathize with the plight of another woman who does not have the time to accomplish all that she would like, and gain assistance in struggling with the problems of depression and war. Paper presented at Hofstra Univ. Conference, 4-6 Mar. 1982.
Beasley presented a similar paper in July 1982 to the Association for Education in Journalism meeting at Ohio Univ. An abridged version of this paper issued as "Eleanor Roosevelt Wrote Her Column, "My Day," 6 Days a Week for Over 25 Years." *Media Report to Women* 10 (1 Oct. 1982): 11.

F1743 ---. *Eleanor Roosevelt and the Media: A Public Quest for Self-Fulfillment*. Urbana: Univ. of Ill. Pr., 1987. xi + 240p. Index. Notes.
ER's exposure to the media and her use of it to promote FDR, social reform, the role of women, and her own self-fulfillment. Beasley draws from published material and interviews which she conducted. The notes are a source to contemporary newspaper accounts of ER as First Lady.

F1744 ---. "Eleanor Roosevelt's Vision of Journalism: A Communications Medium for Women." *Presidential Studies Quarterly* 16 (Winter 1986): 66-75. Notes.
She used her White House press conferences as well as "My Day" and her magazine articles to communicate with women, to bring women's issues to the public's attention, and to provide a means for women to communicate with her and in turn with other women. The theme is expanded in Beasley's *Eleanor Roosevelt and the Media*.

F1745 Beasley, Maurine, and Paul Belgrade. "Eleanor Roosevelt: First Lady as Radio Pioneer." *Journalism History* 11 (Autumn/Winter 1984): 42-45. Notes.
ER made commercial broadcasts during the White House years because she wanted to demonstrate that it was possible for a woman to be rewarded financially, to donate her earnings to charity, and to pursue a career of her own.

F1746 Bilsborrow, Eleanor Janice. "The Philosophy of Social Reform in the Speeches of Eleanor Roosevelt." Diss. Univ. of Denver, 1957. viii + 271p. Bibliography. Notes.

Her effectiveness in promoting social reform is considered through an analysis of 20 of her speeches.

F1747 Butler, Jessie Haver. *Time to Speak Up: A Speaker's Handbook for Women.* 2nd rev. ed. New York: Harper, 1957. xvii + 255p. Index.
   Contains a series of references to ER as a public speaker and subject of interviews. Praise for her ability to speak extemporaneously. Provides examples of her success in responding to difficult questions (pp. 8, 18, 107-8, 139, 227-28).

F1748 "A Call from Hyde Park." *Time* 53 (13 June 1949): 79-80, 83.
   Upset that the editors of the *Ladies' Home Journal* wanted her to revise *This I Remember*, ER switched the serialization of the book as well as her column "If You Ask Me" to the rival *McCall's*. Also includes a discussion of the content of *This I Remember*.

F1749 Carson, Saul. "On the Air: Soap and the Roosevelts." *New Republic* 123 (25 Dec. 1950): 21.
   NBC signed ER for a radio talk program after Mary Margaret McBride moved to ABC. While ER deserves high marks for handling the serious topics addressed by the program, less admirable are son Elliott's commercials in which ER's endorsement is used. Also reported in "Opposites." *Time* 56 (9 Oct. 1950): 58. "Maybe 50G per Wk. for Mrs. R." *Billboard* 62 (2 Dec. 1950): 1, 4 predicts the anticipated weekly gross earnings for the program.

F1750 Christopher, Maurine. "Mrs. Roosevelt Brought Dignity to Ad Role." *Advertising Age* 55 (30 Apr. 1984): 54.
   ER's willingness to do commercials made it easier for other public figures to do so. An overview of her career as a radio and television personality.

F1751 "Columns: Two Roosevelt Women Try to Fill Will Rogers's [sic] Shoes." *Newsweek* 7 (4 Jan. 1936): 31-32.
   Cousins ER and Alice Roosevelt Longworth have both begun newspaper columns.

F1752 Cornwell, Elmer E., Jr. *Presidential Leadership of Public Opinion.* Bloomington: Indiana Univ. Pr., 1965. x + 370p. Index. Notes.
   Through "My Day," lectures, and radio addresses, she helped FDR's image (p. 244).

F1753 Crocker, Lionel. "Eleanor Roosevelt on Public Speaking." *Speaker of Tau Kappa Alpha* 36 (Mar. 1954): 17, 25.
   She was a guest at a Tau Kappa Alpha student dinner, and Crocker provides the question-and-answer session he conducted with her. In describing how to handle hecklers she relates her accounts of speaking at the 1940 American Youth Congress and to students at the Univ. of Allahabad. Louis Howe is recognized as the one who taught her how to make a speech.

F1754 Dado, Susanna Sciutto. "Eleanor Roosevelt as a Columnist." Thesis (M.A.) Calif. State Univ., Northridge, 1977. vii + 245p. Bibliography. Notes.
   ER's style of writing helped endear her to the average readers of "My Day," thus enabling her to gain their respect as she sought to use the column to make them more active participants in the democratic process. Columns from seven periods are

examined. Includes an overview of ER's life and career and a review of major writings by and about her.

F1755 Davis, Kenneth S. "FDR as a Biographer's Problem." *American Scholar* 53 (Winter 1983/84): 100-108.
 In the discussion of his decision to attempt a biographical study of FDR, Davis describes *This Is My Story* and *This I Remember* as poignant accounts of her effort to understand the real FDR.

F1756 Denniston, Elinore. Publisher's Note. *Tomorrow Is Now.* By Eleanor Roosevelt. New York: Perennial-Harper, 1964. vii-x.
 While becoming increasingly weak ER pushed herself to finish the first draft of the book. Her recollections of ER at the time *Tomorrow Is Now* was being written.

F1757 [Dilling, Elizabeth K.] *The Octopus.* By Frank Woodruff Johnson [pseud.] Omaha: Dilling, 1940. 256p. Index.
 There are two brief discussions of ER's appearance in the prologue to the movie version of Ernst Toller's "red anti-Nazi" play *Pastor Hall* (pp. 62, 113).

F1758 Dunning, John. "Eleanor and Anna Roosevelt." *Tune in Yesterday: The Ultimate Encyclopedia of Old-Time Radio, 1925-1976.* By John Dunning. Englewood Cliffs: Prentice-Hall, 1976. 181-82.
 ER's prominence as a commentator is demonstrated by her 1948-1949 radio program *Eleanor and Anna Roosevelt.* Discusses programs and media reaction.

F1759 *Expressions: Eleanor Roosevelt on Her Life.* Ed. A.E. Wooley. Cherry Hill: Wooley, 1984. 40p.
 Photographs of an older ER are used to illustrate how she used her hands to communicate. Includes unidentified quotations from her writings arranged according to broad topics.

F1760 Farr, Finis. *FDR.* New Rochelle: Arlington House, 1972. 439p. Index.
 Although her memoirs are important historical documents, ER would have had no career as a writer or speaker had she not been the wife of FDR (p. 399).

F1761 Ferris, Helen. "Mrs. Roosevelt and Children's Books." *Library Journal* 89 (15 May 1964): 2149-51, 2159.
 From 1929 until her death ER was associated with the Junior Literary Guild, and for many years she reviewed potential guild selections. Ferris recalls the qualities which ER prized in books for young girls. Also paged as 23, 25, 33 of Children's Section which can be cited as *School Library Journal* 10 (May 1964).

F1762 Fielding, Raymond. *The March of Time, 1935-1951.* New York: Oxford Univ. Pr., 1978. viii + 359p. Index. Bibliography. Notes.
 ER was portrayed regularly by prominent actresses in the radio news version of *The March of Time* (p. 12) and in the newsreel version with her voice dubbed by actresses over actual newsreel footage (pp. 165, 261).

F1763 "First Lady of Radio: Eleanor Roosevelt." *FDR, The Intimate Presidency: Franklin Delano Roosevelt, Communications, and the Mass Media in the 1930s, an Exhibition to Commemorate the 100th Anniversary of the Birth of the 32nd President* *of the United States, January 1982.* By Arthur P. Molella and Elsa M. Barton. Ed. with the assistance of Spencer P. Crew. Washington: Smithsonian Institution, National Museum of American History, 1982. 54.

Her speaking style and the impact of her public addresses.

F1764 "First Lady's Home Journal." *Time* 29 (8 Mar. 1937): 36.

The *Ladies' Home Journal* has announced that *This Is My Story* will run in installments. A lengthy excerpt is used to substantiate the editors' claim that this is a frank autobiography.

F1765 "First Lady's Week." *Time* 35 (15 Apr. 1940): 17.

Beginning 30 Apr. she will have a twice-weekly fifteen minute radio program, *Sweetheart Toilet Soap Presents Eleanor Roosevelt.* Although *Movie & Radio Guide* has criticized her speaking ability, she ranks second only to FDR as a "radiator."

F1766 Gould, Bruce, and Beatrice Blackmar Gould. *American Story: Memories and Reflections of Bruce Gould and Beatrice Blackmar Gould.* New York: Harper, 1968. x + 330p.

ER is an important figure in the memoirs of the editors of the *Ladies' Home Journal.* The chapter "First Lady" covers the serialized publication of *This Is My Story* and Elliott Roosevelt's involvement in his mother's writing career (pp. 272-85). There is also a discussion of her column "If You Ask Me" and her 1942 trip to England when she was accompanied by the Goulds (pp. 214-36).

F1767 Gutin, Myra G. "Political Surrogates and Independent Advocates: Eleanor Roosevelt." *The President's Partner: The First Lady in the Twentieth Century.* Contributions in Women's Studies, 105. By Myra G. Gutin. New York: Greenwood, 1989. 81-107. Index. Bibliography. Notes.

ER as writer and public speaker during the White House years (pp. 95-98). Lists her radio series (Johns Manville Co.; Simmons broadcasts, 9 July-25 Sept. 1934; Typewriter Educational Research Bureau, Selby Shoes, Ponds, and Sweetheart Soap series) and describes her 1935-1941 lecture series for the W. Colston Leigh Bureau of Lectures and Entertainments. Based on a more detailed section in the author's dissertation "The President's Partner: The First Lady as Public Communicator, 1920-1976," pp. 335-56 (Univ. of Mich., 1983).

F1768 Hamburger, Philip. "Mrs. Roosevelt's Tea Party." *New Yorker* 26 (25 Feb. 1950): 88-89.

For the initial program of her television series ER invited an impressive group of experts to discuss atomic energy. She had too many guests, and there was not enough time for any of them to say much. She should invite them back a couple at a time and continue the discussion under her able guidance.

F1769 Haws, ---. "Air Secrets of the President's Wife." *Radio Guide* 5 (16 Nov. 1935): 4-5, 15, 17.

She is an outstanding radio personality and humanitarian who contributes her earnings to worthy causes, but I had to convince her to rehearse and gauge her remarks to fit the time allotted.

F1770 Herrick, William. "Days Remembered." Rev. of *Eleanor Roosevelt's My Day* [Vol. 1] ed. Rochelle Chadakoff. *Hudson Valley* (July 1989): 32, 73.

Her "My Day" columns for 1936-1945 do not provide much historical insight, but they do reveal ER's "honesty and dignity" and, most importantly, "a humility that speaks of majesty."

F1771 Hershan, Stella K. "Eleanor Roosevelt Roosevelt." Vol. 3 of *American Women Writers: A Critical Reference Guide from Colonial Times to the Present*. Ed. Lina Mainiero and Langdon Faust. New York: Ungar, 1981. 503-5. Bibliography.
   Brief, critical analyses of some of her writings.

F1772 Hunt, Sandra. "Roosevelt, Eleanor." *First Person Female: A Selected and Annotated Bibliography of the Autobiographies of American Women Living after 1950*. American Notes & Queries Supplement. Ed. Carolyn H. Rhodes. Troy: Whitston, 1980. 328-32.
   Hunt uses generalizations about reviews of ER's works (*This Is My Story, This I Remember, On My Own, The Autobiography of Eleanor Roosevelt*, and *My Days*) to conclude that her autobiographical works emphasize her public life and reviewers emphasize her greatness, not her writing style or what she reveals about her life. Hunt feels that ER's writings are a description of how she evolved "into a liberated woman."

F1773 "Huntley TV Show Revised on NBC." *New York Times* 31 Oct. 1959: 39.
   Includes an announcement that taping of *Prospects of Mankind* has begun. The first program will be aired on 11 Oct. on National Educational Television. The series ended in Aug. 1962. For transcripts of programs, see Papers of Henry Morgenthau, III, Eleanor Roosevelt: *Prospects of Mankind*, FDRL. The finding aid for the collection provides the title of each program and the names of guests.

F1774 Hurd, Charles. "Mrs. Franklin D. Roosevelt." *A Treasury of Great American Speeches: Our Country's Life and History in the Words of Great Men*. By Charles Hurd. New York: Hawthorn, 1959. 297-98.
   The address to the 1952 Democratic National Convention aimed at critics of the UN is one of her outstanding speeches about the organization.

F1775 "Just Babies." *Time* 20 (25 July 1932): 24.
   ER will edit Bernarr Macfadden's new magazine *Babies, Just Babies*. Daughter Anna will assist experienced editor and writer ER in approving manuscripts.

F1776 Kretsinger, Geneva. "An Analytical Study of Selected Radio Speeches of Eleanor Roosevelt." Thesis (M.A.) Univ. of Okla., 1941. iv + 167p. Bibliography. Notes.
   Six speeches are used to analyze ER's ability as a radio speaker. Includes list of recordings of her radio speeches available at the Library of Voices of the Audio-Scriptions, Inc., New York (pp. 22-24).

F1777 MacDonald, J. Fred. *Blacks and White TV: Afro-Americans in Television since 1948*. Chicago: Nelson-Hall, 1983. xvi + 288p. Index. Notes.
   Limited attention to the cancellation of Paul Robeson's scheduled appearance on ER's program *Today with Mrs. Roosevelt*. According to MacDonald, after the episode ER distanced herself from Robeson (pp. 52-53, 55).

F1778 Macfadden, Mary, and Emile Gauvreau. *Dumbbells and Carrot Strips: The Story of Bernarr Macfadden.* New York: Holt, 1953. 405p.

A highly critical account of ER's editorship of Bernarr Macfadden's magazine *Babies, Just Babies* (pp. 299-302).

F1779 Marshall, Margaret. "Columnists on Parade, V. Eleanor Roosevelt." *Nation* 146 (2 Apr. 1938): 386-87.

ER comes across in "My Day" as an ordinary citizen. While she can be criticized for her platitudes, she is to be praised for her ability to share in the lives and problems of ordinary citizens. The column will continue beyond the Roosevelt presidency.

F1780 Martin, Sarah L. "A Study of the Communication Techniques Used to Change the Public's Perception of Eleanor Roosevelt as First Lady." Thesis (M.A.) Boston Univ., 1987. 83p. Bibliography. Notes.

Between 1933 and 1940 how the public viewed ER changed because of her success as a communicator. She became an independent figure with a life and agenda separate from that of FDR.

F1781 McBride, Mary Margaret. *Out of the Air.* Garden City: Doubleday, 1960. 384p.

Radio and television personality McBride considers ER as her most noteworthy program guest. She reminiscences about ER and wishes that she could have known her better (pp. 323-32).

F1782 Midgley, Dorothy A. "A Discussion of Eleanor Roosevelt as Personality and Speaker and a Partial Analysis of Speeches Which She Gave While a Delegate to the United Nations." Thesis (M.A.) Univ. of Mich., 1953.

No known extant copy.

F1783 Monchak, Stephen J. "Mrs. FDR Gets Lesson in Guild Affairs." *Editor & Publisher* 73 (28 Sept. 1940): 12.

On 25 Sept. ER attended her first meeting of the Newspaper Guild of New York of which she is a member. She did not speak during the meeting, was on the losing side of two ballotings, and heard FDR criticized at length.

F1784 Morgenthau, Henry, III. "Eleanor Roosevelt at Brandeis: A Personal Memoir." *Brandeis Review* 4 (Fall 1984): 2-5.

The producer of *Prospects of Mankind* recalls working with ER and JFK and other guests who appeared on the program. With only minor differences the same appeared in *Boston Sunday Globe* 14 Oct. 1984: 23. An earlier article by Ruth S. Morgenthau, "Mrs. Roosevelt I Remember." *Imprint* (Brandeis University National Women's Committee) 4 (Spring 1984): 5, is also a recollection of the series as well as a general tribute to ER.

F1785 "Movies Discussed by Mrs. Roosevelt." *New York Times* 10 July 1934: 19.

ER serves as a news commentator at a broadcast from the world's fair in Chicago. Among other topics, she discussed the motion picture industry and expressed pleasure that the industry has appointed its own censor.

F1786 "Mrs. FDR and Coffee." *In Fact* 3 (4 Aug. 1941): 2.

First, the week ER contracted with Sweetheart Soap for a series of radio broadcasts the Federal Trade Commission chastised the company for its advertising claims. Now, she has signed with a coffee concern when prices are high because trade agreements are limiting the import of coffee beans.

F1787 "Mrs. F.D. Roosevelt on Job as an Editor." *New York Times* 22 July 1932: 17.

The first issue of *Babies, Just Babies* will appear in Sept. under ER's editorship. She accepted the position because she has observed that there are many young women who do not know how to care for their babies. A later article, "Mrs. Roosevelt Edits New Publication," which also excerpts her editorial in the first issue, appeared on p. 24 of the *New York Times*, 20 Sept. 1932.

F1788 "Mrs. Roosevelt and the Newspaper Guild." *Christian Century* 57 (28 Aug. 1940): 1044.

Westbrook Pegler continues to attack ER for her membership in the American Newspaper Guild, a group which he considers to be under Communist influence. Instead of resigning as Pegler wants her to do, she has decided to ensure that the organization does not follow any ideological line.

F1789 "Mrs. Roosevelt Feels Overpaid." *New York Times* 27 May 1934: 16.

Her response to a letter expressing doubt that her radio broadcasts are worth $500 per minute is that she agrees. She says that she is paid that much because she is the wife of the President. She intends to continue to making these broadcasts so that she can give the earnings to needy causes. Includes text of her 21 May letter to her critic.

F1790 "Mrs. Roosevelt Filmed for Anti-Nazi Picture." *New York Times* 18 July 1940: 23.

Yesterday she was filmed reading Robert E. Sherwood's prologue to *Pastor Hall*.

F1791 "Mrs. Roosevelt Gives Advice in New Book." *New York Times* 2 Nov. 1933: 19.

About the publication of *It's Up to the Women*. Includes lengthy quotations from the book.

F1792 "Mrs. Roosevelt Starts a Column." *New York Times* 20 July 1933: 21.

In her first *Woman's Home Companion* column she invites her readers to write to her about their problems and concerns. Includes lengthy excerpts from the column. Earlier articles about her acceptance of a contract to write the monthly column are "Mrs. Roosevelt to Write" *New York Times* 11 May 1933: 20 and "Mrs. F.D. Roosevelt Now a Columnist." *New York Times* 8 July 1933: 13.

F1793 "Mrs. Roosevelt to Drop Her Radio Talks on Commercial Programs after Feb. 24." *New York Times* 5 Feb. 1933: 1.

It is believed that she will not engage in commercial radio broadcasts as long as FDR is President.

F1794 "Mrs. Roosevelt to Get Radio Pay." *New York Times* 15 May 1934: 23.

She has decided to resume commercial radio broadcasts with proceeds going to the American Friends Service Committee. Includes extensive remarks by ER explaining her decision.

F1795 "Mrs. Roosevelt's Address." *Southern Workman* 67 (June 1938): 163-64.
Reports on the simplistic style of her address at the Hampton Institute.

F1796 "Mrs. Roosevelt's Advice on Public Speaking: Have Something to Say, Be Honest and Know How to Stop." *Democratic Digest* 17 (Feb. 1940): 33.
Based on a *Washington Post* article about her address to a public speaking class for congressional wives.

F1797 "My Day." *Time* 27 (13 Jan. 1936): 24, 26-27.
ER has launched her daily column, a diary-like account of her opinions and activities. Lengthy excerpts are used to illustrate how unfortunate it is that never before has a First Lady been able to leave such an historic record.

F1798 "Nation's Neighbor." *Time* 32 (5 Sept. 1938): 34.
It is amazing that the busy First Lady manages to turn out "My Day" six days a week, and in her column she has not made any "serious boners."

F1799 Nelson, Doris. "'If You Ask Me': Mrs. Roosevelt and The Ladies' Home Journal." *Markham Review* 14 (1985): 32-35. Notes.
A discussion of the types of questions her readers asked and how she responded to them in her monthly column for the period 1941-49.

F1800 Pegler, Westbrook. "Fair Enough." *New York World-Telegram* 1 June 1940; 6 Aug. 1940; 9 Aug. 1940; 16 Aug. 1940.
A series of Pegler's columns in which he questions ER's qualifications to belong to the Newspaper Guild of New York. He expresses his outrage that her continued involvement gives comfort to Communists.

F1801 ---. "Fair Enough." *New York World-Telegram* 13 July 1942: 13.
A parody of what he considers the banality of "My Day."

F1802 *Radio Broadcasts in the Library of Congress, 1924-1941: A Catalog of Recordings.* Comp. James R. Smart. Washington: Library of Congress, 1982. xiv + 149p. Index.
The first in a projected series of publications which describe holdings of the Motion Picture, Broadcasting, and Recorded Sound Division of the Library of Congress. The index identifies numerous radio broadcasts featuring ER.

F1803 Ranck, Gloria Virginia. "A Study of Selected Speeches by Mrs. Franklin D. Roosevelt on Human Rights." Thesis (M.A.) Univ. of Wash., 1952. ii + 158p. Bibliography. Notes.
A study of ER's "rhetorical method" as exhibited in six speeches made between Feb. 1949 and Feb. 1951.

F1804 Roberts, Cecil. "The Roosevelts." *And So to America.* By Cecil Roberts. London: Hodder and Stoughton, 1946. 247-77.
A discussion of ER in this look at America past and present. His criticism of American newspaper columnists includes ER whose "My Day" he considers as banal, but a subsequent meeting with her left him impressed with her character and spirit (pp. 249-51).

F1805 Rochelle, Ogden J. "Want Something Done? Ask a Busy Person." *Editor & Publisher* 82 (30 Apr. 1949): 82.

When the *Chicago Sun-Times* syndicates *This I Remember* in Jan. 1950 it will reveal more about FDR than the many biographies which have been issued to date. "My Day" is still a popular column, and ER's own prestige and popularity are considerable.

F1806 Roosevelt, Elliott. "My Mother, Eleanor Roosevelt." *TV Screen* 3 (Apr. 1951): 16-19, 58.

Her son discusses ER's current radio and television programs and how she overcame her initial fear of public speaking. He portrays her as an unselfish and humble person who will continue her active public life dedicated to improving understanding among all nations.

F1807 "The Shape of Things." *Nation* 169 (1 Oct. 1949): 312.

When ER discussed the banning of the *Nation* from the public schools in the New York City many papers decided not to run that edition of "My Day." We urge the papers which did not run the column and those which ran it with alterations to take heed of her warning that democracy is jeopardized when we let the few decide what is best.

F1808 Somers, Florence. "Eleanor and Anna Roosevelt." *Redbook* 93 (Aug. 1949): 10.

What they will cover on their daily ABC radio program *Eleanor and Anna Roosevelt*. Anna usually broadcasts live from Los Angeles while ER's participation is recorded in advance.

F1809 Spacks, Patricia Meyer. "Selves in Hiding." *Women's Autobiography: Essays in Criticism*. Ed. Estelle C. Jelinek. Bloomington: Indiana Univ. Pr., 1980. 112-32.

A study of the autobiographies of five women who experienced criticism after realizing fame. ER's writings reveal her sense of duty, her low estimation of her abilities and accomplishments, and how she subordinated her ideas to those of others, particularly those of FDR. Her writings reveal little about "the self" who is being written about.

F1810 Stix, Thomas L. "Mrs. Roosevelt Does a TV Commercial." *Harper's Magazine* 227 (Nov. 1963): 104-6.

ER's last radio and television agent recalls how sponsors found her too controversial. To prove that she was not "death" to a sponsor, she did her famous commercial for margarine. Also recalls her *Prospects of Mankind* series and projects which her death prevented.

F1811 Taubman, Howard. "Tanglewood Hears Mrs. Roosevelt as 'Peter and the Wolf' Narrator." *New York Times* 12 Aug. 1950: 9.

She brought "simplicity and charm" to the presentation and gave the impression of being a grandmother reading to her grandchildren. Review of the 11 Aug. production at Tanglewood. Excerpted as "Mrs. Roosevelt Records." *RCA Victor Picture Record Review* (Dec. 1950): 4. His earlier article "Mrs. Roosevelt Ready for Debut" *New York Times* 3 Aug. 1950: 19 describes her preparation for the production. There is also "Eleanor and the Wolf." *Newsweek* 36 (21 Aug. 1950): 78 which reports that she had been reluctant to undertake the narration.

F1812 "TV Tea Party." *Newsweek* 35 (27 Feb. 1950): 48.

The first NBC program *Today with Mrs. Roosevelt* was a discussion of atomic energy with leading authorities on the subject. Next will be a consideration of a national health policy. There are few others who can command such notable guests and conduct a discussion with as much grace.

F1813 "Unselfish and Helpful?" *Congressional Record Appendix* (11 June 1941): A2815.

Editorial "More About Eleanor" reprinted from the *Bridgeport Life* [Bridgeport, Conn.] provides examples of how she uses her speaking tours to grasp for money. Other examples in Rep. Charles A. Plumley, "Lady Eleanor--Veni, Vidi, Vici. Or Did She?" *Congressional Record Appendix* (10 June 1941): A2770-71.

F1814 *Variety Television Reviews, 1923-1988.* 15 vols. Ed. Howard H. Prouty. New York: Garland, 1989. Index.

Reviews of television series and appearancs. Guest on *Author Meets the Critics* (1923-1950, 15 Feb. 1950 sect.). *Mrs. Roosevelt Meets the Public* series (1923-1950, 4 Oct. 1950 sect.). Guest on *Comedy Hour* with Bob Hope (1923-1950, 27 Dec. 1950 sect.). Guest on *Hallmark Presents Sarah Churchill* (1951-1953, 10 Oct. 1951 sect.). *Prospects of Mankind* series (1957-1959, 21 Oct. 1959; 1960-1962, 28 Sept. 1960, 31 May 1961, 18 Oct. 1961, and 9 May 1962 sects.). Guest on *Frank Sinatra Show* (1960-1962, 17 Feb. 1960 sect.).

F1815 Waggenspack, Beth M. "Anna Eleanor Roosevelt." *American Orators of the Twentieth Century: Critical Studies and Sources.* Ed. Bernard K. Duffy and Halford R. Ryan. New York: Greenwood, 1987. 337-42. Information Sources.

Analysis of the style and content of her public speeches along with an overview of her career.

F1816 Wamboldt, Helen Jane. "A Descriptive and Analytical Study of the Speaking Career of Anna Eleanor Roosevelt." Diss. Univ. of Southern Calif., 1952. iv + 408p. Bibliography. Notes.

"Public speaking was the most important single tool in Eleanor Roosevelt's career" (p. 361), a career which demonstrates that women can be effective public speakers. Constitutes a detailed, derivative account of her life and speaking career.

Includes the author's interview with Elizabeth von Hesse in which von Hesse recalls how she offered to teach ER "audience control" and describes their intensive early sessions (pp. 182-84). There is also an interview with Elliott Roosevelt in which he describes technical difficulties which resulted in the cancellation of his mother's radio and television programs for the period 1950-1951 (pp. 406-7).

F1817 "WNBA Skinner Medal Given to Eleanor Roosevelt." *Publishers Weekly* 179 (6 Mar. 1961): 27-28.

On 24 Feb. ER was awarded the 1961 Women's National Book Association's Skinner Award for "outstanding contribution to the world of books." Excerpted remarks by Herbert R. Mayes, editor of *McCall's*; Helen Ferris, formerly with the Junior Literary Guild; and Cass Canfield, Harper & Bros., praise ER's contributions to the printed word. Remarks of Mayes and Ferris also excerpted in Alice Sankey, "First Lady of the World." *Elementary English* 38 (May 1961): 346-47.

THE DEATH OF ELEANOR ROOSEVELT

F1818 American Federation of Labor-Congress of Industrial Organizations. *Proceedings of the Fifth Constitutional Convention of the AFL-CIO, New York, New York, November 14-20, 1963. Vol. 1. Daily Proceedings.* N.p.: AFL-CIO, n.d.
  Text of resolution expressing sorrow over the death of ER and requesting all members to donate at least one dollar to the Eleanor Roosevelt Memorial Foundation (pp. 524-25). Also includes text of brief remarks about her life and accomplishments and the purpose of the foundation by Adlai Stevenson (pp. 124-25), George Meany (pp. 525-26), and Walter Reuther (pp. 526-27).

F1819 "Anna Eleanor Roosevelt." *Publishers Weekly* 182 (19 Nov. 1962): 33-34.
  Quotes from JFK's statement on the occasion of her death. Lists some of her publications.

F1820 Ascoli, Max. "Eleanor Roosevelt." *Reporter* 27 (22 Nov. 1962): 12, 16.
  In celebration that ER lived in our country and our time. A tribute to one for whom saintliness is not inappropriate.

F1821 "Baltimore Tribute to Mrs. Roosevelt." *ADA World* 18 (Jan. 1963): 2.
  When FDR died she exchanged sorrow for new challenges. Now at her death her legacy begins, and her accomplishments can be judged on their own merits, not influenced by "envy, distraction and prejudice" of others. Excerpts remarks of Md. Gov. Theodore R. McKeldin to the Baltimore chapter of the ADA. Complete text in *Memorial Addresses...Anna Eleanor Roosevelt...*, pp. 75-78 (Washington: GPO, 1966).

F1822 Blaustein, Jacob. "Tribute to Mrs. Roosevelt." *AAUN News* 35 (Apr. 1963): 4-5.
  Although she will be remembered for her work in the UN on behalf of human rights and her commitment to improving the rights of all in her own country, she realized that human rights is rooted in everyday actions. The most fitting tributes to her would be a continuation of efforts to provide equal rights and the U.S.'s acceptance of the human rights covenants. Also issued in *Memorial Addresses...Anna Eleanor Roosevelt...*, pp. 67-70 (Washington: GPO, 1966).

F1823 Bohn, William E. "The Passing of a Public Conscience." *New Leader* 45 (26 Nov. 1962): 18-19.
  ER's childhood gave no indication that she would become a renowned figure, nor did her critics appreciate how she was able to reach the ordinary citizen through her articles, speeches, and "My Day" and share with them her efforts for peace, democracy, and social justice.

F1824 Bryant, Arthur. "Our Notebook." *Illustrated London News* 241 (17 Nov. 1962): 778.
  Includes a brief tribute to ER, a public figure who cannot be replaced.

F1825 Buckley, William F. "Mrs. Roosevelt, R.I.P." *National Review* 4 (29 Jan. 1963): 58.

ER was a symbol for an era characterized by oversimplification of the solutions to problems. Her approach was one devoid of reasoning. Readers' reactions appeared in issue for 26 Feb. 1963, p. 173.

F1826 Bugbee, Emma. "Mrs. Roosevelt: Portrait of a Beloved Woman." *Brilliant Bylines: A Biographical Anthology of Notable Newspaperwomen in America.* By Barbara Belford. New York: Columbia Univ. Pr., 1986. 183-87.
Bugbee's remembrance and tribute emphasizes her friend's thoughtfulness and spirit. Appeared originally in the *New York Herald Tribune,* 8 Nov. 1962.

F1827 Coe, Christine Sadler. "Mrs. Roosevelt Called 'First Lady of the World.'" *Washington Post* 8 Nov. 1962, sect. A: 23.
A comprehensive assessment of her life, career, and stature.

F1828 Cofield, Ernestine. "Mrs. Roosevelt Loved by All." *Chicago Defender* 10-17 Nov. 1962, City ed.: 1-2.
She was the friend of many black leaders, and much criticism came her way because of what she tried to do for blacks. Cofield says that "the great humanitarian" is gone.

F1829 Coleman, George M. "Mrs. Roosevelt Is Dead." *Atlanta Daily World* 8 Nov. 1962, City ed.: 1, 5.
Recalls her association with Atlanta personalties.

F1830 Considine, Bob. "A Lady of Great Courage." *New York Journal American* 9 Nov. 1962.
At the time of her death Considine recalls ER during World War II.

F1831 Cooke, Alistair. "Maker of a President: Eleanor Roosevelt." *America Observed from the 1940s to the 1980s.* By Alistair Cooke. New York: Knopf, 1988. 142-44.
A tribute to the woman who "created the thirty-second President of the United States." Appeared originally in the *Manchester Guardian,* 13 Nov. 1962.

F1832 "Death of Mrs. Roosevelt." *Times* [London] 8 Nov. 1962: 12.
Announcement of her death. Contains text of JFK's tribute.

F1833 "Eleanor Roosevelt." *Modern Maturity* 8 (Feb./Mar. 1965): 8-10.
She lived a full and meaningful life, and her activities will be remembered through the Eleanor Roosevelt Memorial Foundation.

F1834 "Eleanor Roosevelt." Editorial. *Pittsburgh Courier* 24 Nov. 1962, Nat'l. ed.: 12.
Her example in the 1930s of promoting improved race relations is needed again today. At her death, blacks mourn the loss.

F1835 "Eleanor Roosevelt." Editorial. *Washington Post* 9 Nov. 1962, sect. A: 16.
ER, the First Lady for all times, was uniquely American in her life and actions. Criticism and hatred were directed at her, but to the end her joy in living and serving her country never waned.

F1836 "Eleanor Roosevelt: A Leader in Practicing Democracy." *Childhood Education* 39 (Jan. 1963): 210-12.
Writings by and about her are used in this tribute to a great advocate of education and its importance to the lives of all citizens.

F1837 "The Eleanor Roosevelt Foundation." *Congressional Record* (14 Jan. 1963): 268-71.
Consideration by the Senate of the establishment of the foundation. Debate in the House of Representatives as "Incorporating the Eleanor Roosevelt Memorial Foundation, Inc." *Congressional Record* (18 Mar. 1963): 4403-6. Both include charter and list of members. Abbreviated versions of both are in *Memorial Addresses...Anna Eleanor Roosevelt...,* pp. 1-8, 102-3 (Washington: GPO, 1966).

F1838 "Eleanor Roosevelt, 1884-1962." *Look* 26 (18 Dec. 1962): 124-25.
Brief tribute noting that her deeds will live on and that maybe one day there will be someone who can take her place.

F1839 "Eleanor Roosevelt, R.I.P." *National Review* 13 (20 Nov. 1962): 381.
Praises her efforts on behalf of women and minorities but bemoans the sentimentality which others have for her memory.

F1840 "An Era Is Ended as Mrs. Roosevelt Dies." *Chronicle of the Twentieth Century.* Ed. Clifton Daniel, et al. Mount Kisco: Chronicle, 1987. 890.
The revered and always optimistic ER has died.

F1841 Everett, Arthur. "FDR Widow Is Dead at 78." *Washington Post* 8 Nov. 1962, sect. A: 1, 25.
She died exactly 30 years after FDR's election to a first term. Includes text of statements by Adlai Stevenson and JFK. Other accounts appeared on this and following days. A chronology of important events in her life (8 Nov., sect. A: 23); reactions of public figures and ordinary citizens to her death (9 Nov., sect. A: 1); reactions of world leaders by Maxine Cheshire (9 Nov., sect. C: 1, 3); what ER wrote about world leaders (9 Nov., sect. C: 1.); announcement of funeral plans (10 Nov., sect. A: 14); and Cheshire's account of the funeral and burial (11 Nov., sect. A: 1-2).

F1842 "A First Lady Dies." Editorial. *Evening Star* [Washington] 8 Nov. 1962, sect. A: 12.
Her energy, frankness, and commitment will be remembered.

F1843 "First Lady of the World." *Christian Century* 79 (21 Nov. 1962): 1408.
This "champion of the little people" was respected throughout the world, but equally important is how she maintained dignity and poise in the face of vicious personal attacks.

F1844 Fleeson, Doris. "Mrs. Roosevelt's Love for People." *Evening Star* [Washington] 9 Nov. 1962, sect. A: 17.
A moving tribute to a woman of love, a full participant in the joys and sorrows of life. She was beloved by people everywhere. Also as "She Hated Sin, Loved the Sinner." *Boston Globe* 9 Nov. 1962, Morning ed.: 6.

F1845 Fleming, F. James. "Some Reminiscences of Mrs. Roosevelt." *Crisis* 70 (Jan. 1963): 17-19.
Fleming first met ER during the White House years. He considers an appropriate epitaph the statement in a 1942 letter to FDR informing him that if he could not help, the writer would contact ER.

F1846 Fowlkes, William A. "A Great Woman Has Passed." *Atlanta Daily World* 11 Nov. 1962, City ed.: 4.
She was the foremost American woman social reformer. FDR was often stopped by political considerations, and that is when ER picked up the cause and pursued it until she succeeded.

F1847 "Friend Recalls Rise of Mrs. Roosevelt." *New York Times* 27 Nov. 1962: 29.
We are all better because of her. Her "simplicity and humanity" made her great.

F1848 "From and about Ambassador Stevenson." *AAUN News* 35 (Oct. 1963): 7.
About Stevenson's letter to AAUN members urging them to contribute to the AAUN through the Eleanor Roosevelt Memorial Foundation. Quotes from his letter of tribute to the memory of ER.

F1849 "Goodbye Mrs. Roosevelt!" *New York Amsterdam News* 17 Nov. 1962: 1-2.
Her burial is the occasion to recall her associations with Marian Anderson, Mary McLeod Bethune, and Walter White. Quotes from Roy Wilkins' telegram to the Roosevelt family ("she brought to American Negro citizens a sense of their worth, their dignity and their potentiality as human beings").

F1850 "A Great Lady." *Commonweal* 77 (23 Nov. 1962): 221.
ER was a great person who earned the title "First Lady of the World" because of her work for the less fortunate and her efforts to achieve human rights for all.

F1851 "A Great Woman Leaves Us." *War/Peace Report* (Dec. 1962): 3.
The memory of ER will be with us always. Her work for peace was an inspiration.

F1852 "Her Final Reminiscence." *McCall's* 90 (Feb. 1963): 4.
Tribute praising her as a person and a contributor to *McCall's*.

F1853 "Her Glow Warmed the World." *Newsweek* 60 (19 Nov. 1962): 47, 50.
An account of her death and burial outlining the life of the shy little girl who became a world figure. Includes excerpts from tributes by JFK and Adlai Stevenson together with the reactions of ordinary citizens.

F1854 Hoey, Jane. "A Tribute to Eleanor Roosevelt." *The Social Welfare Forum, 1963: Official Proceedings, 90th Annual Forum, National Conference on Social Welfare, Cleveland, Ohio, May 19-24, 1963*. New York: National Conference on Social Welfare by Columbia Univ. Pr., 1963. xvii-xxii.
The greatest tribute to her memory would be an increase in the number of persons who work to help those in need and pursue "world peace, democracy, and social justice." Followed by remarks by Anna Roosevelt Halsted who spoke of ER as the young settlement house worker who continued to expand her social consciousness.

F1855 Hornaday, Mary. "Mrs. Roosevelt: A Career for Peace." *Christian Science Monitor* 8 Nov. 1962, Eastern ed.: 3.

She worked for peace and, as with all of her other endeavors, she did so out of a sense of obligation.

F1856 "In Memoriam: Anna Eleanor Roosevelt, 1884-1962." *Negro Digest* 12 (Dec. 1962): 34-35.

A woman who never experienced poverty devoted her life to improving conditions of people everywhere. Recalls her Oct. 1943 *Negro Digest* article "If I Were a Negro" and reprints it in part. States that she "readily agreed" to write the article.

F1857 "Israel Mourns Eleanor Roosevelt." *Israel Digest* 5 (23 Nov. 1962): 3

Israel has a special place in her heart for ER. Named for her are a lecture hall at Hebrew Univ., a day care center, and a wing of the Beit Gordon Museum of Natural History. Includes excerpts from messages of Itzhak Ben-Zvi, David Ben-Gurion, and Golda Meir in which they remember her defense of Israel and support of democratic ideals throughout the world.

F1858 Jamison, R.H. "An Illustrious Woman." *Railway Carmen's Journal* 68 (May 1963): 15.

In spite of her critics she continued to be a compassionate figure. She was a union member, and she believed in and supported the union movement. We will remember her humanitarianism.

F1859 "Jews Pay Tribute to Mrs. Roosevelt." *New York Times* 30 Nov. 1962: 23.

She cared about others, be they the neighbors next door or peoples in distant countries. Excerpts remarks by New York Mayor Robert Wagner at meeting of American Jewish Congress, 29 Nov., New York.

F1860 Johnson, Lady Bird. *A White House Diary*. New York: Holt, Rinehart and Winston, 1970. x + 806p. Index.

The entry for 9 Apr. 1964 describes her thoughts when she addressed a meeting of the Eleanor Roosevelt Memorial Foundation. She recalled ER as one who considered the needs of each person as important and could not remain silent when something needed to be said (pp. 104-6). A partial text of Mrs. Johnson's address is in Stella K. Hershan, *The Candles She Lit: The Legacy of Eleanor Roosevelt*, pp. 105-6 (Westport: Praeger, 1993).

F1861 Johnson, Lyndon B. "Letter to Adlai E. Stevenson Agreeing to Serve as an Honorary Trustee of the Eleanor Roosevelt Memorial Foundation." *Public Papers of the Presidents of the United States: Lyndon B. Johnson, Containing the Public Messages, Speeches, and Statements of the President, 1963-64, Book 1--November 22, 1963 to June 30, 1964*. Washington: GPO, 1965. 247-48.

It is appropriate that the foundation emphasize human rights as a memorial to one who was an inspiration to me for over 30 years. Text of 28 Jan. 1964 letter.

F1862 Kennedy, John F. "Letter to the Executive Director, American Association of the United Nations." *Public Papers of the Presidents of the United States: John F. Kennedy, Containing the Public Messages, Speeches, and Statements of the President, January 1 to November 22, 1963*. Washington: GPO, 1964. 268.

His letter of 7 Mar. 1963 to Clark Eichelberger includes a tribute to ER whose legacy he feels will meet the test of time. Reprinted as "President Sends Message." *AAUN News* 35 (Apr. 1963): 1.

F1863 ---. "Remarks at the Ceremony Marking the Issuance of the Eleanor Roosevelt Commemorative Stamp." *Public Papers of the Presidents of the United States: John F. Kennedy, Containing the Public Messages, Speeches, and Statements of the President, January 1 to November 22, 1963.* Washington: GPO, 1964. 779-80.

This stamp is a fitting memorial to ER since its presence in homes throughout the country will remind us of the role which she played in helping the country survive one of its most difficult periods. Remarks made at the White House, 11 Oct. 1963. Also includes text of remarks by Adlai Stevenson about the Eleanor Roosevelt Memorial Foundation and its emphasis on promoting human rights.

F1864 ---. "Remarks upon Signing Bill Incorporating the Eleanor Roosevelt [Memorial] Foundation." *Public Papers of the Presidents of the United States: John F. Kennedy, Containing the Public Messages, Speeches, and Statements of the President, January 1 to November 22, 1963.* Washington: GPO, 1964. 339-40.

As she worked to improve life for the less fortunate her influence extended beyond the White House. Text of remarks to Adlai Stevenson at White House ceremony for signing Public Law 88-11, 23 Apr. 1963. On the formation of the presidential committee which preceded the foundation, see "Kennedy Honors Mrs. Roosevelt with a Group to Press Her Aims." *New York Times* 15 Nov. 1962: 32 and "Plans Made to Continue Mrs. Roosevelt's Work." *New York Times* 28 Nov. 1962: 35.

F1865 ---. "Roosevelt Day Tribute." Editorial. *ADA World* 18 (Feb. 1963): 2.

We do not grieve her loss. Instead, we look to the future as she always did. She viewed the ADA as an organization dedicated to furthering the needs of humanity and FDR's ideals. A message for the 1963 Roosevelt Day Dinners.

F1866 ---. "Statement by the President on the Death of Eleanor Roosevelt." *Public Papers of the Presidents of the United States: John F. Kennedy, Containing the Public Messages, Speeches, and Statements of the President, January 1 to December 31, 1962.* Washington: GPO, 1963. 823.

JFK's sentiments about the death of "one of the great ladies in the history of this country" who was also "an inspiration and a friend." "Her memory and spirit will long endure." Accompanied by additional information: a committee was formed on 14 Nov. to consider ways of pursuing some of ER's interests; ER is not to be replaced as chair of the President's Commission on the Status of Women.

The statement is reprinted in numerous sources.

F1867 King, Martin Luther, Jr. "Epitaph for Mrs. FDR." *New York Amsterdam News* 24 Nov. 1962: 11, 14.

ER, the humanitarian, was one for the ages. She would have been a great person regardless of the era in which she lived.

F1868 Langton, York. "Have You Honored Mrs. Roosevelt with a New AAUN Member?" *AAUN News* 35 (May 1963): 7.

A progress report on the membership drive, a message of tribute from George McGovern, and Langton's brief tribute.

F1869 Louchheim, Katie. *By the Political Sea*. Garden City: Doubleday, 1970. xii + 293p. Index.
Includes an account of ER's funeral and the author's recollections of ER's life (pp. 121-27).

F1870 ---. "Tribute to a Great Lady." *Department of State News Letter* (Mar. 1963): 44-45.
A longtime friend's recollections of ER beginning with the New Deal years. Also in *Memorial Addresses...Anna Eleanor Roosevelt...*, pp. 40-43 (Washington: GPO, 1966).

F1871 MacLeish, Archibald. "Eleanor Roosevelt: 1884-1962." *Nation* 195 (17 Nov. 1962): 317-18.
To her the world and its problems were human, not abstractions. She gave herself--her life as a fellow human being--to the world. Reissued as "Eleanor Roosevelt" in his *A Continuing Journey*, pp. 227-80 (Boston: Houghton Mifflin, 1967).

F1872 ---. "Tribute to a 'Great American Lady.'" *New York Times Magazine* 3 Nov. 1963: 17, 118-19.
Like Abigail Adams, ER was an American woman who found it easy to feel and think. Reissued as "Mrs. Roosevelt: An Anniversary" in his *A Continuing Journey*, pp. 281-85 (Boston: Houghton Mifflin, 1967).

F1873 McCardle, Dorothy. "Mrs. Roosevelt's Dream Is Becoming a Reality." *Washington Post* 11 Oct. 1963, sect. D: 1.
Adlai Stevenson has announced that the International Institute of Human Rights is being founded under the auspices of the Eleanor Roosevelt Memorial Foundation. A fund drive will begin to finance the Institute and the construction of the Eleanor Roosevelt wings of the Franklin D. Roosevelt Library.

F1874 McGill, Ralph. "They Still Write about Mrs. FDR." *Atlanta Constitution* 15 Nov. 1962: 1.
Ordinary people are sending letters of condolence. While ER walked with the great, she endeared herself to all because of the tribulations which she faced as wife and mother. When others suffered from poverty and prejudice, she was there to help.

F1875 McGrory, Mary. "Shy Girl--Renowned Woman." *Boston Globe* 8 Nov. 1962, Morning ed.: 1-2.
With grace she dedicated her life and energy to doing for others. Highlights of her life, criticisms which were directed toward her, and the respect which she enjoyed in later life. Issued in Evening ed. (pp. 1, 39) as "Mrs. F.D.R.--Friend of Underdog, Critic of Upstart V.I.P.s."

F1876 McHugh, John F. *The Death of Eleanor Roosevelt*. Rooseveltiana from the Private Collection of Dr. John F. McHugh. Allentown: McHugh, 1962. 238p.
Consists of photocopies of editorials and newspaper accounts. "Reminiscence of Eleanor Roosevelt" (pp. 1-6). Available at FDRL.

F1877 Mead, Margaret. "Mrs. Roosevelt." *Redbook* 120 (Jan. 1963): 6.
ER's greatest impact was on the lives of children and the less fortunate. She was a wife and mother who tried to make a better life for all children, not just her own.

F1878 *Memorial Addresses in the House of Representatives Together with Tributes on the Life and Ideals of Anna Eleanor Roosevelt.* 88th Cong., 1st Sess. House Document, 152. Washington: GPO, 1966. ix + 112 + 1p.
Proceedings in Congress related to the establishment of the Eleanor Roosevelt Memorial Foundation together with memorial tributes presented in the House and Senate. Included are resolution by the President's Commission on the Status of Women, "A Tribute to a Lady" by Helen Bullard from *Plum* (Associated Plumbing Contractors of Georgia), editorial from the *AFL-CIO News*, statements from several groups of New York Democratic voters, statements by numerous members of Congress, and reprinting of tributes by others including an address by Edward G. Robinson.

F1879 "Memorial Ceremony." *UN Monthly Chronicle* 3 (May 1966): 69-70.
On behalf of the Eleanor Roosevelt Memorial Foundation Thomas K. Finletter presented a granite bench to the UN on 23 Apr. in memory of ER. Remarks by Finletter, U Thant, and Arthur J. Goldberg. ER's commitment to make the business of the UN relevant to everyday life was recalled by UN representative Goldberg.

F1880 "Memories of Eleanor Roosevelt." *Sepia* 12 (Jan. 1963): 70-72.
Copy not examined.

F1881 Meyer, Donald. "Eleanor Roosevelt--1884-1962." *New Republic* 147 (17 Nov. 1962): 8.
At ER's death an excerpt from Meyer's review of *On My Own* from *New Republic* 139 (6 Oct. 1958): 17-18 is reissued as a tribute.

F1882 Michaels, Ruth Gruber. "Eleanor Roosevelt, 'First Lady.'" *Hadassah Magazine* 43 (Dec. 1962): 4-5.
ER is remembered as the "Queen of America," the supporter of the Jewish state and Youth Aliyah.

F1883 "Mrs. Anna Eleanor Roosevelt, Oct. 11, 1884-Nov. 7, 1962." *Senior Scholastic* (Teachers' ed.) 81 (28 Nov. 1962): 22.
Excerpts tributes by JFK, Adlai Stevenson, and U Thant plus editorials from the *St. Louis Post Dispatch*, the *New York Herald Tribune*, and the *Christian Science Monitor.*

F1884 "Mrs. Eleanor Roosevelt." Editorial. *Atlanta Daily World* 10 Nov. 1962, City ed.: 6.
She will have a lasting impact on American life. When we think of how FDR improved life for all, we will also remember ER.

F1885 "Mrs. Eleanor Roosevelt." *Times* [London] 8 Nov. 1962: 14.
She had a positive impact on her country. In politics she had a "sense of noblesse oblige." But her political skill was diminished because of her devotion to certain ideals. She could be self-righteous and was not without prejudices. Also in

Obituaries from the Times, 1961-1970, pp. 684-85 (Reading: Newspaper Archive Developments, 1975).

F1886 "Mrs. FDR Ends Her Day." *America* 107 (17 Nov. 1962): 1081.

She pursued many admirable causes: fought for racial equality, worked for the less fortunate, and made a valiant defense against communism. However, she would have had more admirers if it had not been for the "wrongheadedness with which she embraced certain public policies." For readers' reactions, see 107 (1 Dec. 1962): 1162-63.

F1887 "Mrs. Franklin D. Roosevelt." *AAUN News* 34 (Nov. 1962): 3, 5.

Tributes by AAUN officials Herman Steinkraus and Clark Eichelberger.

F1888 "Mrs. Franklin D. Roosevelt." Editorial. *Crisis* 69 (Dec. 1962): 607.

A belief in the value of all human beings made her great, and that belief is what made her support civil rights and other unpopular causes.

F1889 "Mrs. R." *AAUN News* 34 (Nov. 1962): 4.

To AAUN staff she will always be known as a kind woman who worked to strengthen the UN, not to bring distinction to herself.

F1890 "Mrs. Roosevelt." Editorial. *New York Journal American* (8 Nov. 1962): 22.

A tribute to a remarkable life.

F1891 "Mrs. Roosevelt." Editorial. *New York Times* (8 Nov. 1962): 38.

She served FDR well, broke precedents as First Lady, and was a world figure with a multitude of interests. But more than anything else she was a humanitarian.

F1892 "Mrs. Roosevelt: A Remembrance." *AAUN News* 35 (Nov. 1963): 3.

Residents of the cities which she visited on behalf of the UN will always remember her. She would want us to continue our support of the UN and the cause of peace.

F1893 "Mrs. Roosevelt Dies at 78 after Illness of Six Weeks." *New York Times* 8 Nov. 1962: 1, 34.

This obituary which includes an overview of her life and activities was the first of numerous articles about her death and burial which appeared between 8 and 11 Nov. Her role as UN delegate (8 Nov.: 34); JFK's order for flags to fly at half staff and announcement of funeral plans (9 Nov.: 1, 25); memorial service at the UN (10 Nov: 10); and funeral and burial including text of graveside eulogy (11 Nov.: 1, 87). Paid death notices inserted by organizations and individuals (8 Nov.: 38, 9 Nov.: 35, 10 Nov.: 25, and 11 Nov.: 89). Major accounts are reprinted in *Great Lives of the Century as Reported by the New York Times*, pp. 248-51 (New York: Times Books, 1977).

F1894 "Mrs. Roosevelt Honored." *AAUN News* 35 (Mar. 1963): 1.

AAUN officials have been named to the Eleanor Roosevelt Foundation Committee to coordinate efforts in her memory. Purposes of the Eleanor Roosevelt Memorial Foundation are listed.

F1895 "Mrs. Roosevelt Is Dead after Long Illness." *Evening Star* [Washington] 8 Nov. 1962, sect. A: 1.

A series of articles follows about her life, death, and burial. "Eleanor Roosevelt Chose a Life of Usefulness" is a detailed look at her life and career (8 Nov., sect. A: 4); "Kindness Was the Key" (8 Nov., sect. A: 4); UN tribute including text of Adlai Stevenson's eulogy (9 Nov., sect. A: 1, 6); funeral and burial (10 Nov., sect. A: 1, 15).   There is also Mary McGrory, "Eleanor Roosevelt Rests." *Sunday Star* [Washington] 11 Nov., sect. A: 1, 3.

F1896 "Mrs. Roosevelt (1884-1962)." *Boston Globe* 8 Nov. 1962, Morning ed.: 14.
    She was subjected to years of harsh criticism but emerged as the "best loved woman in the world." Among those who loved her were the young soldiers she visited during the war and the less fortunate she tried so hard to help. Signed "Uncle Dudley."

F1897 "NAACP Tributes to Mrs. Eleanor Roosevelt." *Crisis* 69 (Dec. 1962): 597-99.
    Blacks loved and trusted her, because as "the first lady for civil rights for all Americans" she was an inspiration and untiring advocate of human rights for all. Reissue of statements by Stephen Gill Spottswood, Arthur B. Spingarn, and Roy Wilkins and a resolution by the NAACP.

F1898 "Notes and Comments." *New Yorker* 38 (17 Nov. 1962): 41-42.
    ER was like that one schoolteacher who stands out above all others in our minds. She made the world her classroom, and as students we often fell short of her expectations.

F1899 Patterson, Eugene. "Eleanor Roosevelt: A Lasting Glow." *Atlanta Constitution* 9 Nov. 1962: 4.
    Mrs. Roosevelt is gone, but her example will always be with us. Patterson remembers when she spoke at the 1960 Democratic National Convention on behalf of Adlai Stevenson as the right candidate, not the popular one. This was typical of her, since she always stood for what was right in spite of public opinion.

F1900 Peck, Sidney M. *Anna Eleanor Roosevelt: In Memorium (October 11, 1884-November 7, 1962).* Milwaukee, n.p., 1962. 9p.
    Tribute to ER as a symbol of hope. Text of chapel service on 29 Nov. 1962 at Milwaukee-Downer College.

F1901 Pegler, Westbrook. "Eleanor Roosevelt." *American Opinion* 6 (Feb. 1963): 1-10.
    To Pegler ER was a fraud and a liar whose death is no cause for mourning. On pp. 78-79 of the Sept. issue are readers' reactions in support of Pegler's views.

F1902 Perkins, Frances. "Address by the Honorable Frances Perkins, Former Secretary of Labor." *Official Report of the Proceedings of the Democratic National Convention...August 24 through August 27, 1964.* Washington: Democratic National Committee, 1968. 348-52.
    A tribute to ER for the type of person she was, the help which she provided to FDR, and the symbol which she became for what is best about being an American.

F1903 ---. "Tribute to the Memory of Mrs. Franklin D. Roosevelt by the Honorable Frances Perkins..." *Congressional Record* (18 Feb. 1963): 2432-33.

In praise of the life she led and the impact which she had. Transcription of extemporaneous remarks to Democratic National Committee, Washington, 19th Jan. Also issued in *Memorial Addresses...Anna Eleanor Roosevelt...*, pp. 108-13 (Washington: GPO, 1966).

F1904 Perlmutter, Emanuel. "10,000 Attend Memorial Service for Mrs. Roosevelt." *New York Times* 18 Nov. 1962: 71.
   ER is remembered at service at Cathedral of St. John the Divine on 17 Nov. Includes excerpts from Adlai Stevenson's eulogy.

F1905 Pick, Hella. "Women Talking." *Guardian* [Manchester, Eng.] 20 Apr. 1964: 8.
   About fund-raising luncheon for the Eleanor Roosevelt Memorial Foundation. Discusses remarks by Lady Bird Johnson, Adlai Stevenson, and others about ER's efforts to improve race relations in everyday life.

F1906 Pickett, Clarence E. "Eleanor Roosevelt." *Friends Journal* (Dec. 1, 1962): 504-5.
   She was a generous supporter of the work of the American Friends Service Committee, and when she became a world figure she worked to correct the problems which plagued people everywhere while continuing her concern for the needs of her fellow citizens.

F1907 Polier, Justine Wise. "As I Knew Mrs. Roosevelt." *Petal Paper* [Petal, Miss.] 10 (Jan. 1963): 1-2.
   Polier remembers her long association with ER. Recalled is her commitment to helping Jewish refugees, to Israel, and to improving the quality of that inner feeling which all persons have about themselves. Reprinted from *Congress Bi-weekly*.

F1908 Reading, Stella, Lady. "Mrs. Eleanor Roosevelt." Letter. *Times* [London] 12 Nov. 1962: 12.
   Her greatness came from her character, serenity, and courage. People and their rights dominated her thinking and her life. She "will be remembered throughout the ages." A moving tribute from a friend.

F1909 Roberts, Chalmers M. "Eleanor Roosevelt: As 'Rover's Rangers' Remember Her." *Washington Post* 10 Nov. 1962, sect. A: 13.
   "Rover" was ER's Secret Service code name during the war years, and "Rover's Rangers" were those who tried to keep up with her. Roberts recalls with admiration the exhausting days which ER spent in England 20 years earlier visiting U.S. soldiers and British workers. She won a place in our hearts forever.

F1910 Robertson, Nan. "Mrs. Roosevelt's Doctor Recalls Her Kindness in Tearful Eulogy." *New York Times* 21 Nov. 1962: 23.
   She personified "modesty, courage, and warmth." Lengthy excerpts of address by David Gurewitsch to Federation of Jewish Philanthropies Women's Division, New York, 20 Nov.

F1911 Roche, John P. "Eleanor Roosevelt." Editorial. *ADA World* 18 (Jan. 1963): 2.
　　Her family was mankind; therefore, our hearts go out to the world at her passing.

F1912 *Roosevelt and Frankfurter: Their Correspondence, 1928-1945.* Annotated by Max Freedman. Boston: Little, Brown, 1967. xiv + 772p. Index.
　　A dying Frankfurter writes to the recently deceased ER: you were vital to FDR, and FDR was vital to me. Therefore, your death is like losing part of me (p. 29).

F1913 "Roosevelt, (Anna) Eleanor." *Current Biography Yearbook, 1963.* New York: Wilson, 1964. 362.
　　Brief statement of her activities issued on the occasion of her death.

F1914 "Roosevelt Stamp Rite Licked Him." *Washington Post* 12 Oct. 1963, sect. C: 9.
　　ER's grandson Hall Delano Roosevelt, age 4, received the first ER commemorative stamp from JFK at a White House ceremony on 11 Oct. Adlai Stevenson spoke about his hopes for the success of the Eleanor Roosevelt Memorial Foundation in realizing ER's commitment to human rights.

F1915 Rusk, Dean. *Department of State Bulletin* 48 (14 Jan. 1963): 51.
　　She did not hate, but she could be indignant over poverty and prejudice. A confidence in mankind continued throughout her life, and that life and our memory of it are great events of our time. Text of address, Washington Cathedral, 15 Nov. Issued under the general title "Eleanor Roosevelt Memorial Service Held at Washington Cathedral."

F1916 Sachar, Abram L. *The Many Lives of Eleanor Roosevelt: An Affectionate Portrait.* Waltham: Brandeis Univ. Pr., 1963. [8]p.
　　Brandeis president provides a portrait of the life, work, and legacy of ER. Text of address, Ford Hall Forum, Boston, 17 Mar. 1963.

F1917 "She Was Eleanor." *Time* 80 (16 Nov. 1962): 28-29.
　　There were many tragedies in the life of this woman who became a crusader for the rights of others. In her later years she was judged by her "heart and her humanity," not by the causes which she supported.

F1918 Smith, Merriman. "...She Found Truth; It Made Her Free..." *Boston Sunday Globe* 11 Nov. 1962: 9.
　　Detailed description of the funeral and burial. Includes excerpts from the eulogy.

F1919 Smith, Richard C. Letter. *Christian Century* 80 (9 Jan. 1963): 53.
　　At ER's death a former resident of Scotts Run, W. Va. writes in remembrance of her as the "First Lady of Miners."

F1920 Sobol, Louis. "The World Loses a Friend." *New York Journal American* 8 Nov. 1962: 23.
　　The lead item in his column is a tribute to the woman many considered to be a friend.

F1921 Sokolsky, George. "Eleanor Roosevelt." *Washington Post* 13 Nov. 1962, sect. A: 15.

Her early work in the settlement houses of New York established her life-long role as a social worker. Her involvement changed conditions for the less fortunate, blacks in particular, but she was not an original thinker.

F1922 Stevenson, Adlai E. "Her Journeys Are Over." *Looking Outward: Years of Crisis at the United Nations*. Ed. with commentary by Robert L. and Selma Schiffer. New York, Harper & Row, 1963. 290-95.

We mourn the loss of ER the person, but her deeds will live on. Text of eulogy presented at memorial service, Cathedral of St. John the Divine, New York, 17 Nov. 1962. Also issued as "Eulogy on Eleanor Roosevelt." *Representative American Speeches, 1962-1963*, 178-83 (New York: Wilson, 1963) and as "Eleanor Roosevelt." *Progressive* 27 (Jan. 1963): 30-32. Also in *The Papers of Adlai E. Stevenson*, v. 8, pp. 342-46 (Boston: Little, Brown, 1979) and in *Memorial Addresses...Anna Eleanor Roosevelt...*, pp. 32-36 (Washington: GPO, 1966).

F1923 ---. *The Papers of Adlai E. Stevenson*. Vol. 8. Ed. Walter Johnson, et al. Boston: Little, Brown, 1979. xxv + 885p. Index. Notes.

Stevenson served as chair of the Eleanor Roosevelt Memorial Foundation. This volume contains numerous letters and statements related to establishing objectives for the foundation and raising the funds required to pursue them (pp. 384-85, 425, 433-34, 461-62, 505-6, 521, 543-44, 585, 617).

F1924 ---. "She Would Rather Light Candles: The Death of Eleanor Roosevelt." *Looking Outward: Years of Crisis at the United Nations*. Ed. with commentary by Robert L. and Selma Schiffer. New York: Harper & Row, 1963. 113-15.

She gave us strength and faith in the future and ourselves. In a sense the UN is a tribute to her. Statement to the UN General Assembly, 9 Nov. 1962. Also issued as "United Nations Pays Tribute to the Memory of Mrs. Roosevelt." *Department of State Bulletin* 8 (14 Jan. 1963): 48, 50 and in *The Papers of Adlai E. Stevenson*, v. 8, pp. 339-40 (Boston: Little, Brown, 1979). Excerpts issued as "Eleanor Roosevelt." *Saturday Review* 45 (24 Nov. 1962): 23 and in numerous other publications.

F1925 ---. "Tribute to the Honorable Eleanor Roosevelt." *Official Report of the Proceedings of the Democratic National Convention...August 24 through August 27, 1964*. Washington: Democratic National Committee, 1968. 108-10.

ER's legacy is the example which she set of working for a better America and a better world for all. Text of address, 27 Aug. 1964. Also issued in *The Papers of Adlai E. Stevenson*, v. 8, pp. 613-15 (Boston: Little, Brown. 1979). In *Memorial Addresses...Anna Eleanor Roosevelt...*, pp. 99-101 (Washington: GPO, 1966) as "She Was a Lady for All Seasons."

F1926 Thant, U. "Address at Memorial Tribute to Eleanor Roosevelt at Philharmonic Hall, Lincoln Center." *Public Papers of the Secretaries-General of the United Nations, Volume VI: U Thant, 1961-1964*. Selected and ed. with commentary by Andrew W. Cordier and Max Harrelson. New York: Columbia Univ. Pr., 1976. 480-82.

To all of her activities she brought "affectionate humanitarianism." Her wish that there would be a declaration of human rights as well as a legally binding covenant formed the approach which the UN continues to take with human rights. Text of remarks, 21 Oct. 1963. Excerpted as "Homage to Eleanor Roosevelt." *United Nations Review* 10 (Dec. 1963): 28 and "Eleanor Roosevelt: A Lifetime of Dedication to Human Rights." *Unesco Courier* 16 (Dec. 1963): 15.

F1927 "Tribute to Mrs. Roosevelt." *Southern Patriot* 21 (Mar. 1963): 4.
As read by Anne Revere, Aubrey Williams' tribute at a Southern Conference Educational Fund reception praised ER for her work with the SCEF and her practical approach to problems and claimed that her virtues are those which are valued most in mankind. A great friend is gone.

F1928 "Tributes to Mrs. Roosevelt." *AAUN News* 34 (Nov. 1962): 6.
Excerpts the remarks of Adlai Stevenson, JFK, U Thant, and others.

F1929 "United Nations Pays Tribute to the Memory of Mrs. Roosevelt." *Department of State Bulletin* 48 (14 Jan. 1963): 48-50, 52-59.
Text of statements made in the General Assembly, 9 Nov. Excerpts issued as "Mrs. Eleanor Roosevelt...A United Nations Tribute." *United Nations Review* 9 (Dec. 1962): 27-28.

F1930 Wallace, Robert. "A Great Lady Is Gone." *Life* 53 (16 Nov. 1962): 50.
ER faced life and its problems, hers and those of all peoples. She will be in our hearts forever.

F1931 Wechsler, James A. "Remembrance." *Congressional Record* (8 Nov. 1963): 21534-35.
The greatest tribute is in the midst of crises during the year since she died to wish that ER were still here to help solve them. Reprinted from the *New York Post,* 7 Nov. 1963.

F1932 Welch, Robert. "Pegler on Bigotry." *American Opinion* 6 (Nov. 1963): 13-21.
ER could never have been first lady of the world, because she was never a lady. He uses as an example the difficulty she found herself in with the wife of Earl Miller and how she got out of the difficulties which ensued.

F1933 White, Poppy Cannon. "Mrs. 'R.'" *New York Amsterdam News* 24 Nov. 1962: 11, 14.
A poignant tribute by the widow of Walter White. ER is remembered for her kindness to ordinary people.

F1934 Wilkins, Roy. "There Was Only One!" *New York Amsterdam News* 17 Nov. 1962: 11, 14.
It was ER, more than FDR, who changed the country to the benefit of black citizens.

F1935 "Women in Public Life." Editorial. *Christian Science Monitor* 9 Nov. 1962, Eastern ed.: 22.
ER was a woman of character and conscience, and her life demonstrated the potential which women have. Using arguments which ER herself often put forward, women are urged to learn how to function in the public world which men have created.

F1936 "World in Mourning for Mrs. Roosevelt." *New York Journal American* 8 Nov. 1962: 1, 12.

The first of several accounts which appeared about her death. "She Cared About the Poor People." (8 Nov.: 12); a photo tribute entitled "Anna Eleanor Roosevelt--'First Lady of the World.'" (8 Nov.: 11); UN tribute (9 Nov.); "Leaders Attend Rites Today for Mrs. Roosevelt." by Mort Young (10 Nov.: 1); account of funeral and burial (11 Nov.: 1); and "In the Church--Simple Rites for a 1st Lady." by Pierre J. Huss. (11 Nov.).

ELEANOR ROOSEVELT CENTENNIAL

F1937 Adams, Bruce, and Margaret Engel. "Celebrating a Roosevelt Retreat." *Washington Post* 30 Sept. 1984, sect. E: 1-3.

ER's Val-Kill will be opened as a National Historic Site on the 100th anniversary of her birth. Includes tips for the traveler to Hyde Park and Val-Kill and a lengthy discussion of ER's life there.

F1938 Blyth, Myrna. "The Legacy of Eleanor Roosevelt." *Ladies' Home Journal* 101 (Oct. 1984): 2.

It is appropriate that Geraldine Ferraro is a candidate for Vice President in this the centennial year of ER's birth. ER's association with the *Ladies' Home Journal* and the challenges which she faced in her life.

F1939 Bronson, Susan. "Eleanor." *US* (22 Oct. 1984): 21-23.

Bronson provides a few facts about the life and work of ER as an introduction to statements by nine prominent women (Jane Alexander, Dianne Feinstein, Geraldine Ferraro, Betty Friedan, Nancy Kassebaum, Jeane Kirkpatrick, Jean Stapleton, Gloria Steinem, and Liv Ullmann). The statements praise ER, a child of privilege, who devoted much of her life to helping the less-advantaged and ER, the continuing inspiration for so many modern women.

F1940 Burke, Fran. "Eleanor Roosevelt, October 11, 1884-November 7, 1962--She Made a Difference." *Public Administration Review* 44 (Sept./Oct. 1984): 365-72.

A centennial year tribute which traces her emergence as a public figure and calls for more research on the influence which she had on 20th century American life.

F1941 Chafe, William H. "The Greatness of Eleanor Roosevelt." *Eleanor Roosevelt: An American Journey*. Ed. Jess Flemion and Colleen M. O'Connor. San Diego: San Diego State Univ. Pr., 1987. 1-9. Note on Sources.

A celebration of the significance of ER's life. Chafe also addresses ER's personal life and in particular her relationships with Earl Miller and Lorena Hickok.

F1942 Corry, John. "A Documentary in Praise of a Memorable First Lady." *New York Times* 25 Nov. 1984, sect. 2: 23.

The television documentary to be broadcast tonight is a success. It would have been easy for the aristocratic ER to have removed herself from the concerns which typical citizens can have during periods of economic despair, but she did not. The program includes taped portions of the "Eleanor Roosevelt Centennial Conference" held Oct. 1984 at Vassar.

F1943 Derian, Patricia M. "Eleanor Roosevelt." *Human Rights and the Helsinki Accord: Focus on U.S. Policy*. Headline Series, 264. By William Korey. New York: Foreign Policy Assoc., 1983. [3-4].

An explanation of the Helsinki Accord is a fitting centennial tribute to one who helped organize the Foreign Policy Assoc. and whose dedication to the principles of "equality, liberty, social justice and democracy" still guides us today.

F1944 De Wan, George. "Eleanor the Indomitable." *Newsday* 11 Oct. 1984, pt. 2: 3-5.

Centennial tribute to her life and work.

F1945 [DeWitt, Madlyn]. *The Centenary of Anna Eleanor Roosevelt, 1884-1984: Final Report of the Eleanor Roosevelt Centennial Commission*. N.p.: The Eleanor Roosevelt Centennial Commission, [1991?]. 129p.

The most comprehensive source for the activities of the commission and all events associated with the centennial celebration.

F1946 DiBacco, Thomas V. "Mrs. Roosevelt's Public Mission." *Christian Science Monitor* 11 Oct. 1984, Eastern ed.: 16.

She was the most important female political figure of the 20th century. She helped the less fortunate at home, and in the post-war period made human rights throughout the world her primary concern.

F1947 "Eleanor Roosevelt." *This Constitution: A Bicentennial Chronicle* 4 (Fall 1984): 51.

Recognition of her centennial year and events which are planned.

F1948 "Eleanor Roosevelt: A Woman Without Precedent." *OAH Newsletter* 12 (Feb. 1984): 5.

Announcing the publication of *Without Precedent: The Life and Career of Eleanor Roosevelt* and various events which are scheduled in celebration of the centennial of her birth.

F1949 *Eleanor Roosevelt Centennial, 1884-1984*. Poughkeepsie: Eleanor Roosevelt Centennial Commission, n.d. 1 folder.

Includes a description of the traveling exhibit about ER. Intended as curriculum material.

F1950 "Eleanor Roosevelt: 100 Year." *Feminist Teacher* 1 (Fall 1984): 21.

About the centennial, teaching resources which are available, and books and films on her life and work.

F1951 *An Eleanor Roosevelt Portfolio*. Commemorative ed. Hyde Park: Eleanor Roosevelt Center at Val-Kill, 1984. 9 posters (28 x 36cm.) in portfolio.

Photographs from FDRL are used to illustrate her many activities.

F1952 *The Eleanor Roosevelt Tradition: Its Significance for Today and Tomorrow*. Washington: Americans for Democratic Action, 1984. 29p.

Program for the ADA conference 23-24 June 1984 includes photographs of ER and numerous brief articles about her. Available in Subject Files Relating to the Eleanor Roosevelt Centennial Commission, Box 7, New York State Archives.

F1953 "Eleanor Roosevelt: Vignettes of a League Member." *Junior League Review* (Fall 1984): 6.
Various recollections of ER on the occasion of her centenary.

F1954 "Eleanor Roosevelt's Career Began with Women's Political Networks of the Early 1920s." *Media Report to Women* 12 (July/Aug. 1984): 15.
A discussion of *Without Precedent: The Life and Career of Eleanor Roosevelt*. On the same page is "LWV Work Provided ER Experience and New Contacts" which is a discussion of *In League with Eleanor: Eleanor Roosevelt and the League of Women Voters, 1921-1962*.

F1955 "Eleanor Roosevelt's Centennial & Val-Kill." *American History Illustrated* 19 (Oct. 1984): 6.
The Eleanor Roosevelt National Historic Site will be dedicated on 11 Oct., and the traveling exhibit "The Roosevelt Special" is touring N.Y. and other northeastern states. Brief account of how ER utilized Val-Kill as a home and furniture factory.

F1956 "Eleanor Roosevelt's 100th Birthday Observed." *UN Chronicle* 21 (1984): 88.
On 11 Oct. UN General Assembly President Paul J.F. Lusaka presented a tribute to ER in which he recognized her responsibility for framing the Universal Declaration of Human Rights and her efforts to see that all persons "'are treated as human beings.'"

F1957 Elshtain, Jean Bethke. "Eleanor Roosevelt as Activist and Thinker, the Life of Duty." *Halcyon* 8 (1986): 93-114. Notes.
ER was a "lady," she pursued Christian values, and like Jane Addams her primary objective was social reform not feminism. Paper presented at the Eleanor Roosevelt Centennial Conference, Reno, Nev., 25-27 Oct. 1984.

F1958 *ERVK Newsletter* (Eleanor Roosevelt Center at Val-Kill).
Undated "centennial edition" includes several articles about ER's life at Val-Kill. Included are "Val-Kill a Reflection of Eleanor Roosevelt," "The Saving of Val-Kill" by Joyce C. Ghee, and "First Ladies' Tribute" with comments by Lady Bird Johnson, Betty Ford, Rosalynn Carter, and Nancy Reagan.

F1959 *Establishing a Commission on the Eleanor Roosevelt Centennial*. U.S. Congress. House of Representatives. 98th Cong., 1st Sess. Report 98-398, pt. 1. Washington: GPO, 1983. 6p.
The commission was charged with encouraging and recognizing "appropriate observances and commemorations" of the centennial of ER's birth and to provide advice about those events. The legislation also called for completing the work on the Eleanor Roosevelt Historic Site to the extent that it can be made available for visitors on the 100th anniversary of her birth.
For the text of the joint resolution which led to the formation of the commission, see *Miscellaneous Boundary Adjustments, Public Land Conveyances, Commemoration and Ceiling Increases*, pp. 2-6 (Washington: GPO, 1984). The resolution became Public Law 98-162 and is contained in *United States Statutes at Large*, v. 97, pp. 1013-15 (Washington: GPO, 1985).

F1960 Faber, Harold. "Eleanor Roosevelt's Home Dedicated as Historic Site." *New York Times* 12 Oct. 1984, sect. B: 1, 10.

A series of events on 11 Oct. was highlighted by the dedication of Val-Kill as a National Historic Site. In his address N.Y. Gov. Mario Cuomo said that the way in which she worked for others should still impress us today.

F1961 ---. "An Upstate Focus for Eleanor Roosevelt Centennial." *New York Times* 3 Nov. 1983: 54.
About events planned for her centennial year, in particular efforts to restore Val-Kill.

F1962 Fascell, Dante B. "Eleanor Roosevelt: First Lady of the World." *Congressional Record* (2 Oct. 1984): 28808.
A tribute to her activities on the world scene.

F1963 Feighan, Edward F. "In Celebration of Anna Eleanor Roosevelt." *Congressional Record* (10 Oct. 1984): 31762-63.
A tribute to her commitment to human rights.

F1964 "First Lady of the World." *McCall's* 112 (Oct. 1984): 10.
Tribute to the woman who emerged as a figure loved around the world.

F1965 Franklin D. Roosevelt Library. Vertical File.
The library holds material about centennial events. Includes newspaper articles, programs, proclamations, etc. Unpublished papers about ER in the same file include one by Dorothy Kemp Roosevelt, the widow of ER's brother Hall Roosevelt.

F1966 Gargan, Edward A. "Eleanor Roosevelt's Vision of U.S. Imbues Parley." *New York Times* 17 Oct. 1984, sect. B: 2.
The conference at Vassar was a celebration of ER's beliefs as she pursued them and how they should be pursued today. Excerpts various papers presented at the conference, 13-16 Oct. There is also Richard Higgins, "Conference Opens with Tributes to ER." *Boston Sunday Globe* 14 Oct. 1984.

F1967 Gates, David. "An Independent Woman: A Hundred Years after Her Birth, ER Is Rediscovered." *Newsweek* 104 (15 Oct. 1984): 91-92.
ER will be celebrated with the dedication of the Eleanor Roosevelt National Historic Site and other events. Discussion of current ER scholarship undertaken by Blanche Wiesen Cook and Lois Scharf. Gates' tribute is to ER the independent person.

F1968 Goodman, Ellen. "Remembering the Power of an Idealist." *Los Angeles Times* 9 Oct. 1984, sect. 2: 5.
Her greatness came from character and principle. Her strong sense of duty and conscience, not an attempt to overcome her private problems, was why she created a public life for herself. A syndicated column which appeared on a variety of dates with different titles.

F1969 Green, Bill. "The 100th Birthday of Eleanor Roosevelt." *Congressional Record* (2 Oct. 1984): 28812.
Her many accomplishments make her an example to us all.

F1970 Hareven, Tamara K. "Eleanor Roosevelt: Humanitarian Reformer." *Eleanor Roosevelt: An American Journey.* Ed. Jess Flemion and Colleen M. O'Connor. San Diego: San Diego State Univ. Pr., 1987. 155-71. Note on Sources.

Her admirers and detractors were equally intense about their feelings. ER herself was as complex and contradictory as the feelings others had about her, but Hareven believes that there was a central theme to ER's life and work: humanitarianism.

F1971 Hoff-Wilson, Joan. "Did Eleanor Roosevelt Make a Difference?" *TWU Magazine* (Texas Woman's University) 2 (Fall 1984): 3-9.

She can be considered the unofficial Vice President for both FDR and HST. She changed the role of First Lady forever. There was never an American woman like her, and, because of the circumstances of her life, the conditions of her era, and the way in which women now view their roles, her role will never be duplicated. She was a "superwoman," and her accomplishments as both First Lady and UN delegate are still without parallel. Text of address, Eleanor Roosevelt symposium, Texas Woman's Univ., 11 Oct. 1984.

An edited version appeared in *Texas Humanist* (Nov./Dec. 1984): 33-37.

F1972 ---. "Eleanor Roosevelt: A Centennial Remembrance and Reappraisal." *Social Education* 48 (Nov./Dec 1984): 521.

ER's career provides a good example for young girls of today, and her activities can make her the center of classroom attention to the women's movement and social reform legislation.

F1973 ---. "The Relevance of Eleanor Roosevelt." *Eleanor Roosevelt: An American Journey.* Ed. Jess Flemion and Colleen M. O'Connor. San Diego: San Diego State Univ. Pr., 1987. 351-64. Note on Sources.

Covers many aspects of ER's career and establishes her place in the women's and social reform movements. ER as unofficial Vice President to FDR and HST, the model for subsequent first ladies, the stateswoman, as an opponent of the Equal Rights Amendment, and most importantly as a humanitarian.

F1974 Howlett, Ruth B. "An Encounter." *Christian Science Monitor* 11 Oct. 1984, Eastern ed.: 16.

Recalls seeing the First Lady alone on the streets of New York and how she and her friends admired her.

F1975 Kennedy, Shawn G. "At a Picnic, Roosevelts Recall Their First Lady." *New York Times* 14 Oct. 1984: 46.

Many family members gather at Val-Kill to remember ER and how time she spent there was such an important part of her life.

F1976 Kennelly, Barbara B. "In Honor of Eleanor Roosevelt." *Congressional Record* (12 Oct. 1984): 32566.

Her example is still a challenge to us all.

F1977 Kernan, Michael. "Eleanor Roosevelt, Pioneer." *Washington Post* 13 Sept. 1984, sect. E: 1, 17.

In a comprehensive look at her career her triumphs are remembered along with the criticism which she received. Discusses the opening of the Smithsonian exhibit which includes newsreel footage and actress Jean Stapleton portraying ER in an imaginary interview.

F1978 Klemesrud, Judy. "Assessing Eleanor Roosevelt as a Feminist." *New York Times* 5 Nov. 1984, sect B: 12.

Excerpts of remarks before the American Assoc. of University Women and other groups by Bella S. Abzug, Betty Friedan, Margaret Papandreou, Esther Peterson, Dorothy S. Ridings, Lois Scharf, Laurie Shields, and Gloria Steinem. All except Scharf conclude that ER was a feminist in spite of her refusal to support the Equal Rights Amendment. To Scharf ER was a "'social refomer' rather than a true feminist." Her efforts to advance the status of women through words, actions, and example are cited.

F1979 Lammerding, Betsey. "Eleanor Roosevelt: 'First Lady of the World.'" *Akron Beacon Journal* 7 Oct. 1984, sect. D: 1, 4.

Akron, Ohio residents recall ER. Also reports on 8 Oct. program about ER at the Univ. of Akron with Estelle Linzer, Robert Zangrando, and others to be participating.

F1980 Lammers, A. "Eleanor de Goede (1884-1962)." *Spiegel Historiael* 19 (1984): 438-43.

The life and work of a woman around whom there was an aura of holiness. A centennial tribute. In Dutch.

F1981 Lash, Joseph P. "The Reaches of Conscience." By Joseph P. Lash with Patrick McCaffrey. *Social Education* 48 (Nov./Dec. 1984): 528-30.

On the occasion of the centennial of ER's birth Lash responds to questions about ER's philosophy and career.

F1982 Levy, William Turner. "Mrs. Roosevelt: A Very Warm Friend." *Los Angeles Times* 11 Oct. 1984, sect. 5: 1, 26.

Levy, Episcopal priest and university professor, recalls his casual friendship with ER in the latter part of her life.

F1983 Linzer, Estelle. "Eleanor Roosevelt Centennial Observance, 1884-1984." *WFUNA Bulletin* (World Federation of United Nations Associations) 31 (Sept. 1984): 7-8.

Excerpts from ER's speeches on human rights are used as a tribute. The text is rearranged in the unsigned "Eleanor Roosevelt--The Champion of Human Rights." *The Concert and United Nations Ball Inaugurating the 1984 National UN Day Program*, pp. 8-9 (New York: United Nations Association of the United States of America, 1984).

F1984 "MASC and ERVK Honor Eleanor Roosevelt." *MASC Notes* (Mid-Hudson Arts and Science Center, Poughkeepsie, N.Y.) (Mar./Apr. 1984): 1-2.

Centennial events associated with Val-Kill.

F1985 McCarthy, Abigail. "Message at Campobello: Eleanor Roosevelt & Human Rights." *Commonweal* 111 (7 Sept. 1984): 458-59.

Although her efforts to make a place for women in public life were important, ER is remembered more for her struggle for human rights. Reports on Campobello celebration of her centennial including Barbara Jordan's call for the long overdue ratification of the "Charter of Human Rights" as the perfect memorial to ER.

F1986 McHugh, John F. *A Report of the Eleanor Roosevelt Centennial, 1984.* Rooseveltiana from the Private Collection of Dr. John F. McHugh. N.p.: n.p., [1985?]. n.pag.
Discussion of centennial celebrations with a calendar of events worldwide. Photocopies of articles from newspapers and periodicals. Announcements of programs planned. Available at FDRL.

F1987 Mitchell, Henry. "Memories of Eleanor." *Washington Post* 3 Feb. 1984, sect. E: 1, 4.
Reports on a reception held by the Eleanor Roosevelt Centennial Commission. Members of the Roosevelt family and friends and associates recall ER in private conversations.

F1988 Morrison, Howard Alexander. *Eleanor Roosevelt: First Person Singular.* Washington: Smithsonian Institution, 1984. [21]p.
Catalog of the exhibition. For the announcement of the opening of the exhibition, see "This Week, Community Events September 13-19." *Washington Post* 13 Sept. 1984, sect. Md.: 6. Pamela Kessler, "Mrs. Roosevelt Makes Herself into 'Eleanor.'" *Washington Post* 21 Sept. 1984: 45 is about the exhibition. *Update*, the annual publication of the Smithsonian Institution Traveling Exhibition Service, describes the exhibit, e.g., see 1987 ed.

F1989 Moynihan, Daniel Patrick. "The Centennial of Eleanor Roosevelt's Birth." *Congressional Record* (5 Oct. 1984): 30480-81.
Member of JFK's Commission on the Status of Women and of the Eleanor Roosevelt Centennial Commission, Sen. Moynihan honors the memory of the woman who did so much to improve the status of the underprivileged, disenfranchised, and oppressed.

F1990 ---. "Eleanor Roosevelt's Centennial." *Congressional Record* (12 Oct. 1984): 32444.
He repeats much of his 5 Oct. remarks in this call for remembering ER's vision of an active and responsible government working with the help of responsible citizens.

F1991 Neal, Steve. "Recalling Our Finest First Lady." *Chicago Tribune* 11 Oct. 1984: 27.
Evidence of ER's courage. Compares opposition to Geraldine Ferraro's candidacy for the vice presidency with criticism which ER received and expresses regret that ER was not the Democratic nominee for Vice President in 1948.

F1992 Proxmire, William. "A Tribute to Eleanor Roosevelt." *Congressional Record* (9 Feb. 1984): 2475.
Confirmation by the Senate of human rights documents would honor her memory.

F1993 Radcliffe, Donnie. "Roosevelt Reunion." *Washington Post* 10 Oct. 1984, sect. D: 1, 10.

Nancy Reagan honors the memory of ER at a White House luncheon while Rep. Pat Schroeder and other demonstrators claim that President Reagan's policies go against everything which ER believed in, an opinion echoed by presidential candidate Walter Mondale. Mrs. Reagan remembers being a fan of ER while not always agreeing with her. Another account of the luncheon is "One First Lady Honors Another." *New York Times* 10 Oct. 1984: 21. "Roosevelt Luncheon Protested." *USA Today* 10 Oct. 1984 describes the demonstration.

F1994 Rauh, Joseph L., Jr. "Golden Footprints." *New Republic* 191 (15 Oct. 1984): 10-12.
A tribute by one of the founders of the Americans for Democratic Action. ER played a vital role as helpmate to FDR. The effects of her dedication to civil rights and liberties, women's rights, and aid for the less fortunate can still be seen, and up until the very end she continued to serve others. Also issued in *Congressional Record* (5 Oct. 1984): 30481.

F1995 Reagan, Ronald. "Statement on Signing a Bill to Commemorate the Centennial of the Birth of Eleanor Roosevelt." *Public Papers of the Presidents of the United States: Ronald Reagan, 1983, Book II-July 2 to December 31, 1983*. Washington: GPO, 1985. 1621.
We are honoring a First Lady who worked to help humanity during and after her years in the White House. Text of brief statement on signing Senate Joint Resolution 139 enacted as Public Law 98-162, 21 Nov. 1983.

F1996 Reiter, Ed. "Eleanor Roosevelt Centennial." *New York Times* 7 Oct. 1984, sect. 2: 34.
A bronze medal has been struck to honor the centennial of her birth. Also includes a summary of her life and work.

F1997 "A Remarkable Woman's Life of Faith." *Family Circle* 97 (24 Jan. 1984): 31, 34.
A tribute to the ER's philosophy presented in her own words.

F1998 Remnick, David. "Memories of Eleanor." *Washington Post* 15 Oct. 1984, sect. C: 1, 4.
His centennial tribute is also a report on the Vassar conference "The Vision of Eleanor Roosevelt: Past, Present and Future." He quotes from the remarks of participants Arthur M. Schlesinger, Jr., Joseph Lash, Joseph L. Rauh, Jr., and Marque Mirningoff. Also describes other events scheduled for the centennial year.

F1999 Richards, Ann. "Texas Treasurer Calls for Involvement." *TWU Magazine* (Texas Woman's University) 2 (Fall 1984): 9-11.
She has been elevated to sainthood, because ER's life inspires us to be and do more. Her example should encourage women to become more involved in public affairs while her belief that human rights and equality begin in the home and at school and work should guide us in our daily lives. Text of address "Women in Politics: A Personal Perspective," Eleanor Roosevelt symposium, Texas Woman's Univ., 11 Oct. 1984.

F2000 Roark, Anne C. "E.R.--The History Book Is Reopened." *Los Angeles Times* 8 May 1984, sect. I: 1, 20-21.

Events in remembrance of ER during her centennial year. Roark discusses the scarcity of writings about ER and the problems associated with her and other women as subjects of serious biography. She concludes that those now writing about ER see scholarship about her as a blending of public and social history. Based in part on interviews with others who have written about ER.

F2001 Sarbanes, Paul S. "On the Centennial of Eleanor Roosevelt --'First Lady of the World.'" *Congressional Record* (11 Oct. 1984): 32071-72.
Sen. Sarbanes' tribute to the inspiration which ER provided introduces Nathan Miller's centennial tribute to her life, work, and ideals, "Eleanor Roosevelt--First Lady of the World," from the *Baltimore Sun,* 11 Oct.

F2002 Schneider, Claudine. "A Tribute to Eleanor Roosevelt." *Congressional Record* (12 Oct. 1984): 32568.
We should pursue the her dream of a better life for all.

F2003 Sine, Richard L. "Issue Marks Eleanor Roosevelt Centennial." *New York Times* 23 Sept. 1984, sect. 2: 36.
A commemorative stamp will be issued at an 11 Oct. ceremony. A brief summary of her life and career is included.

F2004 "The Spirit Is Alive." Editorial. *Los Angeles Times* 12 Oct. 1984: sect. 2: 4.
The importance of ER to students of America and humanity. Her spirit lives on.

F2005 Strout, Richard. "Eleanor Roosevelt and Those Unbelievable Days." *Christian Science Monitor* 28 Sept. 1984, Eastern ed.: 14.
As a centennial tribute Strout recalls what he wrote in 1939 about her attendance at a hearing of the Dies committee when leaders of the American Youth Congress were questioned.

F2006 Subject Files Relating to the Eleanor Roosevelt Centennial Commission. 8 boxes.
An extensive collection at the New York State Archives of minutes and press releases of the commission, programs of events held, typewritten copies of remarks made at events, publications issued during the centennial year, and a large number of newspaper articles about ER and centennial celebrations. As of 1993, there was no finding aid.

F2007 "Taste, Waste, and Excellence." *New York Times* 14 Oct. 1984, sect. 4: 22.
ER was a role model for other women and raised the nation's conscience. A section in the editorial column "Topics."

F2008 "Tributes to Eleanor Roosevelt." *Social Education* 48 (Nov./Dec. 1984): 542.
Statements by Jimmy Carter, Mario Cuomo, Gunnar Myrdal, and Arthur M. Schlesinger, Jr., plus statements made at the time of ER's death by Archibald MacLeish, Jawaharlal Nehru, and Adlai Stevenson.

F2009 Trueheart, Charles. "Joseph Lash." *Publishers Weekly* 226 (19 Oct. 1984): 49-50.
In the early 1940s there was a counterintelligence fear that ER was being duped by young revolutionaries. Lash claims that youths learned insights from her, she did

not learn from them. Lash denies that he had any romantic involvement with ER, and he cannot accept the idea that ER might have had a lesbian relationship with Lorena Hickok.

F2010 Urquhart, Brian. "Thoughts on Mrs. Roosevelt and Human Rights." *Eleanor Roosevelt: An American Journey.* Ed. Jess Flemion and Colleen M. O'Connor. San Diego: San Diego State Univ. Pr., 1987. 251-52.
She made lasting impressions in the UN and, through her belief in the human possibilities, on the world.

F2011 Ware, Susan. "The Legacy of Eleanor Roosevelt." *Second Century Radcliffe News* (Feb. 1985:): 9.
Her greatest legacy would be for us to finish the work which she began. She made the New Deal more "humane" and served as a model for women who realize the benefits which can result when they exercise "political strength."

F2012 Watrous, Hilda R. *Eleanor Roosevelt: Some of Her Days in Onondaga County.* Syracuse: Onondaga County Public Library, 1984. [11]p.
Collection of brief statements about visits which ER made to the Syracuse, N.Y. area published on the occasion of her centenary.

F2013 Winkler, Karen J. "Publication of Book 'Without Precedent' Marks Eleanor Roosevelt's Centennial." *Chronicle of Higher Education* 28 (18 Apr. 1984): 7-8.
This new book signals the beginning of interest by scholars on ER's impact. Discusses some of the essays contained in the book.

MISCELLANEOUS TRIBUTES AND ASSESSMENTS

F2014 Abrams, Irwin. *The Nobel Peace Prize and the Laureates: An Illustrated Biographical History, 1901-1987.* Boston: Hall, 1988. xiii + 269p. Index.
Abrams believes that ER would have been a strong candidate for the prize. She was nominated in 1947, but instead the prize went to the Society of Friends with the help of a letter of nomination from her. There was no recipient in 1948 (p. 23). Also see, "Appendix A: Eleanor Roosevelt and the Nobel Peace Prize" in Lash's *Eleanor: The Years Alone.*

F2015 *The All Texas 1956 Roosevelt Day Dinner: Honoring the Memory of Franklin Delano Roosevelt: Featuring the Testimonial of Texas to the First Lady of the World, Mrs. Franklin D. Roosevelt, Dallas, Texas, January the Sixteenth, Nineteen Hundred and Fifty-six.* Dallas, n.p., n.d. [16]p.
Copy not examined.

F2016 Allen, Hugh. *Roosevelt and the Will of God.* New York: Lifetime Editions, 1950. 280p. Notes.
Allen relies on Biblical scripture and Catholic theology to discredit Masonry and one of its own--FDR. ER is not spared either. He claims that she was trying to lead the country into communism, chides her for making too much of an unhappy childhood, and refers to her as "Cassandra of Campobello." Describes her early relationship with Joseph Lash and devotes attention to selected "My Day" columns. Includes excerpt from Hamilton Fish's attack on ER as an anti-Catholic in *Catholic News* [Mount Vernon, N.Y.] (6 Aug. 1949): 55-71.

F2017 Arnoll, Kay. "Eleanor Roosevelt." *New Outlook* 5 (Jan. 1952): 4-8.
She explains ER's greatness by discussing what others have written about her.

F2018 Benjamin, Robert S. *Robert S. Benjamin: A Citizen's Citizen.* New York: United Nations Association of the United States of America, 1980. xiii + 164p. Index.
Benjamin's recollections of ER and excerpts from his speeches provide tributes to ER and insight into their friendship with Adlai Stevenson and their work together with the democratic reform movement in New York City, the AAUN, and at Brandeis Univ. (pp. 7-158 passim).

F2019 Bergquist, Laura. "E'Ancora la Donna piu' Ammirata dagli Americani." *Tempo* (date unknown): 14-15.
ER is more popular than ever. In Italian. From photocopy at FDRL. Date lacking.

F2020 Bliven, Naomi. "Mrs. Roosevelt." Rev. of *Love Eleanor: Eleanor Roosevelt and Her Friends* by Joseph P. Lash and *Mother and Daughter: The Letters of Anna and Eleanor Roosevelt.* Ed. Bernard Asbell. *New Yorker* 58 (9 Aug. 1982): 89-94.
Bliven believes that these collections of letters establish ER's ability to understand the important issues of her time and to lead others in finding solutions to the problems. ER emerged as a maker of history, and Bliven regrets that we never had the chance to experience ER the President.

F2021 Boos, John E. *A First Lady Who Went Far: Eleanor Roosevelt.* Albany: Boos, 1961. 139p.
A typescript with original photographs issued in book form. Reprints some later writings by her and includes other material on FDR and the New Deal era. Available at the New York State Archives.

F2022 Chassler, Sey. "The Nine Lives of Eleanor Roosevelt." *Pageant* (Jan. 1951): 145-55.
She is busier than ever, but there are few accomplishments for which she has been responsible. Reasons are given why she has equally strong admirers and detractors.

F2023 DeMott, Benjamin. Rev. of *Eleanor: The Years Alone* by Joseph P. Lash. *Saturday Review* 5 (19 Aug. 1972): 56, 58.
ER used self-discipline to realize her own abilities while dedicating her life to the service of others.

F2024 De Toledano, Nora. "In Defense of Eleanor Roosevelt." *American Mercury* 78 (Feb. 1954): 69-71.
Since ER is not considered to be of great intellect, her failure to see the true colors of Communists is understandable.

F2025 Douglas, William O. "Eleanor Roosevelt." *Being an American.* By William O. Douglas. New York: Day, 1948; Freeport: Books for Libraries, 1971. 89-91.
To honor her is to honor what is best about America: the belief in human rights for all peoples. Based on an address to the National Council of Jewish Women, 15 Mar. 1948.

F2026 *Eleanor Roosevelt National Historic Site: Hearing before the Subcommittee on Parks and Recreation of the Committee on Energy and Natural Resources, United States Senate, Ninety-fifth Congress, 1st Session.* Washington: GPO, 1977. iii + 44p.

29 Apr. 1977 testimony of Representatives Jonathan B. Bingham and Hamilton Fish, Senators Jacob K. Javits, Daniel Patrick Moynihan, and Mark O. Hatfield, Esther Peterson, ER's grandson Curtis Roosevelt, and actress Jean Stapleton on the significance of ER's life and work and how the designation of Val-Kill as a National Historic Site would be an appropriate memorial to her.

F2027 Fairbanks, Douglas, Jr. "Eleanor Roosevelt." *TV Times* [London] 7 (3 May 1957): 10-11.

An affectionate look at the life and opinions of "one of the outstanding personalities, man or woman, of our times."

F2028 Fuller, John G. "Trade Winds." *Saturday Review* 44 (7 Oct. 1961): 12.

As one of the subjects of his column, ER's current robust life is celebrated.

F2029 Galbraith, John Kenneth. "Eleanor the Good." *Esquire* 100 (Dec. 1983): 544-46.

ER was an influential figure because her efforts on behalf of racial equality made it easier for others to follow her lead. She demonstrated that a woman can be a feared political force and an American can be a citizen of the world. Reissued in his *Fifty Who Made the Difference*, pp. 472-75 (New York: Villard, 1984).

F2030 Gallup, George H. *The Gallup Poll: Public Opinion, 1935-1971.* 3 vols. (xliv + 2388p). New York: Random House, 1972. Index.

Ranked fourth as most admired living person in 1946 poll (v. 1, p. 584) and sixth in 1947 (v. 1, p. 633). She was named the most admired woman in the world in 1948 (v. 1, p. 775) and again in 1949 (v. 2, p. 885).

Named the most admired woman in the world in 1951-1956 and 1958-1959 polls (v. 2, pp. 963, 1113, 1200, 1299, 1392, 1462, 1584; v. 3, pp. 1646-47). In 1953 ER ranked first with those age 50 and older and second with all other age groups (v. 2, p. 1035). Was sixth in a 1958 poll of famous persons in history (v. 2, p. 1560). In 1960 and 1961 was named most admired woman in the world (v. 3, pp. 1696, 1747).

F2031 Gammon, Roland. "Eleanor Roosevelt: 'O Lord, Make Me an Instrument of Thy Peace.'" *Faith Is a Star.* Ed. Roland Gammon. New York: Dutton, 1963. 153.

Tribute to her life and work.

F2032 Gansberg, Martin. "1,500 Honor Mrs. Roosevelt at Foundation Dinner." *New York Times* 13 Oct. 1964: 37.

Earl Warren, Adlai Stevenson, U Thant, New York City Mayor Robert F. Wagner, and others honor her memory, New York, 12 Oct. 1964.

F2033 Hancher, Virgil M. "Virgil M. Hancher Presents Eleanor Roosevelt." *I Am Happy to Present: A Book of Introductions.* Comp. Guy R. Lyle and Kevin Guinagh. New York: Wilson, 1953. 240-41.

Someday ER's role in the people's decision to elect five successive Democratic presidential candidates will be recognized. Introduction to an address by ER in Des Moines, Iowa, 14 Mar. 1949.

F2034 Hershan, Stella K. "Liberty Comes to Life." Letter. *New York Times* 4 July 1986: 26.

In 1939 as a young immigrant Hershan associated the meaning of America and the symbolism of the Statue of Liberty with the life of ER.

F2035 ---. "My Visit with Mrs. Roosevelt." *Pleasures in Learning* (New York University. Division of General Education and Extension Services) 10 (Jan. 1962): 5-11.

Hershan learned from the visit that "democracy imposes a great deal of responsibility on the individual."

F2036 Hurst, Fannie. "Eleanor Roosevelt." *Heroes for Our Times*. Ed. Will Yolen and Kenneth Seeman Giniger. Harrisburg: Giniger-Stackpole, 1968. 110-17.

A highly personal account of ER based in part on Hurst's *Anatomy of Me* (Garden City: Doubleday, 1958). One of 12 profiles of heroes and heroines.

F2037 *Intimate Sidelights about Eleanor Roosevelt: An Extended Interview with Dr. Abram L. Sachar, Chancellor of Brandeis University, Nov. 10, 1978*. N.p.: n.p., 1979. 48p.

Copy not examined.

F2038 Isenberg, Nancy G. "Eleanor Roosevelt: Joseph Lash's 'Eternal Mother.'" *Biography* 10 (Spring 1987): 107-15. Notes.

Lash portrays her as a "timeless" figure and as a woman who "stands 'alone of all her sex.'" She is the "eternal mother" with characteristics not unlike those of the Virgin Mary, in contrast with the other women in her life--Sara Roosevelt, daughter Anna, and Lorena Hickok.

F2039 Janeway, Elizabeth. "Last Years of a Pragmatic Saint." Rev. of *Eleanor: The Years Alone* by Joseph P. Lash. *Life* 73 (1 Sept. 1972): 16.

She was the happiest when working to improve the lot of others while seeking nothing for herself in the process. A woman of peace and influence.

F2040 Johnston, Anne Roosevelt. "Grandmere." *Eleanor Roosevelt and the Universal Declaration of Human Rights: An Agenda for Action in 1988*. Hyde Park: The Franklin and Eleanor Roosevelt Institute, 1988. 7-8.

Her granddaughter celebrates ER's life as one of courage. Today we must be just as courageous and strive to make a better world for all. Text of remarks, Hyde Park, N.Y., 7 Nov. 1987.

F2041 Johnston, Laurie. "Eleanor Roosevelt Honored at Hunter." *New York Times* 11 Oct. 1974: 41.

Report on 10 Oct. Hunter College program includes excerpts from daughter Anna's remarks about ER and Bella Abzug's recollection of a 1941 speech at Hunter in which ER promoted ideas which are now fundamental to the women's movement.

F2042 Luce, Clare Boothe. "Address of Hon. Clare Boothe Luce." *Congressional Record Appendix* (24 May 1950): A3942-43.

She "is the best loved woman in the world today." She is a woman of many careers and many virtues as well. No woman has done more good for as long as she has. Text of address presenting ER with the Williamsburg Gold Medal, New York, 21 May 1950.

F2043 MacLeish, Archibald. "What She Was Herself." *New York Times* 4 May 1972: 45.

At the time of ER's death Adlai Stevenson said that the world lost "what she was herself." MacLeish now defines that as humanity--ER was what humanity is.

F2044 Martin, Ralph G. *Cissy.* New York: Simon and Schuster, 1979. 512p. Index. Bibliography. Notes.

ER and the subject of this biography, newspaper publisher Eleanor Medill Patterson, are portrayed as friends with mutual interests. Martin quotes from unidentified writings by Patterson which praise ER's character and work (pp. 323-24, 326-27, 359-60).

F2045 McElvaine, Robert S. *The Great Depression: America, 1929-1941.* New York: Times Books, 1984. xiv + 402p. Index. Notes.

ER's life was one of love. She sought love as a child, and, as an adult, her efforts to help others was part of her continuing search for love (pp. 107, 109-10).

F2046 Mendoza, Miguel Angel. "Ellas Tambien Hacen Historia: Eleanor Roosevelt." *Manana* (Sept. 194-): 20-22.

Her life has been characterized by the desire to serve others. She helped FDR, and she serves her country and the world through her work with the UN. In Spanish. Dated incorrectly as 1943 by FDRL.

F2047 "Mrs. Franklin D. Roosevelt." *Delhi Mirror* 1 (24 Feb. 1952): 7, 10.
Tribute to her accomplishments.

F2048 "Mrs. Roosevelt's Birthday." Editorial. *New York Times* 11 Oct. 1954: 26.
Since the death of FDR, ER has created a life of her own, and her accomplishments make that life outstanding. A tribute on her 70th birthday.

F2049 "National Dinner Honors Mrs. Roosevelt...." *ADA World* 8 (Feb. 1953): 1-2.
At the Roosevelt Day dinner in New York on 6 Feb. 1953 ER was cited "for the nobility and generosity of her great spirit" and "for the courage and wisdom and fierce fidelity with which she has served the people of our country and all the peoples of the earth who live in freedom or who strive for it."

F2050 Nizer, Louis. "Eleanor Roosevelt." *Between You and Me.* Rev. ed. By Louis Nizer. New York: Yoseloff, 1963. 164-67.

She has championed causes when it was unpopular to do so, and in spite of her critics she is loved and respected.

F2051 "1,000 Attend Birthday Party on Oct. 11th." *AAUN News* 26 (Nov. 1954): 1.
ER is honored in New York on her 70th birthday. Dag Hammarskjold provided the tribute.

F2052 Patterson, William D. "The Hour and the Men." *Saturday Review of Literature* 34 (6 Jan. 1951): 10-11.

In a poll of readers ER was named "greatest living American woman" and "greatest woman in the world."

F2053 Rauh, Joseph L., Jr. "Eleanor Roosevelt 'Graced Our Lives.'" *Washington Post* 3 Dec. 1983: 19.
Co-founder of Americans for Democratic Action recalls his association with her. She proved that the actions of one person can make a difference.

F2054 Robinson, Donald. "Eleanor Roosevelt." *The 100 Most Important People in the World Today.* By Donald Robinson. Boston: Little, Brown, 1952. 63-66.
A tribute to her life and work through 1951.

F2055 Roosevelt, Elliott. Foreword. *Christmas 1940.* By Eleanor Roosevelt. New York: St. Martin's, 1986. 7-17.
The world situation at the time ER's short story was written and a tribute to her faith in mankind.

F2056 Sachar, Abram L. *A Host at Last.* Boston: Little, Brown, 1976. 308p. Index.
In this description of the development of Brandeis Univ. by its first president there are several tributes to ER as Brandeis trustee, part-time faculty member, and moderator of television series *Prospects of Mankind* (pp. 47-48, 87-89, 195-96, 267, 298).

F2057 "Salute to Democratic Women Pioneers." *Democratic Digest* 6 (Aug. 1959): 15.
On 20 Oct., the 20th anniversary of Democratic Woman's Day, contributors can add their names to scrolls which will be sent to ER, the originator of the annual event.

F2058 *70th Birthday Dinner in Honor of Mrs. Franklin D. Roosevelt.* New York: Eleanor Roosevelt 70th Birthday Committee, 1954. [22]p.
Includes brief messages from numerous public figures (pp. [6-7, 10-11]) plus excerpts from Henry Morgenthau, Jr.'s plea that we all follow her "selfless high-minded" example (p. [1]) and Clark M. Eichelberger's tribute to her work with the UN and the AAUN (pp. [3-5]). Held in New York, 11 Oct.

F2059 Sheed, Wilfrid. *Clare Boothe Luce.* New York: Dutton, 1982. vii + 183p. Index.
Luce and ER were opposites in their political and social views. But they shared the hindrance of being women, a fierce commitment to their views, and a willingness to make enemies if necessary (pp. 172-73).

F2060 Silver, Philip, and Jan Bart. *Rooseveltiana.* ATA Topical Handbook, 48. Milwaukee: American Topical Assoc., 1965.
Reproductions of postage stamps honoring ER and FDR. Cover title: *Eleanor and Franklin D. Roosevelt Stamps of the World.*

F2061 Stevenson, Adlai E. "An Appreciation." *Tomorrow Is Now.* By Eleanor Roosevelt. New York: Perennial-Harper, 1964. xi-xii.
She doubted her own worth and in the end became the personification of goodness.

F2062 ---. *The Papers of Adlai E. Stevenson*. Ed. Walter Johnson, et al. 8 vols. Boston: Little, Brown, 1972-1979. Index. Notes.

ER is the greatest proponent of democratic ideas, and through her affection for all peoples she is an inspiration. "Gentle" can be used to describe her, but in her case it means strength and compassion. Text of address at Democratic Advisory Council dinner in ER's honor, New York, 7 Dec. 1959 (v. 7, pp. 374-79).

In commencement address, "Fifty Percent of Our Brains," at Radcliffe College, 12 June 1963 he concludes by reflecting that ER's greatness resulted from her commitment to what needed to be done while not seeking praise from others or fearing criticism (v. 8, pp. 414-21). Also issued in his *Looking Outward: Years of Crisis at the United Nations*, pp. 281-89 (New York: Harper & Row, 1963).

F2063 Tetreault, Mary Kay. "Notable American Women: The Case of United States History Textbooks." *Social Education* 48 (Nov./Dec. 1984): 546-50. Bibliography. Notes.

In American history textbooks ER is portrayed as the type of woman whose life is that of "helpmate" to a famous husband.

F2064 "Tribute to Eleanor Roosevelt." *Variety Television Reviews, 1957-1959*. New York: Garland, 1989. 28 Oct. 1959 sect.

Arthur Godfrey and many others pay tribute to ER on her 75th birthday. Review of NBC television broadcast of 25 Oct. For review of tribute on her 76th birthday, see 12 Oct. 1960 sect. of *Variety Television Review, 1960-1962* (New York: Garland, 1989).

F2065 Vidal, Gore. "Eleanor." Rev. of *Eleanor and Franklin* by Joseph P. Lash. *New York Review of Books* (18 Nov. 1971): 3-4.

Less a review of Lash's biography than Vidal's own tribute to ER. Draws upon his personal recollections of her. Reissued in his *Homage to Daniel Shays: Collected Essays, 1952-1972*, pp. 410-24 (New York: Random House, 1972).

F2066 Walter, Claire. *Winners: The Blue Ribbon Encyclopedia of Awards*. Rev. ed. New York: Facts on File, 1982. ix + 916p. Index.

In 1949 ER was the first recipient of the Henrietta Szold Award of Hadassah (p. 650). In 1950 she was a recipient of the Antoinette Perry Award, American Theatre Wing Special Award (p. 240). She was among those honored in 1968, the first year the United Nations Prizes were awarded for contributions toward improving human rights (p. 620).

F2067 Weintraub, Benjamin. "Eleanor Roosevelt--American Humanitarian." *Decalogue Journal* 8 (Jan./Feb. 1958): 3-4.

Her life personifies "American idealism," and she is a leader who does not compromise principle. A tribute to the recipient of the 1957 Decalogue Merit Award presented in Chicago on 22 Feb. A companion article "Nation Acclaims Decalogue 1957 Choice" (p. 5) consists of excerpts from letters commending the selection. Hugo Black, William O. Douglas, Felix Frankfurter, and others praise ER as an humanitarian.

F2068 "Who's Your Favorite Hero?" *Woman's Home Companion* 75 (Nov. 1948): 12.

When readers were asked what famous person they would most like to invite to dinner, ER ranked fourth after FDR, Abraham Lincoln, and Will Rogers.

G

Interviews with Eleanor Roosevelt

1917

G1   "How to Save in Big Homes." *New York Times* 17 July 1917: 3.
Our ten servants have helped me contain the costs of feeding my family and managing my home. The Roosevelts' Washington household is cited as a model by the Food Admin. Based on a 16 July interview.

1922

G2   "Says Miller Angers Women." *New York Times* 7 Aug. 1922: 12.
Women are realizing that progress is not possible under the leadership of N.Y. Gov. Nathan Miller and the Republicans who support a potentially damaging tariff and believe that prosperity is possible only when workers are treated as slaves. Based on a 6 Aug. interview.

1924

G3   Feld, Rose. "Women Are Slow to Use the Ballot." *New York Times* 20 Apr. 1924, sect. 9: 1, 14.
Gaining the vote was easy compared to getting women into the political arena. Since American women have been taught that politics is only a man's concern, they must first learn about government, current issues, and the rules of politics. At the Democratic National Convention women should be able to have an impact because of their involvement with the platform.

G4   "How Men Have Treated Me in Politics." *Buffalo Evening Times* 29 Apr. 1924: 3.
They have treated me quite well.   While many men believe that women have something to offer to public life, others do not think that we are practical enough to succeed in politics. It should be remembered that men and women can look at issues differently. She was in Buffalo for a convention of the National League of Women Voters.

1928

G5   "Mrs. Roosevelt Pleased." *New York Times* 3 Oct. 1928: 12.
FDR accepted the nomination for governor because of his sense of party loyalty. She intends to continue her efforts to support the presidential ticket since FDR is able to do his own campaigning. Based on a 2 Oct. interview.

G6   Rice, Diana. "Mrs. Roosevelt Takes on Another Task." *New York Times Magazine* 2 Dec. 1928: 5, 23.
When she becomes the first lady of N.Y. she does not plan to give up teaching at the Todhunter School or other personal activities. But she would like to give up speech making, an activity which she does not enjoy. She gives her view of the role of women in politics: women must move slowly, learn about people and government, and realize that a woman cannot achieve public office unless she is trusted and respected by other women.

G7   Woolf, S.J. "A Woman Speaks Her Political Mind." *New York Times Magazine* 8 Apr. 1928: 3.
ER says that although women have the vote men have not taken the female political role seriously. She urges women to organize themselves and learn about politics. Woolf concludes that ER personifies the woman who can be interested and involved in public affairs while still being a wife and mother, realizing that involvement begins at home.

1929

G8   Merrill, Flora. "Mrs. Franklin D. Roosevelts' [sic] Opinions on What Tariff Bill Means in the Home." *Democratic Bulletin* 4 (Oct. 1929): 10-11, 31-32.
If the Smoot-Hawley tariff bill is passed, it will result in higher prices for the housewife. Based on an interview published in the *New York World*.

G9   Wyandt, Frieda. "A Governor's Wife at Work." *Your Home* (Sept. 1929): 11-13, 68-69.
An extensive discussion of the objectives of Val-Kill Industries.

1930

G10   Barnard, Eunice Fuller. "Woman's Place: Home or Office?" *New York Times Magazine* 10 Aug. 1930: 1-2, 19.
Unless economic circumstances force her to work, a mother's place is in the home while her children are young. Modern inventions have lessened the physical burdens of the homemaker, but the responsibility can be more demanding than outside work. While the traditional family unit is harder to maintain in this new age, it is no less important. A joint interview with Mrs. Thomas A. Edison.

G11   Purinton, Thelma. "From the Governor's Lady to Rosie O'Grady: What They Think of Radio Furniture." *Radio Retailing* 12 (Nov. 1930): 44-46, 73.
ER gives her views on radio cabinets (p. 44).

G12   Rice, Diana. "Mrs. Roosevelt Tells of Woman-Run Factory." *New York Times* 16 Nov. 1930, sect. 8: 13.

Our Val-Kill enterprise demonstrates that women can be successful in running a manufacturing firm. There is no reason why a woman could not manage a large industrial plant.

G13   Wilson, Florence Yoder. "Christmas Spirit the Year Around." *Needlecraft* 22 (Dec. 1930): 16-17.
Both ER and Nancy Cook were interviewed about ER's success in providing Christmas for the Roosevelt family as well as for the less fortunate. Cook portrays ER as a modest person who does everything well and has the spirit of Christmas all year, and ER gives credit to those who help her maintain a busy schedule.

G14   Wisehart, M.K. "Mrs. Franklin D. Roosevelt Answers the Big Question--What Is a Wife's Job Today? *Good Housekeeping* 91 (Aug. 1930): 34-35, 166, 169-73.
To be a partner and companion is what a modern wife should be ER states in this interview about the modern mother, homemaker, and wife. Condensation issued in *Literary Digest* 106 (30 Aug. 1930): 18-19 as "The Modern Wife's Difficult Job."

1931

G15   Magenheimer, Kay. "How I Make My Husband Happy." *Times Union* [Albany, N.Y.] 25 May 1931.
Small courtesies are important. ER also discusses the rearing of her children. Photocopy from FDRL. Page no. lacking.

G16   Tarbell, Ida M. "Portrait of a Lady." *Delineator* 119 (Oct. 1931): 19, 47-48, 50.
As the wife of the Gov. of N.Y. ER blends old traditions with the rights of the modern woman and makes herself accessible to the people. She entertains, tries to help those who write for assistance, and speaks to groups throughout the state. The influence of Marie Souvestre, her involvement with the Todhunter School and Val-Kill Industries, and her life as wife and mother.

G17   Woolf, S.J. "Mrs. Roosevelt of the Strenuous Life." *New York Times Magazine* 11 Oct. 1931: 10.
She believes in maintaining a traditional family life while pursing other activities such as teaching at the Todhunter School where she wants to see her students become better prepared to live in a democracy. Her interest in manufacturing furniture is a vital part of her desire to promote the value of rural life as an alternative to moving to the city in search of a factory job.

1932

G18   Adler, Margaret. "The Candidate at Home." *Review of Reviews* 86 (Aug. 1932): 28-29.
ER discusses FDR's hobbies and praises his strength and stamina.

G19   Barnard, Eunice Fuller. "Mrs. Roosevelt in the Classroom." *New York Times Magazine* 4 Dec. 1932: 1-2, 14.
How she became involved with the Todhunter School, the courses which she teaches, and her method of teaching.

G20 "Daily Work Goes on for Mrs. Roosevelt." *New York Times* 10 Nov. 1932: 4.
Only a few hours after FDR's election ER returned to teaching at the Todhunter School. During the day she was confronted with many questions from the press, but she continued the tradition that the wife of the President does not discuss political matters. In an interview reported here she stated that she was happy that FDR would be able to lead the country, that she approves of knowledgeable women in government, and that she could not discuss what is needed for the country because that is a political matter.

G21 "Girlhood Walk Lure to Mrs. Roosevelt." *New York Times* 17 Dec. 1932: 20.
She recalls as a child using a cane to keep her shoulders upright and straight. Interview conducted at Tivoli estate.

G22 "A Governor's Wife and Her Workshop." *Home Craftsman* (July/Aug. 1932): 82, 90, 93.
The founding of Val-Kill Industries, the type of furniture produced, and the skill which goes into its design and manufacture. An interview with the editors.

G23 Hickok, Lorena. Interviews. Nov. 1932.
Hickok conducted several interviews for the Associated Press soon after the 1932 election. They appeared in newspapers around 9-11 Nov. ER discussed her early life, how she was not seeking a position for herself, and how she planned to continue many of her personal activities. Copies of three interviews as published in the *Boston Post* and other papers are in the Lorena Hickok Papers, Box 14, FDRL.

G24 [Hickok, Lorena]. "Wife Prepares a Supper." *New York Times* 2 July 1932: 4.
One politician in the family is enough. She will help in other ways but will not campaign. She does not know what kind of role she would have as First Lady. A 1 July interview in Albany conducted as ER prepares to scramble eggs in celebration of FDR's nomination.

G25 Rodger, Sarah-Elizabeth. "Eleanor Roosevelt: Portrait of a Lady on Her Birthday." *Junior League Magazine* 19 (Nov. 1932): 14-15.
On her 48th birthday ER discusses a variety of issues. Prohibition has not worked, and when it comes to an end I hope that the upper classes make moderation the acceptable behavior. Women should learn about the issues and vote. Persuasion and patience, these are FDR's best qualities. My advice to the young is to marry for love.

1933

G26 Hager, Alice Rogers. "The Vibrant First Hostess of the Land." *New York Times Magazine* 14 May 1933: 6, 14.
ER as homemaker and the Roosevelts' daily life in the White House.

G27 Hickok, Lorena. "Company-Loving Roosevelts Expected to Keep White House Latchstring Out." *Feature Service* (5 Jan. 1933).
They plan to entertain informally and to ask dinner guests to stay overnight. Photocopy from FDRL. Page no. lacking.

G28 [---]. "Crowd Mind Read by Mrs. Roosevelt." *New York Times* 5 Mar. 1933: 7.

On inauguration day ER speaks about the warm reception which the crowd gave FDR's address and how her first weeks will be spent making the White House a home for her family. She provides a glimpse at the type of First Lady she thinks that she will be: a simplified approach to entertaining, she plans to do a lot of reading and to continue writing, and as a homemaker she wants to set an example for other women.

G29 Juno, Irene. "In the Air with Our Flying First Lady." *Good Housekeeping* 96 (June 1933): 26-27, 162.

In an airborne interview ER expresses her confidence in the safety of air travel and how it will change the future.

G30 Leighton, Isabel. "Eleanor Roosevelt--A Recent Portrait." *Ladies' Home Journal* 50 (Mar. 1933): 25, 75-76.

As First Lady ER does not plan to sacrifice her personal interests and she hopes that her children will be able to maintain their freedom. There is also a discussion of her earlier political activities as well as a plea for women to simplify housework in order to pursue activities and interests interests outside the home.

G31 "Mrs. Roosevelt Interviewed by Washington Co-Ed." *Washington College Bulletin* 11 (Nov./Dec. 1933): 18-19.

Since the road to success is harder for women, attending a small college can provide the opportunity for making contacts which will be valuable later.

G32 Rowe, Bess M. "Mrs. Roosevelt Speaks: She Sends a Message to Farm Women." *Farmer's Wife* (July 1933): 5, 24.

ER challenges the rural family to expand its horizons and acknowledge the relationship between the farm and the rest of the country and the world. To survive in these times all homes must adopt the pioneer attitude and make a fresh start.

G33 Stein, Hannah. "Should a Wife Support Herself?" *Every Woman* 1 (July 1933): 3.

If there are young children, the woman should be at home. It becomes a personal decision when the children are older.

1934

G34 Crosby, Pennell. "Mrs. Roosevelt Speaks to Wives of Electrical Workers." *Journal of Electrical Workers and Operators* (July 1934): 302, 324.

The homemaker can make a contribution to the labor movement by participating in the activities of union auxiliaries and by helping to promote the realization that labor and management must work together to achieve higher wages, increased productivity, and a speedy economic recovery.

G35 Love, Everetta. "Mrs. Roosevelt Discusses Radio." *Radioland* (Apr. 1934): 12-13, 56.

Radio should be educational, and children should not be exposed to violence in radio programs.

G36   Schwimmer, Rosika. "Frau Praesident Roosevelt." *Zuricher Post* [Zurich] 17 July 1934.

ER discusses her press conferences, dinner guests, and the origins of her social consciousness.   An interview conducted at the White House.   In German.   From photocopy at FDRL.   Page no. lacking.

1935

G37   "Mrs. Roosevelt Is 'Perturbed' by Verdict in Hauptmann Case." *New York Times* 23 Feb. 1935: 1, 7.

It is possible to have no sympathy for Bruno Richard Hauptmann but still be distressed that an innocent person could be convicted on circumstantial evidence. Based on 22 Feb. interviews in Baltimore and New York.

1936

G38   Dando, Ellen Ann. "An Interview with Eleanor Roosevelt." *Reflector of Central Junior High School, Saginaw, Michigan* (Christmas number 1936): [11].

She was glad to be able to slip out by herself today and take a walk wearing the hat which she uses as a disguise. Miss Dando concludes that the woman who spends so much time trying to learn more about other citizens is ideal for the role of First Lady.

G39   "Mrs. Roosevelt Refuses Election Forecast; Outcome Is 'On Lap of the Gods,' She Declares." *New York Times* 9 Oct. 1936: 18.

This year the voters are concerned with the issues. She has no idea how the election will go.

1937

G40   Grusd, Edward E. "The 'First Lady' Talks." *B'nai B'rith Magazine* (Dec. 1937): 126-27.

Minorities should be allowed to make their own unique gifts to the American heritage. Groups which are subject to discrimination should seek support from the majority of American people who are not prejudiced. Peace will come first through positive relations within our own country. The young and the old are facing similar problems which might be solved through a change in thinking that "success" means only material gain. Interview in Champaign, Ill., where she was a speaker in the lecture series of the B'nai B'rith Hillel Foundation at the Univ. of Ill.

G41   Herrick, Genevieve Forbes. "When the First Lady of the Land Entertains: An Interview." *Democratic Digest* 14 (Sept. 1937): 16-17.

Numerous questions about White House entertaining.

G42   "Mrs. Roosevelt Sees Peace Oath Danger." *New York Times* 3 June 1937: 27.

Students should not sign an oath against bearing arms when we may face war. All countries must work together to achieve peace. Interviewed on 2 June NBC radio program.   Her statements were supported in the editorial column "Topics of the Times." *New York Times* 4 June 1937: 22.

G43 "President's Wife Tells of Memories." *New York Times* 25 Feb. 1937: 17.

It was "exciting" to write *This Is My Story*. I tried to keep it simple and truthful. Now I would like to write a play.

1939

G44 Pew, Marlen E., Jr. "Mrs. FDR Tells of Writing While Hostess to Royalty." *Editor & Publisher* 72 (17 June 1939): 32.

During the visit of the British royal couple she found the time to write "My Day" the same way she does every day by planning ahead and organizing her time which is how all women accomplish as much as they do.

G45 Woolf, S.J. "Energy: Mrs. Roosevelt Tells How She Conserves It." *New York Times Magazine* 28 May 1939: 3, 10.

ER states that she accomplishes so much because she likes what she is doing and does not worry about mistakes and what others think about her. Describes her mail and the influence which Louis Howe had upon her.

1940

G46 Bromley, Dorothy Dunbar. "The Future of Eleanor Roosevelt." *Harper's Magazine* 180 (Jan. 1940): 129-39.

ER has given the American people a new conception of what a First Lady should do. While reluctant to be in the public eye, she is part of a great political team and has served as an inspiration to a generation of young girls.

If FDR is not President after 1940, his successor should offer a post to ER who will be a public force for many years to come. An abridged version issued in *Reader's Digest* 36 (Feb. 1940): 7-11.

In her account of the interview Bromley attributes to ER the view that the American people support involvement in a European war. This caused ER to announce that Bromley had applied a general statement to a specific situation. Bromley then challenged ER through her *New York Post* column. The texts of these two statements as reported in the *New York Times* of 19 and 20 Dec. are reproduced as "Mrs. Roosevelt and Mrs. Bromley." *Harper's Magazine* 180 (March 1940): two unnumbered pages. A discussion of the situation appeared as "Mrs. Roosevelt's War Views Attacked by Rival Columnist." *Newsweek* 15 (1 Jan. 1940): 27.

G47 "Interview with Eleanor Roosevelt--Charter Member, New York League." *Junior League Magazine* 26 (Mar. 1940): 10-11.

Junior Leaguers are in a position to understand the problems of today and to help solve the economic problems facing other young Americans. Pleased that a chapter president will attend the upcoming Citizenship Institute of the Youth Congress. Reissued in *Junior League* 58 (Spring 1971): 53-54.

G48 McLaughlin, Kathleen. "The First Lady's View of the First-Lady Role." *New York Times Magazine* 21 Jan. 1940: 3, 20.

Speculation continues about ER's influence over FDR, and in this interview ER regrets that she does not stay quiet when she appears in public with him. Although she enjoys her travels and public speaking, she does not see her actions as a model for future first ladies. ER on party politics and women running for public office.

G49   ---.   "No Campaigning, First Lady States." *New York Times* 19 July 1940: 1, 5.

She came to speak to the delegates to the Democratic National Convention because friends asked her to. It is hard to imagine why anyone seeks the presidency in these troublesome times; they are so difficult that FDR will not be able to campaign. Based on an interview given to McLaughlin and other reporters in Chicago, 18 July.

G50   Ryan, Edward.   "Eleanor Roosevelt on 20-30." *Twenty-Thirtian* 14 (June 1940): 7, 12.

The young men of 20-30 are the ones which are being asked to fight the war, a war which must be concluded with a fair and lasting peace. An interview conducted by the editor of *Twenty-Thirtian* on a train between Ogden, Utah and Denver, Col.

1941

G51   Furman, Bess.   "Eleanor Roosevelt, Civilian Defense Volunteer, Goes to Work." *Democratic Digest* 18 (Nov. 1941): 4-5, 34.

She faces her greatest challenge as assistant director of the Office of Civilian Defense. An interview with ER about citizens' roles in the civilian defense effort. Also excerpts a 4 Mar. 1933 interview with Lorena Hickok in which ER calls for all people to share while they face the future with courage.

G52   Goldberg, Rose C.   "First Lady in Her Own Right: An Interview with Eleanor Roosevelt." *Echo* (Hunter College) (Mar. 1941): 3-5.

ER states that the problems of youth are universal and that present conditions make these problems worse. She also said that at last our government represents all people including women.

1942

G53   Cairns, Julia.   "I Meet Mrs. Roosevelt." *Weldon's Ladies' Journal* (Jan. 1943): 23.

ER has asked us to be kind to American military personnel but do not offer them luxuries. What women in this country are doing for the war effort will serve them well later. Based on an interview conducted during her Oct.-Nov. 1942 trip to England.

G54   Luxford, Nola.   "Mrs. Roosevelt Talks to the Women of New Zealand." *New Zealand Free Press* 3 (22 July 1942): 1.

In an informal interview ER discusses how she schedules her time, the need to sacrifice in time of war, and the work of Sister Kenny. Luxford describes ER's Washington Square apartment and discusses the praise and criticism which ER receives as First Lady.

1943

G55   Callahan, North.   "The First Lady Speaks on 'Voice of the Army.'" *Army Life and United States Army Recruiting News* (Nov. 1943): 10-11.

All who have loved ones fighting in the Pacific should be proud of their courage. ER is interviewed about her trip to the South Pacific.

1944

G56 McLaughlin, Kathleen. "Mrs. Roosevelt Wants 'Just a Little Job.'" *New York Times Magazine* 8 Oct. 1944: 16, 40-42.

At 60 she still has her same vitality, but now many of her thoughts and actions are concerned with the war. She is grateful for the opportunity to observe the war effort directly, to visit servicemen and to report on what she has seen and heard. To live in the White House means always placing public before private life, and she thinks that her activities as First Lady may set the norm for those who follow her. If FDR is not re-elected she would like to get a job, perhaps one in publishing, which would allow her to measure her effectiveness. She is guarded about the country's ability in the post-war world to provide equal opportunity for all.

1945

G57 Cox, Corolyn. "A Maker of World History." *Canadian Home Journal* (Jan. 1945): 8-9.

An interview about women's role in maintaining peace. ER states that Canadians and Americans can make a difference by working together and showing Europe how the two countries live together in peace and harmony. Cox describes ER as "the outstanding female figure on the world stage today" and looks forward to seeing her in the White House for another four years.

G58 Wollen, Carol. "Mrs. Roosevelt Discusses Housing in Recent Interview with Chronicle." *Vassar Chronicle* 8 Sept. 1945: 1.

Many problems in our society are a result of poor housing, and as a nation we should try to improve living conditions in all areas of the country. She also praised the college's Summer Institute, in which she was a participant during the 11 July-8 Aug. program on community organization. Based on an interview conducted 4 Sept.

G59 Woolf, S.J. "Eleanor Roosevelt of Washington Square." *New York Times Magazine* 23 Sept. 1945: 16, 41.

Woolf found the recently widowed ER to be the same enthusiastic and caring woman he had interviewed on earlier occasions. She plans to continue writing and to work for groups and causes of interest to her. The extent to which many of FDR's ideas are now accepted is of great comfort and satisfaction to her.

1946

G60 Martin, Ralph G. "Number One World Citizen." *New Republic* 115 (5 Aug. 1946): 139-40.

ER on European refugees, returning U.S. veterans and their problems, and hope for the UN and the support which it should receive from veterans.

G61 Woolf, S.J. "The New Chapter in Mrs. Roosevelt's Life." *New York Times Magazine* 15 Dec. 1946: 15, 52-53.

Based on an interview conducted at the end of ER's first year as a UN delegate, a role which she finds more restrictive than that of First Lady. Woolf devotes more attention, however, to assessing how her views have remained constant during the 25-year period he has interviewed her. She still believes that it is important for women to learn more about history and government before getting involved in politics, that it is in our country's best interest to help alleviate discontent in Europe and to accept the fact that democracy can take more than one form, and that there is always the need for government to recognize individuals and their problems.

1947

G62   "Mrs. Roosevelt und die Menschenrechte." *Sie und Er* 23 (12 Dec. 1947): 1-3.
She talks about her work with the UN and the origins of her racial consciousness. In German. Signed "F.v.S."

G63   Oleson, Helmer O. "Franklin D. Roosevelt's Adventure in Stamp Collecting." *Stamps* 232 (1 Sept. 1990): 310, 320.
FDR was fascinated with stamps. While she recognizes the educational value of the hobby, she is not a collector herself. Reprint of an interview from the 27 Dec. 1947 issue of *Stamps*.

G64   "A Visit with Mrs. Roosevelt Two Years after Her Husband's Death." *PM's Sunday Picture News* 6 Apr. 1947: 2.
The American people miss hearing FDR's voice and the feeling of security which he provided. He also gave the citizens of other countries hope that the war would be won.

1948

G65   "Gesprek met Mevrouw Roosevelt." *Vrij Nederland* [Amsterdam] 3 Jan. 1948.
Copy not examined. In Dutch.

G66   Rosenau, James N. "An Estimate of Franklin D. Roosevelt Based upon His Personal Letters." Senior Project, Bard College, 1948. xv + 302p.
Rosenau, who co-edited the second volume of FDR's personal letters, interviewed ER when he was writing this paper. She responds to questions about FDR's family, friends, associates, early political activities, and the development of his social conscience. Excerpts of interviews (pp. 278-302).

G67   Ruys, A. Ch. "Op Bezoek bij Mrs. Roosevelt." *Groene Amsterdammer* [Amsterdam] 12 Juni 1948.
Copy not examined. In Dutch.

1949

G68   *Meet the Press*. 8 Apr. 1949.
Copy of transcript not examined.

1950

G69   Thompson, Era Bell. "How the Race Problem Embarrasses America." *Negro Digest* (Nov. 1950): 52-54.
As a society and a nation we are judged by the way in which we treat minorities. It is now time to move faster to end all discrimination. The UN has made progress in the area of human rights, but true human rights will be achieved only when individuals believe in and practice it. Based on an interview.

G70 Williams, Charl Ormond. "This I Believe about Public Schools." *Nation's Schools* 45 (Mar. 1950): 31-36.

To ER public schools provide not only an education but also the means for our children to grow up as healthy citizens in a democratic society. A long-time friend asks ER a number of questions about public education.

1951

G71 Wamboldt, Helen Jane. "Interview: Mrs. Franklin D. Roosevelt - Helen Jane Wamboldt." "A Descriptive and Analytical Study of the Speaking Career of Anna Eleanor Roosevelt." By Helen Jane Wamboldt. Diss. Univ. of Southern Calif., 1952. 401-5.

In the early years Louis Howe impressed upon her the importance of accepting invitations to speak in FDR's place. Making a speech is still a frightening experience and something which will never be enjoyed.

1952

G72 "Mrs. FDR Gives Her Views on Negro Problems." *Detroit Compass* 10 Feb. 1952.

The petition to the UN charging the U.S. with genocide against blacks is of no effect because any such charges can be responded to by her or alternate delegates Edith Sampson and Channing Tobias. But the petition may interest some in this country who would be pleased with this type of genocide. Morally, intervention in the U.S. by the UN on behalf of blacks could be justified. Article constitutes part of an interview conducted by William A. Rutherford. Available on fiche no. 004,370 of the New York Public Library's *Schomburg Center Clipping File, 1925-1974.*

G73 Spetter, I. "Op Bezoek bij...." *Vrij Nederland* [Amsterdam] 25 Oct. 1952.
Copy not examined. In Dutch.

1953

G74 "Mrs. Roosevelt Finds U.S. Prestige Sagging." *New York Times* 3 Aug. 1953: 15.

Upon her return from a world tour she reports that Asian nations fear the military power of the U.S., not that of the Soviet Union. Everywhere I was asked about Sen. Joseph McCarthy, a figure whose tactics remind some of Hitler or Stalin.

G75 Rosenthal, A.M. "On Dealing with the Russians." *New York Times Magazine* 18 Jan. 1953: 10, 27, 30.

ER recalls her experiences with Soviet delegates at the UN. She wishes that as a nation we would be less fearful about the Russians and more positive about what we have to offer the rest of the world.

1954

G76 Bendiner, Robert. "Eleanor Roosevelt at a Youthful 70." *New York Times Magazine* 10 Oct. 1954: 17, 40, 42, 44.

Her schedule is as busy as ever, and with no family responsibilities she feels that she can take on whatever obligations she likes. She is committed to the UN since it is all that prevents us from having to live in a "jungle" atmosphere with the rest of the world. Maintaining our military strength is important she thinks, but it is equally important that we have pride in our democratic way of life and try to make other countries want the same.

G77   "Curb on M'Carthy [sic] Put Up to Senate." *New York Times* 12 Apr. 1954: 10.

On *Meet the Press* of 11 Apr. she called upon the Senate to control the actions of Sen. Joseph McCarthy. She denied "that communists had infiltrated the government" under the Democrats and was noncommittal on the current political candidacies of sons James and Franklin.

G78   Olmedo, Tomas. "La Senora Roosevelt nos Habla de la Mujer." *Temas* (Mar. 1954): 53-58.

Women in Latin American countries should become more involved in the affairs of their countries. All women want peace, and women should claim their rightful place in public life along with men and work toward achieving a peaceful world. In Spanish.

1955

G79   Debnam, W.E. Addenda. *Segregation*. Raleigh: Privately printed, 1955. [7]p.

A Nov. 1952 interview with ER broadcast over the Smith-Douglas radio network. ER and Debnam discuss her remark in a 1950 "My Day" column that a visit to the South makes her sad, his reaction published as *Weep No More, My Lady*, current economic and racial conditions in the South, and the effect which poor race relations can have on the image of the U.S. An addendum to the text of a discussion between Debnam and Roy Wilkins.

G80   Gu, J. "Frau Eleanor Roosevelt." *Sie und Er* (22 Sept. 1955): 59.

Her many activities including extensive travel leave little time to spend with her family. In German.

G81   Marx, Hilde. "Delegates in the Workshop of Peace." *This Day* (Oct. 1955): 10-13.

The UN has a better chance to succeed than the League of Nations. The presence of women on the political scene has made men more conscientious. These are among the comments which are attributed to ER in an article based in part on Marx's interview (pp. 11-12).

G82   "Reporters Meet Eleanor Roosevelt." *Billtown Banner* (Williamsport High School, Williamsport, Pa.) 4 (1 Apr. 1955): 1, 4.

Find the courage to stand for something. ER gave this advice to a group of students when she was interviewed on 24 Feb. about her work with the UN, "the only 'machinery' working for world peace today."

G83   Sheridan, Michael. "The Best Times of Our Lives." *Family Circle* 47 (Aug. 1955): 21, 51, 53, 57, 60.

After reviewing the various periods of her life, ER concludes that the best time is always the present.

G84   Simon, Gene. "Mrs. FDR Genuinely Fond of People, Simon Finds." *Valley Daily News* [Tarentum, Pa.] 4 Apr. 1955: 1, 12.
The UN must use peace-keeping forces to protect the borders between Israel and its Arab neighbors. The young democratic nation deserves support.

G85   "West Is Cautioned by Mrs. Roosevelt." *New York Times* 20 Sept. 1955: 35.
The ideological battle between the West and the Soviets is still very much alive. We will have to work in Asia to promote our beliefs. Interview after her return from Bangkok.

1956

G86   "Age, Health, and Politics." *Journal of Lifetime Living* 21 (Apr. 1956): 24-27.
Age is not a factor in holding public office. ER's responses to written questions plus editorial comment.

G87   "Eleanor Roosevelt, Margaret Chase Smith." *Face the Nation: The Collected Transcripts from the CBS Radio and Television Broadcasts*. Vol. 2, 1956. New York: Holt, 1972. 354-60.
The two guests discuss the presidential election and current conditions in the Middle East and Europe. Transcript of 4 Nov. television interview.

G88   "Housing for Everybody." *Co-op Contact* (United Housing Foundation Community Services) 1 (May 1956): 1-2.
ER discusses how segregation knows no geographical boundaries and how equal access to housing can help bring full employment, reduce juvenile deliquency, and end segregation in schools and churches.

G89   "Mrs. Roosevelt Talks." *New York Times* 17 Sept. 1956: 19.
Candidate Adlai Stevenson has not explained what he means by ending the military draft. In the future we will need a highly trained, mobile army with many technicians who may not be in the military, said ER. She also called for the North to desegregate their neighborhoods. Informal interview given after 16 Sept. appearance on *Meet the Press*. Transcript of *Meet the Press* appearance not examined.

1957

G90   "Contribution to North Africa's Welfare." *Alliance Review* 12 (Dec. 1957): 3-4.
Interview about her trip to Morocco where she visited schools of the Alliance Israelite Universelle. Also issued in Spanish as "La Contribucion de la Alianza al Bienestar de Notre Africa." *Revista de la Alliance* 32 (Julio 1957): 5-6.

G91   Kutner, Nanette. "Eleanor Roosevelt Today." *American Weekly* (6 Oct. 1957): 10-11, 13.
ER discusses her public and private life in an interview conducted in New York and at Val-Kill.

G92   *Lehman Project, Eleanor Roosevelt*. New York Times Oral History Program, Columbia University Oral History Collection, pt. 2, no. 160. Glen Rock: Microfilming Corp. of America, 1975. 1 microfiche (18 p.) Index.

She talks about Herbert Lehman as FDR's Lt. Gov. and as a U.S. Senator. Interview conducted by Joseph F. Wall.

G93   *Meet the Press* 1 (20 Oct. 1957): 1-8.
ER is interviewed about her trip to Russia, her interview of Nikita Khrushchev, the need for national leadership, and the 1960 presidential election.

G94   Rowan, Carl T. "The Most Remarkable Roosevelt." *Minneapolis Morning Tribune* 4 Sept.-21 Sept. 1957.
Rowan interviewed ER over the course of several days.

G94a   Pt. 1. "There Won't Be a First Lady--Just Plain, Ordinary Mrs. Roosevelt." 4 Sept. 1957: 1, 10.
He assesses her activities as First Lady, cites the honors and tributes which she received and the criticisms leveled at her.

G94b   Pt. 2. "Waves of Hatred Fail to Subdue Mrs. F.D.R." 5 Sept. 1957: 1, 15.
A discussion of some of the writings severely critical of her, in particular those by Westbrook Pegler.

G94c   Pt. 3. "Unhappy Childhood Teaches Her the Fears and Needs of Others." 6 Sept. 1957: 1, 12.
Residents of Hyde Park find ER contradictory: how someone with her background can be so humble and how she could have deserted her family's politics and become such a liberal. Rowan feels that the tribulations and fears of her childhood have had the greatest impact on ER's adult actions and attitudes.

G94d   Pt. 4. "Mrs. F.D.R. Knew Tragedy of Alcohol in Those Close to Her." 7 Sept. 1957: 1, 9.
Alcoholism in her family--her father and brother and her mother's brothers--has been an undeniable influence on her thinking; however, she came to realize that prohibition was unworkable and to accept alcohol in moderation.

G94e   Pt. 5. "F.D.R.'s Mother Tried to Block His Marriage." 9 Sept. 1957: 1, 9.
Sara Roosevelt opposed the marriage, and ER felt dominated by her for many years. ER feels that she did not intrude into FDR's political activities, and she attributes his success to an ability to look at issues historically.

G94f   Pt. 6. "How Does Mrs. Roosevelt Explain the Troubles of Her Children?" 10 Sept. 1957: 1, 9.
Her children have had problems because of having to live in the public eye and since she left too much of their upbringing to servants. To her divorce is preferred to the continuation of an unhappy marriage.

G94g   Pt. 7. "Mrs. Roosevelt Tells Her Views of F.D.R.'s Greatest Contribution." 11 Sept. 1957: 10.
Since FDR the people have considered government to be responsible for their well-being. That was his greatest contribution. She is modest about the influence which she had over New Deal policies and does not think that she was ahead of FDR on social issues.

G94h Pt. 8. "As Saleswoman for New Deal, Mrs. Roosevelt Led All the Rest." 12 Sept. 1957: 6.

Through her writing and speaking it was ER who did the most to promote New Deal programs. FDR was both leader and symbol. She believes that to improve conditions for all more of the wealth will have to be shared.

G94i Pt. 9. "Ike--'Nice Man, Poor Leader'; Nixon 'Anything to Get Elected.'" 13 Sept. 1957: 6.

Her opinions about President Eisenhower, Richard Nixon, and John Foster Dulles. Eisenhower does not have the background to lead our foreign policy and relies too heavily on Dulles. Nixon will do anything to achieve the presidency.

G94j Pt. 10. "Give ALL Citizens Their Rights and the Race Problem Will Fade." 14 Sept. 1957: 9.

Although ER's position on racial equality has brought her more criticism than any other issue, often she has been a moderate in her views. She feels that a coalition of progressive Republicans and northern Democrats will come about only if "some bold young man" emerges. In 1957 she could not see such a person.

G94k Pt. 11. "Roaming World or Busy at Home, Mrs. F.D.R. Sets a Pace That Thrills." 16 Sept. 1957: 9.

Her energy and stamina are legendary. Wartime trips to England and the South Pacific, her work with the UN and the American Association for the United Nations, and her speaking and writing obligations.

G94l Pt. 12. "Gracious Mrs. F.D.R. Has Sense of Humor and Biting Wit." 17 Sept. 1957: 9.

Anecdotes about her wit and humor and her short-lived desires to lead a quite life.

G94m Pt. 13. "Mrs. F.D.R.'s 'Helping Hand' Gives Away a Million." 18 Sept. 1957: 8.

The sources of her current income. Since the 1930s the beneficiaries of her generosity have included the American Association for the United Nations, the American Friends Service Committee, the Wiltwyck School, and individuals.

G94n Pt. 14. "Religion Has Nothing to Do with Any Specific Creed." 19 Sept. 1957: 15.

Praying for peace and having religious beliefs is more important than attending church. Also includes examples of how she feels that others have taken advantage of her.

G94o Pt. 15. "Despite Controversy, Mrs. F.D.R. Is World's Most Honored Woman." 20 Sept. 1957: 13.

A variety of tributes. 1955--Franklin medal from the Philadelphia City Council, Nansen medal, and Philip Murray Award. 1957--United Auto Workers Freedom Award. From her 70th birthday celebration quotations from the remarks of Archibald MacLeish, Helen Keller, A Philip Randolph, and Frank Lloyd Wright. Extensive interviews with former daughter in-law Faye Emerson (ER is the best of everything but still a woman with shortcomings) and newspaper publisher John S. Knight who recalls his 1937 tribute (others criticize her, but they can never come close to matching her greatness).

G94p   Pt. 16. "F.D.R. Death 'Ends Story,' but Widow Continues Work." 21 Sept. 1957: 4.

After FDR's death ER put aside her personal sorrow and resumed a full life. The overriding objective of her service with both the UN and the American Association for the United Nations was to seek peace for all.

1958

G95   Bugbee, Emma.   "Mrs. Roosevelt Shrugged Off Presidency 'Vision.'" *New York Herald Tribune* 1 Feb. 1958: 4.

An interview conducted after the opening of *Sunrise at Campobello*.   In the early years of FDR's illness she did not believe Louis Howe's prediction that FDR would someday achieve the presidency.   She wanted him to return to public life but with no particular office in mind.   She did not find the portrayal of herself realistic, but the play succeeds in presenting the drama of a polio victim trying to return to an active life.

G96   "Eleanor Roosevelt." *Equity* 43 (Oct. 1958): 10-14.

An interview about her trip to Russia.   Complements her report issued as "Mrs. Roosevelt Reports on Her Trip to Russia."

G97   *Meet the Press* 2 (26 Oct. 1958): 1-8.

Responds to questions about the U.S. Senate race in New York, the 1960 presidential election, right to work laws, and whether the U.S. should recognize China and support its admittance to the UN.

G98   Peters, Kenneth.   "Delinquents Can Destroy Us!" *National Police Gazette* 163 (Nov. 1958): 10, 26.

Soon after her return from Russia ER granted this interview in which she looks to strong leadership for a program to overcome the dangers of juvenile delinquency. She calls for a national program involving the schools and law enforcement agencies aimed at getting "young people on the right track," more inspiring teachers, and greater recognition for scientists as encouragement for youth to pursue scientific careers.

G99   Unger, Art.   "I Had to Grow Up Quickly!" *Datebook* 2 (Aug. 1958): 20, 46, 48-49.

ER on her problems as a teenager and the problems facing youth today.

G100   *Vrij Nederland* [Amsterdam] 8 Mar. 1958.

Copy not examined.   In Dutch.

1959

G101   Burns, James MacGregor, and Janet Thompson Burns. "Mrs. Roosevelt at a Remarkable 75." *New York Times Magazine* 4 Oct. 1959: 19, 38, 40, 42.

In a conversation with this idealistic woman who has learned that patience and toughness are needed in dealing with the problems of the world are her recollections of the role which she played in the Roosevelt White House (a prod and a sounding board) and her views on the struggle between communism and democracy (it is more economic and cultural than militaristic).

1960

G102   Nordell, Rod. "Mrs. Roosevelt Talks about What She Likes and Where She Is 'Lost.'" *Christian Science Monitor* 10 Mar. 1960, Atlantic ed.: 13.
She learned to appreciate the value of reading from her father. Children who learn to enjoy reading when young will gain much from the experience. She cannot possibly read all of the books which are sent to her.

1961

G103   Brandle, Lowell. "Dialogue: Mrs. Roosevelt." *Sunday St. Petersburg Times* 29 Oct. 1961: 8-9.
Questions and answers about fear, anti-Communist sentiment, the Republican Party, President Eisenhower as a leader, and the responsibilities of living in a democracy.

1962

G104   "Faith, Home, and Charity, These Three." *Faith Is a Star.* Ed. Roland Gammon. New York: Dutton, 1963. 154-57.
Like a church the UN is only an instrument. What is more important is one's concern for fellow human beings as demonstrated by how one lives. Sees a struggle between communism and democracy and the need for Americans to rise to the challenge. Based on a 1962 interview with Gammon.

G105   "Veinte Minutos con Eleanor Roosevelt." *Temas* (May 1962): 12-14.
A discussion with Rosemarie Perez and Alvaro Gomez about U.S. relations in Latin America. The success of the Alliance for Progress depends on the U.S. as well as the nations which will benefit most from it. She does not favor military intervention in Cuba. In Spanish.

G106   Whedon, Peggy. *Always on Sunday: 1,000 Sundays with "Issues and Answers."* New York: Norton, 1980. xvi + 272p.
On 26 Aug. 1962 she was interviewed on ABC's *Issues and Answers* by the author. Although ill, she was forceful in her defense of pending legislation which would give women job equality and of urging industry to remain competitive with other nations (pp. 155-58).

UNDATED

G107 "Will Your Child Live a Successful Life?" *Family Circle* 64 (Jan. 1964): 25-36.
Based on interviews with ER conducted by the staff of *Wisdom.*

H

Eleanor Roosevelt in Recordings, Films, and Computer Software

RECORDINGS AND FILMS OF RADIO AND TELEVISION APPEARANCES

Recordings

H1   *A Conversation with Eleanor Roosevelt*. Audiocassette. Center for Cassette Studies, 197-.
   William Atwood interviews ER. A recording of 8 Mar. 1959 NBC television program.

H2   *Day of Infamy: Pearl Harbor, Dec. 7, 1941*. Phonodisc. Kalmar K444-1, 1978; Audiocassette. Kalmar, 1987.
   Includes ER's radio program for 7 Dec.

H3   *Eleanor Roosevelt: 1945 Radio Program, 5/8/45 VE Day Speech*. Audiocassette. Audio Archives, 197-.

H4   Franklin D. Roosevelt Library.
   The library holds many recordings of her radio series. Finding aids which list the content of individual programs are available at the library.

H5   *Hello World!* Phonodisc. William Mayer, composer. Words by Susan Otto. RCA Victor, 1960?
   ER did the narration when it was performed on the CBS television program *Let's Take a Trip*, 11 Nov. 1956.

H6   Library of Congress. Motion Picture, Broadcasting, and Recorded Sound Division.
   The library holds numerous recordings of ER's radio program *Current Events* for the Pan-American Coffee Bureau and of her 1944-53 appearances on Mary Margaret McBride's radio programs and on numerous other programs. Recordings are listed in James R. Smart, *Radio Broadcasts in the Library of Congress, 1924-1941* (Washington: Library of Congress, 1982) or in the library's Recorded Sound Catalog Supplement card file.

H7 *Life in the White House*. Audiocassette. Center for Cassette Studies, n.d. 30 min.
Radio broadcast of 2 May 1940 in which ER describes life in the White House.

H8 *Meet the Press*.
Recordings of her appearances of 8 Apr. 1949, 11 Apr. 1954, 16 Sept. 1956, 20 Oct. 1957, and 26 Oct. 1958 are available at the Library of Congress. Those for 11 Apr. 1954 and 16 Sept. 1956 are also available at FDRL.

H9 *My Husband and I: Eleanor Roosevelt Recalls Her Years with F.D.R.* Phonodisc. Columbia, 1965.
Excerpts her interview in *F.D.R.*, the ABC-TV series. For a discussion of the interview and for excerpts, see Helen Roach, *Spoken Records.* 3rd ed., pp. 32-33 (Metuchen: Scarecrow, 1970).

H10 *A Quarter-Century of Meet the Press on NBC-TV*. Phonodisc. NBC, 1973? 46 min.
Includes an appearance by ER.

H11 Roosevelt, Eleanor. *Speeches*. Audiocassette. National Archives and Records Service, 1981? 89 min.
Radio addresses and panel discussions from the period 1939-44.

H12 *This I Believe*. Phonodisc. Columbia SL 192, 1951-1953; Help, 1951-1953.
In 65 broadcasts Edward R. Murrow presents famous guests who discuss their philosophies of life. ER is included.

Films

H13 *Eleanor Roosevelt*. Motion Picture. Wisdom Series, 2. Encyclopaedia Britannica Films, 1960. 30 min. b & w.
ER discusses citizenship, politics, and FDR with William Atwood. Broadcast on NBC-TV 8 Mar. 1959. See the 18 Mar. 1959 sect. in *Variety Television Reviews, 1957-1959* (New York: Garland, 1989) for a review which describes her as being honest and candid in her responses.

H14 *Eleanor Roosevelt*. Motion Picture. WQED-TV (Pittsburgh), 195-. 30 min. b & w.
ER discusses her life in a four-part interview broadcast as part of the series *Heritage*. Available at FDRL and the Library of Congress.

H15 *Eleanor Roosevelt's World: Excerpts from Eleanor Roosevelt's Prospects of Mankind Television Series*. Videocassette. 90 min. b & w.
Available at Brandeis Univ.

H16 *Face the Nation*. Motion Picture. CBS News, 1956. b & w.
ER and Margaret Chase Smith are interviewed on 4 Nov. 1956. Available at FDRL.

H17 *F.D.R.* Videocassette. ABC, 1965.
Television series including interview with ER. Broadcast Jan.-Sept. 1965. For a discussion of her involvement, see Tim Brooks and Earle Marsh, *The Complete Directory to Prime Time Network TV, 1946-Present*, p. 188 (New York: Ballantine, 1979).

H18 *Meet the Press.* Motion picture. NBC. 30 min. b & w.
Films of ER's appearances on 16 Sept. 1956, 20 Oct. 1957, and 26 Oct. 1958 are available at the Library of Congress.

H19 *The Mike Wallace Interview.* Motion Picture. 1957. b & w.
Wallace questions ER about politics and current events. Broadcast 23 Nov. 1957. For a review, see the 27 Nov. 1957 sect. in *Variety Television Reviews, 1957-1959* (New York: Garland, 1989).

H20 Museum of Television and Radio (formerly Museum of Broadcasting).
A small number of films of ER's television series are listed in *Subject Guide to the Radio and Television Collection of the Museum of Broadcasting.* 2nd ed. (New York: The Museum, 1979).

H21 *Our Foreign Policy Objectives.* Motion Picture. KETC-TV (St. Louis), 1959. 30 min. b & w.
ER and Harold Stassen discuss foreign policy. Broadcast in 1959 as part of the series *The Search for America.* Available at the Library of Congress.

H22 *Prospects of Mankind.* Motion Picture. WGBH-TV (Boston), 1959-1962.
In her television series ER discussed international issues with guests. Available at FDRL. For a review, see 28 Sept. 1960 sect. in *Variety Television Reviews, 1960-1962* (New York: Garland, 1989).

H23 *Reading Out Loud.* Motion Picture. Westinghouse Broadcasting-American Library Assoc., 1960. 30 min. b & w.
ER reads a Rudyard Kipling story to her grandchildren. Broadcast in 1960. Available at FDRL and the Library of Congress.

H24 *Relations with Our Western Allies.* Motion Picture. KETC-TV (St. Louis), 1959. 30 min. b & w.
ER and Walt and Elspeth Rostow in discussion. Broadcast in 1959 as part of the series *The Search for America.* Available at the Library of Congress.

H25 *Youth Wants to Know.* Motion Picture. NBC and National Public Relations Dept. of the American Legion. 30 min. b & w.
This series of discussions between high school students and prominent figures was broadcast on NBC beginning in 1951. Date of ER's appearance unknown. Available at the Library of Congress.

RECORDINGS AND FILMS FEATURING ELEANOR ROOSEVELT

Recordings

H26 *...But the Women Rose....* Vol. 2. Phonodisc. Folkways FD 5536, 1971. 80 min.
ER and others speak. Narrated by Phyllis Dolgin, et. al.

H27 *Churchill in His Own Voice and the Voices of His Contemporaries.* Phonodisc.
Caedmon TC 2018, 1965. 126 min.
ER is among those included.

H28 *Eleanor Roosevelt in Conversation with Arnold Michaelis.* Phonodisc. MGM
E3648 RP, 1958; Record Communications RCT-102, 1958; Xerox XRP1001c, 1972;
Audiocassette. Xerox, 197-.
Notes on container by Adlai Stevenson.

H29 *Eleanor Roosevelt in Conversation with Ben Grauer.* Phonodisc. Modern Voices
Series. Prod. Ben Grauer. Riverside RLP 7012, 1957. 60 min.
She discusses a variety of subjects on 2 June 1957.

H30 *Eleanor Roosevelt: Private Life--Public Service.* Audiocassette. Time Educational
Program, 1985. 30 min.
The conversation with Arnold Michaelis.

H31 *Eleanor Roosevelt Reads.* Phonodisc. Spoken Word SW-114, 196-.
She reads portions of Charles Dickens' *A Christmas Carol.*

H32 *F.D.R. Speaks: Authorized Edition of Speeches Delivered by Franklin Delano
Roosevelt.* Phonodisc. Washington Records-Crown, 1960.
Introduction by ER.

H33 Franklin D. Roosevelt Library.
The library has extensive holdings of recordings which feature ER. Available is
an annotated chronological finding aid *Eleanor Roosevelt: Recorded Speeches and
Interviews, 1933-1962.*

H34 *Human Rights.* Phonodisc. Prod. Howard Langer. Folkways FH 5524, 1958.
Includes Harold Langer's interview with ER on the drafting of the Universal
Declaration of Human Rights. Printed text of interview included. For a discussion,
see Helen Roach, *Spoken Records.* 3rd ed., p. 33 (Metuchen: Scarecrow, 1970).

H35 *Israel Speaks: Selections from the Speeches of Abba Eban.* Phonodisc. United
Artists UAL 9002, 1959.
ER reads narration written by Millard Lampell.

H36 Library of Congress. Motion Picture, Broadcasting, and Recorded Sound
Division.
Recordings of various speeches and events featuring ER during the period
1933-1941 are held at the Library of Congress. Entries are listed in James R. Smart,
Radio Broadcasts in the Library of Congress, 1924-1941 (Washington: Library of
Congress, 1982) or in the library's Recorded Sound Catalog Supplement card file.

H37 *The Life and Times of Eleanor Roosevelt*. Phonodisc. Personality Series. Audio Fidelity AFLP-704, 1966.
  ER speaks.

H38 *Major Issues Facing the United Nations Sixteenth General Assembly*. Audiotape. Prod. American Assoc. for the United Nations. Audio Techniques, 1961. 14 min.
  An interview with ER and Clark Eichelberger.

H39 *The Man from Oliver Street. Royal Visitors*. Audiocassette. Voices of Yesterday, 75,77. Mich. State Univ. 001400, 197-. 14 min.
  Includes ER on the visit of the British royal family.

H40 *Mrs. Roosevelt's Guided Tour of the Roosevelt Home*. Audiocassette. Hyde Park Historical Assoc.-Acoustiguide. 20 min.
  Available at FDRL.

H41 *My Life with FDR: Eleanor Roosevelt Judges FDR's Years in the White House*. Audiocassette. Forum Associates, 195-.; Forum Associates, 1970. 29 min.

H42 *Peter and the Wolf*. Phonodisc. Boston Symphony Orchestra. Sergey Prokofiev, composer. Serge Koussevitzky, conductor. RCA Victor Red Seal, 195-.
  ER narrates.

H43 *Peter and the Wolf*. Phonodisc. Dutchess County Philharmonic Orchestra. Sergey Prokofiev, composer. Ole Windingstad, conductor. Dutchess County Philharmonic Society, 1957.
  Available at FDRL.

H44 *[United Nations. Part 2: History of the First Five Years, 1945-1950]*. Audiotape. Tribune Records, 1946. 55 min.
  ER and others.

H45 *War and Peace*. Audiocassette. Creative Learning Center, 197-.
  Includes a wartime speech by ER.

Films

H46 Franklin D. Roosevelt Library
  Motion picture and video holdings which feature ER are accessible through the finding aid *Non-Newsreel Film of Mrs. Roosevelt's Activities* and through sections in finding aids to videorecordings which feature FDR. Numerous entries lack dates and other details.

H47 *Great Speeches*. Vol. 6. Videocassette. Alliance Video, 1991. 120 min. col. and b & w.
  Includes a speech by ER before the UN.

H48 *Hobby-Lobby*. Motion Picture. Fox-Movietone, 1940; Columbia, 1940.
  According to Ruby Black in *Eleanor Roosevelt* (p. 117) ER appeared in three movie shorts beginning 3 May 1940. James Kearney in *Anna Eleanor Roosevelt: The*

Evolution of a Reformer (p. 227) states that she appeared in support of David Elman's radio program *Hobby-Lobby*.

H49 *Mrs. Roosevelt: Her Life in Pictures*. Motion Picture. Editorial Films, 195-. col.
   Using photographs from FDRL, ER tells her life story. Produced for *McCall's*. Available at FDRL. Based on the film is Richard Harrity and Ralph G. Martin, *Eleanor Roosevelt: Her Life in Pictures* (New York: Duell, Sloan and Pearce, 1958).

H50 *NBC Chronolog*. Motion Picture. NBC News, 1972. b & w.
   Home movies of the Roosevelts at Hyde Park, Campobello, and elsewhere. Filmed by Nancy Cook. Narrated by Marion Dickerman. Broadcast 28 Jan. 1972. Available at FDRL.

H51 *Pastor Hall*. Motion Picture. Prod. James Roosevelt. Charter-United Artists, 1940. 97 min. b & w.
   Begins with a prologue written by Robert E. Sherwood and delivered by ER. She calls for religious tolerance in this film which was considered to be anti-Nazi propaganda. Text of prologue is in Box 3039, ER Papers, FDRL. For reviews, see 12 June and 31 July sects. in *Variety Film Reviews, 1938-1942* (New York: Garland, 1983).

H52 *Training Women for War Production*. Motion Picture. National Youth Admin., 194-. col.
   Narration by ER.

RECORDINGS AND FILMS ABOUT ELEANOR ROOSEVELT

Recordings

H53 *Anna Eleanor Roosevelt*. Phonodisc. Women of Courage, 2. Dog Day Records 000549, 1985.
   Her achievements. Aimed at elementary school students. Notes and song lyrics on container.

H54 *Eleanor Roosevelt*. Audiocassette. Mark 56 Records Educational Series. Mark 56 Records, 1982.

H55 *Eleanor Roosevelt*. Audiocassette. Great Women of America. Classroom World Productions, 1967.

H56 *Eleanor Roosevelt*. Audiocassette. The Minds Eye. Great American Women. By Susan Shaffer and Erik Bauersfeld. Jabberwocky 005900, 1981. 59 min.
   Dramatization of her political and humanitarian activities.

H57 *Eleanor Roosevelt Oral History Project*. [Hyde Park: The Franklin D. Roosevelt Library], n.d. n.pag.
   Information sheets for oral histories. The library holds tape recordings of interviews and transcriptions in manuscript form. As part of the celebration of her centenary several small oral history collections were produced. See Madlyn DeWitt, *The Centenary of Anna Eleanor Roosevelt, 1884-1984*, p. 26 (N.p.: The Eleanor Roosevelt Centennial Commission, [1991?]).

H58 *Eleanor Roosevelt: Public and Private Personality.* Audiocassette. Conversations from Wingspread R-156. Johnson Foundation, 1974. 28 min.
  Dan Price and Estelle Linzer discuss ER.

H59 *Eleanor Roosevelt Remembered.* Audiocassette. National Public Radio AT-84-10-11, 1984. 30 min.
  A centennial remembrance. Includes recordings of ER speaking.

H60 *Eulogy of Mrs. Franklin D. Roosevelt.* Phonodisc. United Nations, UNSP62B, 1962?
  Narrated by Adlai Stevenson.

H61 *Joseph Lash Discusses Eleanor and Franklin, His Book about the Roosevelts' Complex Relationship.* Audiocassette. Center for Cassette Studies 27925, 197-. 27 min.

H62 *The Roosevelts of Hyde Park.* Audiocassette. Literary Guild's First Edition Series. Jeffrey Norton 40019, 1975. 55 min.
  A 1973 discussion about ER and FDR with Heywood Hale Broun, Elliott Roosevelt, and James Brough.

H63 *Val-Kill: A Small Place.* Audiotape with slides. 20 min.
  Available through the Eleanor Roosevelt Center at Val-Kill.

Films

H64 *American First Ladies.* Motion Picture. By Edward Walsh and Craig Fisher. Prod. Craig Fisher. NBC News-McGraw-Hill, 1967. 24 min. col.
  The lives of the first ladies. Narrated by Bill Ryan. Available at the Library of Congress.

H65 *Backstairs at the White House.* Videocassette. NBC, 1979. Prod. Fred Friendly. col.
  Based on novel of the same title by Gwen Bagni and Paul Dubov. Television broadcast of Jan.-Feb. 1979.

H66 *CBS News Special Report: First Lady, Mrs. Eleanor Roosevelt.* Motion Picture. CBS, 1962. 30 min. b & w.
  Broadcast 7 Nov. 1962 on the occasion of her death. Available at the Museum of Television and Radio, New York.

H67 *Eleanor and Franklin.* Motion Picture. Talent Associates, 1976-1977; Videocassette. Time Life Multimedia, 1976; Motion Picture. Lucerne, 1976. ca. 400 min. col.
  The adaptation of Lash's *Eleanor and Franklin* with Jane Alexander as ER and Edward Herrmann as FDR. Pt. 1 *(Early Years)* and pt. 2 *(Rise to Leadership)* broadcast by ABC 11-12 Jan. 1976. Pt. 3 *(Eleanor and Franklin: The White House Years)* broadcast 13 Mar. 1977.
  For reviews, see the 14 Jan. 1976 and 16 Mar. 1977 sects. in *Variety Television Reviews, 1974-1977* (New York: Garland, 1989).

H68   *Eleanor: First Lady of the World*. Videocassette. CBS, 1982. 120 min. col.;
Columbia TriStar Home Video, 1992. 96 min. col.
   Jean Stapleton portrays ER as UN delegate. Based on story by Rhoda Lerman.
Broadcast 12 May 1982. For reviews, see Arthur Unger, "Jean Stapleton Superb as
Eleanor Roosevelt." *Christian Science Monitor,* Eastern ed.: 23; John J. O'Connor,
"TV: Movie on Eleanor Roosevelt." *New York Times* 12 May 1982, sect. C: 32; and
the 19 May 1982 sect. in *Variety Television Reviews, 1978-1982* (New York: Garland,
1989).

H69   *Eleanor: In Her Own Words*. Videocassette. Written by Russell Vandenbroucke.
Prod. Judith Rutherford James. KCET-TV (Los Angeles) and Tapes Media Enter-
prises, 1987. 60 min.
   Lee Remick as ER. For review by Elisabeth I. Perry, see *Journal of American
History* 74 (Dec. 1987): 1113-14. A description is in *Arts on Television, 1976-1990:
Fifteen Years of Cultural Programming Supported by the National Endowment for the
Arts*, p. 85 (Washington: GPO, 1991).

H70   *Eleanor Roosevelt*. Motion Picture. Biography Series. Prod. David L. Wolper.
Official Films, 1963; Sterling Educational Films, 1963; Videocassette. Coronet, 1990?
30 min. b & w.
   ER from a shy young girl to world figure. Broadcast in 1962 as part of program
Biography. Available at the Library of Congress. Also issued in Spanish.

H71   [*Eleanor Roosevelt*]. Videocassette. Truly American, 22. Prod. Ohio Dept. of
Educ. Great Plains National Instructional Television Library, 1978. 20 min. col.
   Produced as school teaching aid.

H72   *Eleanor Roosevelt: An Uncommon Woman*. Videocassette. Legends. Prod. Alan
P. Sloan. Pepperwood, 1980. 30 min. b & w and color.

H73   *Eleanor Roosevelt: First Lady of Dutchess County*. Videocassette. 40 min.
   Available through the Eleanor Roosevelt Center at Val-Kill.

H74   *Eleanor Roosevelt: First Lady of the World*. Filmstrip. Society for Visual
Education, 1974. 58 fr. col.

H75   *Eleanor Roosevelt: First Lady of the World*. Videocassette. Prod. Karine
Erlebach. National Audiovisual Center, 1985. 22 min. col.
   ER as a world figure and her life at Val-Kill. Produced for the National Park
Service, U.S. Dept. of the Interior.

H76   *Eleanor Roosevelt: Humanitarian*. Filmstrip with Audiocassette. Popular
Science Audio-Visuals, 1970. 42 fr. col.
   ER as social reformer and humanitarian. Accompanied by teacher's guide.

H77   *The Eleanor Roosevelt Story*. Motion Picture. By Archibald MacLeish.
Macmillan Films, 1965; Fleetwood, 1965; Videocassette. United Home Video, 1987.
90 min. b & w.
   The award-winning documentary on her life. Narrated by Eric Sevareid, Mrs.
Francis Cole, and MacLeish. For reviews, see 20 Oct. 1965 sect. in *Variety Film
Reviews, 1964-1967* (New York: Garland, 1983); Arthur Knight, "Let Us Now Praise

Famous Men." *Saturday Review* 43 (4 Dec. 1965): 74; and Bosley Crowther, "Screen: 'The Eleanor Roosevelt Story.'" *New York Times* 9 Nov. 1965: 50.

An interview with Sidney Glazier about the making of the film is A.H. Weiler, "Story of Mrs. Roosevelt's Life to Be Told in Full-Length Film." *New York Times* 23 June 1964: 25.

H78 *Eleanor Roosevelt: The UN Years*. Videocassette. Speaking of History. Institute for Research in History, 1984. 28 min. col.

Marietta Tree and Pauline Frederick discuss ER as UN delegate.

H79 *The Eleanor Roosevelt We Remember*. Motion Picture. Jewish Theological Seminary of America-NBC, 1964. 30 min. b & w.

Based on the book of the same title by Helen Gahagan Douglas.

H80 *Eva Peron, Amelia Earhart, Eleanor Roosevelt*. Videocassette. Video Library of Biography. Prod. David Wolper. Easton Pr. Video, 1989. 60 min. b & w. and col.

Narrated by Mike Wallace.

H81 *Famous Americans, Group 2*. Filmstrip. Clearvue, 1967. 4 filmstrips. col.

ER and others.

H82 *First Ladies*. Videocassette. Prod. Louis Barbash. Public Media Video FIR 05, 1989; LumiVision LVD9006, 1989; MPI Home Video MP 1867, 1989; Eastman Kodak KV-1106V, 1989; Home Vision, 1991. 60 min. col.

The lives of the first ladies. Features gowns from the collection at the Smithsonian Institution. Narrated by Nancy Dickerson. Also issued with *Presidents* on laserdisc (MPI, 199-).

H83 *First Lady: A Lady of Firsts*. Videocassette. Prod. Ricki Green. WETA-TV (Washington), 1984? 60 min.

Jean Stapleton provides narration for photographs, newsreels, and home movies.

H84 *The First Lady of the World*. Motion Picture. Prod. Harry Rasky. Hearst Metrotone News-B.C.G. Films, 1962. 53 min. b & w.

Her life and work. Broadcast as part of program *Perspective on Greatness*. Narrated by Celeste Holm. Available at the Library of Congress.

H85 *First Lady of the World: Eleanor Roosevelt*. Motion Picture. ACI Films, AIMS Media, 1974; Videocassette. ACI Films, AIMS Media, 1974 and 1985. 25 min.

H86 *The Legacy of Eleanor Roosevelt*. Videocassette. Democratic National Committee, 1984. 10 min.

Narrated by Barbara Jordan.

H87 *News Parade of the Year 1962*. Motion Picture. Castle Films, 1962. 9 min. b & w.

Includes a remembrance of ER.

H88   *Remembering Eleanor Roosevelt: The Politics of Conscience*. Videocassette. ARCO Forum of Public Affairs, Mar. 3. John F. Kennedy School of Government, Harvard Univ., 1984. 240 min. col.

H89   *Soul of Iron*. Motion Picture. By Rhoda Lerman. Tandem, 197-. 15 min.
  A monologue with Jean Stapleton as ER.

H90   *Sunrise at Campobello*. Motion Picture. Prod. Dore Schary. Warner, 1960; Videocassette. Warner Home Video, 1985. 144 min. col.
  The movie version of Schary's play. Stars Greer Garson as ER and Ralph Bellamy as FDR. For review, see 21 Sept. 1960 sect. in *Variety Film Reviews, 1959-1963* (New York: Garland, 1983).

H91   *The World of Eleanor Roosevelt*. Motion Picture. 1964. 60 min.
  Stars of stage and screen pay tribute. Adlai Stevenson gives a eulogy. Broadcast 3 May 1964. For a review, see the 6 May 1964 sect. in *Variety Television Reviews, 1963-1965* (New York: Garland, 1989).

COMPUTER SOFTWARE

H92   Maas, David. *Interviews with History*. Computer Diskette. Educational Publishing Concepts, 1987. 7 computer disks + loose-leaf binder. sd., col.
  Events and personalities in American history. ER is among those featured.

H93   Maas, David, and Jean Dietsch. *Modern America*. Computer Diskette. Historical Perspectives. Educational Publishing Concepts, 1987. 2 computer disks + guide. sd., col.
  Program enables students to interview ER and Martin Luther King, Jr.

I

Writings about Eleanor Roosevelt for Younger Readers

BOOKS

I1   Adler, David A. *A Picture Book of Eleanor Roosevelt*. New York: Holiday House, 1991. [30]p.
   Her life and work for the very young reader with illustrations by Robert Casilla.

I2   Blassingame, Wyatt. *Eleanor Roosevelt*. A See and Read Beginning to Read Biography. New York: Putnam's, 1967. 64p.
   The life and career of ER for the very young reader.

I3   Davidson, Margaret. *The Story of Eleanor Roosevelt*. New York: Scholastic, 1968. 138p.; New York: Four Winds, 1969. 146p. Bibliography.
   A biography emphasizing ER's public life.

I4   Eaton, Jeanette. *The Story of Eleanor Roosevelt*. New York: Morrow, 1956. 251p. Bibliography.
   Her life and work up to 1954. For junior and senior high school students.

I5   *The Eleanor Roosevelt Centennial, 1884-1984: A Curriculum Handbook*. Helena: Office of Public Instruction, n.d. 32p. Bibliography.
   Contains a chronology of her life, biographical sketch, discussion of her activities in Montana, and classroom exercises.

I6   *Eleanor Roosevelt Centennial, 1884-1984: Eleanor Roosevelt Curriculum Kit K-6*. Santa Rosa: National Women's History Project, 1983. 16p. + Poster. Bibliography.
   Includes "Eleanor Roosevelt Biography" by Nancy Aldinger Naki (pp. 2-7) followed by questions and activities about ER's life and work.

I7   Faber, Doris. *Eleanor Roosevelt: First Lady of the World*. Women of Our Time. New York: Viking Kestrel, 1985; New York: Puffin, 1986. 57p.
   ER's life and career with emphasis on the pre-White House years.

I8   Freedman, Russell. *Eleanor Roosevelt: A Life of Discovery*. New York: Clarion, 1993. 198p. Index. Bibliography.
   Her life and career. Includes "Eleanor Roosevelt Photo Album" (pp. 169-83).

I9 Gilbert, Miriam. *Shy Girl: The Story of Eleanor Roosevelt, First Lady of the World*. Doubleday Signal Books. Garden City: Doubleday, 1965. 144p.
  Childhood of ER.

I10 Goodsell, Jane. *Eleanor Roosevelt*. A Crowell Biography. New York: Crowell, 1970. 38p.
  A biography for elementary school readers.

I11 Graves, Charles P. *Eleanor Roosevelt: First Lady of the World*. A Discovery Book. Champaign: Garrard, 1966; New York: Dell, 1968; New York: Dell, 1975. 80p.
  ER overcame shyness to become "first lady of the world." For elementary school readers. Also issued in *Women with a Cause*, pp. 134-65 (Champaign: Garrard, 1975).

I12 Hickok, Lorena A. *The Story of Eleanor Roosevelt*. Signature Books. New York: Grosset & Dunlap, 1959, 180p.
  ER's life and career up through the adoption of the Universal Declaration of Human Rights. Emphasis is on the pre-White House years.

I13 Jacobs, William Jay. *Eleanor Roosevelt: A Life of Happiness and Tears*. New York: Coward-McCann, 1983. 108p. Index. Bibliography.
  Her life and career.

I14 Johnson, Ann Donegan. *The Value of Caring: The Story of Eleanor Roosevelt*. ValuTales. La Jolla: Value Communications, 1977. 63p.
  An invisible friend 'Granny' is always there in this story of ER's life and work for the very young reader. Accompanied by statement of historical facts.

I15 Knapp, Sally. *Eleanor Roosevelt: A Biography*. New York: Crowell, 1949. 185p. Index.
  Biography derived from newspaper articles, "My Day," *This Is My Story* and Ruby Black's *Eleanor Roosevelt*. ER reviewed the manuscript.

I16 Lazo, Caroline. *Eleanor Roosevelt*. Peacemakers. New York: Dillon, 1993. 64p. Bibiliography.
  Her life and career with emphasis on the UN years.

I17 Lee, Myrra. *Great American Lives: Eleanor Roosevelt*. Lakeside: DBA Interact, 1986. 41p.
  A "this is your life" format. Includes guide for teacher and script for students to play roles of ER, FDR, and others.

I18 McAuley, Karen. *Eleanor Roosevelt*. World Leaders Past & Present. New York: Chelsea House, 1987. 116p. Index. Bibliography.
  Candid account of the life and career of ER. For the mature young reader.

I19 McKown, Robin. *Eleanor Roosevelt's World*. New York: Crosset & Dunlap, 1964. 93p.
  ER's life plus accounts of contemporary events and personalities are presented in words and photographs.

I20   Richards, Kenneth C. *Eleanor Roosevelt*. People of Destiny: A Humanities Series, 12. Chicago: Childrens, 1968. 95p. Index. Bibliography.
Her life and work. Quotes extensively from her published writings.

I21   Sabin, Francene. *Young Eleanor Roosevelt*. Mahwah: Troll, 1990. 48p.
Her childhood with a brief summary of her adult life.

I22   Tierney, Tom. *Franklin D. Roosevelt and His Family: Paper Dolls in Full Color*. New York: Dover, 1990. 16 plates + 3 p.
Formal and casual attire from the White House years. Includes a description of each plate and brief biographical sketches of ER and FDR.

I23   Toor, Rachel. *Eleanor Roosevelt*. American Women of Achievement. New York: Chelsea House, 1989. 111p. Further Reading.
Her life, philosophy, and accomplishments.

I24   Weidt, Maryann N. *Stateswoman to the World: A Story about Eleanor Roosevelt*. A Carolrhoda Creative Minds Book. Minneapolis: Carolrhoda, 1991. 64p. Bibliography.
A story for the younger reader which discusses her father's alcoholism and FDR's affair with Lucy Mercer.

I25   Weil, Ann. *Eleanor Roosevelt: Courageous Girl*. Childhoods of Famous Americans. Indianapolis: Bobbs-Merrill, 1965; New York: Aladdin, 1989. 200p.
An account of ER's childhood and life up to her marriage.

I26   Whitney, Sharon. *Eleanor Roosevelt*. An Impact Biography. New York: Watts, 1982. Index. For Further Reading.
ER's life and work were driven by a sense of duty and the compassion which she felt for her fellow human beings. For the mature young reader.

I27   ---. *Totty: Young Eleanor Roosevelt*. New Orleans: Anchorage, 1992. vi +65p.
A play about ER, Allenswood classmates, and Marie Souvestre.

I28   Winner, David. *Eleanor Roosevelt: Defender of Human Rights and Democracy*. People Who Have Helped the World. Milwaukee: Gareth Stevens, 1991. 68p. Index.
Her life and accomplishments and what she did to help others.

SECTIONS OF BOOKS AND PERIODICAL ARTICLES

I29   Anthony, Carl Sferrazza. "Eleanor Roosevelt." *America's Most Influential First Ladies*. By Carl Sferrazza Anthony. Minneapolis: Oliver, 1992. 67-83.
Her life before the White House years and the breadth of her activities as First Lady.

I30   Anticaglia, Elizabeth. "Eleanor Roosevelt." *12 American Women*. By Elizabeth Anticaglia. Chicago: Nelson-Hall, 1975. 184-207. Bibliography.
Biographical profile.

I31   Baker, Gretta. "Here's My Favorite." *Scholastic: The American High School Weekly* 40 (4-9 May 1942): 6.

In a interview conducted in a New York taxi ER discusses her favorite books, poems, art, music, and radio programs.   Confirms her confidence in America's youth.

I32   Bassett, Margaret. "Anna Eleanor Roosevelt Roosevelt." *Profiles & Portraits of American Presidents & Their Wives*. By Margaret Bassett. Freeport: Wheelwright, 1969. 340-53. Bibliography.
Interpretation of the life and career of ER.

I33   Blumberg, Rhoda. "Anna Eleanor Roosevelt Roosevelt." *First Ladies*. Updated ed. A First Book. By Rhoda Blumberg. New York: Watts, 1981. 45-46.
ER as First Lady.

I34   Bolton, Sarah K. "Eleanor Roosevelt, Humanitarian." *Lives of Girls Who Became Famous*. Rev. ed. By Sarah K. Bolton. New York: Crowell, 1949. 295-307.
Biographical profile.

I35   Brin, Ruth F. "First Lady and Diplomat: Eleanor Roosevelt." *Contributions of Women: Social Reform*. By Ruth F. Brin. Minneapolis: Dillon, 1977. 124-50. Bibliography.
Biographical profile.

I36   Calkins, Virginia. "Friend of Children." *Cobblestone* 7 (Nov. 1986): 12-13.
All of her life ER helped less fortunate children.

I37   Carratello, John, and Patty Carratello. "Eleanor Roosevelt." *Great Americans*. By John Carratello and Patty Carratello. Huntington Beach: Teacher Created Materials, 1991. 98-104.
A biographical sketch and classroom activities.

I38   Cavanah, Frances. *They Lived in the White House*. Philadelphia: Macrae Smith, 1959. 191p.
ER as a grandmother (pp. 154-61).

I39   Chaffin, Lillie, and Miriam Butwin. *America's First Ladies* [Vol. 2]. A Pull Ahead Book. Minneapolis: Lerner, 1969. 83-88.
Brief account of the life of ER.

I40   "The Columnists Speak Their Minds." *Senior Scholastic* 51 (3 Nov. 1947): 18-20.
As one of the three columnists covered by the article, ER is that one who pleads causes.   Provides an overview of her current activities and excerpts a "My Day" column in which she argues for the value of feeding the world's hungry.

I41   Commager, Henry Steele. *Crusaders for Freedom*. Garden City: Doubleday, 1962. 240p. Index.
Throughout her life ER considered it her duty to obtain and protect basic freedoms for all, including children.   Her greatest contribution was the drafting of the Universal Declaration of Human Rights.   For the advanced reader (pp. 229-32).

I42   Conta, Marcia Maher. "Eleanor Roosevelt." *Women for Human Rights*. By Marcia Maher Conta. Milwaukee: Raintree, 1979. 34-41.
   ER was a different kind of First Lady.

I43   "Cornering the Columnists." *Scholastic: The American High School Weekly* 32 (26 Mar. 1938): 20E.
   Describes "My Day" as a personal diary and ER as a professional when it comes to preparing her column.

I44   Curtin, Andrew. "Eleanor Roosevelt." *Gallery of Great Americans*. By Andrew Curtin. New York: Watts, 1965. 79.
   Biographical sketch for the young reader.

I45   Daugherty, Sonia. "Eleanor Roosevelt." *Ten Brave Women*. By Sonia Daugherty. Philadelphia: Lippincott, 1953. 136-47.
   ER's life from 1945 through 1953.

I46   "Eleanor Roosevelt." *Women of the Month Display Kits*. Set I. Santa Rosa: National Women's History Project, 198-. 24" x 10" poster.
   Poster and biographical sketch for the classroom.   One of 23 posters.

I47   "Eleanor Roosevelt: First Lady of the World." *Cobblestone* 7 (Nov. 1986).
   The entire issue is devoted to her.   In addition to articles the following are included: letters from readers in response to May 1986 challenge to guess her identity (pp. 2-3); introduction entitled "Eleanor Roosevelt: First Lady of the World" (pp. 4-5); "Eleanor Roosevelt Crossword" (p. 34); "Val-Kill Diorama" by Deborah Lerme Goodman (pp. 39-41); "Ebenezer's Teasers" about ER (p. 42); "Roosevelt Number Game" by Jennifer Scott (p. 43); books and films about ER, places to visit and a list of related articles in earlier issues (pp. 44-46).

I48   Ennis, John, and Jean Ennis. "Mrs. Roosevelt Was Here." *Cobblestone* 7 (Nov. 1986): 24-25.
   In 1943 ER visited a wounded John Ennis in New Zealand.   At first there was resistance to her wartime visits, but that soon changed.

I49   Faber, Doris, and Harold Faber. "Eleanor Roosevelt." *Great Lives: American Government*. By Doris Faber and Harold Faber. New York: Scribner's, 1988. 211-18.
   Her life.

I50   "First Lady: The Wife of the President of the United States." *Calling All Girls* 1 (Dec. 1941): 1-10.
   The life of ER and her activities as First Lady presented in comic strip fashion.

I51   Forsee, Aylesa. "Citizen of the World: Eleanor Roosevelt." *American Women Who Scored Firsts*. By Aylesa Forsee. Philadelphia: Macrae Smith, 1958. 159-81.
   One of 10 biographical sketches of American women.

I52   Franz, Leslie. *America's First Ladies Coloring Book*. New York: Dover, 1991. 42p.
   ER is included (p. 33).

I53   Freedman, Russell. *Franklin Delano Roosevelt*. New York: Clarion, 1990. 200p. Index.
    Her private life (pp. 26-28, 47, 53, 56-57), emergence as a public figure (pp. 71-73), and as First Lady (pp. 113-18). For the advanced reader.

I54   Gilfond, Henry. "Eleanor Roosevelt: A Woman for All Seasons." *Heroines of America*. By Henry Gilfond. New York: Fleet, 1970. 70-77. Index.
    ER worked for the underprivileged everywhere. An overview of her life.

I55   Graves, Charles P. "Eleanor Roosevelt: First Lady of the World." *Women with a Cause*. Target Series. Ed. Bennett Wayne. Champaign: Garrard, 1975. 134-65. Index.
    ER overcame shyness and became "first lady of the world." Also issued as a separate publication *Eleanor Roosevelt: First Lady of the World* (Champaign: Garrard, 1966).

I56   Hickok, Lorena A. *The Road to the White House: F.D.R., the Pre-presidential Years*. Philadelphia: Chilton. 1962. xiii + 145p. Index.
    The emergence of ER and the role which she played in FDR's life before the White House years.

I57   ---. *The Story of Franklin D. Roosevelt*. New York: Grosset & Dunlap, 1956. xii + 177p.
    Includes coverage of ER as young bride and mother and as wife of the President (pp. 81-174 passim).

I58   Hiebert, Roselyn, and Ray Eldon Hiebert. *Franklin Delano Roosevelt: President for the People*. Immortals of History. New York: Watts, 1968. 246p. Index. Further Reading.
    ER's early married life (pp. 49-54, 57-63) and helping a crippled FDR return to public life (pp. 103-12).

I59   Kamenetsky, Karen J. "A Visit to Hyde Park." *Cobblestone* 7 (Nov. 1986): 35-38.
    The Roosevelt home, the library and museum, and Val-Kill.

I60   Kelen, Emery. "Anna Eleanor Roosevelt." *Fifty Voices of the Twentieth Century*. By Emery Kelen. New York: Lothrop, Lee & Shepard, 1970. 132-34.
    A brief biographical sketch followed by a few unidentified statements by her.

I61   Kenworthy, Leonard. *Twelve Citizens of the World: A Book of Biographies*. Garden City: Doubleday, 1953. 154-75.
    Using ER's visit to India to demonstrate her success in overcoming shyness and in developing into one of the most admired persons in the world, Kenworthy then traces ER's life and career up to the 1952 trip.

I62   Lawson, Don. "F.D.R.'s Wife and Sons in Politics." *Famous American Political Families*. By Don Lawson. New York: Abelard-Schuman, 1965. 116-27. Index. Bibliography.
    Overview of the life ER (pp. 116-20).

163   Lieser, Julia F. "Eleanor Roosevelt." *Outstanding American Women*. By Julia F. Lieser. Indianapolis: Youth Publications/The Saturday Evening Post, 1977. 22-23.
    Louis Howe's influence on ER's development as a public figure. Overview of her public and private life.

164   Marvin, Isabel R. "What I Learned from Eleanor Roosevelt." *Cobblestone* 7 (Nov. 1986): 28-29.
    In 1940 she interviewed ER for a school newspaper, and in the process ER taught her how to be a reporter.

165   McKissack, Patricia, and Frederick McKissack. "Eleanor Roosevelt." *The Civil Rights Movement in America from 1865 to the Present*. By Patricia McKissack and Frederick McKissack. Chicago: Childrens, 1987. 170.
    A "cameo" highlighting her civil rights activities.

166   Melick, Arden Davis. "Anna Eleanor Roosevelt: First Lady of the World." *Wives of the Presidents*. Hammond Profile Series. By Arden Davis Melick. Maplewood: Hammond, 1972. 70-73.
    Biographical sketch. Later eds. issued 1977 and 1985.

167   Merriman, Eve. *The Real Book about Franklin D. Roosevelt*. Garden City: Garden City, 1952. 191p. Index.
    ER as the wife of FDR (pp. 70-71, 84, 87-89, 93, 104, 116, 119) with only a brief reference to her activities as First Lady (p. 148).

168   Meyer, Edith Patterson. "Two Workers for Peace and Progress." *Champions of Four Freedoms*. By Edith Patterson Meyer. Boston: Little, Brown, 1966. 211-33.
    The lives of ER and FDR illustrate their commitment to eliminate fear and want.

169   Parks, Lillian Rogers, and Frances S. Leighton. *It Was Fun Working at the White House*. New York: Fleet, 1969. 208p.
    Abridged ed. for young readers of *My Thirty Years Backstairs at the White House*. "There Can Be Only One Mrs. 'R'" (pp. 102-16) and "Mrs. 'R' in Peace and War" (pp. 117-35) are accounts of ER and FDR.

170   Patton, Sally J. "Eleanor Roosevelt, United States." *Reflections on Women in Monarchies and Democracies*. Rev. ed. By Sally J. Patton. Tucson: Zephyr, 1991. 33-43.
    The life of ER with classroom exercises for children in grades 5-8. Published originally, Sausalito: Patton Pending, 1983.

171   Peare, Catherine Owens. *The FDR Story*. New York: Crowell, 1962. 245p. Index.
    ER's early life (pp. 6-7, 13-14, 33-34, 46-48), engagement and early married life (pp. 51-59, 61), emergence as a public figure (pp. 153-55), and as First Lady (pp. 150-52).

172   Pettit, Jayne D. "First Lady of the World." *Cobblestone* 7 (Nov. 1986): 20-23.
    She tried to make life better for others during both world wars, through New Deal programs, and by correcting social injustices.

I73 Plopper, Julie, and Ellen Tull. *First Ladies of the United States.* Indianapolis: Youth Pub., 1978.
Copy not examined.

I74 Plude, Catherine. "Eleanor Roosevelt and Louis Howe." *Cobblestone* 7 (Nov. 1986): 16-19.
Howe's role in ER's emergence as a public figure.

I75 Rappaport, Doreen. "Having Learned to Stare Down Fear." *American Women: Their Lives in Their Words.* By Doreen Rappaport. New York: Crowell, 1990. 220-21.
Her prior contacts with women leaders were critical to her success in convincing FDR to appoint women to public office and to support issues of importance to women.

I76 "Rating the First Ladies." *Scholastic Update* 115 (13 May 1983): 31.
Features ER and Abigail Adams as the two top-rated first ladies. Includes a brief biographical sketch of ER.

I77 Roberts, Russell. "Life after the White House." *Cobblestone* 7 (Nov. 1986): 30-33.
After FDR's death she devoted herself to work with the UN and to improving civil rights in this country.

I78 "Roosevelt, Eleanor." *Significant American Social Reformers and Humanitarians.* Ed. Gilbert Miekina. Chicago: Childrens, 1975. 62.
A comprehensive sketch for younger readers. Also issued in *Significant American Women*, p. 49 (Chicago: Childrens, 1975).

I79 Ross, George E. "Eleanor Roosevelt." *Know Your Presidents and Their Wives.* By George E. Ross. Chicago: Rand McNally, 1960. 65.
ER as wife, mother, and public figure.

I80 Sandak, Cass R. *The Franklin Roosevelts.* New York: Crestwood House, 1992. 48p. Index. Bibliography.
Contains several sections about ER: "Young Eleanor," "Eleanor and Franklin," "The Family and Politics," "A New Kind of First Lady," and "First Lady of the World."

I81 Smith, Margaret Chase, and H. Paul Jeffers. "Eleanor Roosevelt: Honor to All of Us." *Gallant Women.* By Margaret Chase Smith and H. Paul Jeffers. New York: McGraw-Hill, 1968. 114-23. Index.
Summary of her life and work.

I82 St. George, Judith. *The White House: Cornerstone of a Nation.* New York: Putnam's, 1990. 160p. Index. Bibliography.
Anecdotes about ER as First Lady (pp. 108-11, 114).

I83 Sullivan, Wilson. *Franklin Delano Roosevelt.* New York: American Heritage-Harper & Row, 1970. 153p. Index. Further Reference.
Limited attention to ER's private and public life.

184   Taylor, Ethel R. "When Eleanor Roosevelt Was Your Age." *American Child-hood* 32 (Nov. 1946): 10-11, 63-64.
A story written in the second person about ER's life and activities as a young child.

185   Thayer, Judy. "Women Only in the White House." *Cobblestone* 7 (Nov. 1986): 26-27.
ER's women only press conferences.

186   Thomas, Henry. Franklin Delano Roosevelt. *Lives to Remember.* New York: Putmam's 1962. 191p. Index. Bibliography.
Childhood, courtship, and early married life (pp. 25, 33-36, 38, 48-49, 51). As First Lady (pp. 70, 80, 82, 86, 99, 103, 111-12, 174-76).

187   Traub, Carol G. "The Hardest Volunteer Job." *Cobblestone* 13 (Mar. 1992): 8-12.
ER's interests as First Lady and the extent to which she was symbolic of the modern woman who pursues interests independent of her husband's are described in this broad examination of first ladies (p. 10).

188   *20th Century American Women.* Instructor Curriculum Materials, 470. Dansville: Instructor Pubs., 1977. 10 posters (40 x 30 cm.) + Teacher's Guide.
ER is one of 20 women featured. Includes brief biographical sketch. A later ed. features 14 women including ER (Jackson: Weber Costello, 1985).

189   Wadsworth, Virginia Evarts. "An Extraordinary Beginning." *Cobblestone* 7 (Nov. 1986): 6-11.
ER's early life.

190   Wells, Debby. *Little Me and This Big World.* Ed. and comp. Betty Wells. [New York]: Psychological Library, 1963. 42p.
Letters written by a young girl to world figures and the responses which she received. Letter to ER as a friend of children from one who is concerned about the dangers of life today. ER advised her to lead a good life and trust in God (pp. 28-29).

191   "Who's Who among U.S. Leaders." *Senior Scholastic* 57 (4 Oct. 1950), pt. 2: 23.
Brief biographical sketch.

192   Witty, Paul A. "Eleanor Roosevelt, First Lady of the World." *Highlights* 32 (June/July 1977): 44-45.
Her life.

193   Wolfgarth, Maureen. "Eleanor as Teacher." *Cobblestone* 7 (Nov. 1986): 44-46.
Her association with the Todhunter School.

J

Eleanor Roosevelt in Fiction, Poetry, and Song

FICTION

J1   Bagni, Gwen, and Paul Dubov. *Backstairs at the White House*. New York: Bantam, 1979. 469p.
A novel based on *My Thirty Years Backstairs at the White House* by Lillian Rogers Parks. It is the basis of the Jan.-Feb. 1979 television dramatization of Park's book. ER is portrayed on pp. 314-401 passim. Script version (Hollywood: Ed Friendly Productions, 1979).

J2   Baker, Russell. "Some Tears for Il Duce." *New York Times* 29 Sept. 1979: 19.
The column devoted to a work of fiction about ER is also assumed to be fiction itself. ER is a character in an off-Broadway play, *Benito*. In this musical about Mussolini ER sings "Don't Cry for Franklin's White Collars," a real show-stopper claims Baker.

J3   Bingham, June. *Triangles: A Play about the Roosevelts*. Louisville: Aran Pr., 1989. 55p.
About ER, FDR, Lucy Mercer, Anna Roosevelt, Sara Roosevelt, Alice Roosevelt Longworth, and Louis Howe. Copy not examined. For a review, see Walter Goodman, "The Stage: 'Triangles,' Women in F.D.R.'s Life." *New York Times* 30 Oct. 1986, sect. C: 18.

J4   Bolt, Jonathan. *First Lady*. Lyrics by John Forster and music by Thomas Tierney.
Features ER, FDR, Sara Roosevelt, Alice Roosevelt Longworth, Marie Souvestre, and Louis Howe. Copy not examined. For a review, see Herbert Mitgang, "Theatre: 'First Lady' at Promenade." *New York Times* 28 Oct. 1984: 64.

J5   Chakovsky, Alexander. *Unfinished Portrait*. Moscow: Progress, 1988. 259p.
A fictionalized account of international relations toward the end of World War II which centers around the portrait being painted of FDR on the day he died. Lucy Mercer is a central character. ER, a minor one. Translated from the Russian ed. *Neokonchenyi Portret* (Moscow: Progress, 1988).

J6   Charyn, Jerome. *The Franklin Scare*. New York: Arbor House, 1977. 326p.
FDR gives Oliver Beebe, sailor and sometime barber, a room in the White House. This satirical account of Washington in 1944-45 also has as central characters ER, J. Edgar Hoover, and Fala.

J7   Cook, Fannie. "Zorella's Hat." *New Republic* 103 (23 Dec. 1940): 866-67.
Her husband will not let Zorella kept her new hat after the black sharecropper couple were invited to the White House to see ER. When they discovered that the First Lady was wearing a hat identical to Zorella's, the husband concluded that the hat was too fine for his wife.

J8   Goldsmith, Gloria. *Womanspeak*. Denver: Pioneer Drama Service, 1976. 19p.
ER and other noteworthy women converse with a present day woman in this one act play. ER talks about the problems of youth (pp. 16, 18).

J9   Kaminsky, Stuart M. *The Fala Factor: A Toby Peters Mystery*. New York: St. Martin's, 1984. 174p.
When she thinks that Fala has been stolen and replaced with an imposter, ER hires Toby Peters to find him.

J10   Kessner, Zelda Ellen, and Winnie Newman. *Eleanor: A Musical Biography Based on the Life of Eleanor Roosevelt*. Book and lyrics by Zelda Ellen Kessner and Winnie Newman. Music by Maxine Topper Myers. New York: Open Stage, 1974. 32p. Mimeographed.
Features ER, Marion Dickerman, Nancy Cook, Sara Roosevelt, Alice Roosevelt Longworth, and Marie Souvestre. Available in Subject Files Relating to the Eleanor Roosevelt Centennial Commission, Box 7, New York State Archives.

J11   Lerman, Rhoda. *Eleanor: A Novel*. New York: Holt, Rinehart, and Winston, 1979. 297p.
ER during the period 1918-1921. Excerpts issued as "In Which I Leave Aunt Dora's Party and Join a Picket Line." *Ms* 7 (Mar. 1979): 57-59, 84, 86 and "The Summer Eleanor Roosevelt Danced with Passion." *Self* 1 (June 1979): 70-71. A musical adaptation by Gretchen Cryer and Rhoda Lerman was produced in Willamstown, Mass. For a review, see "Eleanor (Don't Frighten the Horses)." *Variety* 324 (3 Sept. 1986): 132.

J12   Roosevelt, Elliott. *A First Class Murder*. New York: St. Martin's, 1991. 261p.
Sept. 1938 on board the liner Normandie. ER, Malvina Thompson, Jack Benny, Mary Livingston, Henry Luce, Charles Lindbergh, and a young JFK confront murder and international intrigue while traveling to New York. ER and JFK work together to solve the case.

J13   ---. *The Hyde Park Murder*. New York: St. Martin's, 1985. 231p.
It is 1935 and ER plays detective. Features FDR, Joseph Kennedy, Fiorello La Guardia, Louis Brandeis, and Sara Roosevelt.

J14   ---. *Murder and the First Lady*. New York: St. Martin's, 1984. 227p.
First in the series of mysteries featuring ER. This one takes place on the eve of World War II and also portrays FDR, Missy LeHand, Harry Hopkins, and J. Edgar Hoover.

J15 ---. *Murder at Hobcaw Barony*. New York: St. Martin's, 1986. 233p.
ER as detective at Bernard Baruch's South Carolina estate. Also on hand are Tallulah Bankhead, Humphrey Bogart, Joan Crawford, Walter Winchell, Darryl Zanuck, and FDR.

J16 ---. *Murder at the Palace*. New York: St. Martin's, 1988. 179p.
ER helps solve a murder during her 1942 trip to England. King George VI and Queen Elizabeth are also portrayed.

J17 ---. *Murder in the Blue Room*. New York: St. Martin's, 1990. 215p.
In the spring of 1942 FDR is preoccupied with war in the Pacific while ER solves the mystery surrounding the death of two young women. Stephen Early, Everett Dirkson, Harry Hopkins, Nelson Rockefeller, and a controversial Washington radio commentator are in this mystery about the First Lady.

J18 ---. *Murder in the Oval Office: An Eleanor Roosevelt Mystery*. New York: St. Martin's, 1989. 247p.
In the summer of 1934 a southern congressman is found dead in the oval office. Suicide or murder? ER solves the murder with a supporting cast of FDR, Missy LeHand, Louis Howe, J. Edgar Hoover, and Sally Rand.

J19 ---. *Murder in the Red Room*. New York: St. Martin's, 1992. 249p.
The second term begins, and while FDR is accused of trying to pack the Supreme Court ER solves two murders involving call girls, pimps, and federal lawyers. Brief appearances by George Patton, Amelia Earhart, and Alice Roosevelt Longworth.

J20 ---. *Murder in the Rose Garden*. New York: St. Martin's, 1989. 232p.
A double murder involving illicit sex and the powerful in Washington in 1936 is solved by ER. Missy LeHand offers assistance.

J21 ---. *Murder in the West Wing: An Eleanor Roosevelt Mystery*. New York: St. Martin's, 1993. 247p.
In early 1936 two associates of the late Huey P. Long as well as his fictional illegitimate daughter figure in two murders. A dying Louis Howe helps ER solve the mystery. FDR, Missy LeHand, and Harry Hopkins are also around.

J22   ---. *The President's Man*. A "Blackjack" Endicott Novel. New York: St. Martin's. 1991. 245p.
FDR's first nomination seems a certainty, and there is a threat on his life because of his support for the repeal of prohibition. When disparaging remarks are made about ER, Jack "Blackjack" Endicott comes to her defense.

J23 ---. *The White House Pantry Murder*. New York: St. Martin's, 1987. 229p.
A body is found in a White House refrigerator while Winston Churchill is visiting during Christmas 1941. FDR, Harry Hopkins, and Henrietta Nesbitt are also there while ER works to solve the mystery.

J24 Roosevelt, James. *A Family Matter*. By James Roosevelt with Sam Toperoff. New York: Simon and Schuster, 1980. 316p.

Roosevelt presents a fictionalized account of the Manhattan Project, and he and FDR are the central characters. Two sections featuring ER are revealing accounts of the relationship between mother and son (pp. 63-70, 172-76).

J25 Schary, Dore. *Sunrise at Campobello: A Play in Three Acts*. New York: Random House, 1958. [viii] + 109p.
The highly-acclaimed dramatization of FDR's crippling illness, the efforts of ER and Louis Howe to return FDR to public life, and the emergence of ER. Also featured are Sara Roosevelt, the Roosevelt children, and Al Smith. Covers the period Aug. 1921-June 1924. Also issued New York: New American Library, 1958 and 1960; 43 *Theatre Arts* (Nov. 1959): [33]-58; Acting ed., New York: Dramatists Play Service, 1961.

J26 Stadd, Arlene. *Eleanor*. 48p.
Script of a one character play. Toured the country staring Eileen Heckart. For an article about the writing of the play, see Arlene Stadd, "The Real Eleanor, On and Off the Stage." *Chicago Sun-Times* 4 July 1976. The play and the article are available in Subject Files Relating to the Eleanor Roosevelt Centennial Commission, Box 7, New York State Archives. Reviews by Glenna Syse from the *Chicago Sun-Times* and Linda Winer from the *Chicago Tribune* are reprinted in *Variety* 283 (28 July 1976): 65 as "Chicago Welcomes Eileen and Eleanor."

J27 Vonnegut, Kurt. *Deadeye Dick*. New York: Delacorte, 1982; New York: Dell, 1985. xiii + 240.
While visiting war plants in Midland City, Ohio ER has lunch on Mother's Day 1944 with young Rudy Waltz and his family (pp. 55-61).

J28 Williams, David J. *Eleanor Roosevelt's Niggers*. Davenport: Coral Reef-Neptune, 1976. 223p.
A fictionalized account of the World War II 761st Tank Battalion which was known as "Eleanor Roosevelt's Niggers." Treatment of ER is limited to the foreword and a few brief references.

POETRY

J29 Appell, Laurie. "Eleanor Roosevelt (1884-1962)." *Huddle Lights* (June 1963): 9.
The death of ER and a tribute to her life.

J30 Boaz, Frances Coffin. "Mrs. Franklin D. Roosevelt." *If Appollo Listens In*. By Frances Coffin Boaz. Dallas: Tardy, 1936. 62.
A short poem in appreciation of the woman who is inspiring others.

J31 Eiku. "She Stays Tall." *Petal Paper* [Petal, Miss.] 10 (Feb. 1963): 3.
In memory of ER.

J32 Harrison, Edna L. "First Lady (to Mrs. Eleanor Roosevelt)." *Ebony Rhythm: An Anthology of Contemporary Negro Verse*. Ed. Beatrice M. Murphy. New York: Exposition, 1948; Freeport: Books for Libraries, 1968; Great Neck: Granger, 1982; Salem: Ayer, 1988. 79-80.
ER who works for peace and the rights of all.

J33 Hull, William D., II. "Mrs. F.D.R." *Sewanee Review* 48 (Jan. 1940): [33].
Her activities as First Lady.

J34 McGroarty, John S. "The Lady Eleanor."
Included in *Congressional Record* (25 Mar. 1936): 4341 and also in collection of anecdotes about ER's travels and legendary energy in "White House Traveler." *Christian Science Monitor Magazine* 25 Nov. 1939, Atlantic ed.: 4. Also in George Wolfskill and John A. Hudson, *All But the People: Franklin D. Roosevelt and His Critics, 1933-39*, pp. 37-45 (New York: Macmillan, 1969).

J35 Newton, Cosette Faust. "Eleanor Roosevelt." *War-Blown*. By Cosette Faust Newton. Dallas: Kaleidograph, 1941. 102.
She knows life's pains and appears to move among us with ease.

J36 [Pegler, Westbrook]. *Lady I*. New York: Privately printed at the Sign of St. Christopher, 1942. 4p.
In the first person style of "My Day" Pegler parodies ER's reporting of her activities and portrays her as an adovcate for labor goons. Copy held by the Univ. of Ore. examined. Copy inscribed by Pegler and includes handwritten textual changes.

J37 Sec. "In Memory." *Reporter* 27 (22 Nov. 1962): 12.
That the world is a lonelier place without her is the conclusion of a poem written at the time of her death.

J38 Smith, Hilda Worthington. "Eleanor Roosevelt in Committee." *Poems*. By Hilda Worthington Smith. Washington: Merkle, 1964. 98.
A tribute to her humanitarianism.

SONG

J39 Humphrey, Brian. "Clover and Thistle (A Song for Eleanor)." Lyrics by Jeanne Junge. *Women of Courage Songbook*. 3rd ed. St. Paul: Dog Day Records, 1985. 12-13.
In tribute to ER's belief that peace begins with the individual.

Author Index

Abell, George, F487
Abell, Tyler, F1717
Abels, Margaret D., F1028
Abramowitz, Mildred, F1295-96
Abrams, Irwin, F2014
Adamic, Louis, F930
Adams, Bruce, F1937
Adams, David, F174
Adams, Frank S., F1297
Adams, Val, F1736-38
Adler, Bill, B223a, B504
Adler, David A., I1
Adler, Margaret, G18
Adler, Nancy J., F397
Aglion, Raoul, F931
Aguiar, Jose, F490
Aikman, Lonnelle, F716
Aldrich, Bernice, D76
Alexander, Charles, F103
Alexander, Jane, F1939
Alexander, Will W., F717, F1145
Allen, Frederick Lewis, F491
Allen, Hugh, F2016
Allen, Robert S., F659-61
Alsop, Joseph, E14, F175-76, F398,
　F718
American Federation of Labor-
　Congress of Industrial Organizations
　(AFL-CIO), F1068, F1818
Americans for Democratic Action
　(ADA), F1952
Amidon, Beulah, E15, E61
Anderson, Alice E., F37
Anderson, Colleen, F1093
Anderson, Jervis, F1146

Anderson, Mary, F1029
Anderson, Peggy, F1176
Andrews, Charles H., B390
Anthony, Carl Sferrazza, F178-80,
　F399, F721-23, F1147, F1674, I29
Anthony, Susan B., II, F1234
Anticagila, Elizabeth, I30
Antler, Joyce, F386
Apeland, Nils M., B462, B566
Appell, Laurie, J29
Aptheker, Herbert, F1447
Arbeiter, Jean S., F918, F1668
Arnoll, Kay, F2017
Arocena, Berta, F38
Asbell, Bernard, B34, F181, F724,
　F1030
Asbury, Edith Evans, F182
Ascoli, Max, F1820
Atwell, Mary Welek, F39, F1443
Austin, Warren, B368, F1437
Ayres, B. Drummond, Jr., F725

Baal-Teshuva, Jacob, B497
Badger, Anthony J., F1148, F1235
Bagni, Gwen, H65, J1
Baillargeon, Patricia, F1604
Baird, A Craig, D104a, F1740-41
Baker, Augusta, E77
Baker, Gretta, I31
Baker, Harry J., F40
Baker, Russell, J2
Ballou, Robert O., B29, B531
Banner, Lois W., F1236
Barber, James David, F183
Barclay, Sarah, F1070

Barnard, Eunice Fuller, G10, G19, F400
Barnett, Lester, F494
Barrett, Mary L., E130
Barrett, Patricia, E151
Barron, Gloria J., F401
Barry, Judy, F495
Bart, Jan, F2061
Barton, Elsa M., F1763
Bartusek, Libushka, B208
Baruch, Bernard M., B368, F1071
Barzman, Sol, F41
Barzun, Jacques, E43
Bassett, Margaret, I32
Bates, Daisy, B486
Bauersfeld, Erik, H56
Bauman, John F., F1072
Baxendale, Hadley V., F37
Bealle, Morris A., F496, F1612
Beard, Mary R., E6
Beard, Timothy, F184
Beasley, Maurine, F726-29, F925, F1106, F1742-45
Beaton, Cecil, F934
Becker, May Lamberton, E53
Becker, Susan D., F1237
Bedell, Jane, F1447
Beebe, Ann, E128
Beezer, Bruce G., F1073
Belford, Barbara, F730
Belgrade, Paul, F1745
Bell, Jack, F1677
Bell, Margaret, B67
Bendiner, Robert, G76
Benet, Stephen Vincent, E44
Benet, William Rose, F107
Benjamin, Louise Paine, F497
Benjamin, Robert S., F2018
Benson, George A., F498
Berger, Jason, F1, F42-43
Berger, V., F499
Bergquist, Laura, F185, F2019
Berman, William C., F1149
Bethune, Mary McLeod, F1150, F1163
Bickerstaff, Joyce, F1151
Bilbo, Theodore G., F1477
Biles, Roger, F1031
Bilsborrow, Eleanor Janice, F1746
Bingham, June, J3
Bird, Caroline, F1238
Birmingham, Stephen, F26, F186

Bishop, Jim, F731
Black, Allida M., F1152-53
Black, Ruby A., B198, F2, F500-504, F1239
Blair, Emily Newell, E17, F402, F505
Blassingame, Wyatt, I2
Blaustein, Jacob, F1822
Bliven, Bruce, F506
Bliven, Naomi, F2020
Bloch, Leon Bryce, E45
Blodgett, Bonnie, F187
Bloom, Sol, F732
Bloom, Vera, F507
Bloxom, Marguerite D., A5
Blum, John Morton, B464, F733-34, F936, F1155
Blumberg, Rhoda, I33
Blyth, Myrna, F1938
Boardman, Bess, B252
Boaz, Frances Coffin, J30
Bodin, Jean, B514
Boettcher, Thomas D., F1205
Boettiger, Anna Roosevelt, see Roosevelt, Anna
Boettiger, John R., B27c, F188
Bogardus, Emory S., E84
Boggs, Ronald James, F1349
Bohn, William E., F1823
Bokhari, Ahmed S., E85
Boller, Paul F., Jr., F44, F735
Bolles, Blair, F1075
Bolt, Jonathan, J4
Bolton, Sarah K., I34
Boos, John E., F2021
Borland, Hal, E54
Boulard, Garry, A1
Bourne, Russell, F789
Boutilier, Mary, F281
Bowen, Croswell, F189
Bowie, Walter Russell, F45
Brandle, Lowell, G103
Brandon, Henry, F366
Breig, Joe, F1614
Breitman, George, pseud., F1202
Breitman, Richard, F937
Brickell, Herschel, E8
Bricker, John, D244b
Briller, Sara Welles, F1238
Brin, Ruth F., I35
Brogan, D.W., E18, E135, F508

Bromley, Dorothy Dunbar, G46
Bronson, Susan, F1939
Brooks, Gertrude Zeth, F109
Brooks, Patricia, F741
Brooks, Tim, H17
Brough, James, F23, F25, F190
Broughton, Nick, E46
Broun, Heywood, F509
Brown, Christine M., F404, F736
Brown, Claude, F1156
Brown, Earl, F1157
Brown, Margaret Warren, E143
Brown, Richard C., B507
Bruns, Roger, F1344
Bryan, Joseph, III, F968
Bryant, Arthur, F1824
Buck, Pearl S., F797
Buckley, William F., Jr., F1032,
   F1825
Buell, Ellen Lewis, E126, E144
Bugbee, Emma, F46, F191, F511-17,
   F737, F1826, G95
Bullard, Helen, F1878
Bunche, Ralph J., F1158
Burke, Fran, F1940
Burlingham, Lloyd, F1074
Burnham, James, E87
Burnham, Louis, F1159
Burnham, Philip, F1373
Burns, Bert, F397
Burns, Helen, E152
Burns, James MacGregor, F193, F405-
   6, F738-39, F938, F1240, F1561,
   F1679, G101
Burns, Janet Thompson, G101
Burns, Stewart, F1561
Burt, Nathaniel, F194
Burton, Dennis A., A8
Bussey, Charles J., F47
Butler, Jessie Haver, F1747
Butler, Paul M., F1680
Butterfield, Roger, F48, F791
Butturff, Dorothy Dow, F740
Butwin, Miriam, I39
Bye, George T., F1076
Byrne, Thomas R., E114

Cadden, Joseph, F1298
Cahn, Robert, F1645
Cairns, Julia, G53
Calkins, Virginia, I36

Callahan, North, G55
Calvert, Paul, F663
Calvin, Floyd G., F1160
Cancino, Francisco Cuevas, B422
Cannon, Poppy, F741, F1161, F1933
Carmichael, Donald Scott, B338
Carmody, Deirdre, F195
Carney, Anne E., F1241
Caroli, Betty Boyd, F49, F742-43
Carratello, John, I37
Carratello, Patty, I37
Carroll, Lewis, B77
Carskadon, T.R., F1077
Carson, Gerald, E149
Carson, Saul, F1749
Carter, Elmer F., F1162
Carter, Jimmy, F1444, F2008
Carter, John Franklin, F519
Carter, Rosalynn, F1958
Casilla, Robertm, I1
Cassin, Rene, F110, F1562
Cates, John M., Jr., F1552-53
Cavanah, Frances, I38
Chadakoff, Rochelle, B36
Chafe, William H., F50-51, F1033,
   F1941
Chaffin, Lillie, I39
Chakovsky, Alexander, J5
Chamberlain, John, F744, F1615
Chandler, Douglas, F312
Chartrand, Philip, F1457
Chartrand, Rita, F1457
Charyn, Jerome, J6
Chassler, Sey, F2022
Cherkasky, Shirley, F814
Cheshire, Maxine, F1841
Childs, Marquis W., F520, F940
Christman, Henry M., B490
Christoper, Maurine, F1750
Christopherson, Marie, F541
Churchill, Allen, B203b, B380a,
   F196, F407, F745
Clapp, Elsie Ripley, F1079-80
Clapper, Olive Ewing, F198, F942
Clapper, Raymond, F521-22, F1035
Clark, Delbert, F523
Clark, Electra, F746, F1242
Clark, Judith Freeman, F52, F1243
Clark, William Lloyd, F524
Clawson, Mary, B449
Clayton, Frederick, F199, F1616

Clemens, Cyril, B361
Close, Kathryn, F1333
Coe, Christine Sadler, F1827
Cofield, Ernestine, F1828
Cohen, Magda, F1639
Cohen, Meg, F747
Cohen, Michael J., F1617
Cohen, Miriam, F1244
Coit, Margaret L., E115, F1081
Coleman, George M., F1829
Collier, Fred, F200
Collier, Peter, F1682
Collins, Jean E., F748
Commager, Henry Steele, B474, I41
Conkin, Paul K., F1083
Connally, Tom, D178
Conrad, Peter, F201, F1036
Considine, Bob, F1830
Conta, Marcia Maher, I42
Converse, Florence, E19
Coode, Thomas H., F1072, F1084
Cook, Blanche Wiesen, F3, F114,
   F202, F408, F749, F1245, F1299,
   F1336, F1619-20
Cook, Fannie, J7
Cooke, Alistair, F1831
Cooke, Robert John, F4
Cooney, John, F1352
Cooper, Ethel A., F750
Cornwell, Elmer E., Jr., F1752
Corr, Maureen, F203
Corrado, Anthony J., F53
Corry, John, F1942
Costigan, James, F17
Costopoulos, Liz, F204
Cousins, Margaret, F910
Cousins, Norman B., E36
Cowan, Holly, F1085
Cowles, Gardner, D237
Cox, Corolyn, F1037, G57
Cox, James M., F1038
Cox, John Stuart, F1336
Craig, Barbara, F751
Crew, Spencer C., F1763
Crocker, Lionel, F1753
Crosby, Pennell, G34
Crossman, R.H.S., E136
Crowell, Paul, F1353
Crowther, Bosley, H77
Culbertson, Mary Haeseter, F527
Culligan, Glendy, F409

Cuomo, Mario M., F2008
Current, Gloster B., F1164
Curtin, Andrew, I44

Dado, Susanna Sciutto, F1754
Dales, Douglas S., F1354, F1683
Dalfiume, Richard M., F1165
Dalgliesh, Alice, E145
Dall, Anna Roosevelt, *see* Roosevelt,
   Anna
Dall, Curtis B., F207
Daly, Macdonald, F208
Dando, Ellen Ann, G38
Daniel, Clifton, F1596, F1840
Daniel, Margaret Truman, F908-10
Daniell, Constance, F1606
Daniels, Jonathan, F209-11, F752
Daniels, Roger, F1086
Danker, Anita, F1246
Darling, Edward, F54
Daugherty, Sonia, I45
Davidson, Frank B., B201
Davidson, Margaret, I3
Davis, Ann, F1247
Davis, Clare Ogden, F410
Davis, Elmer, E37
Davis, Kenneth S., F5, F212-15,
   F411, F753-54, F1755
Davis, Lenwood G., F1166
Davis, Mary Gould, E80
Davis, Maxine, F412, F530, F1300
Dawe, Nancy Anne, F216
DeBenedetti, Charles, F413
Debnam, W.E., F1167, G79
De Bruin, Elizabeth, F1621
Decker, Mary Bell, B382
DeGregorio, William A., F115
Deguchi, Yasuo, B21a
De Kruif, Paul, F1088
Delano, Daniel W., Jr., F217
De Mare, Marie, B416
DeMott, Benjamin, F2023
Denniston, Elinore, B26, F1756
Derian, Patricia M., F1943
Dermody, Eugene M., F85
Des Marteau, Genie Lynn, F1039
De Toledano, Nora, F2024
Deuss, Jean, E137
De Wan, George, F1944
Dewey, Ralph Francis, E1355
DeWitt, Madlyn, F1945

De Witt, William, B20
DiBacco, Thomas V., F1946
Dickens, Charles, H31
Dickerson, Robert B., Jr., F116
Dies, Martin, F1301
Dietsch, Jean, H93
Diller, Daniel C., F55, F755
Dilling, Elizabeth K., F533-34, F1757
Diogenes, F535-37
Donahue, Elizabeth, F539-40
Donaldson, Betty, F218
Donaldson, Norman, F218
Dos Passos, John, F56
Douglas, Emily Taft, F57
Douglas, Helen Gahagan, F6, F228, H79
Douglas, William O., E102, F2025
Downey, Kenneth, B371
Downs, Robert B., F58
Dows, Olin, F219
Driscoll, Kate, F417
Duberman, Martin Bauml, F1166
Du Bois, W.E.B., F1447-48
Dubov, Paul, H65, J1
Dubowski, Donald Edward, F1067
Ducas, Dorothy, F542
Duffill, Alma, F220
Duffy, Bernard K., F1815
Duffy, Martha, F756
Dunning, John, F1758
Dykeman, Wilma, F1040

Eade, Charles, B415
Eads, Jane, D56
Eagles, Charles W., F1168
Eastman, John, F222
Eaton, Allen H., B399
Eaton, Anne T., E3
Eaton, Jeanette, I4
Edelstein, Pauline, A2
Edwards, India, F1449
Egan, Leo, F1685
Eichelberger, Clark M., F1450, F1887
Eichelberger, Robert L., F947
Eiku, J31
Eisen, Jack, F814
Eisenhower, Dwight D., B368
Ekirch, Arthur A., Jr., F418
Eleanor Roosevelt Centennial Commission, F1945, F1949

Eleanor Roosevelt Center at Val-Kill, F379, F1951, F1958
Eleanor Roosevelt Memorial Foundation, F224, F1946
Eleanor Roosevelt 70th Birthday Committee, F2058
Ellickson, Katherine P., F1249
Elshtain, Jean Bethke, F419, F1042, F1957
Elting, M.L., E20
Elwood, Ann, F226
Emblidge, David, B36
Engle, Margaret, F1937
Engle, Paul, E109
Ennis, Jean, I48
Ennis, John, I48
Erikson, Joan M., F227
Ernst, Morris L., F1043
Erskine, Helen Worden, F760
Essary, Helen, F546-49
Evans, Ernestine, F63, F550
Evans, Sara M., F1250
Everett, Arthur, F1841

Fabbri, Dennis E., F1084
Faber, Doris, F228-29, I7, I49
Faber, Harold, F230, F1960-61, I49
Fairbanks, Douglas, Jr., F2027
Fairfax, Beatrice, F551
Farley, James A., F552, F761
Farmer, Susan J., F762
Farr, Finis, F1760
Fascell, Dante B., F1962
Fasulo, Linda M., F1451
Fay, Bernard, F951
Fayerweather, Margaret Doane, B103
Feighan, Edward F., F1963
Feingold, Henry L., F952
Feinstein, Dianne, F1939
Feld, Rose C., E9, E107, G3
Feldman, Trude B., F1626
Felsenthal, Carol, F232
Fenton, John H., F313
Ferraro, Geraldine, F1939
Ferrell, Robert H., F1664
Ferris, Helen, B18, B28, B541, B575, F1761
Fielding, Raymond, F1762
Fields, Alonzo, F763

Fields, W.C., F764
Filler, Martin, F233
Findling, John, F123
Finney, Ruth, F554
Fischer, Louis, F767
Fish, Hamilton, F365
Fishel, Leslie H., F1173
Fisher, Craig, H64
Fisher, Dorothy Canfield, B401, F1252
Fishman, Jack, B498, F958
Flanagan, Hallie, F1096
Fleeson, Doris, F1844
Fleming, F. James, F1845
Fleming, William, F1564
Flemion, Jess, F7, F235-36, F420,
    F768-69, F1627
Flynn, Edward J., B494, F770
Flynn, Elizabeth Gurley, F560
Flynn, John T., F561, F771, F1304
Fogel, Nancy A., F237
Foner, Philip S., F1253
Forbush, Gabrielle, F344
Ford, Betty, F1958
Foreman, Clark, F1174
Forrest, Ralph, F1319
Forrester, E.L., F1170
Forsee, Aylesa, I51
Forster, John, J4
Fowler, Robert Booth, F1254
Fowlkes, William A., F1846
Fox, J. DeWitt, F238
Fox, Victor J., F1688
Fox-Genovese, Elizabeth, F386
Frank, Anne, B400
Frank, Sid, F772
Franken, Rose, F563
Franklin, Jay, F564-65
Franklin, P.L., F566, F1097
Franklin and Eleanor Roosevelt
    Institute, F1563
Franklin D. Roosevelt Library, A6-7,
    A11, F1965, H33, H46, H57
Franz, Leslie, I52
Frazer, Heather T., F961
Free, Ann Cottrell, F773
Freedman, Max, F886, F1912
Freedman, Russell, I8, I53
Freeman, Lucy, E108
Freidel, Frank, F17, F241, F422,
    F774-76
French, Paul Comly, B182

Friedan, Betty, F1939
Friedman, Saul S., F962
Frooks, Dorothy, F777
Fuchs, Lawrence H., F1689
Fuentes, Jodi, F125
Fuller, John G., F2028
Furman, Bess, E117, F242, F567-70,
    F778-80, F1098-1102, G51
Furman, Lucile, F1098-1102
Furnas, Helen, F571
Furnas, J.C., F243

Galbraith, John Kenneth, F118,
    F423, F1690, F2029
Gallagher, Hugh Gregory, F424
Gallick, Rosemary, F173
Gallup, George H., F572-73, F2030
Gammon, Roland, F2031, G104
Ganin, Zv, F1453
Gannon, Robert I., F1356
Gansberg, Martin, F2032
Gardner, Mona, F574
Gardner, Richard N., F1454-55,
    F1566
Gargan, Edward A., F1966
Garraty, John A., F126
Garrett, Evelyn, F575, F963
Garrison, Webb, F244, F781
Garson, Robert A., F1175
Gates, David, F1967
Gauvreau, Emile, F1778
Geddes, Donald Porter, B315a
Geertz, Hildred, B502
Gellermann, William, F1305
Gelman, Eric, F391
Gentry, Kurt, F1336
George, Elsie L., F425, F1255
Gerlinger, Irene Hazard, F127
Ghee, Joyce C., F1958
Gibber, Frances, F8
Gibbs, Margaret, F1176
Gies, Joseph, F245, F782
Gilbert, Miriam, I9
Gilfond, Henry, I54
Gill, Brendan, F246
Gilliam, Dorothy, F1177
Ginna, Robert Emmett, F791
Gioseffi, Daniela, B518
Gitlitz, Susan, F964
Gladstone, Valerie, F783
Gladwin, Lee A., F1103

Goldberg, Richard Thayer, F426
Goldberg, Rose C., G52
Golden, Harry, F1178
Goldman, Harry Merton, F784
Goldsmith, Gloria, J8
Goode, Bill, F576
Goodfriend, Joyce D., B33-35
Goodman, Charles, F965
Goodman, Deborah Lerme, I47
Goodman, Elizabeth B., F247
Goodman, Ellen, F1968
Goodman, Walter, F1306, J3
Goodsell, Jane, I10
Goodwin, Betty, D160
Goodwin, Doris Kearns, F785
Gordon, Evelyn, F487
Gordon, Keith V., F577
Gordon, Linda, F1046
Gosnell, Harold F., E64, F427
Gould, Beatrice Blackmar, F1766
Gould, Bruce, F1766
Gould, Jack, F1737
Gould, Jean, F428, F1632
Gould, Leslie A., B202, F1307
Gould, Lewis L., F786-90
Graff, Robert D., F791
Grafton, David, F248
Graham, Gladys, E31
Graham, Hugh Davis, F249
Graham, Otis L., Jr., F240, F421,
    F1044
Grammatico, Angelina Carmela, F1567
Grant, James, F1081
Grant, Philip A., Jr., F1357
Grantham, Dewey W., F1158
Graves, Charles P., I11, I55
Gray, Joao, F1465
Green, Bill, F1969
Green, James Frederick, F1568
Green, Jerald R., F792
Green, Thomas L., F1180
Greenbaum, Fred, F1181
Greenbaum, Lucy, D185, E57
Greenbie, Sydney, F251
Greenblatt, Robert B., F252
Greene, Thomas F., E153
Griffin, Isabel Kinnear, F579-80
Grobin, Allen N., F348, F468
Gruber, Ruth, F966
Grusd, Edward E., G40
Gu, J., G80

Gulick, Dorothy, F253
Gunther, John, F254, F793
Gup, Ted, F794
Gurewitsch, A. David, F9, F224-25
Gurewitsch, Edna P., F256
Gutin, Myra G., F795, F967, F1047,
    F1767

Haber, Paul, F581
Hacker, Jeffrey H., F257
Hager, Alice Rogers, F429, G26
Hahn, Lorena B., F1456
Haid, Stephen Edward, F1104
Hailey, Foster, F796
Halamandaris, Val J., F65
Hall, Helen, E58
Halle, Rita S., F582
Halsey, William F., F968
Halsted, Anna Roosevelt, see
    Roosevelt, Anna
Hamilton, Thomas J., E82, E103
Hamburger, Philip, F1768
Hamby, Alonzo L., F1691
Hammer, Armand, F259
Hammer Galleries, F260-62, F397
Hancher, Virgil M., F2033
Hanegbi, Yehuda, F1633
Hareven, Tamara K., F10, F66-67,
    F1048, F1970
Harley, J. Eugene, F1435
Harriman, Kathleen, F969-70
Harris, Theodore F., F797
Harrison, Cynthia, F386, F1256
Harrison, Edna L., J32
Harrity, Richard, F11, H49
Hart, James D., F129
Hart, Scott, F950
Hartman, Violet, F430
Hartmann, Susan M., F1257
Hart-Mathews, Jane de, F1087
Hassett, William D., F798
Hatch, Alden, F263, F431, F799
Hatch, Jane M., F61
Hauptman, Laurence M., F1105
Haws, --, F1769
Hay, Peter, F264
Hayward, Tamerin Mitchell, F68
Hazen, Davis W., F583
Healy, Diana Dixon, F69
Heath, Mary, F265
Heath, Monroe, F130

Hecht, Marie B., F870
Heckscher, August, F971
Hellman, Geoffrey T., F584
Helm, Edith Benham, B414, F800
Hendrick, James P., F1540-41
Hennefrund, Bill, F266
Herbert, Elizabeth Sweeney, F267
Herrick, Genevieve Forbes, E41,
    F585, G41
Herrick, William, F1770
Hershan, Stella K., F12-13,
    F1771, F2034-35
Herzberg, Max J., F131
Heseltine, Guy, F268
Hess, Stephen, F269
Heuvel, Jean Vanden, F366
Hickok, Lorena A., B22, B488, F14,
    F70, F801, F1106, F1632, G23-24,
    G27-28, G51, I12, I56-57
Hicks, Donald R., F1569
Hicks, Granville, F802
Hiebert, Ray Eldon, I58
Hiebert, Roselyn, I58
Higgins, Richard, F1966
Hildebrandt, Fred H., F586
Hill, C.P., F270
Hill, Ruth Edmonds, F1154
Hinding, Andrea, A17
Hine, Darlene Clark, F1182
Hodges, Margaret, F271
Hoey, Jane, F1854
Hoff, Henry B., F184
Hoffecker, Savin, B483
Hoffman, Clare E., F945, F1309
Hoff-Wilson, Joan, F35, F1259,
    F1634, F1971-73
Hofstadter, Bernice K., F803
Holborn, Louise W., F1457
Holcombe, Arthur N., F1570
Holland, Bobby, F272
Holman, Frank E., F1571
Holme, Bryan, B512
Holmes, John Haynes, E38
Holmes, Kathleen Sexton, D91, F587
Hoover, Irwin Hood (Ike), F588
Hornaday, Mary, E32, E65, E89,
    E110, E154, F70, F589-94, F1855
Horne, Gerald, F1447
Horne, Lena, F1163
Horneman, Mary Ann, F133
Horowitz, David, F1682

Horton, Mildred McAfee, B26c
Howard, James T., F972
Howard, James W., B115
Howard, Jean, E119
Howe, Louis M., F596
Howe, Quincy, B424
Howlett, Ruth B., F1974
Hudson, John A., J34
Huie, William Bradford, F1310
Hull, Harwood, F667
Hull, William D., II, J33
Humphrey, Brian, J39
Humphrey, John P., F1569, F1578-
    79
Humphrey, Kelly N., F804
Humphries, Jane, F1260
Hunt, Irma, F274
Hunt, Sandra, F1772
Hurd, Charles W., F597, F805-6,
    F1322, F1774
Hurley, Patrick J., F1114
Hurst, Fannie, F526, F598, F807,
    F2036
Hurteau, Laure, F1635
Hurwitz, Howard L., F134
Huss, Pierre J., F1936
Hymowitz, Carol, F1261
Hynes, Betty, F599

Ickes, Harold L., F1109
Ingersoll, Nelson,, B305
Isenberg, Nancy G., F2038

Jacobs, William Jay, I13
Jackson, Alice, F974
Jackson, Charlotte, E146
Jackson, Ronald Vern, F276
Jaffe, Eli, F277
Jamison, R.H., D264a, F1858
Janeway, Elizabeth, E66, E132,
    F1065, F1458, F2039
Jeffers, H. Paul, I81
Jeffreys, Susan Fort, E11
Jeffries, Ona Griffin, F808
Jensen, Amy La Follette, F809-10
Jessup, Philip C., F1459
Johnson, Ann Donegan, I14
Johnson, Frank, pseud., F1757
Johnson, George, F15
Johnson, Gerald W., E155, F278,
    F603, F1049

Johnson, Lady Bird, F1860, F1958
Johnson, Lyndon B., F1050, F1861
Johnson, M. Glen, F1580-81
Johnson, Marilyn, F811
Johnson, Walter, F359, F812, F1483, F1727, F1923, F2062
Johnston, Anne Roosevelt, F2040
Johnston, Laurie, F2041
Jones, Barry O., F138
Jones, Edward Stafford, F604
Josephson, Emanuel M., F813, F1637
Junge, Jeanne, J39
Junior Literary Guild, F368, F372
Juno, Irene, G29

Kahn, Alfred, J., B499
Kahn, E.J., Jr., F248, F279, F1460, F1695
Kamenetsky, Karen J., I59
Kaminsky, Stuart M., J9
Kamp, Joseph P., F605
Kane, Albert E., E90
Kane, Joseph Nathan, F139
Kaplan, Frances Bagley, F1233
Karsh, Yousuf, F280, F317
Kartini, Raden Adjeng, B502
Kassebaum, Nancy, F1939
Katz, Mary Lynn, F920
Katzin, Alfred, F1398
Kaufman, Natalie Hevener, F1582
Kava, Beth Millstein, B514
Kearney, James R., F16, F1183
Keil, Sally Van Wagenen, F975
Kelen, Emery, I60
Keliher, Alice, B459
Keller, Helen, B395
Kelly, Rita Mae, F281
Kemp, Barbara H., A3, F814
Kenneally, James J., F1262
Kennedy, David M., F386
Kennedy, Edward M., F1696
Kennedy, John F., F1263, F1862-66
Kennedy, Shawn S., F1975
Kennelly, Barbara B., F1976
Kent, George F606
Kenworthy, Leonard, I61
Kernan, Michael, F1977
Kessler, Pamela, F1988
Kessner, Zelda Ellen, J10
Keyes, Frances Parkinson, E22, F607-8
Keyssar, Helene, F1020

Kiernan, R.H., F282
Kifer, Allen Francis, F1184
Kilpatrick, Carroll, F885
Kimball, Warren F., F941
King, Florence, F386, F815
King, Martin Luther, Jr., F1867
Kingdon, Frank, F816
Kintner, Robert, F176
Kiplinger, W.M., F609
Kirby, John B., F1185
Kirk, Elise K., F817
Kirkendall, Richard S., F818
Kirkpatrick, Jeane, F1939
Klapthor, Margaret Brown, F140, F819
Kleeman, Rita Halle, F283
Klehr, Harvey, F820
Klein, Barbara Hope, F68
Kleinerman, Lois B., F821
Klemesrud, Judy, F822, F1978
Klots, Allen, F14
Kluckhohn, Frank L., F568
Knapp, Sally, I15
Knight, Arthur, H77
Knox, E.V., E138
Knox, Paul, F610
Koenig, Louis W., F823
Kohlhoff, Dean, F824
Kohn, George C., F284
Kohn, Hans, D226, F1461
Kol, Moshe, B453
Korey, William, F1583
Kornbluh, Joyce L., F1111, F1311
Koykku, Arthur S., F141
Kraft, Joseph, F1697
Kraut, Alan M., F937
Kretsinger, Geneva, F1776
Krock, Arthur, F611-12, F825, F1264
Krueger, Thomas A., F1186
Kulkin, Mary-Ellen, F156
Kunin, Madeleine M., F1051
Kupferberg, Tuli, F17
Kurth, Peter, F1638
Kutner, Nanette, F613, G91

Lachman, Seymour P., F1358
La Follette, Suzanna, E12
Lait, Jack, F826
Lammerding, Betsey, F1979
Lammers, A., F1980

Lampell, Millard, H35
Lamson, Peggy, F1462
Land, Emory Scott, F976
Langton, York, F1868
Laning, Edward, F1112
Lape, Esther Everett, F433
Larson, Jeanne, B517
Lash, Joseph P., B33, B35, B369, F17-20, F71-72, F285-87, F827-29, F977, F1265, F1981, H67
Lash, Trude W., F1639
Laski, Harold J., F1312
Lasky, Victor, F1640, F1698
Laughlin, Nancy Bartlett, F1385
Lavine, Harold, F1699
Lawrence, William H., F615
Lawson, Don, I62
Lazell, Louise T., D58, F616
Lazo, Caroline, I16
Lee, Myrra, I17
Lehmann-Haupt, Christopher, F223
Leighton, Frances Spatz, F867-69, I69
Leighton, Isabel, F344, G30
Le Maistre, Ian, E91
Lenroot, Katherine F., D115a
Leonard, Thomas M., F830
Lerman, Rhoda, H68, H89, J11
Lester, DeeGee, A12
Letts de Espil, Courtney, F831
Leuchtenburg, William E., F832
Levy, William Turner, F1982
Lewis, Dorothy Roe, F833
Lewis, Ethel, B160
Lewis, Fulton, Jr., F1313
Lewis, Grace Hegger, F434
Lewis, Jack, F288
Libby, Bill, F26
Library of Congress, A4, A13
Lieser, Julia F., I63
Lightman, Marjorie, F35
Lilienthal, David E., F289
Lima, Oscar de, F1463
Lindley, Betty, F1314-15
Lindley, Ernest K., F435, F617, F1315
Lindsay, Rae, F73
Lingeman, Richard R., F979
Linzer, Estelle, F1607, F1983
Lippman, Theo, Jr., F290
Lisio, Donald J., F1114
Littell, Norman M., F291, F834,
Logan, Logna B., F143

Lohbeck, Don, F1114
Lombard, Helen, F980
Long, Tania, F981
Longworth, Alice Roosevelt, F618-19, F707
Looker, Earle, F436
Loos, John L., F64
Loots, Barbara Kunz, F835
Lottman, Eileen, F17
Louchheim, Katie S., F1700, F1869-70
Love, Everetta, G35
Lovell, Mary S., F836
Lovell, P.M., D255
Lowenstein, Allard K., B484, F1478
Lowitt, Richard, F1106
Lubitsh, A. Cypen, F492
Luce, Clare Boothe, F1642, F2042
Ludwig, Emil, F292, F437
Luxford, Nola, G54
Lyndon, Neil, F259
Lynn, Kenneth C., F223, F351, F386
Lyons, Eugene, F1316-17

Maas, David, H92-93
MacDonald, Bernice, E111
MacDonald, J. Fred, F1777
MacDougall, Curtis D., F1701
Macfadden, Mary, F1778
Macgregor, Frances Cooke, B13
MacKaye, Milton, F438, F947
MacKenzie, Catherine, F620
MacKenzie, Compton, F439
Macksey, Joan, F144
Macksey, Kenneth, F144
MacLeish, Archibald, F21, F440, F1871-72, F2008, F2043, H77
Maddox, Brenda, F386
Maga, Timothy P., F982
Magenheimer, Kay, G15
Magill, Frank N., F64
Maine, Basil, F293, F441, F621
Malik, Charles, B360, F1502, F1511, F1515, F1523, F1534, F1585
Mallon, Paul, F622
Manchester, William, F74, F837
Mandigo, Pauline E., D60
Maney, Patrick J., F295, F1188
Mangione, Jerre, F1115
Manly, Chesly, F1464
Mannes, Marya, F1052

Manning, Marjorie, F623
Manzon, Jean, F1465
Marbury, Elizabeth, F442
Maria, Fern, F323
Marlow, Joan, F75
Marsh, Earle, H17
Marshall, John David, E120
Marshall, Margaret, E50, F1779
Marston, William Moulton, F624
Martin, George, F838
Martin, George W., F625
Martin, John Bartlow, F1702
Martin, Louis, F1189
Martin, Prestonia Mann, F1318
Martin, Ralph, F983
Martin, Ralph G., F11, F1703, F2044,
   G60, H49
Martin, Sarah L., F1780
Marvin, Isabel R., I64
Marx, Hilde, G81
Maslow, Abraham H., F296
Mason, Lucy Rudolph, B403, F1116
Massey, Michael J., F1704
Mathes, Miriam S., E127
Mathews, Thomas, F1117
Mathews, Tom, F1228
Matson, Howard, F297
Matthews, Glenna, F1033
Matthews, Herbert L., F1643
Matthews, J.B., F839
Mayer, Allan J., F840
Mayer, William, H5
Mayo, Edith F., F841
Maze, John, F1140
McAllister, Dorothy S., F626
McAuley, Karen, I18
McBride, Katherine Elizabeth, D189
McBride, Mary Margaret, F1781
McCardle, Dorothy, F1873
McCarten, John, F627
McCarthy, Abigail Q., F842-44, F1985
McClure, Ruth K., F298
McConnell, Burt, F76
McConnell, Jane, F76
McDonald, William F., F1118
McDonough, Aloysius, F1466
McElvaine, Robert S., F299, F443,
   F1089, F2045
McGarvey, G.A., F1119
McGill, Ralph, F1608, F1874
McGovern, George, F1868

McGroarty, John S., J34
McGrory, Mary, F1875, F1895
McGuire, Phillip, F1190
McHenry, Robert, F122
McHugh, John F., F1876, F1986
McJimsey, George, F845
McKeever, Porter, F1705
McKeldin, Theodore R., F1821
McKinzie, Richard D., F1120
McKissack, Frederick, I65
McKissack, Patricia, I65
McKown, Robin, I19
McLaughlin, Isabel, E4
McLaughlin, Kathleen, D99a, F628-
   29, F984, G48-49, G56
Mead, Margaret, F1233, F1877
Means, Marianne, F77
Meany, George, F1818
Medved, Michael, F846
Meehan, Lina di Nogarole, Countess,
   F300
Mehling, Harold, F301
Mejia, Aimee S.B. de Ramos, F630
Melick, Arden Davis, F772, I66
Melton, Harve L., F1191
Meltzer, Milton, F1319
Melvin, Bruce, B227
Mendoza, Miguel Angel, F2046
Menendez, Albert J., F847
Menz, Katherine B., F397
Meredith, Ellis, E13, F631, F985
Merrill, Flora, G8
Merriman, Eve, I67
Mesta, Perle, F848, F1645
Metcalfe, Ralph, F1163
Meursinge-Warnsinck, Catherina,
   F1121
Meyer, Donald, E121, F444, F1881
Meyer, Edith Patterson, I68
Meyer, Peter, F1586
Meyer, Robert S., F1706
Meyers, Joan, F1694
Michaels, Ruth Gruber, F1882
Micheels-Cyrus, Madge, B517
Midgley, Dorothy A., F1782
Miekina, Gilbert, I78
Milburn, Frank H., F78
Miller, Edward, F79
Miller, Hope Ridings, F302
Miller, Merle, F1676

Miller, Nathan, F303-4, F445, F849-50,
    F1467, F1707, F2001
Miller, William M., F851
Millstein, Beth, B514
Minton, Bruce, F1319
Miringoff, Marque-Luisa, F1266
Mitchell, Henry, F223, F925, F1987
Mitchell, Jack, F305
Mitgang, Herbert, F306, J4
Mohr, Lillian, F852
Molella, Arthur P., F1763
Moley, Raymond, F853-54
Monchak, Stephen J., F1783
Montana. Office of Public Instruction,
    I5
Montgomery, Ruth, F855
Moorstern, Betty, F632
Morales, Jose G., B281
Morgan, Edward P., B402
Morgenthau, Henry, III, F446, F856,
    F1784
Morgenthau, Ruth S., F1646, F1784
Morris, Dan, F146
Morris, Elisabeth Woodbridge, B113
Morris, Inez, F146
Morris, Lloyd, E23
Morris, Sylvia Jukes, F307
Morrison, Allan, F1192
Morrison, Howard Alezander, F1988
Morrison, Margaret L., A5
Morse, Arthur D., F962
Mortimer, Lee, F826
Moscow, Warren, F857
Moser, Leo John, F1567
Moses, Belle, F308, F435
Mouckley, Florence, F310
Mower, A. Glenn, Jr., F1587
Moynihan, Daniel Patrick, F1989-90
Mueller, Jean, F79
Mueller, Merrill, F970
Muller, Herbert J., F1711
Mundt, Karl E., F1316
Murphy, Aileen O'B., E128
Murphy, Beatrice M., J32
Murray, Pauli, F1198-99
Museum of Broadcasting, H20
Museum of Television and Radio, *see*
    Museum of Broadcasting
Myers, Maxine Topper, J10
Myers, R. David, A5
Myhra, David, F1122

Myrdal, Gunnar, F2008

Naki, Nancy Aldinger, I6
Nash, Gerald D., B506
National Women's History Project,
    F119, I6, I46
Neal, Steve, F1991
Nehru, Jawaharlal, F2008
Neighbors, Aileene Herrbach, B509
Nelson, Doris, F1799
Nelson, Michael, F91
Nesbitt, Henrietta, F649, F858-60
Nevins, Allen, F1712
Newcombe, Jack, B203c, B203e
Newman, Winnie, J10
Newton, Cosette Faust, J35
Nichols, Jeannette P., E68
Nichols, Lewis, F1713
Nipson, Herbert B411a
Nixon, Robert G., F862
Nizer, Louis, F2050
Nolde, O. Frederick, B357
Nordell, Rod, G102
Northcroft, Dora, F80
Nowlan, Alden, F319

Oakes, John B., F1322
O'Brien, Steven G., F149
O'Connor, Colleen M., F7, F1474
O'Connor, John J., H68
O'Day, Caroline, F320, F478
Odum, Howard W., F1200
Ogden, August Raymond, F1323
Oleson, Helmer O., G63
Olmedo, Tomas, G78
Olsen, Kirstin, F150
O'Reilly, Kenneth, F1324
O. Rundle Gilbert Auctioneer, F331
Osborn, George C., E122
Ostromecki, Walter A., Jr., F863,
    F1475
O'Sullivan, John, F961
O'Sullivan, Judith, F173
Osur, Alan M., F1201
Otto, Susan H., H5
Oursler, Fulton, F864

Pace, Dixie Ann, F81
Paletta, Lu Ann F82
Palmer, Alan, F151
Palmer, Charles F., F1123

Palmer, Gretta, F1656
Palmer, Phyllis, B136
Papanek, Hanna, F865
Park, Edwards, F866
Parke, Richard H., F1364-67
Parker, Albert, F1202
Parker, Maude, F656
Parks, Lillian Rogers, F867-69, I69, J1
Parmet, Herbert S., F870, F1715-16
Parrish, Michael E., F1056
Parrish, Thomas, F1004
Parsons, Frances Theodora, F321
Parten, Ailese, F871
Partnow, Elaine, B515
Parton, Margaret, E157
Partridge, Bellamy, F657
Pasley, Virginia, F658
Paterson, Judith, F1269
Patterson, Eugene, F1899
Patterson, James T., F1124
Patterson, William D., F2052
Patton, Lillian, F322
Patton, Sally J., I70
Patton, Thomas, F322
Peare, Catherine Owens, I71
Pearson, Drew, F210, F659-61, F1717
Peck, Mary Gray, F662
Peck, Sidney M., F1900
Pederson, Kern, F152
Peebes, Jacqueline Neel, F872
Pegler, Westbrook, F663-64, F873,
    F945, F1171, F1676, F1800-1801,
    F1901, J36
Penkower, Monty Noam, F1006,
    F1125, F1657
Pepper, Claude D., F874
Perkins, Frances, D88a, F324, F452,
    F665, F875-76, F1902-3
Perlmutter, Emanuel, F1904
Perney, Linda M., F325
Perry, Elisabeth Israels, F453-55,
    F461, H69
Peters, Kenneth, G98
Peterson, Esther, F1270-71
Peterson, Virgilia, E123, E133
Pettit, Jayne D., I72
Pew, Marlen E., Jr., G44
Pfeffer, Leo, F1388
Pfeffer, Paula F., F1203
Phillips, Ethel C., D251
Pick, Hella, F1905

Pickard, M. Fortescue, F326
Picker, Jean S., B23
Pickett, Clarence E., F1126, F1906
Piechowski, Michael M., F378
Pierce, Bessie Louise, F83
Pierce, Eleanor G., F327
Pilat, Oliver, F877
The Pilgrims, F1446
Pitcaithley, Dwight T., F375
Pitt, David E., F1325
Plavner, Murray, F1330
Plopper, Julie, I73
Plude, Catherine, I74
Plumley, Charles A., F1813
Polier, Justine Wise, F1907
Pope, Linda Karen Gunter, F1127
Pothens, Philip, B375
Potter, E.B., F968
Potter, Jeffrey, F328
Powell, V., E124
Powers, Richard Gid, F1336
Pratt, Virginia Anne, F1590
Prescott, Orville, E93
Prideaux, Tom, F459
Prindiville, Kathleen, F84
Pringle, Henry F., F670
Prokofiev, Sergey, H42-43
Prouty, Howard H., F1814
Proxmire, William, F1992
Pruden, Edward Hughes, F878
Purinton, Thelma, G11
Putnam, George Palmer, F671

Rabinowitz, Dorothty, F879
Race, Edward Nathan, F22
Radcliffe, Donnie, F880, F1993
Ralph, J.P., F460
Ranck, Gloria Virginia, F1803
Rand, Clayton, F672
Randolph, Mary, F673
Rappaport, Doreen, B520, I75
Rauh, Joseph L., Jr., F1994, F2053
Raven, Susan, F154
Rawick, George Philip, F1328
Read, Mary Dodge, E70
Reading, Stella, F1908
Reagan, Nancy, F1958
Reagan, Ronald, F1995
Redding, Jack, F1719
Reddy, John, F1658
Reeves, Thomas C., F1720

Reifert, Gail, F85
Reilly, Michael F., F881
Reiman, Richard A., F1329
Reiter, Ed, F1996
Remnick, David, F1998
Reston, James B., F1477
Reuther, Walter, F1818
Reyes, Karen C., F332
Reyher, Rebecca, B340, B342, B346
Rice, Diana, G6, G12
Rice, Millard Milburn, F1129
Rich, Doris, F836
Rich, Wilbur C., F1151
Richards, Ann, F1999
Richards, Kenneth C., I20
Richardson, Anna Steese, F462
Richardson, Eudora Ramsay, F463
Richardson, G. Dexter, F1130
Ripley, Josephine, E125, F544
Ritchie, Donald A., F1010
Rixey, Lilian, F333
Roach, Helen, H9, H34
Roark, Ann C., F2000
Roberts, Cecil, F1804
Roberts, Chalmers M., F1909
Roberts, Gary Boyd, F334
Roberts, Russell, I77
Robertson, E. Guy, F882
Robertson, Nan, F1910
Robertson, Stephen L., F55, F755
Robey, Ralph, F1011, F1131
Robinson, Donald, F86, F2054
Robinson, Edward G., F1878
Robinson, Felix G., F1132
Robinson, Nehemiah, F1592
Robinson, Phyllis, F971
Robinson, Sophia M., B264
Roche, John P., F1721, F1911
Rochelle, Ogden J., F1805
Rodger, Sarah-Elizabeth, G25
Rodgers, Agnes, F1113
Rogers, Joseph W., E94
Rollins, Alfred B., F464
Rollyson, Carl, F335, F883
Rolo, Charles J., E95
Rondon, Alberto, F674
Roosevelt, Anna (daughter), B34,
    F206, F258, F528-29, F884, F1854
Roosevelt, Archie, F1330
Roosevelt, Dorothy Kemp, F1965

Roosevelt, Eleanor, B1-575, C1-350,
    D1-274, F17, F772, F1569
Roosevelt, Elliott (father), B4
Roosevelt, Elliott (son), B11a, B203d,
    B324, B339, B352, B369, F23-25,
    F336, F465-66, F1012, F1806,
    F2055, J12-23
Roosevelt, Felicia Warburg, F337
Roosevelt, Franklin D., B16, B118,
    B338-39, B352, B369, B419, F338-
    41
Roosevelt, James (son), F26, F342,
    F467, J24
Roosevelt, Patricia Peabody, F343
Roosevelt, Sara D., F344
Rosen, Ruth, F887
Rosenau, James N., B352, B383,
    B386-88, B393, B396-97, E71, G66
Rosenbloom, Morris V., B408
Rosenfeld, Megan, F223
Rosenman, Samuel I., F347, F888
Rosenthal, A.M., G75
Roskolenko, Harry, E96
Ross, George E., I79
Ross, Irwin, F1659
Ross, Ishbel, F676, F889
Ross, Leland M., F348, F468
Ross, Mary, E25
Ross, Shelly, F349
Rosskam, Edwin, B198
Rothchild, Florence, F1057
Rowan, Carl T., G94
Rowe, Bess M., G32
Rubin, Merle, F386
Ruchames, Louis, F1207
Rusher, William A., E140
Rusk, Dean, F1915
Russell, Francis, F469
Russell, James Earl, B435
Ruys, A. Ch., G67
Ryan, Edward, G50
Ryan, Halford R., F1815

Sabath, Adolph J., F890
Sabin, Francene, I21
Sachar, Abram L., F1916, F2056
Sadler, Christine, F92
Sakanishi, Shio, F27
Salisbury, Harrison E., B458
Salmond, John A., F1058, F1209,
    F1332

Sandak, Cass R., I80
Sandifer, Durward V., F1546
Sandifer, Irene Reiterman, F28
Sankey, Alice, D267, F1817
Sarbanes, Paul S., F2001
Scarlett, William, B332
Schain, Josephine, E39
Scharf, Lois, F29, F93, F1273-75,
    F1479, F1723
Schary, Dore, H90, J25
Scherman, Katharine, E42
Schick, Frank L., A16
Schlesinger, Arthur M., Jr., B424,
    E72, F223, F350-52, F470, F891,
    F1133, F1210, F1480, F2008
Schneider, Claudine, F2002
Schneiderman, Rose, F1134, F1211
Schorr, Daniel, F353, F892
Schriftgiesser, Karl, F94
Schroeder, Eileen E., F95
Schuck, Joyce, F893
Schutz, Susan Polis, B511
Schwarz, Jordan A., F1135
Schwimmer, Rosika, G36
Scime, Joy A., F1276
Scobie, Ingrid Winther, F894
Scott, Anne Firor, B510
Scott, Janet, F471
Scott, Jennifer, I47
Seagraves, Eleanor R., F354, F379
Sealander, Judith, B519
Seale, William, F895
Sears, John F., F355
Sec, J37
Seder, Florence M., F1277
Seeber, Frances M., A15, F1278
Severen, Bill, F896
Shaffer, Ellen, F897
Shaffer, Susan, H56
Shalett, Sidney, F342, F467
Shapiro, Alan, F31
Shapiro, Herbert, F1212
Shattuck, Frances M., F1728
Shaw, Albert, F679
Sheean, Vincent, E73
Sheed, Wilfrid, F2059
Sheerin, John B., F1379
Shelton, Isabelle, F1213
Shelton, Willard, F1724
Sheridan, Michael, G83
Sherman, E. David, F356

Sherwood, Robert E., F898, H51
Shivvers, Martha E., F96
Shore, Rima, F162
Short, Clarice, E74
Sibley, John, F357
Siegel, Mary-Ellen, F156
Silver, Philip, F2060
Simon, Gene, G84
Simpkins, Arthur Lee, F1163
Simsarian, James, F1545, F1547,
    F1557
Sine, Richard L., F2003
Singer, Kurt, F1482
Sister Mary Hugh, S.M., E147
Sitkoff, Harvard, F1214-16
Slocum, William J., F881
Smart, James R., F1802, H6, H36
Smith, A. Merriman, F899, F1918
Smith, Don, F97
Smith, Elaine M., F1217
Smith, Gerald L.K., F682, F900,
    F1725
Smith, Helena Huntington, F472,
    F683-84
Smith, Hilda Worthington, F1279,
    J38
Smith, Huston, B470
Smith, Lillian, E158
Smith, Margaret Chase, I81
Smith, Marie, F901
Smith, Rembert Gilman, F685
Smith, Richard C., F1919
Smithsonian Institution. Traveling
    Exhibition Service, F1988
Snowman, Daniel, F30
Snyder, Louis L., F158
Soames, Mary, F1016
Sobol, Louis, F1920
Sochen, June, F1280-81
Sokolsky, George, F1921
Somers, Florence, F1808
Sosna, Morton, F1218
Southern Conference for Human
    Welfare, D82
Spacks, Patricia Meyer, F1809
Spence, Benjamin A., F1018
Spencer, Gwen Morton, F1019
Spetter, I., G73
Spingarn, Arthur B., F1897
Spottswood, Stephen Gill, F1897
Springer, Gertrude, F1333

Stadd, Arlene, J26
Stallone, Carol N., F121
Stansell, Christine, F386
Stapleton, Jean, F1939
Steele, A.T., E97
Stegner, Wallace, B482a
Stein, Hannah, G33
Stein, Shifra, B81a
Steinberg, Alfred, F31-32, F159, F1726
Steinem, Gloria, F1939
Steinkraus, Herman, F1887
Stern, Elizabeth Gertrude, F687
Sternsher, Bernard, B519
Stevens, Austin, F1369
Stevenson, Adlai E., F359, F1059, F1483, F1727, F1818, F1863, F1922-25, F2008, F2061-62, H28
St. George, Judith, I82
Stidger, William L., F360, F474
Stiles, Lela, B417, F475
Stirling, Nora, F797
Stix, Thomas L., F1810
Stoddard, Hope, F98
Stoessinger, John George, F1484
Stokely, James, F1040
Stokes, Anson Phelps, F1219, F1370
Stokes, Thomas L., F1477
Stone, Kirk, F99
Stones, Betty, F1409
Storey, Walter Rendell, F361
Storm, Carson, F362
Stout, Wesley, F1136
Straight, Michael, F1334
Strayer, Martha, F689, F1220
Strom, Sharon Hartman, F29
Strong, Tracy B., F1020
Strout, Richard, F2005
Stuart, Campbell, D198
Studebaker, J.W., D65
Sullivan, Michael John, F364
Sullivan, Wilson, I83
Swain, Martha H., F1282-83
Swift, Hildegarde Hoyt, B485
Swing, Raymond, F1060
Syse, Glenna, J26

Tabouis, Genevieve, F902
Tananbaum, Duane, F1593
Tarbell, Ida M., E26, G16
Taubman, Howard, F1811

Taylor, Ethel R., I84
Taylor, Helene Scherff, E75
Taylor, Millicent, E134
Taylor, Paul C., F476
Tead, Ordway, E51
Teague, Michael, F366
Teichmann, Howard, F367
Teltsch, Kathleen, F1485
Tenney, Elizabeth Mackintosh, F1662
Tetreault, Mary Kay, B230a-b, F2063
Thant, U, F1926
Thayer, Judy, I85
Theoharis, Athan G., F1336
Thomas, Bert, F1021
Thomas, Henry, I86
Thompson, Charles A.H., F1728
Thompson, Darryl, F369
Thompson, Dorothy, F692
Thompson, Era Bell, B411a, G69
Tice, D.J., F187
Tierney, Thomas, J4
Tierney, Tom, I22
Tillett, Gladys Avery, F1487
Tillett, Paul, F1693
Tinling, Marion, F371
Tobias, John, B483
Todhunter School for Girls, F273
Tolley, Howard, F1595
Tooley, Jo Ann, F866
Toor, Rachel, I23
Toperoff, Sam, J24
Topp, Sylvia, F17
Tor, Regina, B25, B505, B532-35
Torres, Louis, F374-75
Traub, Carol G., I87
Trent, Nan, E150
Trohan, Walter, F376, F905
Trotter, Zoe Pauline, F1663
Trueheart, Charles, F2009
Truett, Randle Bond, F906
Truman, Harry S., F907-8, F1488, F1664
Truman, Margaret, F908-10
Trumbull, Robert, E98
Tufty, Esther Van Wagoner, F1061
Tugwell, Rexford G., F377, F479, F911-12
Tull, Ellen, I73
Tuller, Carol, D134

Tully, Grace, F913
Turim, Gayle, F866
Tuve, Jeanette E., F1284
Tyndale, Hall, F697
Tyska, Cynthia A., F378

Ullmann, Liv, F1939
Unger, Arthur, G99, H68
United States. Congress. Joint
    Committee on Tax Evasion and
    Avoidance, F365
United States. Federal Emergency
    Relief Administration, D30
United States. National Archives and
    Records Administration, A9
United States. National Park Service,
    F117
Urquhart, Brian, F1158, F1447, F2010

Van Deman, Ruth, F699
Vandenbroucke, Russell, H69
Verdoodt, Albert, F1600
Vernoff, Edward, F162
Vidal, Gore, F1729, F2065
Villard, Oswald Garrison, F700-701
Villareal, Maximiano Marmito, F702
Viscardi, Henry, B465
Vishinsky, Andrei, D176
Vonnegut, Kurt, J27
Voss, Carl Hermann, F1669

Wadsworth, Virginia Evarts, I89
Waggenspack, Beth M., F1815
Waldrop, Frank, F1023
Waldrup, Carole Chandler, F100
Walker, Turnley, B409, F381
Wallace, Henry A., F914
Wallace, Robert, F1930
Walley, Dean, B508
Walsh, Edward, H64
Walter, Claire, F2066
Walton, Richard J., F915, F1731
Wamboldt, Helen Jane, F1816, G71
Wander, Meghan Robinson, F240,
    F421, F1044
Wandersee, Winifred D., F101, F1339
Ward, A.C., F163
Ward, Barbara, E141
Ward, Geoffrey C., F33-34, F382-86
Ware, Susan, F481-82, F916, F1285-
    86, F2011

Warren, Ruth, F1063
Waterhouse, Helen, F917, F1931
Watkins, T.H., F1140
Watrous, Hilda R., D1-2, F483,
    F2012
Watson, Lee Rae, F387
Weart, William G., F1667
Weaver, Robert C., F1222
Wechsler, James A., F1340, F1931
Weeks, Edward, E76
Weidt, Maryann N., I24
Weil, Ann, I25
Weil, Martin, F1024, F1492
Weiler, A.H., H77
Weintraub, Benjamin, F2067
Weiser, Marjorie P.K., F918, F1668
Weiss, Katherine Sigler, F705
Weiss, Max, F1341
Weiss, Nancy J., F1223
Weissman, Michaele, F1261
Welch, Robert, F1932
Wells, Debby, I90
Wells, H.G., F706
Welshimer, Helen, D97
Welter, Barbara, F919
West, J.B., F920
Westin, Jean, F921
Whedon, Peggy, G106
Whipple, Wayne, F707
White, Betty, F922
White, Graham, F1140
White, Leonard, B334
White, Lyman Cromwell, B452
White, Poppy Cannon, F741, F1161,
    F1933
White, Robert M., II, F945
White, Walter, F1225-27
White, William S., F923-24
White, W.L., E60
White House Conference on Rural
    Education, B322, F1141
Whitehead, James L., F102
Whitehurst, Ben, F709
Whiteman, Marjorie M., F1601
Whiting, Frances, F389
Whitman, Alden, F1493
Whitman, John Pratt, F1142
Whitney, Sharon, I26-27
Wier, Alison, F154
Wilkins, Roy, F1228-29, F1897,
    F1934

Williams, Aubrey, F1343, F1927
Williams, Barbara, F1287
Williams, Charl Ormond, F1288, G70
Williams, David J., J28
Williams, Dennis A., F391
Williams, Paul, F1586
Wilson, Florence Yoder, G13
Wilson, James Q., F1697
Wilson, Vincent J., F170
Winer, Linda, J26
Winfield, Betty Houchin, F926-28
Winkler, Karen J., F2013
Winner, David, I28
Winslow, Mary N., F1029
Winslow, Thacher, B201
Wise, James Waterman, B233, B330
Wise, Stephen S., F1669
Wisehart, M.K., G14
Witty, Paul A., I92
Wolf, Ann M., F711, F929
Wolfgarth, Maureen, I93
Wolfskill, George, J34
Wollen, Carol, G58
Wolley, A.E., F1759
Woloch, Nancy, F1289
Wolters, Raymond, F1230
Women's City Club of New York, F461
Wood, Wilma H., F1292
Woodbury, Clarence, F393
Woodruff, Caroline S., F713
Woods, Catherine, F1066

Woods, Katherine, E28, E33, E40
Woolf, S.J., G7, G17, G45, G59, G61
Woolley, Mary E., F1293
World Peace Foundation, F433
World Youth Congress, F1347
Wotkyns, Eleanor Roosevelt, F394
Wreszin, Michael, F1344
Wright, Emily L., F395-97
Wright, James L., F714
Wyandt, Frieda, G9
Wyatt, Euphemia Van Rensselaer, E29
Wyatt, Marshall, F327
Wyman, David S., F1026-27

Yarnell, Allen, F1734
Yerby, Frank, F1163
Yorck, Ruth E., F1495
Young, G. Aubrey, E52
Young, G. Gordon, F715
Young, Mort, F1936
Young, Rose, B122
Youngs, J. William T., F36
Yust, Walter, B347

Zangrando, Joanna Schneider, F1231
Zangrando, Robert L., F1231-32
Zarina, F1671
Zelman, Patricia G., F1294
Zinsser, Caroline, F1143
Zwierlein, Frederick J., F1377

Subject Index

AAUN, *see* American Association for
   the United Nations
abortion, C135, C350
Abzug, Bella, F1978, F2041
accidents in the home, D148
Acheson, Dean, C220, C227, C266,
   D211, F1430-31, F1629
ACLU (American Civil Liberties
   Union), F1392
ADA, *see* Americans for Democratic
   Action
Adamic, Louis, F930
Adams, Abigail, F1872, I76
Adams, Josephine Truslow, C285,
   F820
Addams, Jane, B127, D51, F700,
   F1042, F1957
Adenauer, Konrad, C342
Adler, Cyrus, B211
adoption, C138, C155, C163, C180,
   C184, C187, C210
The Adventure of America (Tobias and
   Hoffecker), B483
AFL-CIO (American Federation of
   Labor-Congress of Industrial
   Organizations), D240, D264, F1068
Africa, B484, C329, C343, D180; *see
   also* under names of countries
African Academy of Arts and
   Research, D180
Afro-Americans, *see* Black Americans
agriculture, *see* farms and farming
Air Transport Association, F602
air travel, B143, B187, F471, F602,
   F615, F671, F751, G29, G209

alcohol and alcoholism, C97, C129,
   C154, C313, C349, F249, F524,
   G94d, I24
Alexander, Jane, H67
Alexander, Margaret Walker, F1154
Alexander, Will W., F717, F1040
Algeria, C346
Alice's Adventures in Wonderland
   (Carroll), B211
aliens, B219, B247
Allen, Florence Ellinwood, F1284
Allenswood, F202, I27
Alliance for Progress, G105
American Association for the United
      Nations (AAUN),
   -ER, tributes to, F1822, F1848,
      F1868, F1889, F1892, F1928,
      F1983
   -ER's activities with, B418, B427-
      32, B434, B440, B491, D215-16,
      D225, D227, D237, D249, D260,
      D265, F1450, F1603-9, F1627,
      F2018, G94k, G94m, G94p
American Civil Liberties Union,
   F1392
American Federation of Labor-
   Congress of Industrial
   Organizations (AFL-CIO), D240,
   D264, F1068
American Friends Service
   Committee, F1094, F1794, F1906,
   G94m
American Indians, *see* Native
   Americans
American Legion, F978

American Newspaper Guild, F1068,
  F1739, F1783, F1788, F1800
American Peace Award, B40, B45,
  F413, F433, F461
The American Presidency (Laski), B228
American Student Union, C98
American Unity and Asia (Buck), B251
American Youth (Winslow and
  Davidson), B201
American Youth Congress, B202, C98,
  F1298, F1336
  -congressional hearings on, F595,
  F1301-2, F1306, F1322-23, F1335,
  F1337, F1344
  -ER's support of, B220, B224, C238,
  C242, F595, F1058, F1297, F1307,
  F1309, F1313, F1316-17, F1322-24,
  F1328, F1330, F1334-35, F1337,
  F1339-40, F1342, F1345-46
  -meetings of, D86, F1159, F1297,
  F1304, F1307, F1313, F1317,
  F1330, F1334, F1346, F1753, G47
American Youth Today (Gould), B202
Americans for Democratic Action
  (ADA), B421, B450
  -ER on, B356, C163, C284, D221
  -ER, tributes to, F1724, F1821,
  F1865, F1911, F1952
  -ER's activities with, B424, B443,
  D192, D199, D209, D221, D223,
  D229-30, D235-36, D241, D247,
  F1673, F1679, F1681, F1687,
  F1714, F2053
America's Town Meeting of the Air,
  B382
Anderson, Marian, D94, F1152-53,
  F1162, F1164, F1169, F1187, F1195,
  F1197, F1214, F1219-20, F1849
Anderson, Mary, F1029
Anne Alive! (Fayerweather), B103
Anti-lynching Bill, *see* Costigan-
  Wagner Anti-lynching Bill
anti-Semitism, C99, C155, C157, C295,
  F638, F1637
Arab nations, C320, D224, G84
Arthurdale, F554c, F1071, F1077,
  F1081, F1083-85, F1091-92, F1104,
  F1107-8, F1121, F1127, F1129,
  F1132-33, F1135-37, F1139, F1142
  -criticism of, F1073, F1075, F1084,
  F1091, F1103, F1110

  -ER on, B120, B132, B139, C14,
  C137, F1071, F1110
  -ER's visits to, C11, C14, C26,
  F1070, F1076, F1092, F1107,
  F1137
  -school, F1073, F1077, F1079-80
  see also subsistence homesteads
artificial insemination, C155
arts and crafts, ER's appreciation of,
  B241, C18, C278, C334, D43,
  D101, F251, F298, F361, F395,
  F817, F1087, F1112, F1119-20; *see
  also* Val-Kill Industries
As He Saw It (Elliott Roosevelt, son),
  B324, C160
Asia, B19, B251, C244, D223, D232,
  E84-98, G74, G85; *see also* under
  names of countries
Associated Country Women of the
  World, D57
atheists and atheism, ER on, C181,
  C236, C260, C304
Atlanta, Ga., F1123
atom bomb, *see* nuclear weapons
atomic energy, D239, F1768; *see also*
  nuclear weapons
Atwood, William, H1, H13
*The Autobiography of Eleanor
  Roosevelt* (ER), E135-41
The Azores, C343

Babies, Just Babies, F1775, F1778,
  F1787
Bachrach, Louis F., F216
Backstairs at the White House, H65
Baillargeon, Patricia, F1604
Baldwin, Roger, F1462
Bankhead, Tallulah, J15
Barden, William, F1371
Barden Bill, F1349-92
Barnett, Etta Moten, F1154
Baruch, Bernard M., B408, C219
  -Arthurdale and, F1071, F1081,
  F1104, F1135
  -ER's relationship with, F1081,
  F1135
  -in fiction, J15
Bataan, C121
Battle, George Gordon, F1034
Beasley, Maurine, F925
Beaton, Cecil, F934

Beauty Behind Barbed Wire (Eaton),
    B399
Bellamy, Ralph, H90
Bemelmans, Ludwig, B454
Ben-Gurion, David, C333, F1857
Ben-Zvi, Itzhak, F1857
Benny, Jack, J12
Berlin, C346
Bethune, Mary McLeod, F1849
  -ER's relationship with, F1150-51,
    F1154, F1168, F1177, F1214,
    F1217, F1222, F1295
Bible and Bible study, C188, C226,
    C259, C284, C288
Bierly, Kenneth, F1676
Bill of Rights, B218, B233, D104, D122
Bingham, Jonathan B., F2026
Biography (television program), H70
birth control, C186, C300
Birth of a Baby (motion picture), F555,
    F692
Black, Hugo, F2067
Black, Ruby A., F607, F871, F1117
Black, Shirley Temple, F1451
Black Americans, B267, B269, B314,
    F1148, F1154
  -contributions of, D42, D48, D64,
    D103
  -education of, B207, C127, D42,
    D62, D64, D94, D151, F1159,
    F1213
  -employment of, D141, D151
  -ER on, B267, B270, B273, B349,
    B359, B411, B445, C127, C188,
    C228, C301, D81, E60, F1197, G40
  -ER's prejudice against, F902,
    F1170, F1222
  -ER's public appearances with,
    F1158, F1191, F1204, F1206
  -in the military, C106, C121, C139,
    F1004, F1165, F1182, F1190,
    F1201, F1205
  -New Deal programs and, C7
  -racial equality of, C94-96, C105,
    C125, C130, C132-33, C135, C148,
    C165, C169, C176, C182, C246,
    C275, C280-81, C286, C304-5,
    C325, C332, C350, G69, G94j,
    I65, I77
    --ER's efforts for racial equality
      of, B263, B267, B298, B316,

B332, B373, B469, C241, D48,
    D64, D93-94, D104, D141,
    D147, D151, D174, D193,
    D209, D220, D223, D265,
    F902, F1028-29, F1031, F1044,
    F1047, F1144-1232, F1648,
    F2029; *see also* Roosevelt,
    Eleanor--criticism and ridicule
    of
  -United Nations and, F1212,
    F1447-48, F1635, G69, G72
  -World War II and, B251, D105,
    F1004, F1146, F1157, F1164,
    F1199, F1201, F1227, F1229
  see also March on Washington
    (1941); Costigan-Wagner Anti-
    lynching Bill
Blatch, Harriot Stanton, F1272
Blevins, Frank, F327
Bloom, Sol, D190, F732
Bogart, Humphrey, J15
Boettiger, Anna Roosevelt, *see*
    Roosevelt, Anna
Boettiger, John R. (son-in-law), F188
Bok, Edward, B40
Bok Prize, *see* American Peace
    Award
bomb shelters, C326, C341, C344-45
Bonus March and Bonus Marchers,
    F1086, F1114, F1138
boxing, C347
Boys' Club of America, C189
Brandeis, Louis, B234
  -in fiction, J13
Brandeis University, F313, F392,
    F1670, F2018, F2037, F2056
Bricker Amendment, F1582, F1593
Bridges, Harry, C100, F1612
Bromley, Dorothy Dunbar, G46
Brotherhood of Sleeping Car Porters,
    F1204
Brough, James, H62
Broun, Heywood Hale, H62
Browder, Earl, C285, F820
Brown, Claude, F1156
Brown, Darrel E., F696
Browne, Mary K., B290
Brutal Mandate (Lowenstein), B484
Bryn Mawr College, F345
Buck, Pearl S., B251, D114, F797
Buckley, William F., Jr., E158

Budenz, Louis, F1640
Bugbee, Emma, F191, F730, F748
Bullitt, William, C182
Bulloch family, F390
Bunche, Ralph, C347, F1447
Bush, Barbara, F729
Butler, Hugh, C126
Butler, Sarah Schuyler, F410
"By Eleanor Roosevelt," B131
Byrd, Richard E., D72
Byrnes, James, C305

Calder, Linnea, F266
Calvert, Paul, F663
Camp Fire Girls, D87
Camp Tera, B97, C29, F1338
camping, C47
Campobello (as Roosevelt home), B456,
    B501, C30, F191, F247, F259, F266,
    F285-86, F319, F352, F371
Canadian-U.S. relations, G57
cancer, C164, C319, D257
Canfield, Cass, F1817
Cannon, Poppy, F1161
capital punishment, C233, C245, C324
The Captains and the Kings (Helm),
    B414
Caroli, Betty Boyd, F903
Carter, Rosalynn, F725, F735, F880
Castro, Fidel, C321, C337
Catholics and Catholicism, F692,
    F1614
    -ER as an anti-Catholic, F1364,
    F1376
    -ER as critic of, F2016
    -ER on, C190, C253, C301
    -schools, federal aid to, F1349-92;
    see also Roosevelt, Eleanor--
    criticism and ridicule of
Catt, Carrie Chapman, F662, F1254
CCC, see Civilian Conservation Corps
censorship, C104, C119, C233, C313,
    C332, C340
census, C205, D108
Chambers, Whittaker, F1640
Chandler, Douglas, F312
Chaney, Mayris, F944, F950, F996
Chang, P.C., F1497, F1597
character, ER on, B64, B72, B102,
    C275

charities, B105, B117, B133, C314,
    D15
Chiang Kai-shek, C254, C332
Chiang Kai-shek, Mme., C117,
    C162, C184, C246, F590, F614,
    F797, F860, F963, F1642
Child Labor Amendment, B141,
    C36, C45, C72, D5, F1078
child rearing, ER on, B72, B75, B90,
    B102, B115, B170, C105, C107,
    C110-11, C137, C139, C141, C145,
    C149-50, C152-53, C155-57, C159,
    C161-63, C165, C170, C172, C174-
    76, C178-81, C183, C190, C193,
    C201, C207, C210, C213, C229,
    C269-70, C290, C293, C322, C345,
    C347
childbearing, ER on, C103, C112-13,
    C116, C120, C124, C143, C145,
    C274
children, B72, B75, B78, B90, B98-
    99, B102, B104, B110, B115,
    B170, B212, B323, B331, B426,
    B487, B499, C1, C40, C99-100,
    C113, C116, C147, C152, C208,
    C261, C279, C317, C325, D35,
    D88, D115, D124, D159, F1028,
    F1244, G70, I36, I41, I90
    -books and reading and, B66, B73,
    B77, B195, B479, C147, D267,
    G102
    -health of, B110, B124, B146,
    B246, D21, D29, D46, D69,
    D144; see also health care--
    mothers and infants and
    -home life of, B66, B68, B85, B89,
    B193, B389, C51, C62, C314,
    D29, D75
    see also education; Child Labor
    Amendment; Roosevelt, Eleanor-
    -children of
China, B19, B143, C121, C205,
    C208, C249, C279, C288, C297,
    C334, C341, C348, G97
Christian Science Monitor, C296
Christmas,
    -as celebrated by Roosevelt family,
    B31, B80, B86, B144, C12, C34,
    C315, C327, C339, F362, F847,
    G13

-ER on, B11, B31, B80, B86, B144-45, B163, B203, C315, C327, C339, D77, D113, E42
-ER's customs, C317, F316, F332
Christmas: A Story (ER), E42
A Christmas Carol (Dickens), H31
Churchill, Clementine, F941, F958, F1016
Churchill, Sarah, B498, F1814
Churchill, Winston S., B415, B503, C102, C160, C177, C210, C212, C297, C299, D179, F904, F930, F958, F977, F980, F1016, F1664, H27
-in fiction, J23
CIO (Congress of Industrial Organizations), B403, D161
Citizenship Institute, G47; *see also* American Youth Congress-- meetings of
civil liberties, B437, D104, D122, D219
civil rights movement, *see* Black Americans--racial equality of
civil service laws, C325
Civilian Conservation Corps (CCC), B157, B201, C6-7, C63, C69, C86, F1064
Clapp, Elsie, F1104
Clapper, Raymond, B215, F942
Clemens, Samuel L., B361
Clinton, Hillary Rodham, F749, F785, F815, F841, F880, F887, F892
Cochran, Jacqueline, F975
Cole, Mrs. Frances, H77
college attendance, *see* education-- higher
Collier, Fred, F200
Collier-Thomas, Bettye, F1177
Columbia Syndicate, B88
comic books, ER on, C258-59
Commission on Civil Rights, *see* President's Commission on Civil Rights
Commission on Human Rights, B327, B345, B350, B354-55, B367, B377, B391-92, C208, D206, D210, F1394, F1452, F1456, F1458, F1460, F1489, F1496-1602
Commission on the Status of Women, *see* President's Commission on the Status of Women

Committee on the Investigation of Un-American Activities, *see* United States. Congress. House. Committee on the Investigation of Un-American Activities
Common Sense, D132
Commonwealth College, F605
Communists and communism, B470, C182, C188, C208, F744, F1612, F1614-15, F2016, F2024
-ER identified with, C222, F534, F605, F682, F685, F771, F813, F839, F1212, F1309-10, F1317, F1328, F1331, F1335, F1342, F1464, F1647, F1676, F1688, F1788, F1800
-ER on, B191, B353, B462, B469, B482, B518, C66, C76, C95, C116, C122, C144, C166, C171, C173-75, C183-85, C187-88, C191, C195, C202, C205, C223, C231, C238, C240-45, C247, C249, C253, C257, C265, C270, C272, C333, C335, C344, C346, D92, D207, D219, D230, D254, D264, F690, F1110, F1297, F1625, F1638, F1640, F1665, F1709, F1714, G77, G101, G103-4
compulsory service for youth, B230, B303, C92, C115, C127, C138, C148, C175, D199, F1298, F1319; *see also* draft (military)
Conference on Emergency Needs of Women, D30, F1118
Conference on the Cause and Cure of War, D32, D50, D54
Congress (U.S.), ER on, C17, C45, C92
Congress of Industrial Organizations, B403, D161
Congress of Youth, F1307
Connally, Tom, F1476
conscientious objectors, C107, C129, C146, C212, C347, F961, F1664
conservation in wartime, B235, C84, C102, C104-5, C109-10, C113-16, C118-20, C122, C124, C127-31, C133, C138, C140, C142, C144
conservation of natural resources, B373, B485, C65, C73, D58

consumers, B121, B177, C67, C73
Cook, Blanche Wiesen, B48, F783,
　F1299
Cook, Nancy, B70, C18, F5, F212,
　F215, F311, F320, F328, F395-96,
　F478, G13, H50
　-in fiction, J10
Coolidge, Calvin, B50
Cooper, Ethel A., F750
Cooperative League, B171
Corr, Maureen, F203
corruption, ER on, C302, C348
Costigan-Wagner Anti-lynching Bill,
　D93, F1046, F1181, F1223, F1228,
　F1232
Cousins, Norman, B259
Cowles, Anna Roosevelt, F333
Crawford, Joan, J15
credit unions, B274
cremation, C222
crime, ER on, B200, C28, D44; *see
　also* juvenile deliquency
Crusade in Europe (radio program),
　D213
Cuba, B480, C321, C325, C344, G105
Cuomo, Mario M., F1960
Curie, Marie, C107
curiosity, ER on, B126
Czechoslovakia, B208

Dabney, Virginius, B267, F1218
Dag Hammarskjold (Lash), B478
Dall, Anna Roosevelt, *see* Roosevelt,
　Anna
Dall, Curtis, F225, F2026
Daniel, Margaret Truman, F910
Daniels, Jonathan, F752
Daniels, Josephus, F209, F885
DAR, *see* Daughters of the American
　Revolution
Daughters of the American Depression,
　F1082
Daughters of the American Revolution
　(DAR), C240, C299, C345, F1187
　-ER's resignation from, F572, F1152-
　53, F1162, F1164, F1169, F1176,
　F1195, F1219-20
Davies, Marion, C220
Davis, Elmer, D235
Davis, James J., B219
Dawson, William, C331

death, ER on, C223, C279
Debnam, W.E., G79
De Gaulle, Charles, C210, C320,
　F931
demagogues, ER on, C326
democracy, B493, D92, F1642
　-as alternative to communism,
　B348, B469, B482, B518, C166,
　C191, C244, D264, E41, E43,
　G101, G104
　-ER as a democrat, E52, F502,
　F1379
　-minorities and, D81-82, D103,
　D151, D189, D193, D209, D223
　-nature of, B12, B305, B469, C76,
　D110, E44, E49, E51
　-role of citizens in a, B89, B191,
　B193, B206, B217, B228, B247-
　49, B254, B293, B319, B351,
　B373, B384, B389, B433, B451,
　B466, C71, C78, C80, D76, D81,
　D123, D159, D165, D168, D189,
　D207, D227, E46-48, E50, E52,
　F322, F1197, F2035, G103
　-spirituality and, B294, D255, E43
　-U.S. as a democracy, B348, B470,
　C153, C161, C166, C183, C188,
　C258, D76, D82, D103, D125,
　D160, D193, D204, D206, D212-
　13, D217, D227, D233, D266,
　G76
　-in the world, D116, D150, D154,
　D200, D206-7, D213, D223,
　D255, D266, G61, G76
Democracy Reborn (Wallace), B294
Democratic Advisory Council, F2062
Democratic Digest, D55, F1278
Democratic National Convention
　-1912, C322, F441
　-1920, C322
　-1924, F402, F414, F442, F473, G3
　-1932, C322
　-1936, D55
　-1940, C322, D99, F615, F682,
　F753, F818, F857, F870, F875,
　F896, F915, G49
　-1952, C322, D222, F1774
　-1956, C322, D245, F1684, F1720,
　F1728
　-1960, C318, C321, D262, F1674,
　F1703, F1729, F1899

-1964, F1925
Democratic Party, B42, B49, B326, C84, C128, C133, C138, C171, C186, C206, C234, C270, C276, C300, C325, C338, D4, D144, D181-82, F473
Democratic Party. Women's Division, B43, B60, B351, C86, D6, D55, D98, D117, F400-401, F414, F451, F458, F463, F473; *see also* Women's National Democratic Club
Democratic Party (N.Y.) Democratic Committee. Women's Division, B42, B48, D79, F454, F486
Democratic Women's Day, B351, D90, D98, D131, D144, D146, F531-32, F626
De Sapio, Carmine, C269, C330, C340, F1683, F1712
De Seversky, Alexander, C108
Dewey, Frances, F495, F497
De Witt, William, reviews of his writings, E99-104
Dewson, Mary W. (Molly), B150, D373, F401, F425, F481-82, F1124, F1247, F1278
The Diary of a Young Girl (Frank), B400
Dickerman, Marion, B70, C18, F5, F212, F215, F395-96, F478, H50
-in fiction, J10
Dickerson, Nancy, H82
Dies, Martin, C256, F986, F1301-2, F1305-6, F1337
Dies Committee, *see* United States. Congress. House. Committee on the Investigation of Un-American Activities
Dirkson, Everett, J17
disarmament, B182, C200, C345, D261, F1638
discrimination, B247, B469, C135, C152, C286, D143, D193, F1149, F1153, F1158-59, F1167, G40, G69
District of Columbia, *see* Washington, D.C.
divorce, ER on, B164, C97, C101, C121, C125, C136, C141-42, C151, C154, C206, C254, C314, C338, C340, C342, F555, F692, G94f
Dixon-Yates Project, C264

Dolgin, Phyllis, H26
domestic workers, B69, B136, B342, C37, C55, C67, C71, C131, C141, C152, C165, C178, C306, F902, F1170, G1
Dominican Republic, C290
Douglas, Helen Gahagan, C273, F894, F980, F1678
-ER, recollections of, F6
Douglas, Melvyn, F950, F980, F1045
Douglas, William O., F2067
Dow, Dorothy, F740
draft (military), B239, B244, B303, C91-92, C104, C108, C110-12, C117, C121-22, C124, C129, C132-33, C136, C139, C144, C158, C180, C185, C211, D136, G89; see also women--in the military
Draft Commission on Freedom of Information, F1394, F1509, F1512
Draft Convention on the Supression of the Traffic in Persons and of the Exploitation of the Prostitution of Others, F1410
Dubner, Nancy, F225
Du Bois, W.E.B., F1447
Dubowski, Donald Edward, F1067
Ducas, Dorothy, F748
Dulles, John Foster, C266, C296, G94i
Dunne, Irene, C292

Earhart, Amelia, C204, F671, F836, F975
-in fiction, J19
Early, Stephen, F519, F1214
-in fiction, J17
Easter, B110, B147, D124
Eban, Abba, H35
economic policies and programs, C3, C72, C85, C117, C299-300, D17
Edison, Mrs. Thomas A., G10
education, B64-66, B118-19, B138, B155, B165, B248, B292, B368, B384, B451, C67-68, C85, C136, C154, C169, C199, C205, C300, C302, C318, D11, D22-23, D58, D67, D143-44, D250, D272, F322, F1303, F1532, G70
-financial support for, D166, D253

-higher, B232, B287, B362, B406, C109, C115, C120, C124, C156, D163, C167, C188, C196, C204, C225, C302, C349, D171, D189
-rural, B322, D156-57, D162
-special, D38
see also schools; teachers; women--education of; Black Americans--education of
Eichelberger, Clark M., F2058, H38
Eichelberger, Robert L., F947
Einstein, Albert, F962
Eisenhower, Dwight D., C260, C329
-as President, C239, C248, C254, C265, C272, C278, C282, C285, C303, C321, C324, F1593, G94i, G103
--ER's criticism of, C289, C291, C293, D241, D247, F42
Eisenhower, Mamie D., C263, C281, C306, F867
Eisler, Hanns, C171, C214, C252, F923, F1306
Eleanor and Franklin (Lash), F756, F861, F879, H61, H67
Eleanor and Franklin (television program), F922
Eleanor Clubs, C109, F902, F1175, F1200, F1208
Eleanor: First Lady of the World (television program), H68
Eleanor in Her Own Words (television program), H69
Eleanor Roosevelt (Hickok), F223
Eleanor Roosevelt Centennial, F7, F20, F35, F1937-2013, H59, H88
-centennial celebrations, F1945, F1947-48, F1960-61, F1965, F1967, F1984-86, F1998, F2000
Eleanor Roosevelt Centennial Commission, F1945, F1959, F2006
Eleanor Roosevelt Center at Val-Kill, H63, H73, F379; *see also* Val-Kill
Eleanor Roosevelt, 1884-1933 (Cook), F386, F783
Eleanor Roosevelt Farm Women's Association, F1079
Eleanor Roosevelt: Her Life in Pictures (Harrity and Martin), E117
Eleanor Roosevelt Institute for Cancer Research, D257

Eleanor Roosevelt Memorial Foundation, F1818, F1833, F1837, F1848, F1860-61, F1863-64, F1873, F1878-79, F1894, F1914, F1923,
Eleanor Roosevelt National Historic Site, *see* Val-Kill--as Eleanor Roosevelt National Historic Site
Eleanor Roosevelt Oral History Project, H57
The Eleanor Roosevelt Story (motion picture), F459, H77
The Eleanor Roosevelt We Remember (Douglas), H79
Eleanor Roosevelt's Book of Common Sense Etiquette (ER), E149-50
Eleanor: The Years Alone (Lash), F1721
electoral college, C325, C331
Elizabeth (of England), C113, F963; *see also* George VI and Elizabeth (of England)
Elizabeth II (of England), C243
Elman, David, H48
Emergency Peace Campaign, D72
Emerson, Faye, G94o
employment, B213, B292, B305-6, B308, B310, C70, C80, C89, C199, C335, D163, D169, F1090, F1146, F1224, F1229; *see also* Black Americans--employment of; handicapped persons--employment of; older Americans--employment of; women--employment of
Encampment for Citizenship, B493
Ennis, John, I48
Equal Rights Amendment, B325, B381, D188, F408, F1061, F1237, F1239, F1249, F1256, F1259, F1978
ethics, ER on, C108, C169, C325-26, C331
etiquette, ER on, B29, B189, B438, B487, B531, C318, E149-50

Face the Nation (television program), G87, H16
Fadiman, Clifton, D101
Fair Employment Practices Commission, F1058
A Fair World for All (Fisher), B401
faith healers, C286

Fala, C166, C199, C213, C307, C336, F208, J6, J9

Farley, James A., C168, C194, C246, C322, F552, F761, F891

farms and farming, B114, B120, B194, B205, C39, C46, C59, C71, C87, C104, C116, C190, C270, C299-300, C309, C329, C346, D57, D100, D258, D265, G32

Fascists and fascism, C66, C76, C95, C122, D194

Faubus, Orval E., C305

FBI, C175, C257, C308, F1208
-ER, files on, F794, F1200, F1336
see also Hoover, J. Edgar--ER, relationship with

FDIC (Federal Deposit Insurance Corporation), F1064

F.D.R. (television program), F791, F1736, H9, H17

F.D.R. Columnist (Carmichael), B338

F.D.R.: His Personal Letters, B339, B352, B369

FDR Speaks (Commager), B474

fear, ER on, B183, B206

Federal Art Project, F1112, F1118-19

Federal Deposit Insurance Corporation (FDIC), F1064

Federal Emergency Relief Administration, F1111

Federal Theatre Project, C68, F1087, F1096

Federal Writers' Project, F1115, F1125

Federation of Business Women, D80

Feiner, Ben, Jr., F48, F791

feminism, see Roosevelt, Eleanor--as a feminist

Ferber, Edna, D117

Ferebee, Dorothy Boulding, F1154

Ferraro, Geraldine, F1938, F1991

Ferris, Helen, F1817
-reviews of her writings, E77-83, E142-48

Feuchtwanger, Lion, F12

Feuchtwanger, Marta, F12

Fields, Alonzo, F763

Fifth Amendment, C246

Finland, F987

Finletter, Thomas K., F1683

first ladies, see Roosevelt, Eleanor--as First Lady; under names of other first ladies

Fischer, Louis, F767

Fish, Hamilton, F365, F2016, F2026

Fisher, Dorothy Canfield, F1045

Fitzgerald, F. Scott, F265, F1050

Fitzgerald, Zelda, F265

Flanagan, Hallie, F1118

flying, see air travel

Flynn, Edward J., C322, F770, F1352

Fogg, Robert, F751

food, ER on, B188, B235, C94, C114, C126, C173, C205, D138, D142; see also Roosevelt, Eleanor--recipes of

Food for Europeans, C172

Food for Peace, C338

For Finland, Inc., F987

foreign born groups, B326, C85, C127, C134; see also Japanese-Americans

foreign policy, B58-59, B470, C84, C89, C167, C170, C174, C182, C300, C302, D241, D247, F403, F1634

Foreign Policy Association, F1943

Formosa, C332

Fosdick, Harry Emerson, D72

Foster Parents' Plan, F939

Four Freedoms, C125, D122

Foxx, Redd, F1205

France, C151, C224, C253, F931
-U.S. relations with, B385, D191

Franco, Francisco, C193, F1660

Frank, Anne, B400

Frankfurter, Felix, F886, F1912, F2067

Franklin D. Roosevelt Library, A8, A10-11, A15-16, F1873, F1965, H4, H33, H46, H57, I59

fraternities, C215, C286

Frederick, Pauline, H78

Free World, B256

freedom of speech, C171, C173, C177, C187, D234

Freedom's Charter (Nolde), B357

Freidel, Frank, C273

Friedan, Betty, F1978

Friends of Children, D124
From the Eagle's Wing (Swift), B485
From the Morgenthau Diaries (Blum), B464
Frooks, Dorothy, F777
Fujikawa, Anna Rosenberg, F1655
Fulbright, J. William, C341
Fuller, Margaret, B67
Fundamentals in the Education of Negroes (conference), D64
furniture, manufacturing of, *see* Val-Kill Industries

Gaitskell, Hugh, D261
Gallup Poll, F572, F2030
gardens and gardening, C54
Garner, John Nance, C23, F1169
Garson, Greer, C324, H90
Gaulle, Charles de, C210, C320, F931
Gellhorn, Edna, F883
Gellhorn, Martha, F335, F883, F1072
Gellhorn, Walter, D228
General Federation of Women's Clubs, D187
George VI and Elizabeth (of England), C166, C209, F934
-in fiction, J16
-U.S. visit of, B496, F491, F548, F551, F570, F575, F577, F715, F717, F808, F858, F860, F901, G44, H39
Georgia Warm Springs Foundation, C165
Georgia Woman's Democratic Club, F1062
Germany, B328, C126, C133, C136, C140, C150, C190, C258, C287, C324, C343
Getting Acquainted with Your Children (Howard), B115
Ghee, Joyce,, F225
Gilman, Charlotte Perkins, F1127
Girl Scouts, B331, C60, C260
Give Us These Tools (Viscardi), B465
Glazier, Sidney, F440, H77
Goa, C343
Godfrey, Arthur, F2064
Golden, Harry, F1178
Golden Gate Bridge, B157
Gomez, Alvaro, G105
Good Neighbor Policy, B422, D84

Gould, Beatrice Blackmar, F1656
Gould, Bruce, F1656
Goya, Francisco, etchings of, F792
G.P.A. Healy, American Artist (De Mare), B416
Graham, Billy, C288
Grauer, Ben, H29
Great Britain, B276, B286, B288, C75, C288, D124, D145, D198, F1411
Gridiron Widows, F488, F553, F607
Gromyko, Andrei, C157
Growing Toward Peace (ER), E126-29
Gunther, John, C274, F1045
Gurewitsch, A. David, F256, F335, F1910
-ER, recollections of, F9

Haiti, C297
Hall, Mary Livingston, F227
Hall family, F186
Halsey, William F., F968
Halsted, Anna Roosevelt, *see* Roosevelt, Anna
Halsted, Diana Hopkins, F845, F898
Hammarskjold, Dag, B478, F2051
Hammer, Armand, F259
Hammer, Victor, F259
Hammer Galleries, F397
Hampton Institute, D81, F1201
handicapped persons, B465, D69
-employment of, C189
Happy Times in Czechoslovakia (Bartusek), B208
Harding, Warren G., B50
Harriman, Averell, C255, C269, C280-81
Harrison, Earl, F1640
Harvard University, C274
Hassett, William D., F798
Hatch Act, C88
Hatfield, Mark O., F2026
Hauptmann, Bruno Richard, G37
health care, C97, C107, C143, C289, D143, F1064
-for the elderly, C329
-financing of, B51, C66, C68, C151, C157, C189, D136
-for mothers and infants, B51, B146, B246, C57, C68, D21,

D46, D156; *see also* children--
health of
Healy, G.P.A., B416
hearing aids, D271
hearings, congressional, ER as subject
of, F365; *see also* Roosevelt, Eleanor-
-testimony of
Hearst, William Randolph, C220
Heckart, Eileen, J26
Height, Dorothy L., F1154
Helm, Edith B., B414, F542, F570,
F613, F616, F660, F684, F789, F800
Hemingway, Ernest, F883
Henricks, Namee, F1105
Heritage (television program), H14
Herrmann, Edward, H67
Hickok, Lorena A., F195, F228, F354,
F728, F1106
-on ER, E110, F14, F70, F801, I56
-ER compared to, F2038
-ER, interviews with, G23-24, G27-
28, G49
-ER's relationship with, F195, F202,
F214, F223, F226, F228, F252,
F299, F305, F310, F349, F364,
F370, F383, F391, F1072, F1106,
F1245, F1941
-reviews of her writings, E109-11
Highlander Folk School, F605, F1178
Hill, John Warren, D228
Hiss, Alger, C227, C268, C280, F1640
Hitler, Adolf, C95, C111, C147, C256,
D137, F905, G74
Hobby-Lobby (radio program and
motion picture), H48
Hoffa, James, C308
holidays, B258, C48, C50, C56; *see
also* Christmas; Easter
Holm, Celeste, H84
homosexuals, C211; *see also* lesbianism
Hoover, Herbert C., B57-58, D244a,
C195, C228, C265, C269, F833,
F1114
Hoover, Irwin Hood (Ike), C8
Hoover, J. Edgar, C211
-ER, relationship with, F794, F1324,
F1336
-in fiction, J6, J14, J18
see also FBI--ER, files on
Hoover, Lou H., F412, F429, F693,
F867, F903, F1113

Hope, Bob, F1814
Hopkins, Diana, F845, F898
Hopkins, Harry, C198, D30, F860,
F898, F1060, F1106, F1109
-ER's relationship with, F813,
F823, F834, F845-46, F875
-family of, C109
-in fiction, J14, J17, J21, J23
housing, B210, B240, C27, C69,
C161-62, C324, C345, D143, D169,
F1054, F1102, F1123, F1251,
F1399, G58, G88
Howe, Louis M., B48, B417, C322,
F519, F753, F860, G95
-Arthurdale and, F1084, F1104
-ER's emergence and, B394, F5,
F399, F421, F431, F441, F464-
66, F469-70, F475, F479, F1753,
G45, G71, I63, I74
-in fiction, J3-4, J18, J21, J25
Hoyle, Marguerite, C256
Hull, Cordell, C81, D84
human rights,
-ER as proponent of, B357, B384,
D203, D215, D251, F1409,
F1444-45, F1452, F1458, F1460,
F1463-65, F1467, F1469-70,
F1474-76, F1478, F1482, F1488,
F1496-1602, F1822, F1946,
F1956, F1963, F1983, F1985,
F1999, F2019, F2025, G69, H34
-role of United Nations in, B327,
B344, B350, B354-55, B358,
B367, B377, B391-92, B401,
D197, D252, G69
see also Commission on Human
Rights; Universal Declaration of
Human Rights
Human Rights Day, D215
Hungary, C282
hunger in the U.S., C329
Hunting Big Game in the Eighties
(Elliott Roosevelt, father), C286,
E1-2
Hurley, Patrick, F1086, F1114
Hurst, Fannie, F526, F677, F807
Hutchings, Robert Maynard, B406
Hyde Park, N.Y., F1416; *see also*
Franklin D. Roosevelt Library;
Springwood; Val-Kill; Val-Kill
Industries

hydrogen bomb, *see* nuclear weapons

Ickes, Harold L., C247, C259, F1140
-on ER, F1109
If You Ask Me (ER), E56-60
"If You Ask Me," B20, B30, B230,
B297, B314, B359, B439, B512,
E105-8, F638, F1588, F1748, F1766,
F1799
immigrants and immigration, B452,
C265, C316, F1411
In Your Hands, D251
income tax,
-ER on, C107, C113, C141, C151,
C199, C246, C288, C306, C333,
F1264
-evasion of and ER, F365
India, B19, B375, D223, D232, E84-98,
F1648, F1652, F1671-72, I61
India and the Awakening East (ER),
C256, E84-98
infantile paralysis, *see* Roosevelt,
Franklin D.--illnesses and disability
of
intelligence tests, C218
Internal Revenue Service (U.S.), C333
International Brotherhood of Electrical
Workers, D125
International Council of Women, D185
International Court of Justice, F1410
International Institute of Human
Rights, F1873
International Ladies' Garment
Workers Union, D167
International Rescue Committee, C265
International Student Assembly, D140
International Student Service, B237,
C98, F1319, F1336
International Union of Students, B462
International Women's Day, D183,
D186
intolerance, B213, B321
Ireland, C281
Israel, B426, B449, B453, C245, C333,
D224
-ER, tributes to, F1633, F1857
-ER's support of, B490, B497, D243,
D246, F1610, F1857, F1882, G84,
H35

-establishment of, C180, F1418,
F1421, F1453, F1459, F1617,
F1657, F1669; *see also* Palestine
Issues and Answers (television
program), G106
It Seems to Me (ER), E105-8
Italy, C253
It's Up to the Women (ER), E6-13,
F68, F916, F1273, F1791
Izvestiia, D183

Jackson, Robert H., F365
Japan, B455, C140, C157, C195,
C242
Japanese Americans, B271, B399,
C134
Java, B502
Javits, Jacob K., F2026
The Jew in American Life (Wise),
B330
Jews and Judaism, F1191
-ER on, B169, B258, B282, B330,
C99, C101-2, C105, C107, C111,
C121, C126, C218, C261, C333,
D116, E60, F638, G40
see also anti-Semitism; refugees--
Jewish
John Birch Society, C350
John Martin's Book, B84
Johnson, Lady Bird, B504, F722,
F788, F1905
Johnson, Lyndon B., C293, D269,
F1222, F1726
Jones, Jesse, C223
Jordan, Barbara, F1985, H86
Jordan, C245
Juliana (of the Netherlands), C267
Junior Americans of the United
States, F1308
Junior League, B76, B167, F705,
G47
Junior Literary Guild, B195, F368,
F372, F1761, F1817
Justice Dept. (U.S.), *see* United
States. Dept. of Justice; United
States. Attorney General
juvenile delinquency, B458, C124,
C168, C194, C255, C258-59, C314,
C316, C334, D228

juvenile literature, *see* younger
  readers, writings for

Kahn, Alfred J., D228
Kaiser, Edgar, F1143
Kasenkina, Mme., C182
Keller, Helen, B395, F287, G94o
Kemp, Maida Springer, F1154
Kennedy, Jacqueline, B492, B504,
  F722, F775, F868
Kennedy, John F. (JFK), C265, C295,
  F1727, F1784
  -ER, tributes to, F1263, F1862-66
  -ER's criticism of, F1682, F1698,
    F1703, F1708, F1720, F1728
  -ER's 1960 meeting with, F1694,
    F1696, F1698, F1703, F1716,
    F1720
  -ER's relationship with, F1689-90,
    F1696, F1703, F1717, F1729
  -in fiction, J12
  -as President, C331, C333-34, C337-
    38, C343, C346-47, D273, F78,
    F1178, F1256, F1294, F1483,
    F1674, F1689; *see also* President's
    Commission on the Status of
    Women
Kennedy, Joseph P., F1682
  -in fiction, J13
Kennedy, Robert F., F1238
Kenny, Sister, C128, G54
Khrushchev, Nikita, C292, C298,
  C316, C328-29, C337, C346, F1636,
  G93
Kidd, Gordon, F237
King, Martin Luther, Jr., H92
  -ER, tributes to, F1867
King Features, B88
Kingdon, Frank, F1034, F1045
Kinsey report, C209, C243
Kipling, Rudyard, H23
Kirkpatrick, Theodore, F1676
Knight, John S., G94o
Korea, C212-13, C234, C323, D211,
  F1629

labor strikes, C93, C101, C103, C112,
  C125, C261, C307, C312, C333,
  C341, C343, F1134
labor unions, B298, C104, C107, C114-
  15, C119-20, C123, C131, C148,
    C156, C203, C238, C308, C334-
    35, C341, D44, D167
  -ER's support of, B293, B328,
    B403, B472, C68, C254, D25,
    D71, D83, D125, F1029, F1068,
    F1092, F1116, F1134, F1211,
    G97
  -role of, B298, B316, C249, C254,
    D83, D240, D264, G34
  see also right to work laws;
    workers; under names of labor
    unions
Ladies' Home Journal, C188-89,
  F1748, F1764, F1766, F1799,
  F1938
Ladies of Courage (ER), E109-11
La Guardia, Fiorello, F940, F954,
  F971, F1010, F1207
  -in fiction, J13
Land, Emory Scott, F976
Landis, James M., F1010
landlords, C113
Landon, Theo, F566, F710
Lane, Rose Wilder, B199
Langer, Howard, H34
language universal, ER on, C165,
  C193, C317
languages foreign, ER on, B232,
  B285, B451, C208, C304, C318-19,
  C323, C349
Lape, Esther Everett, F433
Lash, Joseph P., F977, F980
  -on ER, B48, F17-20, F71-72, F757
  -ER centennial and, F1998
  -ER's relationship with, F1301,
    F1324-25, F1336, F2009, F2016
  -writings, discussions of, A1, F17,
    F2038, H61
  -youth movement and, C98, C256,
    F1301, F1319, F1325, F1337
Latin America, G78
  -U.S. relations with, B242, B281,
    B285, B422, C80, C126, C321,
    C333, D134, F674, G105
Laugier, Henri, F1496
League of Nations, D177, F403,
  F1620, G4, G81
League of Women Voters, B37-39,
  B41, B52, C24, C59, D2, D15,
  D26, D29, D102, D109, F483-84
Lebanon, C302

LeHand, Missy,
  -FDR's relationship with, F25, F252,
    F349, F364
  -as FDR's secretary, F460, F519,
    F542, F660
  -in fiction, J14, J18, J20-21
Lehman, Herbert H., C250, C265,
    C281, F1366, F1372, F1390, F1683,
    F1712, G92
Leibowitz, Samuel S., C316
Lend-lease, F1298
Lerman, Rhoda, F223, H68
lesbianism, F202, F223, F226, F228,
    F299, F364, F391, F2009
Let's Take a Trip (television program),
    H5
Letters from Jerusalem (Clawson), B449
Levy, Adele Rosenwald, D259
Lewis, John L., C125, F1309
liberals and liberalism, C79, D193,
    D241, F29, F540, F1032, F1379,
    F1685, F1687, F1691, F1704,
    F1714
  -ER on, C178, C190, C229, C238,
    C340, D193, D241
liberty, ER on, B380, C80
libraries and librarians, B436, D67,
    F1002
Library of Congress, F1802, H6, H36
Life of Lorena Hickok (Faber), F195,
    F202, F223, F228, F370, F383, F391,
    F1245
Lillian Wald (Duffus), B166
Lincoln, Abraham, B315, F2068
Lindbergh, Charles, C95
  -in fiction, J12
Linzer, Estelle, F1606, F1979, H58
literacy tests, C344
Littell, Norman M., F834
Little Rock, Ark., B486, F1171
Livingston, Mary, J12
Livingston family, F186
L.L. Bean, F253
Lodge, Henry Cabot, C261
The Long Shadow of Little Rock
    (Bates), B486
Longworth, Alice Roosevelt, F1751
  -on ER, F190, F232, F337, F366-67
  -in fiction, J3-4, J10, J19
The Lord's Prayer, C290
lottery, C169, C232, C304, C325, C341

Love, Eleanor (Lash), F383, F2020
Lowenstein, Allard K., B484
loyalty tests, C175
Luce, Clare Boothe, B261, C321,
    F1710, F2059
Luce, Henry, J12
Ludlow Amendment, B199, C66,
    C81
Ludwig, Emil, B148
Lusaka, Paul J.F., F1956
Luxembourg, B376
lynching, *see* Costigan-Wagner Anti-
    lynching Bill

Macfadden, Bernarr, F1775, F1778
Macgregor, Frances Cooke, reviews
    of her writings, E53-55
Mack, Mrs. Norman E., F510
MacLeish, Archibald, D101, G940,
    H77
MacVane, John, D232
Madison, Dolley, F628, F908
Malik, Charles, F1497, F1597
The Man Behind Roosevelt (Stiles),
    B417
Mangione, Jerre, F1115
manners, *see* etiquette
March of Dimes, C296
March of Time, F1762
March on Washington (1941), F1058,
    F1157, F1190, F1201-3, F1207
Margaret Fuller (Bell), B67
Marie Antoinette, F22
Mark Twain and Franklin Roosevelt,
    B361
marriage, ER on, B75, B156, B423,
    C61, C93, C95-97, C99-100, C102,
    C110, C119, C121, C125, C132,
    C136, C138, C140, C151-52, C155-
    57, C159, C164-65, C169-73, C179,
    C187, C189, C193, C207, C209,
    C220, C230, C269, C278, C285,
    C300, C313, C350, F1348, G14,
    G25
marriage, interracial, ER on, C96,
    C159, C168, C202, C274, C278
Marshall, George C., F1004, F1421
Marshall, Thurgood, C280
Marshall Plan, C175, C192, C201
Martha (of Norway), F364, F376
Marx, Karl, C207

Maslow, Abraham, F10, F378
Mason, Lucy Randolph, F1116, F1209
maturity, ER on, C241
Maxwell, Elsa, C294
Mayes, Herbert R., F1817
McBride, Mary Margaret, F1749, H6
McCall's, C189, F1748
McCarran-Walter Immigration Act,
   C265
McCarthy, Joseph, C169, C221, C238-
   39, C250, C252-53, C276, D217,
   D236, F1649, F1676, F1698, F1720,
   G74, G77
McCloy, John, F1165
McCrary, Jinx Falkenberg, D221
McDuffie, Elizabeth, F641
McIntyre, Marvin, F519
McLaughlin, Kathleen, F748
McNaught Syndicate, B88
Mead, Margaret, D114
medical profession, C341
Meet the Press (radio and television
   program), G68, G77, G89, G93,
   G97, H8, H10, H18
Meir, Golda, B490, F1857
Meitner, Lise, F1025
Mendell, Brooks, B370
Mendes-France, Pierre, C259
mental illness, C194, C349
mental retardation, C164
Mercer, Lucy Page, F354
   -FDR's relationship with, F175,
      F178, F181, F190, F198, F210-11,
      F226, F232, F241, F274, F284,
      F295, F302, F304-5, F328, F349,
      F351, F364, F376, F409, F420-21,
      F423, F444, I24
   -in fiction, J3, J5
Merchant Marine, C206
Mesta, Perle, B376, F848
Meyer, Mrs. Eugene, F1321
Meyer, Frank, C285
Michaelis, Arnold, H28, H30
Michener, James, D232
Middle East, C227, D224, D246,
   F1646; *see also* Israel; Palestine
militarization of U.S. economy, C192
military in post-war era, B303, B385,
   C348, D199, G74, G76, G89
milk, B121

Miller, Earl, F215, F252, F376,
   F408, F1932, F1941
Miller, Emma Guffey, F1248
Miller, Merle, F1676
Miller, Nathan, G2
Mindszenty, Joseph, C194, C202,
   F1624
minimum wage, C64, C70
Mirningoff, Marque, F1998
Mitchell, Billy, C107
Mobilization for Human Needs,
   B105, B117, C10, C32, D31, F1277
Mondale, Walter F., F1993
Monnet, Jean, F1646
Monroe Doctrine, C333
Montgomery, Ala., B445
Moore, Marianne, B261
The Moral Basis of Democracy (ER),
   E43-52
morale, ER on, B265, B267, C98,
   C131, C145, D121, D123, D127
morality, ER on, C108, C115
Morgan, Edith Hall (Mrs. Forbes),
   B394
Morgenthau, Elinor, F446, F856
Morgenthau, Henry, Jr., B464,
   F365, F733-34, F2058
Morse, Wayne, C286
Moses, Belle, F435
Mosinee, Wisc., C205
Moskowitz, Belle, F452-53
Mother & Daughter (Asbell), F306,
   F383, F2020
mothers-in-law, ER on, C176-77,
   C310
motion pictures, ER on, B92, C332
Moynihan, Daniel Patrick, F2026
Mrs. F.D. Roosevelt's Home Crafts
   Project, F361
Mrs. R. (Steinberg), E117
Muir, John, B485
Munich Conference, C74
Murray, Pauli, F1198-99, F1222
Murrow, Edward R., H12
Museum of Broadcasting, *see*
   Museum of Radio and Television
Museum of Radio and Television,
   H20
music, B186, B317, C7, C129, D130,
   F817

Mussolini, Benito, J2
"My Day," A15, B9, B36, B131, B172,
 B216, B281, C97, E30-33, F584,
 F604, F777, F815, F1015, F1017,
 F1742, F1744, F1751, F1798,
 F2016, G44, I40, I43
-critiques of, E27, E46, E91, E135,
 F625, F700, F1779, F1801, F1804,
 F1807
-parodies of, F510, F1801
-significance of, B36, E32, F506,
 F611, F615, F679, F753, F1278,
 F1653, F1742, F1752, F1754,
 F1770, F1779, F1797, F1805,
 F1823
My Days (ER), E30-33
*My Thirty Years Backstairs at the White
 House* (Parks), I69, J1

NAACP, *see* National Association for
 the Advancement of Colored People
Nation, F1807
National Association for the
 Advancement of Colored People
 (NAACP), C280, D48, D150,
 F1212, F1447-48
-ER, tributes to, F1897
-ER's involvement in, D94, F1161,
 F1164, F1226, F1228
National Business Women's Week, D60
National Citizens Commission for the
 Public Schools, B368
National Committee for American
 Education, C185
National Committee for an Effective
 Congress, F1706
National Conference of Students in
 Politics, F1328
National Conference on the Cause and
 Cure of War, B212
National Conference on the Education
 of Negroes, D42
National Consumers League, D16,
 F1259
National Education Association, F1066
National Emergency Committee
 Against Mob Violence, F1149
National Foundation for Infantile
 Paralysis, C128, C198
National Issues Committee, F1676,
 F1681

National Labor Relations Board, C73
National League of Women Voters,
 see League of Women Voters
National Negro Congress, F1159
National Organization of Women for
 Equality in Education, F1213
National Recovery Administration
 (NRA), D36
National Training School, F680
National Urban League. D62, D105
National Woman's Democratic Law
 Enforcement League, F485
National Youth Administration
 (NYA), B201, F1055, F1058,
 F1168, F1217, F1295-96, F1315,
 F1329, F1339, F1343, H52
Native Americans, C108, C188,
 F550, F1105
NATO, C190, C282, C323, C342
Nazis and nazism, C76, C122, C126,
 C136, C241, C343, D194, F560,
 F820, F1003, H51
Negro Youth Conference, D93
Negroes, *see* Black Americans
Nehru, Jawaharlal, C343, D223,
 F1652
Nehru, Pandit, B375
Nesbitt, Henrietta, C191, F527,
 F570-71, F858-60
-in fiction, J23
neutrality laws, C81
Nevins, Allen, F796
New Deal programs, C89; *see also*
 Black Americans--New Deal
 programs for; women--New Deal
 programs and; young Americans--
 New Deal programs for; under
 names of programs
*The New Program of the United States
 Committee of International Student
 Service*, B237
New York City, B47, C205, C233,
 C308, C319, C332, C337, C343,
 F461
New York Committee of Democratic
 Voters, F1697
New York Herald Tribune Forum on
 Current Problems, D49, D61, D70,
 D85, D92, D103, D153
New York Herald Tribune High
 School Forum, D184

New York Herald Tribune Women's
  Conference on Current Problems,
  D24, D44
New York League of Women Voters,
  see League of Women Voters
New York State Archives, F2006
Newman, Ruby, F494
Newspaper Guild of New York, see
  American Newspaper Guild
Nicholson, Mrs. Jesse W., F485
Nicolson, Marjorie Hope, B287
Nigeria, C341
Nightingale, Florence, C107
Nixon, Richard M., C268, C273, C291,
  C303, C319, C321, C329, G94i
No Time for Tears, B390
Nobel Peace Prize, F1128, F2014
North American Newspaper Alliance,
  B88
North Atlantic Pact, C190
North Atlantic Treaty Organization,
  see NATO
NRA (National Recovery
  Administration), D36
nuclear weapons, B420, C150-51,
  C201, C205, C210, C244, C256,
  C267, C277, C291, C303, C309,
  C326, C342, C345-46, D218, D239,
  D261, F1005, F1025, F1629, F1632;
  see also atomic energy
nurses and nursing, D46, F1182
NYA, see National Youth
  Administration

OCLC, A13-14
O'Day, Caroline, C21, F478, F518,
  F668, F777
O'Dwyer, William, C217, C268, F1353
Office of Civilian Defense,
  -criticism of ER's role with, F940,
    F942, F944, F950, F979-80, F996
  -ER's activities with, B255, D143,
    F935, F954, F956, F967, F971,
    F995, F1002, F1010, G51
Ohio State University, B240
older Americans, C152, C158, C164,
  C324, C329, C342
  -employment of, C41, C60, C69,
    C197
Oleomargine Act, C141
Olivia (Bussy), F202

Olivier, Marcel, F1128
On My Own (ER), E112-25
Onassis, Jacqueline, see Kennedy,
  Jacqueline
Oppenheimer, Robert, C258
Opportunity, B207
Organization for Rehabilitation
  Through Training (ORT), D116
Ottenberg, Mrs. Louis, F1476
Oumansky, Constaine, F980
Oursler, Fulton, F864
Overstreet, Harry A., F1348
Oxnam, G. Bromley, F1387

Palestine, C150, C158, C176, C180,
  F1418, F1421, F1440, F1453; see
  also Israel--establishment of
Pan-American Coffee Bureau, D128,
  H6
Pan American Union, B218
Panama Canal, C255
Pandit, Vijaya, F1641
Papandreou, Margaret, F1978
Parks, Lillian Rogers, F867
parochial schools, see schools,
  parochial
Parran, Thomas, D96
Parsons, Frances Theodora, F321
Partners: The United Nations and
  Youth (ER), E77-83
Pasternak, Boris, C306
Pastor Hall (motion picture), F1757,
  F1790, H51
Patterson, Eleanor Medill, D74,
  F2044
Patton, George, J19
peace, B25, B400, B442, B461, B517,
  C99, C134, C235, D51, D84,
  D90, D241, D274, E35, E38,
  F1054, F1254, G94n, G94p
  -role of citizens, B10, B253, B362,
    C67, C148, D54, D80, D144,
    D150, D178, D187, D255, D274,
    E36, E40
  -role of nations, B303, B307, B316,
    B470, C201, C239, D50, D72,
    D78, D135, D161, D187, D198-
    99, D255, G40, G42
  -spirituality and, B196, B318, E37
  -United Nations and promotion of,
    B182, B366, B379, B405, C97,

C101, C149, C197, D207, D222,
D237-38, D242, D248, D252, E37
see also women--as peacemakers and
peacekeepers
Peace Corps, C333, C341
peace marches, C335
Peace Through Strength (Rosenbloom),
B408
Pearl Harbor, C103-4, C106, C112,
C251, C255
Pecora, Ferdinand, F1045
Pegler, Westbrook, C123, C184, C231,
C255, C305
-ER, criticism of, C103, C263, F279,
F390, F627, F664, F704, F873,
F877, F945, F1171, F1372, F1676,
F1788, F1800-1801, G94b, J36
-ER, praise of, F663
Perez, Rosemarie, G105
Perkins, Frances, C322, F838, F875-
76, F896, F1028, F1246-47, F1278
-oral history of, F452, F838, F875
Perkins, Maxwell, F418
Perspectives on Greatness (television
program), H84
Peter and the Wolf (Prokofiev), F1811,
H42-43
Peterson, Esther, D270, F1287, F1294,
F1978, F2026
pets, ER on, C222; *see also* Fala;
Roosevelt, Eleanor--pets of
Pickett, Clarence, F1640
The Pilgrims, D179
Pinchot, Cornelia, F1166
Pins and Needles, F784
Pius XII, Pope, C99, F1368
planned parenthood, C130, C151
Planned Parenthood League, C139
Plavner, Murray, B220
Poland, B261, C140
polio, *see* Roosevelt, Franklin D.--
illnesses and disability of
polio vaccine, C320
Political Citizens Association, C163
poll-tax, C90, F1224
Porter, Mary Gurley (Polly), F482
Portugal, C343
Postal Service (U.S.), C205, C334
Pour la Victoire, B262
Prasad, Rajendra, F1652

prayer, ER on, C110, C134, C189,
C277, C290, C300, C333, G94n
prejudice, ER on, B233, B263, B316,
C167, C289, C348, D128, F1149,
F1153, F1158-59, F1167, G40
presidency, ER on, B122, B228,
C130, C146, C197, C202, C206,
C230, C284-85, C301, C313, C330,
D201
President's Commission on Civil
Rights, C174
President's Commission on the Status
of Women, B489, D273, F1878
-ER as chair of, D270, F1233,
F1238, F1249, F1256-57, F1263,
F1269-71, F1287, F1294, F1866
-report of, F1233, F1263, F1270
press, ER on the, B218, B270, C162,
C291, C334, C343, C348, F1485;
see also Roosevelt, Eleanor--press
conferences and relations with the
press
Price, Dan, H58
prisons, prisoners, and parolees,
B130, B134, B214, C108, C112
Progressive Citizens of America,
F1731
Progressive Party, F1701, F1709,
F1730, F1734
Prohibiting Poverty (Martin), F1318
prohibition, B49, C95, C283, C313,
D8, D10, D18, F450, F485, G25,
G94d
propaganda, ER on, C61, C91, C344
Prospects of Mankind (television
program), D261, D268, D273,
F1773, F1784, F1810, F1814, H15,
H22
prostitution, C100, F1410
psychoanalysis, C230
public opinion polls, ER on, C77
public speaking, ER on, C76, D112,
D133
Puerto Rico, C49, C84, F1117,
F1415
Putnam, George P., F671, F836

Quakers, *see* Society of Friends
Quebec Conference (1944), F960,
F1016

quiz shows, C317
Qunitanilla, Luis, F792

race relations, *see* Black Americans
radio, C77, C116, C119, C146, G11
    G35
Rand, Sally, J18
Randolph, A. Philip, F1146, F1202-3,
    F1207, G94o
Rauh, Joseph L., Jr., F1998
Rawalt, Marguerite, F1269
reading, ER on, C142, C176-77, C183,
    C219, D67; *see also* children--books
    and reading and
Reagan, Nancy, F828, F844, F1993
Reagan, Ronald, F1993
recreation, B204, C40, D27, D37
Red Cross, B284, B290, B300, C103,
    C106, C124, C137, C142, C145,
    C222, D107, D200, F982
Reedsville, W. Va., *see* Arthurdale
refugees, B264, B452, C80-81, C265,
    D165, D246, F966, F1018, F1393,
    F1395-97, F1402, F1408, F1411,
    F1440, F1442, F1457, F1484,
    F1644, G60
-Jewish, B258, F937, F952, F962,
    F967, F1006, F1026-27, F1907
see also United Nations High
    Commissioner for Refugees
Refugees at Work (Robinson), B264
Reilly, Michael F., F881
religion, ER on, B93, B185, B191,
    B233, B249, B263, B294, B312, C93,
    C96-97, C102-3, C105, C130, C132,
    C142, C154, C167, C170-71, C183-
    84, C187, C206, C212, C218, C221,
    C234, C242, C245-46, C272, C286,
    C295, C319, C332-33, D104, D149,
    D204, G94n; *see also* Roosevelt,
    Eleanor--religious beliefs of
Remick, Lee, H69
rent control, C321
Republican Party, B49-50, B59, B372,
    C128, C171, C186, C206, C270,
    C274, C276, C281, C302, C325,
    C338, D4, D182, F403, F710,
    F1130, F1675, F1681, G103
-in New York, B49, D182, F1290, G2
Research Libraries Group, A14

Research Libraries Information
    Network, A13-14
retirement, ER on, C216, C233
Reuther, Walter, C294, C298
Rhee, Syngman, C323
Rickenbacker, Eddie, C117
Ridings, Dorothy S., F1978
right to work laws B472, C303; *see
    also* labor unions
Ripley, Tenn., F1221
RLIN, A13-14
The Road to the White House
    (Hickok), B488
Robeson, Paul, C196, F1166, F1777
Robinson, Joseph T., B159
Rockefeller, Nelson, J17
Rogers, Will, F1751, F2068
"Rollins Antimated Magazine," F526
Rollins College, F526
Roosevelt, Alice, *see* Longworth,
    Alice Roosevelt
Roosevelt, Anna (daughter), B34,
    B144, B163, B175, F354, F860,
    F884, F1722, F1758, F1775,
    F1808, F2041
-ER compared to, F2038
-ER, recollections of, F206, F258,
    F1854
-in fiction, J3, J25
-oral history of, F258
-private life of, B34, F188
see also Roosevelt, Eleanor--
    children of
Roosevelt, Anna Hall (mother),
    B394, B495, C333, F227, F249
Roosevelt, Archie, B220
Roosevelt, Betsey Cushing, F248
Roosevelt, Curtis, F225, F2026
Roosevelt, Edith Kermit, F307
Roosevelt, Eleanor (ER),
-addresses and speeches of, B153,
    D1-274, F461, F1154, F1157,
    F1164, F1186, F1208, F1256,
    F1291, F1307, H2-3, H11, H33,
    H36, H45, H47
    --on the drafting of the
        Universal Declaration of
        Human Rights and the
        covenants, F1496-1559,
        F1572-77, F1592, F1594,
        F1600

--in the United Nations, F1393-99, F1402-5, F1407-8, F1410-12, F1415-16, F1435-42, F1489-90

-archival material, A7-17

-autobiographical writings of, B8, B17, B24, B27-28, B91, B93, B158, B223, B334, B337, B340-42, B346, B364, B378, B383, B386-88, B394, B396-97, B415, B446, B451, B456-57, B476, B495-96, B498, B501, B506, B508-10, B514, B519-20, E14-29, E61-76, E112-25, E135-41

-awards and prizes, C241, D89, D189, D267, D272, F1034, F1045, F1053, F1062, F1066, F1068, F1128, F1308, F1320, F1644, F1667, F1817, F2014, F2042, F2066-67, G94a, G94n

-bibliographies, A1-6

-biographical sketches of, F37-173, F874

-biographical works about for younger readers, I1-13, I15-21, I23-26, I28-30, I32-35, I37, I39, I42, I44-46, I49-51, I53-58, I60-63, I65-66, I68, I70-71, I73, I76-81, I83, I86, I88, I91-92

-biographies of, F1-6, F8-34, F36

-birthday tributes to, F392, F1179, F1452, F1680, F1685, F2048, F2051, F2058, F2064, G94n

-book reviews by, B166, B228, B251, B294, B478, B493

-candidacies (suggested) of, C75, C203, C269, C301, F508, F583, F596, F829, F1686, F1710, F1991

-cartoons, comic strips, and jokes about, C94, F152, F769, I50

-centenary of, see Eleanor Roosevelt Centennial; Eleanor Roosevelt Centennial Commission

-childhood and youth of, B91, B334, B337, B446, B495, C206-7, C217, E29, F178, F190, F196, F199, F211, F213, F235, F241, F245, F249, F263, F274, F278, F283, F292-93, F295, F304, F308, F333, F348, F350, F377, F423, F554e, F1178, F1569, F2016, G21, G94c,

G99, I9, I25, I71, I80, I84, I86, I89

-children of, B170, B340, B342, B346, B456, B496, C131, C135, C194, C208, C218, C221, C235, C247, C253, C265, C271-72, C283, C291, C304, C309, C318, F196, F254, F304, F324, F347, F922, F1310, F1480, G15, G30, G94f; see also under names of children

-clothing and appearance of, B476, C255, F220, F309, F315, F363, F452, F599, F601, F632, F637, F643, F645, F647, F650, G38, H82, I22

-coloring book about, I52

-as a columnist, F1792; see also "If You Ask Me"; "My Day"

-columns of, C1-350

-commercials and advertisements by, C230, C310, F602, F1737, F1749-50, F1810

-as a communicator, F736, F1735-1817, F1823

-computer software about, H92-93

-conferences, as subject of, F7, F822, F1942, F1957, F1966, F1971, F1979, F1998-99

-criticism and ridicule of, B295, C103, C140, C196, C236, F198, F432, F834, F865, F877, F1114, F1310, F1676, F1725, F1991, F2016, F2022, F2024, F2050, G94a-b

--at death, F1825, F1885-86, F1901, F1921, F1932

--as First Lady, C232, C263, F314, F330, F496, F498, F510, F524, F536-38, F555, F561, F572, F581, F603, F605, F625, F627-28, F651, F653, F661, F677, F682, F685, F697, F731, F742, F744, F750, F771, F777, F786-87, F792, F813, F815, F826, F844, F873, F877, F880, F887, F892, F899-900, F903, F927, F929, F1191, F1372, G45, G54

--parochial schools, on aid to,
   F1357, F1372-73, F1376-77,
   F1379
--racial equality, efforts toward,
   B411, F625, F672, F826, F834,
   F886, F1159, F1167, F1170-71,
   F1176, F1187, F1191, F1196,
   F1198, F1200, F1204, F1208,
   F1213, F1221
--as social reformer, F496, F672,
   F711, F742, F786, F826, F834,
   F929, F1032, F1035-36, F1038,
   F1046, F1075, F1089, F1103,
   F1109-10, F1131, F1155,
   F1159, F1167, F1170-71,
   F1173, F1175, F1196, F1198,
   F1202, F1204, F1206, F1213-
   14, F1218, F1221, F1223,
   F1258, F1264, F1297-98,
   F1309, F1316-17, F1327-28,
   F1330-31, F1342, F1447,
   F1828, G94j
--as United Nations delegate,
   F1447-48, F1464, F1466,
   F1471, F1477, F1482, F1571,
   F1578, F1588
--as world figure, F1606, F1612-
   15, F1618, F1625, F1631,
   F1637, F1640, F1643, F1647,
   F1651
--during World War II, F940,
   F942-46, F950-51, F976, F978-
   80, F991, F996-97, F1003,
   F1011, F1023-24, F1297-98,
   F1341
--as writer or speaker, D18, E3,
   E5, E12, E19, E45, E67, E73,
   E87, E93, E95, E103, E106,
   E109, E112, E125, E127,
   E137, E151, E155, F625,
   F658, F700, F711, F771,
   F1735, F1737, F1788, F1800-
   1801, F1813, J36
-death of, F179, F218, F304, F343,
   F356, F373, F377, F1632, F1702,
   F1705, F1818-1936, H60, H66,
   H87, J29, J31, J37
--funeral and burial of, F179,
   F343, F1841, F1853, F1869,
   F1876, F1893, F1895, F1918

-drama about, I27, J1-4, J8, J10-
   11, J25-26
-emergence as a public figure, E16,
   E20, E23, E25-27, E135, F398-
   486, F963, F1235, F1569, G71,
   H67, I53, I56, I63, I71, I74
--impetus for, F405, F409,
   F419-21, F440, F444, F459
-exhibits about, F866, F1949,
   F1955, F1977, F1988
-FDR, as influence on ER, B394,
   C266, F225, F281, F1809
-as a feminist, F408, F476, F511,
   F1060, F1236, F1239, F1245,
   F1247, F1257, F1274, F1280-81,
   F1292, F1978
-in fiction, J1-28
-in fiction for younger readers,
   I14, I27, I84
-in films, H13-25, H46-52
-films about, H64-91
-finances and business interests of,
   C96, C101, C130, C189, C229,
   C248-49, C284, C336, F221,
   F239, F330, F365, F536, F561,
   F573, F682, F711, F771, F813,
   F1769, F1789, F1793, F1813,
   G94m
-as First Lady, F347, F487-929,
   F963, F1235, F1569, G38, H9,
   H17, H64, H67, H82, I29, I33,
   I53, I71, I86-87, J33
--ER's approach to First Lady
   role, F516-17, F554a-b,
   F554f, F573, F580, F582,
   F598, F606, F615, F618,
   F621, F628, F677, F687,
   F694, F701, F710, F727,
   F735, F742-43, F746-47,
   F749, F755, F768, F778,
   F785-90, F795, F803, F811-
   12, F821-22, F828, F832,
   F840-44, F866, F872, F879,
   F887, F903, F909, F919,
   F921, F926-27, G46, H83,
   I42, I80
---ER on her approach, C1,
   C220, C320, D26, D28, D89,
   G24, G28, G48, G56, G61

--predecessors as, *see* Adams,
   Abigail; Hoover, Lou H.;
   Madison, Dolley
--successors as, F554f, F618,
   F743, F786, F803, F832, F843,
   F926; *see also* under names of
   first ladies
-friends of, B33, B35, F175, F200,
   F234, F248, F268, F271, F752,
   F815, F881; *see also* under names
   of friends
-gifts to, C301, F525, F792
-health of, F218, F238, F356
-homes of, C108, B496, F187, F222,
   F371, G54; *see also* Campobello;
   Springwood; Val-Kill; White House
as humanitarian, *see* human rights--
   ER as proponent of; Roosevelt,
   Eleanor--as social reformer;
   Universal Declaration of Human
   Rights
-influence of, E140, F507, F1675,
   F1732, F1742, F1845-46, F1864,
   F2020, H86
   --as First Lady, C229, C247,
      F493, F500, F522, F524,
      F537, F541, F554, F564,
      F576, F609, F617, F653,
      F683, F704, F711, F725,
      F727, F734, F738-39, F758,
      F783, F787, F796, F802,
      F828, F853, F861, F865,
      F873, F876, F880, F889,
      F912, F959, F1006, F1023,
      F1037, F1255, F1260-61,
      G94g-h
   --as social reformer, F201, F552,
      F554c, F565, F592, F648,
      F679, F1035, F1045, F1051-
      52, F1059-60, F1083, F1108,
      F1146-47, F1152, F1164,
      F1173, F1177, F1180, F1185,
      F1216, F1236, F1243, F1248-
      49, F1261, F1271, F1286,
      F1288, F1315, F1864
   see also Roosevelt, Franklin D.--
      ER, as influence on
-interviews, as subject of, A9, F917,
   F1930, G1-107, H1, H8-10, H13-
   14, H16-19, H28-30, H33-34, H38,
   H93, I31, I64

-juvenile literature about, I1-93
-later life of, F178, F185, F236,
   F238, F277, F355-56, F383, F392
-mail of, C35, C312, D26, F512,
   F642, F688, F709, F789, F1089
-married life of, B506, C284, F175,
   F178, F193, F196, F199, F226,
   F235, F240-41, F245, F252,
   F263, F265, F270, F274, F282,
   F293, F295, F303-4, F314, F328,
   F339, F348, F350, F360, F377,
   F437, G1, G16-17, H9, H17,
   H67, I58, I67, I71, I80, I86
-memberships and affiliations of,
   F533-34, F704, F839, F1676,
   F1688; *see also* Communists and
   communism--ER identified with
-in opinion polls and rankings,
   F562, F572-73, F691, F743,
   F765, F783, F2030, F2068, I76
-paper dolls, as depicted by, I22
-as parent, *see* Roosevelt, Eleanor-
   children of
-pension of, C200
-pets of, F208, F489; *see also* Fala
-philosophy of, B12, B26, B54,
   B79, B81-82, B106, B109, B126,
   B183, B295, B299, B321, B343,
   B402, B448, B456, B460-61,
   B471, B475, B504, B511, B516,
   B520, C52, C98, C158-59, C288,
   C291, C317, E33, E43-52, E130-
   34, E151-58, F277, F355, F1292,
   H12, I23
-physical characteristics of, F280,
   F309, F312, F317, F1759
-poetry about, J29-38
-political activities of, E110, F1945-
   62, F2033, F2057, G94c
   --through 1928, B1-3, B37-39,
      B41-44, B48-53, B55-62,
      C179, C289, C322, D1-8,
      F321, F399-400, F402-3,
      F406, F414-15, F421, F425,
      F430, F441-42, F450-51,
      F453-56, F458, F461-63,
      F473, F478, F480-82, F486,
      F735, F761, F818, F827,
      F841, F844, F851, F857,
      F870, F874-75, F891, F896,
      F905, F914-15, G3-4, G30

--1929-1945, B238, C21, C89,
  C91, C322, D9, D13, D55-56,
  D73-75, D79, D90-91, D95,
  D98-99, D109, D117, D131,
  D144, D146, F401, F406,
  F410, F420, F430, F446,
  F476, F481, F508, F518,
  F531-32, F541, F500, F552,
  F565, F578, F583, F587,
  F615, F626, F631, F642,
  F653, F663, F668, F681-83,
  F711, F723, F727, G5, G20,
  G24, G30, G49
--1945-1962, B336, B372, B424,
  B443, C168, C223-24, C226-
  27, C251, C253, C255, C266,
  C270, C272-74, C282, C285,
  C288, C298, C300, C317-18,
  C321-22, C325-26, C332,
  C337, C340, D181-82, D192-
  93, D221-22, D229-30, D241,
  D245, D247, D254, D262-63,
  F539-40, F1453, F1635,
  F1673-1734, F1899, F2018,
  G93, G97, H8, H10, H16, H19
-possessions of, F224, F260-62, F331,
  F397
-press conferences and relations with
  the press, F501, F504, F523, F539,
  F551, F558, F579, F591, F614,
  F650, F676, F689, F726-30, F736,
  F748, F773, F779, F843, F855,
  F872, F875, F899, F902, F905,
  F916, F925, F928, F972, F1017,
  F1061, F1278, F1744, G36, I85;
  see also press, ER on the
-private life of, B33-35, C132, C269,
  F174-397, F452, F783, F860, F869,
  F1028, F1039, F1199, F1245,
  F1569, H50, I38, I53, I57
-psychological interpretations and
  personality of, F10, F214, F227,
  F243, F246, F249, F252, F265,
  F281, F296, F328, F356, F378,
  F383, F385, F488, F519, F604,
  F607, F624, F739, F762, F879,
  F1039, F1042, F1809, F2045,
  F2061-62, I11, I55, I61
-radio and television appearances of,
  F1781, F1814
-radio and television series of,
  C235, F1116, F1738, F1745,
  F1749, F1752, F1758, F1765,
  F1767-69, F1777, F1786, F1789,
  F1793-94, F1802, F1806, F1808,
  F1812, F1814, F1816, H2-4, H6,
  H15, H20, H22; see also
  Prospects of Mankind (television
  program)
-recipes of, B252, B275, B371,
  B463, F379, F527, F741, F859
-in recordings, H1-12, H26-45
-recordings about, H53-63
-religious beliefs of, B93, B196,
  B294, B299, B318, B461, C192,
  C224, C226, C251, E49, E51,
  F1379, F1957, G94n; see also
  religion--ER on
-scholarship, as subject of, F783,
  F841, F1580, F1940, F1948,
  F1954, F1967, F2000, F2013
-secretaries of, C308, C330; see
  also Baillargeon, Patricia; Corr,
  Maureen; Helm, Edith B.;
  Thompson, Malvina
-significance of, F1177, F2015,
  F2020-21, F2023, F2025-29,
  F2031-43, F2045-51, F2053-54,
  F2056, F2058-59, F2061-62,
  F2065, F2067
  --statements at time of her death,
    F1818-24, F1826-28, F1831,
    F1833-36, F1838-47, F1849-72,
    F1874-79, F1883-93, F1895-
    1900, F1902-8, F1910-11,
    F1914-17, F1919-22, F1924-30,
    F1933-36
  --statements during Eleanor
    Roosevelt Centennial, F1939-
    44, F1946, F1952, F1956,
    F1962-64, F1966-73, F1976-81,
    F1985, F1989-91, F1994-96,
    F1998-99, F2001-5, F2007-8
-as social reformer, B135, B435,
  B510, C319, E6-7, E14, F414,
  F565, F1028-1348, F1846, F1921,
  F1978, G36, G62, H76, I26, I28,
  I54, I68, I71
-songs about, H53, J39
-as speaker and lecturer, B147,
  B153, C78, C167, C220, C245,

C249, C320-21, F512, F625, F700,
F753, F886, F1197, F1420, F1740-
41, F1746-47, F1752-53, F1760,
F1763, F1765, F1767, F1774,
F1776, F1782, F1795-96, F1803,
F1806, F1813, F1815-16, G6, G71,
G94k
-as teacher, F205, F273, F313, F322,
F368, F372, F471, G6, G19, I93
-testimony by, D5, D106, D118,
D143, D244, D248, D258, D270-71,
F1290
-travels of, B70, B140, B142, B147-
78, B157, B159, B236, B337, C4-
11, C13-14, C17-20, C22, C26,
C29-34, C83, C266, C346, D47,
F215, F250, F512, F536, F538,
F557, F559, F572, F584, F594,
F623, F655-56, F663, F675, F705,
F714, F764, F835, F1004, F1628,
F1630, F1637, F1665, G56, G80,
J34
--for American Association for
the United Nations (AAUN),
B418, B427, B430-32, B440,
F1606
--Caribbean (1934), C15, C49,
F511, F667, F1117
--Caribbean (1944), F967, F985,
F1000
--England (1942), B276, B286,
C113, F934, F941, F948,
F953, F958, F963, F969-70,
F973, F980-81, F983, F989-90,
F992-94, F999, F1009, F1012-
13, F1016, F1019, F1766,
F1909, G53, G94k
--India and the East (1952), B19,
D232, E84-98, F1647-48,
F1652, F1671-72, G74, I61
--Israel, F1639, F1626
--Japan, B407
--Morocco, G90
--Russia, B467, C292-93, D256,
F1662, G93, G96, G98
--South Pacific (1943), B272,
B296, B300, B304, C123,
D146, D163-64, F932-33,
F945, F947, F949, F957,
F965, F967-68, F972, F974,
F982, F988, F1001, F1008,

F1014, F1022, G55, G94k,
I48
-as United Nations delegate, B336,
B348, C150, C180, C225, C245,
C251, C265, C287, C333, C348,
D176, F540, F550, F1018, F1393-
1602, F1627, G61-62, G75, G81-
82, G94k, G94p, H38, H44, H47,
H68, H78, I16, I45, I77, I80
-as White House hostess, B111,
B137, B140, B142-43, B147-49,
B151, B153, B174, B476, C11,
C13, C16, C24-25, C195, C204,
C336, F491, F505, F521, F524,
F529-30, F538, F549, F554c,
F564, F570, F580, F582, F588,
F593, F597, F608, F610, F619-
20, F629, F652, F662, F670,
F673, F680, F703, F707-8, F713,
F741, F760, F763, F780, F798,
F800, F808, F817, F819, F850,
F856, F858-59, F867-69, F874,
F884, F895, F901, F920, F926,
G26-28, G36, G41, H7, H65, I69
-as wife of Gov. of N.Y., D12,
F347, F404, F417, F435, F449,
F452, F471-72, G6, G16
-will of, F357, F397
-as world figure, F1603-72
-World War I and, F419, F440,
F458, F1138
-World War II and, F930-1027,
H2-3, H45, H51-52
-as writer, C251, C290, C317,
F368, F513, F536, F539, F630,
F1735, F1744, F1754, F1760,
F1766-67, F1809, F1817, G43,
G94k
-writings, reviews of, E1-158,
F1735, F1771-72
-writings, translations of, B521-75,
Roosevelt, Elliott (father), B4, B334,
B394, B495, B508-9, C7, C286,
E1-2, F180, F227, F249, F327,
G94d, G102, I24
Roosevelt, Elliott (son), C95, C99,
C102-3, C118, C256, C322, F23-
25, F336, F466, F1012, F1701,
F1749, F1766, F1806, F1816
-in fiction, J25

-writings, discussions of, B324,
C160, C210
see also Roosevelt, Eleanor--children
of
Roosevelt, Franklin D. (FDR),
-campaigns of, C75, C89, C91, C93,
C119, C226, C228, C246, C305,
C322, D99, D117, F418, F427,
F496, F551, F560, F583, F622,
F628, F711, F761, F807, F827,
F870, F891, F914, F1023, F1169,
G5, G39, G49
-death and burial of, C144, C189,
C268, F217, F514, F568, F639,
F698, F731, F739, F837, F875,
F885, F899-900, F907, F910, F912,
F924,
-ER as aide to, E66, F199, F241,
F265, F268, F278, F306, F398,
F422, F424, F427-28, F431, F434,
F438, F443, F448, F460, F466,
F498, F519-20, F522, F536, F550,
F552, F554c, F560, F567, F592,
F600, F603, F612, F621-22, F625,
F648, F661, F666, F683, F694,
F697, F720, F735, F739, F753,
F757, F774, F793, F799, F821,
F824, F831, F841, F862, F874-76,
F888, F904, F911, F926, F929,
F953, F1034, F1043, F1052, F1229,
F1680, F1742-43, F1752, F1902,
F1912, F1971, F1973, F1993,
F2063, G46, G101, I56, I58, I67
-ER on, B347, B352, B369, B393,
B396-97, B441, B447, B488, G18,
G25, G59, G64, G66, G94e, G94g,
H9, H13, H17, H32
--as President, B100, B202, B315,
B386-87, B390, B411, B421-
22, B444, B464, B474, B481,
C3, C23, C32-33, C94, C96,
C98, C109, C116, C125,
C134, C160, C181-82, C185,
C188, C195-96, C199, C208,
C211-12, C220-21, C223,
C225-29, C234, C237-38,
C241, C246-47, C250-51,
C255, C257, C261, C266-67,
C269-70, C273-74, C285-86,
C291, C297, C304-5, C322,
C334, C348, D198, D201,

D221, G59, G64, G66,
G94g, H41
--private life of, B339, B346,
B361, B383, B388, B390,
B409, B461, C97, C99-100,
C128-29, C132, C135, C142,
C145, C174, C180, C183,
C189, C191, C193-94, C198,
C200, C213, C215-17, C221-
22, C239, C245-46, C248,
C251-52, C259, C262, C271,
C277-78, C283-84, C286-87,
C289, C294-95, C298, C303,
C331, C344, D175, D179,
G18, G25
-ER's influence on, C107, C183,
C220, E71, E76, E136, F270,
F412, F418, F437-38, F443,
F498, F560, F611, F615, F624,
F658, F661, F733, F738-39,
F744, F756-57, F770, F793,
F824-25, F828, F854, F879,
F888, F908, F918, F951-52,
F962, F998, F1052, F1146,
F1173, F1180, F1228, F1309,
F1831, F2020, F2026, F2029,
F2033, F2039, F2054, G48, I75
-ER's relationship with, C97, C99,
C193, C229, C268, F175, F198,
F209, F219, F227, F254, F265,
F281, F305-6, F338-41, F409,
F426, F437, F444, F793, F818,
F834, F922, F929, F953, F1043,
F1192, H62; *see also* Roosevelt,
Eleanor--married life of
-in fiction, J1-2, J3-6, J13-15, J17-
25,
-in films and recordings, H32
-films and recordings about, H7,
H9, H13, H17, H41, H50, H61-
62, H65, H67, H90
-illnesses and disability of, B352,
B390, B496, C142, C145, C191,
C213, C215, C222, C251-52,
C262, C294, C331, F328, F409,
F424, F426, F428, F431, F434,
F731, G95
Roosevelt, Franklin D., Jr. (son),
B70, C95, C99, C102-3, C118,
C256, C290, F189, F223, F388,
F1637, F1701, G77

-in fiction, J25
see also Roosevelt, Eleanor--children of
Roosevelt, Gracie Hall (brother), F249, F291, F358, G94d
Roosevelt, Hall Delano, F1914
Roosevelt, Irene, F397
Roosevelt, James (son), C95, C99, C102-3, C118, C121, C256, F26, F342, F467, F1078, F1637, F1678, F1692, F1722, G77, H62
-in fiction, J24-25
see also Roosevelt, Eleanor--children of
Roosevelt, John (son), B70, B501, C95, C99, C102-3, C118, C204, C234, C254-56, C277, C297, F331, F388, F900
-in fiction, J25
see also Roosevelt, Eleanor--children of
Roosevelt, Patricia Peabody, F343
Roosevelt, Sara Delano, C177, C252, F217, F344, F547
-ER compared to, F2038
-ER's relationship with, B496, F183, F229, F233, F240, F244, F254, F266, F283, F338-39, F344, F360, F384, F426, G94e
-in fiction, J3-4, J10, J13, J25
-influence of, B394, C183, F183, F194, F624
Roosevelt, Theodore, Jr., C100, F201, F329, F437
Roosevelt and the Warm Springs Story (Walker), B409
Roosevelt family ancestry and history, C105, C108, C174, C245, F176, F184, F186, F192, F196-97, F201, F276, F326, F334, F353
Roosevelt in Retrospect (Gunther), C274
Roosevelt y la Buena Vecindad (Cancino), B422
The Roosevelts of Hyde Park (Roosevelt, James), H62
Rosenberg, Anna M., F1655
Rosenman, Samuel I., C229, F888
-oral history of, F347
Rostow, Elspeth, H24
Rostow, Walt, H24
The Ruhr, C151

rural life, B49, B194, B322, C46, D40, D57, D156-57, D162, D258, F1141, G17, G32
Rusk, Dean, D268, F1660
Russell, Bertrand, D261
Russell, Richard B., F1213
Russia, B348, B467, C153, C172, C292, C318, C349, G93; see also Soviet Union
Rutherford, Lucy Page, see Mercer, Lucy Page
Rutherford, William A., G72
Ryan, Bill, H64

Sabin, Mrs. Charles H., F456
Sacco and Vanzetti case, C187
Sachar, Abram L., F2037
Saint-Exupery, Antoine de, F378
Salisbury, N.C., F1208
Sampson, Edith, C228, G72
San Quentin, C112
Sandiver, Durward V., F28
Sandiver, Irene Reiterman, F28
Sane Nuclear Policy, F1632
Santa Claus, C219
satellites, C350
Saudi Arabia, C261
Scharf, Lois, F29, F1978
Scheider, Malvina, see Thompson, Malvina
Schiff, Dorothy, F328
Schlesinger, Arthur M., Jr., F1998
Schneiderman, Rose, F1211, F1246-47
schools, C62, D29
-parochial, F1349-92
-public, B49, B368, C131-32, C166, C183, C185, C188, C199, C234, C290, C330, D11, D156, D168, F1099, G70
see also Arthurdale--school; teachers
Schroeder, Patricia, F1993
scientific research, C293, C295
scientists, G98
Seagraves, Eleanor, F223
-ER, recollections of, F354
Search for America, H21, H24
Secret Service, C267, F56, F781, F881, F1909

segregation, B269, B469, B486, C253, C257-58, C309, C327, F1213, G79, G88-89

self-determination of nations, F1405, F1441, F1528, F1536, F1558

Senate (U.S.), F1582
-ER on, C252, C293, C317

servants, *see* domestic workers

Sevareid, Eric, H77

sex education, C100, C150, C164, C207

sexes, differences between, ER on, B215, C100, C149, C200

Shakers, F369

Shall Not Perish from this Earth (Perry), E51

Shaver, Mrs. Clem, F450

Sherwood, Mary, and family, F271

Sherwood, Robert E., F1790, H51

Shields, Laurie, F1978

The Shook-up Generation (Salisbury), B458

Sinatra, Frank, C340, F1814

Singh, Sirdar, D232

Sister Kenny, C128, G54

Smith, Alfred E., F432, F453
-ER's support of, B44, B50, B57-58, C289, D7-8, F415, F450, F458, F461, F480, G5
-in fiction, J25

Smith, Mrs. Alfred E., B2, D12

Smith, Hilda W., F425, F1111, F1311

Smith, Margaret Chase, G87, H16

Smith Act, C272

Social Register (New York City), C153

Social Security, C59, C61, C69-71, C74, C76, C88, C141, C158-59, C178, C197, C203, C269, C329, D34, F1055, F1064

Socialists and socialism, C185, C122

Society of Friends, F1094, F1103, F2014

sororities, C215, C286

South Africa, C325, C335, D126

The South and southerners, B301, B403, C72, C130, C253, C327, F605, F1167-68, F1170-71, F1175, F1180, F1186, F1189, F1194, F1196, F1204, F1208, F1213, F1218, G79

South Pacific, *see* Roosevelt, Eleanor--travels of--South Pacific

Southern Conference Educational Fund, F1058, F1193-94

Southern Conference for Human Welfare, D82, F605, F1058, F1116, F1144, F1174, F1186, F1218, F1223, F1927

Souvestre, Marie, B394, C100, D60, F227, F243, F293, G16
-in fiction, J4, J10, I27

Soviet Union, B385, B425, B480-81, C140, C181, C183-84, C206, C218, C236, C263, C341, D194, D246, D253, G74, G85
-United Nations and, B507, C216, C225, C239, C261, C336, D244, F1393, F1396, F1402-3, F1407, F1411, F1415, F1437-38, F1442, F1452, F1458, F1485, F1556, F1584, F1615, F1649, G75
-U.S. relations with, B420, B518, C160, C169, C172, C185, C191, C198, C201, C209, C215, C232, C234, C241, C282, C303, C314, C345-46, C350, D172, D199, D268, F1643, F1649, F1651, F1656, F1664, G75, G85
see also Russia

space exploration, C293, C320, C337, C345

Spain, C207, C231, C271, C275
-Civil War, F767, F792, F883

Sparkman, John, C230

Spellman, Francis,
-criticism of, F1357, F1382-83, F1386, F1389-92
-ER, attack on, C299, F1349-92
-ER, earlier relationship with, F1352
-and parochial schools, aid to, F1349-92

spies, C246

Spingarn Medal, D94, F1152, F1164, F1197

Springwood (Roosevelt home, Hyde Park, N.Y.), B16, B496, C129, C137, C143, D175, F217, F233, F242, F275, F325, F384, H40, I59

Stalin, Joseph, C213, C221, C231, C298, F1310, F1613, G74

stamp collecting, ER on, G63

stamps, ER honored on, F1863, F1914, F2003, F2060

Stapleton, Jean, F1977, F2026, H68, H83, H89

Stassen, Harold, H21

State Dept. (U.S.), *see* United States. Dept. of State; United States. Secretary of State

Staupers, Mabel K., F1182

Steichen, Edward, F766

Steinem, Gloria, F1978

Stella Dallas (motion picture), B152

sterilization, C122

Stevenson, Adlai E., C277, C281, C305, C325, F1199, F1483, F1716, F1735, F1905, F2032, H91
  -criticism of, F1689
  -and death of ER, F1922-25, F2043, H60
  -Eleanor Roosevelt Memorial Foundation and, F1861, F1863-64, F1914, F1923,
  -ER's friendship with, F359, F1483, F1702, F1705, F1711, F2018
  -ER's support of, F1899
  -presidential candidacies of, C322, F1689, F1721
    --1952, D221
    --1956, C253, C255, C266, F1677, F1700, F1702, F1705, F1727-28, G89
    --1960, C298, D262, F1693, F1700, F1702, F1705, F1708, F1727

Stiles, Lela, B417

Stimson, Henry, F1165

The Story of My Life (Keller), B395

Stout, Rex, D117

Stowe, Harriet Beecher, C107

Straight, Michael, F1334

Strait, Clarence, C99

strikes and strikers, *see* labor strikes

Strong, Anna Louise, F1020

Stuart, J. Leighton, F1628

student movevment, *see* American Youth Congress; Lash, Joseph P.-- student movement and

subsistence homesteads, B120, C18, C22, C30, F1047, F1064, F1069, F1083, F1094, F1097, F1109, F1122, F1126, F1128-29, F1137, F1140; *see also* Arthurdale

subversive activities, ER on, C83, C92

suicide, C303

Sunrise at Campobello (Schary), C287, C297, C324, C333, F323, G95, H90

Supreme Court (U.S.), *see* United States. Supreme Court

Sweden, C151

syphilis, D96

Taft, Robert A., C227

Talks with Teachers (Keliher), B459

Tammany Hall, C340

tariffs, F403, G2, G8

Taussig, Charles, F1296

Taiwan, C332

teachers, C135, C236, C342, D71
  -compensation of, B412, C42, C127, C156, C166, C199, C328, C335
  -role of, B64, B176, B184, B186, B278, B384, B433, B459, D11, D22-23, D45, D166, D171, D233, D272, F1326, G98
  -training of, B116, C42-43, C204
  see also Roosevelt, Eleanor--as a teacher; schools

televised court proceedings, C329

television, B468, C332

Tennessee Valley Authority (TVA), C18, C22, C264, F1064

textbooks, ER on, C185

Thant, U, F2032

This I Remember (ER), C189, E61-76, F432, F1748, F1755, F1805

This Is America (ER), E53-55

This Is My Story (ER), A1, E14-29, F753, F1755, F1764, F1766, G43

This Is Our Strength (Christman), B490

This Troubled World (ER), E34-40

Thomas, Constance Allen, F1154

Thompson, Dorothy, B261, F1034, F1638

Thompson, Malvina, F294, F354, F503, F513, F542, F546, F563, F591, F660, F684, F740
  -ER on, C205

-in fiction, J12
300,000 New Americans (White), B452
Tito, Josip, B425, C241, F1649
To Win These Rights (Mason), B403
Tobias, Channing, G72
Today with Mrs. Roosevelt (television program), F1166
Todhunter School for Girls, B313, F5, F205, F212, F273, F322, F536, G6, G16-17, G19-20, I93
tolerance, ER on, B213, B321
Tomorrow Is Now (ER), E151-58, F1756
Tonawanda Indian Community House, F1105
Tor, Regina, reviews of her writings, E126-29
Townsend Plan, C100, C184
toys, ER on, C40
Tractors for Freedom Committee, F1632
Tree, Marietta, F1451, H78
trees, ER on, C58
Trujillo Molina, Rafael, C290
Truman, Bess W., F721, F726, F760, F778, F867, F875, F909
Truman, Harry S. (HST), C214-15, C268, C270, C273, C304, C321-22, C325, D244a, F1692, F1710
-on ER, F907-8
-ER's relationship with, F1453, F1479, F1492, F1617, F1664, F1685, F1699, F1704, F1717, F1723, F1971, F1973
-as President, C147, C150, C188, C232, C267, F890, F1416, F1593, --ER's criticism of, F43, F1443, F1691
-as vice presidental choice, C199, F851
Truman, Margaret, F910
tuberculosis, C26
Tugwell, Rexford G., C30, F498
Tully, Grace, F913
TVA, *see* Tennessee Valley Authority
Twain, Mark, B361
Twentieth Century Club of Buffalo N.Y., F510

UN: Today and Tomorrow (ER), E99-104

UNESCO, C231, C236, D205
UNICEF, B413, F1398, F1404, F1435, F1439
Union for Democratic Action, F1731
Union Now, C99
unions, *see* labor unions
Unitarians, ER on, C279
United Nations (UN), C152, C160, C173-74, C176-77, C187-89, C193, C208, C233, C237, C244-45, C249, C255, C260, C271, C275, C299, C324, C328-29, C343, D180, D184, D211, D219, F1532
-and children, C186, F1398, F1404, F1435, F1439
-ER, tributes to, F1879, F1893, F1924, F1929, F1956
-ER's call for organization of nations, B182, B268, B283, C92, C97, C101, E37, F644, F964
-ER's opinions about, B366, B424, C149-50, C197, C200-201, C270, C341, D170, D177, D197, D207, D220, D222, D225-26, D244, F1774, F1782
-role of, B18, B20, B23, B25, B32, B333, B370, B379, B385, B401, B404-5, B410, B434, B507, D174, D190, D218, D233, D238, D244, D248, D252, D260, E77-83, E99-104, E126-29, E151, F1443, F1457, F1462, F1656, G60, G69, G76, G81-82, G84, G104
-U.S. delegation, meetings of, F1417, F1419, F1422-23, F1425, F1427-30, F1432-33
-U.S. support for, B431, B436, B491, C240, D178, D187, D216, D226, D231, D237, D242, D249
-women in, B381, C225, C292, F1413-14, F1456
see also Black Americans--United Nations; Commission on Human Rights; human rights--role of the United Nations in; peace--United Nations and promotion of; Roosevelt, Eleanor--as United Nations delegate; Soviet Union--United Nations and; women--

rights of; under names of United
Nations specialized agencies
United Nations Appeal for Children,
see UNICEF
United Nations Association of the
United States, *see* American
Association for the United Nations
United Nations High Commissioner for
Refugees, F1395-97, F1402, F1457
United Nations Rehabilitation and
Relief Administration, C147
United States. Attorney General, B437
United States. Congress, ER on, C17,
C45, C92
United States. Congress. House.
Committee on the Investigation of
Un-American Activities, C308,
F690, F923, F986, F1306, F2005
-investigation of youth organizations
by, F595, F1301-2, F1306, F1322-
23, F1335, F1337, F1344
United States. Congress. Senate, F1582
-ER on, C252, C293, C317
United States. Dept. of Justice, F690
United States. Dept. of State, C63,
C238, F1024, F1492
-ER's relationship with, F1421,
F1426, F1430-31, F1433, F1447,
F1492, F1578, F1580-81, F1628-30,
F1660, F1665
United States. Internal Revenue
Service, C333
United States. Postal Service, C205,
C334
United States. Secretary of State, role
of, C311
United States. Supreme Court, ER on,
C25, C118, C120, C332
Unity Settlement House, F1178
Universal Declaration of Human Rights
and the covenants,
-drafting of, F1496-1602
-ER on, B20, B344, B350, B354-55,
B357-58, B360, B363, B365, B367,
B374, B391-92, B401, C186, C309,
D196, D201-2, D204-6, D208,
D210, D214, D252, F1458, H34
-ER's role, later assessments of,
F1455-56, F1463-64, F1474, F1491,
F1561-63, F1565-67, F1569, F1578-

83, F1586-87, F1590, F1592-93,
F1595, F1601, I41
University of Allahabad, F1753
University of Moscow, C274
The Untouchables (Southern
Conference Educational Fund),
F1193

Val-Kill
-as Eleanor Roosevelt National
Historic Site, F182, F225, F332,
F374-75, F379, F1444, F1937,
F1955, F1959-61, F1967, F1984,
F2026, H63
-as ER's home, B159, B496, F182,
F230, F242, F267, F332, F371,
F374-75, F379-80, F382, F388,
F394, F396-97, F567, F1955,
F1958, F1975, I59
see also Eleanor Roosevelt Center
at Val-Kill
Val-Kill Industries, B112, C337, F5,
F212, F231, F251, F311, F318,
F320, F330-31, F346, F369, F374-
75, F387, F395-97, F536, G9, G12,
G16-17, G22
Van Loon, Hendrik, D117
Van Renselaer, Martha, D40
Vandenburg, Arthur, F1451
Vanderlip, Mrs. Frank, F433
Vassar College, G58
The Vatican, C225
venereal disease, C100, C131, C154
veterans (World War II), *see* World
War II--soldiers
vice presidency, ER on, C269-70,
C274, C318
Vishinsky, Andrei, B507, F1584
vocational training, B207, C67,
F1326
Vogeler, Robert, C202
Voice of America, C209, F1454
Von Hesse, Elizabeth, C321, F1816
voting, ER on, B443, C79, C127,
C206, C325, C331, C344, D3,
D181
voting rights, C63, C82-83, C111,
C119, C189, C224; *see also* poll-
tax; women--voting rights of

Wagner, Robert F., F461
Wagner, Robert F., Jr., F1859, F2032
Wald, Lillian, B166
Wall, Joseph F., G92
Wall Street Journal, F704
Wallace, Henry A., B294, B353, C180,
    C272, C322, F540
  -on ER, F914, F1476, F1666
  -ER's relationship with, F818, F870,
    F915,
  -ER's split with, F1701, F1709,
    F1722, F1730-31
  see also Progressive Party
Wallace, Mike, H19, H80
Waller, Odell, F1153
Walton, William, F1694
war, ER on, B71, B122, B259, C67,
    C77, C80, C84, C90, C97, C118,
    C149, C153, C157, C163, C170,
    C179, C214, C325, D32, D50, D54,
    D72, D78, D177, D239, D261, E38
  -war, prevention of, B197, C75, C90,
    C325, D50
Warm Springs, Ga., B409, C34, C165,
    C180, F272, F290, F381, F1170
Warren, Earl, C268, F1692, F2032
Washington, D.C., B160, B162, B198,
    C63, C82, C346, D106, F814, F1098-
    1102, F1152, F1251
Washington Monument, B160
Washington, Nerve Center (Rosskam),
    B198
Washington, Nerve Center. Introduction
    (ER), E41
Wechsler, James, F1665
Weep No More My Lady (Debnam),
    G79
welfare, ER on, C70, C87
Wells, H.G., B169, F706
West, J.B., F920
West Virginia, *see* Arthurdale;
    subsistence homesteads
When You Grow Up to Vote (ER), E3-5
White, Earlene, D74
White, Robert M., II, F945
White, Walter, F1161, F1181, F1214,
    F1222-23, F1226, F1228, F1232,
    F1849
White, William Allen, F1045

White House, B223, B317, C2, C6,
    C21, C33-34, C129, C197, F580,
    F597, F646, F699
  -as Roosevelt home, B100, B111,
    B137, B160, B173, B476, C86,
    C216, C240, C248, D59, F527-
    28, F574, F589, F697, F707,
    F809, F847, F858-60, F867,
    F869, F895, F922
The White House (Lewis), B160
White House Conference on Child
    Health and Protection, B89
White House Conference on
    Children, B212, F1333
White House Conference on Children
    and Youth, C207
White House Conference on Children
    in a Democracy, D88, D115
White House Conference on Rural
    Education, B322, D156-57, D162,
    F1141
White House Press Conference
    Association, *see* Roosevelt,
    Eleanor---press conferences and
    relations with the press
*White House Press Conferences of
    Eleanor Roosevelt* (Beasley), F925
White Top Music Festival (Va.),
    F327
Whitney, Betsey Cushing, F248
WHO (World Health Organization),
    B370
widows and widowhood, C301, C320
Wilcox, Francis, F1451
Wilder, Thornton, D117
Wilhelmina (of the Netherlands),
    F551, F963
Wilkins, Roy, F1128, F1849, G79
Williams, Aubrey W., F1194, F1207
  -ER's relationship with, F875,
    F1058, F1295-96, F1332
Williams, Charl Ormond, D60
Williamsburg, Va., C13
Willkie, Edith, F629
Willkie, Wendell, C228, F500, F1204
Wilson, Woodrow, B50, B315
Wiltwyck School for Boys, F1156,
    G94m
Winchell, Walter, C172
  -in fiction, J15

Windsor, Duke and Duchess of, C104
wiretapping, C325
Wirt, William A., F1110
Wirth, Louis, D101
Wisdom, G107
Wolfe, Thomas, D128, F1227
Woman's National Democratic Club,
  see Women's National Democratic
  Club
Woman's Home Companion, F1792
women, B381, B455, C76, C78, C107,
    C131, C182, C188, C208, C304,
    C307, C324, C348, D28, D61, D87,
    D183, D188, E6-13, F462, F473,
    F552, F1028-29, F1031, F1233-94,
    F1742, F1744-45, F2041, G12,
    G14, G44, G52
  -defense effort (World War II) and,
    B230-31, B235, B238, B245, B255,
    B277, B288, B291, B293, B302,
    B304, B313, B489, C102, C105,
    C111, C125, C139, D139, D142,
    D145, D154, D172, F946, F984,
    F997-98, G53, H52
  -economic recovery, role in, B6, C1,
    C37, D33, E8, F585, F916, F1113,
    G47
  -education of, B63, B91, B289, B473,
    B492, D52, D65, D273, G31
  -employment of, B49, B74, B76,
    B156, B178, B306, B308, B310,
    C38, C59-60, C74, C82, C93,
    C130, C132, C151, C155, C193,
    C203, C210, C213, C306, C350,
    D6, D14, D25, D83, D270, D273,
    F1054, F1095, F1101, F1143,
    F1238, F1241, F1251, F1253,
    F1258, F1266, F1273, F1275-76,
    F1288, F1290-91, G10, G33
  -ER and women's network, F425,
    F455, F476, F481-82, F1033,
    F1046, F1235-36, F1243, F1278,
    F1285, I75
  -as homemakers, B6, B68-69, B74,
    B121, B177, B235, C37, C294,
    C331, C343, D41, E8, E10, E13,
    F403, F1234, F1268, F1277, F1280,
    G8, G10, G30, G33-34
  -in the military, B291, C92, C101,
    C103, C106, C112, C114, C119-

    21, C125, C127-28, C137, C207,
    F975, F1182
  -New Deal programs for, B97,
    C60, D30, F1279, F1283, F1286,
    F1289, F1311, F1338
  -as peacemakers and peacekeepers,
    B517, C75, C92, C123, C155,
    C179, C343, D50, D72, D144,
    D160, D172-73, D178, D185-87,
    E9, F1494, G57, G78
  -post-war world and, B283, B289,
    B302, B306, B308-10, C104,
    C134, D149-50, D158, D160,
    D179, D200, F932
  -protective legislation for, B49,
    B51, B325, D6, D80, F1249,
    F1259, F1273, G106
  -public and political roles of, B6,
    B22, B43, B52, B94-95, B123,
    B336, B351, C62, C64, C66,
    C71, C75, C79, C142, C146-47,
    C158, C203, C251, C270, C274,
    C294, C301, C342, D44, D49,
    D55, D73, D95, D263, E7, E9,
    E109-11, F461, F480, F583,
    F586, F609, F622, F633-34,
    F749, F893, F926, F1037, F1236,
    F1241, F1247, F1255, F1261,
    F1280, F1290, F1641, F1733,
    F1935, F1999, F2011, G4, G20,
    G78, G81
    --ER's advice on, B46, B61,
      B71, B83, B96, B107, B179,
      B192, B200, B222, B226,
      B243, C42, C59, D1, D13,
      D39, D56, D74, D98, D109,
      D114, D131, D144, D195,
      F402, F408, F461, F569,
      F583, F893, F1234, F1244,
      G3, G7, G25, G30
  -rights of, and the United Nations,
    F1407, F1410, F1438, F1490
  -voting rights of, B43, B46, B222,
    C211, F450, F463, G3, G7
  see also Equal Rights Amendment;
    President's Commission on the
    Status of Women
The Women (Boothe), B143
"Women Must Learn to Play the
  Game As Men Do" (ER), F402,
  F408

Women's Centennial Congress, D114
Women's City Club of New York, B1,
 B3, B47, B49, B53, B55-56, B62, D9,
 D13, D250, F454-55, F461
Women's Democratic News, B48, F486
Women's National Democratic Club,
 C86, D90-91, F87, F631
Women's National Press Club, F489,
 F515, F669
Women's Trade Union League, D25,
 D28, D83, F1134, F1211, F1253,
 F1262, F1291
Woodward, Ellen, D30, F425, F1118,
 F1246-47, F1278, F1282-83, F1311
Woollcott, Alexander, C94
workers, B108, B209, C37, C61, C68,
 C83, C92, C303, D17, D118, D258,
 F1111, F1124, F1131, G2; *see also*
 labor strikes; labor unions
Workers' Service Program, F1111
Works Progress Administration
 (WPA), C67, C69, C76, C335, D66,
 D111, F554c, F1088, F1095, F1105,
 F1111, F1253,
World Federation of Democratic
 Youth, B462
World Federation of United Nations
 Associations, B430, F1609
World Health Organization (WHO),
 B370
World War I, B260, F1138
World War II, C63, C74-75, C84,
 C94, C139-40, C152, C163, D124,
 F883, F930-1027
 -conditions and attitudes in U.S.
  during, C87, C114, C134, D121,
  D132, D135, D153
 -defense effort in U.S. during, C77,
  C92, C95, C97, C101, C112, C116-
  17, C122-23, C125, C139, D103,
  D137, D143, D152, F943, F955,
  F984, F1002, F1007, F1011, F1015,
  G51, G54
 -post-war, planning for, B253, B257,
  B260, B268, B278, B283, B285,
  B289, B292, B299-301, B305,
  B307-11, B318, B333, C105, D161,
  F930, F964, F999, F1312, G56
 -prisoners of, C121, C125, C136-38,
  C140, C244

 -soldiers in, B259, B266, B276,
  B279, B286, B296, B304, C98,
  C103-4, C106, C114-15, C117-
  19, C131, C137, C141, C143-46,
  C154, D138, D146, D153-54,
  D163-64, D171, F932, F965,
  F982, F994, F1004, F1008,
  F1013, F1023, G42, G53, G55,
  G60, I48
  --allotments for dependents of,
   C113, C120, C122-23, C129,
   C140-41
 -U.S. entry into, C81, C89, C102,
  C109, D127-28, D135, F943,
  F1017, G46
 -war bonds and, B280, C62, C102,
  C105-6, C110, C115, C131,
  C133, C143-44, C152, D167
 -war criminals of, C150
  see also aliens; Black Americans;
   refugees; Roosevelt, Eleanor--
   World War II and; women;
   young Americans
The World We Saw (Decker), B382
World Youth and the Communists
 (Apeland), B462
World Youth Congress, D84, F1327,
 F1347
The World's Favorite Recipes, B398
Wotkyns, Eleanor Roosevelt, F394,
 F397
Wright, Frank Lloyd, F1127, G94o
Wylie, Laura, B113

Yalta Conference, C262
"You Can't Pauperize Children"
 (ER), C147
You Learn by Living (ER), E130-34
Young, Owen D., F480
young Americans, B82, B109, B180,
 B401, B406, B459, B462, B482,
 B493, C67, C77, C82, C85, C97,
 C132, C149, C233, C276, C279,
 C283, C288, D78, D85, D119,
 D133, D219, D235, F1154, I31
 -ER's advice to, B87, B217, B362,
  B373, B451, C68, C191, D63,
  D84, D129, D140, D184, D218,
  D230, G42
 -New Deal programs for, B181,
  B201, C44, F1217, F1295

-problems of, B28, B125, B185,
B201, B204, B212, B217, B224,
B227, B458, C53, C64, C129,
C134, C154, C313, D18, D20, D24,
D33, D53, D58, D68, D70, D86,
D120-21, E142-48, F1047, F1054,
F1064, F1159, F1217, F1295-1348,
G47, G52, G98-99, J8
-World War II and, D140, D150,
G42, G50, G52
see also National Youth
Administration (NYA)
The Young Citizens (Black), B493
Young Communist League, D127,
F946, F1341
Young Democratic Clubs of America,
D75

younger readers, writings for, B5,
B7, B11, B18, B25, B31, B77, B84,
B103, B202, B401, B463, B483,
B488, E3-5, E42, E77-83, I1-93
Your Teens and Mine (ER), E142-48
You're the Boss (Flynn), B494
Youth Aliyah, B453, D243, F1633,
F1882
*Youth Aliyah: Past, Present and
Future* (Kol), B453
Youth-Millions Too Many (Melvin),
B227
Yugoslavia, C242

Zangrando, Robert, F1979
Zanuck, Darryl, J15

About the Compiler

JOHN A. EDENS is Director of Central Technical Services at the University Libraries of the State University of New York at Buffalo. He is the co-editor of *Research Libraries and Their Implementation of AACR2* (1986).

Recent Titles in
Bibliographies and Indexes in American History

The Natural Sciences and American Scientists in the
Revolutionary Era: A Bibliography
Katalin Harkányi, compiler

Changing Wilderness Values, 1930–1990: An Annotated Bibliography
Shelley Anne Osterreich, compiler

The American Indian Ghost Dance, 1870 and 1890:
An Annotated Bibliography
Shelley Anne Osterreich, compiler

The Immigration History Research Center: A Guide to Collections
Suzanna Moody and Joel Wurl, compilers and editors

Sports Ethics in America: A Bibliography, 1970–1990
Donald G. Jones with Elaine L. Daly

Horace Greeley: A Bio-Bibliography
Suzanne Schulze

Roosevelt Research: Collections for the Study of Theodore,
Franklin, and Eleanor
DeeGee Lester

The 1960's: An Annotated Bibliography of Social and Political
Movements in the United States
Rebecca Jackson

The Haymarket Affair: An Annotated Bibliography
Robert W. Glenn, compiler

Bill Clinton's Pre-Presidential Career: An Annotated Bibliography
Allan Metz, compiler

Learning to Behave: A Guide to American Conduct Books Before 1900
Sarah E. Newton

ISBN 0-313-26050-8

90000>

EAN

9 780313 260506

HARDCOVER BAR CODE

DATE DUE